# AMSCO®

## ADVANCED PLACEMENT EDITION
# English Literature
## and Composition

**Abdon**

**McFarlan**

# PERFECTION LEARNING®

# Authors

## Brandon Abdon, Senior Author, Doctor of Arts, English

Brandon Abdon worked for five years as Director of Curriculum, Instruction, and Assessment for the AP* English courses at The College Board, during which time he collaborated with experts from around the country to develop the Course and Exam Descriptions (CEDs) now in use. This work was a culmination of more than 15 years' experience in high schools and universities, teaching both the AP* English Language and Composition and the AP* English Literature and Composition courses as well as college composition and literature and teacher education courses. He has also taught or trained thousands of teachers around the country. He has served as an AP* Reader, led many professional developments, and offered dozens of conference presentations. Currently, he serves as professional development consultant for the Advanced Placement* program and works as an Education Specialist and Curriculum Coach in Cincinnati, Ohio.

## Rebecca McFarlan, Master of Arts, English

Rebecca McFarlan is a National Board Certified teacher who has taught English at both the high school and college level for many years. She has more than three decades of experience teaching both AP* English Literature and AP* English Language courses. She has been a reader and more recently a table leader for the AP* English Literature Exam. She is also a College Board Consultant for AP* English Literature, AP* English Language, and the Capstone AP* Research course. Rebecca served on the College Board's Instructional Development Committee to help develop instructional materials for teachers of AP* Literature. She developed three online workshops for AP* Central, contributed to the AP* Literature Mentor materials, and worked on the development of several PreAP* workshops. Rebecca is also a recipient of the Martha Holden Jennings Master Teacher award.

## Senior Reviewers

**Lisa Schade Eckert**, Ph.D.
Member of AP* Literature Committee
English Professor and Dean, Graduate
  Studies and Research
Northern Michigan University
Marquette, Michigan

**Thomas C. Foster**
University of Michigan—Flint (emeritus)
East Lansing, Michigan

**Will Nash**, Ph.D.
Professor of American Studies
  and English and American Literatures
Middlebury College
Middlebury, Vermont

## Reviewers

**Jenni Aberli**, B.A., M.A.T., Ed.S.
National Board Certified Teacher
High School English Language Arts
  Curriculum Lead
Jefferson County Public Schools
Louisville, Kentucky

**Susan Barber**, Ed.S.
AP* Literature Teacher
AP* Reader
College Board Consultant
Grady High School
Atlanta, Georgia

**Jerry W. Brown**, B.M.E., M.M.E.
College Board Consultant, Reader,
  Table Leader
AP* English Language and Literature Teacher
Georgetown, Texas

# Contents

Essential Question: *How do structure and contrast contribute to the development of ideas in a poem?*

Essential Question: *How do poets create connections among specific words and phrases to convey meaning?*

Essential Question: *What are the functions of similes and metaphors?*

Essential Question: *How do chronological interruptions in the plot as well as characters' contradictions and inconsistencies affect readers' experiences?*

Essential Question: *How do a narrator's tone, syntax and perspective reveal biases and reliability?*

# Preface

*AMSCO® English Literature and Composition: AP® Edition* develops skills and concepts necessary for both introductory level college courses in Literature in English and on the Advanced Placement® English Literature and Composition exam. While the Course and Exam Description (CED) released by the College Board in 2019 is not a redesign of the course, it does—for the first time in the seventy-five-plus year history of the course—provide specific skills and knowledge that students need to use to demonstrate the important concepts related to writing. The CED also—again, for the first time—suggests an order for teaching those skills and concepts to provide foundations on which students and teachers can build. This book is organized around those skills and concepts and their suggested order, providing students the opportunity to work with a diverse array of authors and poets, a variety of text types and difficulties, and texts both old and new. Users of this book will closely read and analyze texts they encounter and also engage in writing their own texts using literary skills they are studying. In this way, students can learn by doing—a creative approach that has often been lost in the world of skills-focused education.

This book fills the gap between test prep handbooks and costly English textbooks and anthologies. Most important, while it uses the CED as a framework and provides exam practice, it focuses on making students more literate—that is, better readers and writers. It is thorough enough to be a student's go-to book, especially if used in conjunction with other print and online resources. It can be read and practiced gradually over an entire course, reviewed in just a few weeks with the built-in review tools, or used in some combination of the two.

First, thanks go to my parents and grandparents as readers and my gran as a (and my!) teacher. Next, I would like to thank my co-writer and colleague Becky McFarlan for her mentorship, kindness, and patience; English professors Will Nash, David Kirkland, Michael Wood, Julie Cyzewski, Jennifer Fletcher, David Miller, Jim Egan, Tarshia Stanley, Erin Suzuki, Kim Coles, Tom Foster, Lisa Eckert, Erica Still, Warren Carson, Les Burns, and the late Bruce Holle for their inspiration; and my friends and colleagues Timm, Lauren, and Darrin for picking up their phones. Thanks to the reviewers who are listed on pages i–ii, and to Rudy, Amy, Kristina, Erik, Kathy, Minaz, Carlos, Eileen, Dana, Tony, Terri, Kay, Enithie, Brian, and so many others—you're all in here. Special thanks go to John Williamson and Brian Robinson as colleagues and mentors.

Not enough can be said about Carol Francis (the editor of this work) and her team, who fought through the pandemic and other challenges to keep this project on pace while maintaining professionalism, grace, and the patience of Job. And, of course, thanks to AMSCO/Perfection Learning and Steve Keay for believing in us and our work.

But more than anything, thanks to Jeep; the rest of Becky's family; and Angie, Hilton, and Dorian for the sacrifices that allowed this book to become a reality.

*Brandon Abdon, Senior Author, May 2021*

# Introduction

*"I did not know if the story was factually true or not,
but it was emotionally true."*

Richard Wright, *Black Boy*

Literature captures us: it is an art like painting or sculpture or music, and the authors are artists. All artists are observers of humanity, and they all draw on their unique experiences as they create their artworks and represent those experiences.

Like much other art, literature does not always look familiar. For example, at first look, a French countryside painted by Claude Monet may not seem especially relevant to you if you have never seen a French countryside. A song from ancient China may not seem to communicate to you if you have no knowledge of ancient China. Literature from a hundred years ago or a poem written last week by someone with experiences different from your own may not seem to speak to you. So why read it you if you cannot connect with it?

Before attempting to answer that, think about what you *can* connect to: the song you have on repeat on your playlist, the movie you watch over and over again, that picture you chose to make the lock screen on your phone. You see something about yourself in these and you want them at hand—to help you think about who you are. Stories can work the same way. You relate to a story your friend told because it had people, events, or situations in it you recognized. You may enjoy certain shows or films for the same reason. They speak to you.

Stories we encounter in our everyday lives sometimes play out the way we want them to or at least in a predictable manner. Literature also plays out that way sometimes, but more often than not, reflecting the realities of life, it includes complications. Sometimes the main characters don't end up together in a good relationship. Sometimes the family falls apart after the father dies. Sometimes the girl and her best friend grow up but also grow apart until they meet again—with unfortunate results. Sometimes the character wakes up and has turned into a bug, but no one cares because they never cared about him in the first place. Sometimes all the characters hate their jobs until something tragic happens and they all end up somewhere better. Sometimes the son finds out he needs to take revenge for his father's death but spends so much time thinking about what to do that he ends up doing nothing at all, and then he is killed in a fight over his dead girlfriend by her brother, and everyone else dies except his best friend who wants to kill himself but doesn't.

Those are examples from just novels, plays, and short stories. While it uses the same literary elements and techniques of prose (novels and short stories), poetry concentrates the language and experiences into lines and stanzas and (sometimes) rhymes to emphasize certain feelings or ideas. Poetry is painting with words, but because it is so compressed and often doesn't have the narrator that a story does, it may seem harder to read. It is not. It does take practice to read poetry, but the practice pays off. Literature challenges you to really think about the complexities of life and relationships and yourself.

Just as you may be able to hear a song or see a piece of art with which you cannot personally connect, you may still be able to appreciate the talent that created it and recognize that, even though it looks different from your experience, it has something in common with yours.

That brings us back to the quote. Often, literature that at first looks unfamiliar still speaks to you because it captures lived experiences common to most people. It captures emotions and values—which are at the root of what we care about most. So the "truthiness" of literature doesn't matter (after all, it is fiction) as much as how it makes you feel.

You feel as you do in response to literature because those authors—like any other artists—have made thoughtful choices in constructing a text. By accepting the challenge of the Advanced Placement® English Literature and Composition course, you have chosen to become a scholar of how authors make these choices and why. "How" authors make choices centers on the literary tools and techniques they use in their writing. "Why" authors make those choices concerns the effect of those choices on the reader. The conclusions you draw after examining these choices and the emotions or values they convey is your interpretation. The goal of literary analysis is to state this interpretation and then defend it using your reasoning about the text (so the reader of your interpretation understands your thinking) and information from the text (to show the reader of your essay how the details in the text support your interpretation).

Most college students take a literature course like this one at some point early in their college career. At many colleges, such a course is a cornerstone of what is often called a liberal arts or humanities course of study. The point—as mentioned above—is that you come to appreciate literature as an art that captures humanity. You may not become a literature major or an author, but you will likely come to recognize the role such art plays in societies. Like the composition or college writing course represented by the AP® English Language and Composition course—a companion to this literature course—the goal of this course is for college students to sharpen their reading and writing skills to become accomplished members of the community of thinkers. This book will allow you the space to explore texts that may seem both familiar and alien—all in an attempt to help you better understand how creativity, and the humanity expressed through it, illuminate hearts and minds.

Because this course is also about composition, this book will give you many opportunities to write and rewrite. Writing is a process, and all authors, columnists, bloggers, and poets follow that process in some way. For example, when writing this book, my co-author Becky McFarlan and I drafted parts, shared them with others, took feedback, made revisions, improved what we were doing, and then shared our work again, just as all writers do. While this course culminates in an exam, that exam captures the type of reading and writing that you do in college and expects that you produce the best first draft that you possibly can. This should always be the goal—but in the real world, you would be able to revisit that draft and improve it. For this reason, this course provides instruction and practice in the process of writing, revising, rethinking, drafting again, reviewing, sharing with peers, and finally finishing a polished draft. This book will regularly challenge you to consider how what you are learning will affect your writing process and the works you have written.

Throughout the book, you will also be challenged to exercise your own creativity. From dialogue to poetry, you will regularly have the opportunity to create on your own. Such creating is not just to help you engage your creative mind but also to reinforce what you are learning about the literature you are reading: If you can do it and practice it and make choices about what you are creating, then you will be able to better recognize those choices in the work of other authors. Also, if all you ever focus on are the voices and choices of other authors, then you will never learn to value your own voice.

---------------

## The English Literature and Composition Course

Congratulations on accepting the challenge to become a scholar in one of the subjects that will give you a window into yourself as well as into the soul of the world. *AMSCO® English Literature and Composition: Advanced Placement® Edition,* developed to align with the latest course and exam description from the College Board, will help you build mastery of the fundamental concepts of literature. This introduction explains the course design and test format. In the nine skills-building units that follow, you will find extensive discussions of the enduring understandings for the course that are the broad concepts most important to reading and writing; diverse readings and tasks that both teach and challenge you to apply skills and knowledge; a number of practice questions and prompts to help you get used to what and how you will be asked to complete tasks on the exam; and multiple opportunities to address your own growth as a reader and writer and not just a test taker.

The College Board's Advanced Placement® Program started in 1955. The AP® English Literature and Composition course was one of the original courses, and, while it has changed somewhat over the years, it has mostly remained in its current format since the 1970s. In 2019, this exam attracted one of the largest number of test takers, with more than 380,000 students taking it around the world. More than 3,000 colleges accepted these scores and awarded either credit in place of course work or advanced placement into a higher-level college course meant to make students even stronger writers and scholars.

This course may not be for only those who are going to college straight out of high school. The skills that make for better readers and writers—and better critical thinkers in general—are essential as people are daily exposed to a variety of media that seek to get their attention and sway their opinion. Also, skills related to empathizing with others, appreciating their perspectives, and interacting with others' ideas make everyone better members of a complex and diverse society.

The exam is given in early May, but you must register near the beginning of the year. Check your school's guidance department or the College Board's website for details, fees, and deadlines.

## Design of the Course

The College Board published the new course and exam description (CED) in 2019. Though the course has not been redesigned, it has been articulated and focused so that there is little question about the skills and knowledge necessary for the course. These skills, knowledge, and understandings are all directly drawn from previous exams and course descriptions and verified by college professors and writing experts from around the country. The CED focuses on depth rather than breadth and offers detailed enduring understandings meant to clarify the conceptual learning expected in the course. In fact, these enduring understandings and the big ideas they define are important for literature in general, not just texts read in this course. They include

1. Character
2. Setting
3. Structure
4. Narration
5. Figurative Language
6. Literary Argumentation

However, literature does not reside in any one of these alone; it incorporates skills and knowledge from all of the big ideas. For this reason, the CED has outlined units that introduce material at appropriate points, encourage practice, and then build on that in later units by repeating the same skills but with new knowledge and an expectation of a more sophisticated understanding.

Literary elements and techniques are the overwhelming focus of the CED—that is, understanding "how" something in the text works and "why" it is included. Since reading texts and writing about them are not about test taking, to hone these skills you have to write a lot, read a lot, and write and read different texts. Rather than preparing for a test, you will be learning the necessary skills for reading and writing—which will happen to serve you well when you do take the exam. Some practice with test examples and the process of thinking through an exam is necessary—that is why we have practice questions in this book—but a course that teaches only for the test won't help you use those skills in different settings.

The course is designed for depth, not breadth. The texts used in the course should be considered in the same way. You may benefit more from reading a few longer texts and several shorter texts in depth than from reading more texts in a cursory way: depth over breadth; understanding over knowledge.

# English Literature and Composition Content

This course is a college-level, introductory literature course. The key word here is "introductory." Many colleges have only about 45 hours of class work for a course, so they are able to focus on development of the most essential skills and understandings in the course. With an average of 140 hours of instruction in a school year, high schools have the opportunity to teach these same skills in much more depth, with much more practice and much more teacher feedback. Overarching questions addressed in this course include the following: How do details and description in a text reveal perspectives? How do the perspectives of characters, narrators, and speakers affect an interpretation? How do literary elements and techniques affect an interpretation? And what makes for a successful written argument about literature?

**Enduring Understandings** The course content is developed from enduring understandings—statements that synthesize the important concepts in a discipline area and have lasting value even beyond that discipline area. For example, the College Board has articulated this enduring understanding (EU) derived from the big idea of "narration":

> "A narrator's or speaker's perspective controls the details and emphases that affect how readers experience and interpret a text."

Why is that an enduring understanding? It states the fundamental concept that all authors and readers know (whether consciously or not) about how a narrator or speaker works in a text. Every single student who takes any class on literature should clearly understand this concept at the end of that class. Without this understanding, a reader would have trouble recognizing how different perspectives affect a text and might—in the real world—struggle with understanding perspectives of different people. Each unit in this book begins with a listing of the enduring understandings relevant to that unit.

**Skills** To help students fully develop those enduring understandings, the College Board has also articulated skills, or the tasks that students are expected to demonstrate to show that they understand the concepts within the big ideas and enduring understandings. For example, following is a skill related to the enduring understanding above:

> "Explain how a narrator's reliability affects a narrative."

This skill ties to the enduring understanding by providing a specific task that students must do as they read any text and then proceed to interpret and analyze it. A student unaware of this expectation may not be able to examine the character and perspective of a narrator or how that narrator affects the story—an essential aspect of reading and analyzing texts. Each unit begins with a list of the skills tied to the unit's enduring understandings

**Essential Knowledge** Being able to fulfill the learning objectives and demonstrate the skills requires content knowledge. The College Board has homed in on what it and its panel of teachers and professors consider essential knowledge (EK) to achieve that purpose. Here is an example of essential knowledge tied to the above skills:

"Some narrators or speakers may provide details and information that others do not or cannot provide. Multiple narrators or speakers may provide contradictory information in a text."

This essential knowledge statement outlines one of the ideas you need to know to fulfill the learning objective, so you can focus your study on the truly relevant information. A reader who does not know this essential knowledge and cannot recognize it in a text may be confused by the different voices or by the different information being provided. In other words, knowing this EK will help make the reading clearer—this is true of most of the EKs.

Literature courses rely on interpretation of literary texts as art. This approach differs from that of the AP® English Language and Composition course, which focuses on rhetoric and composition. Rhetoric, or how language affects us and how we can use language to affect others, differs from the study of literature. Nobel Prize-winning Irish poet William Butler Yeats may have summed up the differences between literature and rhetoric better than anyone else in this statement:

*"Out of the quarrel with others we make rhetoric; out of the quarrel with ourselves we make poetry."*

*Interpretation* is an old word. It comes from a Latin word that can mean both "understand" and "explain." Those are indeed the tasks you need to do as you interpret a text: develop an understanding of it and then explain that understanding. An interpretation must be accompanied by an explanation; without it, the person reading or hearing the interpretation won't understand how you arrived at your interpretation. Sometimes good interpretations arrived at thoughtfully are dismissed because the writer has not supplied a clear explanation. An interpretation must be supported by the reasoning of the person making it and with information from the text that supports that reasoning.

When literature courses began at American universities in the mid-1800s, their goal was to have students read the texts that helped shape the United States and its "literary tradition." This tradition was never really defined until the early 20th century when some schools started talking about the "canon" (a word used to describe a collection of books deemed sacred by a religion) of literature. Even then the lists differed across the country and continued to evolve. The problem was that the people making the lists all tended to have similar experiences: they were wealthy, educated, and almost completely white and male. They tended to value what 1) reflected their experience and 2) resembled what they had been taught by their teachers. As the country changed socially, economically, and racially, many people who previously had been prevented from attending schools and colleges began doing so. Still, literature courses focused on the canon determined decades before. In the 1960s and 1970s, however, some universities began to revise or add to the lists, recognizing their lack of diversity. But change is slow and the allegiance to the old canon was strong.

Today, many literature scholars and English teachers recognize the value of literature that reflects the diversity of the country and even the world. While many still see value in what have come to be called "canonical" texts, most of those same people also see the need to include texts by traditionally underrepresented groups of people.

This book provides an array of texts by people from an array of backgrounds. Some of them could be considered "canonical," while some may have never been taught in an AP® Literature classroom before. Included here as the focus of literature is, among others, a humorous short story about triumph over prejudice, a traditional short story about an Appalachian farm family, Shakespearean poetry, Victorian drama, and contemporary Native American poetry. The authors have taken the commitment to diversity very seriously, trying to do their part to encourage better understanding and cooperation in our society.

**Reading in the Course** Focus on depth and variety instead of on breadth and a single style or genre. Consider this course a "Literature Appreciation" course in which you encounter a variety of text types from a variety of places. The goals are to help you 1) appreciate the value of literature to all cultures and to society in general and 2) become better readers and smarter consumers of any text you should encounter when you leave the course.

As longtime teachers, consultants, college instructors, and curriculum coaches, the authors of this book want to encourage students to think about the following guidelines for reading.

- **Comprehension** sometimes gets left at the door in AP® English Literature. Take the time you need to understand the literal meaning of what you are reading. Talking about what you read in small groups may help you achieve this understanding. Save close reading for the next step, not the first step.

- **Deeper reading** often involves studying fewer longer texts (novels or plays) to allow time for you to practice the skills you need through close reading activities. Excerpts or short stories are also acceptable texts for close reading.

- **Student choice** can be important in motivating you. The final question on the AP® exam allows you to choose a work on which to base a response to a prompt. When possible, read what interests you.

- **Summer or independent reading** (if done) should encourage interest and motivate reading. Choose texts that will interest you enough so that you will want to read. Talk about what you read with friends or family members.

- **Lists of literary techniques or books** from the Internet can be overwhelming. Avoid them. Read what is in the CED (and in this book) and use a mix of texts that you find engaging and (at times) challenging.

**Writing in the Course** While you will write throughout this course, what and how you write will differ from unit to unit. Although there are ample multiple-choice questions for practice, you will also write in response to a variety of tasks and prompts, including those that suggest ways you can use the reading skills you are learning to create your own texts. Near the end of each unit, you will then encounter writing activities that build across the entire course as your skills accumulate.

As you write in the course, you should make a practice of reflecting back on the lessons you have learned with previous writing tasks and activities and consider how you can use those skills with the next writing task. Helping you transfer those skills to new situations and use them to make better decisions as you write are the goals of this course.

So it is worth explaining the differences among the writing you will do in the course, the writing you will do on the AP® exam, and the writing you will do in the real world. In most classes, writing is assigned and its purpose is to assess what you know and how well you can express it. This writing is usually not "real-world" writing, but you can learn and practice the skills necessary for real-world writing and also learn to value writing as a process of mistakes and collaboration and revision. The AP® exam offers you one instance and demands you respond with as much as you can to show what you know and understand. Though it attempts to give you as much information as you will need to be successful, it is still not a real situation with a real audience and any real consequences beyond getting a certain score. It is a good way to test reading and writing skills, but it is not the goal of any literature course. Real-world writing and reading always happen within a context—a situation—and any reader and writer must be skilled enough to pay attention to that situation and make choices that will make their message successful in that context. The hope is that students of this course will be able to take the skills they learned and sharpened in the imagined situations of the classroom and the exam and transfer them to the real world.

## The Design of This Book

This book explains college-level writing and reading in the most straightforward terms and with many memorable analogies and examples for understanding. It is the result of experiences in teaching both the AP® course and college literature courses, working directly with the College Board, serving as a Reader for the AP® Exams, and engaging with real-world scholarship in literature and literacy. All of these provide perspective for much of the explanation that follows.

The unit sequence in this book corresponds to the order in the CED. However, the units' main points and concepts can be understood in isolation. As with any skills-based book, there is overlap among the units, and we have included cross-references where it was appropriate.

## Nine Units

This book contains nine units:

**Unit One: Elements of Fiction** introduces the fundamentals parts of stories with which many students are likely familiar but may not have studied in depth. As the first unit, it provides the foundation upon which all other units will build as it also offers prompts and activities that encourage practice of fundamentals before expecting a more advanced performance in later units.

**Unit Two: Poetry and the Shift** moves away from the more familiar world of stories and what is expected in most stories to the (sometimes) unique world of poetry. Still an early unit, it continues to offer some foundational skills but begins to emphasize the importance of a text's structure and the significance of shifts in texts.

**Unit Three: Extending the Scope** starts to take concepts established in the first two units and expand on them in application to novels and drama. Development of characters and conflicts feature prominently here as the importance of perspectives and values in literature become clearer.

**Unit Four: Nuance and Complexity** begins to explore more deeply the traits that make some stories and poems more literary than others. The focus is on being able to apply skills to texts that are more nuanced and complex than those in earlier units. Most skills for the course have been introduced by this point, and the rest of the course will focus on improving upon what has already been presented.

**Unit Five: Multiple Meanings** builds on the previous unit. Poems in this unit rely on the stability of their patterns and structures while exploring complicated topics with multiple ways of interpreting them.

**Unit Six: Disruption and Disparity** shows how interruptions to the patterns and structures of texts complicate literature even further. Difference, inconsistencies, contrasts, and contradictions feature heavily as students learn to acknowledge where ideas don't connect and examine those disparities as ripe for analysis.

**Unit Seven: Deepening Complexity** presses students to the next level of interpretation as they build on the disruptions of the previous chapter and begin to see even more complex possibilities. Many of the fundamentals from unit one have remained unchanged to this point, but now settings will change and contradict, narrators may be unreliable, and the plot may not be in chronological order.

**Unit Eight: Language and Ambiguity** goes beyond the essential elements and delves into the very minute and particular techniques involving words and organization of ideas in poetry. While previous units have addressed word choice and structure and syntax, this unit deals very specifically with poems that break structural expectations and provide unpredictable and, at times, confusing words and images.

**Unit Nine: Interactions of Elements** ends the book almost where it began: exploring the different elements and techniques of literature but now looking deeply at how they all interact in a text to create specific effects.

## In Each Unit

Each unit relies on certain organizing factors that help make this book useful and make information easier to find.

**The Unit Overview** does exactly what its name suggests—it provides a high-level explanation of concepts to be explored in the unit. More important, it offers a scenario or example that helps to illustrate the significance of the material in that unit.

**Anchor Texts** are the primary texts that the different parts of the unit will refer to as new skills and knowledge are introduced and applied. These include short stories, poems, or excerpts from novels or plays. Their use fosters rereading and close analysis.

**"What Do You Know?"** is an essential tenet of this book. It asks you to challenge yourself to answer questions that the book hasn't yet covered but that will prepare you to learn by asking you to think about the anchor texts. Don't worry if these are difficult—view this as productive frustration. You usually don't know what you don't know until you know you don't know it.

The **Parts** of the unit are where the learning and practice happen. These also include very specific **essential questions** that focus learning and are answerable with the skills and content being covered. In these parts are smaller sections that break down specific essential knowledge in ways to help with the application of that knowledge and understanding its relationship with the EUs and Skills. Also within each part are **checkpoints** with practice tasks specific to the content in that part as well as AP® Exam-style questions that are likewise specific to the content in that part.

**Creating on Your Own** is where the skills for the AP® course become so much more. Here you are asked to apply the content from different parts of the unit to your own creative writing. In these sections, you are revisiting, revising, and refining your own writing as you work through the book. These skills are essential to being an effective writer in school and in life.

**Apply What You Have Learned** tasks occur at the end of each part and ask you to take the skills, knowledge, and understandings that you have been practicing and apply them to a different text or part of a text to provide you with more practice. This feature also helps to improve the way skills transfer from both this book and this course into the real world.

**The Writer's Craft** or **The Critic's Craft** are special sections occurring once in each unit. These encourage ways of thinking about reading or writing that will enrich your learning experience.

**The Unit Review** provides more opportunity for practice. This section offers full reading and analysis texts with **Multiple-Choice** sets that are aligned to material from the unit as well as questions aligned to other units for expanded practice. There are also practice **Free-Response Questions** of each type—Poetry Analysis, Prose Fiction Analysis, and Literary Argument.

# The Exam

You can earn college credit or placement into a different college course (depending on the institution you attend) for your work in the course upon your successful performance on the national AP® English Literature and Composition exam given in early May. This three-hour test consists of 55 five-option multiple-choice questions and 3 free-response questions. You will have 60 minutes (1 hour) to complete the multiple-choice questions and then 120 minutes (2 hours) for the free-response questions. The free-response questions are worth 55% of the score, with the multiple-choice worth the remaining 45%. A talented team of college faculty and experienced AP® teachers draft the questions and create the exam each year. The exam questions are also field-tested with actual college students and then revised accordingly to ensure they are testing what is necessary for the college-level course. A parallel practice exam is included at the end of this book. On the test, you can earn a score of 1 through 5. The College Board considers a score of 3 as "qualified," but some colleges require a 4 or even a 5 for consideration for credit. To learn more about how colleges regard the exam, check out this website: https://apstudent. collegeboard.org/creditandplacement/search-credit-policies.

## Multiple-Choice Questions

The 55 multiple-choice questions always have five options, A through E. There will be one correct answer. The questions are designed to test your reading analysis skills. The exam includes five sets of questions with eight to thirteen questions per set. Each set is preceded by a passage of prose fiction, drama, or poetry of varying difficulty. The multiple-choice section will always include at least two prose fiction passages (this may include drama) and at least two poetry passages.

Reading the passage completely is essential. Be especially careful not to think you understand it until you have finished it completely. Pay close attention to shifts in the passage (more on this later in the book) as they often indicate what the actual purpose of the passage may be. If you read the passage and have trouble understanding it, you might use the questions to help guide your understanding. Sometimes, even reading the questions first can be a helpful strategy. As with most multiple-choice tests, determine exactly what the question is asking and then select the best answer. If an early option in (A) or (B) looks extremely obvious, continue to read and consider the remaining options to confirm or reconsider your first impressions. For questions you cannot immediately answer, use the process of elimination. Rule out and actually mark through the unlikely options to narrow your choices. Finally, as the directions on the exam will remind you, "pay particular attention to the requirements of questions that contain the words NOT, LEAST, or EXCEPT."

When you see a challenging question, remember time is limited. You have a little over a minute and a half per question—and this allotment includes time for reading the passage and the question and then going through the answers. Some questions will take you less time, some will take you more. Skip the occasional tough question (be sure to leave that spot blank on the answer form) and continue through the test. Return and answer those challenging questions after you have gone through all 55. Since there is no added penalty for guessing, if you do not know the answer, make your best guess. Never leave any responses blank.

In 2021, the College Board began offering digital exams as well as paper and pencil exams. The College Board provides opportunities to practice the digital exam through AP® Central.

If you're just beginning your preparation, the example questions that follow may be challenging. Don't worry if you do not know the correct answer; the following nine units will teach you. These examples are to expose you to the formats of the questions. You could elect to revisit these questions as part of your review as exam day approaches.

## EXAMPLES

### Prose

*Please note that this passage is not as long as an actual exam passage. Also note that a code in small type follows each question. These codes do not appear on the exam but are included here to help you see how your understanding of the skills and concepts is assessed. You can refer to the Course and Exam Description to understand these codes, but you do not need to know them.*

**Questions 1–4. Read the passage carefully before you choose your answers.**

(1) This was Heathcliff's first introduction to the family. On coming back a few days afterwards (for I did not consider my banishment perpetual), I found they had christened him "Heathcliff": it was the name of a son who died in childhood, and it has served him ever since, both for Christian and surname. Miss Cathy and he were now very thick; but Hindley hated him: and to say the truth I did the same; and we plagued and went on with him shamefully: for I wasn't reasonable enough to feel my injustice, and the mistress never put in a word on his behalf when she saw him wronged.

(2) He seemed a sullen, patient child; hardened, perhaps, to ill-treatment: he would stand Hindley's blows without winking or shedding a tear, and my pinches moved him only to draw in a breath and open his eyes, as if he had hurt himself by accident, and nobody was to blame. This endurance made old Earnshaw furious, when he discovered his son persecuting the poor fatherless child, as he called him. He took to Heathcliff strangely, believing all he said (for that matter, he said precious little, and generally the truth), and petting him up far above Cathy, who was too mischievous and wayward for a favourite.

(3) So, from the very beginning, he bred bad feeling in the house; and at Mrs. Earnshaw's death, which happened in less than two years after, the young master had learned to regard his father as an oppressor rather than a friend, and Heathcliff as a usurper of his parent's affections and his privileges; and he grew bitter with brooding over these injuries. I

sympathised a while; but when the children fell ill of the measles, and I had to tend them, and take on me the cares of a woman at once, I changed my idea. Heathcliff was dangerously sick; and while he lay at the worst he would have me constantly by his pillow: I suppose he felt I did a good deal for him, and he hadn't wit to guess that I was compelled to do it. However, I will say this, he was the quietest child that ever nurse watched over. The difference between him and the others forced me to be less partial. Cathy and her brother harassed me terribly: he was as uncomplaining as a lamb; though hardness, not gentleness, made him give little trouble.

1. In the context of the passage, sentence 3 in paragraph 2 ("He took . . . favourite.") contrasts others' treatment of Heathcliff in order to

   (A) demonstrate how undeserving Heathcliff was of the treatment he was getting

   (B) explain why Hindley was so bitter about the relationship between his father and Heathcliff

   (C) emphasize the narrator's foolish treatment of Heathcliff

   (D) explain why Cathy was considered untrustworthy

   (E) demonstrate how the other characters justify their treatment of Heathcliff

Unit 4/ EU STR-1 / Skill 3.D / EK STR-1.T

2. In paragraph 3, sentence 6 ("Cathy ... trouble."), the simile claiming Heathcliff "was as uncomplaining as a Lamb" is complicated by

   (A) the narrator's previous descriptions of Heathcliff and how gentle he could be

   (B) the narrator's previous descriptions of Hindley (the young master) as "bitter with brooding"

   (C) the pity most of the other characters displayed for Heathcliff

   (D) the clause that follows it specifying that the trait of "gentleness" did not explain his behavior

   (E) the earlier image of Heathcliff as "the quietest child that ever nurse watched over"

Unit 7 / EU FIG-1 / Skill 6.A / EK Fig-1.AE

3. The narrator in the passage speaks from the point of view of

   (A) the mother of the family who has lost one of her children

   (B) a member of the household who is close with the family

   (C) a servant who wishes to undermine and ruin the family

   (D) the eldest sibling who has been tasked with raising the others

   (E) an outsider who is nevertheless knowledgeable about the family

Unit 1 / EU CHR-1 / Skill 4.A / EK NAR-1.B

**4.** In the context of the passage, all of the following indicate the other characters' perspectives toward Heathcliff EXCEPT

    (A) "I wasn't reasonable enough to feel my injustice" (Paragraph 1)

    (B) "petting him up far above Cathy" (Paragraph 2)

    (C) "This endurance made old Earnshaw furious" (Paragraph 2)

    (D) "which happened in less than two years after" (Paragraph 3)

    (E) "a usurper of his parent's affections and his privileges" (Paragraph 3)

Unit 7 / EU CHR-1 / Skill 1.D / EK CHR-1.AD

| # | Answer | Rationale |
|---|--------|-----------|
| 1 | A | While most other statements in the passage show how Heathcliff is neglected or even abused by the family, this sentence offers insight into his nature that seems to show that he was not deserving of such treatment. |
| | | The EK focuses on contrasts among character perspectives, which are revealed in the treatment of Heathcliff by different characters. The skill focuses on how a contrast—in this case, the contrasting perspectives on Heathcliff—functions in a text, while the EU focuses on the broader structure of a text, or how things are arranged. In this case, they are arranged to create that contrast. |
| 2 | D | The simile by itself communicates Heathcliff's nature but would not be accurate if it conveyed that he was gentle and docile like a lamb. For this reason, the author chooses to have the narrator explain that it was not the gentleness that made him less trouble. This qualification affects the simile as it limits some traits that would normally transfer from a lamb to the character, making the understanding of the simile more complicated as regular associations with lambs are not as useful. |
| | | The EK addresses the traits of objects being compared in the simile, and the skill expects that those traits be examined in order to explain their function. In the context of the EU, the associations that would be part of the figurative understanding of the simile are interrupted and complicated. |

| 3 | B | The details provided in the passage make it clear that the narrator is a member of the household. She was away for some reason but then allowed to return and immediately began interacting with the family members again, even caring for them when they were ill. |
| | | The EK explores how the narrator's position in the world of the text affects what the narrator is able to offer. It becomes necessary to distinguish between point of view and perspective to understand how the narrator's role as a character affects what is included in the passage. In the context of the skill and the EU, identifying and understanding the position and perspective of the narrator helps in understanding how and why the narrator affects the reader's experience and interpretation. |
| 4 | D | Very simply, this statement describes the passing of the mother (who wasn't very nice to Heathcliff either) and not his treatment at the hand of any characters. |
| | | The EK relates to how multiple characters in a group relate to another character. The skill demands examination of the specific details and how they reveal nuance in the different character relationships which, in the context of the EU, focuses on the values, beliefs, and biases represented by those characters. |

## POETRY

**Questions 5-8. Read the following poem carefully before you choose your answers.**

We Wear the Mask

We wear the mask that grins and lies,
It hides our cheeks and shades our eyes,—
This debt we pay to human guile;
With torn and bleeding hearts we smile,
5    And mouth with myriad subtleties.

Why should the world be over-wise,
In counting all our tears and sighs?
Nay, let them only see us, while
We wear the mask.

10    We smile, but, O great Christ, our cries
To thee from tortured souls arise.
We sing, but oh the clay is vile
Beneath our feet, and long the mile;
But let the world dream otherwise,
15    We wear the mask!

**5.** In the context of the poem, the hyperbole in line 4 ("With ... smile,") has the effect of

(A) illustrating the progress made by the speaker and his people

(B) emphasizing the suffering of the speaker and his people in contrast with their appearance

(C) contrasting the struggles of the people with the struggles of the speaker

(D) illustrating the physical harm done to the speaker and his people and how they try to disguise it

(E) emphasizing the tragic experiences of the speaker over those of his people

Unit 5 / EU FIG-1 / Skill 5.B / EK FIG-1.N

**6.** Which of the following best describes the relationship—and the effect of that relationship—between lines 10 and 12?

(A) They each start with something positive and end with a negative to illustrate the useless hopes of the speaker and his people.

(B) They share imagery that combines to illustrate the suffering of the speaker and his people.

(C) They contradict one another to demonstrate the complexity and frustration faced by the speaker and his people.

(D) Line 12 rephrases line 10 to reiterate the experiences of the speaker and his people.

(E) Line 10 only makes sense when read with line 12 to demonstrate the constant cycle of oppression felt by the speaker and his people.

Unit 2 / EU STR / Skill 3.C / EK STR-1.E

**7.** In the context of the poem, the repetition of the word "world" in lines 6 and 14 could best be said to indicate that

(A) the world in general may care about others even though many individuals do not

(B) the speaker's people cannot understand how they fit into the rest of the world

(C) the world only cares about his people as a group and not him individually

(D) the speaker intends to speak for the entire world

(E) the speaker sees himself and his people as separate from the rest of the world

Unit 2 / EU FIG-1 / Skill 5.B / EK FIG-1.C

**8.** The speaker relies on the extended metaphor of the mask throughout the poem to illustrate which of the following?

(A) That showing emotion is unacceptable

(B) That only those unaffected by emotion can rise to power

(C) That weakness comes from emotion

(D) That the people hide their suffering

(E) That society would rather tell people how they feel

Unit 5 / EU FIG-1 / Skill 6.B / EK FIG-1.U

| # | Answer | Rationale |
|---|--------|-----------|
| 5 | B | While labeling a hyperbole is not the point here, knowing what one is and how it works is absolutely necessary. The question assumes this knowledge and skill; being able to recognize how the exaggeration and imagery work in that line helps to emphasize the suffering of the people. |
| | | The EU/Skill/EK relies on naming the element and then being able to—as the skill demands—explain how it functions in the text. The context of the EU is an understanding that hyperbole is not a literal statement. |
| 6 | A | The two lines are grammatically and topically parallel and each starts with something that could and should be seen as a sign of hope but then resolves with something that is not. They even both start with the collective pronoun "we" and then an "s" word followed by a comma and then a conjunction ("but") to counter the hope. |
| | | The EU/Skill/EK combination emphasizes the relationship between arrangement in a poem and its ideas. The skill expects students to explain the function of any structures in the context of the EU, which describes how the arrangement of all parts of a text might affect interpretations. |
| 7 | E | This word appears in two lines fairly far apart in the context of this poem, but those lines also rhyme and have different end-rhyme words that look very similar. In both cases, the speaker refers to the "world" as apart from the people and those end rhyme words emphasize the otherness. |
| | | The EU/Skill/EK relationship relies on the ideas that get emphasized by repeated words but also includes the context of their use. The skill expects explanation of how those repeated words function in the text. The EU is broader and gets at the associations the words carry and how those associations affect the interpretation of the text. |

| 8 | D | The extended metaphor of the mask essentially *is* the poem and the details and imagery surrounding it illustrate that there is an abundance of suffering that people feel the need to hide. |
| | | The EU/Skill/EK relationship is about how what is happening in the general text affects the metaphor—in this case the details related to suffering beneath the mask. The skill expects students to explain the function of metaphors in the context of the EU, which focuses on how comparisons like metaphors work in the text. |

## Free-Response Questions

The free-response question (FRQ) section of the exam consists of three prompts you must respond to in 120 minutes, about 40 minutes per response. Within that time you will need to read the prompts and plan your response, so develop a strategy to use your time in ways that best suit you.

There are three different free-response prompts on the exam: Poetry Analysis, Prose Fiction Analysis, and Literary Argument, often called the Open Question. The first two are essentially the same kind of prompt but with different types of literature. The third asks you to use a text you have read to respond to a prompt and defend an argument.

These responses are often called "essays," but they differ from what you may be writing as essays in the actual course or in other classes. The goal of these FRQs is to respond to the prompt in a timely manner, showing that you have all of the necessary skills, knowledge, and understanding to produce effective writing. You do not need to worry much about the style of your writing on these responses as long as your claim, your reasoning, your organization, and your use of evidence from the texts is solid. Introductions and conclusions. are not required. While they may help, they may also cut into your allotted time to develop a successful argument.

Your goal in responding to the Free-Response Questions is to write the best possible first draft you can. The readers of your exam will expect that level of writing when they score your essays in June, knowing there is little time during the exam to revise and polish.

**Scoring the FRQ** involves using a rubric that analyzes certain parts of your response to see if you have earned points across three different rows:

Row A: Thesis (0–1 point)

Row B: Evidence and Commentary (0–4 points)

Row C: Sophistication (0–1 point)

**Total possible points**: 6

Though there are a total of 6 points possible, getting 4 or 5 out of 6 is still a good score. The points get more difficult to earn as you move down the rubric, meaning that the thesis point should be the easiest to earn while the sophistication point is the most difficult. In fact, the sophistication point relies on so many different parts of the response working together that it is not only difficult, but *very* difficult, to get. A score of 1 in Row A, 4 in Row B, and 0 in Row C would earn total score of 5/6—which is a very good score.

**Poetry and Prose Analysis Essays** These type of free-response questions give you a passage to read and a prompt to respond to using your analysis of the entire passage or poem. You will be provided with a brief introduction to the passage. You will then be asked to "read the passage carefully" and then analyze how the author uses "literary elements and techniques" to develop something "complex" in the text. Don't miss that part—you must address complexity.

Below are the actual details about your response as they will appear on the exam.

In your response you should do the following:

- Respond to the prompt with a thesis that presents a defensible interpretation.

- Select and use evidence to support your line of reasoning.

- Explain how the evidence supports your line of reasoning.

- Use appropriate grammar and punctuation in communicating your argument.

The rubric below shows additional details for each of the three rows. For even more detail, visit the College Board website and search for the latest scoring rubrics.

| Specifics for Scoring the Poetry and Prose Fiction Analysis Prompts |
|---|
| **A. THESIS** (0–1 point) |
| 1 point: |
| Responds to the prompt with a thesis that presents a defensible interpretation of the poem or passage. |
| 0 points for any of the following: |
| • There is no defensible thesis. |
| • The intended thesis only restates the prompt. |
| • The intended thesis provides a summary of the issue with no apparent or coherent claim. |
| • There is a thesis, but it does not respond to the prompt. |

## B. EVIDENCE AND COMMENTARY (0–4 points)

### 4 points:

| EVIDENCE | COMMENTARY | LITERARY ELEMENTS |
|---|---|---|
| Provides specific evidence to support all claims in a line of reasoning. | Consistently explains how the evidence supports a line of reasoning. | Explains how multiple literary elements or techniques in the poem or passage contribute to its meaning. |

### 3 points:

| EVIDENCE | COMMENTARY | LITERARY ELEMENTS |
|---|---|---|
| Provides specific evidence to support all claims in a line of reasoning. | Explains how some of the evidence supports a line of reasoning. | Explains how at least one literary element or technique in the poem or passage contributes to its meaning. |

### 2 points:

| EVIDENCE | COMMENTARY |
|---|---|
| Provides some specific, relevant evidence. | Explains how some of the evidence relates to the student's argument, but no line of reasoning is established, or the line of reasoning is faulty. |

### 1 point:

| EVIDENCE | COMMENTARY |
|---|---|
| Provides evidence that is mostly general. | Summarizes the evidence but does not explain how the evidence supports the student's argument. |

### 0 points:

| EVIDENCE |
|---|
| Simply restates thesis (if present), repeats provided information, or offers information irrelevant to the prompt. |

> **C. SOPHISTICATION** (0–1 points)
>
> 1 point:
> Demonstrates sophistication of thought and/or develops a complex literary argument by doing any of the following:
>
> 1. Identifying and exploring complexities or tensions within the poem or passage.
>
> 2. Illuminating the student's interpretation by situating it within a broader context.
>
> 3. Accounting for alternative interpretations of the poem or passage.
>
> 4. Employing a style that is consistently vivid and persuasive.
>
> 0 points:
> Does not meet the criteria for one point.

**The Literary Argument (or Open Question)** This is the third free-response question on the exam. It provides an opportunity to base your response on a text of your choice. There will be a list of texts you can choose from below the prompt, but you need not base your response on one of those texts. You are not expected to quote a text, but you are expected to know the text you choose well enough to make specific references to it. While all of the essays are arguments as you are trying to prove your interpretation, this one is the most argumentative as you are also arguing that your chosen text is a great choice to use to answer this prompt.

Like the first two FRQs, this prompt will provide you with a brief introduction to a topic—such as relationships, money, home, or family—but then ask you to develop the topic using a text of your choice.

The instructions for the third FRQ are very similar to the others.

In your response you should do the following:

- Respond to the prompt with a thesis that presents a defensible interpretation.
- Provide evidence to support your line of reasoning.
- Explain how the evidence supports your line of reasoning.
- Use appropriate grammar and punctuation in communicating your argument.

The rubric on the next page shows additional details for each of the three rows of the Literary Argument scoring guide. For even more detail, visit the College Board website and search for the latest scoring rubrics.

## Specifics for Scoring the Literary Argument (Open Question)

### A. THESIS (0–1 point)

1 point:

Responds to the prompt with a thesis that presents a defensible interpretation of the selected work.

0 points for any of the following:

- There is no defensible thesis.
- The intended thesis only restates the prompt.
- The intended thesis provides a summary of the issue with no apparent or coherent thesis.
- There is a thesis, but it does not respond to the prompt.

### B. EVIDENCE AND COMMENTARY (0–4 points)

4 points:

| EVIDENCE | COMMENTARY |
| --- | --- |
| Provides specific evidence to support all claims in a line of reasoning. | Consistently explains how the evidence supports a line of reasoning. |

3 points:

| EVIDENCE | COMMENTARY |
| --- | --- |
| Provides specific evidence to support all claims in a line of reasoning. | Explains how some of the evidence supports a line of reasoning. |

2 points:

| EVIDENCE | COMMENTARY |
| --- | --- |
| Provides some specific, relevant evidence. | Explains how some of the evidence relates to the student's argument, but no line of reasoning is established, or the line of reasoning is faulty. |

1 points:

| EVIDENCE | COMMENTARY |
| --- | --- |
| Provides evidence that is mostly general. | Summarizes the evidence but does not explain how the evidence supports the student's argument. |

0 points:

| EVIDENCE |
| --- |
| Simply restates thesis (if present), repeats provided information, or offers information irrelevant to the prompt. |

**C. SOPHISTICATION** (0–1 points)

1 point:

Demonstrates sophistication of thought and/or develops a complex literary argument by doing any of the following:

1. Identifying and exploring complexities or tensions within the poem.

2. Illuminating the student's interpretation by situating it within a broader context.

3. Accounting for alternative interpretations of the selected work.

4. Employing a style that is consistently vivid and persuasive.

0 points:

Does not meet the criteria for one point.

## Exam Weighting and Review

The College Board has published an explanation of which topics receive the most emphasis on the exam. The table below shows that "weighting." The percentages show the spread of questions on the exam. For example, questions on short fiction will make up between 42 and 49% of the exam.

| Exam Weighting | |
|---|---|
| Short Fiction (Units 1, 4, and 7) | 42–49% |
| Poetry (Units 2, 5, and 8) | 35–45% |
| Longer Fiction or Drama (Units 3, 6, and 9) | 15–18% |

## Review Schedule

Set up a review schedule as you prepare for the exam in the weeks before the test. Start a study group with some of your classmates to intensify your review by talking about the concepts and quizzing one another.

On the next page is a sample of an eight-week review schedule, including information on the units in this book that cover the content to review. Because AP® tests are given during the first two full weeks of May, this review schedule assumes you begin your review in mid-March.

The schedule is based on the weight given to each genre on the exam. Since short fiction receives the most weight, you should spend the most time reviewing that. You may follow the review schedule below or you may alter it to focus on areas that you know you need more review time. You may also want to review the units in the reverse order from the chart on the next page, so the EUs, Skills, and EKs related to short fiction are the freshest in your mind.

| Proposed Review Schedule | | |
|---|---|---|
| Week 1 | Short Fiction | Unit 1 |
| Week 2 | Short Fiction | Unit 4 |
| Week 3 | Short Fiction | Unit 7 |
| Week 4 | Review of Short Fiction | Units 1, 4, and 7 |
| Week 5 | Poetry | Unit 2 |
| Week 6 | Poetry | Unit 5 |
| Week 7 | Poetry | Unit 8 |
| Week 8 | Longer Fiction and Drama | Units 3, 6, and 9 |

## Other Review Suggestions

Use every possible way to make the material your own—read it, take notes on it, talk about it, create visualizations of it, and relate the ideas in this book to your prior experience and learning. In other words, think about how it connects to ideas in your other courses and to your personal life experiences. The following approaches will help you accomplish this goal:

- Start preparing for the AP® English Literature and Composition exam the **first day of class.**

- Form a **weekly study group**. Use the **Essential Question** from each unit part as the starting point for your discussion, focusing on how the material you learned during the week helps to answer that question. Ask questions about anything you do not understand. The weekly meetings ensure that you will prepare on a regular basis, and they also give you a chance to speak about and listen to the concepts you are learning in addition to reading and writing about them.

- **Work collaboratively** in other ways, such as doing the open-response activities in the Checkpoints.

- Use the **techniques of the cognitive scientists** (cognitive psychologists) at http://www.learningscientists.org/. They offer free and more detailed information on the six strategies outlined on the next page, which have been proven in research to help people learn.

| Research-Based Learning Strategies | |
| --- | --- |
| Distributed Practice | **Spread out** your studying over the entire course in manageable amounts. |
| Retrieval | After every class or on another regular schedule, close your book and try to recall the important points, using a practice called **retrieval**. You can use the graphic organizer that accompanies the Reflect on the Essential Question feature at the end of each chapter as a framework. Fill in whatever you can't retrieve from memory alone by going back into the book for the missing pieces. Whether you use sample multiple-choice questions, flash cards, or an online program such as Quizlet, take the time to test yourself with a friend or on your own. |
| Elaboration | When studying, **ask yourself questions** about what you are reading. How does this material connect to other material in the chapter? As you learn material, elaborate on it by connecting it to what you are experiencing in your daily life. |
| Interleaving | Few exams go in the order of how topics are presented in the text. The AP® Literature and Composition exam certainly does not. When you study, **interleave** the material. Switch up the order of your review. For example, when reviewing Chapters 1–3, change the order of your study. Switch it up to 2, 1, and 3. Then during your next review session, follow a different order—3, 2, and 1, for example. Use this technique only occasionally. |
| Concrete Examples | Write down all **concrete examples** your teacher uses in class. Note the examples given in this book. Use these examples to understand the application of the abstract concepts and ideas you are studying. |
| Dual Coding | Use **dual coding**, different ways of representing the information. Take notes or write reflections on a segment of text. Then create a visual representation of the same knowledge using graphic organizers, concept maps, drawings with labels, or other graphics. |

## Exam Day

Wake up in time to relax and eat a normal breakfast. If you are doing the written exam (that is, not on a computer), then bring two #2 pencils for the multiple-choice section, two black or blue ink pens for the free-response section, and a watch. Wear comfortable clothing suitable for a cold or hot testing room. Do not bring any books, laptops, cell phones, or any other connective device.

## Overall Scoring and Credit

The exams are scored in early June and reported back to you and your high school in mid-summer. You can earn between 0 and 6 points.

Many colleges award credit for a score of 3 or better; some require a 5; and occasionally prestigious universities do not recognize AP® exam performance. The College Board equates a score of 5 to an A in a college-level class; a 4 to an A-, B+, or B; and a 3 to roughly a B-, C+, or C.

Be realistic about expectations: In 2019, just over 6 percent of those taking the exam earned a score of 5. Of the nearly 400,000 students who took the exam in that year, no students earned all of the possible points. A score of 3 is realistic to qualify for credit, but for some people, a score of 2 will be honorable.

## A Final Note

"When I look back, I am so impressed again with the life-giving power of literature. If I were a young person today, trying to gain a sense of myself in the world, I would do that again by reading, just as I did when I was young."

—*Maya Angelou*

In your conscientious, rigorous, and intellectual study of literature as you prepare for college, leave space for the literature you read to "slide through your brain and go straight to your heart," to paraphrase another famous quote by writer Maya Angelou. It will have lasting rewards.

Brandon Abdon
Becky McFarlan

# UNIT 1

# Elements of Fiction

## [Short Fiction I]

**Part 1: Characters and Characterization**
**Part 2: Setting**
**Part 3: Plot**
**Part 4: Narrators and Speakers**
**Part 5: Writing About Literature I**

---

### ENDURING UNDERSTANDINGS AND SKILLS: Unit 1

## Part 1 Characters and Characterization

**Understand**

Characters in literature allow readers to study and explore a range of values, beliefs, assumptions, biases, and cultural norms represented by those characters. (CHR-1)

**Demonstrate**

Identify and describe what specific textual details reveal about a character, that character's perspective, and that character's motives. (1.A)

## Part 2 Setting

**Understand**

Setting and the details associated with it not only depict a time and place, but also convey values associated with that setting. (SET-1)

**Demonstrate**

Identify and describe specific textual details that convey or reveal a setting. (2.A)

## Part 3 Plot

**Understand**

The arrangement of the parts and sections of a text, the relationship of the parts to each other, and the sequence in which the text reveals information are all structural choices made by a writer that contribute to the reader's interpretation of a text. (STR-1)

**Demonstrate**

Identify and describe how plot orders events in a narrative. (3.A)
Explain the function of a particular sequence of events in a plot. (3.B)

## Part 4  Narrators and Speakers

### Understand

A narrator's or speaker's perspective controls the details and emphases that affect how readers experience and interpret a text. (NAR-1)

### Demonstrate

Identify and describe the narrator or speaker of a text. (4.A)

Identify and explain the function of point of view in a narrative. (4.B)

## Part 5  Writing About Literature I

### Understand

Readers establish and communicate their interpretations of literature through arguments supported by textual evidence. (LAN-1)

### Demonstrate

Develop a paragraph that includes 1) a claim that requires defense with evidence from the text and 2) the evidence itself. (7.A)

**Source:** *AP® English Literature and Composition Course and Exam Description*

# Unit 1 Overview

In 2009, Nigerian author Chimamanda Ngozi Adichie gave a TED Talk called "The Danger of a Single Story," which you can easily find and watch on YouTube. In this talk, Adichie discusses the importance of encountering stories from different types of people with different backgrounds and different experiences. She explains that she had grown up on a university campus in Nigeria—an African country influenced greatly by British culture because it was a British colony until the 1960s. As a child, she also read a lot. But the stories Adichie read were not from Africa. Instead, they were stories of White British children. When she eventually started to write, also as a child, she wrote about what she was reading. Her characters were White, they had blue eyes, they played in the snow, they drank ginger beer: all things that she, as a Black African child, had never done or experienced. She had only experienced those things through the stories that she read. The problem was that she was not encountering any stories that spoke to her own experiences.

Stories are ways of capturing experiences and allowing other people to participate in them. The details of a story show readers where to focus their attention. The characters of a story face problems and choices that affect them in some way. The setting of a story often affects how the events in the story, or the plot, play out. And the narrator of the story shapes how the reader feels about what is happening, as well as about the people the events affect. These elements—characters, setting, plot, and narrators—work together to capture and share experiences.

For these reasons, stories are powerful. Stories inspire emotion, causing readers to learn, laugh, cry, get angry, or get nervous, all because of the connection to an experience.

Adichie's story continued to develop. She began encountering African stories with characters who looked like her and who ate food she had eaten and who had experiences similar to her own. She realized that those British stories, though they were a part of who she was, were not capturing the experiences of everyone. Other stories from other places captured important experiences of people different from White British children. Through this process, Adichie discovered the danger of a single story—that if we experience only stories of a certain type, we will not develop diverse ways of seeing the world and ourselves. No one story captures all experience. Everyone has different experiences based on who they are, where they come from, and how they see the world.

Despite the diversity of people's experiences, however, literature—often defined as writing of excellent expressive quality that conveys complex ideas with lasting value—can sometimes rise above differences and speak clearly and inspiringly to readers no matter what their background. For this reason, readers can study and explore a range of values, beliefs, assumptions, biases, and cultural norms represented by diverse characters in literature.

**Literature and Complexity** One element that sets literature apart from ordinary communication is complexity. Literature, rich with stories whether in prose or poetry, often raises difficult questions. Complicated people and stories create dilemmas for the characters as well as for the readers, who may have even more questions after reading a particularly challenging text. Unlike many TV shows that introduce a dilemma that simple characters can resolve neatly in 23 minutes, literature tackles the complexities of life and carries readers along a winding path to try to make sense of them.

The focus of this unit is short fiction, including short stories. Short fiction is prose, not poetry. It differs from some other kinds of literature in that it can be read in a single sitting, has relatively few characters, and portrays the events surrounding a single main incident or situation. This unit focuses on analyzing a text to identify specific details that reveal a character's perspective and motives and the story's setting; identifying and understanding the narrator or speaker of a text; and writing a paragraph about a work of literature that includes a defensible claim supported by evidence.

To help you develop the skills of literary analysis and interpretation, this book will give you practice in

- close reading, a careful identification of the literary devices and other details that shape a text's purpose and theme

- analyzing literature, the identification of the role and impact of the literary elements, along with an explanation of how these elements interact to make a cohesive whole

- composing a literary argument, the creation of your own written interpretation of a text by creating an argument supported with textual evidence

- creating your own literary texts

To provide this practice, each unit includes

- an "anchor text," a high-quality written piece for you to analyze carefully, respond to in writing, and show comprehension of by answering AP®-style multiple-choice questions. An anchor icon like the one below accompanies each of these texts.

- analysis activities that provide practice in interpreting the tools writers use to create meaning—character, setting, structure, narration, and figurative language. You will also answer multiple-choice questions on the anchor text that are similar to those found on the AP® test.

- writing prompts like those you will see on the AP® exam to provide practice in creating your own arguments about literature

 **Short Story**
**"THE APPROPRIATION[1] OF CULTURES" by Percival Everett**

Following is a short story published in 1996 by author and distinguished professor Percival Everett. The anchor icon next to the heading tells you that this is a reading you will return to throughout this unit. The story focuses on the wealthy and educated Daniel Barkley and his encounters with people of varied cultures in the state of South Carolina.

1      Daniel Barkley had money left to him by his mother. He had a house which had been left to him by his mother. He had a degree in American Studies from Brown University which he had in some way earned but had not yet earned anything for him. He played a nineteen-forty Martin guitar[2] with a Barkus-Berry pickup[3] and drove a nineteen-seventy-six Jensen Interceptor[4] which he had purchased after his mother's sister had died and left him her money, she having had no children of her own. Daniel Barkley didn't work and didn't pretend to need to, spending most of his time reading. Some nights he went to a joint near the campus of the University of South Carolina and played jazz with some old guys who all worked very hard during the day, but didn't hold Daniel's condition against him.

2      Daniel played standards[5] with the old guys, but what he loved to play was old-time slide tunes.[6] One night, some white boys from a fraternity yelled forward to the stage at the black man holding the acoustic guitar and began to shout, "Play *Dixie*[7] for us! Play *Dixie* for us!"

---

1 **appropriation:** the taking of something for one's own use, typically without the owner's permission
2 **1940 Martin guitar:** an acoustic guitar worth tens of thousands of dollars
3 **Barkus-Berry pickup:** a microphone-like device that amplifies sound
4 **1976 Jensen Interceptor:** an expensive sports car
5 **standards:** tunes and songs well known among jazz musicians and fans
6 **old-time slide tunes:** songs in a style of guitar playing in which a bottleneck-shaped object is placed over a finger of one hand and slid along the strings while the other hand plucks the strings. The style is associated with the blues.
7 *Dixie*: Also known as "I wish I was in Dixie" or "Dixieland," "Dixie" is an American song from before the Civil War. It recalls the desire of a fictitious Black enslaved man to return to his plantation home in the American South. It eventually came to be known as the national anthem of the Confederate States during the American Civil War.

3    Daniel gave them a long look, studied their big-toothed grins and the beer-shiny eyes stuck into puffy, pale faces, hovering over golf shirts and chinos. He looked from them to the uncomfortable expressions on the faces of the old guys with whom he was playing and then to the embarrassed faces of the other college kids in the club.

4    And then he started to play. He felt his way slowly through the chords of the song once and listened to the deadened hush as it fell over the room. He used the slide to squeeze out the melody of the song he had grown up hating, the song the whites had always pulled out to remind themselves and those other people just where they were. Daniel sang the song. He sang it slowly. He sang it, feeling the lyrics, deciding that the lyrics were his, deciding that the song was his. *Old times there are not forgotten . . . .* He sang the song and listened to the silence around him. He resisted the urge to let satire ring through his voice. He meant what he sang. *Look away, look away, look away, Dixieland.*

5    When he was finished, he looked up to see the roomful of eyes on him. One person clapped. Then another. And soon the tavern was filled with applause and hoots. He found the frat boys in the back and watched as they stormed out, a couple of people near the door chuckling at them as they passed.

6    Roger, the old guy who played tenor sax, slapped Daniel on the back and said something like "Right on" or "Cool." Roger then played the first few notes of *Take the A Train*[8] and they were off. When the set was done, all the college kids slapped Daniel on the back as he walked toward the bar where he found a beer waiting.

7    Daniel didn't much care for the slaps on the back, but he didn't focus too much energy on that. He was busy trying to sort out his feelings about what he had just played. The irony of his playing the song straight and from the heart was made more ironic by the fact that as he played it, it came straight and from his heart, as he was claiming southern soil, or at least recognizing his blood in it. His was the land of cotton and hell no, it was not forgotten. At twenty-three his anger was fresh and typical, and so was his ease with it, the way it could be forgotten for chunks of time, until something like that night with the white frat boys or simply a flashing blue light in the rearview mirror brought it all back. He liked the song, wanted to play it again, knew that he would.

8    He drove home from the bar on Green Street and back to his house where he made tea and read about Pickett's charge at Gettysburg[9] while he sat in the big leather chair which had been his father's. He fell asleep and had a dream in which he stopped Pickett's men on the Emmitsburg Road on their way to the field and said, "Give me back my flag."

-------

---

8  *Take the A Train*: a jazz standard associated with the Duke Ellington band
9  **General George Edward Pickett (1825–1875):** a Confederate general during the American Civil War who led an unsuccessful and costly charge during the Battle of Gettysburg

9    Daniel's friend Sarah was a very large woman with a very large afro hairdo. They were sitting on the porch of Daniel's house having tea. The late fall afternoon was mild and slightly overcast. Daniel sat in the wicker rocker while Sarah curled her feet under her on the glider.

10    "I wish I could have heard it," Sarah said.

11    "Yeah, me too."

12    "Personally, I can't even stand to go in that place. All that drinking. Those white kids love to drink." Sarah studied her fingernails.

13    "I guess. The place is harmless. They seem to like the music."

14    "Do you think I should paint my nails?"

15    Daniel frowned at her. "If you want to."

16    "I mean really paint them. You know, black or with red, white and blue stripes. Something like that." She held her hand, appearing to imagine the colors. "I'd have to grow them long."

17    "What are you talking about?"

18    "Just bullsh*tting."

19    Daniel and Sarah went to a grocery market to buy food for lunch and Daniel's dinner. Daniel pushed the cart through the Piggly Wiggly[10] while Sarah walked ahead of him. He watched her large movements and her confident stride. At the checkout, he added a bulletin full of pictures of local cars and trucks for sale to his items on the conveyer.

20    "What's that for?" Sarah asked.

21    "I think I want to buy a truck."

22    "Buy a truck?"

23    "So I can drive you around when you paint your nails."

-------

24    Later, after lunch and after Sarah had left him alone, Daniel sat in his living room and picked up the car-sale magazine. As he suspected, there were several trucks he liked and one in particular, a nineteen-sixty-eight Ford three-quarter ton with the one thing it shared with the other possibilities, a full rear cab window decal of the Confederate flag. He called the number the following morning and arranged with Barb, Travis's wife, to stop by and see the truck.

-------

25    Travis and Barb lived across the river in the town of Irmo, a name which Daniel had always thought suited a disease for cattle. He drove around the maze of tract homes until he found the right street and number. A woman in a housecoat across the street watched from her porch, safe inside the chain-link fence around her yard. From down the street a man and a teenager who were covered with grease and apparently engaged in work on a torn-apart Dodge Charger mindlessly wiped their hands and studied him.

---

10 **Piggly Wiggly:** A grocery store chain found across much of the Southeastern and Midwestern United States

26    Daniel walked across the front yard, through a maze of plastic toys and knocked on the front door. Travis opened the door and asked in a surly voice, "What is it?"

27    "I called about the truck," Daniel said.

28    "Oh, you're Dan?"

29    Daniel nodded.

30    "The truck's in the back yard. Let me get the keys." He pushed the door to, but it didn't catch. Daniel heard the quality of the exchange between Travis and Barb, but not the words. He did hear Barb say, as Travis pulled open the door, "I couldn't tell over the phone?"

31    "Got 'em," Travis said. "Come on with me." He looked at Daniel's Jensen as they walked through the yard. "What kind of car is that?"

32    "It's a Jensen."

33    "Nice looking. Is it fast?"

34    "I guess."

35    The truck looked a little rough, a pale blue with a bleached out hood and a crack across the top of the windshield. Travis opened the driver's side door and pushed the key into the ignition. "It's a strong runner," he said. Daniel put his hand on the faded hood and felt the warmth, knew that Travis had already warmed up the motor. Travis turned the key and the engine kicked over. He nodded to Daniel. Daniel nodded back. He looked up to see a blonde woman looking on from behind the screen door of the back porch.

36    "The clutch and the alternator are new this year." Travis stepped backward to the wall of the bed and looked in. "There's some rust back here, but the bottom's pretty solid."

37    Daniel attended to the sound of the engine. "Misses just a little," he said.

38    "A tune-up will fix that."

39    Daniel regarded the rebel flag decal covering the rear window of the cab, touched it with his finger.

40    "That thing will peel right off," Travis said.

41    "No, I like it." Daniel sat down in the truck behind the steering wheel. "Mind if I take it for a spin?"

42    "Sure thing." Travis looked toward the house, then back to Daniel. "The brakes are good, but you got to press hard."

43    Daniel nodded.

44    Travis shut the door, his long fingers wrapped over the edge of the half-lowered glass. Daniel noticed that one of the man's fingernails was blackened.

45    "I'll just take it around a block or two."

46    The blonde woman was now standing outside the door on the concrete steps. Daniel put the truck in gear and drove out of the yard, past his car and down the street by the man and teenager who were still at work on the Charger. They stared at him, were still watching him as he turned right at the corner. The truck handled decently, but that really wasn't important.

47     Back at Travis's house Daniel left the keys in the truck and got out to observe the bald tires while Travis looked on. "The ad in the magazine said two-thousand."

48     "Yeah, but I'm willing to work with you."

49     "Tell you what, I'll give you twenty-two hundred if you deliver it to my house."

50     Travis was lost, scratching his head and looking back at the house for his wife who was no longer standing there. "Where abouts do you live?"

51     "I live over near the university. Near Five Points."

52     "Twenty-two hundred?" Travis said more to himself than to Daniel. "Sure I can get it to your house."

53     "Here's two-hundred." Daniel counted out the money and handed it to the man. "I'll have the rest for you in cash when you deliver the truck." He watched Travis feel the bills with his skinny fingers. "Can you have it there at about four?"

54     "I can do that."

-------

55     "What in the world do you need a truck for?" Sarah asked. She stepped over to the counter and poured herself another cup of coffee, then sat back down at the table with Daniel.

56     "I'm not buying the truck. Well, I am buying a truck, but only because I need the truck for the decal. I'm buying the decal."

57     "Decal?"

58     "Yes. This truck has a Confederate flag in the back window."

59     "What?"

60     "I've decided that the rebel flag is my flag. My blood is southern blood, right? Well, it's my flag."

61     Sarah put down her cup and saucer and picked up a cookie from the plate in the middle of the table. "You've flipped. I knew this would happen to you if you didn't work. A person needs to work."

62     "I don't need money."

63     "That's not the point. You don't have to work for money." She stood and walked to the edge of the porch and looked up and down the street.

64     "I've got my books and my music."

65     "You need a job so you can be around people you don't care about, doing stuff you don't care about. You need a job to occupy that part of your brain. I suppose it's too late now, though."

66     "Nonetheless," Daniel said. "You should have seen those redneck boys when I took *Dixie* from them. They didn't know what to do. So, the g\*ddamn flag is flying over the State Capitol.[11] Don't take it down, just take it. That's what I say."

67     "That's all you have to do? That's all there is to it."

68     "Yep." Daniel leaned back in his rocker. "You watch ol' Travis when he gets here."

---

11 Between 1962 and 2015, the battle flag of the Confederate States of America—sometimes known as the rebel flag—flew at the South Carolina capitol in Columbia.

69    Travis arrived with the pickup a little before four, his wife pulling up behind him in a yellow TransAm. Barb got out of the car and walked up to the porch with Travis. She gave the house a careful look. "Hey, Travis," Daniel said. "This is my friend, Sarah." Travis nodded hello. "You must be Barb," Daniel said. Barb smiled weakly. Travis looked at Sarah, then back at the truck and then to Daniel. "You sure you don't want me to peel that thing off the window?"

70    "I'm positive."

71    "Okay."

72    Daniel gave Sarah a glance, to be sure she was watching Travis's face. "Here's the balance," he said, handing over the money. He took the truck keys from the skinny fingers.

73    Barb sighed and asked as if the question was burning right through her. "Why do you want that flag on the truck?"

74    "Why shouldn't I want it?" Daniel asked.

75    Barb didn't know what to say. She studied her feet for a second, then regarded the house again. "I mean, you live in a nice house and drive that sports car. What do you need a truck like that for?"

76    "You don't want the money?"

77    "Yes, we want the money," Travis said, trying to silence Barb with a look.

78    "I need the truck for hauling stuff," Daniel said. "You know like groceries and—" He looked to Sarah for help.

79    "Books," Sarah said.

80    "Books. Things like that." Daniel held Barb's eyes until she looked away. He watched Travis sign his name to the back of the title and hand it to him and as he took it, he said, "I was just lucky enough to find a truck with the black power flag already on it."

81    "What?" Travis screwed up his face, trying to understand.

82    "The black power flag on the window. You mean, you didn't know?"

83    Travis and Barb looked at each other.

84    "Well, anyway," Daniel said. "I'm glad we could do business." He turned to Sarah. "Let me take you for a ride in my new truck." He and Sarah walked across the yard, got into the pickup and waved to Travis and Barb who were still standing in Daniel's yard as they drove away.

85    Sarah was on the verge of hysterics by the time they were out of sight. "That was beautiful," she said.

86    "No," Daniel said, softly. "That was true."

-------

87    Over the next weeks, sightings of Daniel and his truck proved problematic for some. He was accosted by two big white men in a '72 Monte Carlo in the parking lot of a 7-11 on Two Notch Road.

88    "What are you doing with that on your truck, boy?"[12] the bigger of the two asked.

89    "Flying it proudly," Daniel said, noticing the rebel front plate on the Chevrolet. "Just like you, brothers."

90    The confused second man took a step toward Daniel. "What did you call us?"

91    "Brothers."

92    The second man pushed Daniel in the chest with two extended fists, but not terribly hard.

93    "I don't want any trouble," Daniel told them.

94    Then a Volkswagen with four black teenagers parked in the slot beside Daniel's truck and they jumped out, staring and looking serious. "What's going on?" the driver and largest of the teenagers asked.

95    "They were admiring our flag," Daniel said, pointing to his truck.

96    The teenagers were confused.

97    "We fly the flag proudly, don't we, young brothers?" Daniel gave a bent arm, black power, closed-fist salute. "Don't we?" he repeated. "Don't we?"

98    "Yeah," the young men said.

99    The white men had backed away to their car. They slipped into it and drove away.

100    Daniel looked at the teenagers and with as serious a face as he could manage, he said, "Get a flag and fly it proudly."

-------

101    At a gas station, a lawyer named Ahmad Wilson stood filling the tank of his BMW and staring at the back window of Daniel's truck. He then looked at Daniel. "Your truck?" he asked.

102    Daniel stopped cleaning the windshield and nodded.

103    Wilson didn't ask a question, just pointed at the rear window of Daniel's pickup.

104    "Power to the people," Daniel said and laughed.

-------

105    Daniel played *Dixie* in another bar in town, this time with an R&B dance band at a banquet of the black medical association. The strange looks and expressions of outrage changed to bemused laughter and finally to open joking and acceptance as the song was played fast enough for dancing. Then the song was sung, slowly to the profound surprise of those singing the song. *I wish I was in the land of cotton, old times there are not forgotten . . . . Look away, look away, look away . . . .*

-------

106    Soon, there were several, then many cars and trucks in Columbia, South Carolina, sporting Confederate flags and being driven by black

---

**12 boy:** a term historically used as a racially derogatory term toward Black men whom racists saw as unworthy of being called "sir"

people. Black businessmen and ministers wore rebel flag buttons on their lapels and clips on their ties. The marching band of South Carolina State College, a predominantly black land grant institution in Orangeburg, paraded with the flag during homecoming. Black people all over the state flew the Confederate flag. The symbol began to disappear from the fronts of big rigs and the back windows of jacked-up four-wheelers. And after the emblem was used to dress the yards and mark picnic sites of black family reunions the following Fourth of July, the piece of cloth was quietly dismissed from its station with the U.S. and state flags atop the State Capitol. There was no ceremony, no notice. One day, it was not there.

107    *Look away, look away, look away . . . .*

 **What Do You Know?**

This unit will explore how details in a text reveal characters and settings. It will also examine the significance of a sequence of events in the plot of a narrative, as well as how to interpret a work's point of view and the narrator's and characters' perspectives. Before you learn new skills and information, assess what you already know. Answer the following questions about "The Appropriation of Cultures." Don't worry if you find these challenging. Answering questions on a subject before formally learning about it is one way to help you deepen your understanding of new concepts.

## CLOSE READING

1. What are a few key details about each of the main characters? What do those details convey about the characters? What are some things readers don't know about the characters that could have been told?

2. What are some of the values that might be associated with different settings in the story (the bar, Daniel's house, Travis's house)? What details indicate these values?

3. What are the cause-and-effect incidents in the plot? What occurs that causes other things to occur?

4. What do readers know about the narrator of the story? What are some details in the story that reveal the perspective of the narrator?

5. What is the narrator's point of view? How might that point of view influence what the narrator relates about the events of the narrative? How might the story be different if told from a different point of view or by a different narrator (say, one that is a character in the story)?

## INTERPRETATION

1. What bigger idea or theme might the story be about? What might it be saying about something beyond the story?

2. What are the most important pieces of information in the text that would support your idea about what the story is about (that is, your interpretation)?

**Source:** Niday Picture Library / Alamy Stock Photo

Painting of Confederate soldiers furling the Confederate battle flag after the 1865 surrender to Robert E. Lee at Appomattox Courthouse, VA. (Richard Norris Brooke, Furling the Flag, 1872. Oil on canvas.) The Confederate flag largely disappeared after the war until the 1950s and 1960s when the civil rights movement gained strength. It was reintroduced to signal support for White supremacy.

*Research the events of the summer of 2017 in Charleston, South Carolina, that led to the vote to remove the Confederate flag from the South Carolina State House grounds. Write a paragraph or discuss in a group how the meaning attached to a symbol can change quickly.*

# Characters and Characterization

**Enduring Understanding and Skill**

## Part 1

### Understand

Characters in literature allow readers to study and explore a range of values, beliefs, assumptions, biases, and cultural norms represented by those characters. (CHR-1)

### Demonstrate

Identify and describe what specific textual details reveal about a character, that character's perspective, and that character's motives. (1.A)
See also Units 2, 3, 4 & 6

**Source:** *AP® English Literature and Composition Course and Exam Description*

**Essential Question:** How do details in a text reveal character, perspectives, and motives?

A **character** is someone who actually does things in a work of literature. Characters make choices that affect themselves and other characters and cause things to happen in the story. Without characters and the actions they take, stories would have no way of moving forward. More important, characters often reflect something about real people and real experiences, providing insight into the human condition. Characters are a key element of literature: they invite readers to connect their lives to stories and experience events and relationships vicariously.

| KEY TERMS | | |
|---|---|---|
| character | perspective | motives |
| details | bias | |

# 1.1 The Details that Create Characters | CHR-1.A, CHR-1.B

The author of a story reveals characters in different ways. The process of shaping readers' impressions of characters is called *characterization*. Authors use description, dialogue, and behavior to reveal characters. Description can come from a speaker, a narrator, or the characters themselves.

## Description, Dialogue, and Behavior

Sometimes an author reveals characters through description—writing whose purpose is to help readers vividly see or understand a character. Authors may use *direct characterization* by providing **details**, pieces of specific information, the reader learns directly from the narrator or other characters. For example, a narrator might say, "Daniel was unpredictable," telling readers directly about an attribute of the character.

Sometimes an author reveals characters through dialogue, or conversations between characters, and behavior, or the things characters do. The method of revealing character by letting readers observe what the character does or says is called *indirect characterization*. For example, a writer might show Daniel saying certain things or doing certain things that a reader might not have predicted from the character—agreeing to play "Dixie" and then delighting in it, for example—and readers can then draw conclusions from this detail of his behavior. During an initial reading of a text, a reader takes in all of those details and forms a general impression. Then a close reader looks back and considers how specific details of description, dialogue, and behavior contribute to that impression and possibly suggest bigger ideas.

**Source:** Getty Images

The author does not provide many details about Daniel, but the narrator lets readers know that Daniel drives an expensive 1976 Jensen Interceptor (similar to the model shown above). A number of different cars and trucks are mentioned throughout the story, each providing a detail about the characters who drive them.

As you read the following passage from "The Appropriation of Cultures," look for the details about characters that are revealed through description, dialogue, and behavior. What impression do they create?

| Description/ Behavior | Daniel's friend Sarah was a very large woman with a very large afro hairdo. They were sitting on the porch of Daniel's house having tea. The late fall afternoon was mild and slightly overcast. Daniel sat in the wicker rocker while Sarah curled her feet under her on the glider. |
|---|---|
| Dialogue | "I wish I could have heard it," Sarah said. |
| | "Yeah, me too." |
| | "Personally, I can't even stand to go in that place. All that drinking. Those white kids love to drink." Sarah studied her fingernails. |
| | "I guess. The place is harmless. They seem to like the music." |
| | "Do you think I should paint my nails?" |
| | Daniel frowned at her. "If you want to." |
| | "I mean really paint them. You know, black or with red, white and blue stripes. Something like that." She held her hand, appearing to imagine the colors. "I'd have to grow them long." |
| | "What are you talking about?" |
| | "Just bullsh*tting." |
| Description/ Behavior | Daniel and Sarah went to a grocery market to buy food for lunch and Daniel's dinner. Daniel pushed the cart through the Piggly Wiggly while Sarah walked ahead of him. He watched her large movements and her confident stride. At the checkout, he added a bulletin full of pictures of local cars and trucks for sale to his items on the conveyor. |

Table 1-1

Most readers would probably note that the description of Sarah and the information the author includes about Daniel's observations of her paints a picture of a strong woman, confident about who she is and comfortable with Daniel. Analytical readers learn to identify or notice the details that help convey or create such impressions. For example, Sarah's large afro could convey that she embraces her physical self and heritage; her feet curled as she sat on the glider indicate her ability to relax and be at ease; her attention to her fingernails while she talks to Daniel displays a nonchalant, no-worries attitude to the situation; Daniel's observation about her behavior makes a statement to the reader about who she is. Another detail of interest to Sarah's character is her thinking about painting her nails with red, white, and blue stripes.

## Says Who?

Characterization is affected by who is doing the describing. A speaker, a narrator, or the characters themselves may offer the descriptive details, each possibly providing a different slant. Always ask, "Says who?" when evaluating a description of a character. For example, characters may be overly negative when describing characters they do not like or overly positive about those they love very much. A narrator may have a neutral viewpoint, or a narrator may be *unreliable*—someone whose credibility is suspect. The source of the information about a character is therefore a key consideration in forming an impression of a character. Bias, or an uneven, unfair viewpoint (see page 20), often creeps into even the smallest detail and can affect the way a reader sees a character. For a full depiction of a character, readers need to consider details provided from a variety of sources.

The chart below shows the tools authors use in characterization. You can remember these tools with the help of the word *STEAL*, which is spelled by putting together the first letter of each of the tools.

| STEAL for Examining Characters | |
| --- | --- |
| **Tools of Characterization** | **Questions to Ask** |
| **S**peech | • What does the character say?<br>• What does the character reveal about himself or herself and others in dialogue with other characters?<br>• Does the character tell readers about himself or herself directly, or is someone else telling readers about the character?<br>• Are readers told what the character said, or do they see the character actually say it? |
| **T**houghts | • What is the character thinking?<br>• How do readers know what that character is thinking? Who tells them?<br>• Do the character's actions or words match his or her thoughts? |
| **E**ffects on others | • How do others react to the character?<br>• What does the character do to other characters?<br>• What do other characters do to that character?<br>• Who tells the reader these things? |
| **A**ctions | • How does that character behave?<br>• Does the behavior match the speech and/or thoughts?<br>• Does behavior of the character change?<br>• Does the character choose to not do something? |
| **L**ooks | • What details describe the appearance of the character?<br>• Does that appearance change based on who is describing?<br>• What impression does that description create? |

Table 1-2

 **Remember:** Description, dialogue, and behavior reveal characters to readers. Descriptions of characters may come from a speaker, narrator, other characters, or the characters themselves. (CHR-1.A–B)

## 1.1 Checkpoint

*Reread the short story "The Appropriation of Cultures" on pages 4–11. Then complete the open-response activity and answer the multiple-choice question.*

1. On separate paper, recreate Table 1-2 on the previous page based on "The Appropriation of Cultures." Choose one character from the story and answer as many of the questions as you can in column 2 to examine characterization.

2. Daniel says, "Tell you what, I'll give you twenty-two hundred if you deliver it to my house" (paragraph 49). What does this dialogue most likely reveal about Daniel's character?

   (A) Daniel is generous with his money.

   (B) Daniel does not like to exert too much effort.

   (C) Daniel feels sorry for Travis and wants to help him out.

   (D) Daniel takes some pleasure in subverting racial power.

   (E) Daniel wants to impress Sarah with his wealth.

### Creating on Your Own

*(These sections encourage you to become an author yourself. Don't worry about "getting it right" or even revising right now. Just write and get ideas on paper.)*

Imagine a conversation about a controversial topic. Maybe people are arguing. Maybe someone is simply explaining something to another. Write out the conversation in a dialogue. What can a reader learn about the different people involved from what you write? Revise what you have written to include some descriptions and behavior. Try to include a mix of showing who the characters are and telling who they are. Save your work.

# 1.2 Perspective | CHR-1.C, CHR-1.D

People are the sum of their backgrounds and experiences. The situations they face, the people they encounter, and the events they walk through shape who they are and how they see the world. The way people see and understand the world is called perspective.

In literature, **perspective** is the way narrators, characters, or speakers understand their circumstances.

## Factors that Inform Perspective

Perspective is informed, or influenced, by the characters' background, personality traits, biases, and relationships. A character's perspective is also both shaped and revealed by relationships with other characters, the events of the plot, and the ideas expressed in the text. People's (and characters') perspectives motivate, or drive, them to take (or avoid) certain actions. Background, personalities, biases, and relationships all influence the perspective of speakers, narrators, and characters. Their perspectives, in turn, influence their **motives**—their reasons for doing and saying the things they do.

**Background and Experience** Consider the table below. How have the things that are part of Daniel's background and experiences in "The Appropriation of Cultures" influenced his perspective, and how do they motivate him?

| Examining Character Perspectives—Daniel | | | |
|---|---|---|---|
| Experiences prior to the beginning of the story (if we know) → | How may these experiences have affected Daniel's perspective and motivated him? | Experiences during the story → | How might these have affected Daniel's perspective and motivated him? |
| • He had a lot of money left to him by his mother.<br>• He earned a degree in American Studies from an Ivy League university.<br>• He played jazz guitar some nights because he wanted to.<br>• He has experienced the feeling of seeing the "blue light" of the police behind him. | • He wasn't struggling or facing much adversity because he had money.<br>• His education shaped his perspective on American culture.<br>• His appreciation for music may have meant he valued other types of arts, too, and knew the power of artistic expression.<br>• He may have felt fear of, and anger about, racial profiling by police officers. | • He was asked to play "Dixie," a song often associated with racism and bigotry.<br>• He hears Sarah bring up painting her nails red, white, and blue while he is still thinking about playing "Dixie."<br>• He is accosted by "two big white men" who are confused by the flag decal on his truck. | • He played the song his way and shocked everyone; he saw the power of thwarting expectations.<br>• The color imagery may have made him think about doing with the rebel flag what he had done with the song.<br>• He sees that his use of the flag is getting attention and confusing people, just as his way of playing "Dixie" confused the frat boys in the bar. |

Table 1-3

**Personality Traits** Good writers create realistic characters who have their own complex personalities. These individual personality traits can also influence characters' perspectives. Consider the following sentences from the narrator of "The Appropriation of Cultures."

- "When he was finished, he looked up to see the roomful of eyes on him. One person clapped. Then another. And soon the tavern was filled with applause and hoots. He found the frat boys in the back and watched as they stormed out, a couple of people near the door chuckling at them as they passed." (paragraph 5)

- "Daniel played *Dixie* in another bar in town, this time with an R&B dance band at a banquet of the black medical association." (paragraph 106)

In both of these examples—100 paragraphs apart—Daniel shows that he is not afraid to challenge people and that he knows the power that music and culture can have. These personality traits—introduced early in the story and reinforced near the end—help shape Daniel's perspective. Daniel's willingness to challenge others' perspectives, an aspect of his personality, drives the action.

Reread paragraphs 69–86 in "The Appropriation of Cultures" and pay close attention to the details included about Travis and what those details may reveal about his character. Through a close reading of those paragraphs, you likely learn that Travis is a man of his word who, though he is still confused by Daniel, offers to help him by removing the flag decal. Because he wants—or maybe needs—the money for the truck, Travis wants to remain willfully ignorant about why Daniel wants the decal to remain.

The chart below shows the relationship between Travis's character traits and his perspective.

| Travis's Personality Traits | Textual Evidence | How Travis's Personality Traits Inform His Perspective |
|---|---|---|
| True to his word and wants to be helpful | "Travis arrived with the pickup a little before four . . ." (paragraph 69) just as Daniel requested in paragraph 49. <br><br> "You sure you don't want me to peel that thing off the window?" (paragraph 69) | He just wants to keep to his word to deliver the truck and collect the money. He likely knows that the flag can be offensive, particularly to African Americans, because it represents a society that enslaved people. So he offers to remove it, which he probably sees as being helpful. |
| Willfully ignorant | " 'Yes, we want the money,' Travis said, trying to silence Barb with a look." (paragraph 77) <br><br> " 'What?' " Travis screwed up his face, trying to understand." (paragraph 81) <br><br> "Travis and Barb looked at each other." (paragraph 83) | Because of the money involved, Travis does not see the need to question Daniel's motives for buying the truck or keeping the flag. Though he clearly doesn't understand something, he either doesn't care enough to ask or is afraid of losing the money. |

Table 1-4

**Biases and Relationships** Because well-developed characters usually have unique perspectives and personalities, they also carry something that all readers also carry and cannot escape: bias. **Bias** is the inclination to like, dislike, or just have an opinion about something or someone based on experiences. When examining how a character develops in a story, pay close attention to the possible biases in the perspectives of the characters.

Bias in characters is often influenced by their relationships and their interactions with other characters. For example, in "The Appropriation of Cultures," Sarah's description of Daniel's interactions with Travis would likely differ from Barb's because the two women have different relationships with the two men. Both would be biased toward the person to whom they are closest. The descriptions of the interactions between Daniel and Travis would also likely differ because Sarah observes the interaction as a Black woman and Barb as a White woman, each with a bias based on her background and experiences.

The diagram below shows how Sarah's relationship and interactions with Daniel may have influenced her perspective on him.

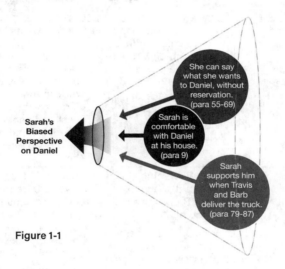

Figure 1-1

While Sarah has a carefree and honest relationship with Daniel, Barb's relationship with Travis stands in stark contrast. The conversation between Barb and Travis when Daniel arrives to see the truck is mostly unheard. But what Daniel and Sarah *do* hear (she "couldn't tell over the phone"—in response to a question about Daniel being Black, paragraph 30)—and Travis's attempt to "silence Barb with a look") all point to his having a controlling influence over her. Later in the story, in contrast, Daniel looks to Sarah not to silence her but to engage her help in thinking of reasons why he needs the truck (paragraph 78). Daniel also makes a point of holding "Barb's eyes until she looked away" (paragraph 80), intentionally exerting a kind of power often historically asserted by a White person over a Black person, demonstrating a bias as someone who may have been on the receiving end of that exercise of power.

# Shaping Perspective

The perspectives of the characters in "The Appropriation of Cultures" have been shaped by their relationships with one another, their environment, the events that unfold in the plot, and the ideas in the text. The table below provides examples.

| Influences | Textual Evidence | How the Influence Shapes Perspective |
|---|---|---|
| Relationships | "Daniel Barkley had money left to him by his mother. He had a house which had been left to him by his mother. He had a degree in American Studies from Brown University which he had in some way earned but had not yet earned anything for him. He played a nineteen-forty Martin guitar with a Barkus-Berry pickup and drove a nineteen-seventy-six Jensen Interceptor which he had purchased after his mother's sister had died and left him her money, she having had no children of her own." (paragraph 1) | Although the details are few, they suggest that Daniel's relationship with his parents may have helped him develop a sense of himself in the world. His parents probably nurtured his musical and academic interests. These relationships likely helped Daniel develop the perspective that he was a person of worth. |
| Environment | "One night, some white boys from a fraternity yelled forward to the stage at the black man holding the acoustic guitar and began to shout, 'Play *Dixie* for us! Play *Dixie* for us!' (paragraph 2)<br><br>"Daniel gave them a long look, studied their big-toothed grins and the beer-shiny eyes stuck into puffy, pale faces, hovering over golf shirts and chinos. He looked from them to the uncomfortable expressions on the faces of the old guys with whom he was playing and then to the embarrassed faces of the other college kids in the club." (paragraph 3)<br><br>"At twenty-three his anger was fresh and typical, and so was his ease with it, the way it could be forgotten for chunks of time, until something like that night with the white frat boys or simply a flashing blue light in the rearview mirror brought it all back." (paragraph 7) | Daniel has grown up in the South amidst racial prejudice, as shown by the attempt of the frat boys to prod him to do something they thought would humiliate him and the possibility of profiling by police officers. His environment has given Daniel a perspective that people with racial privilege in a culture of widespread racism can cause him harm. At the same time, the embarrassment of the other college kids in the club shows that Daniel's environment also includes fair-minded people, so while he has an angry perspective, he can forget about it "for chunks of time." |

*continued*

| Influences | Textual Evidence | How the Influence Shapes Perspective |
|---|---|---|
| Events | "And then he started to play. He felt his way slowly through the chords of the song once and listened to the deadened hush as it fell over the room. He used the slide to squeeze out the melody of the song he had grown up hating, the song the whites had always pulled out to remind themselves and those other people just where they were. Daniel sang the song. He sang it slowly. He sang it, feeling the lyrics, deciding that the lyrics were his, deciding that the song was his. Old times there are not forgotten . . . ." (paragraph 4) | While the event that starts the story in motion is the insulting request of the frat boys that Daniel play "Dixie," the event that shapes Daniel's perspective is the way he finds himself singing it. His perspective on racial symbols shifts as a result of that event. This is the first example of Daniel's appropriation of a racial symbol to overcome the power such symbols have to perpetuate racism. The act of appropriation is so important that it is reflected in the title of the story. |
| Ideas | "What in the world do you need a truck for?" Sarah asked. She stepped over to the counter and poured herself another cup of coffee, then sat back down at the table with Daniel.<br><br>"I'm not buying the truck. Well, I am buying a truck, but only because I need the truck for the decal. I'm buying the decal."<br><br>"Decal?"<br><br>"Yes. This truck has a Confederate flag in the back window."<br><br>"What?"<br><br>"I've decided that the rebel flag is my flag. My blood is southern blood, right? Well, it's my flag." (paragraphs 55–60) | Daniel's perspective is shaped by the idea that he first discovers in the bar—that objects or symbols (or songs) that have been infused with meaning only have that meaning because people have agreed on that meaning. Daniel takes that idea and decides to attach his own meaning to Confederate symbols and spread that meaning when he can. |

**Table 1-5**

## Revealing Perspective

The relationships, environment, and plot events in a story also *reveal* characters' perspectives. For example, suppose a character in a story is a man who had been bullied as a child. The relationships he had with people who hurt him shaped his perspective, likely making him see the world as something of a threat. That perspective, in turn, is revealed as he interacts gruffly with people, assuming the worst of them. When they respond with hostility, his worldview or perspective is reinforced.

But suppose he meets a person who treats him with extraordinary kindness despite his gruffness. That unexpected act of kindness now softens him and begins to reshape his perspective. The next time he encounters someone, he is less gruff and more trusting. That changed behavior is revealing of his changed perspective.

An unexpected act of kindness or a helping hand when needed can take the edges off gruffness and reshape a person's perspective.

In "The Appropriation of Cultures," Daniel's perspective has been shaped by his relationships and environment and the events and ideas in the story, but it is also *revealed* through those same elements as he continues his mission throughout the story to appropriate symbols of Southern racism. His perspective as a person with the upper hand is revealed in his relationship with Travis and Barb. It is revealed in his environment when he drives around proudly with the decal on his truck. The events of his encounters with other motorists and his fascination with the idea of appropriation also reveal his shifted perspective.

**Remember:** Perspective is how narrators, characters, or speakers understand their circumstances, and is informed by background, personality traits, biases, and relationships. A character's perspective is both shaped and revealed by relationships with other characters, the environment, the events of the plot, and the ideas expressed in the text. (CHR-1.C–D)

## 1.2 Checkpoint

*Review the short story "The Appropriation of Cultures" on pages 4–11. Then complete the open-response activities and answer the multiple-choice questions.*

1. Find textual evidence in the story that shows Daniel's relationship with Sarah. Then complete the chart below, adding more rows as needed. One row is done for you.

| Analysis of Daniel's Relationship with Sarah | | |
|---|---|---|
| **Textual Evidence** | **How It Shapes Daniel's Perspective** | **How It Reveals Daniel's Perspective** |
| "Daniel's friend Sarah was a very large woman with a very large afro hairdo. . . . 'So I can drive you around when you paint your nails.'" (paragraphs 9–24) | Daniel's first response to Sarah wanting to paint her nails is to frown. But he shortly changes his perspective to support her idea and even wants to drive her around in a truck. | Daniel sees confidence in the "large movements" of Sarah as she walks in front of him in the Piggly Wiggly. That sense of Sarah reveals his perspective that striding out into the world with confidence is valuable. |
| | | |
| | | |
| | | |

2. Write two to three sentences explaining how Daniel's relationship with Travis both shapes and reveals Daniel's perspective.

3. In "The Appropriation of Cultures," which part of Daniel's experiences most likely has the greatest influence on his perspective?

   (A) Having an education

   (B) Being friends with Sarah

   (C) Driving a 1976 Jensen

   (D) Not having a job

   (E) Being a musician

4. Sarah says to Daniel, "You need a job so you can be around people you don't care about, doing stuff you don't care about. You need a job to occupy that part of your brain. I suppose it's too late now, though." (paragraph 65) What does this statement suggest about the possible bias in Daniel's perspective?

    (A) Daniel has lost his opportunity to be open minded about others.

    (B) Daniel's perspective is biased because he has been belittled about not having a job.

    (C) Daniel lacks perspective because his brain is too occupied with his own concerns.

    (D) Daniel's perspective on White people is biased because of the environment of the South.

    (E) Daniel's perspective on working people may be biased because he does not have to work.

**Creating on Your Own**

Look back at the dialogue you wrote in the last Creating on Your Own activity. Choose one of the characters in the dialogue and spend five to ten minutes writing a background on that person, including experiences, relationships, and environment. What details about that person's experience are important to understanding his or her perspective? Save your work.

# Part 1   Apply What You Have Learned

Review "The Appropriation of Cultures" on pages 4–11. Write a paragraph that identifies specific textual details related to a character and describes how those details reveal that character and that character's perspective and/or motives in the story.

**Reflect on the Essential Question** Write a brief response that answers this essential question: *How do details in a text reveal character, motives, and perspectives?* In your answer, correctly use the key terms listed on page 13.

# Setting

**Essential Question:** What textual details reveal a story's setting?

The location of an event affects how it is perceived. Consider the act of praying. A reader would perceive a character praying in a church as normal. A character praying in the middle of a restaurant may be a less common sight but still not unheard of. But readers would perceive a character kneeling and praying at midnight in the middle of a busy street during a thunderstorm as something quite out of the ordinary. The location and time of the scene and even the weather dramatically affect the perception of the character's act of praying. Readers use descriptive details the author provides about the location of the action, or the **setting**, to build their understanding of the story and the characters in it. Setting details are an essential part of a story. Settings, like characters, offer points of connection for readers.

---

**KEY TERMS**

| | | |
|---|---|---|
| setting | place | values |
| time | | |

---

**Source:** Getty Images

*What do the details in this photo convey about the setting?*

# 2.1 Time and Place | SET-1.A

Setting includes the **time** and **place** of the events in the text. *When* something happens matters as much as *where*. For example, readers expect a character to wake from deep sleep in the morning. But if a character wakes from deep sleep sometime after everyone else has had dinner, then something interesting, or at least unexpected, is happening. The setting has captured the reader's attention.

## The When and the Where

Readers use the experiences they have had with different times and places to imagine themselves in the settings the author describes. As they do, they recognize the **values**—concepts of enduring worth and importance—and principles associated with the time and place of the story. Consider the settings mentioned above: church, restaurant, busy street, morning, after dinner, thunderstorm. Readers will associate a variety of experiences with those details of setting that may call to mind certain values. For example, the values of peace and faith might be associated with a church.

How characters interact with a setting can also reveal their values. For example, the "frat boys" stand apart from others in the way they interact with the setting of the bar, a place where musicians gather for the pleasure of playing together, and listeners come to enjoy music and feel some camaraderie. The frat boys' attempt to disrupt the easy friendliness shows they value a sense of superiority over the fellowship other patrons seem to value.

In addition to conveying associations and even values to the readers, setting also affects the characters. For example, after leaving the bar, Daniel arrives home and settles in with a cup of tea to read "while he sat in the big leather chair which had been his father's." He seems completely at ease in his home, and strength that comes from that kind of comfort may have made it possible for him to dream he reclaimed the flag from General Pickett. Similarly, the experience of watching Sarah stride with confidence as they shop suggests a dignity about her that contrasts with the environment of the Piggly Wiggly with its silly name, perhaps inspiring Daniel to decide to buy the magazine with cars for sale. Close readers pay attention to how the details of settings influence characters.

Contrast, such as that between Sarah's proud confidence and the down-home nature of the grocery store, is often a key part of setting. Sarah seems so large and impressive, all the more so in contrast to the store named Piggly Wiggly, which conjures diminutive and silly surroundings.

The occurrence of an unusual event in usual, or ordinary, settings presents another kind of contrast. Read the following example of an unusual awakening from the first two paragraphs of Franz Kafka's novella, or short novel, *The Metamorphosis*. The words in bold are details of a usually normal morning scene.

> As Gregor Samsa **awoke one morning** from uneasy dreams he found himself transformed in his **bed** into a gigantic insect. He was lying on his hard, as it were armor-plated, back and when he lifted his head a little he could see his dome-like brown belly divided into stiff arched segments on top of which the **bed quilt** could hardly keep in position and was about to slide off completely. His numerous legs, which were pitifully thin compared to the rest of his bulk, waved helplessly before his eyes.
>
> What has happened to me? he thought. It was no dream. His **room, a regular human bedroom**, only rather **too small**, lay **quiet** between the **four familiar walls.**

Here, Gregor *awakes* in his bed, with his *quilt*, in his *bedroom*—but it is *too small* in the *four familiar walls* of what the reader will soon discover is the house he shares with his parents and sister. The reader is reminded that this is just "a regular human bedroom," where a most irregular inhabitant, a human-sized insect, would not normally be expected. The setting challenges readers' expectations and upends the values normally associated with the scene, making readers wonder how and why this situation is happening. That clash of the readers' expectations with the surprises of the unfolding scene makes readers want to keep reading to find an explanation. The situation chart on the next page shows that clash detail by detail.

| Situation | | |
|---|---|---|
| Gregor has awoken and found himself turned into a giant bug. | | |
| The text says . . . | Readers say . . . | Therefore . . . |
| Setting details from text (textual evidence of time and place) | Values or things associated with those setting details | What is the effect of the setting on the situation of the text? |
| One morning | Should be a time of renewal, a fresh start to a new day. | Gregor's transformation is unexpected because there is no indication he was prepared for it. The room is too small, and he is on his back on the bed, about to slide off. Also, that he is in a familiar place with something so strange happening may really drive home how unexpected this was. Nothing about the setting seems to indicate that such a strange thing would happen. |
| Bed and bed quilt | Rest, comfort | |
| Bedroom—too small | Place of one's own, but this one is not big enough for him | |
| Four familiar walls | A place that he knows well | |

Table 1-6

Had this extraordinary event taken place in a magical cave, or had Gregor dreamed he had been visited by an evil wizard in his bedroom, the reader—and Gregor—might have been better prepared for what happened. However, everything about the setting suggests a normal night at home.

 **Remember:** Setting includes the time and place during which the events of the text occur. (SET-1.A)

## 2.1 Checkpoint

*Review the short story "The Appropriation of Cultures" on pages 4–11. Then complete the open-response activity and answer the multiple-choice question.*

1. In "The Appropriation of Cultures," the following details describe aspects of the settings. Make a chart like the situation chart above to help you examine how both time and place in these textual details suggest certain values or associations and what those might convey about the situation of the text.

   - "Some nights he went to a joint near the campus of the University of South Carolina and played jazz with some old guys who all worked very hard during the day, but didn't hold Daniel's condition against him." (paragraph 1)

- "They were sitting on the porch of Daniel's house having tea. The late fall afternoon was mild and slightly overcast. Daniel sat in the wicker rocker while Sarah curled her feet under her on the glider." (paragraph 9)

- "A woman in a housecoat across the street watched from her porch, safe inside the chain-link fence around her yard. From down the street a man and a teenager who were covered with grease and apparently engaged in work on a torn-apart Dodge Charger mindlessly wiped their hands and studied him." (paragraph 26)

- "Daniel played *Dixie* in another bar in town, this time with an R&B dance band at a banquet of the black medical association. The strange looks and expressions of outrage changed to bemused laughter and finally to open joking and acceptance as the song was played fast enough for dancing." (paragraph 106)

2. In "The Appropriation of Cultures," which of the following details of the settings reveals the most about what Daniel values?

    (A) "played jazz with some old guys who all worked very hard during the day" (paragraph 1)

    (B) "The late fall afternoon was mild and slightly overcast." (paragraph 9)

    (C) "A woman in a housecoat across the street watched from her porch." (paragraph 25)

    (D) "The blonde woman was now standing outside the door on the concrete steps." (paragraph 46)

    (E) "this time with an R&B dance band at a banquet of the black medical association" (paragraph 105)

**Creating on Your Own**

Review the conversation and the character(s) you wrote about in previous Creating on Your Own activities. Then write for five to ten minutes creating the setting of this conversation. Consider these questions: Where is this conversation taking place? Why is it taking place where it is? What does the setting say about the people and/or the conversation? Save your work.

Review "The Appropriation of Cultures." Write a paragraph that identifies specific details related to the time and place of a setting or settings in the story and describe how those details create a setting. Also explain how that setting may relate to the situation of the story.

**Reflect on the Essential Question**  Write a brief response that answers the essential question: *What textual details reveal a story's setting?* In your answer, correctly use the key terms listed on page 26.

**Source:** Getty Images

*How does the outdoor nighttime setting affect your impression of the conversation these people are having? What values and associations do you bring to this setting? What story might unfold in this setting?*

# Part 3

# Plot

**Enduring Understanding and Skills**

## Part 3

### Understand
The arrangement of the parts and sections of a text, the relationship of the parts to each other, and the sequence in which the text reveals information are all structural choices made by a writer that contribute to the reader's interpretation of a text. (STR-1)

### Demonstrate
Identify and describe how plot orders events in a narrative. (3.A)
Explain the function of a particular sequence of events in a plot. (3.B)

See also Units 4, 6 & 7

**Source:** *AP® English Literature and Composition Course and Exam Description*

**Essential Question:** How does the plot order the events of the narrative, and how does a particular sequence of events in a plot function?

The novel *Native Son* (1940) by Richard Wright is about the struggles, hopes, and tragedies of Bigger Thomas, a young Black man trying to make his way despite the racial oppression that shapes his life. At the beginning of the novel, readers learn that Bigger's family is poor and lives in a rat-infested one-room apartment in racially segregated Chicago. However, Bigger soon lands a job with the Daltons, a White family. Bigger's taking a new job sets off a series of incidents and events that lead him—and the reader—through the rest of the book. That one event, or cause—taking the job at the Daltons' house—affects the events of the story all the way to the very last page. No matter their length (short stories, novellas, or novels), stories are all cause and effect—something happens that causes something else to happen that causes two other things to happen, and so on to the end.

The connection of events that lead the characters and reader through the story is called plot. Professor Alan Cheuse and writer Nicholas Delbanco refer to plot as "an artful arrangement of incidents." Consider the graphic on the next page depicting this "artful arrangement" of a story.

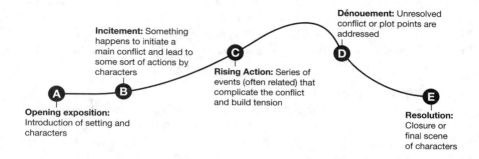

Figure 1-2

plot                          dramatic situation              sequence
cause-and-effect              exposition

# 3.1 An Artful Arrangement of Incidents
### | STR-1.A, STR-1.B

**Plot** is the progression of events in a narrative. The events throughout a narrative are connected, with each event building on the others, often with a **cause-and-effect** relationship. That is, one event causes another, which causes another. Typically, characters in stories face conflicts or challenges that put barriers between them and their goals or desires. The **dramatic situation** of a narrative includes the setting and action of the plot and the way the narrative develops to place characters in those conflicts.

The development of stories often involves the rising or falling fortunes of a main character or set of characters. Plot and the **exposition,** or background information and explanation, that accompanies it focus readers' attention on the parts of the narrative that matter most to its development, including characters, their relationships, and their roles in the narrative, as well as setting and the relationship between characters and setting.

## Connected, Sequenced Events

A concept in physics called "the butterfly effect" states that if a butterfly flaps its wings in Tokyo, then there will be a hurricane in Florida; the slightest movement of the wind by a butterfly in Japan will cause other wind changes which may move a small cloud into a larger one changing the course of that cloud which eventually becomes a part of the weather system that might have brought a hurricane to the Bahamas but now will hit Florida instead.

Of course, you can never know for certain the effects of a single butterfly's wings. But the point is very simple: the smallest causes can lead to the largest effects.

The plot of a story relies on a similar concept. The action and events of a story cause a ripple effect of more actions and events to which the characters must react. Consider the example from *Native Son* with Bigger Thomas and his new job. Had Bigger never taken the new job with the Daltons (had that butterfly never flapped its wings) then the rest of the story would not have happened.

## Dramatic Situation

You might be drawn to a character based on description, dialogue, or behavior, and you may become interested in a character's journey through the story because of a memorable setting. But nothing will pull you into a story so you identify with a character—see and feel yourself in the shoes of that character—as effectively as conflict. The conflict can be between characters (teenagers and their parents, for example), between different parts of a character (the part that wants to do the right thing and the part that is tempted away from doing the right thing), and between a character and the environment (a young African American man in conflict with a segregated city). Readers connect strongly and sympathetically with characters facing a conflict. Conflict is at the heart of a story's dramatic situation. In a story's dramatic situation, characters and setting are tightly intertwined in a sequence of cause-and-effect events in the plot that leads to and develops the conflict that will affect characters' changing fortunes.

Consider the example of Richard Wright's *Native Son* (see page 32). None of the parts of the dramatic situation can be changed without significantly changing—or even eliminating—the story itself. If Bigger Thomas (character) were removed, then the story would not move forward, since it is Bigger who makes the choices that drive the plot. If Bigger's nature as a large but afraid Black man were changed, then the rest of the story would also change. If Bigger doesn't need a job or if he doesn't get the job with a White family (plot), then he may not be pushed to make the decisions he makes. Finally, if 1930s Chicago (setting) was not a racially segregated city that oppressed Black people, then Bigger might not behave the way he does.

**Source:** Getty Images

Although the figurative flap of a butterfly's wings can set a story in motion, at each "ripple," characters have a chance to make choices that determine the next effect and that reveal new information about their characters.

## The Dramatic Situation of Richard Wright's *Native Son*

CHARACTER:
Bigger
Thomas

SETTING:
Racially
segregated
Chicago

PLOT
INCIDENT:
New job with
White family

Figure 1-3

The dramatic situation of the novel places Bigger in direct conflict with other characters, the society, and even himself. If one event in the story is left out, the entire story may fall apart. Literature relies on these connected aspects of a dramatic situation to develop complexity in all aspects of the story. Experienced readers come to recognize how all of these parts of the dramatic situation build upon one another, affect one another, and drive the development of the story as a whole.

Typically, stories are told from beginning to end. The first sequence of events functions as the impetus for the story, the things that happened to set the story in motion. The sequence of events in the middle of the story functions as a way to show how characters run into conflicts or challenges and try to resolve them. The final sequence of events in a story functions as a way to bring the story to a close.

**Remember:** Plot is the sequence of events in a narrative; events throughout a narrative are connected, with each event building on the others, often with a cause-and-effect relationship. The dramatic situation of a narrative includes the setting and action of the plot and how that narrative develops to place characters in conflict(s), and often involves the rising or falling fortunes of a main character or set of characters. STR-1.A–B

### The Writer's Craft: The Shape and Structure of Stories

Author Kurt Vonnegut once presented an idea about stories and plots, explaining that "stories have shapes which can be drawn on graph paper" and claiming that most stories fit into only a few such shapes. These are all built around how characters encounter good or bad fortune over time throughout the story. The outcomes are often the result of choices or incidents with a cause-and-effect relationship. The shape of a story depends on the characters' responses to conflict.

Vonnegut imagined a simple graph, with the horizontal x-axis representing the time of the story, from beginning to end, and the vertical y-axis representing a character's fortunes, from glowing good health and wealth at the top to misery and poverty at the bottom. About halfway between would be a not especially good but not especially bad starting point. The following graph shows what Vonnegut calls "the man in the hole" story: character starts out fine, encounters a conflict (falls in a hole), struggles to get out and succeeds, and is better for the experience.

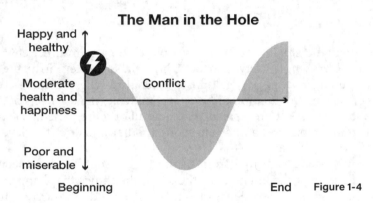

**The Man in the Hole**

Figure 1-4

Of course, the hole does not have to be a hole; it can be any conflict that forces the fortunes of the character to fall—a lost job, a lost love, a lost limb.

Once he established the basic shape of plot, Vonnegut went on to explore different ways that plot can shape different kinds of stories. The different events or incidents—or plot points—are those that characters encounter on their movement between good and bad fortune. The most important events often follow the turning point in the change of fortune where characters encounter conflict, succumb, and then try to rise above it.

Vonnegut said that such story shapes could be generated by computers. Experts in artificial intelligence have found that computer analyses of story plots do in fact correlate very closely to Vonnegut's story shapes. Not only that, but computers can use those story shapes to generate novels.

Following are three common patterns. The ∞ symbol indicates forever.

## Boy Meets Girl

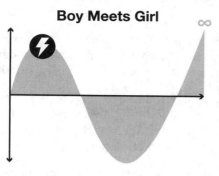

In this pattern, something good happens to raise a person's fortune (a boy meets a girl, for example). Then something happens that causes the loss of that good fortune (the girl falls in love with someone else) and the person's fortune sinks. Finally, the person finds a way to overcome misfortune and end up even better than when he started (the boy and girl are reunited and inherit a fortune).

**Figure 1-5**

## Creation Story

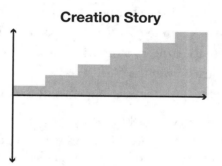

This pattern follows the creation story in the Bible: God created light, then the sky, then the land, and so on. Each step in the story line elevates a person's fortune—one success leads to another. This pattern is more common in non-Western cultures.

**Figure 1-6**

This pattern starts out like the creation story. At the beginning, Cinderella is miserable, working hard for her stepmother and sisters. Once the fairy godmother arrives, her fortune keeps rising: dress, shoes, carriage, meeting the prince and falling in love. When midnight strikes, her fortunes fall even lower than before since now she has known love and lost it. But when her glass slipper matches the one the prince found, she returns to her happiest state and stays there.

**Figure 1-7**

## Cinderella

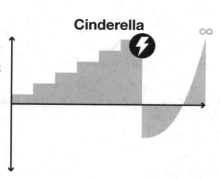

### Use the Writer's Craft

Choose one of the story shapes to help you think of a plot for a story. Recreate the story shape on separate paper. For the main character, choose a character (in a book, on TV, or in real life) you know well. Then plot the key events on the story shape. Finally, write a brief synopsis of your story.

## 3.1 Checkpoint

*Review "The Appropriation of Cultures" on pages 4–11 and complete the open-response activities and answer the multiple-choice questions.*

1. Which of the story shapes on pages 36–37 describes the plot of "The Appropriation of Cultures"? Explain your answer by identifying the points of conflict and how they shape Daniel's rise or fall.

2. Review the dramatic situation diagram (Figure 1–3). Then identify the indispensable parts of the story "The Appropriation of Cultures." Explain in writing or discuss with a partner how the story would change if you eliminated one part of the dramatic situation.

3. Which of the following events from "The Appropriation of Cultures" causes the most effects throughout the plot?

    (A) Daniel plays music in the bar near the campus of the university.

    (B) The frat boys ask him to play "Dixie."

    (C) Daniel goes to the grocery store with Sarah.

    (D) Travis and Barb deliver the truck.

    (E) Daniel is stopped by the big White men in the Monte Carlo.

4. Which of the following best describes the dramatic situation of the story?

    (A) While relaxing on his porch, Daniel's friend Sarah influences him to take control of symbols traditionally used for oppression. In doing so, Daniel comes into conflict with many people who simply do not understand.

    (B) Daniel earns a degree from an Ivy League college but is unable to use his degree to get a job because of racial discrimination. He begins playing music, which allows him to change the culture of racism.

    (C) Travis and Barb desperately need the money from the sale of the 1968 Ford truck but are reluctant to sell to Daniel because he is Black and racial tension runs high.

    (D) Daniel's mother was able to make and save a lot of money despite the racial discrimination in South Carolina during her lifetime. She passed this money along to him, but he is wasting it and not getting a job.

    (E) In a racially charged South Carolina, Daniel notices that taking control of the song "Dixie" takes away some of its power, so he decides to do the same with another symbol, the rebel flag. As he does, he comes into conflict with others who are only confused.

**Creating on Your Own**

Review the writing you have done about the conversation, the characters, and the setting in the previous Creating on Your Own activities. Make a bulleted list of possible occurrences in the plot, including a dialogue. What is the story shape? That is, what sets the story in motion? What might happen in the middle to change the direction of the story? How might the story end? Save your work.

# 3.2 Plot, Exposition, and Sequence | STR-1.C

Plot is more than simply the connection and progression of events through a sequence, or order. The arrangement of the parts and sections of a text, the relationship of the parts to each other, and the sequence in which the text reveals information are all structural choices made by a writer that contribute to the reader's interpretation of a text. For example, some writers might begin telling a story right in the middle of the action and work backward and forward in time to fill out the events of the plot. Some might begin telling a story at the end, so readers know the outcome but wonder how it happened. Writers make deliberate and intentional choices about how to present the plot of a story in order to communicate as effectively as possible with readers.

## Exposition

Take another look at the "Man in the Hole" story shape on page 36. The story could be told just as it is in the illustration:

- The main character (character)
- gets in trouble (plot) by falling in a hole (setting) (This is the dramatic situation.)
- but gets out of it again (plot)
- and ends up better for the experience (resolution)

On the basis of this simple outline, readers may sympathize with the main character's problem. But without details from the author that explain relationships between characters and decisions that led to this dramatic situation and that paint a setting in which readers can picture themselves, most readers would not be much invested in the story.

Fortunately, in well-crafted and developed stories, all of these details become available to the reader in the exposition provided in the text. The exposition does exactly what the word suggests—it "exposes" to the reader certain things that are not obvious from the dramatic situation. Exposition works with plot to focus the attention of the reader on specific details of the incidents, characters, and setting. These details influence the reader's experience with the story.

For example, the exposition of the man-in-the-hole story might explain that the main character is a wealthy businessman in the construction industry, that he is married to a stay-at-home wife, and that he employs seasonal migrant workers in his company. The exposition might also reveal that the man has a very high opinion of himself and a lower opinion of everyone else.

The chart below shows some of the questions the exposition of a story might answer.

| Possible Questions Answered by Exposition |
| --- |
| • Who are all the characters? |
| • What relationships do the characters have? |
| • What role do the characters play in the story? |
| • What is the setting, and what role does it play in the story? |

Table 1–7

## Structural Choices and Sequence

Typically, stories are told from beginning to end. The first sequence of events functions as the impetus for the story (a man falls in a hole), the things that happened to set the story in motion. The sequence of events in the middle of the story (the man figures out how to get out of the hole) function as a way to show how characters run into conflicts or challenges and try to resolve them. The final sequence of events in a story (the man gets out of the hole having learned new lessons) functions as a way to bring the story to a close.

However, writers make structural choices to highlight certain parts of the narrative or characters' traits, motivations, and growth. The **sequence** in which the events of the story unfold is one key choice a writer makes. For example, suppose the man-in-the-hole story begins when the man is already in the hole: "Total darkness enveloped him. His back hurt from the fall, and he wondered if he'd broken a wrist." The writer could continue describing the condition of the man in the hole and, only after that is well established, rewind to show how the man ended up there: "The day had started out so well. The crisp autumn air filled the lungs and spirit of the well-dressed man with energy and optimism. Never had a man been so assured of the good fortune that seemed to follow him wherever he went. He heard squawking above and looked up to see the V-shaped pattern of migrating geese, pitying them for their need to work so hard and travel so far to survive. But he looked up for a little too long. . . ." By beginning with the terrible situation he ends up in, the writer helps focus readers' attention on the contrast between the character's arrogant attitude and the fate that, literally, befalls him. Maybe, while the man is in the hole—first desperate and frightened and later accepting of his fate and determined to get out of the hole—through exposition he thinks back to ways he has interacted with people in his life: his wife, who does all the household chores and childcare; his brother and business partner, whom he has cheated; and the migrant laborers who work for his company, whose recent request for a raise he flatly denied.

By their nature, stories have a beginning and an end. But writers thoughtfully choose in which sequence to present the plot points between the start and end of a story to highlight the most significant parts of the story's development.

**Remember:** Plot and the exposition that accompanies it focus readers' attention on the parts of the narrative that matter most to its development, including characters, their relationships, and their roles in the narrative, as well as setting and the relationship between characters and setting. STR-1.C

## 3.2 Checkpoint

*Review "The Appropriation of Cultures" on pages 4–11 and complete the open-response activity and answer the multiple-choice question.*

1. Below are the plot points in the story in the order in which they're told. Choose one or more events from the end of the story and explain in writing how the story would change if it (or they) were the first thing the reader learned. Evaluate what the story would gain or lose by that change in its effect on the reader.

   - Frat boys ask for "Dixie" and Daniel sings.
   - Daniel drives home and dreams.
   - Sarah visits Daniel at home.
   - Sarah and Daniel go to the grocery store.
   - Daniel decides to buy the truck, or rather, the decal.
   - Daniel arranges with Travis to see the truck.
   - Daniel meets Travis and Barb and takes the truck for a test drive.
   - Daniel tells Travis he'll pay extra for him to deliver the truck.
   - Daniel and Sarah have a dialogue about buying the truck and its relation to the flag flying over the state capitol.
   - Travis arrives with the truck.
   - Barb asks Travis why Daniel wants to leave the decal on.
   - Daniel reveals to Travis that he believes it's the Black power flag.
   - Daniel encounters two big White men.
   - Black teenagers arrive, and Daniel tells them the meaning of the decal "with as serious a face as he could manage."
   - The White men leave without trouble.
   - Daniel encounters lawyer Ahmad Wilson, and they have a friendly conversation.
   - Daniel plays "Dixie" again, this time at a meeting of Black professionals.
   - Daniel's idea spreads until the Confederate flag has no more association with confederacy and is quietly taken down from the capitol.

**2.** Which of the following best explains how the plot and exposition work together to focus readers on the parts of the narrative that matter most to its development?

    (A) Beginning with the experience in the bar, the story shows how Daniel feels less and less intimidated by encounters with White people.

    (B) The exposition about Daniel's not having a job shows that he has time to pursue his ideas about the meaning of symbols.

    (C) With each step in the story, Daniel seems to gain more strength and assurance about attaching his own meaning to Confederate symbols and spreading that meaning.

    (D) The plot and exposition work together to show Travis and Barb and all other White people in a negative light while presenting Daniel as a positive figure.

    (E) The exposition at the end focuses attention on how the efforts of one determined person can bring about a big social change.

**Creating on Your Own**

Review the previous writing you have done. Think about the occurrences you listed as part of your plot. Consider what you will convey through exposition and what you will convey through plot and dialogue. Also determine how you will sequence the events in the plot to focus readers' attention on the most important parts of the narrative. Write a rough draft of your story and save your work.

**Source:** Getty Images

# Part 3 Apply What You Have Learned

Carefully review "The Appropriation of Cultures." Write a paragraph that identifies specific aspects of the dramatic situation and explains how the relationship between those aspects—and the exposition provided throughout the story—contribute to the development of the story. Your paragraph should do the following:

1. Identify the specific parts of the dramatic situation in the story (do not just list what a dramatic situation is, but give specifics from this story).

2. Explain how different specific aspects of this story's dramatic situation relate to and affect one another and tie to the big ideas in the text.

3. Explain how specifics from the exposition of this story bring attention to particular aspects of the story and the ideas in the text.

4. Use a strong concluding sentence that makes a final statement about the ideas in the text and what the dramatic situation specifically tells readers about those ideas.

Avoid simply summarizing the story. The key to avoiding a simple summary is to make sure you relate textual details to the *ideas* you see in the text, not just to the events. If you are writing about *what* happened, you are summarizing; if you are writing about *why* it happened and *how* it relates to the ideas involved, then you are writing about the text.

You may want to structure your paragraph in this pattern:

> A number of aspects contribute to the dramatic situation in "The Appropriation of Cultures." These include [identify and explain them here]. In the dramatic situation, the relationship between those aspects is [identify the relationship and explain how it is central to the story here]. In addition, the exposition of the story functions to [explain the purpose of the exposition here]. [Add a strong concluding sentence.]

**Reflect on the Essential Question** Write a brief response that answers the essential question: *How does the plot order the events of the narrative, and how does a particular sequence of events in a plot function?* In your answer, correctly use the key terms listed on page 33.

# Narrators and Speakers

**Enduring Understanding and Skills**

## Part 4

### Understand
A narrator's or speaker's perspective controls the details and emphases that affect how readers experience and interpret a text. (NAR-1)

### Demonstrate
Identify and describe the narrator or speaker of a text. (4.A)
Identify and explain the function of point of view in a narrative. (4.B)

**Source:** *AP® English Literature and Composition Course and Exam Description*

**Essential Question:** Who is the narrator or speaker in a story, and how does point of view function in a narrative?

Close readers pay attention to who is telling the story, because stories with different emphases emerge from different storytellers. Earlier in the unit you read about experience and perspective. Everyone has a perspective—the way they see things—that comes from their background. The backgrounds and experiences of the fictional characters you meet in literature, including the person telling the story, contribute to individual, inescapable bias.

The person telling the story, the **narrator**, is sometimes overlooked. Yet, a narrator's perspective directly affects the details included in the story, and it influences how the reader reacts to the story. An author uses a narrator to communicate certain details in a certain way.

Similarly, point of view, the narrator's stance in relation to the events of the story, affects how a storyteller tells the story. If the narrator is not a participant in the story, the story is told from the third-person point of view, and the narrator has some distance from the characters and actions. If the narrator is a participant in the story, it is told from the first-person point of view, and the narrator is right in the thick of the action. Each point of view has the potential for bias.

To help gain a good understanding of a story, close readers consider point of view and what it reveals about the narrator's perspective and involvement in the events of the story.

# 4.1 Narrators and Their Perspectives | NAR-1.A, NAR-1.B, NAR-1.C

Narrators or speakers in stories relate accounts to readers and establish a relationship between the text and the reader. Readers come to know the voice of the person telling the story even if the narrator is not actually a character in the story. However, the speaker or narrator is not necessarily the author.

As you read in Part 1, **perspective** refers to how narrators, characters, or speakers see their circumstances. **Point of view** refers to the position from which narrators or speakers relate the events of a narrative. Were they participants or eyewitnesses, or do they have a distance from the story in either time or space?

## Relating to the Reader

Consider how the narrator relates to the readers in this excerpt from a collection of short stories by Tim O'Brien called *The Things They Carried*, published in 1990. The book focuses on soldiers from the Vietnam War and their experience before, during, and afterward.

### Excerpt 1 (Curt Lemon)

It happened, to me, nearly twenty years ago, and I still remember that trail junction and those giant trees and a soft dripping sound somewhere beyond the trees. I remember the smell of moss. Up in the canopy there were tiny white blossoms, but no sunlight at all, and I remember the shadows spreading out under the trees where Curt Lemon and Rat Kiley were playing catch with smoke grenades. Mitchell Sanders sat flipping his yo-yo. Norman Bowker and Kiowa and Dave Jensen were dozing, or half dozing, and all around us were those ragged green mountains.

Except for the laughter things were quiet.

At one point, I remember, Mitchell Sanders turned and looked at me, not quite nodding, as if to warn me about something, as if he already knew, then after a while he rolled up his yo-yo and moved away.

It's hard to tell you what happened next.

They were just goofing. There was a noise, I suppose, which must've been the detonator, so I glanced behind me and watched Lemon step from the shade into bright sunlight. His face was suddenly brown and shining. A handsome kid, really. Sharp gray eyes, lean and narrow-waisted, and when he died it was almost beautiful, the way the sunlight came around him and lifted him up and sucked him high into a tree full of moss and vines and white blossoms.

In this short passage, the narrator establishes a relationship with the reader, establishes a perspective, and reveals a point of view.

- By immediately saying "it happened to me," the narrator establishes a relationship with the reader and creates a sense that the story really happened.

- The perspective or way the narrator sees his circumstances is revealed mostly by the words used to describe different parts of the situation. Details relating to relaxation and rest, "tiny blossoms," "dozing," or "half dozing," the "yo-yo," and the smoke grenade game all suggest a restful and worry-free perspective (despite the tragedy that would come in the last paragraph).

- The narrator tells the story as a character who is there, providing details that would likely only be available to someone who was actually in the war with the other characters. The narrator uses *first-person point of view* with such pronouns as *me* and *I*, giving the reader a feeling of connecting directly with him.

As you read a story, analyze the narrator by asking the questions in the chart below.

| Questions to Analyze Narrators | |
|---|---|
| How does the narrator establish a relationship with the reader? | • What information are you given to pull you into the story?<br>• Why are you given that particular information? |
| What is the narrator's perspective? | • What details let you know how the narrator sees his or her circumstances?<br>• What do those details tell you about the narrator? |
| What is the narrator's point of view? | • What is the position of the narrator in relation to the story itself?<br>• Is the narrator directly involved?<br>• Did the narrator see it happen or just hear about it?<br>• What is the narrator's role in the story? |

Table 1-8

An experienced reader realizes that the narrator tells the story, not the author. Even if the narrator claims to also be the author, a reader should be skeptical. Consider the stories in *The Things They Carried* by Tim O'Brien. In other stories in the book, readers learn that the character of the narrator is also named Tim. It soon becomes difficult for a reader to distinguish between Tim the narrator and Tim the author. Tim the author even served in Vietnam. But the stories he has written are fictional. Often, readers of the book are shocked when, after finishing the book, they are reminded that it is fiction.

**Remember:** Narrators or speakers relate accounts to readers and establish a relationship between the text and the reader. Perspective refers to how narrators, characters, or speakers see their circumstances, while point of view refers to the position from which a narrator or speaker relates the events of a narrative. A speaker or narrator is not necessarily the author. (NAR-1.A–C)

## 4.1 Checkpoint

*Review "The Appropriation of Cultures" on pages 4–11. Then complete the open-response activity and answer the multiple-choice question.*

1. The narrator in the story is not a character but could still be said to have a perspective on the characters. With a partner, discuss the following questions using specific details from the story to drive your discussion.

   - What is the narrator's relationship to the events of the story?

   - How does the narrator establish a relationship between the characters and the reader?

   - What details help the narrator establish a relationship with the reader?

   - How does the narrator view the circumstances of the story?

2. In "The Appropriation of Cultures," which of the following statements best describes how the narrator establishes a relationship between the text and the reader?

   (A) The narrator pulls readers in by emphasizing tense conflicts.

   (B) The narrator sets the tone for a story that is whimsical and imaginary.

   (C) The narrator relates the story through the point of view of a distant, objective set of eyes.

   (D) The narrator uses humor early in the story to engage readers.

   (E) The narrator appeals to readers by conveying the seriousness of the story.

**Creating on Your Own**

Review your story draft. Who is the narrator? What would happen if the narrator changed and became one of the characters? Consider rewriting part of your dialogue from the perspective of this different narrator. Save your work.

# 4.2 Narrators and Point of View

| NAR-1.D, NAR-1.E, NAR-1.F, NAR-1.G, NAR-1.H, NAR-1.I

The point of view of narrators, characters, or speakers in a text determines what information and details they can and cannot provide, depending on their level of involvement and intimacy with the details, events, or characters. Narrators can tell a story at a distance from the characters, observing their actions and words and peering into their thoughts and feelings. Narrators may also be characters, and their role as characters may influence their perspective. For example, if a narrator is also a character in a story, he or she cannot know the thoughts of another person, just as people in real life cannot know what other people are thinking, nor can they provide descriptive details about setting or other characters except through a limited point of view. The chart below shows different kinds of narrators and their relationship to the characters.

| Types of Narrators (Points of View) | Relation to Characters and Events | Effect on Perspective |
|---|---|---|
| **First-person narrator** (Uses first-person pronouns such as I, we, and me) | Involved in the story | Events and other characters shape their perspective and they can only tell their own thoughts and feelings |
| **Third-person narrator** (Uses third-person pronouns such as he, she, and they) | Outside observer | Events and characters may not affect the narrator's perspective |
| · **Third-person observational** | Describes only what can be observed, not inner thoughts and feelings; often narrates mainly from the perspective of one character | Affects the reader's relationship to the characters, since readers develop a bond with the character from whose perspective the narrator tells the story |
| · **Third-person all-knowing** | Knows everything about all the characters and settings | |

Table 1-9

## Understanding Narrative Perspective

As you read the following excerpt, also from Tim O'Brien's collection of short stories, *The Things They Carried*, try to identify the perspective of the narrator.

## Excerpt 2 (Jimmy Cross)

In the first week of April, before Lavender died, Lieutenant Jimmy Cross received a good-luck charm from Martha. It was a simple pebble, an ounce at most. Smooth to the touch, it was a milky white color with flecks of orange and violet, oval-shaped, like a miniature egg. In the accompanying letter, Martha wrote that she had found the pebble on the Jersey shoreline, precisely where the land touched water at high tide, where things came together but also separated. It was this separate-but-together quality, she wrote, that had inspired her to pick up the pebble and to carry it in her breast pocket for several days, where it seemed weightless, and then to send it through the mail, by air, as a token of her truest feelings for him. Lieutenant Cross found this romantic. But he wondered what her truest feelings were, exactly, and what she meant by separate-but-together. He wondered how the tides and waves had come into play on that afternoon along the Jersey shoreline when Martha saw the pebble and bent down to rescue it from geology. He imagined bare feet. Martha was a poet, with the poet's sensibilities, and her feet would be brown and bare, the toenails unpainted, the eyes chilly and somber like the ocean in March, and though it was painful he wondered who had been with her that afternoon. He imagined a pair of shadows moving along the strip of sand where things came together but also separated. It was phantom jealousy, he knew, but he couldn't help himself. He loved her so much. On the march, through the hot days of early April, he carried the pebble in his mouth, turning it with his tongue, tasting sea salt and moisture. His mind wandered. He had difficulty keeping his attention on the war. On occasion he would yell at his men to spread out the column, to keep their eyes open, but then he would slip away into daydreams, just pretending, walking barefoot along the Jersey shore, with Martha, carrying nothing. He would feel himself rising. Sun and waves and gentle winds, all love and lightness.

**Identifying and Describing Narrators** You may notice that though this story is from the same book as the previous excerpt, the narrator of this excerpt is different. The narrator is not a character in the story with first-hand knowledge of the events. Instead, this narrator knows things that no one could know simply by being there and being a part of the narrative. This narrator is able to reveal the thoughts and feelings of the character Jimmy Cross. This ability makes him a third-person, outside, **all-knowing narrator** even though the inner details conveyed are about only one person. Some all-knowing narrators provide insight into the thoughts of a number of characters.

In the excerpt on page 45 about Curt Lemon, the narrator was also limited in knowledge about the other characters but still able to report the events as the narrator-as-character experienced them. He is a **first-person narrator**, involved in the story directly. The narrator in the Jimmy Cross excerpt, however, tells the story from a removed third-person perspective. He does not take part in the action of the story, nor is he affected by the events. However, he does relay information that the reader needs in order to better understand Jimmy Cross and his circumstance.

The level of detail provided by a **third-person narrator** may vary—from the all-knowing example in the Jimmy Cross excerpt to a limited, strictly observational point of view. A third-person **observational narrator** does not delve into a character's inner life but instead relates only those events and details that the character can observe.

In contrast, first-person narrators are themselves characters. They take action, they interact with other characters, they face conflicts, they have experiences, and they have developed unique perspectives.

Because of a first-person narrator's involvement in the story, close readers seek to understand the perspective of a narrator as they read the story so they can recognize situations in which information might be biased based on the narrator's relationship with the events of the narrative.

At the same time, third-person narrators may not be affected by the events of the narrative at all. They may even tell a story from "long, long ago" and "far, far away." Or, like the narrator in the Jimmy Cross excerpt, they may tell the story through the eyes and mind of one character without being affected by the events or thoughts that trouble Jimmy Cross.

| Excerpts from *The Things They Carried* | Point of View | Information the Narrator Does or Does Not Have as a Result of the Point of View |
|---|---|---|
| Curt Lemon excerpt | First-Person | • **HAS:** Facts about the step-by-step events of the situation<br>• **HAS:** Details about other soldiers' behaviors<br>• **HAS:** Details related to setting<br>• **DOES NOT HAVE:** Any character's thoughts |
| Jimmy Cross excerpt | Third-Person (all-knowing) | • **HAS:** Jimmy's mindset and thoughts<br>• **HAS:** History about Jimmy and Martha |

Table 1-10

**The Function of Point of View** What role does point of view play in a story? Put simply, a story's point of view filters the details the narrator shares with the readers, which in turn affect the readers' attitudes toward the characters and events and may even shape how the narrator feels.

One way to examine the function of point of view is to consider how a story might change if told from a different point of view. For example, if the Curt Lemon excerpt were told from the point of view of Curt Lemon, then it might focus on the fun of the moment and the break it provided from the horrors of the war. It might end abruptly at the moment of his death without explanation to the reader about why, or it might change from the fun of the moment to the pain or peace or relief the character might feel at the moment of death. And what if the Jimmy Cross excerpt were told in the first-person point of view with Jimmy himself narrating? Maybe readers wouldn't learn as much about why he does what he does or how he feels about Martha because maybe Jimmy can't be honest with himself or readers.

Of course, readers can never know. As literature professor Will Nash at Middlebury College in Vermont has said, "we can never assume more than the text gives us." You can, however, explore possibilities like these, if only to better understand why authors chose the perspectives and points of view of the narrators and characters.

**Remember:** The point of view contributes to what narrators, characters, or speakers can and cannot provide in a text based on their level of involvement and intimacy with the details, events, or characters. Narrators may also be characters, and their role as characters may influence their perspective. First-person narrators are involved in the narrative; their relationship to the events of the plot and the other characters shapes their perspective. Third-person narrators are outside observers. Their knowledge about events and characters may range from observational to all-knowing, which shapes their perspective. The outside perspective of third-person narrators may not be affected by the events of the narrative. (NAR-1.D–I)

## 4.2 Checkpoint

*Review "The Appropriation of Cultures" on pages 4–11. Then complete the open-response activity and answer the multiple-choice questions.*

1. Point of view often reveals the level of intimacy the narrator has with the events and characters of the story. On separate paper, complete the table below identifying the narrator's point of view in the text and what the narrator can and cannot provide to the reader because of that point of view.

| Point of View | What specific information does the narrator have or not have as a result of the point of view? |
|---|---|
|  |  |

2. In "The Appropriation of Cultures," which of the following statements best describes the relationship between the characters and the narrator?

   (A) The narrator has roughly equal knowledge of all the characters.

   (B) The narrator regards all the characters seriously.

   (C) The narrator acts as a character in the story.

   (D) The narrator tends to share Daniel's perspective.

   (E) The narrator can share the thoughts of all characters.

3. The most significant effect of the point of view in this story is that

   (A) readers can witness the events and decide how they feel about them

   (B) readers learn to trust the narrator

   (C) readers get more details about different characters' personalities

   (D) readers better understand different characters' motivations

   (E) readers can better recognize the needs of different characters

**Creating on Your Own**

The writing you have done throughout this unit is the beginning of your own short story—and maybe even more. Take some time to write your story, using the different parts that you developed throughout this unit to guide you. Feel free to change and revise as you go. For example, maybe you could provide more details to reveal characters and their perspectives. Maybe you could refine the details you provide about the setting so they invite richer associations. Maybe your plot would become stronger if you related the events out of the usual order. Experiment. No one writes beautiful first drafts! Save your work.

# Part 4  Apply What You Have Learned

Closely reread the short story "The Appropriation of Cultures" on pages 4–11. Write a paragraph that describes the perspective of the narrator in this story. Explain how perspective and point of view differ and how each affects readers of this story. Use textual evidence to support your explanation. When you cite examples, be sure to show how they serve as evidence in your explanation. Avoid just retelling events or dialogue from the text. Use them to make interpretations instead.

**Reflect on the Essential Question**  Write a brief response that answers the essential question: *Who is the narrator or speaker in a story, and how does point of view function in a narrative?* In your answer, correctly use the key terms listed on page 45.

# Part 5

# Writing About Literature I

> ### Enduring Understanding and Skill
>
> ## Part 5
>
> ### Understand
> Readers establish and communicate their interpretations of literature through arguments supported by textual evidence. (LAN-1)
>
> ### Demonstrate
> Develop a paragraph that includes 1) a claim that requires defense with evidence from the text and 2) the evidence itself. (7.A)
>
> **Source:** *AP® English Literature and Composition Course and Exam Description*

**Essential Question:** How can you communicate your interpretation of a work of literature in a paragraph that asserts a claim and supports it with evidence?

Experienced students of literature read and think about texts in their own unique and individual way. The goal of the AP® English Literature and Composition course is to learn how to develop an interpretation of a text, not to learn the teacher's or professor's interpretation of a text. Developing your own interpretation requires close reading and analysis.

Interpretation begins with observing the whole and then breaking down the parts—or analyzing. As you are developing an interpretation, slow down, look closely, analyze the parts, and try to understand exactly what is in the text and how the parts all work together. Begin with the close examination of the key elements of a story—characters, setting, plot, and narrator.

**Interpretation and Claims about Literature** Unit 1 began by exploring with Chimamanda Ngozi Adichie the "danger of a single story." Reading literature is different for everyone because no two people have the same experience. People will see different meanings as they read because of the varied experiences they bring to the text. Consider the anchor text for this unit, "The Appropriation of Cultures." For one reader, Daniel's experiences in the bar near the beginning may emerge as the most noticeable or important feature because that reader has had a group of people attempt to embarrass him or her. Another reader may see the southern setting as very important because that reader grew up in the South. Still another reader will connect with the confusion that Travis and Barb face because that reader has also been confused by issues surrounding race and equality. There is no right or wrong way to connect to a text as long as you can put your finger on details in the text—that is, not assume what isn't there—and explain how those details in the text make you connect to something in your experience. Once you connect to some of the details in a text, you then explore through close reading what the text may be saying about those details. Your interpretation, or explanation of the meaning, begins to develop at this point.

By returning to a text for close reading, you begin to piece together your own interpretation and find details in the text that you might use to support it. Because this sort of literary analysis often brings to the surface details that might be glossed over during a first reading, you may find yourself changing the interpretation you had after your first reading.

**Communicating Your Interpretation** The most common way students argue for their interpretation of literature is by writing essays. The word *essay* comes from the French word *essai*, meaning "a trial" or "an attempt," which came to refer to a brief literary composition. An essay will test or prove the soundness of a claim. In your literary argument, you are not trying to prove that yours is the only interpretation; instead, you are arguing that your interpretation can be defended with evidence from the text. Before you write a full essay, however, you will convey your literary argument in a paragraph.

---

**KEY TERMS**

| | | |
|---|---|---|
| analysis | argument | evidence |
| interpretation | claim | commentary |

---

# 5.1 Making a Claim Based on Textual Details | LAN-1.A

In literary **analysis**, writers read a text closely to identify details related to characters, setting, plot, and narration. In combination, these details lead readers to develop an **interpretation**, or explanation of meaning, of an aspect of the text.

Literary analysis begins with reading. Throughout Unit 1, you have read different texts carefully and repeatedly. You have read about how characters are shaped and revealed through textual details and evidence and how the details of the setting contribute to characters' actions and readers' impressions. You have also read about the sequence of events in a plot and the function of certain sequences of events within a story—to set the story in motion, to introduce the complications and conflicts that affect a character's rising or falling fortunes, and to resolve the problems or conflicts at the end of the story. Finally, you read about the role of the narrator and how the details from a first-person or third-person narrator reveal the narrator's relationship to the characters and events and filter the story for the reader. Those are a lot of details to keep in mind, and literature is complex, so close readers often use several processes to help keep details straight.

## Two Processes for Close Reading: Rereading and Annotating Texts

One process experienced readers use is to read a text a number of times. They read a text the first time to try to comprehend what is being said. They want to meet the characters, get to know the narrator, see the setting, and understand what is happening in the plot. Then, on a second time through, readers return to the text to look more closely at details. They might not reread the entire text—just specific sections that require more attention or that caught their eye as something interesting, confusing, important, or surprising.

Another process close readers use is annotating texts, or making notes to remind themselves of the details they find. Readers can annotate texts they own or have permission to mark. More and more, texts are available in digital form that allow virtual annotations.

The close reading guide below shows one suggested way to carry out these two processes as you read and analyze a text. You will have many opportunities to use these processes in this course.

| Suggested Close Reading Guide | | |
|---|---|---|
| **Read** | **Focus** | **Questions to Ask** |
| **First Reading** | • Comprehension<br>• Key ideas and details | • What is happening?<br>• What characters are most interesting?<br>• What questions do I have?<br>• What problems remain? |
| **Second Reading** | • Review marks and add new ones<br>• Make notes<br>• Connect different parts of the text | • Why did something happen?<br>• Why did they say/do/not do this?<br>• Why is the narrator/character giving that detail?<br>• How does this detail relate to another aspect or part of the text?<br>• What other ideas do you have about the details in the text? |
| **Third (and further) Readings** | • Ask new questions or raise problems<br>• Develop an interpretation<br>• Explore language that requires a figurative, rather than literal, reading (See Unit 2.) | • Why does this matter beyond the text?<br>• Could there be more to this than is in the story?<br>• Why did the author/narrator choose these words rather than more common ones?<br>• What questions do I still have? |

**Table 1-11**

## From Details to Big Ideas

In the introduction to this unit, you read that literature can touch on big ideas and emotions that speak to a wide variety of readers with diverse backgrounds. These universal ideas and emotions include family, friendship, honor, evil, love, hatred, pain, joy, disgust, anger, happiness, worry, fear, anxiety, comfort, loss, relief, and many others that humans think about and experience in their own unique ways.

Once readers have read, reread, and analyzed all or parts of a text, they have probably started to notice patterns of details in the text that relate to certain universal or big ideas. In "The Appropriation of Cultures," for example, readers may notice that they are never directly told Daniel's race. Details throughout offer hints, and by the end of the story there is little doubt, but that conclusion relies completely on a collection of different details provided throughout the story. That Daniel's race is only slowly revealed or suggested in the story could cause a reader to consider ideas relating to race—stereotyping, prejudice, diversity, and culture, for example. Other details and experiences may lead readers to big ideas about family, friendship, wealth, and freedom. Only when readers begin to explain what the story says or implies about those ideas are they really providing an interpretation of the text.

## Examining Complexity

As you read in the Unit 1 Overview, literature "conveys complex ideas with lasting value." The complexity and lasting nature of the ideas are really what make literature into literature. Because life is rarely simple and one dimensional, literature that truly captures experience is rarely simple and one dimensional. Readers analyzing a text first identify big ideas in the text and then consider the complexity of those ideas. Often, examining complexity begins with looking at ideas that appear in opposition or in tension. For example, the way Daniel is stereotyped because of his race and the freedoms he has as a human being put the ideas of prejudice and freedom in opposition.

**Source:** Getty Images

As you make lists of different universal ideas or big ideas in a text, think about the traditional Chinese Yin and Yang. This symbol represents unity of opposites. That is what you aim for in your thematic statement as you address complexity in a text.

Consider the details in "The Appropriation of Cultures" that might lead readers to the universal or big ideas of "prejudice" and "freedom." In multiple situations, Daniel encounters prejudice but uses what he has available to him—freedom of speech and expression—to push back against it.

What could the story be saying to a reader about the themes of prejudice and freedom? The answer depends on a reader's perspective. But a reader might make the following statement:

> **Thematic Statement**: Overcoming prejudice requires making the most of the freedoms you have.

This thematic statement—a statement about what the text may be saying about some universal idea—emerges from both the reader's experiences and the details in the text. It usually grows out of tension between two or more ideas in the text. A writer's claim about a text grows out of this statement.

 **Remember:** In literary analysis, writers read a text closely to identify details that, in combination, enable them to make and defend a claim about an aspect of the text. (LAN-1.A)

## 5.1 Checkpoint

*Closely reread "The Appropriation of Cultures" on pages 4–11. Then complete the open-response activity and answer the multiple-choice question.*

1. On separate paper, make a chart like the one below, adding as many rows as you want. Identify one or more big ideas by looking for patterns of evidence that point to them. Record those in the chart.

| Possible Big Ideas | Details that Point to the Big Idea |
|---|---|
| | |

2. The story "The Appropriation of Cultures" as a whole might be best represented by which of the following thematic statements?

   (A) Stereotypes shape our assumptions about equality.

   (B) Stereotypes force us to accept who we are.

   (C) People reject prejudice when faced with their own rejection.

   (D) The only way to defeat prejudice is with prejudice.

   (E) Prejudice and stereotypes are the same thing.

**Composing on Your Own**
Using your chart as a guide, develop a possible thematic statement about "The Appropriation of Cultures" or another story you are studying.

# 5.2 Developing and Supporting a Claim | LAN-1.B

A literary **argument** requires more than a thematic statement. It requires a **claim**, an assertion that the textual evidence in the story will support. A claim about a text needs to be tied to the text directly, as in the statement below.

> **Claim:** Daniel's experiences in "The Appropriation of Cultures" illustrate how overcoming prejudice requires making the most of the freedoms you have.

While this is not the only claim possible on these ideas or on this story, it does meet the following requirements of a claim.

- *It is arguable*—that is, it is not just a fact about the text. The statement "Daniel resists prejudice" is more of a fact in the text than an interpretation. Few would or could argue with that statement based on the facts in the text. Although it addresses the universal idea of prejudice, it is not an interpretation, it is not complex, and it does not draw meaning from the idea beyond the story itself. In contrast, "Daniel's experiences in 'The Appropriation of Cultures' illustrate how overcoming prejudice requires making the most of the freedoms you have" is a claim. Other readers may argue with it, seeing the roles prejudice and freedom play in the story in a different light. For example, a reader might make the claim that Daniel tries to use his freedoms to overcome prejudice, but in doing so he is being controlled by the prejudice and is not actually free. That would certainly be an acceptable and complex interpretation.

- *It is defensible* with information from the text. That is, the textual **evidence** you have found supports the claim. A reader who makes a different claim, such as the one in the previous paragraph about being controlled by prejudice, may rely on the same evidence that the first claim uses, but the evidence may be interpreted in different ways. As long as the interpretation is reasonable, it defends the claim. The differences between claims about a work of literature may be small, but literature is complex, and small differences are still arguable differences. A reader builds an argument around his or her claim that demonstrates and proves it by defending it with textual evidence.

As you develop a claim, be sure you can answer yes to all the following questions.

| Checklist: Developing a Claim about Literature |
| --- |
| Does your claim . . . |
| - address universal ideas or big ideas that contrast or are in tension with one another? |
| - build on a thematic statement that says something about those ideas? |
| - link the text (and/or specifics from the text) to the thematic statement? |
| - present a defensible interpretation—that is, can you use information from the text as evidence to support it? |
| - present an arguable interpretation—that is, could someone reasonably disagree? |

Table 1-12

## Using Textual Evidence to Support a Claim

Just as a thematic statement is not a claim until it is tied directly to the text, details and other information from the text are not evidence until they are clearly connected to a claim. Evidence does not connect to or prove the claim on its own. It requires **commentary**, or explanation of the writer's thinking, to support the claim. To defend an interpretation, writers need to explain clearly how the evidence that led them to their claim illustrates their thinking about the claim. In other words, they need to explain the reasoning for how and why that evidence justifies that claim—why they included the pieces of evidence they did. The explanation of how the evidence supports the claim is known as the line of reasoning. (See Unit 3.) The chart below shows the process of thinking about the text, creating an interpretation, showing the evidence that justifies it, and then explaining the thinking that led to that interpretation.

### From Reading a Text to Writing an Argument About It

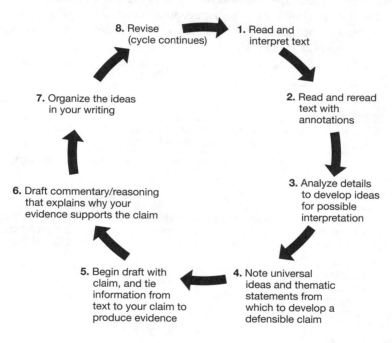

8. Revise (cycle continues)

1. Read and interpret text

2. Read and reread text with annotations

3. Analyze details to develop ideas for possible interpretation

4. Note universal ideas and thematic statements from which to develop a defensible claim

5. Begin draft with claim, and tie information from text to your claim to produce evidence

6. Draft commentary/reasoning that explains why your evidence supports the claim

7. Organize the ideas in your writing

Figure 1-8

**Remember:** A claim is a statement that requires defense with evidence from the text. (LAN-1.B)

## 5.2 Checkpoint

*Review "The Appropriation of Cultures" on pages 4–11 and complete the following open-response activity.*

Below are statements about "The Appropriation of Cultures." Read each one and decide whether it meets the requirements of a claim. Explain each answer.

1. Sarah and Daniel are good friends.

2. Sarah's function in the story is to provide a contrast to Daniel.

3. Daniel pushes back on symbols of White supremacy.

4. Daniel feels superior to Travis in almost the same way the frat boys feel superior to Daniel.

### Composing on Your Own

Using your previous work, on separate paper complete a graphic organizer like the one below for "The Appropriation of Cultures" or another story. You may use the claim already stated for "The Appropriation of Cultures" or you may develop a new one. One example of evidence and commentary is provided for you as an example. It is based on the claim stated on page 58.

| Text: | | |
|---|---|---|
| Universal Ideas: | | |
| Thematic Statement: | | |
| Claim: Daniel's experiences in "The Appropriation of Cultures" illustrate how overcoming prejudice requires making the most of the freedoms you have. | | |
| Evidence from Text | Evidence from Text | Evidence from Text |
| Daniel plays "Dixie" in the bar and makes it his own. | | |
| Commentary/Explanation of why information from text supports claim | Commentary/Explanation of why information from text supports claim | Commentary/Explanation of why information from text supports claim |
| As a musician, Daniel is free to perform as he wishes. Though the "frat boys" are behaving with prejudice when they ask a Black band to play "Dixie," Daniel freely chooses to play it in his own way, deflating the prejudice in the request. | | |
| Concluding Sentence: | | |

# 5.3 Writing a Paragraph of Literary Argument | LAN-1.C

The process described in Figure 1-8 for developing a literary argument, sometimes called an open approach, starts "from scratch"—that is, the reader completes all the stages outlined in the circle. In some circumstances, though, including on the AP® exam, you will be asked to focus on a certain aspect of the text or you will be given an idea (similar to a universal idea) and asked to analyze how a text comments on that idea. Developing your skill with the open approach will give you a good grounding in responding to a focused prompt as well. Beginning by writing a clear and effective paragraph of literary argument will likewise prepare you well for longer literary analyses.

## Purpose and Audience

When you write literary analysis, just as when you write anything, take your purpose and audience into consideration. Possible purposes and audiences for writing a literary analysis are:

- to clarify your own interpretation of literature (audience: yourself)

- to make a convincing argument to classmates and other readers who know the story or other work of literature well (audience: your classmates and other readers familiar with the work)

- to demonstrate for your teacher or an examiner how well you can establish a claim and defend it with textual evidence (audience: teacher or examiner who knows the work of literature)

In each case, your audience is familiar with the work. You do not, therefore, need to provide a summary of the work or provide details that are unrelated to your argument. You need only identify the work early in your writing, as the claim on page 58 does. This guideline holds true for a literary analysis of any length—it allows you to get down to the business of stating and defending your claim right away.

## Components of a Paragraph of Literary Analysis

The main components of a paragraph of literary analysis are the claim and the textual evidence that supports it. Those components correspond to the components of any good paragraph: a topic sentence and a body of supporting sentences. Stand-alone paragraphs, including those providing literary analysis, also often have a concluding sentence.

The table on the next page shows how the parts of a standard stand-alone paragraph correspond to the parts of a stand-alone paragraph of literary analysis.

| Standard Paragraph | Paragraph of Literary Analysis |
|---|---|
| Topic sentence states main idea | Claim asserts interpretation |
| Body of sentences providing details that support the topic sentence | Evidence supporting the claim and commentary explaining how the evidence ties to the text |
| Concluding sentence | Concluding sentence |

Table 1-13

Although the topic sentence or claim can appear anywhere in the paragraph, in a stand-alone paragraph it is usually most effective at the beginning.

Read the following very short story, "Sticks," by George Saunders. Then read the paragraph of literary analysis that follows it and note its components.

### STICKS

Every year Thanksgiving night we flocked out behind Dad as he dragged the Santa suit to the road and draped it over a kind of crucifix[1] he'd built out of a metal pole in the yard. Super Bowl week the pole was dressed in a jersey and Rod's helmet and Rod had to clear it with Dad if he wanted to take the helmet off. On the Fourth of July the pole was Uncle Sam, on Veteran's Day a soldier, on Halloween a ghost. The pole was Dad's only concession to glee. We were allowed a single Crayola from the box at a time. One Christmas Eve he shrieked at Kimmie for wasting an apple slice. He hovered over us as we poured ketchup saying: good enough good enough good enough. Birthday parties consisted of cupcakes, no ice cream. The first time I brought a date over she said: what's with your dad and that pole? and I sat there blinking.

We left home, married, had children of our own, found the seeds of meanness blooming also within us. Dad began dressing the pole with more complexity and less discernible logic. He draped some kind of fur over it on Groundhog Day and lugged out a floodlight to ensure a shadow. When an earthquake struck Chile he lay the pole on its side and spray painted a rift in the earth. Mom died and he dressed the pole as Death and hung from the crossbar photos of Mom as a baby. We'd stop by and find odd talismans from his youth arranged around the base: army medals, theater tickets, old sweatshirts, tubes of Mom's makeup. One autumn he painted the pole bright yellow. He covered it with cotton swabs that winter for warmth and provided offspring by hammering in six crossed sticks around the yard. He ran lengths of string between the pole and the sticks, and taped to the string letters of apology, admissions of error, pleas for understanding, all written in a frantic hand on index cards. He painted a sign saying LOVE and hung it from the pole and another that said FORGIVE? and then he died in the hall with the radio on and we sold the house to a young couple who yanked out the pole and the sticks and left them by the road on garbage day.

---

1 **crucifix:** a representation of a cross

| Paragraph of Literary Analysis | Components |
|---|---|
| <u>In "Sticks" by George Saunders, Dad's changing decorations of the pole reflect his gradual realization that he has lost his chance for generous family love.</u> At first, Dad's dressing of the pole is playful, "his only concession to glee." It was also, at least at the beginning, a family affair. The family "flocked" behind Dad with the Santa suit, suggesting a family connectedness, and dressing the pole was a holiday tradition. At the same time, however, the narrator provides examples of his father's stinginess (limiting crayons and ketchup, for example). By the second paragraph, the distance between the father and his family grows, and the dad's dressing of the pole becomes darker and more bizarre. Maybe feeling the ground shifting beneath his own feet as his family moves on (the grown kids who feel his "meanness blooming" inside themselves "stop by" rather than really visit), he marks the earthquake in Chile with the pole. When his wife dies, completing his isolation, the father mourns by dressing the pole as Death. He then seems to begin a reflection on his life by leaving talismans of his younger days and everyday mementos of his wife. His final acts with the pole—creating offspring connected by strings—seem to be frantic efforts to create the connected family he never achieved. He looks for love and forgiveness but then dies alone, having missed his chance for a family of generous love. | **Claim:** highlights tension between what was and what could have been<br><br>**Textual evidence**<br><br>**Commentary** showing the tie between the evidence and the idea of family in the claim<br><br>**Textual evidence** supporting claim by identifying ungenerous acts<br><br><br>**Textual evidence** (how the pole was used) and commentary explaining how that reflects distance within the family<br><br><br><br><br><br>**Textual evidence** (creating connected family) with commentary explaining how it relates to the idea of family in the claim |

 **Remember:** In literary analysis, the initial components of a paragraph are the claim and textual evidence that defends the claim. (LAN-1.C)

## 5.3 Checkpoint

1. How do the components in a standard paragraph correspond to those in a paragraph of literary analysis?

2. What is the difference between evidence and commentary? Use examples from the paragraph of literary analysis above in your explanation.

**Composing on Your Own**

Use your chart from the previous Composing on Your Own activity to draft your own paragraph of literary analysis.

# Part 5  Apply What You Have Learned

Closely read the following story, "The Kiss," by Kate Chopin. Using the skills and strategies you have learned in this unit, write a single paragraph that makes a defensible claim about an interpretation of the text and that provides evidence and commentary that explains how the evidence justifies the claim.

## THE KISS

1      It was still quite light out of doors, but inside with the curtains drawn and the smoldering fire sending out a dim, uncertain glow, the room was full of deep shadows.

2      Brantain sat in one of these shadows; it had overtaken him and he did not mind. The obscurity lent him courage to keep his eyes fastened as ardently as he liked upon the girl who sat in the firelight.

3      She was very handsome, with a certain fine, rich coloring that belongs to the healthy brune[1] type. She was quite composed, as she idly stroked the satiny coat of the cat that lay curled in her lap, and she occasionally sent a slow glance into the shadow where her companion sat. They were talking low, of indifferent things which plainly were not the things that occupied their thoughts. She knew that he loved her—a frank, blustering fellow without guile enough to conceal his feelings, and no desire to do so. For two weeks past he had sought her society eagerly and persistently. She was confidently waiting for him to declare himself and she meant to accept him. The rather insignificant and unattractive Brantain was enormously rich; and she liked and required the entourage[2] which wealth could give her.

**Source:** Getty Images

---

1 **brune:** brunette
2 **entourage:** people attending a person of stature

4     During one of the pauses between their talk of the last tea and the next reception the door opened and a young man entered whom Brantain knew quite well. The girl turned her face toward him. A stride or two brought him to her side, and bending over her chair—before she could suspect his intention, for she did not realize that he had not seen her visitor—he pressed an ardent, lingering kiss upon her lips.

5     Brantain slowly arose; so did the girl arise, but quickly, and the newcomer stood between them, a little amusement and some defiance struggling with the confusion in his face.

6     "I believe," stammered Brantain, "I see that I have stayed too long. I—I had no idea—that is, I must wish you good-bye." He was clutching his hat with both hands, and probably did not perceive that she was extending her hand to him, her presence of mind had not completely deserted her; but she could not have trusted herself to speak.

7     "Hang me if I saw him sitting there, Nattie! I know it's deuced[3] awkward for you. But I hope you'll forgive me this once—this very first break. Why, what's the matter?"

8     "Don't touch me; don't come near me," she returned angrily. "What do you mean by entering the house without ringing?"

9     "I came in with your brother, as I often do," he answered coldly, in self-justification. "We came in the side way. He went upstairs and I came in here hoping to find you. The explanation is simple enough and ought to satisfy you that the misadventure was unavoidable. But do say that you forgive me, Nathalie," he entreated, softening.

10     "Forgive you! You don't know what you are talking about. Let me pass. It depends upon—a good deal whether I ever forgive you."

11     At that next reception which she and Brantain had been talking about she approached the young man with a delicious frankness of manner when she saw him there.

12     "Will you let me speak to you a moment or two, Mr. Brantain?" she asked with an engaging but perturbed smile. He seemed extremely unhappy; but when she took his arm and walked away with him, seeking a retired corner, a ray of hope mingled with the almost comical misery of his expression. She was apparently very outspoken.

13     "Perhaps I should not have sought this interview, Mr. Brantain; but—but, oh, I have been very uncomfortable, almost miserable since that little encounter the other afternoon. When I thought how you might have misinterpreted it, and believed things"—hope was plainly gaining the ascendancy over misery in Brantain's round, guileless face—"Of course, I know it is nothing to you, but for my own sake I do want you to understand that Mr. Harvy is an intimate friend of long standing. Why, we have always been like cousins—like brother and sister, I may say. He is my brother's most intimate associate and often fancies that he is entitled to the same privileges as the family. Oh, I know it is absurd, uncalled for, to tell you this; undignified even," she was almost weeping, "but it makes so much

---

3 **deuced:** extremely

difference to me what you think of—of me." Her voice had grown very low and agitated. The misery had all disappeared from Brantain's face.

14    "Then you do really care what I think, Miss Nathalie? May I call you Miss Nathalie?" They turned into a long, dim corridor that was lined on either side with tall, graceful plants. They walked slowly to the very end of it. When they turned to retrace their steps Brantain's face was radiant and hers was triumphant.

15    Harvy was among the guests at the wedding; and he sought her out in a rare moment when she stood alone.

16    "Your husband," he said, smiling, "has sent me over to kiss you."

17    A quick blush suffused her face and round polished throat. "I suppose it's natural for a man to feel and act generously on an occasion of this kind. He tells me he doesn't want his marriage to interrupt wholly that pleasant intimacy which has existed between you and me. I don't know what you've been telling him," with an insolent[4] smile, "but he has sent me here to kiss you."

18    She felt like a chess player who, by the clever handling of his pieces, sees the game taking the course intended. Her eyes were bright and tender with a smile as they glanced up into his; and her lips looked hungry for the kiss which they invited.

19    "But, you know," he went on quietly, "I didn't tell him so, it would have seemed ungrateful, but I can tell you. I've stopped kissing women; it's dangerous."

20    Well, she had Brantain and his million left. A person can't have everything in this world; and it was a little unreasonable of her to expect it.

**Reflect on the Essential Question**  Write a brief response that answers the essential question: *How can you communicate your interpretation of a work of literature in a paragraph that asserts a claim and supports it with evidence?* In your answer, correctly use the key terms listed on page 54.

---

4  **insolent:** arrogant and disrespectful

# Unit 1 Review

## Section I: Multiple Choice

## Section II: Free Response

---

## Section I: Multiple Choice

Questions 1–11. Read the following passage carefully before you choose your answers.

1     What happy hours Mary and I have passed while sitting at our work by the fire, or wandering on the heath-clad hills, or idling under the weeping birch (the only considerable tree in the garden), talking of future happiness to ourselves and our parents, of what we would do, and see, and possess; with no firmer foundation for our goodly superstructure than the riches that were expected to flow in upon us from the success of the worthy merchant's speculations. Our father was nearly as bad as ourselves; only that he affected not to be so much in earnest: expressing his bright hopes and sanguine[1] expectations in jests and playful sallies,[2] that always struck me as being exceedingly witty and pleasant. Our mother laughed with delight to see him so hopeful and happy: but still she feared he was setting his heart too much upon the matter; and once I heard her whisper as she left the room, 'God grant he be not disappointed! I know not how he would bear it.'

2     Disappointed he was; and bitterly, too. It came like a thunder-clap on us all, that the vessel which contained our fortune had been wrecked, and gone to the bottom with all its stores,[3] together with several of the crew, and the unfortunate merchant himself. I was grieved for him; I was grieved for the overthrow of all our air-built castles: but, with the elasticity of youth, I soon recovered the shock.

3     Though riches had charms, poverty had no terrors for an inexperienced girl like me. Indeed, to say the truth, there was something exhilarating in the idea of being driven to straits,[4] and thrown upon our own resources. I only wished papa, mamma, and Mary were all of the same mind as myself; and then, instead of lamenting past calamities we might all cheerfully set to work to remedy them; and the greater the difficulties, the harder our present privations, the greater should be our cheerfulness to endure the latter, and our vigor to contend against the former.

---

1  **sanguine:** optimistic
2  **sallies:** flights of fancy
3  **stores:** supplies
4  **straits:** confining circumstances

4    Mary did not lament, but she brooded continually over the misfortune, and sank into a state of dejection from which no effort of mine could rouse her. I could not possibly bring her to regard the matter on its bright side as I did: and indeed I was so fearful of being charged with childish frivolity, or stupid insensibility, that I carefully kept most of my bright ideas and cheering notions to myself; well knowing they could not be appreciated.

5    My mother thought only of consoling my father, and paying our debts and retrenching our expenditure by every available means; but my father was completely overwhelmed by the calamity: health, strength, and spirits sank beneath the blow, and he never wholly recovered them. In vain my mother strove to cheer him, by appealing to his piety, to his courage, to his affection for herself and us. That very affection was his greatest torment: it was for our sakes he had so ardently longed to increase his fortune—it was our interest that had lent such brightness to his hopes, and that imparted such bitterness to his present distress. He now tormented himself with remorse at having neglected my mother's advice; which would at least have saved him from the additional burden of debt—he vainly reproached himself for having brought her from the dignity, the ease, the luxury of her former station to toil with him through the cares and toils of poverty. It was gall and wormwood[5] to his soul to see that splendid, highly-accomplished woman, once so courted and admired, transformed into an active managing housewife, with hands and head continually occupied with household labours and household economy. The very willingness with which she performed these duties, the cheerfulness with which she bore her reverses, and the kindness which withheld her from imputing the smallest blame to him, were all perverted by this ingenious self-tormentor into further aggravations of his suffering.

---

1.   Which detail from the passage reveals the narrator's ignorance of her family's situation?

(A) She and Mary would wander "on the heath-clad hills" (paragraph 1).

(B) She "laughed with delight" (paragraph 1).

(C) She thought "there was something exhilarating" about their poverty (paragraph 3).

(D) "[S]he brooded continually" (paragraph 4).

(E) She thought only of paying "debts and retrenching our expenditure" (paragraph 5).

---

5 **wormwood:** something bitter

2. In relation to the first paragraph, the second paragraph indicates a shift from
   (A) a loving family to a fearful and lost family
   (B) the joys of childhood to the realities of young adulthood
   (C) the severity of the father to his patience and joy
   (D) concerns that the girls will never marry to worries about money
   (E) the hopes and joys of the family to the tragedy of their lost wealth

3. The narrator's perspective on the events of the passage is most affected by
   (A) her mother's selfless devotion to the family, especially her father
   (B) the pain she experienced before the beginning of the passage
   (C) the loss of her parents in a shipwreck
   (D) her family's poverty
   (E) her close relationship with the characters and events of the narrative

Questions 4 and 5 are covered in Unit 2.

4. The word choice in paragraph 2 ("It came like a thunder-clap on us all") emphasizes what about the experiences of the narrator's family?
   (A) The overwhelming shock of losing their fortune
   (B) Their inability to weather bad situations
   (C) Their fear of not being able to keep up appearances
   (D) Their concerns about other families trying to be better than them
   (E) The enduring pain of losing a child

5. The relationship of the first sentence of the passage and the last sentence of the passage is best expressed in which of the following statements?
   (A) The "hours Mary and [the narrator] passed while sitting" (paragraph 1) are contrasted with the hours that they must now work.
   (B) "The only considerable tree in the garden" (paragraph 1) must now be chopped for fire wood.
   (C) The mother's attempts to behave with "cheerfulness" and "kindness" (paragraph 5) are contrasted with images of true cheer and "happiness" (paragraph 1).
   (D) The "aggravations of [the father's] suffering" (paragraph 5) are all due to the girls' playing in "the garden" (paragraph 1).
   (E) The mother's "cheerfulness" (paragraph 5) is as great as the girls' "happy hours" (paragraph 1).

Questions 6 and 7 are covered in Unit 3.

6. What do the details of the setting in paragraph 1 ("What ... parents") establish about the social and cultural situation of the family?

   (A) The family regularly takes advantage of the people who own land around them.

   (B) The family enjoys gardening but not trees.

   (C) The family is wealthy enough to have leisure time to enjoy the things around them.

   (D) The family is so accustomed to being wealthy that they have never worked.

   (E) The father often ignores or neglects the children.

7. Which of the following is the best possible defensible interpretation of the passage as a whole?

   (A) Siblings stand beside one another, regardless of what happens in a family.

   (B) Parents will generally give anything for their children.

   (C) Even family is bothersome sometimes, and everyone needs space to maintain family relationships.

   (D) Despite any hardship, a family generally supports and cares for one another.

   (E) Wealth changes people.

Question 8 is covered in Unit 4.

8. Based on their interactions with the setting in the first sentence of the passage ("What ... speculations."), the narrator and Mary can initially be described as

   (A) spoiled girls with complete disregard for others

   (B) carefree children, naïve to any concerns about poverty

   (C) ignorant children who fail to notice important things around them

   (D) delightful girls certain to marry into wealthy families

   (E) characters meant to represent the author and her sisters

9. This narrator's reliability is most directly affected by

   (A) her sister Mary's perspective

   (B) her mother's devotion to her father

   (C) her distance from the events of the passage as her family suffered

   (D) her direct involvement with, and suffering through, the events of the passage

   (E) her interactions with her mother and how those affected her relationship with her father and sister

10. Which of the following lines best demonstrates the mother's complexity?

    (A) Paragraph 2, sentence 1 ("Disappointed … himself.")

    (B) Paragraph 3, sentence 3 ("I only … myself;")

    (C) Paragraph 5, sentence 1 ("My mother … available means;")

    (D) Paragraph 5, sentence 2 ("In vain … and us.")

    (E) Paragraph 5, sentence 6 ("The very … suffering.")

11. Showing how Mary "brooded continually over the misfortune, and sank into a state of dejection" establishes which of the following relationships between her and the narrator as characters?

    (A) Mary is a contrast to the narrator who seems generally unaffected by the family's change in situation.

    (B) Mary and the narrator fall into bitter conflict over the family's circumstances.

    (C) The narrator is a stronger person than Mary.

    (D) Mary fails to find a husband and blames the narrator for her misfortunes.

    (E) The narrator and Mary are essentially the same character but with different motivations.

## Section II: Free Response

**Question 1 is a poetry analysis and will be introduced in Unit 2.**

### Question 2: Prose Fiction Analysis

On pages 67–68 is an excerpt from *Agnes Grey,* a novel written in 1847 by Anne Brontë. In the passage, a young girl explains the reactions of her family members to a sudden fall into poverty.

Read the passage carefully. Then, in a well-written paragraph that makes a defensible claim and develops commentary to explain how the evidence supports the claim, analyze the narrator's perspective on the dramatic situation of the passage.

In your response you should do the following:

- Respond to the prompt with a claim that presents a defensible interpretation.
- Select and use evidence to support your line of reasoning.
- Explain how the evidence supports your line of reasoning.
- Use appropriate grammar and punctuation in communicating your argument.

### Question 3: Literary Argument—Character Values and Motivations

Characters in works of literature often reveal their values by the things they say and do. Often, those same values work to motivate a character to do something or not do something.

Choose a work of fiction in which a character's behavior is clearly based on his or her values. Then, in a well-written paragraph, make a defensible claim about the values of that character and support that claim with evidence from the text and well-developed commentary. Do not merely summarize the plot.

In your response you should do the following:

- Respond to the prompt with a claim that presents a defensible interpretation.
- Provide evidence to support your line of reasoning.
- Explain how the evidence supports your line of reasoning.
- Use appropriate grammar and punctuation in communicating your argument.

# UNIT 2

# Poetry and the Shift

[Poetry I]

**Part 1: Characterization**
**Part 2: Structure, Contrasts, and Shifts**
**Part 3: Relationships Among Words**
**Part 4: Similes and Metaphors**
**Part 5: Writing About Literature II**

---

**ENDURING UNDERSTANDINGS AND SKILLS: Unit 2**

## Part 1 Characterization

**Understand**

Characters in literature allow readers to study and explore a range of values, beliefs, assumptions, biases, and cultural norms represented by those characters. (CHR-1)

**Demonstrate**

Identify and describe what specific textual details reveal about a character, that character's perspective, and that character's motives. (1.A)

## Part 2 Structure, Contrasts, and Shifts

**Understand**

The arrangement of the parts and sections of a text, the relationship of the parts to each other, and the sequence in which text reveals information are all structural choices made by a writer that contribute to the reader's interpretation of a text. (STR-1)

**Demonstrate**

Explain the function of structure in a text. (3.C)
Explain the function of contrasts within a text. (3.D)

## Part 3 Relationships Among Words

**Understand**

Comparisons, representations, and associations shift meaning from the literal to the figurative and invite readers to interpret a text. (FIG-1)

**Demonstrate**

Explain the function of specific words and phrases in a text. (5.B)

# Unit 2 Overview

Chances are you recognize a poem when you see one. How do you know? Is this a poem?

### HOW A SNOWFLAKE FORMS

A snowflake begins to form when a particle of dust becomes coated in water vapor high in the Earth's atmosphere. That coating makes it heavier and it begins to fall. As it falls, more water vapor comes in contact with it and the ice begins forming into a six-sided crystal. Each new layer of water vapor adds intricacies to the hexagonal crystal, and no two snowflakes are ever the same. By the time it hits the ground, a snowflake has formed into its final shape.

Is this a poem?

### SNOWFLAKES

Not slowly wrought, nor treasured for their form
In heaven, but by the blind self of the storm
Spun off, each driven individual
Perfected in the moment of his fall.

You probably knew right away that the first example is not a poem and the second is—it is a poem by former U.S. Poet Laureate Howard Nemerov. You probably recognized it by the way it is presented on the page—in distinct lines—and possibly by the rhyme of line 2 with line 1 and line 4 with line 3. You might also note that the words in the first prose example are chosen and arranged to suggest straightforward, common speech. The words in the poem, however, are not chosen or arranged to reflect common speech. Instead, they are arranged for their meanings, sounds, rhymes, rhythms, and emotional impact.

Even though it is easy to recognize, poetry is hard to define. Samuel Johnson, an 18th-century English writer, went so far as to say, "To circumscribe poetry by a definition will only show the narrowness of the definer." While some poets turned to metaphor to define poems ("imaginary gardens with real toads," wrote poet Marianne Moore), Nemerov developed a thoughtful, literal definition of poetry: "literature that evokes a concentrated imaginative awareness of experience or a specific emotional response through language chosen and arranged for its meaning, sound, and rhythm." Understanding each part of this definition will help you put it all together. Poetry is

- "literature that evokes a concentrated imaginative awareness of experience" =
  Poetry is literature—artistic writing—that creates in readers' imaginations an intense sense of having an experience.

- "or a specific emotional response" =
  Poetry evokes certain feelings in readers resulting from carefully crafted details.

- "through language chosen for its meaning" =
  The words in poems are chosen carefully for their meanings (both denotative and connotative). Words in poems often have more than one meaning.

- [through language chosen for its] "sound" =
  Poets choose words that have relationships between their sounds, such as starting with the same letter or ending with a similar sound.

- [through language chosen for its] "rhythm" =
  Poets choose words whose pronunciation creates a beat or meter in the readers' ears.

Despite the differences between prose like the short story you read in Unit 1 and poetry like Nemerov's "Snowflakes," the skills and strategies a reader needs to analyze and interpret a poem are very similar to the skills and strategies you learned in Unit 1. Like characters in fiction, characters in poems reveal their perspectives and biases through details. Like structure in fiction, structure in poetry—the relation of the parts to one another and to the whole—conveys and amplifies meaning. However, poetry relies more on "language chosen and arranged for its meaning, sound, and rhythm" than does prose. This unit will help strengthen the skills you need to analyze and interpret a poem and to share your interpretation in writing.

The following poem, published in 1987, recounts the thoughts of a White speaker during her chance encounter with a Black commuter. Before you read, take a minute to get an impression of the poem by noting the title (above) and scanning the poem. Then read it carefully to get a general understanding of it. Almost all poetry needs to be read more than once because so much is packed into so few words. Poetry is also meant to be heard, so try to read every poem aloud at least once. You will have many opportunities to return to this poem throughout this unit.

The boy and I face each other.
His feet are huge, in black sneakers
laced with white in a complex pattern like a
set of intentional scars. We are stuck on
5    opposite sides of the car, a couple of
molecules stuck in a rod of light
rapidly moving through darkness.
He has the casual cold look of a mugger,
alert under hooded lids. He is wearing
10   red, like the inside of the body
exposed. I am wearing dark fur, the
whole skin of an animal taken and
used. I look at his raw face,
he looks at my fur coat, and I don't
15   know if I am in his power—
he could take my coat so easily, my
briefcase, my life—
or if he is in my power, the way I am
living off his life, eating the steak
20   he does not eat, as if I am taking
the food from his mouth. And he is black
and I am white, and without meaning or
trying to I must profit from his darkness,
the way he absorbs the murderous beams of the
25   nation's heart, as black cotton
absorbs the heat of the sun and holds it. There is
no way to know how easy this
white skin makes my life, this
life he could take so easily and
30   break across his knee like a stick the way his
own back is being broken, the
rod of his soul that at birth was dark and
fluid and rich as the heart of a seedling
ready to thrust up into any available light.

This unit will focus on differences between poetry and prose—specifically, how the structures of poetry contribute to meaning and interpretations. It will also explore the importance of word choice and simile and metaphor. Before you learn new skills and information, assess what you already know. Answer the following questions about "On the Subway." Don't worry if you find these challenging. Learning scientists have found that answering questions on a subject before formally learning about it is one way to help you deepen your understanding of new concepts.

## CLOSE READING

**1.** What details reveal the narrator's perspective and biases?

**2.** How does the poem's structure show relationships among ideas?

**3.** What contrasts highlight key ideas in the poem?

**4.** What words, phrases, or clauses had a strong impact on you?

**5.** Where do similes and/or metaphors help convey an idea artfully?

## INTERPRETATION

**1.** What bigger idea or theme might the poem be about? What might it be saying about something beyond the poem?

**2.** What are the most important details in the text that would support your idea about what the poem is about (that is, your interpretation)?

**Source:** Getty Images

# Part 1

# Characterization

**Enduring Understanding and Skill**

## Part 1 Characterization

### Understand
Characters in literature allow readers to study and explore a range of values, beliefs, assumptions, biases, and cultural norms represented by those characters. (CHR-1)

### Demonstrate
Identify and describe what specific textual details reveal about a character, that character's perspective, and that character's motives. (1.A)

See also Units 1, 3, 4 & 6

**Source:** *AP® English Literature and Composition Course and Exam Description*

**Essential Question:** How do the specific textual details of a poem reveal the nature of a character and that character's perspective and motives?

Characters in poetry, as in prose, allow readers to study and explore a range of values, beliefs, assumptions, biases, and cultural norms. Authors shape readers' impressions of characters and bring them to life through **details**—pieces of specific information about characters' physical descriptions, words, thoughts, and actions. These details are at the core of analyzing characters and their perspectives and motivations: How do they see the world? What drives them? The details provide the evidence to answer these questions.

| KEY TERMS | | | |
|---|---|---|---|
| details | perspectives | biases | motives |

# 1.1 Details that Reveal Character, Perspectives, and Biases | CHR-1.E

Poet Rita Dove has said that "poetry is language at its most distilled and most powerful." Out of all the rich and abundant qualities every actual person has, a poet distills them—boils them down to their essence—to reveal a character that conveys the poet's vision and message. From those distilled details, poets also reveal characters' **perspectives,** the way characters see and understand the world. The details also reveal characters' **biases,** the inescapable inclinations to like, dislike, or just have an opinion about something or someone based on experiences. The words characters use, the details they provide in the text, the organization of their thinking, the decisions they make, and the actions they take all reveal their character, perspectives, and biases.

The following poem by African American poet Marilyn Nelson tells the story of the poet's mother on her first day of teaching at an elementary school on an Air Force base in Kansas just four months after the landmark Supreme Court decision, *Brown v. Board of Education of Topeka, Kansas*, paved the way for integration of schools throughout the nation.

### THE CHILDREN'S MOON

In my navy shirtwaist dress[1] and three-inch heels,
my pearl clip-ons[2] and newly red-rinsed curls,
I smoothed on lipstick, lipstick-marked my girls,
saluted and held thumbs-up to my darling Mel,
5    and drove myself to school for the first day.

Over the schoolyard a silver lozenge
dissolved into the morning's blue cauldron.
Enter twenty seven-year-old white children.
*Look, children,* I said as they found their desks:
10    *The children's moon![3] A special good luck sign!*

We pledged allegiance, and silently prayed.
George Washington watched sternly from his frame.
I turned to the blackboard and wrote my name.
I thought I heard, *She's the REAL teacher's maid!*
15    I thought I heard echoes of history.
But when I turned, every child in the room
had one hand up, asking, *What is the children's moon?*

---

1 **shirtwaist dress:** a style of dress popular in the 1950s that borrows some elements of men's shirts, such as a collar, buttons down the front, and cuffed sleeves
2 **clip-ons:** earrings that clip onto the ear lobe
3 **children's moon:** a moon visible in the morning sky when children are awake to see it

# Textual Details that Reveal Character

The poem "The Children's Moon" tells a simple story of a teacher going to class on the first day of school. As the character of the teacher begins the story, though, she doesn't simply say, "I got dressed, kissed my daughters goodbye, waved to my husband, and went to school." Instead, she provides descriptive details that reveal the nature of her character through the choices she makes. For example, she explains her wardrobe choices in vivid detail: not just a dress and good shoes but a "navy shirtwaist dress and three-inch heels." The chart below shows these and other details of her appearance and what they may reveal about her character.

| Details | What They May Reveal about Character |
| --- | --- |
| *Clothing:*<br>navy shirtwaist dress<br>three-inch heels<br>pearl clip-ons | She chooses to dress in a formal but not fancy way in the popular style of the day, suggesting she takes her job and her position of authority in the classroom seriously. The button-down dress conveys an almost military neatness, especially with the word *navy* describing it, even though that word refers to a dark blue color. These details convey the sense of a disciplined person. |
| *Hair and make-up:*<br>newly red-rinsed curls<br>lipstick | The narrator has "newly" applied a red rinse to her hair, suggesting she did so for the start of school and conveying her concern about looking as good as she can for her job. The last detail she mentions, lipstick, is the finishing touch to her carefully thought through appearance. |

Table 2-1

On the face of it, lines 3–5 just finish the first part of the story—the narrator leaves her family and heads for school. However, the words and actions in those lines reveal even more about the narrator, as the chart below shows.

| Words and Actions | What They May Reveal about Character |
| --- | --- |
| *Saying goodbye:*<br>lipstick-marked my girls<br>saluted<br>held thumbs up | The expression "lipstick-marked" instead of simply "kissed" conveys the idea that the narrator is leaving an impression on her daughters, aware of her role in raising them well. The word *saluted*, especially near the word *navy*, reinforces the military discipline the woman appears to have. Holding thumbs up conveys a sense of confidence and optimism. |
| *Going to school:*<br>drove myself to school | The narrator doesn't get a ride to school—she explicitly drives herself to school. The detail of this action adds *independent* and *self-sufficient* to the words that describe the narrator. |

Table 2-2

## Details that Reveal Perspective and Bias

Characters also reveal their perspectives and biases through textual details, including the decisions they make and the way they think. For example, the reader experiences the classroom through the perspective of the teacher. She stands at the front of the room while the children take their seats facing her; readers see the class through her eyes. She also shows her perspective when she decides to point out the children's moon, "a special good luck sign!" Readers can take from that decision that the teacher has hopeful expectations.

Readers learn about the teacher's bias as well. When she turns her back to her students to write her name on the blackboard, she imagines she hears students disrespecting her authority, saying that she is not the real teacher, but instead is the real teacher's maid. She believes she hears "echoes of history." That bias is possibly the result of her lived experiences as an African American in the 1940s and 1950s. However, the children's interest in the moon when she turns back to see them puts those concerns to rest.

The table below summarizes the decisions and way of thinking that reveal the perspective and bias of the teacher.

| Decision | What It May Reveal about Perspective |
|---|---|
| *Pointing out the children's moon as students take their seats facing her* | The teacher stands at the front of the class in a position of authority even though a long history of racial inequality in the country preceded this moment. The teacher chooses to point out the children's moon, which reveals her upbeat and optimistic perspective. |
| **Thinking** | **What It May Reveal about Bias** |
| *Imagining that the children are questioning her authority by saying behind her back that she is not the real teacher because she is Black* | The racial prejudice the teacher may have experienced biased her toward believing that White children would not accept her authority and respect her. |

Table 2-3

## Details that Reveal Motivation

When you have determined a character's perspective and bias, you can also determine that character's **motives**—the driving force behind a character's behaviors and actions, since perspective and bias influence motivation. Close readers focus on four types of details to determine motives: what a character says and thinks and how a character acts and reacts. To help you recall what to look for when analyzing characters, remember **STEAL** (see Unit 1).

| S | Speech—What does the character say? |
|---|---|
| T | Thoughts—What is the character thinking? |
| E | Effects on others—How do others interact with or react to the character? |
| A | Actions—How does the character behave or act? |
| L | Looks—What details describe the character? |

Table 2-4

In "The Children's Moon," you have already seen an analysis of what the teacher says and thinks and how the teacher acts. How do you think the teacher *reacts* when she sees the hands of the students and hears the question on all their minds? All the rest of the details in the poem point to the likelihood that she is very pleased and very relieved that the children are focused on the moon and not dwelling on and possibly not even noticing the racial difference between them and their teacher.

Putting all these details together, a reader may surmise that the teacher's motives are to exert her appropriate authority, present a positive attitude, tamp down her own bias, and seek a productive learning environment in the educational world after *Brown* v. *Board of Education.*

**Remember:** Characters reveal their perspectives and biases through the words they use, the details they provide in the text, the organization of their thinking, the decisions they make, and the actions they take. (CHR-1.E)

Source: Getty Images

The Moon is visible in daylight most days, but the best times to see the "children's moon" are close to the first and last quarter.

*What idea might the children's moon represent in the poem?*

## 1.1 Checkpoint

*Reread "On the Subway" on page 76. Then complete the open-response activities and answer the multiple-choice questions.*

1. In the opening lines of "On the Subway," the speaker says *The boy and I face each other.* Focusing on word choice and physical description, explain how this simple sentence might reveal both perspective and bias.

2. Reread these lines from "On the Subway." Then on separate paper complete column three of the table below.

> He has the casual cold look of a mugger,
> alert under hooded lids. He is wearing
> 10   red, like the inside of the body
> exposed. I am wearing dark fur, the
> whole skin of an animal taken and
> used. I look at his raw face,

| Thinking, Decisions, and Actions | | |
|---|---|---|
| **Element from the text** | **Text** | **How it reveals bias** |
| Thinking | *He has the casual cold look of a mugger, / alert under hooded lids.* | |
| **Element from the text** | **Text** | **How it reveals perspective** |
| Thinking | *He is wearing / red, like the inside of the body / exposed. I am wearing dark fur, the / whole skin of an animal taken and / used.* | |
| **Element from the text** | **Text** | **How it reveals bias** |
| Decisions and Actions | *I look at his raw face* | |

3. At the beginning of "On the Subway," which of the following details best represents the speaker's perspective of the situation as a whole?
   - (A) "The boy and I face each other."
   - (B) "His feet are huge, in black sneakers"
   - (C) "We are stuck on / opposite sides of the car"
   - (D) "a couple of / molecules stuck in a rod of light"
   - (E) "He has the casual cold look of a mugger"

**4.** The details about the boy's shoes in lines 2–4 suggest the speaker's bias toward the boy and how the speaker believes the boy may be

(A) a conformist because the boy wears flashy, fashionable sneakers

(B) menacing, as suggested by the size of the boy's feet and the lace "scars"

(C) privileged, since the boy can afford such expensive sneakers

(D) pompous, considering the superior intelligence required for such a complex lace pattern

(E) aloof, due to the boy focusing on his sneakers rather than conversing with the speaker

**Creating on Your Own**

Choose one of the following scenes or think of one of your own. Imagine two characters within that scene and make a STEAL chart for each (see below). Identify the bias that might be present in the scene and "distill" it into only a few well-chosen words, details, or actions that could be the first few lines of a poem. Save your work for later use.

Possible scenes:

| | |
|---|---|
| • A convenience store at closing time<br>• A school cafeteria<br>• Waiting in line to vote | • Moving to a new neighborhood<br>• Playing basketball on a public court<br>• A protest demonstration |

| STEAL Chart to Analyze and Develop Characters | |
|---|---|
| **S**peech—What does the character say? | |
| **T**houghts—What is the character thinking? | |
| **E**ffects on others—How do others interact with or react to the character? | |
| **A**ctions—How does the character behave or act? | |
| **L**ooks—What details describe the character? | |

# Part 1  Apply What You Have Learned

Write a paragraph explaining how the details in "On the Subway" reveal the speaker's perspective and bias. Use details from the text for support.

**Reflect on the Essential Question**  Write a brief response that answers the essential question: *How do the specific textual details of a poem reveal the nature of a character and that character's perspective and motives?* In your answer, correctly use the key terms on page 78.

# Part 2

# Structure, Contrasts, and Shifts

## Part 2  Structure, Contrasts, and Shifts

### Understand
The arrangement of the parts and sections of a text, the relationship of the parts to each other, and the sequence in which the text reveals information are all structural choices made by a writer that contribute to the reader's interpretation of a text. (STR-1)

### Demonstrate
Explain the function of structure in a text. (3.C)
Explain the function of contrasts within a text. (3.D)

**Source:** *AP® English Literature and Composition Course and Exam Description*

**Essential Question:** How do structure and contrast contribute to the development of ideas in a poem?

The word *poem* derives from the Greek word meaning "a thing made," and a poet is a "maker of things." Poets have also been known as "shapers." In *A Midsummer Night's Dream* (Act V, Scene 1), Shakespeare describes how poets imagine "the forms of things unknown" and turn them into shapes, giving "airy nothing" a home and a name. Making something out of "airy nothing" requires some clever tools. You read in Part 1 about the power of words and details as tools to convey meaning. Poets also use structure, or organization, and contrast to give their ideas shape and subtlety.

---

### KEY TERMS

| | | |
|---|---|---|
| structure | contrast | shift |
| stanza | imagery | juxtaposition |

---

# 2.1 Structure | STR-1.D, STR-1.E, STR-1.F

In a poem, the words themselves—expressing physical descriptions of characters, their thoughts and speech, the decisions they make, and the actions they take—reveal much about characters and help convey a poet's vision. The arrangement of those words and the lines they appear in also contribute to the expression of ideas in a poem. The organization and arrangement of lines and groups of lines is the poem's **structure**. The structure of a poem, by connecting and layering ideas through the relative positions and placement of words and lines in the text, affects readers' reactions. Sometimes connecting certain ideas creates a strong emotional response in the reader, an effect poet Dale Wisely calls "the turn of the knife."

While writers of novels and short stories use sentences and paragraphs to move the reader forward, poets use lines and stanzas. A **stanza** is a group of related lines separated from other lines in the poem, sometimes in a way that repeats a rhythm or rhyme scheme. Like paragraphs in a story, stanzas guide readers through a poem. For example, the first stanza in a poem often introduces characters, the setting, situation, and sometimes even the conflict or crisis. From there, each stanza helps to build on and support the ideas presented in the opening stanza.

## Line and Stanza Breaks

In the sketch below, you can no doubt discern a bird, but the artist is careful to have the image reflect the "idea" of a bird rather than a literal bird, relying on the viewer's mind to fill in missing lines. Like poets, some artists want to give form to "airy nothing" without weighing it down with too much literal specificity. To accomplish this same purpose, poets use structural elements to convey subtle meanings, leaving readers to "connect the dots."

**Source:** Getty Images

Poems, like all literature, are open to multiple interpretations.

*How is this sketch like a poem?*

One such structural element is the line break. Compare the first few lines of "The Children's Moon" with those of "On the Subway."

### FROM "THE CHILDREN'S MOON"

In my navy shirtwaist dress and three-inch heels,
my pearl clip-ons and newly red-rinsed curls,
I smoothed on lipstick, lipstick-marked my girls,
saluted and held thumbs-up to my darling Mel,
5    and drove myself to school for the first day.

In "The Children's Moon," the first five lines are one sentence. Each line ends with a punctuation mark that indicates a pause. The commas indicate a slight pause; the period at the end of the last line is a complete stop. That neat, predictable pattern seems to emphasize the neat, put-together nature of the speaker that the words and actions reveal.

### FROM "ON THE SUBWAY"

The boy and I face each other.
His feet are huge, in black sneakers
laced with white in a complex pattern like a
set of intentional scars. We are stuck on
5    opposite sides of the car, a couple of
molecules stuck in a rod of light
rapidly moving through darkness.

In "On the Subway," the first seven lines contain three sentences. The first is short, only one line long, and direct. A period at the end of the first sentence creates a full stop. However, the next two sentences are not as neatly assigned to lines. The second sentence ("His feet are huge . . .") runs over three lines, with no punctuation until the middle of the third line (" . . . intentional scars."). The third sentence runs over four lines. The lack of the neat pattern of lines such as that in "The Children's Moon" may suggest that the runover lines reflect the way the speaker is gradually taking in and making sense of the scene. From the simple "The boy and I face each other," which sets the scene and conflict for the poem, complex thoughts unfold in the mind of the speaker. The reader's pace accelerates following these thoughts because no punctuation at the end of lines forces a pause, and that quickened pace adds a sense of building tension. The third sentence ("We are stuck . . .") expands on the simple idea in the first line but recasts the idea as if the speaker is looking through a microscope, presenting a different perspective.

Stanza breaks function in part to show where one group of related thoughts or ideas ends and another begins. In this way, they contribute to the development of ideas in a poem and the relationships among those ideas. Reread "The Children's Moon" on page 79. Note that there are three stanzas—all but the first separated by a line space between them. The table on the next page shows how each stanza contributes to the development and relationship of ideas.

| Stanza | Development of Ideas | Relationships Among Ideas |
|---|---|---|
| 1 | This stanza introduces and reveals the teacher's character and sets up the situation. | This stanza shows the narrator in her home environment. |
| 2 | Stanza 2 continues the story, showing the narrator arriving at school, noticing the sky, and watching the White children take their seats. She points out the children's moon to them as a sign of good luck. | Between the down-to-earth details of the teacher's preparations for school in the first stanza and the arrival of the White students, the first two lines of the second stanza call attention to something bigger than the schoolyard, bigger than the world itself: the morning sky. The teacher shares that perspective with her students by pointing out the children's moon. |
| 3 | The events in this stanza continue to unfold in chronological order. The school day starts with the pledge of allegiance and continues with a prayer as the nation's first president looks on. The narrator turns her back on the children to write her name on the board and imagines she hears them talking behind her back. | From the expansive perspective of the morning sky, the scene in stanza 3 condenses back into the somewhat rigid confines of the classroom with its regimen of the pledge of allegiance and prayer. The first leader of the nation (in which only White, property-owning males could vote) presides over the classroom as he had presided over the young country. The teacher who seemed so self-assured in her home setting in the first stanza now, in this environment, seems to feel less confident as she wonders if the children are trying to diminish her because of her skin color. |
| 4 | The last stanza, by far the shortest, is the only one with a run over line, perhaps suggesting a more natural flow of understanding between the teacher and students. | Although the teacher was worried about what the children were thinking, they too seem to understand that the interesting thing in that classroom that day wasn't that their teacher was Black but rather that a children's moon, whatever that was, was looking down on them as a sign of good luck. |

Table 2–5

Until that final stanza, readers may expect that the teacher is right about what the students are saying behind her back, that the "echoes of history" are resonating through that classroom. But the ideas in the final two lines, connecting back to the idea of the children's moon, highlight things bigger than any perceived differences between people. The tension that built as the teacher turned her back and wondered what the children were saying is resolved optimistically in the last stanza.

**Remember:** Line and stanza breaks contribute to the development and relationship of ideas in a poem. The arrangement of lines and stanzas contributes to the development and relationship of ideas in a poem. A text's structure affects readers' reactions and expectations by presenting the relationships among ideas of the text via their relative positions and their placement within the text as a whole. (STR-1.D–F)

## 2.1 Checkpoint

*Reread "On the Subway" on page 76. Then complete the open-response activities and answer the multiple-choice questions.*

1. Compare the line breaks in "On the Subway" with those in "The Children's Moon." In what ways are they different? What effect do the different styles of line breaks have on readers?

2. Compare the use of stanzas in "On the Subway" with that in "The Children's Moon." In what way is it different? What effect does the different use of stanzas have on readers?

3. Explain how lines 31–34 of "On the Subway" refer back to earlier lines. How do the relative positions of lines 31–34 and the lines they refer to affect readers' reactions?

4. In "On the Subway," the poem's structure of a single stanza serves primarily to
   (A) reinforce the singular focus on the speaker's and boy's similar life experiences
   (B) contrast the speaker's and boy's clashing attitudes toward public transit
   (C) illustrate the growing divide between socioeconomic classes
   (D) depict the speaker's and boy's mutual distrust of each other
   (E) emphasize how inequality has entwined the speaker's and boy's lives

5. The poem's line breaks, in which complete sentences continue over multiple lines, is best interpreted as representing the speaker's
   (A) persistent confidence in the American dream
   (B) building internal conflict about race
   (C) diminishing concerns about social justice
   (D) heightened awareness of the speaker's intolerance
   (E) growing assurance of the boy's good will

**Creating on Your Own**

Review the first lines of the poem you started. As you think about how those lines might unfold into a complete poem, ask yourself what structure might be most effective in conveying your meaning. Would the ideas be better expressed in stanzas with regular patterns of line breaks, such as those in "The Children's Moon," or would run over or more jagged lines and unpredictable stanza patterns suit the subject better? Write a rough draft of your poem and experiment to find the answer to these questions. Save your work for future use.

# 2.2 Contrasts and Shifts | STR-1.G, STR-1.H, STR-1.I, STR-1.J

In a speech before the United Nations in 2013, Malala Yousafzai, a Nobel Peace Prize winner at age 16 for her advocacy of global education for women, said, "we realize the importance of light when we see darkness. We realize the importance of our voice when we are silenced." In those statements she demonstrated that some ideas are more powerfully understood in contrast to others—light without a contrast to its absence in darkness may not be fully understood. In poetry, where words are relatively few and the reader needs to make connections, contrasts can help illuminate ideas in a way simple description might not. Shifts, or movements of perspective or emphasis, help create these contrasts. Words, structural conventions, or punctuation can signal shifts.

## Contrasts

The word *contrast* derives from the Latin *contrastare*, roughly translating to "stand against." While comparison connects through similarities, **contrast** separates and shows differences in ideas or other elements of a poem. Poets often use contrast to shock and startle us; we expect connections, not contrast. And poets sometimes use our expectations against us—"the turn of the knife"—to create beautiful yet sometimes disturbing comparisons, as in the following poem by Margaret Atwood.

### [YOU FIT INTO ME]

You fit into me
like a hook into an eye

a fish hook
an open eye

**Source:** Getty Images
A hook and eye that fasten two sides of a piece of clothing.

In the first stanza of "[you fit into me]," the image that comes to mind is a hook fitting into an eye on clothing. In stanza two, that image is abruptly contrasted with the painful image of a fish hook fitting into an actual eye.

In "[you fit into me]" the poet uses **imagery**—visually descriptive language—to introduce the startling contrast. Poets introduce contrast in a number of other ways as well, as the table below shows.

| Ways to Introduce Contrast | Explanation | Example |
|---|---|---|
| Focus | The poet refocuses the readers' attention onto a contrasting idea. | The first two lines of the second stanza in "The Children's Moon" introduce contrast by redirecting focus from the teacher's preparation for class to the morning sky. |
| Tone | The poet's tone, or attitude toward the subject or character, changes to show contrast. | In the first stanza of "A Barred Owl" by Richard Wilbur (page 111), parents tell their child, who is wakened by the sound of an owl, that it was just an "odd question from a forest bird" asking the somewhat friendly question "who cooks for you?" At the end of the poem, however, the tone toward that "forest bird" changes as the owl is described as carrying "some small thing in a claw . . . up to some dark branch and eaten raw." |
| Point of View | The poet changes the point of view to show contrast. | The poem "La Migra" (Border Patrol) by Pat Mora (page 112) shows children acting out a pretend encounter of a "Mexican maid" with the border patrol officer. The poem is in two parts.<br>Part 1 begins with the lines "Let's play *La Migra* / I'll be the border patrol. / You be the Mexican maid." Part II begins with the lines "Let's play *La Migra* / You be the Border Patrol. / I'll be the Mexican woman." How the game plays out is very different through each point of view. |
| Perspective of character, narrator, or speaker | A character, narrator, or speaker sees things from a different perspective and ushers in a contrast. | The speaker in "The Children's Moon" turns her back and with that changed perspective a concerning contrast is introduced—are the children talking behind her back about her race? |
| Dramatic situation or moment | The plot takes a surprising turn, creating a contrast. | In Sara Teasdale's two-stanza poem "The Star" (page 113), the first half relates how a star finds a still pool that reflects its light perfectly, unlike "the moving sea" which never gave her a good reflection. The star gives her light to the pool "forever," believing the pool to be "fathomless." The contrast appears in the second half of the stanza: "But out of the woods as night grew cool / A brown pig came to the little pool." The pig gleefully splashes around in the shallow pool, churning up mud. |

*continued*

| Ways to Introduce Contrast | Explanation | Example |
|---|---|---|
| Settings or time | The poem switches settings or moves to a different time, creating a contrast. | "The Children's Moon" begins with the teacher in her home getting ready for the first day of school; the scene change to the schoolyard and classroom creates a contrast. |
| Imagery | The poem provides contrasting visual or other sensory images, such as those in "[you fit into me]." | The poem "At Black River" by Mary Oliver (page 114) opens with the image of an unnamed animal that the reader soon can identify as an alligator (or crocodile) that lies napping, soaking its "dark, slick bronze . . . in a mossy place." When he wakes in "the warm darkness," this Florida "king" paralyzes its prey. The poem ends with the image of the alligator attacking "the bird / in its frilled, white gown, / that has dipped down / from the heaven of leaves / one last time, / to drink." The contrast between the darkness of the beginning and the white, frilled gown of the bird from "the heaven" of leaves is striking. |

Table 2-6

## Shifts and Juxtaposition

Contrast can be introduced in a number of ways, such as through a change in words, a change in structure, or even a change in punctuation. However, in each case it is the result of a shift or juxtaposition or both. A **shift** is a change in tone, point of view, rhyme pattern, thought, image, or emotion. In "You Fit into Me," the contrast in image shows the shift in how the speaker views her relationship; she moves from feeling loved and comforted to pain and discomfort, as shown by the contrasting images of the hook and eye. A shift is often signaled by a word, especially a coordinating conjunction (*for, and, nor, but, or, yet, so*). In Sara Teasdale's poem "The Star," for example, after the star asks the pool to hold her forever, the shift begins with a coordinating conjunction: "But out of the woods as night grew cool / A brown pig came to the little pool."

Poets can also signal shifts through structural conventions, such as starting a new stanza, and punctuation. In Robert Frost's poem "The Road Not Taken," for example, the narrator ponders which of two diverging roads to take through the forest ("Two roads diverged in a yellow wood, / And sorry I could not travel both/And be one traveler, long I stood . . ."). At the end of the poem, however, the narrator has made a decision, and that shift is represented in part by the use of a dash ("Two roads diverged in a wood, and I— / I took the one less traveled by"), the dash serving to cement the decision.

Poets also introduce contrast through **juxtaposition**, the side-by-side positioning of images, lines, ideas, characters, or actions for the purpose of comparing or contrasting. In "[you fit into me]," the contrast results from the juxtaposition of two differing meanings of *hook* and *eye*. It is reinforced through the structural convention of the stanza—the meanings are too different to be in the same stanza.

Following is an example of how you might write an analysis of the effect of the juxtaposition in that poem and its contribution to the speaker's shift in perspective on her relationship:

> At the beginning of Margaret Atwood's poem "[you fit into me]," the speaker compares her relationship with her lover to that of a hook fitting into an eye on clothing, suggesting that, like the hook-and-eye closure working together to secure garments, the lovers "fit into" each other securely in their relationship. However, that image of a hook is juxtaposed in the second stanza with the image of a fish hook, and the eye on clothing suddenly becomes a literal eye. This contrast in images suggests the speaker has new insight on her relationship with the "open eye." The speaker, who was once so connected with her lover, now feels baited and unable to free herself from her lover's hook. A love that initially felt safe and secure has become a never-ending world of pain, as the lack of punctuation in the final line might suggest. The juxtaposition and structural convention of the separation of the stanzas also suggests the distance that has developed in the relationship, for the couple that began as one now find themselves torn in two, unable to reconnect and "fit" into each other.

 **Remember:** Contrast can be introduced through focus; tone; point of view; character, narrator, or speaker perspective; dramatic situation or moment; settings or time; or imagery. Contrasts are the results of shifts or juxtapositions or both. Shifts may be signaled by a word, a structural convention, or punctuation. Shifts may emphasize contrasts between particular segments of a text. (STR-1.G–J)

## 2.2 Checkpoint

*Reread "On the Subway" on page 76. Then complete the open-response activities and answer the multiple-choice questions.*

1. How does juxtaposition contribute to contrast in the poem? Provide examples.

2. What effect does this contrast have on readers? Explain your answer using textual details.

3. Where is the shift in the poem? How is that shift signaled? What might this shift indicate?

4. In "On the Subway," the speaker's and boy's life experiences are contrasted primarily through the imagery of
   - (A) the molecules and rod of light
   - (B) the eating of steak
   - (C) darkness and light
   - (D) the black cotton and heat of the sun
   - (E) the seedling ready to emerge

5. Which of the following best describes the shift in the speaker's perspective from the start of the poem to the end?
   - (A) The speaker's racial prejudice shifts to reluctant tolerance of differences.
   - (B) The speaker's stereotyping of the boy shifts to recognize her complicity in his life condition.
   - (C) The speaker's feelings of superiority over the boy shift to feelings of inferiority.
   - (D) The speaker's fear of the young man shifts to a determination to mentor him.
   - (E) The speaker's sympathy for the young man and his life circumstances shifts to apathy.

**Creating on Your Own**

Return to the draft of the poem you started. Brainstorm a list of possible contrasts contained within your subject that might help convey your ideas. Experiment with one or two of them by trying to work them into the rough draft of your poem. Try introducing them through a word, such as *but* or *though*; a structural convention, such as a new stanza; or punctuation (or even some combination of those). Also consider where you might effectively use juxtaposition. Revise your draft using one or more of these experimental contrasts. Save your work for future use.

# Part 2 Apply What You Have Learned

Write a paragraph discussing how the structure, contrast, and shifts in "On the Subway" contribute to the development of ideas in the poem.

**Reflect on the Essential Question** Write a brief response that answers the essential question: *How do structure and contrast contribute to the development of ideas in a poem?* In your answer, correctly use the key terms on page 85.

# Relationships Among Words

## Part 3 Relationships Among Words

### Understand
Comparisons, representations, and associations shift meaning from the literal to the figurative and invite readers to interpret a text. (FIG-1)

### Demonstrate
Explain the function of specific words and phrases in a text. (5.B)

**Source:** *AP® English Literature and Composition Course and Exam Description*

**Essential Question:** How do poets create connections among specific words and phrases to convey meaning?

In some ways, a poem is like a wind chime. Words in a poem make other words in the poem resonate, just as the metal tubes in a wind chime set off the chime of other tubes. For example, recall the poem "The Children's Moon" (see page 79). In the first stanza the narrator describes putting on a navy shirtdress. In that context, *navy* appears to name a color, a dark blue. However, that color is so named because it is the color of navy uniforms, so the other meaning of *navy*—a branch of the military—is sitting just below the surface. Later in the poem, when the narrator said goodbye to her family, she *saluted* her husband Mel. The use of the word *saluted* sends a vibration back to the word *navy* and brings it up from below the surface, linking the words in the reader's mind.

Source: Getty Images

Poets pay close attention to how words relate to one another in a poem. Words have a grammatical relationship, of course, even in poems that do not use complete sentences. They also relate to one another through repetition of whole words as well as repetition of just the beginning sounds of words. The more connections you can recognize, the more rich and sonorous the poem will be for you.

# 3.1 Antecedents and Referents | FIG-1.A, FIG-1.B

One way a word connects to another is by depending for its meaning on a word that came earlier. For example, if writers use a pronoun in a sentence, such as *they, them, he, she,* or *it,* they provide a noun before it so the pronoun is clearly tied to something and will make sense.

The <u>boys</u> wore *their* backpacks as *they* climbed the mountain trail.

In this sentence, the pronouns are in italics. Readers understand their meaning because they clearly refer back to <u>boys</u>, the noun. In constructions in which the noun precedes the pronoun, the noun is known as the **antecedent.** The pronouns that refer back to it are known as **referents.**

In addition to a single word, antecedents can be phrases or clauses.

**Phrase as antecedent:** The <u>setting sun</u> spread *its* colors across the sky.
**Clause as antecedent:** The trail leader said <u>that the hikers had to clean up each night's campsite</u>. *It* was his number one rule.

In addition to pronouns, referents can include nouns, phrases, or clauses.

**Noun as referent:** Although <u>their</u> legs ached, the *boys* made it to the summit.
**Phrase as referent:** <u>It</u> is a simple activity, but *walking the dog* is good exercise.
**Clause as referent:** Alysa laughed with <u>Claire</u>, *whom she had known* since childhood.

## Referents and Ambiguity

Prose writers are generally careful to make their referents as clear as possible. This is not the case with Dingbang, however, in the exchange below from a cartoon by Wayne E. Pollard chronicling the "writing life."

**Bo:** What are you writing, Dingbang?

**Dingbang:** A poem, Bo. I read an article in *Harper's* about the bad state of poetry and I decided to contribute to it.

*Bo's Café Life* by Wayne E. Pollard

Here, the pronoun *it* refers back to both *Harper's* magazine *and* bad poetry. By having the referent remain ambiguous, the reader does not know if Dingbang means he is contributing a poem he believes is good to uplift the state of poetry or if he is contributing a bad poem to the magazine, adding to the bad state of poetry. The humor arises from the lack of clarity of the referent.

Poets, on the other hand, sometimes see an unclear referent as a possibility to add a layer of meaning through **ambiguity**, a literary device that allows for more than one interpretation. Referents become ambiguous if they can refer to more than one antecedent (as Dingbang's did). Consider the possible ambiguities in the following poem by Joy Harjo.

### REMEMBER

Remember the sky that you were born under,
know each of the star's stories.
Remember the moon, know who she is.
Remember the sun's birth at dawn, that is the
5      strongest point of time. Remember sundown
and the giving away to night.
Remember your birth, how your mother struggled
to give you form and breath. You are evidence of
her life, and her mother's, and hers.
10     Remember your father. He is your life, also.
Remember the earth whose skin you are:
red earth, black earth, yellow earth, white earth
brown earth, we are earth.
Remember the plants, trees, animal life who all have their
15     tribes, their families, their histories, too. Talk to them,
listen to them. They are alive poems.
Remember the wind. Remember her voice. She knows the
origin of this universe.
Remember you are all people and all people
20     are you.
Remember you are this universe and this
universe is you.
Remember all is in motion, is growing, is you.
Remember language comes from this.
25     Remember the dance language is, that life is.
Remember.

Look at lines 7–9:

Remember your birth, how your mother struggled
to give you form and breath. You are evidence of
her life, and her mother's, and hers.

In line 9, the first and second *her* clearly refer back to "your mother" in line 7. The final *hers*, however, is slightly ambiguous. It would be awkward to say "her mother's mother's mother," which is the implied continuation of the generations. But simply saying "hers" is ambiguous. It could refer back to her mother's mother, but it could also suggest in its lack of specificity an echo of the long line of generations past.

Lines 23–24 also contain a referent that could have more than one antecedent.

> Remember all is in motion, is growing, is you.
> Remember language comes from this.

To what does the word *this* refer? If that last line were spelled out without ambiguity, would *this* be followed by *all* or *motion*, or *growing*, or *you*? By leaving the reference to *this* ambiguous, Harjo suggests that it is a mixture of all those possibilities and all the others mentioned in the poem. In that way she unifies a key idea in the poem—that everything and everyone, past and present, is connected.

**Missing Antecedent**  Referents are also ambiguous when no antecedent is present, as in the following poem, "The Death of the Ball Turret Gunner," written in 1945, the year World War II ended. In five tight lines, poet Randall Jarrell tells the story of a young soldier assigned to machine gun duty in the ball turret of a warplane.

### THE DEATH OF THE BALL TURRET GUNNER

> From my mother's sleep I fell into the State
> And I hunched in its belly till my wet fur froze.[1]
> Six miles from earth,[2] loosed from its dream of life,
> I woke to black flak and the nightmare fighters.
> 5     When I died they washed me out of the turret with a hose.

In the line "Six miles from earth, loosed from its dream of life," *earth* is the antecedent for the pronoun referent *its*.

Six miles from <u>earth</u>, loosed from *its* dream of life

However, in the final line of the poem, the pronoun *they* lacks an antecedent.

When I died <u>they</u> washed me out of the turret with a hose.

Because *they* lacks an antecedent to clarify its meaning, readers don't know who "they" are. Jarrell's omission of a clear antecedent for the pronoun *they* creates a sense of ambiguity and relates to Jarrell's theme of the dehumanization of soldiers. Like the gunner, "they" seem to lack identities and serve no purpose other than to do their job—to wash out the unrecognizable remains of the gunner in the turret and prepare it for the next soldier—wash, rinse, repeat.

---

1  Bomber jackets were lined in fur. The gunner may have been sweating with fear, making the fur wet.
2  At six miles above Earth, the temperature is about –40° F, too cold for human survival.

**Remember:** An antecedent is a word, phrase, or clause that preceded its referent. Referents may include pronouns, nouns, phrases, or clauses. Referents are ambiguous if they can refer to more than one antecedent, which affects interpretation. (FIG-1.A–B)

**Source:** Wikimedia

A ball turret in a B-17 plane. Jarrell provided this explanatory note with his poem: "A ball turret was a Plexiglas sphere set into the belly of a B-17 or B-24, and inhabited by two .50 caliber machine guns and one man, a short small man. When this gunner tracked with his machine guns a fighter attacking his bomber from below, he revolved with the turret; hunched upside-down in his little sphere, he looked like the fetus in the womb. The fighters that attacked him were armed with cannon firing explosive shells."

## The Critic's Craft: Three-Column Poetry Chart

Randall Jarrell decided to include a note when he published "The Death of a Ball Turret Gunner" explaining what a ball turret was and how a man looked while he was in it. His note highlights the importance of understanding the literal message of a poem. If you don't know what a ball turret is, the poem will make little to no sense. Making sure you understand the literal meaning of a poem—the "what's-actually-happening-in-this-poem" meaning—is a good place to begin a critical analysis of poetry. During this phase you identify the characters, setting, plot or actions (if there are any), situation, and conflict. You may want to write a literal summary of a poem before moving to interpretation. For "The Death of a Ball Turret Gunner," a literal summary of the poem might be as follows:

This poem tells what happens to a ball turret gunner, a soldier with a machine gun who sits in a round compartment under a plane that rotates completely so he can fire shots in any direction. The poem is told from his point of view. He starts off thinking about his mother and then finds himself hunched inside the ball turret. The plane flies so high that the temperature is very cold, and the fur in the soldier's jacket freezes. He feels like he's in a dream, and when he wakes up, there is gunfire all around him. He is killed, yet he still seems to know what happens to him afterward, which is that his shot-up body is hosed from the turret.

Once you have a good literal understanding of the poem, you can reread it to identify the tools the poet uses. Analyze for STEAL (see pages 16 and 81) and look for contrasts, shifts, repetition, figurative language, sound effects, and poetic techniques that may create ambiguity.

However, simply identifying these tools does not take you all the way to a critical analysis. That requires understanding how and why the poet uses the tools you identified to convey meaning about the characters, theme, and ideas. At this stage of your analysis, you draw conclusions and make assertions about the effect of the tools on the poem.

One way to think about the stages in a critic's analysis is to picture (or actually use) a three-column chart.

| What the Poet Says | What the Poet Does | What the Poet Implies |
|---|---|---|
| **First Reading:** Read for the *literal* meaning. | **Second Reading:** Annotate for the tools the poet uses: STEAL, structure, and figurative language. | **Third and Later Readings:** Draw conclusions/assertions about the effect of the tools used based on the poem (theme, character, and ideas). |
| • Speaker and Point of View: | • STEAL (details of what characters say and think and how they act and react) | • Why did the poet make certain structural choices (stanzas, line breaks)? What do they contribute to the effect and meaning of the poem? |
| • Setting: | • Contrasts/shifts: | • Why did the poet use other poetic tools? What do they contribute to the effect and meaning of the poem? |
| • Character(s): | • Repetition(s): | • How do the patterns of language used contribute to the poem's meaning? |
| • Situation: | • Language: | • What assertion(s) can you make about the poem's meaning and the way the poet conveys it? |
| • Conflict: | • Other poetic techniques: | • How do poetic techniques amplify meaning? |

Table 2–7

Critics also take part in critical conversations with other readers. This community of readers learns from, disagrees with, extends, and in other ways interacts with others who assert claims about a work of literature. Some claims may be only slightly different from others, but some may be significant. For example, while many critics focus on the helpless innocence of the gunner in "The Death of a Ball Turret Gunner," one critic, Brooke Horvath at Kent State University, asks, "In what sense is a ball turret gunner 'innocent' when charged with gunning down enemy aircraft piloted and crewed by young men like himself?" Horvath goes on to assert that the poem suggests "that, in warfare, no one is entirely innocent or helpless, and everyone both victim and victimizer." Part of the critic's craft is reading what other critics have written about a work and synthesizing those ideas with their own.

## Using the Critic's Craft

Choose a poem from among those in the Poetry Gallery on pages 111–114. Complete a three-column chart to develop a critical analysis of that poem. Then talk with your classmates and read what others have written about the poem by searching for an analysis of it online. If anything you hear or read changes your views, write a brief paragraph explaining how and why.

### 3.1 Checkpoint

*Complete the open-response activity and answer the multiple-choice question.*

1. Read the poem below by Emily Dickinson and answer the questions that follow it. You may wish to work with a partner to share ideas and possible interpretations.

**IT'S ALL I HAVE TO BRING TODAY**

It's all I have to bring today
This, and my heart beside—
This, and my heart, and all the fields—
And all the meadows wide—
5     Be sure you count—should I forget
Some one the sum could tell—
This, and my heart, and all the Bees
Which in the Clover dwell.

- What words in this poem create ambiguity?
- What are possible interpretations of those words?

2. The ambiguous antecedents of the words *it* and *this* in "It's all I have to bring today" help the speaker understate

    (A) the few valuable possessions that the speaker can offer

    (B) the urgency for someone to appraise the value of the speaker's offerings

    (C) the reluctance to declare the speaker's love for "you"

    (D) the worth of the speaker's invaluable contributions

    (E) the desire of the speaker to repay "you"

**Creating on Your Own**

Return to the draft of your poem. Identify the antecedents and referents in your poem. Would any benefit from ambiguity? If so, make the necessary changes and explain how the ambiguity would affect a reader's interpretation. Save your work for future use.

## 3.2 Repetition and Alliteration | FIG-1.C, FIG-1.D

Besides creating ambiguity, poets also use techniques for adding emphasis, often through **repetition**—the repeating of words or phrases. They also use a form of repetition known as **alliteration** when they repeat the same letter sound at the beginning of adjacent or nearby words.

    Read the following excerpt from Shakespeare's play *Hamlet*. In this scene, the Ghost of Old Hamlet has returned to speak to his son about the events surrounding Old Hamlet's death at the hands of his own brother, Claudius, the current king of Denmark.

> T'is given out[1] that, sleeping in my orchard,
> A serpent stung me, so the whole ear of Denmark
> Is by a forged process of my death
> Rankly abused.[2] But know, thou noble youth.
> 5    The serpent that did sting thy father's life
> Now wears his crown.

In the selection above, Old Hamlet's Ghost repeats the word *serpent* and uses multiple words that begin with the letter *s* next to or near one another.

> T'is given out that, **sleeping** in my orchard,
> A **serpent stung** me, **so** the whole ear of Denmark
> Is by a forged process of my death
> Rankly abused. But know, thou noble youth.
> 5    The **serpent** that did **sting** thy father's life
> Now wears his crown.

The purpose of this repetition is to focus the audience's attention on the word *serpent* and have them conjure images of snakes in their minds. But Shakespeare takes it a step further. He doesn't want the audience to just picture a snake—he wants them to hear it as well. For this purpose, he uses alliteration. The placement of the words beginning with *s* next to and near one another creates a sound like the hissing of a snake. Shakespeare wants his audience to see Claudius not as a man but as a snake. The repetition of *serpent* and the hissing effect with the alliteration of the *s* sound emphasize a connection between Claudius and the serpent in the Garden of Eden that brought sin into the world.

In "The Death of the Ball Turret Gunner," Jarrell uses alliteration of the letter *f* in the phrase "my wet fur froze." Here, the alliteration may suggest the sound of someone's lips vibrating above chattering teeth in intense freezing temperatures.

Repetition of sounds at the *end* of words is also an effective poetic technique. For example, in "The Death of the Ball Turret Gunner," the repetition of the *k* at the end of *black* and *flak* creates a harsh staccato sound that emphasizes the intensity of the anti-aircraft's fire the speaker hears.

**Remember:** Words or phrases may be repeated to emphasize ideas or associations. Alliteration is the repetition of the same letter sound at the beginning of adjacent or nearby words to emphasize those words and their associations or representations. (FIG–1.C–D)

---

1 **given out:** said
2 **whole ear of Denmark:** Claudius killed King Hamlet by pouring poison in his ear; the ghost says that all of Denmark was harmed by the lie that he was stung by a serpent.

### 3.2 Checkpoint

*Reread "On the Subway" on page 76. Then complete the open-response activity and answer the multiple-choice question.*

1.  On separate paper, make a chart like the one below. Complete the chart by finding examples of repetition and alliteration in "On the Subway" and explaining how they help shape the interpretation of the poem. Compare responses with those of a partner or group members.

| Examples of Repetition | Effect on Interpretation |
|---|---|
|  |  |
| **Examples of Alliteration** | **Effect on Interpretation** |
|  |  |

2.  In the context of the poem, the repetition of the word *stuck* in lines 4 and 6 suggests the speaker and boy's
    - (A) inability to change seats on the subway
    - (B) reluctance to acknowledge their differences
    - (C) tendency to focus on their surroundings rather than people
    - (D) powerlessness to escape their current social status
    - (E) objection to harmful stereotypes

**Creating on Your Own**
Return to the draft of your poem. Are there places you might strengthen it by using repetition and alliteration? If so, revise accordingly. Save your work for future use.

## Part 3   Apply What You Have Learned

Write a paragraph explaining techniques the poet used to connect words and phrases in "On the Subway" and the effect of those techniques on the meaning conveyed.

**Reflect on the Essential Question**  Write a brief response that answers the essential question: *How do poets create connections among specific words and phrases to convey meaning?* In your answer, correctly use the key terms on page 96.

# Similes and Metaphors

**Enduring Understanding and Skills**

**Part 4  Similes and Metaphors**
### Understand
Comparisons, representations, and associations shift meaning from the literal to the figurative and invite readers to interpret a text. (FIG-1)
### Demonstrate
Identify and explain the function of a simile. (6.A)
Identify and explain the function of a metaphor. (6.B)

**Source:** *AP* English Literature and Composition Course and Exam Description*

**Essential Question:**  What are the functions of similes and metaphors?

Poetry communicates through **figurative language**, language whose purpose is to create images and effects on the reader beyond the literal meaning of the words. It accomplishes its purpose through **figures of speech**, expressions that convey a non literal meaning. Two of the most common figures of speech are similes and metaphors, both of which draw comparisons between two subjects, transferring the qualities of one subject to another and shifting meaning from the literal to the figurative.

### KEY TERMS

figurative language          simile                          metaphor
figures of speech

## 4.1 Similes | FIG-1.E, FIG-1.F, FIG-1.G

Recall the poem "[you fit into me]" by Margaret Atwood.

> You fit into me
> like a hook into an eye
>
> a fish hook
> an open eye

The poem uses a comparison in the opening stanza: "You fit into me / *like* a hook into an eye." The comparison to the hook and eye on clothing functions to imply that the speaker sees the relationship in a positive light and feels safe and secure in it. She and her lover "fit" together, similar to how the hook and eye on clothing "fit into" each other, securing the fabric in place.

The figure of speech she uses to make this comparison is a **simile,** a figure of speech that makes a *direct comparison* between two subjects by using the words *like* or *as*. A simile aims to show the relationship between two subjects by focusing on their similarities. In a simile, one subject is "like" another, or one does something in the same way "as" another does it. Similes compare two different subjects to transfer the traits and associations of one to the other.

## The Relationship of the Compared Subjects

However, the transference is not full. Some properties are transferred, but not all of them. In a simile, something is *like* something else, but it is not that thing. The subjects of the comparison might share similarities and qualities, but they are not exactly the same. For example, a poem by Scottish poet Robert Burns begins with these lines:

> Oh my love's like a red, red rose
> Newly sprung in June

The simile here compares the speaker's love to a red rose newly sprung. The qualities that transfer from the rose to the love are likely the intense beauty of the rose (not just red, but red, red) and its freshness—just sprung. However, the features of the red, red rose that likely do not transfer in this context are the thorns, nor does the poet offer any comparison between his love and an inevitably wilting rose.

In the Robert Burns example, the main subject is the speaker's love. The comparison subject is the rose.

Consider how much would be missing if the meaning were conveyed in literal terms: "My love is beautiful and fresh." A reader would have only generalities to respond to with literal language. Now consider how much the simile stirs in readers: they picture an intensely red rose springing up from black earth; they can imagine the fragrance of a rose and the feeling of a warm day in June. Similes function, then, to awaken responses in readers as they transfer qualities of the comparison subject to the main subject.

 **Remember:** A simile uses the words "like" or "as" to liken two objects or concepts to each other. Similes liken two different things to transfer the traits or qualities of one to the other. In a simile, the thing being compared is the main subject; the thing to which it is being compared is the comparison subject. (FIG-1.E–G)

## 4.1 Checkpoint

*Review "On the Subway" on page 76. Then complete the open-response activity and answer the multiple-choice question.*

1. Locate three similes in the poem. For each one, write a sentence or two explaining what qualities transfer from the comparison subject to the main subject and what you can infer about the speaker based on the similes.

2. Which of the following best describes the function of the simile in line 10 of "On the Subway" (reproduced below)?

He is wearing

10       red, like the inside of the body

exposed.

    (A) To portray the young man as threatening

    (B) To suggest the young man is vulnerable

    (C) To highlight the color of the sweatshirt

    (D) To contrast the color of the young man's skin with his clothing

    (E) To show the speaker's hostility toward the young man

### Creating on Your Own
Return to the draft of your poem. What similes have you used already, if any? What was their function? Add one or more similes to your poem to see if you can strengthen the impact on the reader. Save your work for future use.

# 4.2 Metaphors | FIG-1.H, FIG-1.I, FIG-1.J, FIG-1.K

While a simile directly states a comparison between two subjects, a **metaphor** is a figure of speech that *implies* similarities between two (usually unrelated) subjects in order to reveal or emphasize one or more qualities or features about one of them. Sometimes the differences between the two may be as revealing as the similarities. In a metaphor, as in a simile, the subject being compared is the main subject; the subject to which it is being compared is the comparison subject.

To fully understand and interpret a metaphor, be sure to consider its context. The text may determine what qualities are transferred from the comparison subject in the metaphor to the main subject.

## Implicit Comparisons
The word *metaphor* is derived from the Greek, meaning "to transfer." Metaphors make a comparison between two subjects without using the words *like* or *as*, resulting in an *implicit* rather than an explicit comparison. In a metaphor, the two subjects being compared often seem unrelated, but the linkage of the two often surprises, shocks, delights, and even enlightens readers.

Metaphors rely on the experiences and associations readers already have with subjects of the comparison. In "The Death of the Ball Turret Gunner," for example, Jarrell builds the central image of his poem on a metaphor: He compares a soldier in the belly of a plane to a fetus in a mother's womb. The effect of this comparison is to contrast the warmth and safety of a womb to the cold and dangerous belly of a plane. But nowhere in the poem does he state the similarity directly. Instead, he relies on readers' associations to make the comparison. After reading the word *mother's* in the first line, a reader would connect the phrase "hunched in its belly" back to a mother even though the pronoun *its* does not make a link clear. Only after reading the whole poem (possibly several times) does the reader see the comparison between the mother's womb and the ball turret.

> From my mother's sleep I fell into the State
> And I hunched in its belly till my wet fur froze.
> Six miles from earth, loosed from its dream of life,
> I woke to black flak and the nightmare fighters.
> 5    When I died they washed me out of the turret with a hose.

Some metaphors make a comparison by equating two subjects. Consider the famous balcony scene in *Romeo and Juliet*.

> But soft! What light through yonder window breaks?
> It is the east, and Juliet is the sun.
> Arise, fair sun, and kill the envious moon,
> Who is already sick and pale with grief,
> 5    That thou, her maid, art far more fair than she.
> . . .
>
> Two of the fairest stars in all the heaven,
> Having some business, do entreat her eyes
> To twinkle in their spheres till they return.
> What if her eyes were there, they in her head?
> 10   The brightness of her cheek would shame those stars
> As daylight doth a lamp. Her eye in heaven
> Would through the airy region stream so bright
> That birds would sing and think it were not night.

Romeo proclaims that "Juliet is the sun" after seeing Juliet leaning out of her window. Since this scene occurs in the evening, Romeo's comparison implies that Juliet's beauty has the power to transform the darkness to light. Here, the metaphor relies on the context of darkness and the experiences and associations readers have with the sun and its ability to bring light to that darkness; hence, the metaphor transfers properties of the sun, namely its ability to shine brightly, onto Juliet. The linking verb *is* acts as an equal sign: Juliet = the sun.

Sometimes, however, a metaphor requires the reader to unpack the comparison. This type of metaphor states no simple equation between the compared subjects. For example, if Romeo had said "Juliet shines," readers would draw on the experiences and associations they have with subjects that shine and figure out how those associations fit into the context of the text (darkness). A line later, Romeo comments that the moon is envious of Juliet because she is more beautiful and more brilliant than it is. Romeo also claims that the "brightness of [Juliet's] cheek" has the ability to "shame . . . stars," and that "her eye of heaven" would shine so bright that "birds would sing and think it were not night." Readers (or audience members) would have to think about what would make the moon envious, what could outshine the stars, and, ultimately, what is in the heavens (the sky) that would make birds sing? After this unpacking, readers can make the connection between Juliet and the sun: like the sun, Juliet shines.

Unpacking a metaphor is like solving an equation. Sometimes you have all the parts ("Juliet is the sun"), and at other times you only have pieces ("Juliet shines"). You can think of metaphors as an equation in which A = the literal (main) subject and B = the figurative (comparison) subject. In the Juliet examples, the equations would look like this:

| Types of Metaphors | |
|---|---|
| **Both Subjects Named** | **One Subject Named** |
| A = B | A = ? |
| Juliet = the sun | Juliet shines. Therefore Juliet = ? |

Table 2-8

 **Remember:** A metaphor implies similarities between two (usually unrelated) concepts or objects in order to reveal or emphasize one or more things about one of them, though the differences between the two may also be revealing. In a metaphor, as in a simile, the thing being compared is the main subject; the thing to which it is being compared is the comparison subject. Comparisons between objects or concepts draw on the experiences and associations readers already have with those objects and concepts. Interpretation of a metaphor may depend on the context of its use; that is, what is happening in the text may determine what is transferred in the comparison. (FIG-1.H–K).

## 4.2 Checkpoint

*Review "On the Subway" on page 76. Then complete the open-response activity and answer the multiple-choice questions.*

1. Find an example of a metaphor in the poem. After identifying the two subjects, explain in writing how the two subjects are compared. Then explain how readers' associations help the poem convey meaning.

2. Which of the following statements best describes the figurative language in lines 4–7 (reproduced below) in "On the Subway"?

> We are stuck on
> 5      opposite sides of the car, a couple of
> molecules stuck in a rod of light
> rapidly moving through darkness.

   (A) A simile with *We* as the comparison subject

   (B) A simile with *rod* as the main subject

   (C) A metaphor that names both the main and comparison subject

   (D) A metaphor that names only one subject

   (E) One metaphor and one simile

3. In lines 21–26 (reproduced below) of "On the Subway," which of the following associations would best guide a reader's interpretation of the poem?

> And he is black
> and I am white, and without meaning or
> trying to I must profit from his darkness,
> the way he absorbs the murderous beams of the
> 25    nation's heart, as black cotton
> absorbs the heat of the sun and holds it.

   (A) The feeling of a black cotton shirt absorbing rather than reflecting heat

   (B) A knowledge of the country's history of lynchings, police shootings, and slavery

   (C) The impulse of people not socializing with others who are quite opposite from them

   (D) An awareness of how some view the world in straightforward, uncomplicated terms

   (E) A grasp of profit's role in a capitalist society

**Creating on Your Own**

Return to the draft of your poem. What metaphors have you used already, if any? What was their function? What associations would you expect readers to bring to them? What qualities are transferred to the main subject? Add one or more metaphors to your poem to heighten the impact on the reader. Save your work for future use.

## Part 4  Apply What You Have Learned

Choose three similes and/or metaphors from "On the Subway" and write a paragraph explaining the effect of those figures of speech on the meaning conveyed. In your explanation, include discussion of the associations and experiences readers are likely to bring to those comparisons.

**Reflect on the Essential Question**  Write a brief response that answers the essential question: *What are the functions of similes and metaphors?* In your answer, correctly use the key terms listed on page 105.

### POETRY GALLERY

**A BARRED OWL**
**BY RICHARD WILBUR (1921–2017), PUBLISHED IN 2000**

The warping night air having brought the boom
Of an owl's voice into her darkened room,
We tell the wakened child that all she heard
Was an odd question from a forest bird,
5   Asking of us, if rightly listened to,
"Who cooks for you?" and then "Who cooks for you?"

Words, which can make our terrors bravely clear,
Can also thus domesticate a fear,
And send a small child back to sleep at night
10   Not listening for the sound of stealthy flight
Or dreaming of some small thing in a claw
Borne up to some dark branch and eaten raw.

# LA MIGRA
## BY PAT MORA (1942–) PUBLISHED IN 1993

Let's play *La Migra*[1]
I'll be the Border Patrol.
You be the Mexican maid.
I get the badge and sunglasses.
5   You can hide and run,
but you can't get away
because I have a jeep.
I can take you wherever
I want, but don't ask
10   questions because
I don't speak Spanish.
I can touch you wherever
I want but don't complain
too much because I've got
15   boots and kick—if I have to,
and I have handcuffs.
Oh, and a gun.
Get ready, get set, run.

II

Let's play *La Migra*
20   You be the Border Patrol.
I'll be the Mexican woman.
Your jeep has a flat,
and you have been spotted
by the sun.
25   All you have is heavy: hat,
glasses, badge, shoes, gun.
I know this desert,
where to rest,
where to drink.
30   Oh, I am not alone.
You hear us singing
and laughing with the wind,
*Agua dulce brota aqui,*[2]
*aqui, aqui,* but since you
35   can't speak Spanish,
you do not understand.
Get ready.

---

1 *La Migra*: Spanish for border patrol officer
2 *Aqua dulce brota aqui*: Spanish for "sweet water flows from here"

## THE STAR
### BY SARA TEASDALE (1884–1933) PUBLISHED IN 1915

A white star born in the evening glow
Looked to the round green world below,
And saw a pool in a wooded place
That held like a jewel her mirrored face.
5  She said to the pool: "Oh, wondrous deep,
I love you, I give you my light to keep.
Oh, more profound than the moving sea
That never has shown myself to me!
Oh, fathomless as the sky is far,
10  Hold forever your tremulous star!"

But out of the woods as night grew cool
A brown pig came to the little pool;
It grunted and splashed and waded in
And the deepest place but reached its chin.
15  The water gurgled with tender glee
And the mud churned up in it turbidly.
The star grew pale and hid her face
In a bit of floating cloud like lace.

**Source:** Getty Images

## AT BLACK RIVER
### BY MARY OLIVER (1935–2017) PUBLISHED IN 2003

All day
    its dark, slick bronze soaks
      in a mossy place
        its teeth,

5    a multitude
      set
        for the comedy
          that never comes—

its tail
10    knobbed and shiny,
      and with a heavy-weight's punch
        packed around the bone.

In beautiful Florida
    he is king
15    of his own part
      of the Black River,

and from his nap
    he will wake
      into the warm darkness
20        to boom, and thrust forward,

paralyzing
    the thin-waisted fish,
      or the bird
        in its frilled, white gown,

25    that has dipped down
    from the heaven of leaves
      one last time,
        to drink.

# Writing About Literature II

## Part 5  Writing About Literature II

### Understand
Readers establish and communicate their interpretations of literature through arguments supported by textual evidence. (LAN-1)

### Demonstrate
Develop a paragraph that includes 1) a claim that requires defense with evidence from the text and 2) the evidence itself. (7.A)

**Source:** *AP® English Literature and Composition Course and Exam Description*

**Essential Question:** How can you communicate your interpretation of a poem in a paragraph that asserts a claim and supports it with evidence?

If you completed the activities in Unit 1, Part 5, you have already written a paragraph of literary argument. In this unit, the tasks are the same:

- reading closely for textual details that combine to lead to and support a claim about an aspect of the text
- developing an arguable claim supportable with the details from the text
- writing a paragraph of literary analysis with a claim and textual evidence to support it

Because the tasks are the same, the key terms are also the same.

| KEY TERMS | | |
|---|---|---|
| analyzing | claim | evidence |
| argument | interpretation | |

# 5.1 Making a Claim Based on a Poem's Textual Details | LAN-1.A

You have already encountered several strategies for "mining" a literary work for details. These include

- rereading a text
- annotating a text
- creating a three-column analysis chart

Any or all of these can help you isolate and evaluate the details that will help you form and support a claim.

## TP-CASTT and TP-CAST PLUS

Another useful organizer for **analyzing**, or breaking down into its parts, poetry or other literature is known by its acronym, *TP-CASTT*, the first letters of the words *Title, Paraphrase, Connotation, Attitude, Shifts, Title, and Theme*. You can start filling in this template with your first reading of the poem, though some rows will require subsequent readings. The chart below explains more.

| TP-CASTT Template for Literary Analysis | |
| --- | --- |
| Title | What does the title lead you to expect about the poem? |
| Paraphrase | What is the poem literally saying? Write each sentence in your own words. (This task is similar to the first column in the Three-Column Analysis chart.) |
| Connotation | What could the words mean beyond their literal meaning? Look for similes and metaphors, repetition and alliteration, and connotations that might contribute to ambiguity. |
| Attitude | What is the speaker's or narrator's attitude, or perspective, toward the subject? What does this attitude contribute to the meaning of the poem? |
| Shifts | Where are the contrasts, shifts, and juxtapositions in the poem? What is their effect? |
| Title (revisited) | Now that you are familiar with the poem, can you find more or different meaning in the title? How does that meaning affect the poem? |
| Theme | What are the bigger ideas beyond the poem that the details may be reaching toward? Here you can try to develop a thematic statement. |

Table 2-9

Completing the TP-CASTT template is just the beginning of your effort to find meaning in a work of literature. Simply identifying textual evidence is not sufficient to make a literary interpretation. Once you have collected your textual details in each row, your next step is to interpret them, to understand how they work together to convey meaning.

After completing the TP-CASTT chart and devising a thematic statement, you are likely ready to put forward at least a rough idea for a claim that offers an interpretation. The following TP-CAST^PLUS chart provides space for you to write that claim and then connect the details you already noted to your working claim. (This chart eliminates the second "Title" row since you will already have addressed that in the first "Title" row.)

| TP-CAST^PLUS Template for Literary Analysis | |
|---|---|
| Your working claim: | |
| **Title** | What does the title lead you to expect about the poem? |
| **PLUS** commentary | Explain with commentary how your ideas about the title relate to and help support your claim. |
| **Paraphrase** | What is the poem literally saying? Write each sentence in your own words. (This task is similar to the first column in the Three-Column Analysis chart.) |
| **Connotation** | What could the words mean beyond their literal meaning? Look for similes and metaphors, repetition and alliteration, and connotations that might contribute to ambiguity. |
| **PLUS** commentary | Explain with commentary how the connotations and figures of speech relate to and help support your claim. |
| **Attitude** | What is the speaker's or narrator's attitude, or perspective, toward the subject? What does this attitude contribute to the meaning of the poem? |
| **PLUS** commentary | Explain with commentary how the attitude you identified relates to and help supports your claim. |
| **Shifts** | Where are the contrasts, shifts, and juxtapositions in the poem? What is their effect? |
| **PLUS** commentary | Explain with commentary how the contrasts, shifts, and juxtapositions you identified relate to and help support your claim. |
| **Theme** | What are the bigger ideas beyond the poem that the details may be reaching toward? Here you can try to develop a thematic statement. |
| PLUS commentary | Explain with commentary how the theme(s) you identified relate to and help support your claim. |

Table 2-10

See Supporting a Claim with Details from the Text on page 119 for more on providing commentary.

## Complexities

Recall from Unit 1 that thematic statements often grow out of tensions and contrasts in a text, which are also often the source of complexity. For example, the details in "On the Subway" might lead readers to the universal or big ideas of "racism" and "privilege" or possibly "youth" and "adulthood" even though there is no interaction between the characters in the poem.

Big ideas are also known as *universal ideas*, ideas that humans can understand and relate to no matter what their culture, nation, or geography may be. They are central ideas about being human. The table on the next page lists some out of many universal ideas.

| Some Universal Ideas | | |
|---|---|---|
| age | happiness | nature |
| equality | innocence | peace |
| family | justice | racism |
| freedom | kindness | responsibility |
| friendship | loss | sadness |
| generosity | love | war |
| greed | meanness | youth |

Table 2-11

Many if not all universal ideas can be paired with others that show differences. For example:

- age and youth
- innocence and guilt
- war and peace
- happiness and sadness
- justice and injustice

These pairings are often the source of the tension within big ideas.

Although different readers may come up with different ways of turning big-ideas-in-tension into a thematic statement in relation to "On the Subway," the following represent several acceptable ways.

> **Thematic Statement:** White people are slow in recognizing the role their privilege plays in a racist society.

> **Thematic Statement:** Opportunities provided or denied people at a young age affect those people for the rest of their lives.

Though not yet a claim, a thematic statement is a good first step in articulating the big ideas in a poem and the complexities they raise. Overly simplified statements would miss some of the most interesting aspects of a poem. For example, statements such as "Racism is harmful" or "The color of your skin affects the quality of your life," while true, do not reflect the richness of the poem and its exploration of the inner journey of the White woman facing a young Black man on the subway.

 **Remember:** In literary analysis, writers read a text closely to identify details that, in combination, enable them to make and defend a claim about an aspect of the text. (LAN-1.A)

## 5.1 Checkpoint

*Review "On the Subway" or another poem you are studying. Then complete the open-response activities and answer the multiple-choice question.*

1. On separate paper, complete a TP-CASTT chart for "On the Subway" or another poem you are studying.

2. On separate paper, make a chart like the one below, adding as many rows as you want. Identify one or more big ideas by looking for patterns of evidence that point to them. Record those in the chart.

| Possible Big or Universal Ideas | Details that Point to the Big Ideas |
|---|---|
|  |  |
|  |  |

3. The poem "On the Subway" might be best represented by which of the following thematic statements?

    (A) Women, like Black people generally, have been socially and economically oppressed.

    (B) Understanding racism requires taking accountability for one's participation in it.

    (C) Public transportation is a great equalizer of people from different backgrounds.

    (D) Young people have much to teach older generations.

    (E) The unequal power dynamics in racism make it impossible to overcome.

**Composing on Your Own**

Using your charts as a guide, develop a possible thematic statement about "On the Subway" or another poem you are studying.

# 5.2 Supporting a Claim with Details from the Text
| LAN-1.B

A literary **argument** requires a **claim**, a statement dependent on support by evidence from the text. A claim needs to be tied to the text directly, as below.

> **Claim:** In what starts with a stereotyped view, the White woman's ruminations in "On the Subway" show her transformative understanding of racism's causes.

Other claims about this poem are certainly possible. The one above addresses a theme of the poem. Other claims might address other aspects of the poem, such as literary and poetic techniques. The following claim addresses the use of imagery in the poem.

**Claim:** Though the poem takes place entirely inside the head of the woman on the subway, the visceral imagery in "On the Subway" highlights the very real pain of racism.

Both of the claims have the two defining requirements for a claim: they are arguable, and they are defensible. They are arguable because they do not just present a fact about the poem. Instead, they present an **interpretation**, and some people might reasonably disagree with that interpretation. They are defensible because they can be supported with **evidence** from the poem. To make evidence convincing, writers of literary argument show how the evidence supports the claim by providing commentary.

Recall Table 1-12 from Unit 1, a checklist for developing a claim. Analyzing the first claim above will show how it fulfills each requirement.

| Checklist: Developing a Claim about Literature |
|---|
| **Does the claim . . .** |
| • address universal ideas or big ideas that contrast or are in tension with one another? |
| The claim addresses the universal ideas of racial stereotypes and the transformative power of thinking beyond them. |
| • build on a thematic statement that says something about those ideas? |
| The claim builds on the idea expressed in the thematic statement about White people's slowness to recognize their role in perpetuating racism. |
| • link the text (and/or specifics from the text) to the thematic statement? |
| The claim specifically names the poem and refers to the speaker's ruminations that show her gradual change of perception of the young man. |
| • present a defensible interpretation—that is, can you use information from the text as evidence to support it? |
| There is evidence in the poem to support this claim, ranging from her stated, mainly negative, impressions at the beginning to a sincere and painful appreciation of how White society has limited the young man's opportunities. |
| • present an arguable interpretation—that is, could someone reasonably disagree? |
| Someone could have a different interpretation. For example, someone might conclude that all the woman is doing in the poem is exercising her White privilege—she has the luxury to think these matters through—without doing anything meaningful to bring about change and without really changing her thinking at all. |

Table 2-12

## Supporting a Claim with Evidence

If you have analyzed a poem with any of the methods introduced so far (Three-Column Analysis Chart, TP-CASTT, or simply rereading and annotating), chances are you have already collected evidence that led you to your claim. However, evidence alone does not prove your claim.

For example, if you were arguing the claim about the visceral imagery in the poem, your evidence might include the reference to "scars," to the young man's "wearing / red, like the inside of the body / exposed," and to his "raw face." All that "proves," however, is that the poem contains visceral images. Your argument requires *commentary*, or an explanation of your thinking, to support the claim. Writers need to defend their interpretations with clear explanations of the reasoning for how and why that evidence justifies that claim, explaining how the evidence ties directly to the text. The TP-CAST[PLUS] template is especially useful in this stage.

Adding commentary to explain how the evidence of the visceral images supports the claim might look like the following.

> In the very first image in "On the Subway"—the reference to the young man's shoelaces looking like "intentional scars"—the speaker begins what becomes a continuous pattern in the poem: through completely cerebral ruminations she comes to terms with the pain racism inflicts by expressing her thoughts through visceral images. She seems at times intimidated by the young man but at other times aware of his vulnerability, seeing the red color of his clothing as "the inside of the body / exposed" and his face as "raw."

 **Remember:** A claim is a statement that requires defense with evidence from the text. (LAN-1.B)

## 5.2 Checkpoint

*Review "On the Subway" and complete the following open-response activity.*

Below are statements about "On the Subway." Read each one and decide whether it meets the requirements of a claim. Explain each answer.

1. The White woman and young Black man face each other on the train.

2. Though starting out intimidated, the speaker in "On the Subway" develops tenderness for the young Black man facing her.

3. The setting of "On the Subway" is a metaphor for the woman's journey from stereotyping the young man to feeling empathy for his situation.

4. The poem "On the Subway" reveals only the woman's thoughts, not the thoughts of the young man.

**Composing on Your Own**

Using your previous work, on separate paper complete a graphic organizer like the one on the next page for "On the Subway" or another poem you are studying. You may use the claims already stated for "On the Subway" or you may develop a new one.

| Text: | | |
|---|---|---|
| **Universal Ideas:** | | |
| **Thematic Statement:** | | |
| **Claim:** | | |
| Evidence from Text | Evidence from Text | Evidence from Text |
| | | |
| Commentary/Explanation of why information from text supports claim | Commentary/Explanation of why information from text supports claim | Commentary/Explanation of why information from text supports claim |
| | | |
| **Possible concluding sentence:** | | |

# 5.3 Writing a Paragraph of Literary Argument About a Poem | LAN-1.C

All literary arguments share some common features. For example, they all identify the poem or other literary text their argument is about, but they do not provide summaries or simple retellings of the dramatic situation. Writers of literary arguments assume their readers have read the work at the center of the argument.

All literary arguments also include the same basic components: the claim, the textual evidence that supports it, and commentary explaining how the evidence justifies the claim. They also usually include a closing sentence, a statement that brings the argument to a logical close and offers a sense of completion. In a paragraph of literary argument, the claim is usually expressed in the topic sentence. The evidence and commentary make up the body of supporting sentences. The concluding sentence unifies and ends the argument.

For this unit, you will once again be writing a paragraph of literary analysis. Getting more practice in writing a good paragraph will make a longer essay easier to compose.

Read the following poem, "Winter Dusk" by Walter de la Mare. Then read the paragraph of literary analysis that follows it and note its components.

## WINTER DUSK

Dark frost was in the air without,
The dusk was still with cold and gloom,
When less than even a shadow came
And stood within the room.

5      But of the three around the fire,
None turned a questioning head to look,
Still read a clear voice, on and on,
Still stooped they o'er their book.

The children watched their mother's eyes
10     Moving on softly line to line;
It seemed to listen too—that shade,
Yet made no outward sign.

The fire-flames crooned a tiny song,
No cold wind stirred the wintry tree;
15     The children both in Faërie¹ dreamed
Beside their mother's knee.

*continued*

---

1 **Faërie:** fairyland

And nearer yet that spirit drew
Above that heedless one, intent
Only on what the simple words
20    Of her small story meant.

No voiceless sorrow grieved her mind,
No memory her bosom stirred,
Nor dreamed she, as she read to two,
'Twas surely three who heard.

25    Yet when, the story done, she smiled
From face to face, serene and clear,
A love, half dread, sprang up, as she
Leaned close and drew them near.

Photographers use shadows and light to give their compositions a sense of mystery or drama. Similarly, poets use figurative language to build images in their readers' minds and to convey emotions.

*What emotions might shadows convey? Why?*

| Paragraph of Literary Analysis | Components |
|---|---|
| <u>In "Winter Dusk" by Walter de la Mare, contrasts create a tension between the chill and gloom of the world outside and the coziness and warmth of the inside by the fire and highlight the mother's "half dread" when the outside intrudes on the inside.</u> The first stanza establishes the nature of the outside, with "dark frost" in the air and a stillness of "cold and gloom." Even before the reader has a chance to learn what the inside is like, something slips in from that dark and cold outside and stands "within the room." In the second stanza, the presence of that "something less than a shadow" provides a murky contrast to the coziness of the "three around the fire" and the mother's clear voice. Stanza four is the only one that does not include a mention of "that shade," and that stanza paints a picture of comfort and delight, of "fire-flames" crooning "a tiny song," no cold wind intruding, the children lost in the fairyland of the story as they lean against their mother's knee. But the spirit draws nearer as the mother remains intent on the meaning of "the simple words" in her "small story." In stanza 6, the narrator says that the mother had no unspoken sorrow or sad memory that might have conjured the spirit, and while engrossed in her story—an emblem of childhood—she remains "heedless" of the presence of the outside in the room. Only when she finishes the story, smiling face to face with her children, does her "half dread" love spring up, as if she were suddenly aware of the presence in the room, the spell of the innocence of "faërie" broken. In a protective act, she draws her children near, perhaps realizing that despite her best efforts, she will not always be able to keep her children safe and comfortable. Sooner or later, the outside world, with its "cold and gloom," will intrude on their lives. | **Claim:** Contrasts create a tension between the outside world and the safety of parental protection.<br><br>**Textual evidence**<br><br><br><br><br><br>**Commentary** showing the contrast between the murky shadow and the cozy inside<br><br><br><br>**Textual evidence** supporting claim by showing the safety and delights of the fireside scene with "the simple words" of the "small story"<br><br>**Textual evidence** (what the spirit is *not*) and **commentary** explaining the mother's awareness of the contrast between the outside world and her safe home<br>**Textual evidence** (a love of which half is dread) with **commentary** explaining how it relates to the idea of contrasts between inside and outside. |

Table 2-13

 **Remember:** In literary analysis, the initial components of a paragraph are the claim and textual evidence that defends the claim. (LAN-1.C)

## 5.3 Checkpoint

*Answer the following questions.*

1. What features do all literary arguments share?

2. Explain the relationship between evidence and commentary. Use examples from the paragraph of literary analysis above in your explanation.

**Composing on Your Own**

Use your chart from the previous Composing on Your Own activity to draft your own paragraph of literary analysis.

# Part 5 Apply What You Have Learned

Choose one of the poems from the "Poetry Gallery" on pages 111–114 and write a literary argument on an aspect of the poem covered in this unit:

- characterization
- structure
- contrasts and shifts
- relationships among words
- ambiguity
- similes and metaphors

In your response, you should do the following:

- Respond to the prompt with a claim that presents a defensible interpretation.
- Select and use evidence to support your line of reasoning.
- Explain how the evidence supports your line of reasoning.
- Use appropriate grammar and punctuation in communicating your argument.

**Reflect on the Essential Question** Write a brief response to the essential question: *How can you communicate your interpretation of a poem in a paragraph that asserts a claim and supports it with evidence?* In your answer, correctly use the key terms listed on page 115.

# Unit 2 Review

## Section I: Multiple Choice

## Section II: Free Response

## Section I: Multiple Choice

Questions 1–6. Read the following passage carefully before you choose your answers.

1      It was night again. The Waystone Inn lay in silence, and it was a silence of three parts.

2      The most obvious part was a hollow, echoing quiet, made by things that were lacking. If there had been a wind it would have sighed through the trees, set the inn's sign creaking on its hooks, and brushed the silence down the road like trailing autumn leaves. If there had been a crowd, even a handful of men inside the inn, they would have filled the silence with conversation and laughter, the clatter and clamor one expects from a drinking house during the dark hours of night. If there had been music . . . but no, of course there was no music. In fact there were none of these things, and so the silence remained.

3      Inside the Waystone a pair of men huddled in one corner of the bar. They drank with quiet determination, avoiding serious discussions of troubling news. In doing this they added a small, sullen silence to the larger, hollow one. It made an alloy of sorts, a counterpoint.

4      The third silence was not an easy thing to notice. If you listened for an hour, you might begin to feel it in the wooden floor underfoot and in the rough, splintering barrels behind the bar. It was in the weight of the black stone hearth that held the heat of a long dead fire. It was in the slow back and forth of a white linen cloth rubbing along the grain of the bar. And it was in the hands of the man who stood there, polishing a stretch of mahogany that already gleamed in the lamplight.

5      The man had true-red hair, red as flame. His eyes were dark and distant, and he moved with the subtle certainty that comes from knowing many things.

6      The Waystone was his, just as the third silence was his. This was appropriate, as it was the greatest silence of the three, wrapping the others inside itself. It was deep and wide as autumn's ending. It was heavy as a great river-smooth stone. It was the patient, cut-flower sound of a man who is waiting to die.

Question 1 is covered in Unit 1.

1. Which of the following best describes the passage's narrative point of view?
   (A) A character in the narrative relays an opinionated, subjective account.
   (B) A character in the narrative relays an unbiased, objective account.
   (C) A figure outside of the narrative relays a disinterested, objective account.
   (D) A figure outside of the narrative relays a candid, subjective account.
   (E) A figure outside of the narrative relays a comical, subjective account.

2. What is juxtaposed throughout the second paragraph?
   (A) hypothetical situations and reality
   (B) objective facts and the narrator's opinion
   (C) images outside of the inn and images inside of the inn
   (D) the effect of time on the inn
   (E) the men's thoughts and the narrator's insights

3. The repetition of the phrase "If there . . ." in the second paragraph primarily serves to
   (A) contradict the previous paragraph's assertion about the Waystone Inn
   (B) foreshadow the conflict of the men in the next paragraph
   (C) highlight the absent sounds that contribute to the overwhelming silence
   (D) emphasize the sounds that contribute to the rowdiness at the inn
   (E) build the narrator's argument for what the inn should be like

4. The sentence "The man had true-red hair, red as flame" contains which of the following figurative language?
   (A) metaphor
   (B) simile
   (C) personification
   (D) oxymoron
   (E) hyperbole

5. In the sentence, "It was the patient, cut-flower sound of a man who is waiting to die," the antecedent of the word *it* is

   (A) the Waystone

   (B) the third silence

   (C) the man with "true red-hair"

   (D) autumn's ending

   (E) a great river-smooth stone

6. The metaphor in the sentence, "It was the patient, cut-flower sound of a man who is waiting to die," functions by comparing

   (A) silence and death

   (B) patience and the dying man

   (C) cut flowers and death

   (D) silence and the dying man

   (E) cut flowers and the dying man

Questions 7–16. Read the following poem carefully before you choose your answers.

## BETWEEN THE ROCKETS AND THE SONGS
### MARTÍN ESPADA

The fireworks began at midnight,
golden sparks and rockets hissing
through the confusion of trees above our house.
I would prove to my son, now twelve,
5    that there was no war in the sky, not here,
so we walked down the road
to find the place where the fireworks began.
We swatted branches from our eyes,
peering at a house where the golden blaze
10   dissolved in smoke. There was silence,
a world of ice, then voices rose up
with the last of the sparks, singing,
and when the song showered down on us
through the leaves we leaned closer, like trees.
15   *Rockets and singing from the same house,* said my son.
We turned back down the road,
at the end of the year, at the beginning of the year,
Somewhere between the rockets and the songs.

7. The alliteration in line 15 creates the effect of

    (A) "rockets hissing" (line 2)

    (B) "the golden blaze" (line 9)

    (C) "a world of ice" (line 11)

    (D) "the last of the sparks" (line 12)

    (E) "the rockets and the songs" (line 18)

8. Details from which of the following lines reveals the son's perspective on the fireworks?

    (A) "there was no war in the sky, not here" (line 5)

    (B) "We swatted branches from our eyes" (line 8)

    (C) "There was silence" (line 10)

    (D) "the song showered down on us" (line 13)

    (E) "We turned back down the road" (line 16)

9. The metaphor of "a world of ice" (line 11) contributes to the poem by

    (A) suggesting that the fireworks were only imagined and that the night outside their house is cold and still

    (B) establishing a contrast between the "golden blaze" and the cold stillness after the smoke has cleared

    (C) inferring that the fireworks have disrupted the peace and quiet of the speaker and their son's house

    (D) characterizing the speaker and son's relationship as uncaring

    (E) inviting the reader to relate the stillness and emptiness of the situation to war

10. According to the details in the poem, the speaker of this poem might best be described as a parent who is

    (A) harshly critical of others who engage in boisterous activities

    (B) overly protective of his impressionable child

    (C) boldly intrusive in his neighbors' private lives

    (D) gently instructive by teaching through a protected experience

    (E) unintentionally detached from his anxious child

11. The line "We turned back down the road" (line 16) comes after the line "*Rockets and singing from the same house,* said my son" (line 15), most likely because this arrangement suggests that

(A) the fireworks event has ceased its display of "golden sparks and rockets hissing" (line 2)

(B) the son has finally understood "that there was no war in the sky, not here" (line 5)

(C) the speaker has identified the "place where the fireworks began" (line 7)

(D) the evening has become too uncomfortable for the speaker and son in this "silence, a world of ice" (lines 10–11)

(E) the neighbors have concluded the event after their "voices rose up with the last of the sparks, singing" (lines 11–12)

12. At the beginning of the poem, describing the fireworks as "golden" and "hissing" serves primarily to

(A) characterize the fireworks as treacherous by comparing them to sounds associated with animals

(B) suggest that the speaker and son's relationship is particularly close and nurturing

(C) establish the speaker's conflicted feelings about living in his community

(D) propose a complex perspective on fireworks by juxtaposing ideas of beauty and danger

(E) develop imagery that emphasizes the dangers of fireworks

Question 13 is covered in Unit 3.

13. Which of the following is the best possible defensible interpretation of the poem?

(A) Children often learn difficult lessons best through a parent's explanation rather than through their own first-hand experience.

(B) Individuals must frequently accept their fears as obstacles that may not necessarily be overcome but must be confronted nonetheless.

(C) When people give in to their fears, they eliminate opportunities to develop new insights about the world around them.

(D) Individuals who trust loved ones to guide them through frightening experiences often develop new understandings of their world.

(E) Children can mature only when loved ones promote the children's independence and allow them to discover the world on their own.

Question 14 is covered in Unit 4.

14. The speaker's attitude toward the situation of the poem is both
    (A) fearful and defensive
    (B) attentive and curious
    (C) annoyed and disinterested
    (D) fascinated and disappointed
    (E) sympathetic and discouraged

Questions 15 and 16 are covered in Unit 5.

15. When the speaker says, "there was no war in the sky, not here" (line 5), the phrase "not here" could suggest that
    (A) the speaker and son previously lived in a war-torn area
    (B) the son believes that the community in which he lives is entirely safe
    (C) the speaker attempts to assuage his son's fears but does not believe his own words
    (D) the son is too young to understand the destructive forces of war
    (E) the speaker questions whether war might, in fact, be possible in their community

16. Multiple possible meanings of the word *confusion* (line 3) could contribute to all of the following EXCEPT
    (A) the speaker's anxiety as he attempts to console his son
    (B) the tangled crossing of many tree branches above the speaker's house
    (C) the turmoil that the speaker's son feels when observing the fireworks
    (D) the difficulty the speaker and son both experience trying to view the fireworks through the branches
    (E) the neighbors' disoriented voices emanating from the house as they set off their fireworks

## Section II: Free Response

### Question 1: Poetry Analysis

In the poem on page 129 by Latino poet Martín Espada (published in 2006), the speaker and his son are experiencing New Year's fireworks. Read the poem carefully. Then, in a well-written paragraph that makes a defensible claim and develops commentary to explain how the evidence supports the claim, analyze the relationship between the speaker and the son.

In your response you should do the following:

- Respond to the prompt with a claim that presents a defensible interpretation.
- Select and use evidence to support your line of reasoning.
- Explain how the evidence supports your line of reasoning.
- Use appropriate grammar and punctuation in communicating your argument.

### Question 2: Prose Fiction Analysis

Carefully read the selection on page 127 from Patrick Rothfuss's 2007 novel *The Name of the Wind*. Then write a paragraph analyzing how Rothfuss establishes the barkeeper's relationship to the setting through the use of such literary devices as word choice, imagery, selection of details, and figurative language.

In your response you should do the following:

- Respond to the prompt with a claim that presents a defensible interpretation.
- Select and use evidence to support your line of reasoning.
- Explain how the evidence supports your line of reasoning.
- Use appropriate grammar and punctuation in communicating your argument.

## Question 3: Literary Argument—Contrast and Theme

Many works of literature use contrasts to develop thematic complexities. With this idea in mind, choose a poem of literary merit and write a paragraph discussing how the poem's use of contrast contributes to a theme in the poem and an interpretation of the work as a whole. (You may use one of the poems in the Poetry Gallery.) Do not merely summarize the plot.

In your response you should do the following:

- Respond to the prompt with a claim that presents a defensible interpretation.
- Provide evidence to support your line of reasoning.
- Explain how the evidence supports your line of reasoning.
- Use appropriate grammar and punctuation in communicating your argument.

# UNIT 3

# Extending the Scope

[Longer Fiction or Drama I]

## Part 1: Characters, Readers, and Narrators
## Part 2: Setting and Values
## Part 3: Significant Events and Conflicts
## Part 4: Writing About Literature III

---

**ENDURING UNDERSTANDINGS AND SKILLS: Unit 3**

### Part 1  Characters, Readers, and Narrators

**Understand**

Characters in literature allow readers to study and explore a range of values, beliefs, assumptions, biases, and cultural norms represented by those characters. (CHR-1)

**Demonstrate**

Identify and describe what specific textual details reveal about a character, that character's perspective, and that character's motives. (1.A)

**Demonstrate**

Explain the function of a character changing or remaining unchanged. (1.B)

### Part 2  Setting and Values

**Understand**

Setting and the details associated with it not only depict a time and place, but also convey values associated with that setting. (SET-1)

**Demonstrate**

Identify and describe specific textual details that convey or reveal a setting. (2.A)

### Part 3  Significant Events and Conflicts

**Understand**

The arrangement of the parts and sections of a text, the relationship of the parts to each other, and the sequence in which the text reveals information are all structural choices made by a writer that contribute to the reader's interpretation of a text. (STR-1)

**Demonstrate**

Explain the function of a significant event or related set of significant events in a plot. (3.E)

Explain the function of conflict in a text. (3.F)

**Understand**

Readers establish and communicate their interpretations of literature through arguments supported by textual evidence. (LAN-1)

**Demonstrate**

Develop a paragraph that includes 1) a claim that requires defense with evidence from the text and 2) the evidence itself. (7.A)

Develop a thesis statement that conveys a defensible claim about an interpretation of literature and that may establish a line of reasoning. (7.B)

Develop commentary that establishes and explains relationships among textual evidence, the line of reasoning, and the thesis. (7.C)

Select and use relevant and sufficient evidence to both develop and support a line of reasoning. (7.D)

Demonstrate control over the elements of composition to communicate clearly. (7.E)

Source: *AP® English Literature and Composition Course and Exam Description*

# Unit 3 Overview

Award-winning fiction writer Lorrie Moore, author of *How to Become a Writer*, explained that "a short story is a love affair, a novel is a marriage." Literary critic Wayne C. Booth compares novels to "would-be friends" and recognizes that readers "keep company" with narrators and authors. Mohsin Hamid, the author of this unit's anchor text, *Exit West,* describes how novels let you be "inside the character." "You're trying on their personhood and becoming this person . . . [T]he power of fiction is that it lets you be people you aren't." All of these descriptions acknowledge the investment readers make in longer fiction.

In contrast to short fiction and poetry, longer works of fiction and drama have more scope to replicate life's complexities. In longer works, readers encounter multiple ideas, complicated and confounding relationships, and multiple perspectives. Instead of a single conflict, readers encounter several conflicts that will overlap and intersect. Readers are challenged to find the most important meanings among several possibilities as they invest in a "marriage," a "would-be friend," or a character's personhood.

As you "keep company" with narrators and characters in longer fiction, you will likely ask yourself questions like the following:

- What vision of the world does this novel or play present? Do I share that vision or is mine different?

- Why do some characters change (or not change)? How might I behave in such a situation?

- What values motivate the characters' choices? How do they compare to mine?

- What is the social, cultural, and historical situation in which the story takes place? What influence might those situations have on the characters, setting, plot, and narrative structure?

By answering these questions (and more), you will be building an understanding of the work that will enable you to convey your interpretation to a community of readers who know the work as well as you do.

**Novel**
*Exit West* by Mohsin Hamid

The novel *Exit West*, published in 2017, is the anchor text for this unit. Only excerpts are used for instruction in this unit. The novel is written in a realistic style—with one important exception. Characters migrate to faraway places through magical black doors. Once characters go through a door, the story immediately jumps to life in the new location.

Below is a very brief summary of *Exit West* followed by a number of excerpts to which you will be referring throughout this unit. (The paragraph numbers refer to the location of the paragraphs within the chapters.)

**Plot Summary:** The story begins in an unnamed Middle Eastern city on the verge of civil war. Saeed, the only child of older parents, is fairly conservative and lives with his parents. Nadia is estranged from her family, works in an office, and has her own apartment. She meets Saeed in an advanced marketing class and they begin to date.

Clashes between militants and the government become more frequent. Saeed and Nadia hear that there are doors in the city that serve as portals to other places, but most of them are guarded by militants. They hire an agent to help them find one of those doors, and with the agent's help they end up on the Greek island of Mykonos. There they are among many refugees living in tents. Eventually, a young woman helps them escape through another door.

This time they end up in a luxurious London apartment, again with other migrants. As more migrants arrive, hostility erupts between migrants and nativist mobs. The authorities cut off power to the neighborhood where Saeed and Nadia live, and surveillance drones fly overhead at night. The city begins to construct a city surrounding London for the new migrants. Although Saeed and Nadia are on the list to get a home in the new city, they are increasingly unhappy. Nadia suggests they move again.

Their next door takes them to Marin, in California. Saeed begins to worship with a congregation of mostly Black Americans. Although he seems happier, Nadia finds herself thinking of the young woman on Mykonos who helped them find the door to London. Saeed and Nadia separate but meet once a week to go for a walk. Nadia begins to date a woman she meets at work. Saeed ends up falling in love with his preacher's daughter. The two begin to see each other less frequently until they stop meeting altogether.

In the last chapter, 50 years later, they are both back in their original city, which has been partially restored. They have a bittersweet reunion and catch up on each other's lives.

## From Chapter One

1    In a city swollen by refugees but still mostly at peace, or at least not yet openly at war, a young man met a young woman in a classroom and did not speak to her. For many days. His name was Saeed and her name was Nadia and he had a beard, not a full beard, more a studiously maintained stubble,[1] and she was always clad from the tips of her toes to the bottom of her jugular notch[2] in a flowing black robe. Back then people continued to enjoy the luxury of wearing more or less what they wanted to wear, clothing and hair wise, within certain bounds of course, and so these choices meant something.

2    It might seem odd that in cities teetering at the edge of the abyss young people still go to class—in this case an evening class on corporate identity and product branding—but that is the way of things, with cities as with life, for one moment we are pottering about our errands as usual and the next we are dying, and our eternally impending ending does not put a stop to our transient beginnings and middles until the instant when it does.

3    Saeed noticed that Nadia had a beauty mark on her neck, a tawny oval that sometimes, rarely but not never, moved with her pulse.

4    Not long after noticing this, Saeed spoke to Nadia for the first time. Their city had yet to experience any major fighting, just some shootings and the odd car bombing, felt in one's chest cavity as a subsonic vibration like those emitted by large loudspeakers at music concerts, and Saeed and Nadia had packed up their books and were leaving class.

5    In the stairwell he turned to her and said, "Listen, would you like to have a coffee," and after a brief pause added, to make it seem less forward, given her conservative attire, "in the cafeteria?"

6    Nadia looked him in the eye. "You don't say your evening prayers?" she asked.

7    Saeed conjured up his most endearing grin. "Not always. Sadly."

8    Her expression did not change.

9    So he persevered, clinging to his grin with the mounting desperation of a doomed rock climber: "I think it's personal. Each of us has his own way. Or . . . her own way. Nobody's perfect. And, in any case—"

10    She interrupted him. "I don't pray," she said.

11    She continued to gaze at him steadily.

12    Then she said, "Maybe another time."

13    He watched as she walked out to the student parking area and there, instead of covering her head with a black cloth, as he expected, she donned a black motorcycle helmet that had been locked to a scuffed-up hundred-ish cc trail bike, snapped down her visor, straddled her ride, and rode off, disappearing with a controlled rumble into the gathering dusk.

---

1 **stubble:** facial hair growth too short to be considered a beard
2 **jugular notch:** a visible dip in the neck at the throat

14     The next day, at work, Saeed found himself unable to stop thinking of Nadia. Saeed's employer was an agency that specialized in the placement of outdoor advertising. They owned billboards all around the city, rented others, and struck deals for further space with the likes of bus lines, sports stadiums, and proprietors of tall buildings.

15     The agency occupied both floors of a converted townhouse and had over a dozen employees. Saeed was among the most junior, but his boss liked him and had tasked him with turning around a pitch[3] to a local soap company that had to go out by email before five. Normally Saeed tried to do copious amounts of online research and customize his presentations as much as possible. "It's not a story if it doesn't have an audience," his boss was fond of saying, and for Saeed this meant trying to show a client that his firm truly understood their business, could really get under their skin and see things from their point of view.

16     But today, even though the pitch was important—every pitch was important: the economy was sluggish from mounting unrest and one of the first costs clients seemed to want to cut was outdoor advertising—Saeed couldn't focus. A large tree, overgrown and untrimmed, reared up from the tiny back lawn of his firm's townhouse, blocking out the sunlight in such a manner that the back lawn had been reduced mostly to dirt and a few wisps of grass, interspersed with a morning's worth of cigarette butts, for his boss had banned people from smoking indoors, and atop this tree Saeed had spotted a hawk constructing its nest. It worked tirelessly. Sometimes it floated at eye level, almost stationary in the wind, and then, with the tiniest movement of a wing, or even of the upturned feathers at one wingtip, it veered.

17     Saeed thought of Nadia and watched the hawk.

**Source:** Getty Images

*What effect does the hawk (as opposed to a songbird, for example) have on the scene?*

---

3  **pitch:** short for sales pitch, a presentation designed to persuade someone to buy your product or service

18    When he was at last running out of time he scrambled to prepare the pitch, copying and pasting from others he had done before. Only a smattering of the images he selected had anything particularly to do with soap. He took a draft to his boss and suppressed a wince while sliding it over.

19    But his boss seemed preoccupied and didn't notice. He just jotted some minor edits on the printout, handed it back to Saeed with a wistful smile, and said, "Send it out."

20    Something about his expression made Saeed feel sorry for him. He wished he had done a better job.

## From Chapter Two

2    The art in Nadia's childhood home consisted of religious verses and photos of holy sites, framed and mounted on walls. Nadia's mother and sister were quiet women and her father a man who tried to be quiet, thinking this a virtue, but who nonetheless came to a boil easily and often where Nadia was concerned. Her constant questioning and growing irreverence in matters of faith upset and frightened him. There was no physical violence in Nadia's home, and much giving to charity, but when after finishing university Nadia announced, to her family's utter horror, and to her own surprise for she had not planned to say it, that she was moving out on her own, an unmarried woman, the break involved hard words on all sides, from her father, from her mother, even more so from her sister, and perhaps most of all from Nadia herself, such that Nadia and her family both considered her thereafter to be without a family, something all of them, all four, for the rest of their lives, regretted, but which none of them would ever act to repair, partly out of stubbornness, partly out of bafflement at how to go about doing so, and partly because the impending descent of their city into the abyss would come before they realized that they had lost the chance.

3    Nadia's experiences during her first months as a single woman living on her own did, in some moments, equal or even surpass the loathsomeness and dangerousness that her family had warned her about. But she had a job at an insurance company, and she was determined to survive, and so she did. She secured a room of her own atop the house of a widow, a record player and small collection of vinyl,[4] a circle of acquaintances among the city's free spirits, and a connection to a discreet and nonjudgmental female gynecologist. She learned how to dress for self-protection, how best to deal with aggressive men and with the police, and with aggressive men who were the police, and always to trust her instincts about situations to avoid or to exit immediately.

---

4    **vinyl:** musical recordings made on vinyl; records

## From Chapter Five

*The situation in their city was deteriorating. Saeed's mother had been killed, and Saeed and Nadia made arrangements with an agent for them and Saeed's father to leave.*

41    It might seem surprising that even in such circumstances Saeed's and Nadia's attitudes towards finding a way out were not entirely straightforward. Saeed desperately wanted to leave his city, in a sense he always had, but in his imagination he had thought he would leave it only temporarily, intermittently, never once and for all, and this looming potential departure was altogether different, for he doubted he would come back, and the scattering of his extended family and his circle of friends and acquaintances, forever, struck him as deeply sad, as amounting to the loss of a home, no less, of his home.

42    Nadia was possibly even more feverishly keen to depart, and her nature was such that the prospect of something new, of change, was at its most basic level exciting to her. But she was haunted by worries too, revolving around dependence, worries that in going abroad and leaving their country she and Saeed and Saeed's father might be at the mercy of strangers, subsistent on handouts, caged in pens like vermin.

43    Nadia had long been, and would afterwards continue to be, more comfortable with all varieties of movement in her life than was Saeed, in whom the impulse of nostalgia was stronger, perhaps because his childhood had been more idyllic, or perhaps because this was simply his temperament. Both of them, though, whatever their misgivings, had no doubt that they would leave if given the chance. And so neither expected, when a handwritten note from the agent arrived, pushed under their apartment door one morning and telling them precisely where to be at precisely what time the following afternoon, that Saeed's father would say, "You two must go, but I will not come."

\* \* \*

44    Saeed and Nadia said this was impossible, and explained, in case of misunderstanding, that there was no problem, that they had paid the agent for three passages and would all be leaving together, and Saeed's father heard them out but would not be budged: they, he repeated, had to go, and he had to stay. Saeed threatened to carry his father over his shoulder if he needed to, and he had never spoken to his father in this way, and his father took him aside, for he could see the pain he was causing his son, and when Saeed asked why his father was doing this, what could possibly make him want to stay, Saeed's father said, "Your mother is here."

45    Saeed said, "Mother is gone."

46    His father said, "Not for me."

47    And this was true in a way, Saeed's mother was not gone for Saeed's father, not entirely, and it would have been difficult for Saeed's father to

leave the place where he had spent a life with her, difficult not to be able to visit her grave each day, and he did not wish to do this, he preferred to abide, in a sense, in the past, for the past offered more to him.

48      But Saeed's father was thinking also of the future, even though he did not say this to Saeed, for he feared that if he said this to his son that his son might not go, and he knew above all else that his son must go, and what he did not say was that he had come to that point in a parent's life when, if a flood arrives, one knows one must let go of one's child, contrary to all the instincts one had when one was younger, because holding on can no longer offer the child protection, it can only pull the child down, and threaten them with drowning, for the child is now stronger than the parent, and the circumstances are such that the utmost of strength is required, and the arc of a child's life only appears for a while to match the arc of a parent's, in reality one sits atop the other, a hill atop a hill, a curve atop a curve, and Saeed's father's arc now needed to curve lower, while his son's still curved higher, for with an old man hampering them these two young people were simply less likely to survive.

49      Saeed's father told his son he loved him and said that Saeed must not disobey him in this, that he had not believed in commanding his son but in this moment was doing so, that only death awaited Saeed and Nadia in this city, and that one day when things were better Saeed would come back to him, and both men knew as this was said that it would not happen, that Saeed would not be able to return while his father still lived, and indeed as it transpired Saeed would not, after this night that was just beginning, spend another night with his father again.

50      Saeed's father then summoned Nadia into his room and spoke to her without Saeed and said that he was entrusting her with his son's life, and she, whom he called daughter, must, like a daughter, not fail him, whom she called father, and she must see Saeed through to safety, and he hoped she would one day marry his son and be called mother by his grandchildren, but this was up to them to decide, and all he asked was that she remain by Saeed's side until Saeed was out of danger, and he asked her to promise this to him, and she said she would promise only if Saeed's father came with them, and he said again that he could not, but that they must go, he said it softly, like a prayer, and she sat there with him in silence and the minutes passed, and in the end she promised, and it was an easy promise to make because she had at that time no thoughts of leaving Saeed, but it was also a difficult one because in making it she felt she was abandoning the old man, and even if he did have his siblings and his cousins, and might now go live with them or have them come live with him, they could not protect him as Saeed and Nadia could, and so by making the promise he demanded she make she was in a sense killing him, but that is the way of things, for when we migrate, we murder from our lives those we leave behind.

## From Chapter Six

*At this point, Nadia and Saeed are going through the first of the black doors, emerging on the Greek island of Mykonos.*

6  It was said in those days that the passage was both like dying and like being born, and indeed Nadia experienced a kind of extinguishing as she entered the blackness and a gasping struggle as she fought to exit it, and she felt cold and bruised and damp as she lay on the floor of the room at the other side, trembling and too spent at first to stand, and she thought, while she strained to fill her lungs, that this dampness must be her own sweat.

7  Saeed was emerging and Nadia crawled forward to give him space, and as she did so she noticed the sinks and mirrors for the first time, the tiles of the floor, the stalls behind her, all the doors of which save one were normal doors, all but the one through which she had come, and through which Saeed was now coming, which was black, and she understood that she was in the bathroom of some public place, and she listened intently but it was silent, the only noises emanating from her, from her breathing, and from Saeed, his quiet grunts like those of a man exercising, or having sex.

8  They embraced without getting to their feet, and she cradled him, for he was still weak, and when they were strong enough they rose, and she saw Saeed pivot back to the door, as though he wished maybe to reverse course and return through it, and she stood beside him without speaking, and he was motionless for a while, but then he strode forward and they made their way outside and found themselves between two low buildings, perceiving a sound like a shell held to their ears and feeling a cold breeze on their faces and smelling brine in the air and they looked and saw a stretch of sand and low gray waves coming in and it seemed miraculous, although it was not a miracle, they were merely on a beach.

\* \* \*

26  Someone had told them the best times to fish were at dawn and dusk, so they stayed out alone longer than they otherwise might have. It was getting dark when they saw four men in the distance, approaching along the beach. Nadia said they should go, and Saeed agreed, and the couple walked away quickly, but the men seemed to follow, and Saeed and Nadia increased their pace, increased it as much as they could manage, even though Nadia slipped and cut her arm on the rocks. The men were gaining on them, and Saeed and Nadia began to wonder aloud what of their things they could leave behind, to lighten the load, or as an offering that might sate[5] their pursuers. Saeed said perhaps the men wanted the rod, and this seemed more reassuring to them than the alternative, which was to consider what else the men might want. So they dropped the rod, but soon after they rounded a bend and saw a house and outside the house were uniformed guards which meant the house contained a

---

5  **sate:** satisfy

door to a desirable place, and Saeed and Nadia had never before been relieved to see guards on the island, but they were now. They came close, until the guards shouted them to stay back, and there Saeed and Nadia stopped, making it clear they would not try to rush the house, sitting down where the guards could see them, and where they felt safe, and Saeed considered whether to run back and retrieve the rod, but Nadia said it was too risky. They both regretted dropping it now. They watched for a while but the four men never appeared, and the two of them set up their tent right there, but were unable to sleep much that night.

\* \* \*

27    The days were growing warmer, and spring was stuttering into being in Mykonos, with buds and scattered flowers. In all the weeks they had been there Saeed and Nadia had never been to the old town, for it was off-limits to migrants at night, and they were strongly discouraged from going there even by day, except to the outskirts, where they could trade with residents, which is to say those who had been on the island longer than a few months, but the gash on Nadia's arm was beginning to fester, and so they had come to the outskirts of the old town to get it tended to at a clinic. A partly shaved-haired local girl who was not a doctor or a nurse but just a volunteer, a teenager with a kind disposition, not more than eighteen or nineteen years of age, cleaned and dressed the wound, gently, holding Nadia's arm as though it was something precious, holding it almost shyly. The two women got to talking, and there was a connection between them, and the girl said she wanted to help Nadia and Saeed, and asked them what they needed. They said above all they needed a way off the island, and the girl said she might be able to do something, and they should stay nearby, and she took Nadia's number, and each day Nadia visited the clinic and she and girl spoke and sometimes had a coffee or a joint together and the girl seemed so happy to see her.

28    The old town was exquisite, white blocks with blue windows scattered along tawny hills, spilling down to the sea, and from the outskirts Saeed and Nadia could spy little windmills and rounded churches and the vibrant green of trees that from a distance looked like potted plants. It was expensive to stay nearby, the camps there often having migrants with more money, and Saeed was becoming worried.

29    But Nadia's new friend was as good as her word, because very early one morning she put both Nadia and Saeed on the back of her scooter and sped them through still-quiet streets to a house on a hill with a courtyard. They dashed inside and there was a door. The girl wished them good luck, and she hugged Nadia tight, and Saeed was surprised to see what appeared to be tears in the girl's eyes, or if not tears then at least a misty shine and Nadia hugged her too, and this hug lasted a long time, and the girl whispered something to her, whispered, and then she and Saeed turned and stepped through the door and left Mykonos behind.

# From Chapter Seven

*Nadia and Saeed have taken a door from Mykonos to London.*

8      To have a room to themselves—four walls, a window, a door with a lock—seemed incredible good fortune, and Nadia was tempted to unpack, but she knew they needed to be ready to leave at any moment, and so she took out of their backpack only items that were absolutely required. For his part Saeed removed the photo of his parents that he kept hidden in his clothing and placed it on a bookshelf, where it stood, creased, gazing upon them and transforming this narrow bedroom, at least partially, temporarily, into a home.

9      In the hall nearby was a bathroom, and Nadia wanted to take a shower more than anything, more even than she wanted food. Saeed stood watch outside, while she went in and stripped, and observed her own body, leaner than she had ever seen it, and streaked with a grime mostly of her own biological creation, dried sweat and dead skin, and with hair in places from which she had always banished hair, and she thought her body looked like the body of an animal, a savage. The water pressure in the shower was magnificent, striking her flesh with real force, and scouring her clean. The heat was superb too, and she turned it up as high as she could stand, the heat going all the way into her bones, chilled from months of outdoor cold, and the bathroom filled up with steam like a forest in the mountains, scented with pine and lavender from the soaps she had found, a kind of heaven, with towels so plush and fine that when she at last emerged she felt like a princess using them, or at least like the daughter of a dictator who was willing to kill without mercy in order for his children to pamper themselves with cotton such as this, to feel this exquisite sensation on their naked stomachs and thighs, towels that felt as if they had never been used before and might never be used again. Nadia began to put her folded clothes back on but all of a sudden could not bear to, the stench from them was overpowering, and so she was about to wash them in the tub when she heard a banging on the door and realized she must have locked it. Opening up, she saw a nervous and annoyed and dirty-looking Saeed.

10     He said, "What the hell are you doing?"

11     She smiled and moved to kiss him, and while her lips did touch his, his did not much respond.

12     "It's been forever," he said. "This isn't our house."

13     "I need five more minutes. I have to wash my clothes."

14     He stared but did not disagree, and even if he had disagreed, she felt a steel in herself which she knew meant she would have washed them anyway. What she was doing, what she had just done, was for her not about frivolity, it was about the essential, about being human, living as a human being, reminding oneself of what one was, and so it mattered, and if necessary was worth a fight.

15     But the extraordinary satisfactions of the steamy bathroom seemed to have evaporated as she shut the door, and the washing of her clothes,

watching the turbid[6] water flow from them down the drain of the bathtub, was disappointingly utilitarian. She tried to recover her former good mood, and not be angry with Saeed, who she told herself was not wrong in his own way, just out of rhythm with her in this moment, and when she emerged from the bathroom wrapped in her towel, her towels, for she had one around her body and another around her hair, and with her dripping but clean clothes in her hands, she was prepared to let the little confrontation between them go.

16    But he said, looking at her, "You can't stand here like that."

17    "Don't tell me what I can do."

18    He looked stung by this comment, and also angry, and she was angry as well, and after he had bathed, and washed his clothes, which he did perhaps as a conciliatory gesture or perhaps because once he was cleansed of his own grime he too realized something of what she had realized, they slept on the slender single bed together without speaking, without touching, or without touching more than the cramped space demanded, for this one night not unlike a couple that was long and unhappily married, a couple that made out of opportunities for joy, misery.

* * *

28    Nadia experienced the environment of the house as a bit like that of a university dormitory at the start of classes, with complete strangers living in close proximity, many of them on their best behavior, trying to add warmth to conversations and strike poses of friendship, hoping these gestures would become more natural over time. Outside the house much was random and chaotic, but inside, perhaps, a degree of order could be built. Maybe even a community. There were rough people in the house, but there were rough people everywhere, and in life roughness had to be managed. Nadia thought it madness to expect anything else.

29    For Saeed existence in the house was more jarring. On Mykonos he had preferred the outskirts of the migrant camps, and he had grown accustomed to a degree of independence from their fellow refugees. He was suspicious, especially of the other men around, of whom there were many, and he found it stressful to be packed in so tightly with people who spoke in tongues he did not understand. Unlike Nadia, he felt in part guilty that they and their fellow residents were occupying a home that was not their own, and guilty also at the visible deterioration brought on by their presence, the presence of over fifty inhabitants in a single dwelling.

30    He was the only one to object when people started to take for themselves items of value from the house, a position that struck Nadia as absurd, and physically dangerous for Saeed besides, and so she had told him not to be an idiot, said it harshly, to protect him rather than to harm him, but he had been shocked by her tone, and while he acquiesced, he wondered if this new way of speaking to one another, this unkindness that

---

6    **turbid:** cloudy from particles suspended in it

was now creeping into their words from time to time, was a sign of where they were headed.

31      Nadia too noticed a friction between them. She was uncertain what to do to disarm the cycles of annoyance they seemed to be entering into with one another, since once begun such cycles are difficult to break, in fact the opposite, as if each makes the threshold for irritation next time a bit lower, as is the case with certain allergies.

## From Chapter Eight

44      In London, Saeed and Nadia heard that military and paramilitary formations had fully mobilized and deployed in the city from all over the country. They imagined British regiments with ancient names and modern kit[7] standing ready to cut through any resistance that might be encountered. A great massacre, it seemed, was in the offing. Both of them knew that the battle of London would be hopelessly one-sided, and like many others they no longer ventured far from their home.

45      The operation to clear the migrant ghetto in which Saeed and Nadia found themselves began badly, with a police officer shot in the leg within seconds as his unit moved into an occupied cinema near Marble Arch, and then the flat sounds of a firefight commenced, coming from there but also from elsewhere, growing and growing, all around, and Saeed, who was caught in the open, ran back to the house, and found the heavy front door locked shut, and he banged on it until it opened, Nadia yanking him in and slamming it behind him.

46      They went to their room in the back and pushed their mattress up against the window and sat together in one corner and waited. They heard helicopters and more shooting and announcements to peacefully vacate the area made over speakers so powerful that they shook the floor, and they saw through the gap between mattress and window thousands of leaflets dropping from the sky, and after a while they saw smoke and smelled burning and then it was quiet, but the smoke and the smell lasted a long time, particularly the smell, lingering even when the wind direction changed.

47      That night a rumor spread that over two hundred migrants had been incinerated when the cinema burned down, children and women and men, but especially children, so many children, and whether or not this was true, or any of the other rumors, of a bloodbath in Hyde Park, or in Earl's Court, or near the Shepherd's Bush roundabout, migrants dying in their scores, whatever it was that had happened, something seemed to have happened, for there was a pause, and the soldiers and police officers and volunteers who had advanced into the outer edges of the ghetto pulled back, and there was no more shooting that night.

---

7  **kit:** military gear

## From Chapter Nine

*Self-contained episodes of people moving through the magical doors appear throughout the book. The following such episode is placed right after Saeed and Nadia learn of the death of Saeed's father.*

11    For many, adjustment to this new world was difficult indeed, but for some it was also unexpectedly pleasant.

12    On Prinsengracht[8] in the center of Amsterdam an elderly man stepped out onto the balcony of his little flat, one of the dozens into which what had been a pair of centuries-old canal houses and former warehouses had been converted, these flats looking out into a courtyard that was as lush with foliage as a tropical jungle, wet with greenness, in this city of water, and moss grew on the wooden edges of his balcony, and ferns also, and tendrils climbed up its sides, and there he had two chairs, two chairs from ages ago when there were two people living in his flat, though now there was one, his last lover having left him bitterly, and he sat down on one of these chairs and delicately rolled himself a cigarette, his fingers trembling, the paper crisp but with a hint of softness, from the damp, and the tobacco smell reminded him as it always did of his departed father, who would listen with him on his record player to audio recordings of science fiction adventures, and would pack and puff on his pipe, as sea creatures attacked a great submarine, the sounds of the wind and waves in the recording mixing with the sounds of the rain on their window, and the elderly man who was then a boy had thought, when I grow up I too will smoke, and here he was, a smoker for the better part of a century, about to light a cigarette, when he saw emerging from the common shed in the courtyard, where garden tools and the like were stored, and from which a steady stream of foreigners now came and went, a wrinkled man with a squint and a cane and a Panama hat, dressed as though for the tropics.

**Source:** Getty Images

An aerial view of Prinsengracht, one of Amsterdam's most beautiful canals

---

**8  Prinsengracht:** one of four major canals in Amsterdam

13     The elderly man looked at this wrinkled man and did not speak. He merely lit his cigarette and took a puff. The wrinkled man did not speak either: he walked slowly around the courtyard, leaning into his cane, which made scraping noises in the gravel of the footpath. Then the wrinkled man moved to reenter the shed, but before he left he turned to the elderly man, who was looking at him with a degree of disdain, and elegantly doffed his hat.

14     The elderly man was taken aback by this gesture, and sat still, as if transfixed, and before he could think of how to respond the wrinkled man stepped forward and was gone.

15     The next day the scene repeated itself. The elderly man was sitting on his balcony. The wrinkled man returned. They gazed upon each other. And this time when the wrinkled man doffed his hat, the elderly man raised a glass to him, a glass of fortified wine, which he happened to be drinking, and he did so with a serious but well-mannered nod of his head. Neither man smiled.

16     On the third day the elderly man asked the wrinkled man if he would care to join him on his balcony, and though the elderly man could not speak Brazilian Portuguese and the wrinkled man could not speak Dutch, they cobbled together a conversation, a conversation with many long gaps, but these gaps were eminently comfortable, almost unnoticed by the two men, as two ancient trees would not notice a few minutes or hours that passed without a breeze.

17     On his next visit the wrinkled man invited the elderly man to come with him through the black door that was inside the shed. The elderly man did so, walking slowly, as the wrinkled man did as well, and at the other side of that door the elderly man found himself being helped to his feet by the wrinkled man in the hilly neighborhood of Santa Teresa, in Rio de Janeiro, on a day that was noticeably younger and warmer than the day he had left in Amsterdam. There the wrinkled man escorted him over tram tracks to the studio where he worked, and showed him some of his paintings, and the elderly man was too caught up in what was happening to be objective, but he thought these paintings were marked by real talent. He asked if he might buy one, and was instead given his choice as a gift.

18     A week later a war photographer who lived in a Prinsengracht flat that overlooked the same courtyard was the first neighbor to note the presence of this aged couple on the balcony opposite and below her. She was also, not long after, and to her considerable surprise, a witness to their very first kiss, which she captured, without expecting to, through the lens of her camera, and then deleted, later that night, in a gesture of uncharacteristic sentimentality and respect.

\* \* \*

43     The northern summer evenings were endless. Saeed and Nadia often fell asleep before it was fully dark, and before they fell asleep they often sat outside on the ground with their backs to the dormitory, on their phones, wandering far and wide but not together, even though they appeared to

be together, and sometimes he or she would look up and feel on their face the wind blowing through the shattered fields all about them.

44    They put their lack of conversation down to exhaustion, for by the end of the day they were usually so tired they could barely speak, and phones themselves have the innate power of distancing one from one's physical surroundings, which accounted for part of it, but Saeed and Nadia no longer touched each other when they lay in bed, not in that way, and not because their curtained-off space in the pavilion seemed less than entirely private, or not only because of that, and when they did speak at length, they, a pair once not used to arguing, tended to argue, as though their nerves were so raw that extended encounters evoked a sensation of pain.

45    Every time a couple moves they begin, if their attention is still drawn to one another, to see each other differently, for personalities are not a single immutable color, like white or blue, but rather illuminated screens, and the shades we reflect depend much on what is around us. So it was with Saeed and Nadia, who found themselves changed in each other's eyes in this new place.

46    To Nadia, Saeed was if anything more handsome than he had been before, his hard work and his gauntness suiting him, giving him a contemplative air, making out of his boyishness a man of substance. She noticed other women looking at him from time to time, and yet she herself felt strangely unmoved by his handsomeness, as though he were a rock or a house, something she might admire but without any real desire.

47    He had two or three white hairs in the stubble of his beard now, new arrivals this summer, and he prayed more regularly, every morning and evening, and perhaps on his lunch breaks too. When he spoke he spoke of paving and positions and waiting lists and politics, but not of his parents and not anymore of travel, of all the places they might one day see together, or of the stars.

48    He was drawn to people from their country, both in the labor camp and online. It seemed to Nadia that the farther they moved from the city of their birth, through space and through time, the more he sought to strengthen his connection to it, tying ropes to the air of an era that for her was unambiguously gone.

49    To Saeed, Nadia looked much the same as she did when they first met, which is to say strikingly fetching, if vastly more tired. But it was inexplicable that she continued to wear her black robes, and it grated on him a bit, for she did not pray, and she avoided speaking their language, and she avoided their people, and sometimes he wanted to shout, well take it off then, and then he would wince inwardly, since he believed he loved her, and his resentment, when it bubbled up like this, made him angry with himself, with the man he seemed to be becoming, a less than romantic man, which was not the sort of man he believed a man should aspire to be.

50    Saeed wanted to feel for Nadia what he had always felt for Nadia, and the potential loss of this feeling left him unmoored, adrift in a world where one could go anywhere but still find nothing. He was certain that he cared

for her and wished good for her and wanted to protect her. She was the entirety of his close family now, and he valued family above all, and when the warmth between them seemed lacking his sorrow was immense, so immense that he was uncertain whether all his losses had not combined into a core of loss, and in this core, this center, the death of his mother and the death of his father and the possible death of his ideal self who had loved his woman so well were like a single death that only hard work and prayer might allow him to withstand.

51      Saeed made it a point to smile with Nadia at least sometimes, and he hoped she would feel something warm and caring when he smiled, but what she felt was sorrow in the sense that they were better than this and that together they had to find a way out.

\* \* \*

52      And so when she suggested one day, out of the blue, under the drone-crossed sky and in the invisible network of surveillance that radiated out from their phones, recording and capturing and logging everything, that they abandon this place, and give up their position on the housing list, and all they had built here, and pass through a nearby door she had heard of, to the new city of Marin, on the Pacific Ocean, close to San Francisco, he did not argue, or even resist, as she thought he might, and instead he said yes, and both of them were filled with hope, hope that they would be able to rekindle their relationship, to reconnect with their relationship, as it had been not long ago, and to elude, through a distance spanning a third of the globe, what it seemed in danger of becoming.

## From Chapter Ten

*Nadia and Saeed have gone through the third door and are now living in Marin.*

6       One night Nadia brought back some weed a coworker had given her. She did not know how Saeed would react, and this fact struck her as she hiked home. In the city of their birth they had smoked joints together with pleasure, but a year had passed since then, and he had changed since then, and perhaps she had changed too, and the distance that had opened between them was such that things once taken for granted could be taken for granted no longer.

7       Saeed was more melancholic than he had been before, understandably, and also more quiet and devout. She sometimes felt that his praying was not neutral towards her, in fact she suspected it carried a hint of reproach, though why she felt this she could not say, for he had never told her to pray nor berated her for not praying. But in his devotions was ever more devotion, and towards her it seemed there was ever less.

8       She had considered rolling a joint outdoors and smoking the weed by herself, without Saeed, concealed from Saeed, and it had surprised her to be considering this, and made her wonder about the ways in which she was herself putting barriers between her and him. She did not know if these gaps that had been widening were mostly her doing or his, but

she knew she still harbored tenderness for him, and so she had brought the weed home, and it was only when she sat beside him on the car seat they had bartered for and used now as a sofa, that she realized, from her nervousness, that how in this moment he responded to the weed was a matter of portentous significance to her.

9    Her leg and arm touched Saeed's leg and arm, and he was warm through his clothing, and he sat in a way that suggested exhaustion. But he also managed a tired smile, which was encouraging, and when she opened her fist to reveal what was inside, as she had once before done on her rooftop a brief lifetime ago, and he saw the weed, he started to laugh, almost soundlessly, a gentle rumble, and he said, his voice uncoiling like a slow, languid exhalation of marijuana-scented smoke, "Fantastic."

10   Saeed rolled the joint for them both, Nadia barely containing her jubilation, and wanting to hug him but restraining herself. He lit it and they consumed it, lungs burning, and the first thing that struck her was that this weed was much stronger than the hash back home, and she was quite floored by its effects, and also well on her way to becoming a little paranoid, and finding it difficult to speak.

11   For a while they sat in silence, the temperature dropping outside. Saeed fetched a blanket and they bundled it around themselves. And then, not looking at each other, they started to laugh, and Nadia laughed until she cried.

\* \* \*

23   Saeed and Nadia were loyal, and whatever name they gave their bond they each in their own way believed it required them to protect the other, and so neither talked much of drifting apart, not wanting to inflict a fear of abandonment, while also themselves quietly feeling that fear, the fear of the severing of their tie, the end of the world they had built together, a world of shared experiences in which no one else would share, and a shared intimate language that was unique to them, and a sense that what they might break was special and likely irreplaceable. But while fear was part of what kept them together for those first few months in Marin, more powerful than fear was the desire that each see the other find firmer footing before they let go, and thus in the end their relationship did in some senses come to resemble that of siblings, in that friendship was its strongest element, and unlike many passions, theirs managed to cool slowly, without curdling into its reverse, anger, except intermittently. Of this, in later years, both were glad, and both would also wonder if this meant that they had made a mistake, that if they had but waited and watched their relationship would have flowered again, and so their memories took on potential, which is of course how our greatest nostalgias are born.

## What Do You Know?

This unit will explore how details, descriptions, and actions or nonactions reveal characters, some of whom change through the narrative while others remain unchanged, and raise readers' expectations about how characters will behave. It will also explore how setting affects meaning and how significant events drive the story forward or help develop characters and themes.

Before learning the new skills and information this unit presents, assess what you already know. Read the anchor text, *Exit West* by Mohsin Hamid. Then answer the following questions. Don't worry if you find these challenging. Answering questions on a subject before formally learning about it is one way to help you deepen your understanding of new concepts.

### CLOSE READING

1. What are a few key details about Saeed and Nadia? How do these details show changes in each character? Why do you think Saeed and Nadia change as they do?

2. Which characters do not change? How does their static nature contribute to the novel's themes and ideas?

3. What are some of the values that might be associated with different settings in the story? What details indicate these values? You might consider the settings Saeed and Nadia inhabit or some of the places the minor characters appear (The Netherlands, for example).

4. Choose a significant event in the story. What is the relationship of this event to others? Is it a cause of future events or the result of prior events or both?

5. Choose one of the novel's conflicts. It could be tension between groups within society or between two characters. How does your chosen conflict relate to other conflicts?

### INTERPRETATION

1. How do various settings reveal conflicts that cut across multiple cultures and at the same time show conflicts unique to one location?

2. What message may the text convey about clashes between and within different cultures?

# Characters, Readers, and Narrators

**Enduring Understanding and Skills**

## Part 1

### Understand
Characters in literature allow readers to study and explore a range of values, beliefs, assumptions, biases, and cultural norms represented by those characters. (CHR-1)

### Demonstrate
Identify and describe what specific textual details reveal about a character, that character's perspective, and that character's motives. (1.A)

Explain the function of a character changing or remaining unchanged. (1.B)

See also Units 1, 2, 3, 4 & 6

**Source:** *AP® English Literature and Composition Course and Exam Description*

**Essential Question:** What do textual details reveal about characters and their motivation to change or stay the same?

"Books do not simply happen to people. People also happen to books." Those are the words of Louise Rosenblatt, a major proponent of reader response theory, which holds that readers' experiences and texts interact to create meaning. The act of critical reading is a transaction between the words of the author and responses of the reader. Writers make choices aimed at eliciting certain responses from readers.

In Part 1 you will explore not only what the author's descriptions and details reveal about characters, but also how they evoke various responses and expectations from you. You will consider how the narrator's perspective on a character affects your impression of that character. In other words, you will engage in a transactional relationship with the text. This type of critical reading will add to your understanding of complexity in longer works of fiction.

# 1.1 How Readers Get to Know Characters

| CHR-1.F, CHR-1.G, CHR-1.H, CHR-1.I, CHR-1.J, CHR-1.K

Readers have certain expectations of how a character will behave from the descriptions provided of that character. Whether the character meets those expectations or fails to will influence how a reader feels about that character. Details that describe or are associated with a character shape a reader's interpretation of that character. Besides learning about characters through direct description, readers draw inferences about characters' motives from their actions or inactions.

Further, perspectives, or attitudes, play a key role in helping readers get to know characters. For example, the way readers understand a character's perspective depends on the perspective of the narrator or speaker describing the character. Comparisons also illuminate characters. When narrators, characters, or speakers compare another character to something or someone else, they both show their perspective on the compared character and may also reveal a quality of the compared character. Finally, a character's perspective may shift during the story.

## Character Descriptions and Reader Expectations

Despite their differences, short fiction and longer fiction both introduce readers to characters through descriptions as well as through the choices the characters make to act or not act. Readers piece together a character from the accumulation of details provided by a first- or third-person narrator or by other characters. At the beginning of a novel, a character is usually a complete stranger to the reader. The more details and actions ascribed to that character, the more fully focused the reader's knowledge of the character becomes. The more focused the reader's knowledge becomes, the more the reader begins to have expectations of that character.

In *Exit West*, the reader first meets Nadia through this description:

> . . . she was always clad from the tips of her toes to the bottom of her jugular notch in a flowing black robe. Back then people continued to enjoy the luxury of wearing more or less what they wanted to wear, clothing and hair wise, within certain bounds of course, and so these choices meant something.

**Source:** Getty Images

The Quran instructs women to dress modestly, but the ways in which they follow this command vary throughout the Muslim world. Some women wear full-body robes that leave only the hands and eyes exposed, while others cover only their hair with a head covering.

When they first meet her, readers learn that Nadia is covered in a black robe, and they might associate the detail of the black robe with a strict Islamic religious tradition and expect Nadia to behave as a strict Muslim woman. However, the next part of the sentence provides the detail that people can wear "more or less what they wanted to wear," suggesting that people's clothes may not necessarily define other aspects of them. This qualification makes pinning down Nadia somewhat more complicated. Further, her participation in an "evening class on corporate identity and product branding" does not fit expectations for a strictly religious Muslim woman.

In the same way, during the first part of Nadia's conversation with Saeed, details may again suggest that Nadia is strictly religious. She asks Saeed, "You don't say your evening prayers?" Saeed seems to interpret that question as disapproving. But once again, Nadia defies expectations and says, "I don't pray." She turns him down for the date but by leaving the door open for another time, she leaves the impression that she is interested in him as well. Readers might interpret her steady gaze as an effort to size him up.

When Saeed watches her leave and go to the student parking lot, he expects her to put a black cloth on her head, but instead she puts on a helmet and rides off on a motor bike. The unmet expectations of earlier descriptions may make the reader more ready for her taking off on a motor bike than Saeed is. Readers can infer from her action that she is motivated by the drive to be her own person rather than conform to expected norms. The reader is coming to know Nadia as somewhat unconventional through details that shape their interpretation and affect their feelings.

You might use these details, descriptions, and actions to come up with an initial claim about Nadia.

> **Claim based on details, descriptions, and actions:** When readers first meet Nadia and Saeed, one might argue that Nadia is the more complex character because of the unexplained discrepancies among her appearance, her speech, and her actions.

Readers also come to know Saeed through descriptions and details associated with him and his actions. The chart on the next page shows how a reader might interpret those details.

| Details, Descriptions, and Actions of Saeed | Effect on Readers' Feelings and Interpretation |
|---|---|
| "did not speak to her" (Chapter One, paragraph 1) | The detail that Saeed did not speak to Nadia "for many days" suggests he was aware of her and thinking about talking to her. Readers may have a sympathetic feeling about him. |
| "had a beard, not a full beard, more a studiously maintained stubble" (Chapter One, paragraph 1) | The "studiously maintained stubble" suggests Saeed's beard was not primarily for religious purposes and that he is aware of style and appearance. That detail lets readers know he is not strictly religious—while with Nadia there is some uncertainty at first. |
| "Saeed noticed that Nadia had a beauty mark on her neck that sometimes, rarely but not never, moved with her pulse" (Chapter One, paragraph 3) | Readers would interpret his knowing with such detail how and when the beauty mark moves with her pulse as a sign of how attracted he is to her. |
| Decided to ask her out, trying not to come on too strong because of her conservative dress (Chapter One, paragraph 5) | From Saeed's action to ask Nadia out, readers can infer that he is motivated by his attraction to her and has overcome whatever had been holding him back. |
| Does not always say his evening prayers. Explains that praying or not praying is personal. "'Each of us has his own way. Or . . . her own way.'" (Chapter One, paragraphs 6–9) | He admits what Nadia might see as a shortcoming, suggesting he is honest. His explanation also is careful to acknowledge—by using both the masculine and feminine possessive pronouns *his* and *her*—an attitude of equality toward the sexes. |
| Watches her leave and put on the motor bike helmet (Chapter One, paragraph 13) | He seems to be very taken with her and surprised when she does something he does not expect. |

Table 3-1

Using these details, descriptions, and actions, you might develop a claim about Saeed such as the following.

> **Claim based on details, descriptions, and actions**: Saeed seems somewhat caught between the traditions of his religion and the changing norms of everyday life.

## Characters' Actions and Motives

**Motives** are the reasons for doing or not doing something. For real people, the motivation to act or not to act comes from many intersecting forces, both internal and external. Furthermore, as people encounter additional forces, their motives may change. The same holds true for fictional characters. How characters act—or fail to act—provides readers another way to get to know characters. Readers can often infer characters' motives from their actions or inaction.

Think about the forces that propel Saeed and Nadia to act or that stifle them into inaction. Reread paragraphs 14–20 of Chapter One on pages 139–140. The chart below shows examples of Saeed's actions and inactions from that excerpt, along with the possible motives.

| Character | Action | Inaction | Interpretation of Motive |
|---|---|---|---|
| Saeed | | Can't focus on work and doesn't do copious amounts of research for a project | He is motivated by his infatuation with Nadia and lets his emotions control his actions. |
| | | Doesn't customize the soap presentation to meet the client's needs, though he has consistently done so in the past, even though he realizes revenue is important in the sluggish economy | The conflicting forces of his own sense of obligation, the troubled economy, and his infatuation with Nadia intersect. His motives reflect a shift in priorities from business to a relationship. |
| | Lets the hawk distract him from his work. Notices that the hawk works tirelessly, is stationary, then "veers" | | Saeed may be motivated to watch the hawk because he sees himself in the hawk and is considering life choices. He has worked diligently, has lived with his parents, but now thinks of moving. |
| | Slaps together a shoddy presentation and gives it to his boss | | He is still motivated by his obligation to his work and to his boss, though other pressures have led him to lower his standards. |

Table 3-2

An initial claim about Saeed that interprets his actions, inactions, and motivation might be the following.

**Claim based on actions, inaction, and motives:** The tension between fulfilling his duties for his employer and his desire for Nadia causes Saeed to feel guilty.

## Narrator and Character Perspectives

**Perspective** is how narrators, characters, or speakers understand their circumstances. The **narrator** is the voice that tells the story and should not be confused with the author who wrote the story. In poetry, the narrator is often referred to as the **speaker** since poetry is meant to be read aloud. A narrator's perspective is how the narrator perceives what's happening within the story, and it colors how a reader understands a character.

## Narrator Perspectives

Early in the novel *Exit West*, readers get a sense of the narrator's perspective. For example, in paragraph 2 of Chapter One, the narrator pulls back a bit from the story and reveals a broader perspective.

> It might seem odd that in cities teetering at the edge of the abyss young people still go to class—in this case an evening class on corporate identity and product branding—but that is the way of things, with cities as with life, for one moment we are pottering about our errands as usual and the next we are dying, and our eternally impending ending does not put a stop to our transient beginnings and middles until the instant when it does.

How is the reader's understanding of the characters shaped by this narrator's perspective? One way is that the narrator uses the inclusive first person *we* as s/he muses on the oddness of everyday life against a backdrop of "teetering at the edge of the abyss," drawing the reader into the narrator's somewhat distant and philosophical perspective. (See Unit 4 for more on narrative distance.) Readers see the characters as the narrator does, almost as players in a drama. Another way is that the narrator is accepting and nonjudgmental of the characters' idiosyncrasies and leans toward tenderness. Saeed is not ridiculed for his "studiously maintained stubble" and, in paragraph 20 of Chapter One, the reader sees a sensitive side to Saeed when his boss's smile makes Saeed feel sorry for him and wish that he had done a better job. Readers see Saeed and the other characters through the narrator's eyes and with the narrator's attitude.

Following is a possible claim on the effect of the narrator's perspective on readers' understanding.

> **Claim based on narrator's perspective:** The narrator's frequent commentaries on broad truths of life, along with the use of *we* to draw the reader into the narrative perspective, leads the reader to see the characters as part of a timeless global drama.

## Comparisons

Comparisons also help readers understand characters. When narrators, characters, or speakers compare another character to something or someone else, they reveal their perspective on the compared character and may also reveal a quality of the compared character. In the following excerpt, the narrator compares the posture of Saeed and Nadia as they head out to meet their agent.

> Because of the flying robots high above in the darkening sky, unseen but never far from people's minds in those days, Saeed walked with a slight hunch, as though cringing a tad at the thought of the bomb or missile one of them might at any moment dispatch. By contrast, because she wanted not to appear guilty, Nadia walked tall, so that if they were stopped and their ID cards were checked and it was pointed out that her card did not list him as her husband, she would be more believable when she led the questioners home and presented the forgery that was supposedly their marriage certificate. (Chapter Five, paragraph 28)

Following is a possible claim on how a comparison reveals both the narrator's perspective on a character as well as innate qualities of a character.

> **Claim based on narrator's comparison:** The comparison of Saeed and Nadia as they walk through their embattled city sustains the narrator's perspective on Saeed as honest and justifiably afraid and on Nadia as confident and independent, but it also suggests innate qualities that draw Nadia to deception and disguise.

## Shifting Character Perspectives

Characters' perspectives—how they view their circumstances—often change as the narrative progresses. For example, shortly after Saeed's mother dies at the end of Chapter Four, his father—until this point portrayed with a perspective focused on the good and gentle side of life—undergoes an abrupt shift in perspective, even though he tries to deny it (Chapter Five, paragraph 25).

> Saeed's father tarried at [his wife's] grave each evening on the way home [from visiting family]. Once as he stood there he saw some young boys playing football and this cheered him, and reminded him of his own skill at the game when he was their age, but then he realized that they were not young boys, but teenagers, young men, and they were not playing with a ball but with the severed head of a goat, and he thought, barbarians, but then it dawned upon him that this was the head not of a goat but of a human being, with hair and a beard, and he wanted to believe he was mistaken, that the light was failing and his eyes were playing tricks on him, and that is what he told himself, as he tried not to look again, but something about their expressions left him in little doubt of the truth.

Following is a possible claim about how a character's perspective shifts.

> **Claim based on shift in character's perspective:** The perspective of Saeed's father, who has previously viewed his circumstances as happy and satisfying, changes after the violent death of his wife as he begins to recognize the barbarous people and acts in his world.

**Remember:** The description of a character creates certain expectations for that character's behaviors; how a character does or does not meet those expectations affects a reader's interpretation of that character. Details associated with a character and/or used to describe a character contribute to a reader's interpretation of that character. Readers can infer a character's motives from that character's actions or inactions. Readers' understanding of a character's perspective may depend on the perspective of the narrator or speaker. When narrators, characters, or speakers compare another character to something or someone else, they reveal their perspective on the compared character and may also reveal something innate about the compared character. A character's perspective may shift during the course of a narrative. (CHR-1.F–K)

## 1.1 Checkpoint

*Reread the excerpts from* Exit West *on pages 138–152. Then complete the open-response activities and answer the multiple-choice questions.*

1. Focusing on the excerpt from Chapter Two, recreate the chart below to analyze how the action or inaction of Nadia reveals her motives. One row is completed for you.

| Nadia's Action | Nadia's Inaction | Interpretation of Nadia's Motives |
|---|---|---|
| Questioned religion and was irreverent | | Desire to be independent; does not conform to cultural dictates |
| | | |
| | | |
| | | |

2. Using the details from the chart you completed in #1 above, write a claim that highlights the new understanding you gained about Nadia's motivations.

3. Using evidence in *Exit West* from either the excerpts provided or other parts of the book, develop a claim about the changing perspectives of Saeed or Nadia. You may wish to use the following as a template for your claim.

   In Chapter One, Character X perceives the situation as _____.
   However, in later chapters, Character X's perspective shifts to
   _____. [Here you should try to include any shifts in
   Chapters Six and Ten.] Character X's perspective is significant because
   _____.

4. Which of the following statements from Chapter Six best expresses the sense of conflict Saeed feels regarding his decision to leave his home and father behind?

   (A) "was both like dying and like being born"
   (B) "his quiet grunts like those of a man exercising"
   (C) "embraced without getting to their feet"
   (D) "she saw Saeed pivot back to the door"
   (E) "not a miracle, they were merely on a beach"

5. In Chapter Ten, paragraph 8, Nadia considers "rolling a joint outdoors and smoking the weed by herself, without Saeed" because

   (A) she fears it will make him more melancholic

   (B) she selfishly wants to enjoy it alone

   (C) she wants to test his devotion to her

   (D) she wishes to distance herself from him

   (E) her coworker gave the gift to her only

6. Nadia's "jubilation" (Chapter Ten, paragraph 10) derives primarily from her

   (A) relief Saeed isn't melancholic

   (B) hope for an improved relationship

   (C) remembrance of happier times

   (D) surprise at the weed's potency

   (E) feelings of tenderness for Saeed

7. The shift from paragraph 2 to paragraph 3 in Chapter Ten illustrates

   (A) Saeed's growing religious fervor

   (B) repairing a strained relationship

   (C) finding pleasure in a bleak situation

   (D) Saeed's behavior and Nadia's response

   (E) the narrator's change in perspective toward Nadia

**Creating on Your Own**

Hamid uses the motif of doors to represent endings and beginnings in life. In Chapter Six the narrator describes passage through the doors: "It was said in those days that the passage was both like dying and like being born."

1. Reflect on doors that you have passed through. Draw a storyboard of at least six of those doors. Label them with details and descriptions that define the experiences for you. If possible, identify the perspective that changed and the new one that came about as a result of that change.

2. Choose one of the doors from the storyboard. Describe the incident from your perspective at the time it happened, and then retell it from your current perspective. Explain what shifts, if any, resulted from it in the most important relationships in your life.

| 1st day of kindergarten | 13th birthday | First date |
|---|---|---|
| Details and descriptions: | Details and descriptions: | Details and descriptions: |
| Perspective change: | Perspective change: | Perspective change: |

## 1.2 Dynamic and Static Characters
| CHR-1.L, CHR-1.M, CHR-1.N

A **dynamic character**, one who changes and develops over the course of the narrative, often makes choices that directly or indirectly affect the outcome of that narrative. A dynamic character's changes can be visible and external, such as changes in health or social status (see Kurt Vonnegut's story graphs in Unit 1), or they can be internal, psychological, or emotional. Saeed and Nadia experience both kinds of character change in *Exit West*. External changes can cause internal changes, and internal changes can cause external changes.

**Static characters**, those who don't change and are largely unaffected by the events of the narrative, nonetheless contribute to the development of themes and help readers understand the complexities of dynamic characters.

### Dynamic Character Changes and Plot

Characters, not events, are the centerpiece of works of literary merit. A well-written plot is character driven and is the inevitable outcome of character decisions. In particular, the decisions of dynamic characters shape the arc of the plot. The characters' changes and decisions accumulate, causing complications until reaching a crisis, the most intense moment of opposing forces. The crisis reaches a **climax**, the height of the tension and the point at which the main character must make a decision. In well-constructed plots, the decision made by the main character at the climax leads to falling action and then finally to a **resolution**, when the conflicts are resolved, ending the narrative.

For example, in *The Grapes of Wrath* (1939) by John Steinbeck, another famous novel about migrants, the protagonist Tom Joad develops over the course of the novel from a recently released prisoner looking to make the most of every day for himself to a person whose whole life is devoted to helping others. In Chapter Ten he tells his mother about the attitude he developed in prison:

"You can't go thinkin' when you're gonna be out. You'd go nuts. You got to think about that day, an' then the nex' day, about the ball game Sat'dy. That's what you got to do. . . . Whyn't you do that? Jus' take ever' day."

His transformation occurs as he accompanies his family from the Dust Bowl of Oklahoma to the farms and vineyards of California where they believe they can find work. His friend Jim Casy, a former preacher, influences Tom's thinking about helping other people. Tom sees the hardships of the workers and the deceit and greed of the landowners. During a migrant labor strike, at the climax of the story, Casy is beaten to death and Tom kills the man who beat him. Tom's choice forces him to leave his family, since he will be wanted by the police, and he resolves to spend the rest of his life helping workers who have been mistreated at the hands of the wealthy and powerful. As he is saying goodbye, Tom's mother worries that she will not know where he is.

Tom laughed uneasily, "Well maybe like Casy says, a fella ain't got a soul of his own, but on'y a piece of a big one—an' then—"

"Then what, Tom? "

"Then it don' matter. Then I'll be all aroun' in the dark. I'll be ever'where— wherever you look. Wherever they's a fight so hungry people can eat, I'll be there. Wherever they's a cop beatin' up a guy, I'll be there. . . . I'll be in the way kids laugh when they're hungry an' they know supper's ready. An' when our folks eat the stuff they raise an' live in the houses they build— why I'll be there."

Tom's change is mainly emotional and internal. No longer just concerned with taking life a day at a time for himself, he understands that he is more fulfilled—has more of a soul—when he is helping others.

Another character who makes a dramatic change and whose decisions drive the plot is Janie Crawford, the protagonist in Zora Neale Hurston's *Their Eyes Were Watching God*. One review, highlighting the change Janie undergoes, notes that "the novel narrates Janie Crawford's ripening from a vibrant, but voiceless, teenage girl into a woman with her finger on the trigger of her own destiny."

Janie's story relates the decisions and actions that led her into and out of three marriages—first to Logan Killicks, a farmer who treats her like his property; second to Joe Starks, a wealthy and influential property owner who offers material comfort but still limits her independence; and finally, after Starks dies, to her true love, Tea Cake. After Tea Cake is bitten by a rabid dog and goes insane, he tries to shoot Janie. Her previous decisions and the changes they bring give her the strength to kill Tea Cake in self-defense. She is literally "a woman with her finger on the trigger of her own destiny."

In addition to the internal changes Janie goes through as she reaches gradually toward true love and independence, she also experiences external changes as she becomes wealthy after Starks dies.

Not all dynamic characters go through such dramatic changes. In *Exit West*, for example, there are no crisis points such as Janie's decision to shoot Tea Cake in *Their Eyes Were Watching God* or Tom Joad's decision to kill the man who beat Jim Casy to death in *The Grapes of Wrath*. Instead, bound by decency and genuine affection for each other, they make small decisions that eventually lead to going their separate ways.

## Static Characters

Partly to provide a contrast to dynamic characters, static characters tend not to be affected by the events of the narrative, at least not in a transformative way. In *The Grapes of Wrath*, for example, Connie Rivers, the husband of Tom's sister Rose of Sharon, appears to learn nothing from the hardships the family endures and deserts his family when they reach California. In contrast to Tom, Connie continues to think only of his own needs.

In *Their Eyes Were Watching God*, Joe Starks is the driving force behind the growth and prosperity of the town of Eatonville, but he doesn't change. He craves power and control and does not change even when opportunities arise for him to do so. One townsperson sums up the static nature of Joe Starks, wondering how Janie will make out with him given that he "changes everything, but nothin' don't change him." When Joe is on his deathbed, Janie tells Joe the same thing: "Ah knowed you wasn't gointuh lissen tuh me. You changes everything but nothin' don't change you—not even death."

This static character helps to highlight a theme of the novel—that chasing money can deprive a person of finding love. Starks's controlling, unchanging nature is powerful enough to temporarily arrest Janie's quest for love and her insatiable desire to explore new horizons, presenting Janie an opportunity for new learning about what she wants and doesn't want. The death of this static character allows Janie to regain her quest for happiness.

**Remember:** A dynamic character who develops over the course of the narrative often makes choices that directly or indirectly affect the climax and/or the resolution of that narrative. Character changes can be visible and external, such as changes to health or wealth, or can be internal, psychological, or emotional changes; external changes can lead to internal changes, and vice versa. Some characters remain unchanged or are largely unaffected by the events of the narrative. (CHR-1.L–M)

## 1.2 Checkpoint

*Review the excerpts from* Exit West *on pages 138–152 or other parts of the novel. Complete the following open-response activities and answer the multiple-choice questions.*

1. Recreate the chart below. Choose either Saeed or Nadia from *Exit West* and trace the decisions he or she makes in the book. In the left-hand column, summarize the choices and the motivations. In the right-hand column, analyze the impact on the resolution of the story.

| Saeed/Nadia Choices | Impact on Plot |
|---|---|
| | |
| | |
| | |

2. Write a few sentences analyzing whether Saeed's father does or does not change. Include a discussion of how his change or static nature adds meaning to the novel.

3. Which statement best conveys Nadia's changing attitude toward Saeed?

   (A) "She did not know how Saeed would react . . ." (paragraph 6)

   (B) "a year had passed since then, and he had changed . . ." (paragraph 6)

   (C) "Saeed was more melancholic than he had been before . . ." (paragraph 7)

   (D) "She did not know if these gaps . . . were mostly her doing or his . . ." (paragraph 8)

   (E) ". . . he was warm . . . and he sat in a way that suggested exhaustion." (paragraph 9)

**Creating on Your Own**

Choose a different door from your storyboard. How did the incident associated with that door change you or not change you? Tell the story from your perspective. Revise it with details or dialogue that capture both external and internal changes. Creating your own writing will help deepen your understanding of a writer's choices as you make a literary analysis.

# Part 1 Apply What You Have Learned

For both Nadia and Saeed, find three passages that show change. Write a paragraph that analyzes how these changes contributed to the end of their relationship. Include a claim about their drifting apart, evidence from the passages you find, and commentary that connects the evidence to the claim.

**Reflect on the Essential Question** Write a brief response that answers the essential question: *What do textual details reveal about characters and their motivation to change or stay the same?* In your answer, correctly use the key terms listed on page 155.

# Part 2

# Setting and Values

**Enduring Understanding and Skill**

## Part 2

### Understand
Setting and the details associated with it not only depict a time and place, but also convey values associated with that setting. (SET-1)

### Demonstrate
Identify and describe specific textual details that convey or reveal a setting. (2.A)
See also Unit 1

**Source:** *AP® English Literature and Composition Course and Exam Description*

**Essential Question:** How does the social, cultural, and historical situation help shape setting?

In its simplest expression, setting is the time and place in which the events of a narrative unfold. But "time" and "place" have many layers. Suppose, for example, a narrative tells the story of a soldier returning home to New York state (place) after World War II (time). If the soldier is White, the story might go that he buys a home in a newly created suburb with support from the GI Bill, obtains a university degree with support from the GI Bill, gets a decent job as a result, and becomes a good breadwinner for his family while his wife takes care of the kids. He returns to the United States when the war has helped pull the nation out of the Great Depression and economic opportunity abounds.

Now imagine the same setting and basic story—a solder returning from World War II (time) to New York state (place)—but in this narrative, the soldier is Black. Local bank practices have found ways around the GI Bill to deprive the soldier of the opportunities the White veterans enjoy. He is unable to attend college and instead finds a job as a janitor to try to make rent, cut off from the economic good times.

Understanding how characters interact with their setting, then, depends on understanding the social, cultural, and historical forces that have helped shape that setting and the values associated with it. The author reveals those aspects of setting through details in the text.

# 2.1 Social, Cultural, and Historical Details in Setting
## | SET-1.B

Setting includes the social, cultural, and historical situation during which the events of the text occur. The **social situation** of a literary work refers to how individuals or groups relate to others. It may be determined by physical environment, such as school or the workplace or prison; by sex or gender identification; by race; or by economic status. Many young adult novels deal with social situations as teens struggle to fit into society.

The **cultural situation** is shaped by the values, beliefs, customs, and activities shared by a group of people. Often, the cultural situation is shaped by a character's racial or ethnic identity, but it may be shaped by other things as well, such as education or economic status. Social and cultural situations are closely linked. For this reason, they are sometimes referred to as the sociocultural setting.

The **historical situation** refers to the time in which the story takes place, whether it is in the author's present time; in the past, as in historical fiction; or in the future, like most science fiction. Most literature, however, takes place in the time when the author is actually writing it. That "present," though, soon becomes the past, and because good literature is timeless, new readers continue to discover it decades or centuries after it was written.

Sometimes an author intentionally makes the details of a setting ambiguous. In *Exit West*, for example, Mohsin Hamid never identifies the city where Saeed and Nadia meet, nor does he tell readers when the action is supposed to take place. Based on the descriptions of social and cultural situations, readers know that the setting for the novel's opening chapters is a Muslim country, probably in the Middle East. The presence of smartphones and drones tells readers that the time is either the present or the recent past or future. Yet Chapter Twelve takes place half a century later. This shift gives the novel a timeless quality. Parts of the story seem as though they could have been torn from the pages of today's newspaper, while other parts have the surreal feeling of a modern fable. Still others seem like tales from long ago, especially since the narrator often uses the phrase "in those days" to describe customs and relationships.

In contrast to *Exit West*, *The Grapes of Wrath* is set in a very specific time and place. Early in the novel, the author describes the devastating effects of the drought-stricken farmland that came to be called the Dust Bowl. Although that is a physical setting, for readers today it is also a historical, social, and cultural setting, since it recreates the hardships of the 1930s Dust Bowl devastation to farms and the migration of poor, often starving farmers from Oklahoma and other Plains states to California, where they hoped to find work.

| Setting Situations in *The Grapes of Wrath* | | |
| --- | --- | --- |
| **Social** | **Cultural** | **Historical** |
| The social situation of the Joads is the close-knit community of farmers whose land and houses are being bulldozed by big landowners when the farmers can't make their loan payments. | The cultural situation is the lower, generally uneducated economic class the Joads and others belong to. They are used to hard work and value close family ties, but no matter how hard they try they cannot improve their lives if they stay where they are. Part of the American culture is that opportunity awaits for those who pursue it, which is what the Joads try to do. Though Tom is skeptical, his mother is convinced by fliers she has seen that life will be wonderful, with abundant food and work, when they reach California. | The severe dust storms of the 1930s followed on the heels of the already serious Great Depression that began in 1929 when the stock market crashed. The dust killed farm animals and crops and forced more than a million people in the Midwest and on the Southern Plains off their land. The migrants were unwelcome in California and treated more like refugees than people from the same country. |

Table 3-3

**Source:** Library of Congress

During the Great Depression, photographer Dorothea Lange captured images of migrants who fled the Dust Bowl for the "promised land" of California.

In a similar way, details in *Their Eyes Were Watching God* reveal the historical, social, and cultural situations in which Janie finds herself. While Hurston does not give specific dates, readers quickly pick up that the time frame for the story is post–Civil War, because Nanny, Janie's grandmother, was born into slavery but is no longer enslaved. Nanny has her own house in the backyard of "de white folks she worked wid."

Readers can also assume the story takes place before the civil rights movement of the 1960s. Women, and particularly Black women, did not have many opportunities. Nanny tells Janie, "Ah wanted to preach a great sermon about colored women sittin' on high, but they wasn't no pulpit for me."

Today, the use of the word *colored* referring to Blacks is offensive. Words such as *colored* and *negro* conjure memories of segregation. Before the civil rights movement, signs abounded in the South that sent "colored" folks to one line and "whites" to another. Hurston doesn't need to include specific dates for readers to know that the Black people in the novel, and especially Black women, were living in a time where they faced tremendous hurdles to find success, held back by the so-called Jim Crow laws that states enacted to enforce segregation. That Janie finds both financial and emotional stability makes her journey remarkable.

**Remember:** Setting includes the social, cultural, and historical situation during which the events of the text occur. (SET-1.B)

## 2.1 Checkpoint

*Reread the excerpts from* Exit West *on pages 138–152. Then complete the open-response activity.*

1. On separate paper, recreate Table 3-3 for *Exit West*. Although the exact geographic location is unknown, the author does provide a number of details about the social, cultural, and historical setting. Choose the most relevant details to complete the chart. Then write a paragraph identifying possibly conflicting values among the different aspects of the setting.

**Creating on Your Own**
Choose the earliest event from your doors storyboard. Identify the historical, cultural, and social situation in which the event took place. Then answer these questions.

- Have you changed location?
- Have your values changed? If so, how?
- Have the values of society and/or your culture changed? If so, how?

Compare the setting then with the situation as it is today. Tell the story from the perspective of your younger self and again from your current perspective. Save your work.

## The Writer's Craft: The Demands and Opportunities of Genre

If a short story is a "love affair" and a novel is a "marriage," a poem might be thought of as a "kiss." In a very brief experience, a poet tries to distill the power that fiction writers build gradually over pages and pages, chapters and chapters.

The following poem is by Tracy K. Smith, poet laureate of the United States from 2017 to 2019 and professor of creative writing at Princeton University. In 164 words, she captures an essential tension of the immigrant experience. Part of her success in doing so is her choice of setting—at the border—and her narrator, a U.S. officer of Customs and Border Protection. Typically, new arrivals at the U.S. border are asked such questions as "Why are you visiting the United States? Where will you be staying? How long will you be staying? How much money do you have for this trip and who is paying for it?" The questions the officer asks in "The United States Welcomes You" reveal much deeper concerns about the arrival of immigrants.

### THE UNITED STATES WELCOMES YOU

Why and by whose power were you sent?
What do you see that you might want to steal?
Why this dancing? Why do your dark bodies
Drink up all the light? What are you demanding
5   That we feel? Have you stolen something? Then
What is that leaping in your chest? What is
The nature of your mission? Do you seek
To offer a confession? Have you anything to do
With others brought by us to harm? Then
10  Why are you afraid? And why do you invade
Our night, hands raised, eyes wide, mute
As ghosts? Is there something you wish to confess?
Is this some enigmatic type of test? What if we
Fail? How and to whom do we address our appeal?

### Use the Writer's Craft

Think about the emotional impact the poem had on you. Then read the poem again to identify what elements or ideas in the poem evoked those feelings. Recall from Unit 2 that some of the tools poets use are vivid words and details, line and stanza breaks, contrasts, shifts, juxtapositions, relationships among words, repetition and alliteration, and figures of speech, including similes and metaphors.

Then choose one of the door experiences on your storyboard and write a poem about it. Identify an essential tension within your experience. Then try to use the power tools poetry allows to evoke an emotional response in readers.

Source: Getty Images

In literature, doors often symbolize transitions. They may be portals from one place to another, as in *Exit West*. They also symbolize a metamorphosis, or change from one state to another, as in Franz Kafka's story *The Metamorphosis*, as well as passages from one stage of life to another, as in *The Rise of David Levinsky* (on the next page) and your storyboard.

*If doors are symbols of transitions, what might a closed or locked door represent? What about a door that swings open both ways?*

# Part 2 Apply What You Have Learned

Many American novels deal with the immigrant experience. Following are a few passages from one of those books, *The Rise of David Levinsky*, written in 1917 by Abraham Cahan following a period of immigration to the United States by Jews persecuted in Russia. After you read the passages, write a paragraph noting similarities and differences between Cahan's story and Hamid's, especially in the social, cultural, and historical setting and in descriptions of the immigrant experience. The paragraphs are numbered in the order they appear here; the ellipsis marks where sections from the original book have been left out.

1    Sometimes, when I think of my past in a superficial, casual way, the metamorphosis I have gone through strikes me as nothing short of a miracle. I was born and reared in the lowest depths of poverty and I arrived in America—in 1885—with four cents in my pocket. I am now worth more than two million dollars and recognized as one of the two or three leading men in the cloak-and-suit trade in the United States. And yet when I take a look at my inner identity it impresses me as being precisely the same as it was thirty or forty years ago. My present station, power, the amount of worldly happiness at my command, and the rest of it, seem to be devoid of significance.

\* \* \*

2    The immigrant's arrival in his new home is like a second birth to him.

3    Imagine a new-born babe in possession of a fully developed intellect. Would it ever forget its entry into the world? Neither does the immigrant ever forget his entry into a country which is, to him, a new world in the profoundest sense of the term and in which he expects to pass the rest of his life. I conjure up the gorgeousness of the spectacle as it appeared to me on that clear June morning: the magnificent verdure of Staten Island, the tender blue of sea and sky, the dignified bustle of passing craft—above all, those floating, squatting, multitudinously windowed palaces which I subsequently learned to call ferries. It was all so utterly unlike anything I had ever seen or dreamed of before. It unfolded itself like a divine revelation. I was in a trance or in something closely resembling one.

\* \* \*

4    Ten minutes' walk brought me to the heart of the Jewish East Side. The streets swarmed with Yiddish-speaking immigrants. The sign-boards were in English and Yiddish, some of them in Russian. The scurry and hustle of the people were not merely overwhelmingly greater, both in volume and intensity, than in my native town. It was of another sort. The swing and step of the pedestrians, the voices and manner of the street peddlers, and a hundred and one other things seemed to testify to far more self-confidence and energy, to larger ambitions and wider scopes, than did the appearance of the crowds in my birthplace.

5    The great thing was that these people were better dressed than the inhabitants of my town. The poorest-looking man wore a hat (instead of a cap), a stiff collar and a necktie, and the poorest woman wore a hat or a bonnet.

6    The appearance of a newly arrived immigrant was still a novel spectacle on the East Side. Many of the passers-by paused to look at me with wistful smiles of curiosity.

7    "There goes a green one!" some of them exclaimed.

8    The sight of me obviously evoked reminiscences in them of the days when they had been "green ones" like myself. It was a second birth that they were witnessing, an experience which they had once gone through themselves and which was one of the greatest events in their lives.

9    "Green one" or "greenhorn" is one of the many English words and phrases which my mother-tongue has appropriated in England and America. Thanks to the many millions of letters that pass annually between the Jews of Russia and their relatives in the United States, a number of these words have by now come to be generally known among our people at home as well as here. In the eighties, however, one who had not visited any English-speaking country was utterly unfamiliar with them. And so I had never heard of "green one" before. Still, "green," in the sense of color, is Yiddish as well as English, so I understood the phrase at once, and as a contemptuous quizzical appellation for a newly arrived, inexperienced immigrant it stung me cruelly. As I went along I heard it again and again. Some of the passers-by would call me "greenhorn" in a tone of blighting gaiety, but these were an exception. For the most part it was "green one" and in a spirit of sympathetic interest. It hurt me, all the same. Even those glances that offered me a cordial welcome and good wishes had something self-complacent and condescending in them. "Poor fellow! he is a green one," these people seemed to say. "We are not, of course. We are Americanized."

**Reflect on the Essential Question**  Write a brief response that answers the essential question: *How does the social, cultural, and historical situation help shape setting?* In your answer, correctly use the key terms listed on page 168.

# Significant Events and Conflicts

**Essential Question:** How do the writer's structural choices emphasize significant events and conflict?

"Fiction is like a spider's web, attached ever so lightly perhaps, but still attached to life at all four corners."

Virginia Woolf, *A Room of One's Own*

This quotation from Virginia Woolf contains two important ideas: literature is connected to life, and the parts in a work of literature are connected to one another, if ever so lightly. Longer works of fiction and drama have a larger collection of "parts" to connect. From a small scene, such as the one between Saeed and his boss at the beginning of *Exit West* that shows Saeed's sensitivity and conscience, to a dramatic episode such as the nativist attack on immigrants in London, events in a novel unfold as the characters maneuver within them and face their conflicts.

| | | |
|---|---|---|
| events | scenes | internal conflicts |
| conflict | significant event | psychological conflicts |
| episodes | values | external conflict |
| encounters | | |

# 3.1 Plot and the Significance of Events

| STR-1.K, STR-1.L, STR-1.M

Every story, or narrative, is delivered through a series of **events** that relate to a **conflict**, or struggle between opposing forces. Events include **episodes**, single events; **encounters**, meetings between characters; and **scenes**, story lines often conveyed within a chapter. All of these can introduce and develop a plot. A **significant event** is one of special importance to the unfolding of the narrative, to the heightening or resolution of the conflict, and to the development of characters.

**Events that Introduce or Develop the Plot** The function of some events in a narrative is to initiate or develop the plot. These are the events in the cause-and-effect chain that sets the story in motion and extends through the resolution of the conflict. The chart below shows some of these events in *Their Eyes Were Watching God*. They all have a direct impact on the arc of the storyline, and therefore the structure of the narrative, as Janie confronts her conflict, so they are all significant events.

| Selected Significant Events that Function to Begin and Develop the Plot in *Their Eyes Were Watching God* | |
|---|---|
| **Event** | **Relation to Plot/Conflict** |
| Janie kisses a boy close to her age, so her grandmother insists Janie marry an older man, Logan Killicks, who will provide financial security and preserve Janie's reputation. | This event establishes the conflict that will run through the book. It is the initiating event that sets up an opposing force in Janie's struggle to find fulfilling love. |
| Janie, unhappy in her marriage to Logan, leaves him for the more polished and ambitious Joe Starks. | Janie's marriage to Starks is the next big obstacle in her search for love, since she does not find it with Joe, but she does experience new horizons. |
| Joe Starks becomes terminally ill and transfers his fears to Janie by berating her in public. One day she snaps in their store and tells him he is wrong to be so condescending to her. The store is filled with townspeople and Joe is embarrassed. | This marriage is a 20-year struggle for Janie. She still longs for a genuine love that will allow her to grow and develop as a person. Unlike during her experience with Logan, Janie learns to feel with her heart while agreeing with her mouth. When she confronts Joe in the store and later on his deathbed, she finally finds the words to express her emotions. Janie tells Joe he has been so caught up in his ambitions that he has missed the chance to care about others and have them care about him. |

Table 3-4

**Events that Develop Characters or Themes** Not all events related in longer fiction serve the purpose of driving the plot. Some may seem disconnected from the plot or able to stand alone as *their* own complete stories. In most cases, the function of such scenes or episodes is to reveal something about a character or theme. For example, the first half of Chapter Six in *Their Eyes Were Watching God* tells the story of Matt Bonner's old, underfed mule that the town mistreats. Janie feels sorry for the mule, and Joe buys it from Matt. The mule goes from being a target of the town's abuse to mythic stature in the town's folklore. Joe takes all the credit even though it was Janie's empathy for the mule that caused him to buy it.

On the surface, the chapter seems disconnected from the rest of the story. It is an episode that can stand alone as a narrative. However, it functions within the main narrative in part to add depth to the character of Joe Starks. Joe hears Janie express sympathy for the mule and decides to buy it at that time to give it a better life. That action shows Joe's wish to make Janie happy even though he remains domineering. Also, the episode illuminates a theme of the book. The mistreatment of the mule mirrors the mistreatment of Janie by her first two husbands. The mule's death, subsequent funeral, and attack by vultures have connections to Joe's death, his funeral, and behavior of the townspeople whose behavior resembles that of the vultures.

 **Remember:** A story, or narrative, is delivered through a series of events that relate to a conflict. Events include episodes, encounters, and scenes in a narrative that can introduce and develop plots. The significance of an event depends on its relationship to the narrative, the conflict, and the development of characters. (STR-1.K–M)

## 3.1 Checkpoint

*Review the excerpts from* Exit West *on pages 138–152 or answer with examples from other parts of the book. Complete the following open-response activity and answer the multiple-choice question.*

1. Borrowing from Virginia Woolf's spider web metaphor, choose three episodes, encounters, or scenes from *Exit West*. Recreate Table 3-4 and fill in the columns for each selection.

2. In *Exit West*, the episode between the elderly man from the Netherlands and the wrinkled man from Brazil functions as a

    (A) validation of same-sex relationships

    (B) sarcastic portrayal of meddling neighbors

    (C) significant event highlighting the losses that come with age

    (D) thematic commentary on open borders

    (E) celebration of the power of love at all ages

**Creating on Your Own**

Revisit the doors of your storyboard. What is the most significant event represented in your door experiences? What minor events relate to this conflict? Write a memoir that centers on that significant event, using the related events to flesh out your narrative.

# 3.2 Conflict, Tension, and Contrasts

| STR-1.N, STR-1.O, STR-1.P, STR-1.Q

Conflict is tension between competing values either within a character or with outside forces that obstruct a character in some way, known as external conflict. A text may contain multiple conflicts. Often two or more conflicts in a text intersect. A primary conflict can be heightened by the presence of additional conflicts that intersect with it. Inconsistencies in a text—characters behaving in ways that seem to be at odds with previous behavior, for example, or at odds with the setting—may create contrasts that represent conflicts of values or perspectives.

## Internal and External Conflicts

Every time you make a difficult decision, you are working through a conflict—picking a side in the tension between competing **values**, or fundamental beliefs that guide attitude and actions. The conflict can be within one person who struggles with opposing beliefs or wishes. These are called **internal conflicts**, also known as **psychological conflicts**. For example, an internal conflict may arise if many of your friends are getting tattoos and urging you to as well. While you want to, you believe that such a permanent change may not age well. How will it look when you go for a job interview after college, for example? This is a conflict between valuing fitting in with your friends and valuing considering the long-term consequences of your actions. Internal conflicts may be caused by many things, such as doubts about religion, moral dilemmas, and existential struggles to find meaning in life.

The type of conflict changes, however, if you know you want a tattoo but your parents won't allow you to get one. This situation represents an **external conflict**, an outside obstruction to your desires. This type of conflict between people (or characters, in literature) may also result from competing values. In this case, you value the freedom to express yourself through body art and fit in with other friends who are getting tattoos, while your parents value your health and safety and feel an obligation to protect the adult "you" from the youthful "you" who might not be able to evaluate long-term consequences.

External conflicts may not just be between individuals. They may be between people and society, people and nature, people and the supernatural, people and fate, or people and technology.

## Competing Values

Conflict is tension between competing **values**, or fundamental beliefs that guide characters' attitudes and actions. Conflict occurs when characters have values that aren't compatible with one another. Competing values may come from either external or internal sources. In *Exit West*, both Saeed and Nadia struggle with remaining in an unfulfilling relationship. Their values have changed since their initial meeting. Saeed is more devout toward religion and less devoted to Nadia. While living in London, Nadia assimilates by embracing new cultures. She joins the Nigerian council and learns a bit of their language. Saeed, on the other hand, finds solace in a household of Muslims that reminds him of home. By Chapter Ten the competing values have driven them apart.

## Multiple Changing Conflicts

As a narrative progresses, multiple conflicts arise and intersect with one another, thickening a text's complexity. At the beginning of *Exit West*, for example, the external conflict of war is serious, but both sides are clearly defined as militants and nonmilitants—characters are in either one camp or the other. The militants want a religious state. At this point, Saeed and Nadia are in the same nonmilitant camp, but their internal conflicts about religion will continue to intensify throughout the story and will intersect with external conflicts. By the end of the book, their competing values have driven them apart. Saeed has become extremely devout and is drawn to the preacher's daughter in Marin. Nadia remains nonreligious.

These characters' internal conflicts intersect with two of the novel's external and overarching conflicts. Saeed's internal struggle with religion mirrors the militants' desire to create a religious state. Nadia's internal struggles to assimilate intersect with the novel's primary conflict between nativists and those who migrate. The intersection of the internal with the external conflicts helps illuminate the text's message on the topics of religion, politics, and migration. As the two characters have exited westward—first to Mykonos, sometimes thought of as the gateway from the Middle East to Europe, then to London, and then to Marin—they have become freer to be fully themselves.

The chart on the next page shows the interplay of conflicts in Saeed and Nadia. It is followed by claims that draw conclusions about the impact of conflict on character, plot, or theme development.

| Character | Internal Conflicts | External Conflicts | Intersection with Other Conflicts |
|---|---|---|---|
| Saeed | When he goes through the door to Mykonos, he looks back as though he is unsure he wants to continue. He thinks of his father, whom he left behind. (Chapter Six)<br><br>The narrator sums up the internal conflict: "for when we migrate, we murder from our lives those we leave behind." (Chapter Six) | Leaves because of war in his birth city<br><br>Finds anti-migrant sentiment in Mykonos, London, and Marin<br><br>Subjected to physical violence in Mykonos and London: "At night, in the darkness, as drones and helicopters and surveillance balloons prowled intermittently overhead, fights would sometimes break out, and there were murders and rapes and assaults as well." (Chapter Eight) | The narrator brings together the internal and external conflicts. "All over the world people were slipping away from where they had been, from once fertile plains cracking with dryness, from seaside villages gasping beneath tidal surges, from overcrowded cities and murderous battlefields, and slipping away from other people too, people they had in some cases loved, as Nadia was slipping away from Saeed, and Saeed from Nadia." (Chapter Eleven) |
| Nadia | Nadia rebels against cultural norms that maintain women should be submissive, protected by men, and religious. As a young girl she dabbles in art that is abstract, quite different from the religious art in her house. The narrator shares that she had a "constant questioning and growing irreverence in matters of faith" (Chapter Two). She moves into her own apartment. | Her family disowns her.<br><br>She has to wear long black robes to protect herself from men. | When Saeed's father dies, she asks to be part of the prayer circle but does not intend to pray. Her conflict about religion intersects with her conflict about Saeed. She feels she should be close to him, but she felt "for the first time unwelcome. Or perhaps unengaged. Or perhaps both." (Chapter Nine) |

Table 3-5

**Possible Claims about Character, Plot, and Theme Development:**

- In escaping physical violence, Saeed is guilty of emotional violence to himself and to those he loves.

- Migration will continue as long as people live in harsh conditions, but migrants will continue to face hostile environments and personal sacrifice.

- Nadia wears black robes, a cultural symbol of submission and piety, so that she can lead her life as an independent woman.

- Nadia's black robes become a source of irritation to Saeed as he grows more devout and she becomes more independent and they continue to move further apart.

## Inconsistencies and Contrasts

Complex literary characters, like complex people, sometimes act in inconsistent ways that may seem to go against the values they previously defended. In *To Kill a Mockingbird*, for example, the fair-minded Atticus Finch, the attorney who sits guard at the jailhouse to make sure the townspeople don't take the law into their own hands and hurt his client who is inside, agrees at the end of the novel with Sheriff Tate's suggestion that they not pursue charges against the shy Boo Radley for killing the man who attacked Finch's children. In so doing, he and Tate take the law into their own hands. That decision contrasts with Finch's earlier refusal to allow others to do the same. Some critics have argued that the decision to shield Boo Radley reflects the perspective of those who see one set of rules for poor Whites like the man who attacked Finch's children and another set of rules for less poor Whites like the reclusive Boo Radley.

In *Their Eyes Were Watching God*, Tea Cake, the love of Janie's life, beats her. He explains that he was trying to show his dominance over her when he felt threatened by a lighter-skinned man that a neighbor thought would suit Janie better than the dark-skinned Tea Cake. That behavior, though, is inconsistent with Tea Cake's former treatment of Janie. Some readers speculate that the racism associated with skin color unleashes a force in Tea Cake, but most agree it is out of character for him to behave that way. Tea Cake becomes a more complex character as a result of that inconsistent behavior.

Much literature and drama after World War II set up contrasts and inconsistencies about meanings people attach to life. For example, Samuel Beckett's 1953 play *Waiting for Godot* begins with one of the two protagonists saying "Nothing to be done." Most audiences expect action in a play, and when the second protagonist responds, "I'm beginning to come round to that opinion," theater goers might wonder if anything is ever going to happen in the play. At the end, the two characters decide to "go." While the audience doesn't know where they might go, they expect them to move. However, the play ends with the two characters sitting and not moving. Once again, the audience is presented with inconsistencies.

Why would Beckett subject audiences or readers to an entire work where nothing happens? One possible explanation is he is trying to convey the idea that expectations in life are seldom met or the idea that meanings people construct about life are just that—human constructs, not actual inherent meanings.

These inconsistencies or surprises in literature do not offer readers easy answers. Rather, they prod readers to examine their expectations and determine why the author does not meet them. What impact do these inconsistencies have on character and theme? Answers to that question will depend on the textual evidence used to support a claim.

**Remember:** Conflict is tension between competing values either within a character, known as internal or psychological conflict, or with outside forces that obstruct a character in some way, known as external conflict. A text may contain multiple conflicts. Often two or more conflicts in a text intersect. A primary conflict can be heightened by the presence of additional conflicts that intersect with it. Inconsistencies in a text may create contrasts that represent conflicts of values or perspectives. (STR-1.N–Q)

### 3.2 Checkpoint

*Review the excerpts from* Exit West *on pages 138–152 or refer to other parts of the book. Complete the following open-response activity and answer the multiple-choice questions.*

1. Using the information in Table 3-5, write a paragraph that explains the interplay among conflicts in *Exit West*.

2. In the passage below, the narrator's description most clearly serves to highlight which conflict?

   All over the world people were slipping away from where they had been, from once fertile plains cracking with dryness, from seaside villages gasping beneath tidal surges, from overcrowded cities and murderous battlefields, and slipping away from other people too, people they had in some cases loved, as Nadia was slipping away from Saeed, and Saeed from Nadia.

   (A) The end of Saeed and Nadia's relationship
   (B) The environmental and political tragedies behind migration
   (C) The threats that overpopulation and global warming pose to the environment
   (D) The fragility of love in the presence of strife and natural disasters
   (E) The danger that warfare poses to human relationships

3. Which of the following lines from Chapter Twelve of *Exit West* best describes the resolution Saeed and Nadia assign to their relationship?

    (A) "They were former lovers, and they had not wounded each other so deeply as to have lost their ability to find a rhythm together . . . ."

    (B) "Their conversation navigated two lives, with vital details highlighted and excluded."

    (C) "They grew younger and more playful as the coffee in their cups diminished . . . ."

    (D) "Passersby did not pause to look at this old woman in her black robe or this old man with his stubble."

    (E) "He nodded and said if she had an evening free he would take her, it was a sight worth seeing in this life . . . ."

4. In the passage below, which purpose do the descriptive contrasts mainly serve?

> Air strikes were called in by the army on both occasions, shattering Saeed's bathroom window while he was in the shower, and shaking like an earthquake Nadia and her lemon tree as she sat on her terrace smoking a joint. Fighter-bombers grated hoarsely through the sky.

    (A) to highlight the dangers Saeed and Nadia face as migrants

    (B) to portray Nadia as indifferent to the destruction around her

    (C) to portray war's destruction of ordinary life

    (D) to emphasize the different responses people have to war

    (E) to illustrate the fragility of nature in war

**Creating on Your Own**

Return to your doors storyboard. Choose a door you have not yet written about. Identify the internal and external conflicts it represents. What were the competing values behind each of those conflicts? How did they intersect with one another? Create a graphic representation of the intermingling of external and internal conflicts. Try to capture the motivations of each force.

# Part 3   Apply What You Have Learned

Read the final passage from the novel *The Rise of David Levinsky*. (See pages 173–174 for an excerpt from earlier in the book.) Choose one of the conflicts identified in this final passage and write a paragraph that explains how the conflict reveals values and a theme of the novel. (The paragraph numbering continues from the previous excerpt.)

10    Sometimes when I am alone in my beautiful apartments, brooding over these things and nursing my loneliness, I say to myself: "There are cases when success is a tragedy."

11    There are moments when I regret my whole career, when my very success seems to be a mistake.

12    I think that I was born for a life of intellectual interest. I was certainly brought up for one. The day when that accident turned my mind from college to business seems to be the most unfortunate day in my life. I think that I should be much happier as a scientist or writer, perhaps. I should then be in my natural element, and if I were doomed to loneliness I should have comforts to which I am now a stranger. That's the way I feel every time I pass the abandoned old building of the City College.

13    The business world contains plenty of successful men who have no brains.

14    Why, then, should I ascribe my triumph to special ability? I should probably have made a much better college professor than a cloak-manufacturer, and should probably be a happier man, too. I know people who have made much more money than I and whom I consider my inferiors in every respect.

15    Many of our immigrants have distinguished themselves in science, music, or art, and these I envy far more than I do a billionaire. As an example of the successes achieved by Russian Jews in America in the last quarter of a century it is often pointed out that the man who has built the greatest sky-scrapers in the country, including the Woolworth Building, is a Russian Jew who came here a penniless boy. I cannot boast such distinction, but then I have helped build up one of the great industries of the United States, and this also is something to be proud of. But I should readily change places with the Russian Jew, a former Talmud[1] student like myself, who is the greatest physiologist in the New World, or with the Russian Jew who holds the foremost place among American song-writers and whose soulful compositions are sung in almost every English-speaking house in the world. I love music to madness. I yearn for the world of great singers, violinists, pianists. Several of the greatest of them are of my race and country, and I have met them, but all my acquaintance with them has brought me is a sense of being looked down upon as a money-bag striving to play the Maæcenas.[2] I had a similar experience with a sculptor, also one of our immigrants, an East Side boy who had met with sensational success in Paris and London. I had him make my bust. His demeanor toward me was all that could have been desired. We even cracked Yiddish jokes together and he hummed bits of synagogue music over his work, but I never left his studio without feeling cheap and wretched.

---

1  **Talmud:** a book that serves as the main source of Jewish law and theology
2  **Maæcenas:** a man of great wealth in ancient Rome

16    When I think of these things, when I am in this sort of mood, I pity myself for a victim of circumstances.

17    At the height of my business success I feel that if I had my life to live over again I should never think of a business career.

18    I don't seem to be able to get accustomed to my luxurious life. I am always more or less conscious of my good clothes, of the high quality of my office furniture, of the power I wield over the men in my pay. As I have said in another connection, I still have a lurking fear of restaurant waiters.

19    I can never forget the days of my misery. I cannot escape from my old self.

20    My past and my present do not comport well. David, the poor lad swinging over a Talmud volume at the Preacher's Synagogue, seems to have more in common with my inner identity than David Levinsky, the well-known cloak-manufacturer.

THE JEWISH SCHOOL.

A yeshiva is a Jewish educational system that focuses on study of the Talmud, or Jewish law, and the Torah, the first five books of the Hebrew Bible. Traditionally, only males attended yeshivas, although most non-Orthodox yeshivas now also admit females.

**Reflect on the Essential Question** Write a brief response that answers the essential question: *How do the writer's structural choices emphasize significant events and conflict?* In your answer, correctly use the key terms listed on page 176.

# Part
# 4

# Writing About Literature III

**Enduring Understanding and Skills**

## Part 4

### Understand
Readers establish and communicate their interpretations of literature through arguments supported by textual evidence. (LAN-1)

### Demonstrate
Develop a paragraph that includes 1) a claim that requires defense with evidence from the text and 2) the evidence itself. (7.A)

Develop a thesis statement that conveys a defensible claim about an interpretation of literature and that may establish a line of reasoning. (7.B)

Develop commentary that establishes and explains relationships among textual evidence, the line of reasoning, and the thesis. (7.C)

Select and use relevant and sufficient evidence to both develop and support a line of reasoning. (7.D)

Demonstrate control over the elements of composition to communicate clearly. (7.E)

See also Units 1, 2 (Skill 7.A only for Units 1 and 2), 4, 5, 6, 7, 8 & 9

**Source:** *AP® English Literature and Composition Course and Exam Description*

**Essential Question:** How can you communicate in writing an interpretation of a work of literature that asserts a claim and supports it with evidence?

The process of communicating your interpretations of literary works supported by textual evidence is known as *literary analysis*. Unlike other forms of argumentation, literary argument does not call the audience to action or persuade them to change their minds; rather it seeks to engage the audience in an interpretation of literature that presents an interesting and credible perspective.

In this unit you will build skills to write a thesis and develop a line of reasoning, both of which are explained through commentary. The word *thesis* comes from Greek, meaning "to place a proposition." The thesis will propose your argument to the reader and provide a road map or logical line of reasoning for a series of related paragraphs.

| | | |
|---|---|---|
| claims | line of reasoning | associate |
| textual evidence | illustrate | amplify |
| commentary | clarify | qualify |
| thesis statement | exemplify | recursive |

# 4.1 Components of Literary Analysis

| LAN-1.A, LAN-1.B, LAN-1.C

As you closely read a text, details will begin to congeal into ideas that lead to thematic statements, which in turn will lead to **claims**, or assertions. (See Units 1 and 2.) Your claims will be supportable with **textual evidence**, the details you found in the work that can be quoted either directly or indirectly. The evidence you use should reflect your unique interpretations. No single correct interpretation exists, only credible ones that come from readers' critical thinking.

The degree of credibility in your literary analysis comes from three factors. First, your claims must be arguable. In other words, they must go beyond the obvious to statements about the significance of tensions and conflicts with which others may disagree. Second, you need to defend or justify your claims with evidence from the text. Finally, you must logically explain the link between your claims and evidence. This explanation is called **commentary**. Strong literary analyses have commentary that consistently explains or justifies the connections between claims and evidence.

In Units 1 and 2, your task was to write a paragraph of literary analysis. In this and all remaining units, you will be writing an *essay* of literary analysis. The table below shows how the components of a paragraph of literary analysis compare with the components of an essay of literary analysis.

| Paragraph of Literary Analysis | Essay of Literary Analysis |
|---|---|
| Topic sentence that states the claim asserting the interpretation | Introduction that includes the thesis statement (main claim) expressing the writer's interpretation |
| Body of sentences providing evidence supporting the claim and commentary explaining how the evidence ties to the text | Body of supporting paragraphs, each expressing a supporting claim and devoted to a different set of evidence and commentary tying the evidence to the text |
| Concluding sentence | Concluding paragraph |

Table 3-6

**Remember:** In literary analysis, writers read a text closely to identify details that, in combination, enable them to make and defend a claim about an aspect of the text. A claim is a statement that requires defense with evidence from the text. In literary analysis, the initial components of a paragraph are the claim and textual evidence that defends the claim. (LAN-1.A–C)

## 4.1 Checkpoint

The College Board posts sample student essays on its website. You can find them most easily by doing a Google search for AP° English Literature student samples. For the purpose of this activity, it doesn't matter what year the samples are from. Just choose an essay that received a high score. Find, download, and read the student sample. Identify the following components of it, either by making digital notes on the pdf or printing the sample and marking the printed page:

- claim
- three pieces of evidence
- two statements of commentary

**Composing on Your Own**

Throughout this unit, you have been carefully analyzing *Exit West* or another work of longer fiction or drama, focusing on

- how readers get to know characters (details, descriptions, actions)
- the function of changing and unchanging characters
- the setting, including the social, cultural, and historical situation
- significant events in the unfolding of a plot
- multiple and intersecting conflicts
- character inconsistencies

As you have proceeded through this work, what aspect interested you the most? What ideas seemed to always come to the surface of your thinking? What questions did you have? Write freely in answer to these questions and save your work.

## 4.2 Thesis Statement | LAN-1.D, LAN-1.E

Like a claim, a **thesis statement** expresses an interpretation of a literary text and requires a defense through use of textual evidence. How, then, is a thesis different from a claim? One way to think about the difference is to view the thesis statement as the *overarching claim*. In a paragraph of literary analysis, the claim is supported by evidence in the sentences in the body of the paragraph. In an essay of literary analysis, the thesis statement, or overarching claim, is supported by other claims, each of which is the topic sentence of a paragraph of its own. Developing the skill of writing defensible thesis statements is an important step in writing an effective essay.

In fact, thesis statements are so critical to effective essay writing that the rubric for the AP® English Literature and Composition Exam has a separate category for your literary thesis. Thesis statements are critical for several reasons:

- They help organize your thinking.
- They exclude irrelevant information.
- They help you dig more deeply into nuanced meanings of the text, showing your ability to think critically.
- They help the reader follow the logic of your line of reasoning.
- They provide an overarching frame for your supporting claims, evidence, and commentary.

While the best thesis statements reflect the unique perspectives of their writers, most also share certain attributes:

- They demonstrate laser focus and clarity.
- They have an arguable or interesting take: the writer has a position on the topic.
- They enter into a conversation about a theme and tie the theme to the text.
- They convince the audience that the writer has an intimate understanding of the text.
- They show critical thinking through interpretation of the text.
- They have a universal component that goes beyond the text itself.

## Process of Developing a Thesis Statement

A thesis statement is a claim, but it is broad enough to encompass a series of claims that will organize your line of reasoning. It makes sense that the same process of developing a claim can be used to start developing your thesis statement.

| Steps in Developing a Thesis | | |
|---|---|---|
| Universal Ideas → | Thematic Statement → | Thesis Statement |
| These are big ideas and emotions that tend to transcend differences in readers' backgrounds. | Stories can convey a general message about some of these big ideas. | The thematic statement only becomes a thesis statement when it is tied directly to the story and has a defensible proposition. |

Table 3-7

When deciding on possible topics for your thesis, consider aspects of the text that you noticed when reading and annotating. Then ask yourself how those aspects relate to a possible thematic statement and write several thematic statements. Choose one of the statements that most interests you. Finally, write the first draft of a thesis statement, often called a *working thesis*. As you work through developing claims and finding evidence, chances are you will want to revise your thesis to make it more arguable and laser focused. Here is a sample process for developing a thesis for *Exit West*.

| Steps in Developing a Thesis | | |
|---|---|---|
| Universal Ideas → | Thematic Statement → | Working Thesis Statement |
| Throughout time humans have migrated to new locations for better opportunities. | Migrants often face hostile receptions in their new homes. | In Mohsin Hamid's novel *Exit West*, Saeed and Nadia face hostile receptions from nativists. |

Table 3-8

The following thesis is definitely a working thesis and can be improved. It is not arguable. Below is a rubric you can use to evaluate your thesis statements or to give feedback to a peer.

**Working Thesis**: In Mohsin Hamid's novel *Exit West*, Saeed and Nadia face hostile receptions from nativists.

| | Excellent | Acceptable | Missing | Comments |
|---|---|---|---|---|
| Laser Focused and Clear | X | | | It is clear that the paper will focus on both the difficulties and rewards of migration. |
| Arguable and Interesting | | | X | Not much of an argument. Anyone reading the story will say Nadia and Saeed face hostile receptions from the nativists. |
| Familiarity with the Text | | | X | Not convincing. Could do an Internet search and find this information. |
| Critical Thinking/ Interpretation of the Text | | | X | What are the causes? The effects? Does this happen to everyone? |
| Universal Component Greater Than the Text Itself | | X | | The universal is implied, but because it is not accompanied by critical thinking, it becomes obvious and not arguable. |

Table 3-9

Based on the comments in the rubric, a revised thesis might resemble the one below.

> **Revised Thesis**: While Saeed and Nadia do face rejection and aggression from nativists, Hamid does not focus on that conflict but rather sheds light on the personal struggles and sacrifices of migrants.

## Previewing the Line of Reasoning

After reading the revised thesis statement, what might you expect from the rest of the essay? Which topic would you expect to be covered first, and then next, and then after that? Many readers might expect the essay to unfold this way:

**First body paragraph**: evidence of rejection and aggression from nativists that Nadia and Saeed experience (transition)

**Second body paragraph**: evidence of Hamid's focus on personal struggles and sacrifices—maybe with focus on one character or one specific part of the book (transition)

**Third body paragraph**: evidence of Hamid's focus on personal struggles and sacrifices focusing on a different character or different part of the book

If this is indeed how the essay progresses, then the thesis statement will have provided a preview of the organization. It could also preview other arrangements (see Line of Reasoning, page 193). Not all thesis statements need to provide a preview, however.

**Remember:** A thesis statement expresses an interpretation of a literary text and requires a defense through use of textual evidence and a line of reasoning, both of which are explained in an essay through commentary. A thesis statement may preview the development or line of reasoning of an interpretation. This is not to say that a thesis statement must list the points of an interpretation, literary elements to be analyzed, or specific evidence to be used in the argument.

## 4.2 Checkpoint

In your own words, explain what happens at each of the following stages of developing a thesis statement:

- close reading
- universal ideas
- thematic statement
- thesis statement

## Composing on Your Own

Return to the work you did in the previous Composing on Your Own section. Choose an aspect of the literary work you have been studying that holds special interest for you. Think carefully about how you interpret that aspect in relation to the meaning of the whole work. Then go through the steps of developing a thesis statement to express an overarching claim stating your interpretation. You can begin to fill in an organizer like the one below as you work through the process of sketching out an essay of literary analysis. For now, just complete the first four rows. Save your work.

| Text: | | |
|---|---|---|
| Universal Ideas: | | |
| Thematic Statement: | | |
| Thesis Statement: | | |
| Supporting Claim 1: | | |
| Evidence from Text | Evidence from Text | Evidence from Text |
| Commentary explaining how information from text supports claim | Commentary explaining how information from text supports claim | Commentary explaining how information from text supports claim |
| Supporting Claim 2: | | |
| Evidence from Text | Evidence from Text | Evidence from Text |
| Commentary explaining how information from text supports claim | Commentary explaining how information from text supports claim | Commentary explaining how information from text supports claim |
| Supporting Claim 3: | | |
| Evidence from Text | Evidence from Text | Evidence from Text |
| Commentary explaining how information from text supports claim | Commentary explaining how information from text supports claim | Commentary explaining how information from text supports claim |
| Possible concluding sentence: | | |

# 4.3 Line of Reasoning and Commentary

| **LAN-1.F, LAN-1.G**

In each paragraph, commentary links your evidence to your claim. Effective commentary also links each paragraph to the thesis. Your commentary will serve as a map for the reader to follow your **line of reasoning**, the logical sequence of claims that work together to defend the overarching thesis statement.

Look again at the *Exit West* thesis on page 191. ("While Saeed and Nadia do face rejection and aggression from nativists, Hamid does not focus on that conflict but rather sheds light on the personal struggles and sacrifices of migrants.") One line of reasoning might be to classify the types of sacrifices and contributions made by the characters and arrange your claims in accordance with those categories. Another might be to order the claims by location, which would also follow the structure of the novel. The important consideration is that you have a well-thought-out line of reasoning clearly expressed through your commentary.

## Consistent and Explicit Commentary

After determining the order of your claims, use your commentary to:

- explain the significance of the evidence to the claim and thesis
- explain the connections among the thesis, claims, and evidence
- address an interpretation of the work as a whole

Don't assume your reader can readily infer connections among the thesis, claims, evidence, and the meaning of the work as a whole. Make these connections explicit throughout the essay to guide the reader through your argument.

 **Remember:** A line of reasoning is the logical sequence of claims that work together to defend the overarching thesis statement. A line of reasoning is communicated through commentary that explains the logical relationship between the overarching thesis statement and the claims/evidence within the body of an essay. (LAN-1.D–G)

## 4.3 Checkpoint

Return to the sample essay you downloaded from the College Board website or download a new one. Identify the line of reasoning the writer used by listing the supporting claims in the order they are presented. Then evaluate how effectively the commentary ties the evidence to both the supporting claims and the thesis statement.

**Composing on Your Own**

Return to the chart you began in the previous Composing on Your Own activity. Fill in the rest of the chart, checking to be sure you can explain a very clear connection between the evidence and the supporting claims and thesis. Then write a first draft of your essay of literary analysis. Share it with a peer and revise it if necessary to make the commentary explicit and consistent in connecting claims, evidence, and the thesis statement.

# 4.4 Strategic and Sufficient Evidence

| LAN-1.H, LAN-1.I, LAN-1.J, LAN-1.K

After writing your first draft, you may feel that your essay is thin on evidence. Knowing the strategic purposes for which you can use evidence and having a sense of how much evidence is enough will help you flesh out some of the thin parts and strengthen your essay. As you make your claims, determine if they provide an opportunity for any of the following purposes of evidence:

- **Illustrate**, or show or demonstrate something clearly
- **Clarify**, or clear up ambiguities or contradictions
- **Exemplify**, or provide examples
- **Associate**, or draw comparisons
- **Amplify**, or expand through additional evidence or examples
- **Qualify** a point, acknowledging limitations

Understanding the purpose and impact of evidence can strengthen your commentary. The examples in the chart on the next page illustrate how thinking about the strategic use of or reason for the evidence can lead to insightful commentary. As you fill in the boxes in your own chart, you will probably find that you are revising your ideas to make the connections among them clearer and more succinct. The evidence and commentary on the next page relates to this working thesis statement about *Exit West*:

> **Working thesis statement:** While Nadia and Saeed are dynamic characters, the changes they undergo serve to make them more aware of and true to their original selves.

How much evidence you need depends on the nature of your claims. If you claim that throughout the novel, the narrator creates a storytelling style by repeatedly using the phrase "in those days," then you need to provide enough examples of that usage to justify the "throughout the novel" part of that claim. In many cases, though, two or three well-chosen, high-quality examples are likely to be sufficient.

The table below provides examples of claims, evidence, strategic use of evidence (illustrate, clarify, exemplify, associate, amplify, or qualify), and commentary.

| Claim | Evidence | Strategic Use of Evidence | Commentary |
|---|---|---|---|
| Saeed and Nadia differ in their perspective—Nadia looks to the future while Saeed tends to look to the past. | Saeed considers returning home before he reaches Mykonos because he realizes he has lost his father. Nadia has separated from her family even before they leave for Mykonos. | These examples illustrate Saeed's greater ties to family are opposed to Nadia's more independent behaviors. | Saeed's attachment to his old life draws him to a somewhat traditional community of faith, while Nadia's pragmatic outlook allows her to embrace adventure and assimilate into her surroundings. |
| Saeed's guilt at leaving his father makes him increasingly devout to the religion he and his father practiced. | While in London, Saeed is attracted to people of the Muslim faith and in Marin he prays more devoutly. | These examples fit the profile of a devout Muslim. | Saeed grows to resemble those from whom he initially fled. |
| Nadia's black robes become emblematic of her fierce need to live independent of society's expectations. | In her birth city, she uses the robes to keep men from accosting her, but she continues to wear them in Marin because they make people uncomfortable. | Black robes are associated with piety in her birth city but with a religious zeal in Marin. | Nadia is unconcerned with public perception and expectations. |

**Table 3-10**

## A Recursive Process

People take different approaches to the writing process. Some writers first consider the evidence and ask "What is important about this passage?" to formulate a claim. Others might first form an interpretation that results in a claim and then find supporting evidence. Either is a good starting place, but the process will likely move back and forth between those approaches as the writing continues. In other words, the process is **recursive**, or repetitious and somewhat circular. Rather than writing in a linear fashion from beginning to end, you go back frequently to review what you have written before moving on. At each step, you evaluate the effectiveness of your evidence in supporting your claim, developing your thesis, and establishing a logical line of reasoning.

Theoretically, writing could be in a constant stage of revision. New ideas and understandings of evidence could prompt a writer to change parts of a text, including the thesis statement, in a continual effort at refinement. Recall the figure from Unit 1.

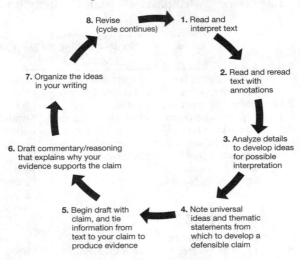

**From Reading a Text to Writing an Argument About It**

1. Read and interpret text
2. Read and reread text with annotations
3. Analyze details to develop ideas for possible interpretation
4. Note universal ideas and thematic statements from which to develop a defensible claim
5. Begin draft with claim, and tie information from text to your claim to produce evidence
6. Draft commentary/reasoning that explains why your evidence supports the claim
7. Organize the ideas in your writing
8. Revise (cycle continues)

**Remember:** Writers use evidence strategically and purposefully to illustrate, clarify, exemplify, associate, amplify, or qualify a point. Evidence is effective when the writer of the essay uses commentary to explain a logical relationship between the evidence and the claim. Evidence is sufficient when its quantity and quality provide apt support for the line of reasoning. Developing and supporting an interpretation of a text is a recursive process; an interpretation can emerge from analyzing evidence and then forming a line of reasoning, or the interpretation can emerge from forming a line of reasoning and then identifying relevant evidence to support that line of reasoning. (LAN-1.H–K)

## 4.4 Checkpoint

Read the two paragraphs of literary analysis in the chart on the next page. The first paragraph is an introduction that includes the thesis. The second paragraph is a body paragraph that follows the line of reasoning set up in the thesis. Identify the elements in this sample by choosing the correct term to label the numbered components. One example is done for you.

**Terms**

- tie to universal idea
- thesis statement
- claim
- evidence
- commentary

| Introductory Paragraph | Components |
|---|---|
| 1) Headlines are filled with stories of the mistreatment of migrants escaping from war and famine. Yet many risk their lives to migrate to what they consider a better location. Many of the news reports focus on the atrocities committed against these migrant groups, but only a few add the personal stories of those trying to migrate. As a result, it becomes easier to see the issue as "us" versus "them." Mohsin Hamid's *Exit West* does the opposite. 2) While Saeed and Nadia do face rejection and aggression from nativists, Hamid minimizes the binary "us" versus "them" to shed light on the personal struggles and sacrifices of migrants. | **1) Tie to universal ideas** Explains the conflict in a broader context and the treatment of it by Hamid<br><br><br><br>2) _____ States that Hamid shifts the focus of his narrative from the external conflicts to internal struggles |
| **Body Paragraph** | **Components** |
| 3) In the first five chapters, the narrator balances violence with personal narratives. 4) A stray bomb kills Saeed's mother and his father grieves for his best friend even when his safety is jeopardized. War eroded their buildings as "neighborhoods fall to the militants in startlingly quick succession" (Chapter Four), but the narrator gives us details about Saeed and Nadia's personal life. They take business classes at the university, Saeed prays with his father on Fridays, Nadia doesn't pray at all, but wears long black robes. 5) By the time Saeed and Nadia leave for Mykonos, we see them as real people determined in their struggle for a better life. 6) As the novel progresses the details of external conflicts become fewer as the focus shifts to personal struggles. 7) In Mykonos, their refugee camp keeps them separated from the natives, but at the same time they can find food, clothing, and shelter. "Here, decent people vastly outnumbered dangerous ones" (Chapter Six). 8) In Mykonos, the narrator begins to focus on the sacrifices of Saeed. He prays daily, especially for his father "who was not with them, and should have been" (Chapter Six). Migration has not provided an escape from the reality of sacrifice. | 3) _____ Interprets the significance of structure<br><br>4) _____ Examples of external and internal conflict<br><br><br><br>5) _____ The external conflicts imposed on ordinary people justify their migration.<br><br>6) _____ Internal conflicts are emphasized<br><br>7) _____ Examples of both external and internal conflicts<br><br>8) _____ Explains that while Mykonos is not as dangerous as their birth city, the internal conflicts remain. |

## Composing on Your Own

On separate paper, complete a graphic organizer like Table 3-10 on page 195 for *Exit West* or another longer work of fiction or drama you are studying. Return to the draft of the essay you wrote in the previous Composing on Your Own activity. Using the chart, identify the purpose and impact of the evidence. Ask yourself the following questions:

- Have I chosen the most effective evidence to achieve my intended purpose?

- Can I strengthen my commentary to more explicitly and consistently connect the claims, evidence, and thesis?

With your graphic organizer and these questions in mind, revise your literary essay. Save your work.

# 4.5 Using the Conventions of Communication
| LAN-1.L

Writers of imaginative literature often intentionally stretch or break conventions of language, whether for character development, emphasis, or some other artistic reason. For example, Zora Neale Hurston's narrative voice is that of a sophisticated, college-educated person, but she went to great pains to faithfully render the dialect her southern Black characters would have used.

The type of writing you do for the AP* Literature course and for college demands that you know and follow the conventions of language so you can communicate clearly with your audience. When you write an academic paper, your audience is educated and expects the rules to be followed. Furthermore, most of the rules are in place because they aid in clarity and shape meaning.

## Key Conventions in Grammar and Mechanics

Below is a list of 10 of the most often misused conventions. If you are unfamiliar with any of them, do a quick Internet search and learn how and why to use the convention correctly. You may want to try explaining the convention to a peer. Then use the list as you do a final edit of your paper before turning it in.

| Ten Grammar and Mechanics Conventions to Know and Follow | | |
|---|---|---|
| | **Incorrect** | **Correct** |
| 1. Subject/verb agreement | A <u>flood</u> of migrants from all over the world <u>have reached</u> the borders of developed nations. | A <u>flood</u> of migrants from all over the world <u>has reached</u> the borders of developed nations. *[The subject, flood, is singular, so it calls for a singular verb, has reached.]* |
| 2. Noun/pronoun agreement | <u>Migrants</u> of different religions bring <u>his or her</u> faith to countries where those religions may be in the minority. | <u>Migrants</u> of different religions bring <u>their</u> faith to countries where those religions may be in the minority. *[The noun migrants is plural, so the pronoun that refers back to it should also be plural.]* |
| 3. Punctuation of subordinate clauses | Even if they make it safely to their new country migrants face many problems. | Even if they make it safely to their new country, migrants face many problems. *[A subordinate clause at the beginning of a sentence should be followed by a comma.]* |
| | Migrants face many problems, even if they make it safely to their new country. | Migrants face many problems even if they make it safely to their new country. *[A subordinate clause at the end of a sentence should not be preceded by a comma.]* |

*continued*

| | Incorrect | Correct |
|---|---|---|
| 4. Fragments | The migrant families <u>traveling</u> long distances. | The migrant families <u>travel</u> long distances.<br><br>*[Write in complete sentences, with the form of the verb that makes a thought complete.]* |
| 5. Run-on sentences | Nadia is a unique <u>character she</u> has an unconventional attitude. | Nadia is a unique <u>character. She</u> has an unconventional attitude.<br><br>Nadia is a unique <u>character; she</u> has an unconventional attitude.<br><br>Nadia is a unique <u>character, and</u> she has an unconventional attitude.<br><br>*[Separate independent clauses with a period or semicolon or join them with a conjunction, but do not run them together.]* |
| 6. Comma splice | Nadia is a unique character, <u>she</u> has an unconventional attitude. | *[Independent clauses cannot be separated by a comma. See above for corrected forms.]* |
| 7. Punctuation of series | The fleeing migrants left behind their plates, <u>pots and pans</u>. | The fleeing migrants left behind their plates, <u>pots, and</u> pans.<br><br>*[Using a comma before the conjunction preceding the last item in a series avoids misunderstandings.]* |
| 8. Tense shifts | Saeed and Nadia <u>go</u> to Mykonos first and then they <u>went</u> to London. | Saeed and Nadia <u>go</u> to Mykonos first and then they <u>go</u> to London.<br><br>*[Avoid tense shifts (from present to past, for example). When writing about literature, the present tense is often preferred.]* |
| 9. Capitalization | *Exit West* begins in an unnamed country in the middle east. | *Exit West* begins in an unnamed country in the Middle East.<br><br>*[If you are uncertain about capitalizing a geographic area, an era, or a social movement, look it up online.]* |
| 10. Titles of Texts | *Exit West* has two protagonists, while the short story <u>The Appropriation of Cultures</u> has only one. | *Exit West* has two protagonists, while the short story "The Appropriation of Cultures" has only one.<br><br>*[Titles of novels or plays are italicized (or underlined if you are writing by hand). Titles of short stories and poems are put in quotes.]* |

**Table 3-11**

## The Power of Punctuation

The presence or absence of punctuation can make a big difference. Take, for example, the following sentence:

> Zora Neale Hurston was a strong spirited woman.

Does it mean that she had a strong spirit? Or that she was both strong and spirited? Punctuation can clarify the meaning. Adding a hyphen between *strong* and *spirited* indicates that she had a strong spirit:

> Zora Neale Hurston was a strong-spirited woman.

Adding a comma between those words indicates that she was both strong and spirited:

> Zora Neale Hurston was a strong, spirited woman.

The proper use of punctuation can help your readers understand your meaning right away instead of leaving them to guess.

 **Remember:** Grammar and mechanics that follow established conventions of language allow writers to clearly communicate their interpretation of a text. (LAN-1.L)

### 4.5 Checkpoint

Exchange your literary essay with that of a peer. Check each other's essays for proper use of linguistic conventions.

**Composing on Your Own**

Revise your literary analysis as necessary to produce an essay that reflects the standards of academic discourse.

# Part 4   Apply What You Have Learned

Return to the sample student essay you downloaded from the College Board website. Review it carefully with an eye for linguistic conventions. Identify three places where one or more of the 10 conventions in Table 3-11 were successfully followed. If there are any places that do not follow linguistic conventions, note them and show how they can be correctly edited.

**Reflect on the Essential Question** Write a brief response that answers the essential question: *How can you communicate in writing an interpretation of a work of literature that asserts a claim and supports it with evidence?* In your answer, correctly use the key terms listed on page 187.

# Unit 3 Review

## Section I: Multiple Choice

Questions 1–5. Read the following passage carefully before you choose your answers.

1    I fully expected to find a Constable[1] in the kitchen, waiting to take me up. But not only was there no Constable there, but no discovery had yet been made of the robbery. Mrs. Joe was prodigiously busy in getting the house ready for the festivities of the day, and Joe had been put upon the kitchen doorstep to keep him out of the dust-pan,—an article into which his destiny always led him, sooner or later, when my sister was vigorously reaping the floors of her establishment.

2    "And where the deuce ha' *you* been?" was Mrs. Joe's Christmas salutation, when I and my conscience showed ourselves.

3    I said I had been down to hear the Carols. "Ah! well!" observed Mrs. Joe. "You might ha' done worse." Not a doubt of that I thought.

4    "Perhaps if I warn't a blacksmith's wife, and (what's the same thing) a slave with her apron never off, *I* should have been to hear the Carols," said Mrs. Joe. "I'm rather partial to Carols, myself, and that's the best of reasons for my never hearing any."

5    Joe, who had ventured into the kitchen after me as the dustpan had retired before us, drew the back of his hand across his nose with a conciliatory air, when Mrs. Joe darted a look at him, and, when her eyes were withdrawn, secretly crossed his two forefingers, and exhibited them to me, as our token that Mrs. Joe was in a cross temper. This was so much her normal state, that Joe and I would often, for weeks together, be, as to our fingers, like monumental Crusaders as to their legs.

6    We were to have a superb dinner, consisting of a leg of pickled pork and greens, and a pair of roast stuffed fowls. A handsome mince-pie had been made yesterday morning (which accounted for the mincemeat not being missed), and the pudding was already on the boil. These extensive arrangements occasioned us to be cut off unceremoniously in respect of breakfast; "for I ain't," said Mrs. Joe,—"I ain't a-going to have no formal cramming and busting and washing up now, with what I've got before me, I promise you!"

---

1  **constable:** a British police officer of the lowest rank

7      So, we had our slices served out, as if we were two thousand troops on a forced march instead of a man and boy at home; and we took gulps of milk and water, with apologetic countenances, from a jug on the dresser. In the meantime, Mrs. Joe put clean white curtains up, and tacked a new flowered flounce across the wide chimney to replace the old one, and uncovered the little state parlour across the passage, which was never uncovered at any other time, but passed the rest of the year in a cool haze of silver paper, which even extended to the four little white crockery poodles on the mantel-shelf, each with a black nose and a basket of flowers in his mouth, and each the counterpart of the other. Mrs. Joe was a very clean housekeeper, but had an exquisite art of making her cleanliness more uncomfortable and unacceptable than dirt itself. Cleanliness is next to Godliness, and some people do the same by their religion.

1. The primary purpose of the passage is to
   (A) describe the orderly atmosphere of the house
   (B) characterize Joe as a threat to the house's cleanliness
   (C) develop the relationship between the speaker and Joe
   (D) reveal conflict among Mrs. Joe, the speaker, and Joe
   (E) intensify the mystery surrounding the robbery

2. What does the following sentence from the end of the first paragraph indicate?

   Joe had been put upon the kitchen doorstep to keep him out of the dust-pan,—an article into which his destiny always led him, sooner or later, when my sister was vigorously reaping the floors of her establishment.

   (A) Mrs. Joe demanded work from her husband.
   (B) Joe enjoyed sweeping floors but did so inadequately.
   (C) The narrator desires to protect Joe from undue criticism.
   (D) Joe rushed to leave the house as Mrs. Joe cleaned.
   (E) Mrs. Joe liked to clean without being interrupted.

3. In context, paragraph 4 portrays Mrs. Joe's
   (A) resentment toward her station in life
   (B) resentment toward the demands of the holiday
   (C) concern for the narrator's welfare
   (D) desire to hear Christmas carols
   (E) desire to get the house ready for the holiday

4. The shift in paragraph 5
   (A) highlights the narrator's sense of humor
   (B) illustrates Joe's public and private attitude to his wife
   (C) portrays Mrs. Joe as cranky and unreasonably demanding
   (D) creates sympathy for Mrs. Joe because of her labor
   (E) establishes the relationship between Joe and the narrator

5. The passage reveals an inconsistency between
   (A) the Christmas season and Mrs. Joe's attitude
   (B) Joe's attitude toward work and his wife's wishes
   (C) the narrator's disappearance and return
   (D) Mrs. Joe's treatment of Joe and the narrator
   (E) Mrs. Joe's housekeeping and her religion

Questions 6–10. Read the following poem carefully before you choose your answers.

**THE NEW COLOSSUS**

Not like the brazen giant of Greek fame,
With conquering limbs astride from land to land;
Here at our sea-washed, sunset gates shall stand
A mighty woman with a torch, whose flame
5   Is the imprisoned lightning, and her name
Mother of Exiles. From her beacon-hand
Glows world-wide welcome; her mild eyes command
The air-bridged harbor that twin cities frame.
"Keep, ancient lands, your storied pomp!" cries she
10  With silent lips. "Give me your tired, your poor,
Your huddled masses yearning to breathe free,
The wretched refuse of your teeming shore.
Send these, the homeless, tempest-tossed to me,
I lift my lamp beside the golden door!"

Questions 6 is covered in Unit 2.

6. The simile in line 1 evokes the feeling that the Statue of Liberty is
   (A) superior to the Greek Colossus
   (B) inferior to the Greek Colossus
   (C) restricted in her power to provide light
   (D) mighty but overpowering to the weak
   (E) mighty but also nurturing

7. Lines 9–14 ("Keep ancient lands . . . golden door") mark a shift from
   (A) weariness to excitement
   (B) disdain to acceptance
   (C) superiority to humility
   (D) supplication to demand
   (E) hypothetical to factual

8. The primary purpose of the poem is to
   (A) compare the United States to the glory of ancient Greece
   (B) welcome immigrants to the United States
   (C) compare tyrannical governments to the United States
   (D) personify an inanimate object with ideals
   (E) offer speculation about the fate of the United States

9. The imagined statement made by the statue in line 9 reveals the speaker's sense of
   (A) indignation
   (B) adoration
   (C) hopefulness
   (D) jubilation
   (E) trepidation

10. Considered as a whole, the poem embodies the cultural values of
   (A) prosperity and capitalism for all
   (B) freedom and opportunity for all
   (C) ending oppression and tyranny
   (D) gender equality and suffrage
   (E) actions speaking louder than words

## Section II: Free Response

### Question 1: Poetry Analysis

In the poem on page 203 by Emma Lazarus, the speaker reflects on the importance of the newly acquired Statue of Liberty. Read the poem carefully. Consider the implied conflicts and the speaker's attitude toward them. Write a thesis statement that captures those conflicts and the speaker's attitude toward those tensions. Then, in a well-written essay that makes defensible claims and develops commentary, explain how the evidence supports the claim.

In your response you should do the following:

- Respond to the prompt with a thesis that presents a defensible interpretation.
- Select and use evidence to support your line of reasoning.
- Explain how the evidence supports your line of reasoning.
- Use appropriate grammar and punctuation in communicating your argument.

### Question 2: Prose Fiction Analysis

Carefully read the selection on pages 201–202 from Charles Dickens's 1867 novel *Great Expectations*. Then write an essay analyzing how the speaker handles the relationship with his overbearing sister who has guardianship of him. Consider his interactions with the other character, Joe, and the speaker's perspective on the situation.

In your response you should do the following:

- Respond to the prompt with a thesis that presents a defensible interpretation.
- Select and use evidence to support your line of reasoning.
- Explain how the evidence supports your line of reasoning.
- Use appropriate grammar and punctuation in communicating your argument.

## Question 3: Literary Argument—Exile and Alienation

Many works of literature have characters who experience exile and/or alienation. This exile or alienation can be external, internal, or both. Choose a character from a work of literary merit that experiences exile or alienation. Write a thesis statement that takes a position on the work's message on this topic. Then write a literary argument that makes supporting claims about the thesis. It should provide apt and specific evidence for that claim along with commentary that ties the evidence to both the claim and thesis. Do not merely summarize the plot.

In your response you should do the following:

- Respond to the prompt with a thesis that presents a defensible interpretation.
- Provide evidence to support your line of reasoning.
- Explain how the evidence supports your line of reasoning.
- Use appropriate grammar and punctuation in communicating your argument.

# UNIT 4

# Nuance and Complexity

[Short Fiction II]

**Part 1:  Nuanced and Contrasting Characters**
**Part 2:  Setting, Mood, and Atmosphere**
**Part 3:  Plot Patterns**
**Part 4:  Narrative Distance and Perspective**
**Part 5:  Writing About Literature IV**

---

**ENDURING UNDERSTANDINGS AND SKILLS:** Unit 4

## Part 1  Nuanced and Contrasting Characters

### Understand

Characters in literature allow readers to study and explore a range of values, beliefs, assumptions, biases, and cultural norms represented by those characters. (CHR-1)

### Demonstrate

Identify and describe what specific textual details reveal about a character, that character's perspective, and that character's motives. (1.A)

Explain the function of contrasting characters. (1.C)

Describe how textual details reveal nuances and complexities in characters' relationships with one another. (1.D)

## Part 2  Setting

### Understand

Setting and the details associated with it not only depict a time and place, but also convey values associated with that setting. (SET-1)

### Demonstrate

Explain the function of setting in a narrative. (2.B)

Describe the relationship between a character and a setting. (2.C)

## Part 3  Plot Patterns

### Understand

The arrangement of the parts and sections of a text, the relationship of the parts to each other, and the sequence in which the text reveals information are all structural choices made by a writer that contribute to the reader's interpretation of a text. (STR-1)

### Demonstrate

Identify and describe how the plot orders events in a narrative. (3.A)

Explain the function of contrasts within a text. (3.D)

## Part 4  Narrative Distance and Perspective

### Understand

A narrator's or speaker's perspective controls the details and emphases that affect how readers experience and interpret a text. (NAR-1)

### Demonstrate

Identify and describe the narrator or speaker of a text. (4.A)

Identify and explain the function of point of view in a narrative. (4.B)

Identify and describe details, diction, or syntax in a text that reveal a narrator's or speaker's perspective. (4.C)

## Part 5  Writing About Literature IV

### Understand

Readers establish and communicate their interpretations of literature through arguments supported by textual evidence. (LAN-1)

### Demonstrate

Develop a thesis statement that conveys a defensible claim about an interpretation of literature and that may establish a line of reasoning. (7.B)

Develop commentary that establishes and explains relationships among textual evidence, the line of reasoning, and the thesis. (7.C)

Select and use relevant and sufficient evidence to both develop and support a line of reasoning. (7.D)

Demonstrate control over the elements of composition to communicate clearly. (7.E)

**Source:** *AP® English Literature and Composition Course and Exam Description*

# Unit 4 Overview

How well do people know you? Are you the same in school as you are at home or at a friend's house? Are you the same whether you are being viewed by a concerned parent, an angry parent, a rivalrous sibling, or a new boyfriend or girlfriend? Are you the same when you go through a difficult time as you are when everything seems to be going your way? Are your values ever in conflict?

**Source:**
Getty Images

In this second unit devoted to short fiction (see Unit 1 for the first), you will be asking these questions about the characters you encounter. What do you know about the characters' values, beliefs, and cultural norms, and how do you know it? Through what perspective(s) do you learn about the characters? How do the characters interact with the settings and dramatic situations in which they find themselves?

As you answer these questions, you will be exploring the complexity that emerges from tensions between competing values within characters themselves, with those of other characters, and with those in the world around them.

You will also explore the structural choices a writer makes when presenting the story's events, or plot, and you will gain practice in developing an interpretation of a work and communicating your interpretation in a well-developed essay.

### Short Story
### "THE SANCTUARY DESOLATED" by Jesse Stuart

The following is a short story published in 1943 by Appalachian author and poet Jesse Stuart. In this text, the narrator—a young boy named Shan—tells a story with a dramatic situation including his grandma, her house, and evolving relationships in his rural family.

1    After Grandpa died Grandma lived alone in her big house that stood upon a knoll[1] surrounded by giant black oaks and hickories. If the house had been a person it would have been a cripple for it was much older than Grandma and she was crippled with rheumatics[2] until she could hardly get about. But Grandma stayed in this big house that had a moss-covered sagging roof and the tops of the two big chimneys were crumbling in the summer wind and rain and the winter freezes. Rosebushes and shrubs grew around the house until you could hardly see the downstairs windows. And when I went to stay with Grandma at night, I always got there before darkness hovered around it. I was afraid of the house and the dense patches of shrub and vines that grew so thick the morning sunlight couldn't filter through them to dry the moss-covered damp walls that were gradually falling to decay.

2    "Your mother can't go on livin' in that house," Pa told Mom. "That house is old. It's ready to tumble in. It's a damp house inside with too many shrubs and vines around it. She must come here and live with us."

---

1  **knoll:** a small hill or mound
2  **rheumatics:** any disease marked by inflammation and pain in the joints, muscles, or fibrous tissue, especially rheumatoid arthritis.

Source: Getty Images

*The second sentence of the story begins "If the house had been a person . . . ." In what ways might a house or some other nonhuman entity be a character in a story?*

3    "But Ma will never leave that house," Mom said. "She was born in it. She was married in it. And her seven children were born in it. Grandpa planted the oaks and hickories around it when he was a young man and Ma and Dad planted the shrubs and rose-vines around it. I was a little girl when they planted part of them. She'll never leave the house, Mick."

4    "But you've never explained it the right way to her," Pa said.

5    "Now you go and see her," Mom said. "If you can do anything with her, I'll be happy. I'd be happy if she'd come here and stay with us. I won't be afraid of the house catching on fire or the roof fallin' in. Just a spark from one of the chimneys or from the flue would set the moss-covered shingles afire. You know that. And the roof is liable to fall any time."

6    I listened to them talk. I liked to go stay with Grandma for she let me run all over the house—except I was afraid to go into a few of the dark rooms upstairs. I was afraid of the attic. I was afraid of snakes and lizards in the attic. But Grandma let me do as I pleased in the big house. She let me run through it fast as I wanted to run—and I couldn't do that in our house. And she let Uncle Jason's boy, Will, do the same thing. She let Uncle Jake's boy, Herbert, do as he pleased too. And she let my sister, Mary, do as she pleased; she let Uncle Jason's girl, Effie, do as she pleased and she let Uncle Jake's girl, Carrie, do as she pleased. We had a good time with Grandma and all of us longed for our turn to go and stay with her.

7    I didn't want Grandma to come and stay with us. I wanted her to stay in the big house so sister Mary and I could go and stay our two weeks out of every six weeks with her. But Pa and Mom didn't want us to stay with her. He'd talked to Uncle Jake, Uncle Jason, Aunt Mallie and Aunt Phoebe about it. They had agreed to get Grandma away from the house and to take her to one of their homes. Each wanted her to stay but they would let her choose just so they could get her out of the old house. Even our

neighbors were talkin' about us for leaving Grandma in such a wreck of a house. People said it was a sin. I heard the boys and girls at school talking about it and they asked me why my Pa and my uncles hadn't fixed the roof. I didn't bother to tell them why but I knew Grandma wouldn't let 'em take a board from the roof and put a new one on. And she wouldn't allow a shrub or a tree cut no matter how near ready it was to fall of old age and she wouldn't allow a rosebush dug up. It was Grandma's house and land and she owned it, every foot of dirt, every shingle on the roof and every root of the rosebushes and every leaf on the tree and not one of her sons or daughters could tell her what to do with it.

8      "I'll go up there now and see her," Pa said to Mom. "I'll explain to her."

9      "I'd like to go with you, Pa," I said.

10     "All right," he said.

11     When Pa put on his hat and stepped out at the door, I followed him. It was good to put my feet in the soft green April grass again after they had been confined in shoes all winter and I walked behind Pa and stepped on every green clump of grass along the path. We lived the closest to Grandma's. If it were not for our own apple orchard and the tall green rye that Pa had sown in the orchard to turn under for a cover crop,[3] we could have seen Grandma's house from our house. We just lived around the slope—not a quarter of a mile. In a few minutes we reached Grandma's house from our house and when we reached the front gate, Pa stood and looked at it. The gate posts had rotted and the gate was ready to tumble over. But Grandma had had Cousin Herbert to nail a wire to the gate post and then nail a wire to an oak tree.

12     "This gate's even ready to fall," Pa said as he opened it carefully to keep it from falling. Then he stood under a front yard oak and looked at the hulk of a tree that held an immense top. Only the outer rim of the tree was sound and the interior of it had rotted and sparrows built their nest up in its hollow. Then Pa looked at the roof—the moss-covered shingle roof and it was as uneven as the ridges on a washboard. It was gradually sinking.

13     "The weight of a snow ten inches deep would cave that roof in," Pa said. "Mother Shelton must move from this house."

14     I didn't say anything to Pa but I hoped that she would tell him that she wouldn't move for I knew if Grandma came to stay with us that she wouldn't be the same Grandma to bake us pies and cakes and to give us money and to let us have the freedom that we didn't get at home.

15     "Well, Mother," Pa said with a big smile as we entered the house, "I thought I'd come up to see how you were feeling."

16     "I feel all right, Mick," she said. "How's everybody down your way?"

17     "All right," Pa told her.

18     "That's fine," Grandma told him.

19     Grandma sat in a big rocker and looked at Pa. She knew that Pa had come to see her about something—maybe moving—and she just sat there and waited for him to ask her and I thought he would.

---

3  **cover crop:** a crop grown for the protection and enrichment of the soil

20     "Your gate needs fixin', Mother," Pa said. "It's about ready to fall."

21     "That gate's all right," Grandma said. "Herbert fixed that gate for me. He fixed it just the way I wanted it fixed."

22     "But what about that big front yard oak?" Pa asked her. "Any windstorm is liable to push it over on the house."

23     "I've got birds that have built in that oak for twenty-five years," Grandma said. "I don't aim to have it cut. Let it fall on the house if it doesn't find some other way to fall."

24     Pa didn't say anything.

25     "Shan, there's some candy in there on the dresser for you," Grandma said.

26     I ran into the front room to get the candy and while I ate candy, I heard Grandma and Pa talking but I couldn't tell what they were saying. Soon as I had finished the candy, I went back where Pa and Grandma were talking.

27     "If you all are afraid that I am going to be found dead in the house some morning," Grandma said, "I don't mind going down to your house and try staying for a while. I'll still be in sight of my house—but I want you to know that I was born in this house and I've lived here all my life and I don't mind to die in this house. I have always expected to die here. I'll have to do it someplace and this house is the best place I know."

28     "But we'll make things comfortable for you, Mother," Pa said in a pleased tone of voice. "Our children love you and I think you'll be happy with us. Sal will fix you a room all to yourself. And when you want to lie down and rest, you won't be bothered."

29     "I've never stayed but three nights away from here in my life," Grandma said. "And I've never been a hundred miles away from here. It may work out all right. I'll try it."

30     When Grandma came to stay with us, Pa had to haul the furniture from her room and put it in the room that Mom had set aside for her in our house. But that was all the furniture that was taken from Grandma's house. She asked Pa to leave the house as she had always kept it. Grandma had never locked her doors and she left the doors unlocked, though Pa and Mom wanted her to lock her doors.

31     "I've not got anything anybody wants," Grandma said. "Jake would never sleep in a house with locked doors. Now that he's gone, I'll leave the house the way he left it."

32     Sister Mary and I did anything for Grandma that she wanted done. And when one of us went to the store, she always gave us money to get candy. And she sent money to Uncle Jake's and Uncle Jason's boys and girls to get candy. I thought that she thought she'd be going back to her old home again and that we'd be a-coming to stay with her. And I hoped that this would happen for it was better to stay in the old house with Grandma than it was to live at home.

33     One morning when I took Grandma a fresh pitcher of water, she poured herself a glass, looked at it—smelled of it—and then she made a face when she tasted it. She took a sip of it and then she gagged.

34    "What's wrong with the water, Grandma?" I asked.

35    "It's not good water," Grandma said. "This water will finish me if I keep on drinking it. Go to my well and draw me a bucket of fresh water and bring it here, Shan."

36    I told Mom and Pa that Grandma couldn't stand the water from our well and Pa said the water in our well was the same kind of sweet water that Grandma had in her well and the wells were not three hundred yards apart. Then Pa and Mom went to Grandma's room to talk to her about the water.

37    "I've drunk water from the same well for eighty-five years," Grandma told Mom and Pa, "and it's hard for me to drink this new water from a well that's not twenty-five years old."

38    "Then we'll carry you water from your well," Mom said.

39    "That will be fine," Grandma said.

40    Then she asked Pa if he'd been around her house many times since she had left. And Pa told her he had been around it every day. I wondered if she would ask him if anybody had opened the unlocked doors and had gone inside and ransacked the house. But she didn't ask Pa anything about the inside of the house. She asked him all about her trees, shrubs, and birds. She even asked Pa if the big oak had fallen yet and Grandma had just been away three days.

41    "Mick, there's one thing I want you to do for me," Grandma said.

42    "What is it, Mother?" Pa asked.

43    "I want you to cut the tall green rye in your young apple orchard so I can see my house," she said. "If you'd do that I could sit in my room and look at my house from this window."

44    "Well, Mother," Pa said, "if you'll just wait about three weeks, I'll plow that rye under. I sowed it in my young orchard for a cover crop and I want it to get its growth—and right now it's a-getting its growth. See, it's a fine crop to fertilize the roots of young apple trees."

45    "Don't think I can wait three weeks," Grandma said.

46    But Pa didn't want to turn it under now so he didn't say anything more to Grandma about it. Next day she asked him when he was going to turn it under or cut it and Pa said that he would do it soon as he plowed another field. And soon as Pa and Mom got off in another room to themselves, Mom told him to wait, that Grandma was a little childish and that she would soon forget about it.

47    But the next day, Grandma asked Pa about when he was going to cut his rye or plow it under. And Pa said that he would do it as soon as he got his plowing done for corn. Grandma didn't like his answer and Pa could tell that she didn't. He didn't want to hurt Grandma and he didn't want to spoil his rye field in his young orchard so he called Mom into another room and talked to her about it. And Mom told him to leave it a few days. And the following day, Grandma told Pa that if he didn't do something about the rye that some morning he would get up and his rye would be blown flat on the ground by a windstorm. Pa wanted to laugh at Grandma's words but he was afraid he would make her mad.

48 "In three more days, I'll plow it under," Pa said.

49 But early next morning, when Pa had fed his team and hitched it to the wagon, he looked at this rye in the young orchard and it was flat on the ground as if a log had been rolled over it. Pa ran inside the house and told Mom and they both went up to the orchard to see if the windstorm had hurt any of the young apple trees but not a tree had been hurt by the wind. Then they went up to Grandma's house to see if the wind had caved in the roof or had blown down the giant hulk of an oak in the front yard or had blown the gate down. There had been a windstorm all right but it hadn't hurt anything but Pa's rye.

50 "I'll tell you, Sal," Pa said just before he drove his team to the field. "I am all upset."

51 After Pa had taken our team to the field, I went into Grandma's room. She was homesick. She would look through our window at her house and still she couldn't see it very well for one of our apple trees was in the path of Grandma's eyes. She told me that she wanted me to cut this young apple tree so she could see her house. I told Mom about it and she told me not to do it.

52 "That's a pretty tree," Mom said. "I know your Pa doesn't want it cut. I know that I don't want it cut."

53 Our young apple orchard was just eight years old and the trees had been carefully trimmed until their tops looked like big green bowls—but now they looked like big white bowls in the blue wind of April for they were white with blooms and the honeybees were flying over their tops and fighting the bumblebees for the fragrance of the blossoms. I wanted to see Grandma get what she wanted but I knew how hard Mom and Pa had worked to get this orchard and how they put fires near the orchard to make great smokes to keep the frosts away so they couldn't fall on the young trees and bite the fruit that was yet in blossoms. I knew that our orchard was the prettiest thing that there was on our farm in April and that it was our money crop. And that if one tree was cut it would hurt the looks of our orchard.

**Source:** Getty Images

54    When Pa came home at noon and had fed his team he came into the house. He was worried about his rye and when Mom told him about Grandma's wanting the young apple tree cut so she could see her house, Pa sat down in his chair. He didn't say anything.

55    "I can't cut one of my flowerin' fruit trees," Pa said. "I've worked too hard to raise that orchard. To cut one tree would ruin the looks of my orchard."

56    "But Ma will forget about it," Mom said.

57    "I'm afraid she won't," Pa said.

58    "Grandma is homesick," I said. "She wants to see her own house."

59    "I'll tell you what we'll do," Pa said, his face growing brighter, "we'll take Mother back to her house and let her look the place over and go around the house again."

60    "Why haven't we thought of that before, Mick?" Mom said.

61    And when Pa told Grandma that he couldn't afford to cut his young tree but that he would haul her back to the house and let her spend the day a-looking it over, Grandma was pleased. Mary and I went with Grandma and we spent the day. Mary took her by one arm and I took her by the other and we helped her every place she wanted to go. Grandma was happy and she laughed and talked to us about her house, her trees, shrubs and rose-vines. She had us to take her to this one and that one and told us when it was planted and the person that planted it. And when Pa came after us late in the afternoon, Grandma didn't want to go but we lifted her on the express-wagon seat and hauled her down to our house.

62    "I think she'll forget about my apple tree now," Pa said, "She had a good day at her old home."

      But the next day when Grandma tried to look at her own home, the tree was in her way and she talked to Mom about having me to chop it down with an ax. But Mom told her the tree was a pretty tree and that it looked good in the orchard white with blooms and when it had borne fruit this year that she would have Pa trim its long branches. But Grandma wanted it cut. And that night she told Pa she wanted him to cut the apple tree or take her back to her old house to live.

63    Pa didn't think anything about the orchard until two days had passed and he had his team harnessed to try to plow the tangled rye under. And when Pa drove his team into the orchard, he stopped his team, threw up his hands and ran to the house.

64    "What's the matter, Mick?" Mom asked.

65    "Who cut that apple tree?"

66    "No one," Mom said. "Has it been cut?"

67    "See for yourself," he told Mom and then Mom went out with him to look at the tree. I sat in Grandma's room with her and watched her look out of the window at her old home. Grandma sat peacefully by the window as if nothing had happened.

68    I saw Pa and Mom standing by the tree. Pa was carefully examining it. And I left Grandma in her room and went to see if the tree had been uprooted in a windstorm. And it had been uprooted by a windstorm that

had just swept the corner of our orchard and hit this tree that Grandma wanted cut. Not a heavy leafed, blossoming branch had been molested on the other trees. And again Pa hurried to Grandma's old home to see if the wind had done any damage there but not a thing had been touched since her house missed the path of the wind.

69      "I don't understand," Pa said. "I think we'd better take Mother back to her own home. I don't know what will happen here next if we don't."

70      Grandma was sitting by the window looking at her own home when
71  Pa and Mom asked her if she wanted to move back.

72      "I never wanted to move here in the first place," Grandma said. "I don't like it here. I'll never like it here. Yes, take me back."

73      I was glad when Pa and Mom took Grandma and her furniture back to the old house and my sister Mary and I went with her to stay. Will, Herbert, Effie and Carrie were glad too. Sister Mary and I hated to see our two weeks pass. We hated to go back home. We would rather have lived with Grandma all the time. But Pa and Mom wouldn't let us do this. And, often, Uncle Jason, Uncle Jake, Pa, Aunt Mallie, Aunt Phoebe and Mom came to see Grandma. But she never went to see one of them. She stayed in her own house and among her old pieces of furniture, her flowers, vines, shrubs, and trees.

74      We spent the spring and summer with Grandma. And autumn came and the leaves started turning. They fell into the drainpipes and clogged them and I climbed on top the house and lifted dead leaves from the drainpipes. Once when I stepped on the shingle-roof, my foot broke through. I had the best times I ever had in my life when I did things for Grandma and I enjoyed the freedom that she gave me. But it made me sad to hear her say that she would die in this house.

75      That hot September night thunder shook the earth and streaks of lightning cut the dark sky into tiny bits. It was a terrible night—a great rush of wind came. And Grandma told Mary and me to leave the house. She said that she would follow us. We didn't want to go at first but she told us to and we did as we were told. And we hadn't more than reached the sidewalk until we heard a mighty crash. Little pieces of oak twigs hit us. We ran out into the yard—out into heavy darkness screamin' for Grandma. But she didn't come. The heavy-topped oak had fallen onto the decaying house and it had crashed through it. When the lightning flashed we could see parts of the hulk of the house standing. Even the doorway that we had come through was crashed.

76      "Let's tell Mom and Pa," Mary said.

77      We followed the path toward home by the lightning flashes and on our way we met Mom and Pa coming in raincoats and carrying lanterns.

78      "The old oak fell on the house," Mary screamed. "Grandma can't get out."

79      Pa sent me with the lantern to run through the darkness and the rain that was now falling in torrents to tell Uncle Jake and Uncle Jason.

And Uncle Jason sent Herbert to tell John Blevins and Uncle Jake sent Will to tell Ernie Tabor what had happened. When I got back to the house, Pa had thrown pieces of broken shingles and joists back from the place where Mary had told him Grandma was when the crash came. And they found Grandma pinned to the floor beneath a joist. She was dead. She had died where she wanted to die and maybe the way she had wanted to die. She had died in her own house, and the oak that Pa had often told her was dangerous and that he wanted to cut for her, had killed Grandma. And even through the mighty storm that raged and out into the vast swirl of wind, darkness, and rain, her birds flew from the hollow of the oak, chirruping a pensive melancholy dirge for her.

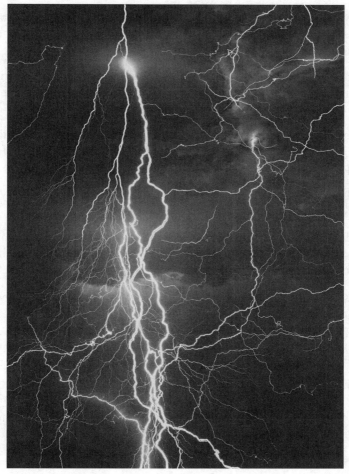

**Source:** Getty Images

This unit will explore complexities associated with each aspect of a story—characters, setting, plot, and narration—that affect readers' interpretations. You may already know something about these topics. Assess what you know by reviewing the anchor text on pages 209–217 and answering the following questions. Some questions may be challenging, but according to scientists who study learning, answering questions on a subject before formally learning about it is one way to help you deepen your understanding of new concepts.

## CLOSE READING

1. Identify a few key details about each of the main characters. What do these details reveal? What are some things readers don't know about the characters?

2. What characters could be said to be contrasting? Why? You might first consider what common ground they have and then consider the differences that make them contrasting.

3. How do the broad setting and the more narrow, individual settings within it affect the story? Consider how the characters and the plot develop within those multiple settings.

4. Other than characters, what are some other contrasts in the story? How could they relate to bigger ideas?

5. What does the reader know about the narrator? What are some details in the story that reveal the perspective of the narrator? What is that perspective?

6. What is the narrator's point of view? How might that point of view influence what he relates about the events of the narrative? How might the story be different if told from a different point of view or by a different narrator, perhaps one who is not also a character in the story?

## INTERPRETATION

1. What bigger idea or theme might the story be about? What might be the meaning of the work as a whole?

2. What is the most important textual evidence that would support your idea about what the story is about (that is, your interpretation)?

# Nuanced and Contrasting Characters

## Part 1:  Nuanced and Contrasting Characters

### Understand
Characters in literature allow readers to study and explore a range of values, beliefs, assumptions, biases, and cultural norms represented by those characters. (CHR-1)

### Demonstrate
Identify and describe what specific textual details reveal about a character, that character's perspective, and that character's motives. (1.A)

Explain the function of contrasting characters. (1.C)

Describe how textual details reveal nuances and complexities in characters' relationships with one another. (1.D)

See also Units 1, 2, 3, 6 & 7

**Source:** *AP® English Literature and Composition Course and Exam Description*

**Essential Question:**  How do textual details reveal nuances of characters and a contrast of values between characters?

Think back to the questions at the beginning of this unit: How well do people in various settings and with varying perspectives know you? The answer to those questions depends on what details of your words, actions, and physical description you reveal or present to them. In the same way, you come to understand fictional characters by examining their words, actions, physical descriptions, and thoughts (if the narrator can share them). You may also see that a character viewed through one perspective seems different from that same character viewed through a different perspective. You will see characters interact with other characters, what values motivate them, and how their values may clash with those of other characters or even between parts of themselves. You will also see how their choices influence the cause-and-effect unrolling of the plot.

| KEY TERMS | | |
|---|---|---|
| agency | values | antagonist |
| nuance | protagonist | collective |

# 1.1 Character Agency and Nuance | CHR-1.O, CHR-1.P

The role characters play in a story often relies on their ability to make choices, the reasons for those choices, and the way the characters relate to other characters. Details provided as characters interact and move through the story reveal these aspects of character. They also reveal subtleties about the characters' values.

## Agency and Nuance

**Agency** is the ability to act. A character with agency has the power to make choices. These choices often form the basis of stories:

- characters dealing with the consequences of choices they made in the past
- characters faced with making new choices
- characters who don't have choices but wish they did
- characters who have choices but choose not to act

Sometimes a character exhausts all of his or her choices or gives up in despair. In the story "The Appropriation of Cultures," for example, when the White fraternity boys call out for Daniel's band to play "Dixie," Daniel chooses to play it, but defiantly, not submissively. Later, he chooses to take the Confederate flag—another symbol of racism—and use it to fight the sort of prejudice it represents. In "The Sanctuary Desolated," Grandma makes many choices: she chooses to let the house decay around her, she chooses not to trim the bushes that keep the light out and the trees that threaten to fall on her house, she chooses to go back to the house where she has lived all her life and where she hopes to die. The significance of characters is often revealed through their agency.

Characters' significance is also revealed through nuanced descriptions. **Nuance** is a subtle distinction, a shade of meaning. Nuanced descriptions often rely on the connotation of words—the ideas and feelings readers associate with those words—as opposed to denotation, or their literal meaning. (Connotation has been described as "the aura surrounding a word.") For example, the words *house* and *home* are sometimes used interchangeably. The difference between the words arises partly from the connotations most people associate with these words. The word *house* has few connotations, merely referring to a structure. *Home*, on the other hand, while it can refer to the structure itself, has the connotation of the place where people live and belong. It has a "warm and fuzzy" appeal.

Consider the following description of the White fraternity boys in "The Appropriation of Cultures" (see Unit 1).

> One night, some white boys from a fraternity yelled forward to the stage at the black man holding the acoustic guitar and began to shout, "Play *Dixie* for us! Play *Dixie* for us!"

Daniel gave them a long look, studied their big-toothed grins and the beer-shiny eyes stuck into puffy, pale faces, hovering over golf shirts and chinos. He looked from them to the uncomfortable expressions on the faces of the old guys with whom he was playing and then to the embarrassed faces of the other college kids in the club.

Connotations of some of the descriptive words contribute to nuance. The boys' "puffy" faces that are "hovering" over the preppy clothes suggests something insubstantial—airy, not solid.

To find nuance in "The Sanctuary Desolated" (see pages 209–217), you need to look no further than the title for the first example. The author could have called his story "The Ruined House," but it would not have had the same effect as the title he chose. The word *sanctuary* refers to a refuge or safe place. It can also refer to a sacred or holy place. Grandma views her house and its surroundings as an almost holy place because of the associations she makes with her dead parents and husband and her children. The trees are a refuge for wildlife. The word *desolated* is related to the adjective *desolate*, which means bleak. *Desolated* means ruined—laid waste to or devastated.

If the title seems to have a biblical feel, that may be because it can be found in the Bible in the Book of Daniel. (See Unit 5 for allusions to other literary works or sacred texts.) In Chapter 9, Daniel asks God to restore the "desolated sanctuary," the temple in Jerusalem, after it was defiled by conquering Greeks in 167–164 BCE.

## Choices and Values

Every choice a character makes—every exercise of agency—is motivated by that character's **values**, or fundamental beliefs.

In "The Sanctuary Desolated," for example, Grandma agrees to try living with her daughter and son-in-law even after saying she doesn't really want to leave. Following is the exchange between Grandma and Pa (paragraphs 26–29).

I ran into the front room to get the candy and while I ate candy, I heard Grandma and Pa talking but I couldn't tell what they were saying. Soon as I had finished the candy, I went back where Pa and Grandma were talking.

"If you all are afraid that I am going to be found dead in the house some morning," Grandma said, "I don't mind going down to your house and try staying for a while. I'll still be in sight of my house—but I want you to know that I was born in this house and I've lived here all my life and I don't mind to die in this house. I have always expected to die here. I'll have to do it someplace and this house is the best place I know."

"But we'll make things comfortable for you, Mother," Pa said in a pleased tone of voice. "Our children love you and I think you'll be happy with us. Sal will fix you a room all to yourself. And when you want to lie down and rest, you won't be bothered."

"I've never stayed but three nights away from here in my life," Grandma said. "And I've never been a hundred miles away from here. It may work out all right. I'll try it."

Why does Grandma change her mind and agree to stay with Shan's family? What values motivated that decision? The story provides a few clues. For example, the family seems close. The children of Uncle Jake, Uncle Jason, Aunt Mallie, and Aunt Phoebe take turns staying at Grandma's house. The adults frequently talk (see paragraph 7), suggesting strong connections. In paragraph 26, readers learn that Grandma and Pa had been talking while Shan went to get candy. The first sentence of paragraph 27 suggests that they were talking about how worried the family was about Grandma's safety. Perhaps motivated by the sense of obligation that strong family ties engender, Grandma makes the choice to try living with her daughter and son-in-law. The values of obligation to the living family overrode the values of obligation she felt to the memories of her past family. These conflicting values are nuanced, however, since both relate to the importance of family.

As you look for how the author displays the characters' ability to make choices, ask yourself these questions.

- What details, however small, are provided about the characters?
- How do nuanced descriptions of the characters affect your understanding of them and their actions?
- What conclusions or inferences about the characters can you make based on answers to the above questions?
- What words or phrases in the story helped you reach your conclusion or inference?

One way to organize your analysis is shown in Figure 4-1.

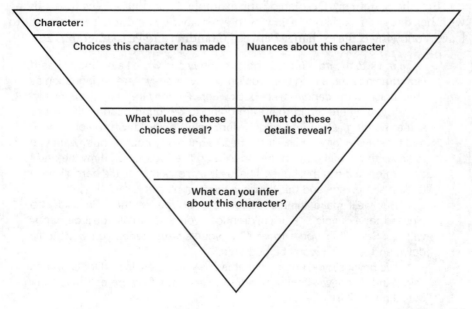

Figure 4-1

**Remember:** The significance of characters is often revealed through their agency and through nuanced descriptions. Characters' choices—in speech, action, and inaction—reveal what they value. (CHR-1.O–P)

## *1.1 Checkpoint*

*Review "The Sanctuary Desolated" on pages 209–217. Then complete the following open-response activities and answer the multiple-choice questions.*

1. On separate paper, recreate the graphic organizer in Figure 4-1 including only the words in bold type. Then choose a different character in the story to fill in the organizer. You may wish to work with a partner to complete this activity.

2. Write a paragraph that identifies the nuances, motives, and values of the character you chose, and then provide the specific details that helped you come to your conclusions. Be sure to explain your thinking through commentary about *how* those details helped you arrive at your conclusion.

3. Which of the following nuances from the story best reveals Grandma's conflict?

   (A) Grandma's house is a "damp house inside with too many shrubs and vines around it." (paragraph 2)

   (B) She felt that Herbert had fixed the gate "just the way [she] wanted it fixed." (paragraph 21)

   (C) When she took a sip of the well water, "she gagged." (paragraph 33)

   (D) She did not think she could "wait three weeks" for Pa to plow the rye. (paragraph 45)

   (E) She explained that she "never wanted to move [to Shan's house] in the first place." (paragraph 72)

4. Which of the following actions taken by a character in the story best reveals what that character values?

   (A) boys and girls at school talking about why Shan's family hadn't fixed Grandma's roof (paragraph 7)

   (B) Shan going into the other room to get candy while Pa and Grandma talked (paragraph 26)

   (C) Grandma telling Mary and Shan to leave the house during the storm (paragraph 75)

   (D) Pa moving Grandma's bedroom furniture to his house (paragraph 30)

   (E) Pa and Mom talking to Grandma about the water (paragraph 36)

**Creating on Your Own**

Write a new dialogue and character interaction from scratch or look back at the creative writing you have done in previous units. Find two or three places to insert small but important nuances about what characters say or do. Consider what each addition reveals about the characters. Save your work.

# 1.2 Protagonists, Antagonists, and Contrasting Values | CHR-1.Q, CHR-1.R, CHR-1.S

Stories have *protagonists* (derived from the Greek word meaning "first actor") and *antagonists* (derived from the Greek word meaning "opponent"). The **protagonist** is usually the main character in a story. The **antagonist** is often another character in conflict with the protagonist. However, the antagonist can also be an internal part of the protagonist, the social or cultural forces in which the protagonist operates, or forces of nature. The struggles between the protagonist and the antagonist often stem from a conflict of values, which creates dramatic tension.

## Protagonists and Antagonists

The distinction between protagonists and antagonists may sound straightforward, and it has often been greatly oversimplified by the idea that the protagonist is the "good guy" and the antagonist is the "bad guy." In some stories, that simple distinction seems to work, at least on first glance: Harry Potter is the main character and he is good; Voldemort is his opponent and he is bad. Typically, the protagonist is mainly moral and likable but flawed. He or she drives the plot through choices made in pursuit of a goal. The protagonist also experiences the consequences of those choices. The antagonist stands in the way of the protagonist's goals, often because of a clash of values. In this example, the antagonist is another character in the story, Voldemort. Antagonists often elicit dislike in readers.

**Collectives as Antagonists** Harry lives in a society, or **collective**, that has prejudice against Muggles—those without magic and wizard blood—and his values call on him to stand up for the rights of all. The prevailing culture, then, is also an antagonist to Harry. Voldemort, though himself not a pure wizard, values a society in which the power belongs only to the Pure-Bloods, so his values and Harry's clash. In "The Appropriations of Cultures," the story in Unit 1, racism is similarly an antagonist to Daniel.

**Internal Conflicts of the Protagonist** In some stories, both the protagonist and the antagonist inhabit the same character. For example, in "The Tell-Tale Heart" by Edgar Allan Poe, the narrator is the protagonist who relates with pride the fastidious way he commits a murder and hides the body under the floorboards in the victim's house. When police arrive after a neighbor reports hearing a scream, the narrator invites them in for a tour, and he is so confident of his handiwork that he invites them into the room where the body is hidden. The police are satisfied and sit for a while and "[chat] of familiar things." The narrator, however, hears the pounding of the victim's heart: it "grew louder—louder—louder! And still the men chatted pleasantly, and smiled. Was it possible they heard not?" In fact, only *he* could hear that sound—the product of his conscience (his antagonist)—and finally driven to distraction by his guilt, he stood up. "Villains!" I shrieked, "dissemble no more! I admit the deed!—tear up the planks! here, here!—It is the beating of his hideous heart!"

**Nature as Antagonist** Humans facing the forces of nature is a common theme in literature. One of the best-known short stories in which the protagonist faces the threats of nature as the antagonist is "To Build a Fire" by Jack London. In that story, the protagonist, a newcomer to the area, ignores warnings from older and experienced residents about the dangers of traveling alone through the Yukon Territory in Canada in extreme cold weather. He puts up a fight to try to stay alive, but he ends up freezing to death. The clash of values is between the sense of superiority or dominance of humans and nature's unremitting insistence on the survival of the fittest—or luckiest.

**Ambiguous Protagonists** In some stories, there may be several characters who fit the description of a protagonist—they drive the plot through choices they make, and they experience the consequences of their choices. In "The Sanctuary Desolated," for example, both Pa (and Mom) and Grandma make choices that determine the plot.

Stories may also have unlikeable or immoral protagonists. In Mary Shelley's novel *Frankenstein*, for example, the scientist and protagonist Victor Frankenstein makes morally questionable choices, first in creating the monster and then in rejecting him. Nonetheless, readers may sympathize with him because of his anguish. However, the sensitive portrayal of the monster elicits more sympathy for him than for his creator, creating ambiguous relationships between the protagonist and antagonist. (See Unit 6.)

## Contrasting Values

The conflicts between protagonists and antagonists often arise as a result of tensions between their different value systems. Which characters readers sympathize with depends on which value systems come closer to their own.

In "The Appropriation of Cultures" in Unit 1, for example, Daniel (the protagonist) values the freedom to express himself and control his circumstances. Society (the antagonist) values maintaining power in the hands of those who have it. The table on the next page shows one way to explore the clash of values between the protagonist and the antagonist.

| Protagonist/Antagonist Values |
|---|
| **Story:** "The Appropriation of Cultures" |

| **Protagonist(s):** Daniel | **Antagonist(s):** general society around him |
|---|---|
| **What does the protagonist(s) value?** | **What does the antagonist(s) value?** |
| Freedom to express himself and control his circumstances; efforts to subvert systemic racism | Power of those in the majority; prejudice and stereotyping because they maintain the idea of superiors and inferiors |

| **Compare the values of each and explain how the different value systems relate, what they say about the character(s), and/or how they affect the story. Do not summarize the plot—talk about the values and the characters, not just what happens in the story.** |
|---|
| Daniel doesn't fit the stereotype that the society around him has created because he is educated and wealthy, but people still stereotype him based on his appearance. He seeks more ways to express who he is and to push back against that prejudice and the system of racism, so he takes over symbols that represent the values of the society that is against him: "Dixie" and the Confederate flag (and the old truck, in a way). His efforts confuse both Black and White people who encounter him with the truck and flag, because he doesn't fit anyone's prejudiced stereotype. |

Table 4-1

 **Remember:** The main character in a narrative is the protagonist; the antagonist in the narrative opposes the protagonist and may be another character, the internal conflicts of the protagonist, a collective (such as society), or nature. Protagonists and antagonists may represent contrasting values. Conflict among characters often arises from tensions generated by their different value systems. (CHR-1.Q–S)

## 1.2 Checkpoint

*Review "The Sanctuary Desolated" on pages 209–217. Then complete the following open-response activity and answer the multiple-choice question.*

1. Recreate the chart above with all the bold words copied and with Pa and Mom as the protagonists and Grandma as the antagonist. (A case can be made for Grandma as the protagonist as well and you may use her as the protagonist and Pa and Mom as the antagonists.) In this activity you will explore conflict between characters rather than between a character and an aspect of society. What will remain the same is the examination of the values and how they relate.

**2.** Besides the antagonist(s) you identified, the most likely additional antagonist in "The Sanctuary Desolated" is

    (A)  a society that is prejudiced against the elderly

    (B)  the force of nature that has brought decay to Grandma's house

    (C)  Uncle Jake and Uncle Jason

    (D)  the traditional society of the rural South

    (E)  the community that gossips about the family

**Creating on Your Own**

Review the conversation and the character(s) you wrote about in the previous Creating on Your Own activity. Consider the values represented by those characters. Spend five to ten minutes writing about the values of each character to help you better understand who they are and what they value. Then revise your writing so that what the characters say and do reflects those values. Since the words and actions of characters (like those of people) are not always consistent with their values, leave room for complexity. Save your work.

# Part 1  Apply What You Have Learned

Carefully examine "The Sanctuary Desolated" to gather textual evidence that reveals Grandma's values and the values of Mom and Pa. Then write a paragraph that uses commentary to explain how the details show the nuances and complexities of each side's willingness or resistance to compromise their values for the sake of the other.

> **Reflect on the Essential Question** Write a brief response that answers the essential question: *How do textual details reveal nuances of characters and a contrast of values between characters?* In your answer, correctly use the key terms listed on page 219.

# Part 2

# Setting, Mood, and Atmosphere

**Enduring Understanding and Skills**

## Part 2  Setting, Mood, and Atmosphere

### Understand

Setting and the details associated with it not only depict a time and place, but also convey values associated with that setting. (SET-1)

### Demonstrate

Explain the function of setting in a narrative. (2.B)

Describe the relationship between a character and a setting. (2.C)

See also Unit 7

**Source:** *AP® English Literature and Composition Course and Exam Description*

**Essential Question:** What is the relationship between a character and a story's setting?

Read the following opening paragraph. What feeling does it convey? What relationship does it establish between the setting and the man?

> Day had broken cold and grey, exceedingly cold and grey, when the man turned aside from the main Yukon trail and climbed the high earth-bank, where a dim and little-travelled trail led eastward through the fat spruce timberland. It was a steep bank, and he paused for breath at the top, excusing the act to himself by looking at his watch. It was nine o'clock. There was no sun nor hint of sun, though there was not a cloud in the sky. It was a clear day, and yet there seemed an intangible pall over the face of things, a subtle gloom that made the day dark, and that was due to the absence of sun. This fact did not worry the man. He was used to the lack of sun. It had been days since he had seen the sun, and he knew that a few more days must pass before that cheerful orb, due south, would just peep above the skyline and dip immediately from view.

As you may know or have guessed, this paragraph is the beginning of Jack London's short story "To Build a Fire." You may have thought the paragraph conveyed a somber, gloomy scene foreboding danger. You may also have thought that the man, telling himself he had to rest only to look at his watch, may not quite be up to the task he has set himself. In this first paragraph London has described the essential qualities of the location and the feelings those qualities awaken in a reader.

---

**KEY TERMS**

atmosphere                    mood                         environment

---

# 2.1 Atmosphere and Mood | SET-1.C, SET-1.D

Part 2 of this unit explores the feelings established by settings, the effect of those settings on readers, and what readers can learn about characters who inhabit the settings.

## Creating Atmosphere

A story's **atmosphere** is created by the descriptions attached to the physical setting. Just as Earth's atmosphere surrounds the planet, a story's atmosphere—or multiple atmospheres if the settings change—surround and color the characters and actions.

Carefully chosen details create an overall effect that awakens feelings in readers that influence their views of the characters.

Reread the opening paragraph of "To Build a Fire." Note that the physical descriptions (exceedingly cold and grey, dim and little-travelled trail, steep bank, intangible pall, subtle gloom) create a cold and forbidding atmosphere. Compare that opening paragraph to the first paragraph in "The Sanctuary Desolated."

> After Grandpa died Grandma lived alone in her big house that stood upon a knoll surrounded by giant black oaks and hickories. If the house had been a person it would have been a cripple for it was much older than Grandma and she was crippled with rheumatics until she could hardly get about. But Grandma stayed in this big house that had a moss-covered sagging roof and the tops of the two big chimneys were crumbling in the summer wind and rain and the winter freezes. Rosebushes and shrubs grew around the house until you could hardly see the downstairs windows. And when I went to stay with Grandma at night, I always got there before darkness hovered around it. I was afraid of the house and the dense patches of shrub and vines that grew so thick the morning sunlight couldn't filter through them to dry the moss-covered damp walls that were gradually falling to decay.

The atmosphere Stuart creates in this opening paragraph could hardly be more different from the atmosphere in "To Build a Fire." This story takes place in a setting with a run-down house, roof sagging with moss, chimneys crumbling, and shrubs and vines overgrowing so thickly around the house that they would not even let in morning sunlight. Instead of a cold and forbidding atmosphere like that in "To Build a Fire," this story creates an atmosphere of decay, and the narrator (Shan) also adds a sense of danger to the house by admitting "I was afraid of the house and the dense patches of shrub and vines . . . ."

## Establishing Mood

**Mood** in literature is the set of emotions that the descriptions and other details of the atmosphere evoke in the reader. The cold and forbidding atmosphere of "To Build a Fire" may evoke a gloomy and foreboding mood. The atmosphere of decay and ruin in "The Sanctuary Desolated" may evoke a depressing or anxious mood. Depending on the atmosphere and the associations or connotations readers bring to authors' words, readers' moods can run the gamut of human emotions—cheerful, romantic, frightened, carefree, hopeful, gloomy, and dozens more.

## Environment and Character

In addition to establishing the atmosphere and evoking a mood, a setting also functions to reveal information about characters in their **environment**, or surroundings. The harshness of the extreme cold in "To Build a Fire," for example, brings to light the man's overconfidence in human ingenuity in the face of natural forces. The sagging house in "The Sanctuary Desolated" mirrors Grandma herself. It is even compared directly to her: "If the house had been a person it would have been a cripple for it was much older than Grandma and she was crippled with rheumatics until she could hardly get about."

Beyond these general revelations, however, the accumulation of details of setting as they are rolled out throughout the story can reveal many more aspects of characters, including their values. Consider what the setting in the following excerpt from "The Appropriation of Cultures," the anchor text from Unit 1, reveals about the characters.

> Travis and Barb lived across the river in the town of Irmo, a name which Daniel had always thought suited a disease for cattle. He drove around the maze of tract homes until he found the right street and number. A woman in a housecoat across the street watched from her porch, safe inside the chain-link fence around her yard. From down the street a man and a teenager who were covered with grease and apparently engaged in work on a torn-apart Dodge Charger mindlessly wiped their hands and studied him.
>
> Daniel walked across the front yard, through a maze of plastic toys and knocked on the front door.

The main characters in this brief excerpt are Daniel and Travis and Barb, but there are other characters as well—the woman in a housecoat and the man and teenager with greasy hands. A character and setting chart like the one on the next two pages will help you draw meaning about the characters from the details of the setting.

| Characters | Setting Details | What the Details Reveal about the Character |
|---|---|---|
| Daniel | "Across the river" | The setting includes a boundary between where Daniel lives and where Travis and Barb live, and Daniel appears to recognize the differences. |
| | "Irmo, a name which Daniel had always thought suited a disease for cattle" | Daniel's disdainful impression suggests he has a superior attitude toward the town. |
| | "maze of tract homes" | Tract homes are many similar affordable houses built on a subdivided tract of land. That they appear as a "maze" to Daniel suggests his lack of familiarity with such housing developments. Daniel appears out of his element in this setting. |
| Travis and Barb | "tract homes" "maze of plastic toys" | Travis and Barb live somewhat modestly. The "maze" of plastic toys, besides revealing that they likely have one or more children, may suggest some disorder to their lives. |
| Woman in housecoat | "A woman in a housecoat across the street watched from her porch, safe inside the chain-link fence around her yard." | A housecoat, a garment stay-at-home women might wear, suggests the woman is not a professional. The chain-link fence, which some view as cheap and unattractive, makes her feel "safe inside" it, suggesting she is fearful of Daniel, possibly because she holds racist stereotypes. |
| Man and teenager | "covered with grease and apparently engaged in work on a torn-apart Dodge Charger mindlessly wiped their hands and studied him" | The man and teenager appear to be working on the car at their home, adding a detail to the emerging picture of Irmo. Their studious curiosity about Daniel may also suggest that they can't understand why he might be in Irmo. That curiosity might be based in prejudice. |

*continued*

| Characters | Setting Details | What the Details Reveal about the Character |
|---|---|---|
| **Explain how these details of setting come together to convey a relationship between the setting and characters and to reveal information about the characters and their values. Do not summarize the plot.** | | |
| The details of the setting in Irmo reveal information about characters, their relationship to the setting, and their values. For example, the people in Irmo live in modest tract houses, suggesting they may also have modest incomes. The houses are also mainly the same as one another. This sameness of the setting may reflect the values of the people who live there: sameness is good; difference is unnerving, suggesting the likelihood of racial prejudice. The people who live in Irmo feel that they belong there. When Daniel enters the scene, however, the people in the setting appear uncomfortable; several watch closely as they keep distance and hide behind fences or doors. Daniel has a different relationship to the setting. He knows he is regarded as different in this community "across the river." While Daniel doesn't appear uncomfortable, he does not have a positive regard for the place, as his comment about the town's name suggests. Daniel's presence in that environment, as part of his plan to own a truck with a Confederate flag decal, reflects what he values: his agency to push back against cultural conventions and subvert racial relationships. | | |

Table 4-2

 **Remember:** A setting may help establish the mood and atmosphere of a narrative. The environment a character inhabits provides information about that character. (SET-1.C–D)

## 2.1 Checkpoint

*Review "The Sanctuary Desolated" at the beginning of this unit. Then complete the following open-response activity and answer the multiple-choice question.*

1. On separate paper, recreate a table like the one on the next page focusing on Grandma as the character and Grandma's house as the primary setting. Identify five details of the setting and explain what they reveal about Grandma and her values.

| Five Setting Details about Grandma's House | What the Details Reveal about Grandma and Her Values |
|---|---|
| 1. | |
| 2. | |
| 3. | |
| 4. | |
| 5. | |

Explain how these details of setting come together to convey a relationship between the setting and characters and to reveal information about the characters and their values. Do not summarize the plot.

2. Which of the following statements best represents the relationship between a character and the environments that character inhabits in the text?

   (A) Mom and Pa living in their own home illustrates how independent they are from the rest of the family.

   (B) Mary always visiting Grandma's house with Shan illustrates that she fears the family history.

   (C) Shan wanting to spend more time at Grandma's illustrates his desire to have more freedom from his parents.

   (D) Cousin Herbert fixing the gate according to Grandma's wishes illustrates his commitment to her and the house.

   (E) Grandma's resistance to living with Mom and Pa illustrates her dislike of her children's choices.

**Creating on Your Own**

Review the conversation and the character(s) you wrote about in previous Creating on Your Own activities. What atmosphere and mood might be effective for this interchange? What setting(s) might be appropriate to reveal more information about the characters, their values, and their relationship to their environment? Experiment with a few ideas and see what settings and atmosphere seem most effective. Save your work.

# Part 2 Apply What You Have Learned

Carefully review "The Sanctuary Desolated" to gather textual evidence about the setting and the aspects of the setting that help establish the atmosphere and mood of the story. Write a paragraph identifying the atmosphere and mood. In your paragraph, explain with commentary what and how the atmosphere and mood contribute to your understanding of a character in the story.

**Reflect on the Essential Question** Write a brief response that answers the essential question: *What is the relationship between a character and a story's setting?* In your answer, correctly use the key terms listed on page 229.

**Source:** Getty Images

# Plot Patterns

## Part 3  Plot Patterns

### Understand

The arrangement of the parts and sections of a text, the relationship of the parts to each other, and the sequence in which the text reveals information are all structural choices made by a writer that contribute to the reader's interpretation of a text. (STR-1)

### Demonstrate

Identify and describe how the plot orders events in a narrative. (3.A)

Explain the function of contrasts within a text. (3.D)

See also Units 1, 2, 6, 7 & 8

**Source:** *AP English Literature and Composition Course and Exam Description*

---

**Essential Question:** What are common dramatic situations and how do contrasts illuminate them?

Are you wanting to write the script for the next blockbuster movie but having trouble thinking of a plot? You could turn to Kurt Vonnegut's story shapes plotted on graph paper for ideas (see Unit 1). Or you could turn to any of the many other collections of basic story plots that writers and critics have identified and categorized based on several thousand years of Western literature. (See "The Writer's Craft" on page 238.) These are the stories that have recurred over the centuries and presented human experience in a relatively small number of patterns that have become familiar to readers, so familiar that readers have expectations of the outcome for each pattern.

One element each of these patterns has in common is conflict. Conflict is often represented through contrasting values and perspectives and is the beating heart of plot.

---

**KEY TERMS**

| | | |
|---|---|---|
| archetypes | conflicts | values |
| contrast | | |

# 3.1 Archetypes and Expectations | STR-1.R

According to some critics, all stories can be categorized into one (or sometimes more) of relatively few basic plots. These basic plot patterns are called **archetypes**, from the Greek word meaning roughly "original pattern or model." (There are also archetypal *characters*, which you will read about in Unit 6.) Following are some of the archetypal stories with examples.

| Selected Archetypal Stories |
|---|
| The Quest  (*The Fellowship of the Ring*) |
| Rags to Riches (Cinderella) |
| Obstacles to Love (*Romeo and Juliet*) |
| Voyage and Return (*Odyssey, Alice in Wonderland*) |
| Pursuit (*The Fugitive*) |
| Battle between Good and Evil (*Batman*) |
| Coming of Age (Initiation) (*To Kill a Mockingbird*) |
| Rivalry (David vs. Goliath) |
| Disaster (or Fall from Power) (*Julius Caesar*) |
| Death and Rebirth (Jesus in the Christian New Testament; Quetzalcoatl in Aztec mythology) |

Table 4-3

If a story starts to take shape according to one of these patterns, readers familiar with that plot pattern have expectations about how the story will continue to develop and end. For example, if a story begins with an innocent man being framed for a crime, readers probably expect he might run away and be pursued and almost caught a few times. While he is fleeing, he also tries to figure out who the real criminal is. After being caught at the end and nearly punished for the crime, evidence comes to light about the real criminal, and the fugitive's name is cleared. But what if one of the officers pursuing the fugitive believes he is innocent and, when he catches the fugitive, starts working with him to find the real criminal? That development would push against readers' expectations and create a level of interest and complexity.

Although some stories follow archetypal patterns that are easily recognizable, many complex stories do not fit neatly and are variations on or combinations of different patterns. For example, one pattern readers might see in "The Sanctuary Desolated" is the "Disaster" story, in which a great power falls after being defeated by an opponent. In this case, Grandma is the great power who is "defeated" by Pa and Mom when they get her to agree to move in with them.

The second half of "The Sanctuary Desolated," however, resembles a typical rivalry story between a superior and inferior rival, with the superior rival winning the object of rivalry. In this case, Grandma is the superior who defeats Pa and Mom—with the help of some unexplained and very targeted windstorms that suggest a kind of supernatural power—and wins the object of the rivalry, her house. Grandma is unhappy because Pa's rye obstructs her view of her house. When he does not honor her request to plow it because that rye is valuable to him as a cover crop for the orchard, a windstorm comes and flattens it but does no other damage. Then Grandma complains that a young apple tree keeps her from seeing her house clearly and asks Pa to cut it down. When her son-in-law once again refuses to honor her request, the tree is uprooted by the wind but, as before, nothing else has been touched. Only then does Pa decide he'd better take Grandma back to her own house before anything else bad happens. His two choices to refuse her requests have led to the very things he was trying to avoid. The superior rival has won, with the help of a supernatural power.

**The Rule of Three** Though not an archetype itself, the "rule of three" is a very common and expected feature of archetypal stories. The rule of three is the idea that groupings of three have both simplicity and completeness. How many stories can you think of that feature a group of three? You will not have trouble coming up with them: the three little pigs, the three musketeers, Ebenezer Scrooge's three ghosts, Aladdin's three wishes from the genie—the list could go on and on.

In "The Sanctuary Desolated," almost every number mentioned is three. More important, Grandma also has three requests of Mom and Pa—1) bring her water from her own well, 2) plow the rye under so she can see her house, and 3) cut the tree so she can see her house. These "threes" lend an air of familiarity to the patterns of the story.

 **Remember:** Some patterns in dramatic situations are so common that they are considered archetypes, and these archetypes create certain expectations for how the dramatic situations will progress and be resolved. Note: For the exam, you are not expected to identify or label archetypes. (STR-1.R)

## The Writer's Craft: Archetypal Dramatic Situations

In 1895, French writer Georges Polti wrote a book listing 36 dramatic situations that he claimed formed the basis of every story or performance, such as a play or opera. His book, *The Thirty-Six Dramatic Situations*, was based on a list attributed to the Italian playwright Carlo Gozzi. It names each of the situations and provides a description of the situation (including variations on it) as well as examples. Most of Polti's 1,200 examples were taken from the stage, ranging from classical Greek theater to Shakespeare and Molière to 19th-century plays that have been long forgotten. (You can view an English translation of the book online at the Internet Archive if you search for "The Thirty-Six Dramatic Situations," or you can search Wikipedia for "The 36 Dramatic Situations" for a good summary. It includes some more modern examples, such as *The Lord of the Rings*, *The Shining*, and *Braveheart*.

Other critics and writers have categorized the basic plots in a different way. For example, Rudyard Kipling (*The Jungle Book*) believed there were 69 basic plots. Ronald Tobias, a writer, documentary filmmaker, and professor, published a book for writers called *20 Master Plots and How to Build Them.* Christopher Booker, using examples from ancient myths all the way to modern TV shows, boiled the number of basic stories down to seven in his book *The Seven Basic Plots: Why We Tell Stories*. Some of these books are used in workshops for professional writers to help them develop and guide their plots.

### Use the Writer's Craft

Choose any of the plot patterns considered basic or archetypal. (See page 236 for selected patterns and/or research some of the titles listed above.) Either in words or in drawings on a storyboard, sketch out the main characters and the key points in the plot. Share your stories with your classmates. If anyone else chose the same basic plot pattern as yours, discuss how the stories differ (or not).

**Source:** Getty Images

### 3.1 Checkpoint

*Review "The Sanctuary Desolated." Then complete the following open-response activity.*

1. Grandma seems to have the help of a supernatural power to win back her house. Many archetypal stories use magic or the supernatural. Think of a story you know that roughly follows one of the archetypal patterns and features magical weapons or other magical or supernatural forces. Then write a paragraph explaining how the presence of magic or the supernatural colors a reader's or viewer's expectations of how the story will develop and end.

**Creating on Your Own**

Review the conversation, character(s), setting, and atmosphere you developed in previous Creating on Your Own activities. What archetypal patterns might you already be following? How might you revise what you have done to follow another pattern or to break the expectations of a pattern? What would following and/or breaking a certain pattern mean to the story you are developing? Experiment with revising your story and then write brief answers to the questions above. Save your work.

## 3.2 Contrasts and Conflicts of Values | STR-1.S, STR-1.T

Comparing—explaining something by showing how it is similar to another more familiar thing—is an essential literary tool, but sometimes the differences are more important (and interesting) than similarities. Juxtaposing images, ideas, characters, or actions (putting them next to or near each other) to create **contrast** or differences is also an essential tool, helping readers see nuance and complexity. Contrast can be introduced through a shift—that is, a change in tone, point of view, thought, image, or emotion. The differences highlighted by a contrast emphasize the traits, aspects, or characteristics that are most important in the subjects being compared.

### Clash of Values

Contrasts often represent **conflicts** or clashes in **values**, or fundamental beliefs, related to the perspectives of characters, narrators, or speakers on ideas represented by a text.

For example, paragraphs 11–29 in "The Sanctuary Desolated" are structured so readers can easily compare the attitudes of Grandma and Pa. The differences between these characters' attitudes conveys much about each character.

| Examining Contrasts in a Text | |
|---|---|
| **What is being contrasted?** Pa's perspective and Grandma's perspective on Grandma's home | |
| **Contrasts** | |
| Pa sees the gate as rotten and falling down. | Grandma sees the gate as fixed just the way she wanted. |
| Pa sees the oak tree as rotten and dangerous. | Grandma sees the tree as a home to birds and as something her husband planted. |
| Pa sees the house as dangerous. | Grandma sees the house as her home. |
| **What do readers learn from these contrasts? What values do they represent?** Pa is most concerned about Grandma's safety, and all he sees around him is death and rot. Grandma, on the other hand, sees life and the way that her history and her family are represented by the things around her. | |

Table 4-4

These contrasts can lead readers to inferences about values and even foreshadow big ideas that may be represented in the text. Pa values safety more than tradition; Grandma values traditions more than her own safety. Even though she agrees to try staying with Shan's family, Grandma says, "I was born in this house and I've lived here all my life . . . . I have always expected to die here."

 **Remember:** The differences highlighted by a contrast emphasize the particular traits, aspects, or characteristics important for comparison of the things being contrasted. (STR-1.S)

## 3.2 Checkpoint

*Review "The Sanctuary Desolated." Then complete the following open-response activity and answer the multiple-choice question.*

1. On separate paper, recreate Table 4-4, this time focused on the contrast between Pa's and Grandma's perspectives of the rye field and the apple tree. Find your answers by looking for textual evidence and then drawing conclusions.

2. Which of the following statements best explains what is revealed through the contrast of Shan (the narrator) and his parents?

   (A) Shan concerns himself more with the safety of his parents than with that of his grandma.

   (B) Shan cares more about his own happiness than about the safety of his grandma.

   (C) Shan worries that he, his sister, and his cousins will be unsafe at Grandma's house unless it is repaired.

   (D) Mom and Pa worry more about Grandma's safety than the safety of their own children.

   (E) Mom and Pa care only about their crops and their children.

**Creating on Your Own**

Review the conversation, character(s), setting, atmosphere, and archetypal plot patterns you developed in previous Creating on Your Own activities. You likely already have framed some contrasts as you have developed the characters and conflict. What contrasts do you recognize? How might you revise your story to enhance or even modify those contrasts? Experiment with revising your story to heighten contrasts and show how your characters' values may clash. Save your work.

# Part 3 Apply What You Have Learned

Think of a story, novel, or movie you know well. In a few paragraphs, answer the following questions about your chosen text or movie.

- What archetype, if any, does it resemble?
- Did the story proceed and end as you expected it would? Explain your answer with details from the story.
- What contrasts are evident in the story? What do they reveal about the characters in the story?
- What is the central conflict in the story? What clashing values are behind the conflict?

If someone else in your class has chosen the same story, compare your responses and discuss similarities and differences.

**Reflect on the Essential Question** Write a brief response that answers the essential question: *What are common dramatic situations and how do contrasts illuminate them?* In your answer, correctly use the key terms listed on page 235.

# Part 4

## Narrative Distance and Perspective

### Part 4 Narrative Distance and Perspective

**Understand**

A narrator's or speaker's perspective controls the details and emphases that affect how readers experience and interpret a text. (NAR-1)

**Demonstrate**

Identify and describe the narrator or speaker of a text. (4.A)

Identify and explain the function of point of view in a narrative. (4.B)

Identify and describe details, diction, or syntax in a text that reveal a narrator's or speaker's perspective. (4.C)

See also Units 6 & 9

**Source:** *AP® English Literature and Composition Course and Exam Description*

---

**Essential Question:** How can you describe narrative point of view and perspective?

The way authors choose to tell their stories has a major impact on the way stories affect readers. One of the first choices authors have to make is what point of view to take. Will their narrator be a participant in the action or merely an observer? Will the story focus on one character or follow several characters? Also, how will the narrator's perspective shape the story? How will the characters' perspectives, or ways of viewing and processing what is going on, motivate them?

---

**KEY TERMS**

| | | |
|---|---|---|
| narrator | relational distance | perspective |
| narrative distance | emotional investment | adjectives |
| physical distance | stream of consciousness | adverbs |
| chronological distance | tone | attitude |

# 4.1 Narrators as Characters or Observers | NAR-1.J

As you read in Unit 1, fiction writers make use of a variety of points of view. The **narrator** or speaker who tells the story may be part of the story or may simply be an observer who reports the action. Stories can be narrated in the first person ("I"), the second person ("you"), or the third person ("he," "she," or "it").

In first-person narratives, the narrator is a character in the story. Narrators who are part of the story either tell about events they recall from the past or describe them as they occur. In "The Sanctuary Desolated," Shan recalls events from his past: "And when I went to stay with Grandma at night, I always got there before darkness hovered around it. I was afraid of the house and the dense patches of shrub and vines that grew so thick the morning sunlight couldn't filter through them . . . ."

The narrator in ZZ Packer's "The Ant of the Self," a story about a tense relationship between a young man and his alcoholic father, describes the events as they occur in the present—including attending the Million Man March on Washington called by Nation of Islam leader Louis Farrakhan in 1995 to project a positive image of Black men. These are the final paragraphs describing the young man's experiences in a railroad station. Notice the present tense.

> I sit down on a wooden bench. The old white woman next to me carefully pours imaginary liquid into an imaginary cup. The man with the kid goes up to the ticket officer, who stops staring into space long enough to say, "May I help you, sir?"
>
> "Do y'all still say 'All aboard'?"
>
> "Excuse me?" the ticket officer says.
>
> "My son wants to know if y'all say 'All aboard.' Like in the movies."
>
> "Yes," the ticket officer says wearily. "We do say 'All aboard.' How else would people know to board the train?"
>
> Now the boy jiggles up and down on his father's back, suddenly animated, as if he's riding a pony. The ticket officer sighs, hands grazing the sides of his face as though checking for stubble. Finally he throws his arms up in a "Sure, what the hell" kind of way, and disappears into the Amtrak offices for what seems like an hour. The father sets the boy down, feet first, onto the ground. An intercom crackles and a voice says:
>
> *"All aboard!"*
>
> The voice is hearty and successful. The boy jumps up and down with delight. He is the happiest I've seen anyone, ever. And though the urge to weep comes over me, I wait—holding my head in my hands—and it passes.

Some writers may also use first person as the main narrative point of view but then occasionally have that narrator address readers directly. A famous example of direct address occurs at the beginning of the last chapter of Charlotte Brontë's 1847 novel *Jane Eyre*: "Reader, I married him." In this case, Brontë's first-person narrator, Jane Eyre, addresses the reader, something she does from time to time throughout her fictional autobiography.

Second-person narration, addressing the reader directly as "you," can be effective in making the reader a character, drawing him or her into the story. Following is the beginning of a short story called "This Story Begins with You" by Rachael K. Jones that uses second-person point of view.

> The story goes that your dad got a new job.
>
> The story goes that you moved 5,000 miles away. You didn't know anyone in your new town, and none of them knew you.
>
> You had a best friend in your old town named Marco, but you left him behind. You had a playground on your old street. A favorite climbing tree. A secret hideout behind the garden shed made from plywood and latticed tree branches, papered with mildewed books the library had thrown out after the classics section flooded.
>
> The story goes that losing all of this felt like a part of you had died. You cried a lot. That bothered your parents. You didn't want them to feel guilty, so after a while you only cried when you were alone.

 **Remember:** Narrators may function as characters in the narrative who directly address readers and either recall events or describe them as they occur. (NAR-1.J)

## 4.1 Checkpoint

*Review "The Sanctuary Desolated." Then complete the open-response activity and answer the multiple-choice questions.*

1. The narrator's or speaker's perspective controls the details and points of emphasis that in turn affect how readers interpret a text. How does the narration of Shan, a young boy at the time of the story, color a reader's experience of the story? Write a paragraph answering this question, using details from the text to support your answer.

2. The narration provided in paragraph 6 of "The Sanctuary Desolated" serves mainly to

   (A) detail the plans for helping Grandma move from her house to Shan's parents' house

   (B) compare Shan's intentions with those of his mother and father and the rest of the family

   (C) explain why Shan didn't want Mary to visit the house with him and Pa

   (D) display the fear that Pa has for Grandma if she stays in the house

   (E) demonstrate Shan's selfish reasons for wanting Grandma to stay in her house

3. As the narrator, Shan is emotionally concerned and involved with the events of the story because

    (A) he wants to have control over the circumstances affecting all of his family members

    (B) Grandma's house is the center of the entire family and those he cares for are saddened by its deterioration

    (C) those events involve all of his closest family members and will affect his own happiness

    (D) no one else cares about his well-being but his Grandma and he wants to care for her

    (E) Mary is still very young and he wants her to have memories of both Grandma and the house

**Creating on Your Own**

Review the conversation, character(s), setting, atmosphere, and archetypal plot patterns you developed in previous Creating on Your Own activities. Review the point of view you have chosen if you have already worked narration into your scene to make sure it's the best choice. If you haven't yet added narration, do so now, being aware that the speaker's or narrator's point of view will affect how readers experience your story. Save your work.

# 4.2 Narrative Distance | NAR-1.K, NAR-1.L

The distance between the narrator and the other elements of a story, such as the characters, setting, and events, is the **narrative distance**. Narrative distance refers to the physical and chronological distance, relationships, or emotional investment of the narrator to or in the events or characters of the narrative.

## Types and Degrees of Distance

A *first-person narrator* who is also the major character in a story has little narrative distance.

A *third-person narrator* has the greatest narrative distance to the characters and settings. A third-person narrator may be one of the following.

- *An outside observer.* Events and characters may not affect the narrator's perspective. This kind of narrator has considerable distance from the characters and settings.

- *An observational narrator.* This narrator can relate only observable information, not thoughts and feelings. This narrator also may tell the story from the perspective of one character with whom readers are likely to develop a strong bond. For this reason, an observational narrator has less narrative distance than an outside observer.

- *An all-knowing narrator.* This narrator knows everything about the characters, including thoughts and feelings, and typically has the least narrative distance.

Narrative distance may change through a text as the narrator zooms in or zooms out on different characters or settings. Mary Shelley's 1818 (revised 1831) novel *Frankenstein; or, The Modern Prometheus*, shows this zooming in and zooming out through its unique narrative structure and neatly demonstrates the various types and degrees of narrative distance.

The novel, the anchor text in Unit 6, tells its story through three first-person narratives arranged in a zooming in and zooming out again pattern.

### Zooming In

- The novel begins with the framing narrative by Robert Walton, an English explorer in the Arctic, who writes letters to his sister in England. When his ship stalls in ice, Walton encounters another traveler, Victor Frankenstein, weak and starving from his travels to the north by land. Walton has **physical distance**; he is far away from where the action of the main story takes place. He also hears Frankenstein's story after it has happened, so he has **chronological distance** as well. As someone just listening to the story of a stranger, Walton also has **relational distance** and limited **emotional investment**.

- The novel continues with the first-person account of Victor Frankenstein, ostensibly conveying his story to Walton. All aspects of the narrative distance decrease as Frankenstein tells his story, though he still has some chronological distance since he is reporting on events in the past, including his childhood. He was physically close to the events he recounts and also close in relationships and emotional involvement.

- The next first-person narrator is the monster himself, whom Frankenstein encounters on a glacier where he went hoping to find renewal in the beauty of nature. Instead he finds the monster he created and then abandoned who demonstrates great intelligence and learning as he recounts his story. The monster's story is therefore embedded in the story Frankenstein is relating to Walton. The monster as narrator has very little narrative distance to the events he relates and has great emotional investment: "Believe me, Frankenstein, I was benevolent; my soul glowed with love and humanity; but am I not alone, miserably alone? You, my creator, abhor me; what hope can I gather from your fellow creatures, who owe me nothing? They spurn and hate me." Readers have a chance to see the relationship of Frankenstein and his creature, as well as their emotional responses to each other, through their own eyes.

### Zooming Out

- After the monster's narration, the narrative voice pulls back in the opposite order in which it began. The scientist Frankenstein resumes his first-person narrative.

- When Frankenstein reaches the point in the story where he met up with Walton, Walton once again takes over as narrator, completing the story.

## Stream of Consciousness

Usually, stories narrated from a first-person point of view are constructed with dialogue, description, and action like those in third-person stories. Sometimes, however, a story—or part of a story—may be told in the form of an *interior monologue*. Interior monologue is constructed like regular spoken monologue, in fully formed sentences, but represents the narrator's train of thought as it might be "heard" by a mind reader. It is closely related to stream of consciousness, which aims to portray the actual messier process of thinking, with all the distractions and chaos that normally enter a person's thought process.

French writer Marcel Proust's novel *Swann's Way* (1913), the first installment of what was to be a seven-volume novel called *Remembrance of Things Past*, starts with the narrator relating a seemingly insignificant event: the eating of a small French cake called a *madeleine* and drinking some tea. Over the course of seven volumes, Proust takes the reader inside the mind and memories of the narrator through **stream of consciousness**, a technique by which the narrator's thoughts, feelings, memories, reactions, and more are presented in a continuous flow.

Stream of consciousness unspools strings of thoughts in a character's or narrator's mind often caused by something that may or may not be related to those thoughts. In the case of Proust, the taste of a small crumb brought back seven volumes of memories. In another text, stream of consciousness might be triggered by the death of someone, or a question, or a simple flash of light.

In the following excerpt from *To the Lighthouse*, author Virginia Woolf takes readers inside her narrator's mind. At the end of the passage, she actually provides a description of the stream of consciousness process through a metaphor of colored lights flashing through the dark space of a mind.

> It didn't matter, any of it, she thought. A great man, a great book, fame—who could tell? She knew nothing about it. But it was his way with him, his truthfulness—for instance at dinner she had been thinking quite instinctively, "If only he would speak!" She had complete trust in him. And dismissing all this, as one passes in diving[1] now a weed, now a straw, now a bubble, she felt again, sinking deeper, as she had felt in the hall when the others were talking, There is something I want—something I have come to get, and she fell deeper and deeper without knowing quite what it was, with her eyes closed. And she waited a little, knitting, wondering, and slowly rose those words they had said at dinner, "the China rose is all abloom and buzzing with the honey bee," began washing from side to side of her mind rhythmically, and as they washed, words, like little shaded lights, one red, one blue, one yellow, lit up in the dark of her mind, and seemed leaving their perches up there to fly across and across, or to cry out and to be echoed; so she turned and felt on the table beside her for a book.

---

1 **diving:** diving into the ocean or another natural body of water

Source: Getty Images

Although stream of consciousness may be somewhat hard to follow, you can make progress if you focus on facts and comprehension first and then try to use what you learn and know about the passage to draw supportable inferences. As you read stream of consciousness passages, ask yourself these questions.

| Questions to Ask to Understand Stream of Consciousness | |
| --- | --- |
| First Focus on Comprehension | • What specific thoughts are you reading?<br>• What has brought these thoughts on? How, if at all, is the cause of the thoughts related to the thoughts themselves?<br>• What specific things do you learn about the narrator, main character, or other characters on a literal level? |
| Then Focus on Inference | • What can you say about the character whose mind you have entered?<br>• What do the meanings in the stream of consciousness add to the interpretation of the text as a whole? |

Table 4-5

 **Remember:** Narrative distance refers to the physical distance, chronological distance, relationships, or emotional investment of the narrator to the events or characters of the narrative. Stream of consciousness is a type of narration in which a character's thoughts are related through a continuous dialogue or description. (NAR-1.K–L)

## 4.2 Checkpoint

Review "The Sanctuary Desolated." Then complete the following open-response activities and answer the multiple-choice question.

1. Complete the following chart to analyze the type and degree of narrative distance Shan has in the story. In the middle column, choose from close, moderate, and distant. Then add textual evidence to support your choice.

| Type of Narrative Distance | Degree of Narrative Distance | Supporting Textual Details or Facts |
|---|---|---|
| Physical | | |
| Chronological | | |
| Relational | | |
| Emotional | | |

2. Read the following passage from *A Portrait of the Artist as a Young Man* by James Joyce, the story of how a young man, Stephen Dedalus, discovers his love for words and ability to create art with them. In this scene, he is in a strict Catholic boarding school as a child. Then answer the questions for understanding stream of consciousness in Table 4-5 on the previous page. (The final question will not apply unless you have read the whole work.)

> He opened the geography to study the lesson; but he could not learn the names of places in America. Still they were all different places that had different names. They were all in different countries and the countries were in continents and the continents were in the world and the world was in the universe. . . .
>
> What was after the universe? Nothing. But was there anything round the universe to show where it stopped before the nothing place began? It could not be a wall but there could be a thin thin line there all round everything. It was very big to think about everything and everywhere. Only God could do that. He tried to think what a big thought that must be but he could only think of God. God was God's name just as his name was Stephen. *Dieu* was the French for God and that was God's name too; and when anyone prayed to God and said Dieu then God knew at once that it was a French person that was praying. But though there were different names for God in all the different languages in the world and God understood what all the people who prayed said in their different languages still God remained always the same God and God's real name was God.
>
> It made him very tired to think that way. It made him feel his head very big.

3. The narration provided in paragraph 6 of "The Sanctuary Desolated" provides what information about Shan's state of mind?

    (A) He fears parts of the house but also longs to stay there.

    (B) He does not care about the house as much as his parents think he does.

    (C) He needs to stay in the house or he fears bad things will happen.

    (D) He wants his parents to fix the house but respects Grandma's desire to leave it as it is.

    (E) He is more dedicated to his cousins than he is to his parents and sister.

**Creating on Your Own**

Reread what you have written in previous Creating on Your Own activities. Experiment with taking readers inside the mind of one of your characters. Teacher and author Barry Lane calls this technique a "thought shot"—slowing down and targeting the specific thoughts running through a character's or narrator's mind. What can you reveal to readers about the character by showing his or her thoughts? Save your work.

# 4.3 Perspective, Description, and Tone
| NAR-1.M, NAR-1.N, NAR-1.O

The narrators', characters', or speakers' backgrounds and perspectives shape the attitude they convey about subjects or events in the text. Perspective is expressed partly through descriptive words, such as adjectives and adverbs, which also qualify or modify the things they describe. The attitude of narrators, characters, or speakers toward an idea, character, or situation emerges from their perspective and may be referred to as **tone**.

## The Influence of Background and Perspective

In literature, **perspective** is the way that narrators or characters understand the world around them. Characters' perspectives are informed by their backgrounds and personalities. They influence their relationships, their motivation, and their choices. In "The Sanctuary Desolated," for example, Grandma and Pa are motivated by their very different perspectives on Grandma's old house and Shan introduces his own perspective as the story's narrator.

Similarly, characters' perspectives help shape their opinions. Just like real people, narrators and characters have biases that shape their opinions. As you will recall, bias refers to a prejudice either for or against something or someone. In "The Appropriation of Cultures," for example, Daniel's bias about poor Whites is revealed when he goes to Irmo to buy a used truck. Unreliable narrators may exhibit bias in the way they choose to include or omit certain information in order to influence their readers.

## Descriptive Language

Daniel's perspective as a wealthy and educated Black man is revealed in part by the words used to describe other characters or settings. The character's or narrator's choice of descriptive words, such as the **adjectives** that describe people, places, or things, or the **adverbs** that modify verbs and adjectives, helps convey perspective.

> "Daniel gave them a long look, studied their <u>big-toothed</u> grins and the <u>beer-shiny</u> eyes stuck into <u>puffy, pale</u> faces, hovering over <u>golf shirts and chinos</u>" (paragraph 3).

In this passage, the narrator provides certain descriptive words and phrases that reveal Daniel's **attitude** about the fraternity boys requesting the song. Think about the connotations of the descriptive words (underlined) in this passage. What attitude do they reveal toward those characters? How do the specific descriptive words and details influence you to view a character, positively or negatively? How do they achieve that effect?

Tone—the attitude of narrators, characters, or speakers toward an idea, character, or situation that emerges from their perspective—is often conveyed through details, diction (choice of words), and syntax (the arrangement of words). Look for the details, diction, and syntax in Shan's description of the family's apple orchard as you try to determine his tone. Pay special attention to the adjectives and adverbs.

> Our young apple orchard was just eight years old and the trees had been carefully trimmed until their tops looked like big green bowls—but now they looked like big white bowls in the blue wind of April for they were white with blooms and the honeybees were flying over their tops and fighting the bumblebees for the fragrance of the blossoms. I wanted to see Grandma get what she wanted but I knew how hard Mom and Pa had worked to get this orchard and how they put fires near the orchard to make great smokes to keep the frosts away so they couldn't fall on the young trees and bite the fruit that was yet in blossoms. I knew that our orchard was the prettiest thing that there was on our farm in April and that it was our money crop. And that if one tree was cut it would hurt the looks of our orchard.

The chart on the next page shows an analysis of Shan's tone.

| Analyzing Tone | | |
|---|---|---|
| **Details** | • Pleasant details about the trees that appeal to the senses—the shape and color of the trees, the fragrance of the blossoms<br>• Vivid details about the work Mom and Pa did to keep the frost away, including details that appeal to the sense of smell (smoky fires) and touch (biting frosts) | |
| **Diction, Especially the Choice of Adjectives and Adverbs** | **Adjectives**<br>• <u>young</u> apple orchard<br>• <u>big green</u> bowls<br>• <u>big white</u> bowls<br>• <u>blue</u> wind<br>• <u>great</u> smokes<br>• <u>young</u> trees<br>• <u>prettiest</u> thing | **Adverbs**<br>• <u>just</u> eight years old<br>• <u>carefully</u> trimmed<br>• how <u>hard</u> Mom and Pa had worked |
| **Syntax** | • Sentences of decreasing length (62 words, 57 words, 24 words, 15 words)<br>• First two sentences both contain *but* to show contrast | |
| **Shan's Perspective and Tone** | Shan's choice of descriptive words conveys his perspective on the orchard and on the request of Grandma to cut one tree down. His adjectives stress the youthfulness of the orchard, possibly about as old as Shan himself. His adverbs stress the care with which Mom and Pa have nursed the orchard. The syntax of the passage also reveals Shan's perspective. The first two long sentences spin out details of the beautiful orchard filled with buzzing life as well as the arduous tasks of keeping the trees safe from frost. The second sentence reveals his divided view of the matter, signaled by the word *but*. He wants his Grandma to get what she wants *but* he realizes the beauty of the orchard as it is and the hard work Mom and Pa have put into it. The final short sentences suggest that he has formed a clearer perspective, favoring not cutting down the tree. | |

Table 4-6

Completing the first three rows of the table above (or doing the mental equivalent) is a necessary step to identifying perspective and the tone that grows out of it. But without the final row, which stitches together the details from the first three rows, there would be no explanation of how the writer created Shan's tone and perspective.

Perspectives and attitudes can appear simply positive or negative, but their complexity often increases through the use of nuanced words and complex syntax, as in the example above.

| Syntactical Ways Writers Show Nuanced Attitudes | |
|---|---|
| • *x* but *y* | "Shan loves the orchard but also loves Grandma." |
| • *x* and *y* | "Shan loves the orchard and also loves Grandma." |
| • while *x*, also *y* | "While Shan loves the orchard, he also loves Grandma." |
| • *xy* | "Shan is lovingly conflicted about the orchard." |

Table 4-7

**Remember:** The narrators', characters', or speakers' backgrounds and perspectives shape the tone they convey about subjects or events in the text. Descriptive words, such as adjectives and adverbs, not only qualify or modify the things they describe but also convey a perspective toward those things. The attitude of narrators, characters, or speakers toward an idea, character, or situation emerges from their perspective and may be referred to as tone. (NAR-1.M–O)

## 4.3 Checkpoint

*Review "The Sanctuary Desolated." Then complete the following open-response activity and answer the multiple-choice questions.*

1. Carefully reread the first paragraph, which shows Shan's attitude toward the house and conveys a tone. On separate paper, recreate Table 4-6, including only the words in bold type and leaving room for you to fill in the rest. Give special care to how you stitch the details together in the last row to show how they create tone.

2. At the beginning of the story, Pa's attitude toward Grandma can best be described as

    (A) concerned but respectful

    (B) respectful but angry

    (C) concerned but annoyed

    (D) cautious and respectful

    (E) concerned and worried

3. In paragraph 12, Shan uses the words *hulk* and *immense* to highlight the

    (A) terrible treatment Pa feared from Grandma when he asked her to move

    (B) worrisome disrepair shown by Grandma's house

    (C) considerable concern Pa had for Grandma's safety

    (D) significant size of the rotten oak tree

    (E) beautiful bushes Grandma had growing around her house

**Creating on Your Own**
Review your work in progress from previous Creating on Your Own activities. Have you included any descriptions that reveal the attitude of a narrator or character toward someone or something in the passage? If so, take time to revise/refine it. If not, spend five to ten minutes planning what you could do to develop an attitude somewhere in your text. Save your work.

# Part 4 Apply What You Have Learned

Think of a story or novel you know well. In a few paragraphs, answer the following questions about your chosen text.

- Who is the narrator?
- From what type and degree of narrative distance does the narrator tell the story?
- What is the effect of that narrative distance on the reader?
- What is the tone of the story?
- What descriptions help create that tone?
- How does the tone reveal the characters' backgrounds and perspectives?

If someone else in your class has chosen the same story, compare your responses and discuss similarities and differences.

**Reflect on the Essential Question** Write a brief response that answers the essential question: *How can you describe narrative point of view and perspective?* In your answer, correctly use the key terms listed on page 242.

**Source:** Getty Images

Visuals express tone as well.

*What tone does this photo of a neglected apple orchard convey? What details led you to your answer?*

# Writing About Literature IV

## Part 5  Writing About Literature IV

**Understand**

Readers establish and communicate their interpretations of literature through arguments supported by textual evidence. (LAN-1)

**Demonstrate**

Develop a thesis statement that conveys a defensible claim about an interpretation of literature and that may establish a line of reasoning. (7.B)

Develop commentary that establishes and explains relationships among textual evidence, the line of reasoning, and the thesis. (7.C)

Select and use relevant and sufficient evidence to both develop and support a line of reasoning. (7.D)

Demonstrate control over the elements of composition to communicate clearly. (7.E)

See also Units 1, 2 (Skill 7.A only for Units 1 and 2), 4, 5, 6, 7, 8 & 9

**Source:** *AP® English Literature and Composition Course and Exam Description*

**Essential Question:** How can you communicate a written interpretation of a work of literature by expressing a thesis statement, using sufficient evidence and commentary to support your line of reasoning, and achieving coherence?

What happens when people talk about books? Take a few minutes and write some answers to that question. Then share your answers with your classmates and create a master list of all the responses.

Chances are your list includes some of these points and maybe others.

- Readers tend to understand the book a bit better.

- Readers have a chance to express their views about the book.

- Readers have a chance to express their views about the subject of the book.

- Depending on the book, readers have a chance to explore meaningful and relevant ideas.

- Readers may question their views about the book after hearing others' ideas.

- Readers may point to details or evidence in the book that lent special meaning to their understanding of it.

- Readers get to know one another better.
- Readers understand how books can be interpreted based on the reader's unique perspective.

Writing about literature and sharing your writing with others have the same effects as talking about books. By the time you sit down to write, you have read the work carefully and noted key details, quotations, descriptions, perspectives, and narration. Each writer will bring together that textual evidence in a unique argument, just as in a book discussion each participant joins the group with a certain idea of the book. When you write about literature, you are not trying to convince readers that yours is the only interpretation. Instead, you are writing to convince fellow readers that your argument is a reasonable interpretation, well supported by the evidence.

---

**KEY TERMS**

| | | |
|---|---|---|
| thesis statement | cohesive | quality |
| line of reasoning | quantity | relevant |
| commentary | sufficient | coherence |

---

# 5.1 Thesis Statement and Line of Reasoning
## | LAN-1.D, LAN-1.E

In some ways, a **thesis statement** is like a destination on a GPS app. It is the "place" to which your literary analysis has led you and the interpretation you now want to defend through the use of textual evidence and a line of reasoning, both of which are explained in an essay through commentary. A thesis statement may give readers an overview of the route you plan to take as you develop your line of reasoning, though not all thesis statements need to provide this preview. A line of reasoning—the logical sequence of claims that together defend the thesis statement—is communicated through commentary that explains the logical relationship between the thesis statement and the claims and evidence within the body of an essay.

## Reaching a Destination Thesis Statement

From Unit 3, you may remember that the narrowing path to a thesis statement requires you to answer the questions in the figure on the following page as you go. (See Unit 3, Part 4.)

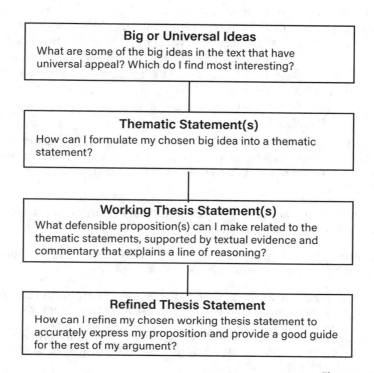

**Big or Universal Ideas**
What are some of the big ideas in the text that have universal appeal? Which do I find most interesting?

**Thematic Statement(s)**
How can I formulate my chosen big idea into a thematic statement?

**Working Thesis Statement(s)**
What defensible proposition(s) can I make related to the thematic statements, supported by textual evidence and commentary that explains a line of reasoning?

**Refined Thesis Statement**
How can I refine my chosen working thesis statement to accurately express my proposition and provide a good guide for the rest of my argument?

Figure 4–2

Even though you refine your thesis at this point, as you write your argument you may want to revise it again—readjust your destination—if you come to understand your evidence in a new light.

## Anticipating the Line of Reasoning

As you are working on refining your thesis statement, you will be drawing on the evidence you collected and the way you have come to understand it through a **line of reasoning**, the logical sequence of claims that work together to defend the overarching thesis statement. Your line of reasoning shows how the evidence relates to your thesis and to other claims you may plan to make in the body of your essay.

Suppose, for example, that you found the multiple references to Grandma's bushes, rose-vines, and trees notable and began to connect those plantings to the different vegetation on Mom and Pa's land—the apple orchard and rye field. You notice that the bushes, rose-vines, shrubs, and trees around Grandma's house are all associated with age and decline, though they are full of memories of the people who planted them. You also notice that youth is repeatedly associated with the apple orchard and that Shan remembers how hard Mom and Pa worked to protect the young trees from the bite of frost. Your line of reasoning is roughly to first establish that the references to the old and young vegetation reveal certain attitudes the characters have. Further, you plan to show how the evidence points to a fundamental difference in attitude between Grandma and her younger family members that relates to their different stages of life.

With this reasoning in mind and following the path shown above, you develop the following thesis statement as a starting point for your essay on "The Sanctuary Desolated."

> **Thesis Statement:** In Jesse Stuart's story "The Sanctuary Desolated," the characters' attitudes toward the vegetation on their land reveal their failure to understand the differing needs of the old and young.

Based on that thesis statement, a reader might expect your essay to make these claims to support your thesis:

> **Supporting Claim 1:** Textual evidence reveals Grandma's attitude toward her vegetation and its association with age.

> **Supporting Claim 2:** Textual evidence reveals Pa, Mom, and Shan's attitude toward their vegetation and its association with youth.

> **Supporting Claim 3:** The difference between attitudes about vegetation is a result of not fully understanding the life stage of different family members.

If this is what your readers anticipate as your reasoning and that is indeed your plan for developing your essay, then your thesis statement has the effect of previewing the development and line of reasoning of your argument, setting your readers' minds for what is to come.

Not all thesis statements need to preview the line of reasoning. Nor does a thesis statement need to list the points in your interpretation, the specific literary elements, such as descriptive details, that you will be focusing on, or the textual evidence you will use.

 **Remember:** A thesis statement expresses an interpretation of a literary text and requires a defense through use of textual evidence and a line of reasoning, both of which are explained in an essay through commentary. A thesis statement may preview the development or line of reasoning of an interpretation. This is not to say that a thesis statement must list the points of an interpretation, literary elements to be analyzed, or specific evidence to be used in the argument. (LAN-1.D–G)

## 5.1 Checkpoint

On separate paper, create a graphic organizer like the one below for "The Sanctuary Desolated" or another work of short fiction you are studying. Add as many solid claims as you can. You will return to this chart as you work toward writing your literary analysis.

| |
|---|
| **Text:** |
| **Big or Universal Ideas:** |
| **Thematic Statement:** |
| **Thesis Statement:** |
| **Supporting Claim 1:** |
| **Supporting Claim 2:** |
| **Supporting Claim 3:** |

### Composing on Your Own

Evaluate your thesis statement and claims from the previous activity. Does your thesis assert an arguable position that can be defended with evidence and commentary? Explain. Look over your claims. Are they in the most logical order? If not, rearrange them until you are satisfied they are in the best possible order. Then review your thesis statement again. Does it preview your line of reasoning? Write a brief explanation of your answer. Save your work.

# 5.2 Line of Reasoning and Commentary
| LAN-1.F, LAN-1.G, LAN-1.M, LAN-1.N

You communicate your line of reasoning through **commentary**, the explanation of your thinking process that shows how you logically connect your overarching thesis statement and the claims and evidence within the body of your essay.

While your thesis statement is like your destination on a GPS, the commentary in the body paragraphs of a written argument is like the map of connecting roads that get you there. Body paragraphs develop the reasoning and justify claims using evidence and providing commentary that links the evidence to the overall thesis.

Like a good set of directions that lead you smoothly from one point to another, effective paragraphs are **cohesive**, linked to provide a unified whole. Body paragraphs often use topic sentences to state a claim and explain the reasoning that connects the various claims and evidence that make up the body of an essay.

## Logical Sequence and Clear Connections

The series of claims outlined above about the vegetation in "The Sanctuary Desolated" is an example of a logically sequenced line of reasoning. Suppose, though, that the claims had been presented in a different order.

> **Claim 1:** Textual evidence reveals Pa, Mom, and Shan's attitude toward their vegetation and its association with youth.
>
> **Claim 2:** The difference between attitudes about vegetation is a result of not fully understanding the life stage of different family members.
>
> **Claim 3:** Textual evidence reveals Grandma's attitude toward her vegetation and its association with age.

You may notice that the order does not flow as logically in this arrangement. Claim 2 in this order depends on understanding the different attitudes, but Grandma's attitude is not addressed until Claim 3 in this order. While it may be possible to argue your thesis statement with the claims in this order, the order does not align with that previewed by your thesis statement.

## Effective Body Paragraphs

In many cases, the body paragraphs unfold in the order suggested by the thesis statement. In the above example (with the logical order of claims), the first paragraph would assert a claim about how Grandma's attitude toward the vegetation on her land is associated with her age. The other sentences would introduce evidence to support that claim. For example:

> References in the story to the plantings on Grandma's land are so numerous and pointed that they call out to readers the value Grandma places on them as well as their associations with age. In the first three paragraphs alone, there are four references to the bushes, rose-vines, and shrubs. Later, when Pa goes back to examine her house after Grandma has moved in with Shan's family, Grandma does not ask about anything on the inside of the house, only about "her trees, shrubs, and birds" (paragraph 40). When the family takes Grandma back to her home to see it, Grandma "was happy and she laughed and talked to us about her house, her trees, shrubs and rose-vines" (paragraph 61). And after Grandma moved back into her house, her family members paid visits to her, but she never visited them. "She stayed in her own house and among her old pieces of furniture, her flowers, vines, shrubs, and trees."

The supporting sentences in that paragraph establish evidence of the numerous references to the vegetation on Grandma's land. However, they do not use commentary to connect that evidence to the claim in the topic sentence, which supports the thesis statement. Commentary serves three main purposes:

- it explains the significance of the evidence to the claim and thesis
- it clearly explains connections among the thesis, claims, and evidence
- it addresses an interpretation of the work as a whole

Note the difference in clarity in the revision below about Grandma's shrubs and vines when commentary (in italics) connects the evidence to the claim and thesis. The sentences are numbered for easy reference.

(1) References in the story to the plantings on Grandma's land are so numerous and pointed that they call out to readers the value Grandma places on them as well as their associations with age. (2) In the first three paragraphs alone, there are four references to the bushes, rose-vines, and shrubs. (3) *While the descriptions are generally negative through the young narrator's eyes, the importance of the plants to Grandma is made clear when her daughter, Shan's mother, says* "Grandpa planted the oaks and hickories around it when he was a young man and Ma and Dad planted the shrubs and rose-vines around it. (4) I was a little girl when they planted part of them." (5) *Shan's mom makes clear that their value to Grandma derives from their long association to generations of her beloved family members, an association only possible with age.* (6) Later, when Pa goes back to examine her house after Grandma has moved in with Shan's family, Grandma does not ask about anything on the inside of the house, only about "her trees, shrubs, and birds" (paragraph 40). (7) *She also wonders if the old oak had fallen yet, possibly because she has a sense that her lifespan and that of the oak are intertwined.* (8) When the family takes Grandma back to her home to see it, Grandma "was happy and she laughed and talked to us about her house, her trees, shrubs and rose-vines" (paragraph 61). (9) *She leads the family around from one plant to another, repeating the history of their planting, apparently clinging to the past perhaps because she knows her future is limited.* (10) And after Grandma moved back into her house, her family members paid visits to her, but she never visited them. (11) "She stayed in her own house and among her old pieces of furniture, her flowers, vines, shrubs, and trees" (paragraph 73).

Commentary also helps create cohesive paragraphs, tying the details together in support of the claim of the paragraph, which in turn supports the overall thesis statement.

**Remember:** A line of reasoning is the logical sequence of claims that work together to defend the overarching thesis statement. A line of reasoning is communicated through commentary that explains the logical relationship between the overarching thesis statement and the claims/evidence within the body of an essay. The body paragraphs of a written argument develop the reasoning and justify claims using evidence and providing commentary that links the evidence to the overall thesis. Effective paragraphs are cohesive and often use topic sentences to state a claim and explain the reasoning that connects the various claims and evidence that make up the body of an essay. (LAN-1.F–N)

## 5.2 Checkpoint

*Review the revised paragraph about the vegetation on Grandma's land. Think carefully about the claim in that paragraph, which is also the topic sentence. Then write one or two different concluding sentences for the paragraph that provide commentary for the final piece of evidence in sentence 11 and help create a cohesive paragraph.*

### Composing on Your Own

Your composing goal for this unit is to write a full literary argument. The following first-draft organizer will help you pull together the evidence you have gathered for each of your claims and develop commentary to show how it supports the claims and thesis statement. Complete it and then write a first draft of your essay. Revise your first draft if necessary to make the commentary explicit and consistent in connecting claims, evidence, and the thesis statement. Save your work.

| Thesis Statement: | | |
|---|---|---|
| **Supporting Claim 1:** | | |
| Evidence from Text | Evidence from Text | Evidence from Text |
| Commentary/Explanation of why information from text supports claim | Commentary/Explanation of why information from text supports claim | Commentary/Explanation of why information from text supports claim |
| **Supporting Claim 2:** | | |
| Evidence from Text | Evidence from Text | Evidence from Text |
| Commentary/Explanation of why information from text supports claim | Commentary/Explanation of why information from text supports claim | Commentary/Explanation of why information from text supports claim |
| **Supporting Claim 3:** | | |
| Evidence from Text | Evidence from Text | Evidence from Text |
| Commentary/Explanation of why information from text supports claim | Commentary/Explanation of why information from text supports claim | Commentary/Explanation of why information from text supports claim |

# 5.3 Well Supported Arguments | LAN-1.H, LAN-1.I, LAN-1.J, LAN-1.K

The most convincing arguments are those that present high-quality and sufficient evidence strategically and purposefully to illustrate, clarify, exemplify, associate, amplify, or qualify a point. However, without commentary to explain a logical relationship between the evidence and claim(s), even strategic and purposeful evidence cannot support a thesis alone.

The process of developing a literary interpretation is recursive—you are likely to repeat certain steps on your way to arriving at a final draft. For example, you will begin by analyzing evidence and forming a line of reasoning. However, as you continue to work on your essay, you will likely look at some of your evidence in a new light as new ideas occur to you. Your new understanding of your evidence, or finding new evidence may lead to revisions in your thesis statement. Those revisions, in turn, may lead you back to the text to look for more evidence to support your revised thesis.

Writers work in different ways. An interpretation can emerge from analyzing evidence and then forming a line of reasoning, or the interpretation can emerge from forming a line of reasoning and then identifying relevant evidence to support that line of reasoning.

## Sufficient, High-Quality Evidence

While all parts of a literary argument make a valuable contribution to the whole, the quantity and quality of evidence and the strategic purposes for it are essential for defending your thesis statement and claims. The **quantity** of evidence required to support your thesis is a matter of judgment—there is no set amount. Use **sufficient**, or enough, evidence to assure your readers that the preponderance of textual evidence supports your view even if there are exceptions. The **quality** of your evidence is determined by how effectively it supports your claim—is it an excellent piece of evidence that makes your point clearly, leaving little room for doubt, or is it a stretch? Effective evidence is also **relevant**, or closely connected, to the point being made.

One way to evaluate the quality of your evidence is to assess how strategic and purposeful it is. (See Unit 3.) In Table 4-8 below, examples from the revised student paragraph on page 261 are indicated with their sentence number.

| Strategic Uses of Evidence | |
|---|---|
| Illustrate | describe or explain (sentences 10 and 11) |
| Clarify | clear up ambiguities or contradictions (sentence 5) |
| Exemplify | provide examples (sentence 6) |
| Associate | draw comparisons (sentence 7) |
| Amplify | expand through additional evidence or examples (sentence 9) |
| Qualify | acknowledge limitations (sentence 3) |

Table 4-8

Clearly understanding the purpose of your evidence will help you provide strong commentary. The example on the next page of one piece of evidence and its accompanying commentary illustrates a strategic use of evidence.

| Claim | Evidence | Strategic Use of Evidence | Commentary |
|---|---|---|---|
| References in the story to the vegetation on Grandma's land are so numerous and pointed that they call out to readers the value Grandma places on them as well as their associations with age. | *". . . Grandpa planted the oaks and hickories around it when he was a young man and Ma and Dad planted the shrubs and rose-vines around it. (4) I was a little girl when they planted part of them."* | This statement *clarifies* the reasons Grandma is so attached to her vegetation and also qualifies the negative impression of it created at the very beginning. | *Shan's mom makes clear that their value to Grandma derives from their long association to generations of her beloved family members, a quality only possible with age.* |

Table 4-9

Writing commentary to explain how your evidence supports the claims that justify your thesis requires you to think very clearly about your subject. You may find yourself making adjustments to your claims or thesis through this recursive process.

**Remember:** Writers use evidence strategically and purposefully to illustrate, clarify, exemplify, associate, amplify, or qualify a point. Evidence is effective when the writer of the essay uses commentary to explain a logical relationship between the evidence and the claim. Evidence is sufficient when its quantity and quality provide apt support for the line of reasoning. Developing and supporting an interpretation of a text is a recursive process; an interpretation can emerge from analyzing evidence and then forming a line of reasoning, or the interpretation can emerge from forming a line of reasoning and then identifying relevant evidence to support that line of reasoning. (LAN-1.H–K)

## 5.3 Checkpoint

*Exchange drafts with a partner. Review your partner's essay by answering the following questions with brief explanations.*

- Is the evidence sufficient?
- Is the evidence of high quality?
- Is the evidence relevant?
- Is the evidence put to good strategic and purposeful use?
- Does commentary connect the evidence to the claim in the paragraph and to the thesis statement?

- Could the commentary be clearer? If so, explain how.

Return your comments and your partner's paper.

**Composing on Your Own**
Carefully read over how your partner answered the questions above about your literary argument. Make revisions as you see fit and save your work.

# 5.4 Achieving Coherence | LAN-1.O, LAN-1.P

**Coherence** is the quality that makes writing logical and consistent. In a coherent sentence, the idea in one clause logically links to an idea in the next. In a coherent paragraph, the idea in one sentence logically links to an idea in the next. In a coherent text, the ideas in one paragraph link logically to the ideas in the next. Writers achieve coherence when the arrangement and organization of reasons, evidence, ideas, or details is logical. Coherence is not just a superficial quality of a text—it is essential to a tight and well-reasoned and supported argument.

Writers achieve coherence when the arrangement and organization of reasons, evidence, ideas, or details is logical. Writers may use transitions, repetition, synonyms, pronoun references, or parallel structure to indicate relationships between and among those reasons, evidence, ideas, or details.

## The Tools of Coherence

The most fundamental tool of coherence is logic. When a reader can understand why one reason, one piece of evidence, one idea, or one detail moves on smoothly to the next, the writer has achieved coherence. Anything that requires readers to think backward to something they just read will have the effect of connecting the writing into a whole.

Coherence starts at the sentence level. Consider the thesis statement:

> References in the story to the vegetation on Grandma's land are so numerous and pointed that they call out to readers the value Grandma places on them as well as their associations with age.

The phrase "so numerous and pointed that" shows a logical relationship: because there are so many references, they call out why Grandma values them. Another phrase that creates coherence in this sentence is "as well as." The meaning of that phrase and what follows it would not make sense without what comes before it. It's another way of saying "and," which is a connector.

The table on the next page shows a variety of ways to make writing smooth and coherent so your reader can follow your argument.

| Ways to Create Coherence | | |
|---|---|---|
| Transitions | **Definition:** words or phrases that help readers move from one thought or idea to another<br>**Examples:** *also, in contrast, similarly, later, the next day, soon after, next, finally, as a result*<br>**Example from the sample paragraph:** Sentence 6 ("Later, . . . ") | |
| Repetition | **Definition:** repeated words or phrases that link each repetition with the one that came before it<br>**Example from the sample paragraph:** The word *references* in sentences 1 and 2; the words *plantings, plants,* and *planted* throughout | |
| Synonyms | **Definition:** words that mean about the same thing as other words<br>**Example from the sample paragraph:** The word *plants* in sentence 3 is a synonym (though more general) for "bushes, rose-vines, and shrubs" in sentence 2. | |
| Pronoun References | **Definition:** pronouns that refer back to a previously named subject linking the pronoun with the noun it replaces<br>**Example from sample paragraph:** The pronoun *her* repeatedly refers to Grandma in sentence 8. | |
| Parallel Structure | **Definition:** the use of the same grammatical structure to link ideas<br>**Example from the sample paragraph:** "Grandpa planted . . . Ma and Dad planted . . . they planted." The parallel structure (subject–verb) not only links the ideas but also links the generations. | |

Table 4-10

Coherence between paragraphs as well as within them is crucial to your readers' ability to follow your line of reasoning. For example, the paragraph following the sample paragraph might begin this way:

> References to the plantings on Mom and Pa's land, on the other hand, are associated with youth.

The phrase "on the other hand" creates coherence by forcing the reader to link back to the first paragraph, in this case to understand a contrast. All the ways to create coherence between sentences also work between paragraphs.

**Remember:** Coherence occurs at different levels in a piece of writing. In a sentence, the idea in one clause logically links to an idea in the next. In a paragraph, the idea in one sentence logically links to an idea in the next. In a text, the ideas in one paragraph logically link to the ideas in the next. Writers achieve coherence when the arrangement and organization of reasons, evidence, ideas, or details is logical. Writers may use transitions, repetition, synonyms, pronoun references, or parallel structure to indicate relationships between and among those reasons, evidence, ideas, or details. (LAN-1.P–O)

## 5.4 Checkpoint

*Once again exchange drafts with a partner. Review your partner's essay by answering the following questions. Provide examples with each answer.*

- Is there coherence within and between sentences?
- Is there coherence between paragraphs?
- Is the evidence put to good strategic and purposeful use?
- What specific ways of creating coherence do you see in this essay?

Carefully read over how your partner answered the questions above about your literary argument. Make revisions as you see fit and save your work.

### Composing on Your Own

Use the organizer below to draft your essay with coherence.

| Introductory Paragraph | | |
|---|---|---|
| Lead in addressing big idea or theme<br>Thesis Statement: | | |
| **Body Paragraph 1** | | |
| Transitional clause or sentence<br>Supporting Claim 1: | | |
| Evidence from Text | Evidence from Text | Evidence from Text |
| Commentary/Explanation of why information from text supports claim | Commentary/Explanation of why information from text supports claim | Commentary/Explanation of why information from text supports claim |
| **Body Paragraph 2** | | |
| Transitional clause or sentence<br>Supporting Claim 2: | | |
| Evidence from Text | Evidence from Text | Evidence from Text |
| Commentary/Explanation of why information from text supports claim | Commentary/Explanation of why information from text supports claim | Commentary/Explanation of why information from text supports claim |
| **Body Paragraph 3** | | |
| Transitional clause or sentence<br>Supporting Claim 3: | | |
| Evidence from Text | Evidence from Text | Evidence from Text |
| Commentary/Explanation of why information from text supports claim | Commentary/Explanation of why information from text supports claim | Commentary/Explanation of why information from text supports claim |
| **Concluding Paragraph** | | |
| Reconnect to thesis | | |

# Part 5 Apply What You Have Learned

Exchange papers with a new partner. Read your partner's essay and answer these questions in writing.

1. What is the thesis statement?

2. What claims support the thesis statement?

3. Is the evidence relevant, sufficient, and of high quality? Explain your answer.

4. How effectively does commentary connect the evidence to the claims and thesis?

5. Identify five places where your partner achieved coherence and the tools used to achieve it.

6. What is one strength of this essay?

7. In what way might this essay be improved?

When your own essay is returned to you, carefully review your partner's evaluation and make revisions that you believe will improve your work.

**Reflect on the Essential Question** Write a brief response that answers the essential question: *How can you communicate a written interpretation of a work of literature by expressing a thesis statement, using sufficient evidence and commentary to support your line of reasoning, and achieving coherence?* In your answer, correctly use the key terms listed on page 256.

# Unit 4 Review

## Section I: Multiple-Choice

## Section II: Free Response

---

## Section I: Multiple Choice

Questions 1–11. Read the passage carefully before you choose your answer.

1    If all the Saturdays of 1982 can be thought of as one day, I met Tracey
     at ten a.m. on that Saturday, walking through the sandy gravel of a
     churchyard, each holding our mother's hand. There were many other
     girls present but for obvious reasons we noticed each other, the
5    similarities and the differences, as girls will. Our shade of brown was
     exactly the same—as if one piece of tan material had been cut to make
     us both—and our freckles gather in the same areas, we were of the
     same height. But my face was ponderous and melancholy, with a long,
     serious nose, and my eyes turned down, as did my mouth. Tracey's
10   face was perky and round, she looked like a darker Shirley Temple,[1]
     except her nose was as problematic as mine, I could see that much at
     once, a ridiculous nose—it went straight up in the air like a little piglet.
     Cute, but also obscene: her nostrils were on permanent display. On
     noses you could call it a draw. On hair she won comprehensively. She
15   had spiral curls, they reached to her backside and were gathered into
     two long plaits, glossy with some kind of oil, tied at their ends with
     satin yellow bows. Satin yellow bows were a phenomenon unknown
     to my mother. She pulled my great frizz back in a single cloud, tied with
     a black band. My mother was a feminist. She wore her hair in a half-
20   inch Afro, her skull was perfectly shaped, she never wore makeup and
     dressed us both as plainly as possible. Hair is not essential when you
     look like Nefertiti.[2] She'd no need of make-up or products or jewelry
     or expensive clothes, and in this way her financial circumstances, her
     politics and her aesthetic were all perfectly—conveniently—matched.
25   Accessories only cramped her style, including, or so I felt at the time,
     the horse-faced seven-year-old by her side. Looking across at Tracey
     I diagnosed the opposite problem: her mother was white, obese,
     afflicted with acne. She wore her thin blond hair pulled back very tightly

---

1   **Shirley Temple:** one of the first popular child actresses in movies
2   **Nefertiti:** a legendary queen of ancient Egypt, noted for her beauty

30     in what I knew my mother would call a "Kilburn facelift."[3] But Tracey's personal glamour was the solution: she was her own mother's most striking accessory. The family look, though not to my mother's taste, I found captivating: logos, tin bangles and hoops, diamanté[4] everything, expensive trainers[5] of the kind my mother refused to recognize as a

35     reality in the world—"Those aren't shoes." Despite appearances, though, there was not much to choose between our two families. We were both from the estates,[6] neither of us received benefits. (A matter of pride for my mother, an outrage to Tracey's: she had tried many times—and failed—to "get on the disability.") In my mother's view it

40     was exactly these superficial similarities that lent so much weight to questions of taste. She dressed for a future not yet with us but which she expected to arrive. That's what her plain white linen trousers were for, her blue-and-white-striped "Breton" T-shirt, her frayed espadrilles, her severe and beautiful African head—everything so plain, so

45     understated, completely out of step with the spirit of the time, and with the place. One day we would "get out of here," she would complete her studies, become truly radical chic, perhaps even spoken of in the same breath as Angela Davis and Gloria Steinem[7] . . . Straw-soled shoes were all a part of this bold vision, they pointed subtly at the

50     higher concepts. I was an accessory only in the sense that in my very plainness I signified admirable maternal restraint, it being considered bad taste—in the circles to which my mother aspired—to dress your daughter like a little whore. But Tracey was unashamedly her mother's aspiration and avatar, her only joy, in those thrilling yellow bows, a frou-

55     frou skirt of many ruffles and a crop top revealing inches of childish nut-brown belly, and as we pressed up against the pair of them in this bottleneck of mothers and daughters entering the church I watched with interest as Tracey's mother pushed the girl in front of herself— and in front of us—using her own body as a means of obstruction,

60     the flesh on her arms swinging as she beat us back, until she arrived in Miss Isabel's dance class, a look of great pride and anxiety on her face, ready to place her precious cargo into the temporary care of others. My mother's attitude, by contrast, was one of weary, semi-ironic servitude, she thought the dance class ridiculous, she had

65     better things to do, and after a few further Saturdays—in which she sat slumped in one of the plastic chairs that lined the left-hand wall, hardly able to contain her contempt for the whole exercise—a change was made and my father took over. I waited for Tracey's father to take over, but he never did. It turned out—as my mother had guessed

70     at once—that there was no "Tracey's father," at least not in the conventional, married sense. This, too, was an example of bad taste.

---

**3**  **Kilburn facelift:** a nonsurgical method of removing unwanted facial wrinkles
**4**  **diamanté:** decorated with artificial jewels
**5**  **trainers:** British term for sneakers, athletic shoes, or tennis shoes
**6**  **estates:** British term for government housing
**7**  **Angela Davis and Gloria Steinem:** powerful activists for racial minorities and women

1. The narrator's perspective throughout the passage might be best described as that of

   (A) an angry feminist

   (B) a bitter critic of parenthood

   (C) a thoughtful daughter

   (D) a kind teacher and student

   (E) an energetic dancer

2. The narrator's perspective on her mother is demonstrated by which of the following lines?

   (A) "Despite appearances, though, there was not much to choose between our two families." (lines 35–36)

   (B) "My mother's attitude, by contrast, was one of weary, semi-ironic servitude," (line 63–64)

   (C) "Cute, but also obscene: her nostrils were on permanent display." (line 13)

   (D) "This, too, was an example of bad taste." (line 71)

   (E) "My mother was a feminist." (line 19)

3. Considering the other details provided about Tracey, the narrator, and their mothers, which element of the setting is likely most significant?

   (A) It takes place "in Miss Isabel's dance class." (line 61)

   (B) There are "plastic chairs that lined the left-hand wall." (line 66)

   (C) They walk "through the sandy gravel of a churchyard." (lines 2–3)

   (D) "There were many other girls present." (lines 3–4)

   (E) "I met Tracey at ten a.m. on that Saturday" (line 1)

4. Which of the following best supports the narrator's assertion that her "mother's attitude, by contrast, was one of weary, semi-ironic servitude"? (lines 63–64)

   (A) "But Tracey's personal glamour was the solution: she was her own mother's most striking accessory." (lines 30–32)

   (B) "In my mother's view it was exactly these superficial similarities that lent so much weight to questions of taste." (lines 39–41)

   (C) "a change was made and my father took over." (lines 67–68)

   (D) "My mother was a feminist." (line 19)

   (E) "... the kind my mother refused to recognize as a reality in the world—'Those aren't shoes.'" (lines 34–35)

5. Which of the following lines from the passage illustrates Tracey's mother's attitude toward Tracey?
   (A) "she thought the dance class ridiculous, she had better things to do" (lines 64–65)
   (B) "She'd no need of make-up or products or jewelry or expensive clothes" (lines 22–23)
   (C) "But Tracey's personal glamour was the solution" (line 30–31)
   (D) "Tracey's mother pushed the girl in front of herself" (line 58)
   (E) "Tracey was unashamedly her mother's aspiration and avatar." (lines 53–54)

6. Which of the following best describes the narrator's perspective on Tracey?
   (A) Jealous of her beauty but curious about her
   (B) Angry, though she is willing to forgive her
   (C) Better than her in nearly every way
   (D) Generally equal, though with different upbringings
   (E) Sad but hopeful

7. Which of the following is the best possible defensible interpretation of the passage as a whole?
   (A) Regardless of what we see, people's realities are complex because some people are genuine while others try to mask who they are.
   (B) Mothers will always judge one another and their parenting style, though it doesn't matter as long as children grow up healthy.
   (C) Daughters and mothers—despite the conflict and differences between them—are often more alike than not.
   (D) Fear of growing old makes some people live through their children while others simply accept aging as fate.
   (E) Complex family situations mean that everyone is raised differently.

Question 8 is covered in Unit 1.

8.  What is the most likely effect of separating the sentence in lines 53–63 from the earlier description of the mothers and daughters arriving at the church where the dance class was held (lines 1–3)?

    (A) It allows for more development of Tracey and the narrator before commenting on Tracey's mother.

    (B) It allows for more development of Tracey's mother at the end of the passage.

    (C) It emphasizes how Tracey's mother treats Tracey.

    (D) It creates a sudden contrast between Tracey and the narrator before comparing the two mothers.

    (E) It shifts from description of the relationship between the narrator and her mother to a focus on criticism of Tracey's mother.

Question 9 is covered in Unit 2.

9.  The shift at line 63 creates a contrast between

    (A) the churchyard and the dance class

    (B) Tracey's style and the criticism of the narrator's mother

    (C) Tracey's advantages and the narrator's struggles

    (D) the different mother-daughter relationships in the passage

    (E) the narrator's father and Tracey not having a father

Question 10 is covered in Unit 3.

10. Of the following, which details are used to create a sense of similarity between Tracey and the narrator?

    (A) "But my face was ponderous and melancholy, with a long, serious nose, and my eyes turned down, as did my mouth." (lines 8–9)

    (B) "Satin yellow bows were a phenomenon unknown to my mother. She pulled my great frizz back in a single cloud, tied with a black band." (lines 17–19)

    (C) "The family look, though not to my mother's taste, I found captivating: logos, tin bangles and hoops, diamanté everything, expensive trainers of the kind my mother refused to recognize as a reality in the world—" (lines 32–35)

    (D) "There were many other girls present but for obvious reasons we noticed each other, the similarities and the differences, as girls will." (lines 3–5)

    (E) "Our shade of brown was exactly the same—as if one piece of tan material had been cut to make us both—and our freckles gather in the same areas, we were of the same height." (lines 5–8)

Question 11 is covered in Unit 5.

11. Allusions to "Shirley Temple" (line 10) and "Nefertiti" (line 22) help to create

   (A) a contrast between temporary childhood fame and legendary status suggesting differences between the speaker's mother and Tracey's mother

   (B) associations between popular culture and ancient history to compare reality with the imaginative

   (C) a comparison between Tracey's mother and the speaker's mother that also comments on the relationship between the speaker and Tracey

   (D) metaphors that illustrate the differences between the speaker's family and Tracey's family

   (E) confusion about the roles that history and pop culture play when someone is describing her experiences to people who do not know

Questions 12–21 refer to the poem "The Man He Killed" by Thomas Hardy, a White English poet.

## The Man He Killed

1      "Had he and I but met
       By some old ancient inn,
       We should have sat us down to wet
       Right many a nipperkin![1]

5      "But ranged as infantry,
       And staring face to face,
       I shot at him as he at me,
       And killed him in his place.

       "I shot him dead because—
10     Because he was my foe,
       Just so: my foe of course he was;
       That's clear enough; although

       "He thought he'd 'list,'[2] perhaps,
       Off-hand like—just as I—
15     Was out of work—had sold his traps—
       No other reason why.

       "Yes; quaint and curious war is!
       You shoot a fellow down
       You'd treat if met where any bar is,
20     Or help to half-a-crown."[3]

---

1  **nipperkin:** a liquor container
2  **'list:** enlist, as in join the military
3  **half-a-crown:** a former British coin and monetary unit

12. The speaker's perspective throughout the poem might be best described as

   (A) regretful but accepting
   (B) angry and vengeful
   (C) lonely but hopeful
   (D) pitiful and hurt
   (E) lost and hopeless

13. The speaker's imagined relationship with the man he killed reveals what about his perspective on war?

   (A) War pits people who might otherwise have been friendly against each other.
   (B) War only happens when it is necessary.
   (C) War forces together people from many backgrounds.
   (D) People accept war as something that cannot be avoided.
   (E) Leaders don't consider who the people are before they send them to war.

14. The speaker's point of view is significant in this poem because

   (A) he speaks with significant knowledge of a man he had never met
   (B) he fails to recognize the problems with the way he is thinking about the man
   (C) he speaks from experience with his own family but not with the family of the man he killed
   (D) he speaks from direct experience in war but not direct experience with the life of the man he killed
   (E) he speaks directly to the man even though the man is dead

15. The comparisons in line 7 and line 14 emphasize what central idea in the poem?

   (A) The two men are nothing alike.
   (B) The speaker is interested in possible similarities between the two men.
   (C) The speaker has lost his faith in humanity.
   (D) War is a reasonable excuse for killing others.
   (E) People are interrelated and they can't know whom they'll meet.

16. Repetition of the word *because* in the third stanza (lines 9–12) likely indicates what about the speaker?

    (A) That he does not know what to say

    (B) That he failed to think about saving the man before he killed him

    (C) That he fears that he may have killed the man for the wrong reasons

    (D) That he is struggling with understanding why he killed the man

    (E) That he resists feeling guilty because he was at war

17. Repetition of the word *foe* (lines 10 and 11) emphasizes what idea that is central to the poem?

    (A) The two men should have been good friends.

    (B) There will always be people fighting.

    (C) The two men were friends forced to fight one another.

    (D) Killing someone in war is morally acceptable.

    (E) The two men were fighting on opposite sides.

18. The word *although* (line 12) most clearly ties to which word(s) in the same stanza (lines 9–12)?

    (A) *because* (lines 9 and 10)

    (B) *foe* (lines 10 and 11)

    (C) *he* (lines 10 and 11)

    (D) *clear* (line 12)

    (E) *enough* (line 12)

19. In the context of the poem, repetition of the word *you* in the fifth stanza (lines 17–20) has which of the following effects?

    (A) It demonstrates how the man tries to speak to the man he killed.

    (B) It shows us how lives can intersect.

    (C) It creates an expectation that he will kill again.

    (D) It acknowledges the family of the man he killed.

    (E) It emphasizes that this could happen to any person as it addresses the reader directly.

20. Where does the most significant shift occur in the poem?

    (A) Line 3

    (B) Line 5

    (C) Line 10

    (D) Line 17

    (E) Line 19

Question 21 is covered Unit 5.

21. Which of the following is the best possible defensible interpretation of the passage as a whole?

    (A) Despite conflicts between leaders, war pits people who may be very much alike against each other, adding to the tragedy.

    (B) People just have to kill others in war.

    (C) Everyone is connected in some way, regardless of the distance between them or the difference in their experiences.

    (D) War means we must sacrifice ourselves for the greater good of our society, regardless of our own values and beliefs.

    (E) In a world where war is a reality, we must be prepared to kill.

## Section II: Free Response

### Question 1: Poetry Analysis

In the poem on page 274, "The Man He Killed" by Thomas Hardy (published 1902), the speaker recalls an experience from war. Read the poem carefully. Then, in a well-written essay, analyze how Hardy uses poetic elements and techniques to develop the complex recollection.

In your response you should do the following:

- Respond to the prompt with a thesis that presents a defensible interpretation.

- Select and use evidence to support your line of reasoning.

- Explain how the evidence supports your line of reasoning.

- Use appropriate grammar and punctuation in communicating your argument.

## Question 2: Prose Fiction Analysis

On pages 269–270 is the opening chapter from *Swing Time*, a 2016 novel by Zadie Smith. In the passage, the narrator describes the first time she met Tracey, the girl who would become her best friend and regularly reappear throughout the novel.

Read the passage carefully. Then, in a well-written essay, analyze how Smith uses literary elements and techniques to create the complex portrayals of the two mothers.

In your response you should do the following:

- Respond to the prompt with a thesis that presents a defensible interpretation.
- Select and use evidence to support your line of reasoning.
- Explain how the evidence supports your line of reasoning.
- Use appropriate grammar and punctuation in communicating your argument.

## Question 3: Literary Argument—Character Inaction

Often, characters in works of fiction are defined by their actions. Sometimes, however, a character's inaction—whether it is a refusal or an inability to do something—can be just as significant.

Choose a work of fiction in which a character's inaction is significant to the development of the story. Then, in a well-written essay, analyze how the character's inaction contributes to an interpretation of the work as a whole. Do not merely summarize the plot.

In your response you should do the following:

- Respond to the prompt with a thesis that presents a defensible interpretation.
- Provide evidence to support your line of reasoning.
- Explain how the evidence supports your line of reasoning.
- Use appropriate grammar and punctuation in communicating your argument.

# UNIT 5

# Multiple Meanings

[Poetry II]

**Part 1: Power of Poetic Structure**
**Part 2: Literal and Figurative Language**
**Part 3: Imagery**
**Part 4: Figures of Speech**
**Part 5: Writing About Literature V**

---

**Enduring Understandings and Skills: Unit 5**

## Part 1  Power of Poetic Structure

**Understand**

The arrangement of the parts and sections of a text, the relationship of the parts to each other, and the sequence in which the text reveals information are all structural choices made by a writer that contribute to the reader's interpretation of a text. (STR-1)

**Demonstrate**

Explain the function of structure in a text. (3.C)
See also Unit 2

## Part 2  Literal and Figurative Language

**Understand**

Comparisons, representations, and associations shift meaning from the literal to the figurative and invite readers to interpret a text. (FIG-1)

**Demonstrate**

Distinguish between the literal and figurative meanings of words and phrases. (5.A)
Explain the function of specific words and phrases in a text. (5.B)
See also Unit 2

## Part 3  Imagery

**Understand**

Comparisons, representations, and associations shift meaning from the literal to the figurative and invite readers to interpret a text. (FIG-1)

**Demonstrate**

Identify and explain the function of an image or imagery. (5.D)
See also Unit 7

## Part 4  Figures of Speech

### Understand

Comparisons, representations, and associations shift meaning from the literal to the figurative and invite readers to interpret a text. (FIG-1)

### Demonstrate

Identify and explain the function of a metaphor. (6.B)

Identify and explain the function of personification. (6.C)

Identify and explain the function of an allusion. (6.D)

See also Unit 2

## Part 5  Writing about Literature V

### Understand

Readers establish and communicate their interpretations of literature through arguments supported by textual evidence. (LAN-1)

### Demonstrate

Develop a thesis statement that conveys a defensible claim about an interpretation of literature and that may establish a line of reasoning. (7.B)

Develop commentary that establishes and explains relationships among textual evidence, the line of reasoning, and the thesis. (7.C)

Select and use relevant and sufficient evidence to both develop and support a line of reasoning. (7.D)

Demonstrate control over the elements of composition to communicate clearly. (7.E)

Source: *AP® English Literature and Composition Course and Exam Description*

# Unit 5 Overview

In her poem "A Valentine for Ernest Mann," Arab-American poet Naomi Shihab Nye has a curious stanza about skunks:

> . . .
>
> Once I knew a man who gave his wife
> two skunks for a valentine.
> He couldn't understand why she was crying.
> "I thought they had such beautiful eyes."
> And he was serious. He was a serious man
> who lived in a serious way. Nothing was ugly
> just because the world said so. He really
> liked those skunks. So, he re-invented them
> as valentines and they became beautiful.
> At least, to him. And the poems that had been hiding
> in the eyes of skunks for centuries
> crawled out and curled up at his feet.
>
> . . .

This stanza captures an idea that runs through so much of modern poetry: that it can be inspired by—and thus be about—*anything*, depending on the perspective of the author. This man found beauty in those skunks, and when he recognized that beauty, all the things beautiful about skunks were realized and appreciated, despite skunks' negative reputation. Skunks happen to also be the perfect vehicle for talking about poetry, how language often works in a poem, and how poems are put together.

**Skunks and Expectations: Structure**  When you hear the word "skunk," certain things are likely to come immediately to mind—the smell and the black and white stripes. Those stripes, meant to serve as a bold warning sign to animals (and people), are unmistakable. Even if you have never seen a skunk in person, you would immediately recognize it and the peril it provides. You would have certain expectations for a skunk based on what you saw.

Poetry is much the same. You may see a poem on the road ahead and want to go the other way as you would with a skunk. As with the skunk, what you see—the structure and organization of a poem on the page—can help you recognize what you are encountering (and possibly the peril it provides, if it is a particularly difficult poem).

For example, if you see a poem with three stanzas and then a shorter final stanza, you may be encountering a sonnet—such as the poems by Spenser on page 324, Shakespeare on page 290, and McKay on page 347. If you see a poem split into two stanzas, you should look for some sort of shift or change when the stanzas change—as in the poem by Nazik al-Malaika on page 327 in which time passes between the two stanzas. As you'll come to see, recognizing patterns in the way some poems are built will sometimes help you as you approach the meaning of the poem.

Patterns, though, only work until they are broken. Take, for example, the *spotted* skunk. It doesn't have the telltale stripe of its popular cousin, but if you were to encounter one, you would likely know immediately that it was some kind of skunk—or at least that it is something you should avoid because it looks enough like a skunk to keep you guessing.

**Source:** National Park Service

As you might have determined with this analogy, which is also an extended metaphor, poems can work the same way. You might see a poem that resembles a familiar pattern but with some kind of difference. As with the skunk, your prior knowledge of what to expect from the structure of some poems can help you with reading others that look similar but not identical. For example, the poem by Wordsworth on page 318 looks like the other sonnets but with some slight differences that deserve your attention, or the poems by Rocha on page 328 and Chan on page 330 in which the poets are playing with the sonnet form but not matching it exactly.

**Literal and Figurative Language** The difference between the literal, what a thing really means, and the figurative, what it may represent or come to represent, depends on how it is used. Literally, skunks are weasel-like mammals that defend themselves with a spray that smells so bad it can induce convulsive vomiting and be smelled by a human more than three miles away. Figuratively, however, a skunk may represent something or someone that cannot be trusted: King Claudius in *Hamlet* says that his "offence is rank. It stinks to high heaven" and few who know the play would disagree in calling Claudius a skunk: Something about him stinks. So it is a surprise when the speaker in Nye's poem explains that a man found poems in the eyes of those skunks.

This skunk metaphor also introduces another set of concepts on which you will focus over the course of this unit: that authors don't always mean what they say. That is, authors use subjects or objects from what they hope is a common experience to communicate some new or interesting perspective to a reader, as Naomi Shihab Nye does in the excerpt from her poem. She draws on many people's knowledge of what a skunk is and what a skunk does in order to surprise the reader when her speaker claims that there are poems in the eyes of a skunk. If you've ever been sprayed by a skunk or smelled one that has been killed on a roadside, then you know that such beauty would be hard to find in a skunk. Because of people's knowledge of or experience with skunks, the idea of their having beautiful eyes startles you. It may almost be funny. In this way, Nye is able to toy with the literal understanding of a skunk and the things you may associate with it and communicate that poetry can come from any inspiration, even the strangest subjects.

In the following poem by English poet and soldier Wilfred Owen (1893–1918), published posthumously in 1920, the speaker describes a gruesome scene and reveals a perspective on war.

## DULCE ET DECORUM EST[1]

Bent double, like old beggars under sacks,
Knock-kneed, coughing like hags, we cursed through sludge,
Till on the haunting flares we turned our backs,
And towards our distant rest began to trudge.
5   Men marched asleep. Many had lost their boots,
But limped on, blood-shod. All went lame; all blind;
Drunk with fatigue; deaf even to the hoots
Of tired, outstripped Five-Nines[2] that dropped behind.

Gas![3] GAS! Quick, boys!—An ecstasy of fumbling
10   Fitting the clumsy helmets just in time,
But someone still was yelling out and stumbling
And flound'ring like a man in fire or lime.[4]—
Dim through the misty panes and thick green light,[5]
As under a green sea, I saw him drowning.

15   In all my dreams before my helpless sight,
He plunges at me, guttering, choking, drowning.
If in some smothering dreams, you too could pace
Behind the wagon that we flung him in,
And watch the white eyes writhing in his face,
20   His hanging face, like a devil's sick of sin;
If you could hear, at every jolt, the blood
Come gargling from the froth-corrupted lungs,
Obscene as cancer, bitter as the cud[6]
Of vile, incurable sores on innocent tongues,—
25   My friend, you would not tell with such high zest
To children ardent for some desperate glory,
The old Lie: *Dulce et decorum est*
*Pro patria mori.*[7]

---

1  **Dulce et Decorum Est:** Latin for "It is sweet and fitting."
2  **Five-Nines:** 5.9 inch artillery shells
3  **Gas:** chemical gases that killed 1.3 million people during World War I
4  **lime:** powdery substance that can produce significant dust; a severe irritant to the skin and the mucus membranes of the eyes, mouth, and lungs
5  **thick green gas:** indicative of chlorine gas used during World War I; this gas stays close to the ground and turns to hydrochloric acid in the lungs.
6  **cud:** partially digested food that returns to the mouth for more chewing in ruminants such as cows
7  **Pro patria mori:** Latin for "to die for one's country"

This unit will explore how poets use structure and language as they develop ideas. Before you learn new skills and information, assess what you already know. Read "Dulce et Decorum Est" again and answer the following questions. Don't worry if you find these challenging. Answering questions on a subject before formally learning about it is one way to help you deepen your understanding of new concepts.

## CLOSE READING

1. Do you recognize any patterns in the poem, of rhyme or line length or images? How could the relationships of those patterns relate to an idea in the poem?

2. What can you say about the four individual stanzas of the poem and how they relate to one another?

3. Are there words or expressions that could have more than one meaning? How would those affect the way you read the poem and think about its ideas?

4. How are objects and people described? What words or phrases are particularly interesting or surprising in the way they are used to describe subjects? What do those descriptions reveal about the speaker's perspective?

5. Where does the poet make comparisons between subjects? How do those comparisons help with the way you see or think about the ideas in the poem?

## INTERPRETATION

1. What bigger ideas are being developed in this poem? What might it be saying about those ideas beyond the poem?

2. What are the most important pieces of information in the text that would support a claim about the poem (that is, your interpretation)?

# Power of Poetic Structure

---

**Enduring Understanding and Skill**

## Part 1  Power of Poetic Structure

### Understand

The arrangement of the parts and sections of a text, the relationship of the parts to each other, and the sequence in which the text reveals information are all structural choices made by a writer that contribute to the reader's interpretation of a text. (STR-1)

### Demonstrate

Explain the function of structure in a text. (3.C)
See also Unit 2

**Source:** *AP® English Literature and Composition Course and Exam Description*

---

**Essential Question:** How do different kinds of poetic structures emphasize ideas and concepts?

Just as effective writers walk readers through certain ideas and present thoughts in a logical order to guide thinking, poets may do the same as they provide images or ideas. Often, a certain structure or a certain rhyme scheme emphasizes an idea in the poem.

Studying the way a poem is put together helps you see the different parts of an idea or ideas in a poem. It also helps you understand a perspective expressed in the poem and a perspective you may form as a reader.

---

**KEY TERMS**

| closed form | stanza | rhyme |
| lines | meter | open form |

---

## 1.1 Closed Forms | STR-1.U

When people think of poetry, they probably think of a text with a certain rhythm, a "feel" to how the words are put together, and then—of course—rhyme. A **closed form** of poetry is one that follows patterns of lines, stanzas, rhythm, and rhyme.

From the earliest childhood nursery rhymes to songs and the jingles you hear on commercials, some patterns in language and rhyme stick in our minds. Before most people could read and write, these patterns helped people remember stories that they could then recite and pass down to others. Much rhythmic and rhyming poetry still plays with that today—even if it plays with it by changing it unexpectedly.

Read aloud this popular poem by American poet Edgar Guest (1881–1959), first published in 1921.

### KEEP GOING

When things go wrong, as they sometimes will,
When the road you're trudging seems all uphill,
When the funds are low and the debts are high,
And you want to smile, but you have to sigh,
5  When care is pressing you down a bit,
Rest if you must—but don't you quit.

Life is queer with its twists and turns,
As every one of us sometimes learns,
And many a failure turns about
10  When he might have won had he stuck it out;
Don't give up, though the pace seems slow—
You may succeed with another blow.

Often the goal is nearer than
It seems to a faint and faltering man,
15  Often the struggler has given up
When he might have captured the victor's cup,
And he learned too late, when the night slipped down,
How close he was to the golden crown.

Success is failure turned inside out—
20  The silver tint of the clouds of doubt,
And you never can tell how close you are,
It may be near when it seems afar;
So stick to the fight when you're hardest hit—
It's when things seem worst that you mustn't quit.

## Lines, Stanzas, Meter, and Rhyme

The elements of poetry that create patterns in closed poems are **lines**, stanzas, meter, and rhyme. A **stanza** is a group of related lines separated from other lines in the poem, sometimes in a way that repeats a rhythm or rhyme scheme.

**Line Breaks** Readers can see where a line ends in print, and those listening to a poem or reading it aloud will detect the end of a line based primarily on its punctuation and how that is expressed in speech. The end of a line is in many cases not the end of a sentence. In fact, in the first stanza of "Keep Going," the complete sentence doesn't end until the final line. All the preceding lines lead up to it with subordinate clauses. "Translated" into regular prose and summarized, the sentence could read: when a lot of things seem to weigh you down, keep going.

Just identifying those line breaks and the punctuation that signals a pause but not a complete stop until the end of the stanza does not really provide much insight into the poem. However, if you stop and think about what the words are saying—and about the title of the poem—you can see that the structure of the poem's lines emphasizes the main point, because the lines themselves just "keep going." The structure amplifies meaning.

**Stanzas and Chunking, or Blocking** The stanza break, the space between groups of lines, often signals a shift in the poem, or at least another way to look at the subject. Often each stanza has its own focus, or idea. But within that stanza, you might also find chunks or blocks of ideas. A table such as 5-1 can help you see the separate ideas. "Keep Going" is not a challenging or complex poem, and the ideas are simple, but you can still see how the ideas chunk in stanzas 2–4.

| Blocks/Chunks of Related Texts | Key Ideas |
|---|---|
| **TITLE:** Keep Going | Don't give up. |
| **STANZA 2**<br><br>Life is queer with its twists and turns,<br>As every one of us sometimes learns,<br>And many a failure turns about<br>10   When he might have won had he stuck it out | Unexpected challenges |
| Don't give up, though the pace seems slow—<br>You may succeed with another blow. | Slow pace of progress |
| **STANZA 3**<br><br>Often the goal is nearer than<br>It seems to a faint and faltering man,<br>15   Often the struggler has given up<br>When he might have captured the victor's cup, | Closer than you think sometimes |
| And he learned too late, when the night slipped down,<br>How close he was to the golden crown. | Learn too late |
| **STANZA 4**<br><br>Success is failure turned inside out—<br>20   The silver tint of the clouds of doubt, | Get over doubts |
| And you never can tell how close you are,<br>It may be near when it seems afar; | Closer than you think |
| So stick to the fight when you're hardest hit—<br>It's when things seem worst that you mustn't quit. | Even in the worst of times, don't quit. |

**Table 5-1**

For a more complex poem, chunking is even more helpful in seeing the ideas in each stanza or part of a stanza. For example, read "Elegy for a Woman of No Importance (or, images from a Baghdad alleyway)" by Nazik al-Malaika in the Poetry Gallery on page 327. Then return to this page to see how it can be blocked to help clarify its meaning.

| Blocks/Chunks of Related Texts | Key Ideas |
|---|---|
| TITLE: Elegy for a Woman of No Importance | Lament for an unknown woman |
| **STANZA 1**<br><br>She died, but no lips shook, no cheeks turned white<br>no doors heard her death tale told and retold,<br>no blinds were raised for small eyes to behold<br>the casket as it disappeared from sight. | Dying alone |
| 5   Only a beggar in the street, consumed<br>by hunger, heard the echo of her life—<br>the safe forgetfulness of tombs,<br>the melancholy of the moon. | Shift to the one person who was aware of her death, a hungry beggar |
| The night gave way to morning thoughtlessly,<br>10   and light brought with it sound—boys throwing stones,<br>a hungry, mewling[1] cat, all skin and bones,<br>the vendors fighting, clashing bitterly,<br>some people fasting, others wanting more,<br>polluted water gurgling, | Shift to daytime and unpleasant and ugly everyday noises. "Thoughtlessly" suggests life went on unchanged without her. |
|            and a breeze<br>playing, alone, upon the door<br>16   having almost forgotten her. | Another shift to a gentle and playful breeze that almost—but didn't—forget her |

Table 5-2

**Meter and Rhythm Meter** is the basic rhythmic structure of poetry, the pattern of accented and unaccented syllables. In the first stanza of "Keep Going," below, the stressed syllables are printed in bold type.

When **things** go **wrong,** as they **some**times **will,**
When the **road** you're **trudg**ing seems **all** uphill,
When the **funds** are **low** and the **debts** are **high,**
And you **want** to **smile,** but you **have** to **sigh,**
5   When **care** is **press**ing you **down** a bit,
**Rest** if you **must**—but **don't** you **quit.**

---

1 **mewling:** whimpering

One of the features of this poem that makes it so accessible is the predictability of its meter. Each line beats out this rhythm: da DUM da DUM da DUM da DUM—except for the last line, which beats out DUM da DUM da DUM da DUM. The first five lines of the stanza "keep going." The final line of this stanza stops that motion through a change in meter that brings the momentum to a standstill—a rest—emphasizing the meaning of the last line. In this way, the poem's metrical structure amplifies its meaning.

In "Dulce et Decorum Est," the meter does not fall into such neat patterns.

> **Bent double, like old beg**gers **under sacks,**
> **Knock**-kneed, **coughing like hags, we cursed** through **sludge**

The rhythm of the first two lines scans this way:

> DUM DUM da | da DUM DUM da | DUM da DUM /
> DUM da | DUM da da DUM | da DUM | da DUM

The irregular pattern helps convey the meaning that, unlike "Keep Going," Owen's war poem relates ideas and images far beyond the normal and accessible.

**Rhyme** Another feature of this poem that makes it easily accessible is the predictability of its rhyme scheme. **Rhyme** is the close similarity in vowel and consonant sounds of the end of words, especially at the ends of lines. One way to analyze the pattern of rhyme is to assign a letter of the alphabet to the lines that rhyme, as below.

> When things go wrong, as they sometimes will, (A)
> When the road you're trudging seems all uphill, (A)
> When the funds are low and the debts are high, (B)
> And you want to smile, but you have to sigh, (B)
> 5  When care is pressing you down a bit, (C)
> Rest if you must—but don't you quit. (C)

You could describe the rhyme scheme of this stanza as AA-BB-CC, in that way showing that lines 1 and 2 rhyme, 3 and 4 rhyme, and 5 and 6 rhyme. Pairs of rhyming lines that form a unit are known as couplets. Rhymes at the ends of sentences are called *end rhymes*.

Using the same method of identifying rhyming lines, the second stanza of "Elegy to a Woman of No Importance" could be notated as follows:

> 5  Only a beggar in the street, consumed (A)
> by hunger, heard the echo of her life (B)
> the safe forgetfulness of tombs, (A)
> the melancholy of the moon. (A)

As you can see, *consumed, tombs,* and *moon* are not perfect rhymes. Words that sound alike but rhyme imperfectly are called *near rhymes*. In a poem with otherwise regular rhymes, near rhymes call attention to themselves and create emphasis on those words. They can also contribute to tone with the close sound of their internal vowels. The *oo* in this poem softens the tone.

Some poets use *internal rhymes*, rhymes between a word in the middle and a word at the end of a line, but they are much more infrequent than end rhymes. Edgar Allan Poe's "The Raven" is the most famous example. The words in bold type are internal rhymes.

> Once upon a midnight **dreary**, while I pondered, weak and **weary**,
> Over many a quaint and curious volume of forgotten lore—
> While I nodded, nearly **napping**, suddenly there came a **tapping**,
> As of someone gently **rapping**, rapping at my chamber door.
> "'Tis some visitor," I muttered, "**tapping** at my chamber door—
> Only this and nothing more."

**The Sonnet** One closed form of poetry makes very strategic use of all of these literary devices—line, stanza, meter, and rhyme. Poets have used this form for hundreds of years.

The *sonnet* (Italian for little song) is almost always easily recognizable, even just by its appearance on the page. Professor and author Tom Foster once said, "if it's square, it's a sonnet."

Sonnets typically have fourteen lines and they often follow certain rhyme schemes and/or metrical patterns.

Consider this sonnet by William Shakespeare. It is structured with three sets of four-line units, called quatrains. It ends with a couplet. The rhyme scheme is identified below. The first and third lines and second and fourth lines in each quatrain rhyme.

### SONNET 22

> My glass[1] shall not persuade me I am old, (A)
> So long as youth and thou are of one date; (B)
> But when in thee time's furrows I behold, (A)
> Then look I death my days should expiate.[2] (B)
>
> 5   For all that beauty that doth cover thee, (C)
> Is but the seemly raiment[3] of my heart, (D)
> Which in thy breast doth live, as thine in me: (C)
> How can I then be elder than thou art? (D)
>
> O! therefore, love, be of thyself so wary (E)
> 10  As I, not for myself, but for thee will; (F)
> Bearing thy heart, which I will keep so chary[4] (E)
> As tender nurse her babe from faring ill. (F)
>
> Presume not on thy heart when mine is slain, (G)
> Thou gav'st me thine not to give back again. (G)

---

1   **glass:** mirror
2   **expiate:** atone for
3   **raiment:** clothing
4   **chary:** carefully

The metrical pattern of sonnets is typically what you see in Sonnet 22: five da DUMS in each line. Each da DUM is called an iamb. Since there are five of them in each line, the technical term for this pattern is *iambic pentameter*. The first line shows the five iambs.

My **glass** | shall **not** | per**suade** | me **I** | am **old**,
So **long** as **youth** and **thou** are **of** one **date**;
But **when** in **thee** time's **fur**rows **I** be**hold**,
Then **look** I **death** my **days** should ex**piate**.

In some ways, a sonnet is like an argument. The first quatrain introduces an idea; the second quatrain develops it, as if building a logical argument. The third quatrain sometimes begins a shift toward a conclusion, and the final couplet drives the point home. The final couplet gets the most emphasis in the sonnet.

The argument in Sonnet 22 might be expressed this way:

| 1st quatrain | I'm not going to believe I'm old until you, my young friend, start showing signs of aging. |
|---|---|
| 2nd quatrain | Your beauty lives in my heart as my heart lives in you. |
| 3rd quatrain | Therefore, be careful not to give your heart that I am taking care of to someone else. |
| Couplet | Because you can't have yours back. |

Table 5-3

When analyzing closed forms of poetry, consider all the possible ways the structure can convey meaning. For example, the start of a new stanza might tell you that the idea is shifting; the way sentences run over from one line to the next before they end might express momentum, as it does in "Keep Going;" rhymes connect the rhyming words, showing a relationship in their meaning; meter, especially when a pattern is broken, may call attention to an important idea; a couplet may almost summarize the meaning of a sonnet. A poem is much more than the words it contains or a paraphrase of it—it is a holistic communication conveying meaning through all of its elements.

 **Remember:** Closed forms of poetry include predictable patterns in the structure of lines, stanzas, meter, and rhyme, which develop relationships among ideas in the poem. (Note: The AP® Exam will not require students to label or identify specific rhyme schemes, metrical patterns, or forms of poetry.) (STR-1.U)

## The Poet's Craft: Breaking Patterns

If you were analyzing the structure of "Dulce et Decorum Est," you might start by looking at the stanza structure. You would find this pattern:

Stanza 1—8 lines
Stanza 2—6 lines
Stanza 3—2 lines
Stanza 4—12 lines

You may not recognize that pattern of closed form, with that grouping of lines, but you do notice that the first two stanzas together are 14 lines, and the second two stanzas are also 14 lines together. You might begin to wonder if this form is related to a sonnet, with its characteristic 14-line structure. One critic, in fact, has called this poem a "sandwich sonnet."

With that in mind, you sketch out the rhyme scheme to test your idea. Through line 12, the poem follows the exact rhyming pattern of a sonnet—ABABCDCDEFEF. The next structure you would expect in a sonnet would be the couplet, the rhyming pair of lines, but the rhyme pattern is GH, not GG as you would expect in a sonnet.

Lines 15 and 16 *look* like a couplet, but they don't rhyme either. They continue the rhyming pattern started in lines 13 and 14.

The rest of the poem follows the expected rhyme of the first 12 lines of a sonnet: IJIJKLKLMNMN.

In comparison to a conventional sonnet, then, "Dulce et Decorum Est" is different in these ways:

- twice the number of lines
- no couplet where you would expect it to be; in fact, no couplet at all
- irregular metrical pattern

There's enough about the poem's form for a reader to associate it with the tidy, proper form of a sonnet. That the poet has broken away from that form, however, may reflect the nature of the subject. Maybe the poem has twice the number of lines because the story of witnessing the gruesome cruelties of war is too big to tell in only 14 lines, or too horrifying to be told with "such high zest" in a standard poetic form as some poets use when they glorify war. Maybe there is no clear couplet because there is no way to summarize the unthinkable terror in two rhyming lines.

Maybe the brutality of war and the narrator's "smothering dreams" upend predictable comforts and cannot be expressed in regular meters. These are all examples of interpretations you can make based on connections between a poem's structure and its meaning. When poets break expected patterns, look for ways those breaks amplify the message of the poem.

(For another example of a sonnet that breaks expected patterns, see "Persephone, Falling" by Rita Dove on page 321.)

**Source:** Getty Images

*How might these interlaced fingers be similar to the middle four lines of "Dulce et Decorum Est"?*

## Use the Poet's Craft

Try writing a poem inspired by "Keep Going" but taking the attitude of Homer Simpson, the dimwitted, lazy, donut-loving character in the long-running animated television show "The Simpsons," as he gives advice to his son Bart.

> **Bart:** You're the one who told me I could do anything if I just put my mind to it!
> **Homer:** Well, now that you're a little bit older, I can tell you that's a crock! No matter how good you are at something, there's always about a million people better than you.
> **Bart:** Gotcha. Can't win, don't try.

In your poem, break expected patterns to reinforce the comic idea "Can't win, don't try."

## 1.1 Checkpoint

*Reread the poem "Dulce et Decorum Est" on page 283. Then complete the open-response activity and answer the multiple-choice questions.*

1. Use the chunking or blocking technique to analyze the groups of ideas in "Dulce et Decorum Est." Use as many rows for each stanza as you need.

| Block/Chunks of Related Texts | Label or Ideas |
|---|---|
| TITLE: | |
| STANZA 1 | |
| | |
| STANZA 2 | |
| | |
| STANZA 3 | |
| | |
| STANZA 4 | |
| | |

2. Which of the following best describes the progression of ideas represented by the structure of stanzas in the poem?

   (A) Personal injury, Paralyzing fear, Loss of memory, Pity for children of dead soldiers

   (B) Chaotic attack, Pain of memory, Recollection of a dream, Dire warning to reader

   (C) Deathly march, Chaotic attack, Haunting memory, Dire warning to reader

   (D) Haunting memory, Sacrifice for others, Dream, Regret and pain

   (E) Horror of war, Fear of attack, Fulfillment of dreams, Glory

3. Which of the following rhymes from the poem most directly relate to the complex perspective being presented on war and dying for one's country?

   (A) "sacks" and "backs" (lines 1 and 3)

   (B) "boots" and "hoots" (lines 5 and 7)

   (C) "light" and "sight" (lines 13 and 15)

   (D) "blood" and "cud" (lines 21 and 23)

   (E) "glory" and "mori" (lines 26 and 28)

**Creating on Your Own**

Think of a saying that you have grown up hearing that you either disagree with or that you think is not helpful. Take five to ten minutes to just write, filling each line of your paper or computer screen all of the way to the end. Don't try to be "poetic"—just write and explain and describe as you go. Don't worry about being "accurate," just write what you see and what you know.

Once you have identified and explained your perspective, make a plan for developing some poetry about it.

1. Make a list of words that rhyme (try for pairs) that relate to the topic and your perspective.

2. Think about the order of your ideas: Where do you want readers to start their thinking? What ideas do you want to leave until the end?

3. Draft some lines that end with those rhyming words. You can try couplets or some other pattern of rhyme—just make sure the rhymes are meaningful.

4. Play with moving some of those lines or words around.

5. Try revising your lines into rhythmic patterns.

## 1.2 Open Forms and Emphasis | (STR-1.V–W)

While closed form poems are structured to follow certain poetic conventions, other poems employ an **open form** structure, sometimes called free form. Open form poetry may still have a structure, and it may follow certain conventions but not others. Think of the range between closed and open form as the range of a door: It can be either closed shut or open, but it can also be open to different degrees and in different ways—ajar, cracked, wide-open, and swinging back and forth, for example. So too are open form poems always attached to some sort of convention—that is, not completely unhinged—but they vary in just how strictly structured they are. "Dulce et Decorum Est" is a closed form, but as you saw it breaks some conventions of closed forms. Open forms usually break even more.

Read aloud this poem by Kentucky author Wendell Berry (1934–) first published in 1994.

## ENEMIES

If you are not to become a monster,
you must care what they think.
If you care what they think,

how will you not hate them,
5    and so become a monster
of the opposite kind? From where then

is love to come—love for your enemy
that is the way of liberty?
From forgiveness. Forgiven, they go

10   free of you, and you of them;
they are to you as sunlight
on a green branch. You must not

think of them again, except
as monsters like yourself,
15   pitiable because unforgiving.

This poem might be like a half open door. Since you have been used to seeing patterns in the previous poems, you might have been surprised to find them missing in this poem. Nonetheless, groups of three line stanzas (called *tercets*) form a pattern, and you will even find some repetition and rhyme, just not as consistently and as patterned as in other poems.

Whereas in closed form poetry a break in structure often signals a point of emphasis, in open forms a point where structure *does* appear has a similar effect. "Enemies" uses conventions of closed form in the following ways:

- the repetitions of "monster" at the ends of lines 1 and 5 and of "think" at the ends of lines 2 and 3
- the near rhyme of "them" and "then" in lines 4 and 6
- the single end rhyme of "enemy" and "liberty" in lines 7 and 8

That end rhyme is especially significant since it shines a light on the two main contrasting ideas in the poem, highlighting their relationship.

## Emphasis

Knowing what an open form is and how it compares to a closed form, knowing that poems often use stanzas, knowing to look for words that rhyme, or paying close attention to the meter and structure of a poem: All of this knowledge is superficial until you examine the effect of these literary elements on the poem, especially as ways to emphasize ideas. Identifying a literary technique is of no use unless you can explain how that technique contributes to an interpretation of meaning.

Think again about the single end rhyme of "enemy" and "liberty" in lines 7 and 8 of "Enemies." As the only rhyme in the poem, it draws attention to the ideas related to the words "enemy" and "liberty." This attention or emphasis helps the poet communicate an idea or even a perspective. In this case, the poem may suggest that loving your enemy is a way to set yourself free.

It isn't the rhyme alone that emphasizes those words and the ideas attached to them—it's their location as well. They appear at the beginning of stanza 3 in the dead middle of the poem, lines 7 and 8 of a 15-line poem. Multiple structures combine here to emphasize these lines and their ideas. The rhyme, the stanzas, the lines, and the structure in general combine to bring attention to those lines. As you read poetry, be attentive to places in poems where multiple structures and techniques appear to be combining for emphasis.

**Remember:** Open forms of poetry may not follow expected or predictable patterns in the structure of their lines or stanzas, but they may still have structures that develop relationships between ideas in the poem. Structures combine in texts to emphasize certain ideas and concepts. (STR-1.V–W)

## Part 1.2 Checkpoint

*Reread the poem "Dulce et Decorum Est" on page 283. Then complete the open-response activity and answer the multiple-choice questions.*

1. Think about the structures of the poem and how they create emphasis at certain points and on certain ideas. In a paragraph, identify the points of emphasis and explain how they may contribute to the ideas in the poem.

2. Which of the following best describes the reason for line 28 remaining shorter than all of the other lines?

    (A) To demonstrate the honorable sacrifices people make when they go to war

    (B) To match the length of the first line of the poem

    (C) To underscore that dying for one's country is the main topic of the poem

    (D) To complete the meter and rhythm of the previous line

    (E) To celebrate the sacrifice that people make when they go to war

3. Which of the following best describes the reason for the rhyme and repetition of the word "drowning" in lines 14 and 16?

(A) The speaker's eyes are so filled with tears that his impaired vision views the scene as if underwater.

(B) That word is essential to the reader's understanding of the suffering involved in dying in a gas attack and the pain of war.

(C) "Drowning" is also a figurative description of how anti-war sentiments can overwhelm someone.

(D) It is a unique way of describing pain in war to readers who were tired of hearing about the war.

(E) Anyone who has choked or nearly drowned would be able to understand the feeling.

**Creating on Your Own**

Review the writing you did in previous Creating on Your Own activities. Consider patterns you created, and then look at how you might break them or alter them to emphasize something in your draft. You might:

1. Interrupt the rhyme scheme by creating an internal rhyme or a non-rhyme or changing the pattern of lines that rhyme.

2. Break the poem into different stanzas or lines.

3. Consider a combination of 1 and 2 in which the lines and rhymes work together.

# Part 1 Apply What You Have Learned

Read the poems in the Poetry Gallery of this unit (or Unit 2 or 8) and choose one to examine more closely. Write a paragraph or series of paragraphs that identifies structural aspects of the poem, examines what the effect of those structures might be, and then explains how those structures and their effect relate to bigger ideas or meaning in the poem. Cite specific line numbers and explain your thinking to your reader.

**Reflect on the Essential Question** Write a brief response that answers the essential question: *How do different kinds of poetic structures emphasize ideas and concepts?* In your answer, correctly use the key terms listed on page 285.

# Literal and Figurative Language

## Part 2  Literal and Figurative Language

### Understand
Comparisons, representations, and associations shift meaning from the literal to the figurative and invite readers to interpret a text. (FIG-1)

### Demonstrate
Distinguish between the literal and figurative meanings of words and phrases. (5.A)

Explain the function of specific words and phrases in a text. (5.B)

See also Unit 2

**Source:** *AP® English Literature and Composition Course and Exam Description*

**Essential Question:** What are the effects of literal and figurative language?

As the skunk example at the beginning of this unit shows, poets often use words in unexpected ways. The narrator of the excerpt about the skunks was talking about actual skunks that are black and white and defend themselves with a violently odorous spray, but you also saw how the term might be used to describe a person. In fact, this usage has become so common that the Merriam-Webster dictionary lists "an obnoxious or disliked person" as the second definition of the word "skunk." It isn't that skunks are necessarily obnoxious or disliked, but in most cases they are to be avoided, and that is likely how the term came to be associated with such people. People who are skunks are to be avoided.

You have no doubt heard other words used in similar ways. One might call a person who betrays a friend a "rat" or refer to someone who displays cowardice as a "chicken." In each case, the traits often associated with those animals are being applied or transferred to the person. Rats are associated with being sneaky, disease-ridden, and unclean and are therefore to be avoided, not unlike the person who betrays friends. Chickens are not cowards, but they are weak and they run away easily. Words such as these with multiple meanings—one literal and one metaphorical—are the shining currency of poetry.

## 2.1 Words with Multiple Meanings | FIG-1.L

Used skillfully, the elements of poetry—lines, stanzas, meter, and rhyme—can add levels of meaning to a poem. The words themselves, however, also add nuance or complexity that contributes to the interpretation of a text. Words with multiple meanings or connotations are especially powerful.

### Literal and Figurative Meanings

Authors and poets use language in different ways. A word or phrase used in a very **literal** way is based on its actual definition. Words used in a **figurative** way keep their literal meaning but also invite readers' associations with it.

*Literal* means "by the letter"—that the word being used means exactly what it is meant to mean, its dictionary definition. *Figurative*, on the other hand, comes from the Old French word *figuratif*—meaning metaphor—and the Latin *figura* meaning to form or shape or create. Figurative language is language that has its meaning formed or shaped by the person using it.

Like *skunk* and *rat* and *chicken*, sometimes the figurative usage of a word becomes so popular that it makes its way into the dictionary and becomes an accepted definition. These cases are still figurative uses of the words because those new definitions originated with the first definition.

### Connotations and Multiple Meanings

Readers' associated understandings of words and their meanings are referred to as **connotations**. Some words are said to "connote" an idea or feeling that is not necessarily its primary definition.

An easy way to remember this idea is to imagine that a connotation is the aura that surrounds a word—the way it feels and the way people feel about it. Words might have a positive connotation or a negative one, but often they express more nuance than those extremes.

In these ways, words can have multiple meanings. They can have literal and figurative meanings but also have different connotations, depending on how they are used and how a reader relates to them.

Poets and authors often rely on this quality of words to create complexities and ambiguous possibilities in their texts. Taking the time to examine those words, their different possibilities, and their relationship to other aspects of the text will open up a number of routes to your understanding of a text.

Read this popular poem by American poet Robert Frost (1874–1963) that was published in 1923.

# STOPPING BY WOODS ON A SNOWY EVENING

Whose woods these are I think I know.
His house is in the village though;
He will not see me stopping here
To watch his woods fill up with snow.

5   My little horse must think it queer
To stop without a farmhouse near
Between the woods and frozen lake
The darkest evening of the year.

He gives his harness bells a shake
10  To ask if there is some mistake.
The only other sound's the sweep
Of easy wind and downy flake.

The woods are lovely, dark and deep,
But I have promises to keep,
15  And miles to go before I sleep,
And miles to go before I sleep.

The dramatic situation of this poem is clear, especially given the title. The pattern of syllables and stanzas and rhymes are all conventional: eight syllables per line (tetrameter), and every second syllable is stressed (iambic tetrameter), four stanzas of four lines each, and a rhyme scheme that sets up the rhyme for the next stanza in the third line of the previous stanza—an act of poetic creation that Frost himself called "reckless."

That last stanza is different, however. Here is where many readers see the conventional nicety of this poem breaking apart. All of these lines rhyme and the last two are repetitions. Based on what you read earlier in this unit and in other units, you probably noted the change in structure, which emphasizes these final lines.

The last three lines of the poem also begin to reach past the dramatic situation of the poem established by the title and move into the life of the speaker beyond this moment. There have been promises made and there is a journey ahead.

But what kind of journey?

The use of "miles" and "sleep" and the entire phrase "miles to go before I sleep" can be read both literally and figuratively in the context of the poem.

| "miles to go before I sleep" (lines 15 and 16) | |
|---|---|
| **Possible Meanings (consider the context of the poem)** | |
| **Literal:**<br>"miles": a long way to travel (especially on horseback and as night is beginning to fall on a snowy night)<br><br>"sleep": rest at the end of a day and after a journey | **Figurative:**<br>"miles": a lot to do in order to accomplish something, especially to fulfill the promises made (in line 14)<br><br>"sleep": rest assured knowing the promises have been kept or some other thing has been accomplished |
| **How these different meanings might affect the reading of the poem** | |
| The poem is just the situation as it is presented, nothing more. The snow is falling, and the speaker takes a break on his long way to travel on a cold, dark evening. | The situation of the poem is a moment of contemplation for the speaker—watching the woods fill up with snow and thinking about promises made and work to do to meet obligations before resting assured that promises have been kept. |

Table 5-4

Both readings make sense at the same time. To limit your reading to only the literal is to ignore the possibilities that poetry—and language in general—provide. So many markers point you to those final lines (the rhyme, the repetition, the literal and figurative possibilities) that you should take the time to carefully examine their effect on the interpretation of the poem.

Multiple meanings of a word may not always divide between literal or figurative. Consider the work *dark* (line 13) in the Frost poem: it could mean literally dark as in devoid of light, but it also has more than one connotation. It could be "dark" as in the unknown, "dark" as in something bad or evil, or it could even bring to mind its opposite—light. On this "darkest evening of the year," *dark* might convey both the unknown depths of the forest and its contrast to the light as the day is ending and the white of the heavy snowfall. The "darkest evening of the year" is the winter solstice, when there is the least amount of daylight. However, it is a turning point, since all the days that follow will get longer and longer. The speaker may feel a sense of turning point, especially with the word *But* at the beginning of line 14.

 **Remember:** Words with multiple meanings or connotations add nuance or complexity that can contribute to interpretations of a text. (FIG-1.L)

## 2.1 Checkpoint

*Reread the poem "Dulce et Decorum Est" on page 283. Then complete the following open-response activities and answer the multiple-choice questions.*

1. As you reread the poem, pay attention to language that can be read both literally and figuratively. On separate paper, recreate Table 5-4 to analyze both kinds of meanings.

2. Read the poem again and consider words that have different connotations or multiple meanings that affect the ideas in the poem. How might multiple meanings affect the interpretation of the poem?

3. In the context of this poem, which of the following is the best literal understanding of the figurative words "old beggars under sacks" (line 1)?

    (A) Weak and pitiful

    (B) Intoxicated and foolish

    (C) Ignorant and irresponsible

    (D) Elderly and miserable

    (E) Pained and witless

4. Within the context of the entire poem, the use of *smothering* in line 17 could serve both to characterize the emotional feeling of the speaker's dreams and

    (A) criticize the feeling of being forced into a war to die for one's country

    (B) contrast the speaker's fears with the glory others find in war

    (C) relate the feeling of the gas, the gas masks, and the war in general

    (D) describe the feeling of glory that overcomes the participants in a battle

    (E) capture the speaker's ability to come to terms with what has occurred on the battlefield

## Creating on Your Own

Review the writing you did in earlier Creating on Your Own activities. Look closely at some of the words or phrases you used and consider revising or emphasizing certain words whose literal meaning could work as well as their figurative meaning to contribute more to the poem. Then, look at words you used or could use to include different or multiple meanings. These are challenging activities, so take your time and consider all of your language. Think about perspectives you are trying to communicate that are especially difficult or uncertain—those areas may be ripe for communicating with more than one meaning. Put your poem aside from time to time and come back to it with a fresh mind and try again. Save your work.

# 2.2 Descriptive Words, Exaggerations, and Understatement | FIG-1.M, FIG-1.N

Note the difference between the following lines and the ones Frost actually wrote.

> The sound is the sweep
> Of wind and snow
>
> The woods are deep.

Of course, what he actually wrote was

> The <u>only</u> <u>other</u> sound's the sweep
> Of <u>easy</u> wind and <u>downy</u> flake.
>
> The woods are <u>lovely, dark</u> and <u>deep</u>

Descriptive words, such as adjectives (underlined above) and adverbs, qualify or modify the things they describe and affect readers' interaction with the text. Other techniques poets use are **hyperbole**, which exaggerates, and **understatement**, which minimizes. Exaggerating or minimizing an aspect of an object focuses attention on that trait and conveys a perspective about the object.

## Modifiers

Language reflects thinking. Grammar shows the relationships between subjects (nouns) and actions (verbs) that the subjects take (predicates). Every other grammatical element is some kind of modifier. As the Frost example above shows, without the modifiers, the narrator's thinking would be hazy to the reader, too general.

The most fundamental way of modifying words is to use adjectives and adverbs. The choices of **adjectives** to describe nouns (things) or **adverbs** to describe verbs (actions) can reveal much about the perspective and attitude of the speaker toward the ideas and events in the text. In the skunk poem on page 280, for example, when the man in the poem describes the skunks as "beautiful," readers learn the most important information about him and recognize his unique perspective. Readers also learn about the speaker's attitude toward the man through the adverb used to describe how he "<u>really</u> liked those skunks." These are small details, but they accumulate through the poem and become significant in what they reveal.

Read this poem by English Poet Percy Bysshe Shelley (1792–1822), published in 1818. Modifiers in this famous poem are critical in revealing the perspective of both the narrator and speaker (the traveler).

## OZYMANDIAS[1]

I met a traveller from an antique land,
Who said—"Two vast and trunkless legs of stone
Stand in the desert. . . . Near them, on the sand,
Half sunk a shattered visage[2] lies, whose frown,
And wrinkled lip, and sneer of cold command,
Tell that its sculptor well those passions read
Which yet survive, stamped on these lifeless things,
The hand that mocked them, and the heart that fed;
And on the pedestal, these words appear:
My name is Ozymandias, King of Kings;
Look on my Works, ye Mighty, and despair!
Nothing beside remains. Round the decay
Of that colossal Wreck, boundless and bare
The lone and level sands stretch far away."

1 **Ozymandias:** an ancient Greek name for Egyptian Pharaoh Ramses II
2 **visage:** face

| Modifier (in *italic* type) | How it Affects Readers' Interactions with Text |
|---|---|
| *antique* land (adjective) | *Antique* can mean old, or old and valuable, or old and not of much practical value today. The last meaning resonates as the reader completes the poem. |
| *vast* and *trunkless* legs (adjectives) | While *vast* suggests the enormity of the legs, *trunkless* immediately undermines the power of the legs by stating they have no body. |
| *half sunk* (adverbs) lies | The face part of the sculpture is already sinking into oblivion. |
| *shattered* visage (adjective) | The face is not just broken; it is shattered. |
| *wrinkled* lip | *Wrinkled* is often associated with old and withered. |
| *cold* command | The ruler's command lacked empathy for those he ruled. |
| *lifeless* things | The sculpture is lifeless, despite the glory it may try to express. |
| *Round the decay / Of that colossal Wreck* (adverb phrases modifying the verb *stretch* and the adjective *colossal* modifying Wreck) | All the modifiers point to the decay and ruin of the once-huge statue. |
| *Boundless and bare, lone and level* modify "sands" (adjectives) | All the modifiers create the vision of an endless desert, emphasizing the irony of the inscription on the monument. |
| **Overall Effect on Reader:** The repeated, persistent modifiers pointing out ruin, decay, and barrenness make the inscription ironic. While Ozymandias lived, he hoped that others would look on his mighty works and despair that they could never create anything so grand. To the traveler and anyone else looking at the ruins in the present, the source of the despair changes: No matter how mighty your earthly creations may be, they will all come to ruin in time. | |

Table 5-5

## Hyperbole and Understatement

Sometimes a writer may take a description a step further to create emphasis or to intensify an attitude or perspective. **Hyperbole**, an exaggerated statement not meant to be taken seriously, provides emphasis for the subject being described. In fact, the word actually means to "overthrow" or "go too far," and that is exactly what a hyperbole does. It takes something too far to emphasize it, as W. H. Auden does in "As I Walked Out One Evening."

> I'll love you, dear, I'll love you
> Till China and Africa meet,
> And the river jumps over the mountain
> And the salmon sing in the street.

Everybody knows that even in an eternity China and Africa will never meet and salmon will never sing in the street. The lines convey through hyperbole how long the speaker's love will last.

Poets also use **understatement,** a literary technique whose purpose is to intentionally make a subject seem less important than it is. Although it is in some ways the opposite of hyperbole, its effect is much the same—to show the real strength or importance of the subject. Read the following poem by Robert Frost.

### FIRE AND ICE

> Some say the world will end in fire,
> Some say in ice.
> From what I've tasted of desire
> I hold with those who favor fire.
> But if I had to perish twice,
> I think I know enough of hate
> To say that for destruction ice
> Is also great
> And would suffice.

The subject of the poem is the destruction of the world, yet the speaker considers the options between fire and ice with the same tone as if they were choices between buying an iOS or an Android phone: "I see the point of those who favor the iOS, but if I could buy two the Android would also be sufficient." Such phrases as "those who favor," "is also great," "And would suffice" are the kinds of phrases used in everyday speech about everyday things. That they are used in the context of the destruction of the world understates the power of desire and hate to destroy the world.

 **Remember:** Descriptive words, such as adjectives and adverbs, qualify or modify the things they describe and affect readers' interaction with the text. Hyperbole exaggerates while understatement minimizes. Exaggerating or minimizing an aspect of an object focuses attention on that trait and conveys a perspective about the object. (FIG-1.M–N)

## 2.2 Checkpoint

*Reread the poem "Dulce et Decorum Est" on page 283. Then complete the following open-response activities and answer the multiple-choice question.*

1. Pay special attention to adjectives and adverbs that modify people and objects you are learning about in the poem. On separate paper, recreate Table 5-5 to examine how some of those modifiers affect your reading or reveal perspectives or attitudes in the poem.

2. Reread the poem again, this time paying particular attention to any examples of hyperbole or understatement. Examine how some of those affect your reading or reveal perspectives or attitudes in the poem.

3. In line 23 ("Obscene . . . cud"), the word *Obscene* most directly indicates that the speaker

   (A) lets the memories of these events greatly affect him and prevent him from living morally

   (B) is offended by the idea of going to war to die for his country

   (C) fears that the gas will cause cancer in him and the other men with whom he is fighting

   (D) expresses worry that the gas will spread unchecked around the battlefield

   (E) finds the pain and cruelty experienced by the other soldier immoral, even in war

**Creating on Your Own**

Review the writing you did in earlier Creating on Your Own activities. Identify a line that needs an adjective for description and choose an adjective that conveys a perspective you intend. Look for another line where exaggeration (hyperbole) or understatement might make your point effectively. Try to make all your choices support the same perspective or set of ideas you are trying to convey. Save your work.

# Part 2 Apply What You Have Learned

Read the poems in the Poetry Gallery of this unit (or Unit 2 or 8) and choose one to examine more closely. Write a paragraph or series of paragraphs in which you identify, examine, and explain how words with multiple meanings, modifiers, and hyperbole or understatement work to affect the reading of the poem and your interpretation of its ideas.

**Reflect on the Essential Question** Write a brief response that answers the essential question: *What are the effects of literal and figurative language?* In your answer, correctly use the key terms listed on page 300.

# Part 3

# Imagery

**Enduring Understanding and Skill**

### Part 2  Imagery

**Understand**

Comparisons, representations, and associations shift meaning from the literal to the figurative and invite readers to interpret a text. (FIG-1)

**Demonstrate**

Identify and explain the function of an image or imagery. (5.D)
See also Unit 7

**Source:** *AP® English Literature and Composition Course and Exam Description*

**Essential Question:** What is the function of imagery?

You encounter the world with your senses, and when they are activated by something familiar, you recall a particular time or place or event associated with what you sense. Sometimes people use the phrase "it brings to mind" to indicate what they are thinking of in relation to what they are sensing. Certain memories and images are brought to the front of the mind by certain triggers of our senses.

Take, for example, the smell of Play-Doh®. Some scientific research has shown that scent is the sense most linked to memory. Play-Doh has its unique smell—if you played with it as a child, you can no doubt recognize it immediately. This unique smell is so important in reminding people of their childhood that Hasbro®, the company that owns Play-Doh, actually trademarked the smell in 2017 so that unique smell would always be associated only with their product.

Like Hasbro, authors and poets know the power of the senses. Though you may often hear the word applied to something you can see, in literature and writing **image** refers to all the sensory perceptions that bring together memories based on earlier experiences with sights, smells, sounds, tastes, textures, and feelings of motion.

An image refers to a single instance in which an author may include a detail that "brings to mind" some association by appealing to sense. **Imagery**, however, is a literary device writers use to present multiple sensory images throughout a text or related texts, often through figurative language.

image                          imagery

# 3.1 Images and Imagery | FIG-1.O, FIG-1.P, FIG-1.Q

Like all other figurative language, imagery works by relying on associations that the reader brings to the text. Poets count on these associations as they provide sensory images in the text. The images awaken those associations as readers bring to mind memories that make the poet's words vividly alive.

Reread the poem "Stopping by Woods on a Snowy Evening" on page 301.

**Source:** Getty Images

Look closely at the images provided throughout this poem. There are images related to seeing ("watch his woods fill up with snow," line 4), to hearing ("gives his harness bells a shake," line 9, and "the sweep / Of easy wind and downy flake" lines 11–12), and possibly even to perceiving motion ("He gives his harness bells a shake," line 9).

Simply identifying the image, though, does not deepen your understanding or interpretation of a poem. That requires examining and explaining how it contributes to meaning in the poem.

Images, like words, can be both literal and figurative based on how they are used in a text. Describing the literal falling of snow or the shake of a horse's harness bells fits appropriately in the context of the poem and helps to develop the situation of the text. Both images might have figurative meaning as well. For example, the mesmerizing quiet of the falling snow in the isolated woods may cause the speaker to stop and contemplate his surroundings in a fresh way;

the jangle of the horse's bells may serve to "shake" the speaker out of his reverie and remind him of everyday doings.

The table below shows one way to examine images in a poem.

| Examining Images | |
| --- | --- |
| **Image** | **Association** |
| **1)** "watch his woods fill up with snow" (line 4) | The slow accumulation of snow on the branches of trees and on the forest floor, seeing it pile against tree trunks as the wind blows it about |
| *What might this image suggest in the context of the poem?* | |
| Stopping to watch the "woods fill up with snow" would take a while as the snow often falls slowly and piles up very slowly, so the speaker would be seeing nature overwhelm the forest. | |
| **2)** "the sweep / Of easy wind and downy flake." (lines 11–12) | Easy wind blowing downy (feather-like) snowflakes makes a noise, but it is a very quiet noise that takes place amidst a general hush and almost seems to emphasize the quiet. |
| *What might this image suggest in the context of the poem?* | |
| These sounds contribute to the hush of the speaker's solitude because there are no other sounds, especially since line 6 provides the detail that there is no "farmhouse near." So this image contributes to the isolation of the speaker. | |
| **3)** "He gives his harness bells a shake" (line 9) | The jangle of the bells is by far the loudest sound in the poem. The speaker interprets this action as the horse asking if there is some mistake in their stopping. |
| *What might this image suggest in the context of the poem?* | |
| The speaker interprets the horse's jangle in a way that suggests the horse is not accustomed to stopping in the woods like this. This interpretation may show that something peculiar or unexpected is happening in the life of the speaker. | |

Table 5-6

Each of these images contributes in its unique way to an understanding of the situation of the poem, but you probably noticed that they all overlap in some way. To talk about them all would be to discuss the *imagery* of the poem. Recall that imagery is a collective term used to describe how the individual images work together in a text. Nonetheless, to truly appreciate the effect of the imagery, you need to see what role each individual image plays in the whole.

 **Remember:** Descriptive words, such as adjectives and adverbs, contribute to sensory imagery. An image can be literal or it can be a form of a comparison that represents something in a text through associations with the senses. A collection of images, known as imagery, may emphasize ideas in parts of or throughout a text. (FIG-1.O–Q)

### 3.1 Checkpoint

*Reread the poem "Dulce et Decorum Est" on page 283. Then complete the following open-response activity and answer the multiple-choice question.*

1. Pay particular attention to individual images and the imagery in general. Examine some of the individual images and what they contribute to the poem and then briefly explain how those images work together as a body of imagery in the poem. You may want to organize your thoughts with a chart like Table 5-6.

2. The image in line 24 ("Of vile . . . tongues") most clearly serves to associate war with

    (A) experience of pain and loss

    (B) destruction of the young and innocent

    (C) glory and sacrifice for one's own country

    (D) victory in the face of considerable odds

    (E) honor given more to those who die than to those who survive

**Creating on Your Own**
Look over the writing you did in previous Creating on Your Own activities. You likely already have several images throughout your writing that help communicate ideas. Review and revise those as you seek to create some consistent imagery.

Also consider developing some different imagery to help communicate multiple perspectives on ideas at the same time. Save your work.

# Part 3 Apply What You Have Learned

Read the poems in the Poetry Gallery of this unit (or Unit 2 or 8) and choose one to examine more closely. Write a paragraph or series of paragraphs in which you identify, examine, and explain imagery, the individual images that comprise it, and how they relate to an interpretation. Be certain to cite specific line numbers and explain your thinking to your reader.

> **Reflect on the Essential Question** Write a brief response that answers the essential question: *What is the function of imagery?* In your answer, correctly use the key terms listed on page 310.

# Figures of Speech

**Enduring Understanding and Skills**

## Part 4  Figures of Speech

### Understand
Comparisons, representations, and associations shift meaning from the literal to the figurative and invite readers to interpret a text. (FIG-1)

### Demonstrate
Identify and explain the function of a metaphor. (6.B)
Identify and explain the function of personification. (6.C)
Identify and explain the function of an allusion. (6.D)
See also Unit 2

**Source:** *AP® English Literature and Composition Course and Exam Description*

**Essential Question:** What is the function of a metaphor, personification, and allusion?

**Source:** Getty Images

*What can you compare to a roller coaster? Also, how could you describe riding a roller coaster to someone who has never ridden one? What unlikely thing could you compare to a roller coaster?*

"You climb, you fall. You rise again only to crash to the bottom while people just scream and cry around you. In the end, though it may make you sick to your stomach, all you can do is smile."

This statement describes the life experience of many people—ups, downs, screams, tears, and smiles as you experience the challenges and joys of life.

This statement also describes riding a roller coaster, climbing the hill, going over the top, and then doing it again as the passengers scream and even cry. You end the ride a little queasy, but you enjoyed the ride.

Life is a roller coaster.

That is a **metaphor**, a figure of speech that implies similarities between two (usually unrelated) subjects in order to reveal or emphasize one or more qualities or features about one of them. In this case, it takes the traits of a roller coaster ride and uses them to communicate a perspective on life. Metaphors and other *figures of speech,* as they are called, make comparisons to help explain unfamiliar things or to describe unique perspectives on a subject. (See Unit 2.) If a metaphor runs through a longer portion of the text with additional details contributing to the comparison, then it is an **extended metaphor.**

Similes are like metaphors, but similes use the words *like* or *as* to make a comparison, while metaphors just state an equivalency: "Life is a roller coaster," not "Life is *like* a roller coaster."

If a figure of speech attributes human qualities to nonhuman subjects, that technique is called **personification.**

If a figure refers to some text, story, or myth or to some other information from a source outside of the main text to highlight a comparison between the original text and the outside text, that figure is an **allusion**.

The key to all these is that the subject being compared has certain traits associated with it that are meant to describe or transfer to the subject with which it is being compared.

These comparisons all rely on figurative language. Life is not literally a roller coaster, but some things people associate with roller coasters help to describe some parts of life. Without figurative language and the associations they bring to mind, no figure of speech would work.

---

**KEY TERMS**

metaphor                personification           allusion
extended metaphor

---

# 4.1 Metaphors | FIG-1.R, FIG-1.S, FIG-1.T, FIG-1.U

Several years ago, astronaut Buzz Aldrin, one of the first people to walk on the Moon, was asked to describe the view of Earth from space. The interviewer had asked Aldrin to do something that was actually very difficult: communicate the awe and grandeur of seeing our planet from space. He replied, "It was a brilliant jewel in the black velvet sky."

How else was he to describe something that fewer than 600 people (as of late 2020) had ever seen? By comparing Earth to the "brilliant jewel" and the backdrop of space to "black velvet," he was able to both describe the uncommon beauty of the scene and communicate his perspective on the precious rarity of Earth and the depth and beauty of space.

This example demonstrates the strength of metaphors. They not only help the reader understand a speaker's perspective, but they also contribute to the reader's own understanding and perspective on the subject or idea being described.

**Source:** NASA

The first photograph of Earth as a whole was taken on Dec. 7, 1972, by scientist-astronaut Harrison H. Schmitt, a member of the Apollo 17 crew on their way to complete NASA's final mission to land on the Moon.

Read this poem by African American author Langston Hughes (1902–1967) published in 1922.

## MOTHER TO HER SON

> Well, son, I'll tell you:
> Life for me ain't been no crystal stair.
> It's had tacks in it,
> And splinters,
> 5  And boards torn up,
> And places with no carpet on the floor—
> Bare.
> But all the time
> I'se been a-climbin' on,
> 10  And reachin' landin's,
> And turnin' corners,
> And sometimes goin' in the dark
> Where there ain't been no light.
> So boy, don't you turn back.
> 15  Don't you set down on the steps
> 'Cause you finds it's kinder hard.
> Don't you fall now—
> For I'se still goin', honey,
> I'se still climbin',
> 20  And life for me ain't been no crystal stair.

The speaker of the poem uses a clear metaphor to address her son, "Life for [her] ain't been no crystal stair[case]." It may be considered a sort of *anti-metaphor* since she is not actually saying life *is* a crystal staircase but saying it *isn't*. However, the comparison still functions as a metaphor. Consider what might be the traits of a crystal staircase:

1. Beautiful

2. Shining / Sparkling

3. Reminiscent of a fairy tale—Cinderella, for example

4. Has stairs—you climb them up or down (but she is going up, lines 9 and 19)

The speaker rejects the first three traits when she says her life "ain't been" that way. The fourth, however, still applies as she explains she's "been a-climbin'" and is "still climbin'. "

If the poem stopped at line 2, Hughes would have provided an effective metaphor for the struggle of the speaker. Life hasn't been beautiful or sparkling, and sometimes you go up and sometimes you go down. But Hughes keeps going; 18 more lines describe climbing stairs that are not crystalline.

In this way, the author goes from using a metaphor to developing an extended metaphor, a metaphor that extends through the text and continues to develop as more details and images are provided. Because of the additional material, extended metaphors allow an author to communicate more of the perspective and often exert more control over the perceptions and perspective of the reader.

Consider the additional details readers learn about the speaker in this poem. Once the speaker has said what her life has *not* been, she describes what it *has* been. The staircase of her life has "had tacks in it, / And splinters, / And boards torn up, / And places with no carpet on the floor— / Bare." This description demonstrates her real perspective on her life.

The staircase of the speaker's life has/is:

1. tacks in it

2. splinters

3. no carpet

4. bare

5. landings

6. corners

7. dark

The details of the extended metaphor provide the traits to transfer to the speaker's life. The first two are pain, the second two could be slips or emptiness or just something hard, while the last three could be the stops and surprises and fears she has encountered. You could connect these details to the life of the speaker in multiple ways, but the point of the poem remains the same as she explains in the final lines of the poem. Just because you hurt and feel empty or alone and there are barriers in your way slowing you down, you cannot quit— she is still going.

This poem allows you to see how a simple metaphor could be effective by itself and also how an extended metaphor can sometimes add depth to a poem's meaning. Authors can decide if they want to control the perspective being developed or to leave their metaphors open for interpretation.

 **Remember:** Metaphorical comparisons do not focus solely on the objects being compared; they focus on the particular traits, qualities, or characteristics of the things being compared. Comparisons not only communicate literal meaning but may also convey figurative meaning or transmit a perspective. An extended metaphor is created when the comparison of a main subject and comparison subject persists through parts of or an entire text, and when the comparison is expanded through additional details, similes, and images. Interpretation of an extended metaphor may depend on the context of its use; that is, what is happening in a text may determine what is transferred in the comparison. (FIG-1.R–1.U)

### 4.1 Checkpoint

*Reread the poem "Dulce et Decorum Est" on page 283. Then complete the following open-response activity and answer the multiple-choice question.*

1. Lines 6 and 7 contain metaphors. Identify them and write a paragraph explaining their effect on the poem.

2. The metaphor in line 7 emphasizes which of the following?

    (A) The stupefying pain and loss of the war effort

    (B) The stumbling and witless exhaustion of the men

    (C) The drunken celebrations when the war is over

    (D) The foolish and irresponsible behavior of the men

    (E) The impaired state of the men who enlisted

**Creating on Your Own**

Review the writing you did in previous Creating on Your Own activities. Look for opportunities to use the strength of a metaphor, or even an extended metaphor, to better communicate or develop a perspective, and then revise to include a metaphor or extended metaphor. Save your work.

# 4.2 Personification | FIG-1.V

A common way of describing subjects, personification does exactly what its name implies: it "person-ifies" the subject it is describing. It gives human traits to the object or concept so that the narrator, speaker, or reader—as a person— can better understand the subject being described. It also adds insight into the person in the poem who is attributing those human qualities and who may be projecting his or her feelings onto the nonhuman subject.

Read this poem written by English poet William Wordsworth (1770–1850) in 1807.

### I WANDERED LONELY AS A CLOUD

    I wandered lonely as a cloud
    That floats on high o'er vales and hills,
    When all at once I saw a crowd,
    A host, of golden daffodils;
 5  Beside the lake, beneath the trees,
    Fluttering and dancing in the breeze.

Continuous as the stars that shine
And twinkle on the milky way,
They stretched in never-ending line
10  Along the margin of a bay:
Ten thousand saw I at a glance,
Tossing their heads in sprightly dance.

The waves beside them danced; but they
Out-did the sparkling waves in glee:
15  A poet could not but be gay,
In such a jocund¹ company:
I gazed—and gazed—but little thought
What wealth the show to me had brought:

For oft, when on my couch I lie
20  In vacant or in pensive mood,
They flash upon that inward eye
Which is the bliss of solitude;
And then my heart with pleasure fills,
And dances with the daffodils.

The title itself, taken from the first line, personifies the cloud as lonely. A cloud cannot be lonely. You may need a minute to even imagine a cloud as lonely, but the image of a single cloud in a vast sky floating "high o'er [valleys] and hills" soon settles in. The personification of the cloud as lonely then brings you to see the speaker as lonely as that cloud. In this way, the first line works as a simile with the personification. Once you accept that a cloud can be lonely, you can transfer that trait back to the speaker.

Personification elsewhere in the poem helps the reader connect emotionally with the images it brings to mind. The "dancing" of the daffodils "tossing their heads" might bring to mind such actions that the reader had witnessed or experienced and elicit the feelings of joy or celebration associated with such dancing. In this way, the adverb "sprightly" emphasizes these positive associations. The personified waves also dance, but not as well as the daffodils, which are again personified in their "glee." All of these instances bring to mind the readers' own associations and help readers understand the perspective of the speaker. At the end, readers see that the speaker's own heart "dances with the daffodils" and can understand some part of his pleasure.

 **Remember:** Personification is a type of comparison that assigns a human trait or quality to a nonhuman object, entity, or idea, thus characterizing that object, entity, or idea (FIG-1.V).

---

1  **jocund:** cheerful or merry

### 4.2 Checkpoint

*Reread the poem "Dulce et Decorum Est" on page 283. Then complete the following open-response activity and answer the multiple-choice question.*

1. Identify instances of personification in the poem. In a paragraph, explain how that personification could affect an interpretation of the poem.

2. In line 8 ("Of tired ... behind"), personification seems to indicate that
   - (A) nothing can frighten these men any more
   - (B) the men no longer care about one another
   - (C) exhaustion controls the men's lives
   - (D) even the weapons are tired of war
   - (E) the enemy is running low on ammunition

**Creating on Your Own**

Once again review the poem you have been developing throughout this unit. Where could you personify a subject or concept to better develop a perspective on it? Try revising a few different places to add personification. Save your work.

# 4.3 Allusion | FIG-1.W

As a figure of speech, allusion is sometimes the most complicated because it requires you to have knowledge of myths or sacred texts; works of art including paintings, music, and other literature; or people, places, or events outside the text. In some ways, this requirement is not so different from that of a metaphor. In the example of the roller coaster, if readers have never seen or even heard of a roller coaster, then they will not understand the metaphor. If readers are not familiar with the outside work to which an allusion refers, it becomes a secretive figure of speech.

Some people who study literature for a living become experts at spotting these. Other readers, whose knowledge of life or literature is more limited, need to rely on footnotes and Google.

Using allusions is a way to connect a text to a certain part of the world or a certain tradition. Like other figures of speech, an allusion works by transferring something about the work being referenced to the subject it is being compared to or the situation of the text in general.

Read the poem on the next page by African American poet Rita Dove (1952–), published in 1995.

# PERSEPHONE, FALLING

One narcissus among the ordinary beautiful
flowers, one unlike all the others! She pulled,
stooped to pull harder—
when, sprung out of the earth
5   on his glittering terrible
carriage, he claimed his due.
It is finished. No one heard her.
No one! She had strayed from the herd.

(Remember: go straight to school.
10  This is important, stop fooling around!
Don't answer to strangers. Stick
with your playmates. Keep your eyes down.)
This is how easily the pit
opens. This is how one foot sinks into the ground.

Now, consider the myth which is the source of the allusion in the poem.

**The story of Persephone from Greek Myth:** Persephone was the goddess of plant life. She was the daughter of Zeus (king of the gods) and Demeter (the goddess of the harvest). One day, she was in a meadow picking flowers with her friends when she encountered a single narcissus flower among the other wildflowers. As she stooped to pick this flower, the ground opened up and she was taken by Hades (god of the underworld and afterlife) so quickly that no others saw it happen. When her mother eventually learned what happened, she was so distraught that her despair killed all of the crops on Earth. Zeus took pity on Earth and forced Hades to return Persephone, but Hades tricked her into eating a pomegranate seed while in the underworld. Because of that act, she was made to spend a third of the year with Hades and only two-thirds of the year on Earth with Demeter. This myth is used to explain the seasons. When the goddess of plant life is in the underworld for three months, everything dies and winter sets in. When she returns, spring comes and then summer, but as she prepares to leave the earth for the underworld, summer gives way to autumn.

You can now probably see how the allusion to Persephone works in the poem. The title is a hint, but the details provided in the two stanzas solidify it. The kidnapping of Persephone becomes a warning from the speaker to the child addressed directly in the second stanza.

This allusion works a bit differently from most other allusions because the poet provides details that let you know what aspect of the myth to focus on. However, other parts of the work alluded to may also be relevant to the poem. The grief of the mother, likely the speaker of the poem, might be similar to that of Demeter if the child she addresses in the second stanza did not listen. This is just one example of how any number of traits related to the origin of the allusion could transfer to the text and your understanding of it.

Source: Getty Images

*These are narcissus flowers, also known as daffodils or jonquils. For another allusion, look up the myth of Narcissus. What meaning might an allusion to Narcissus convey? What perspective might it help communicate?*

 **Remember:** Allusions in a text can reference literary works including myths and sacred texts; other works of art including paintings and music; or people, places, or events outside the text. (FIG-1.W)

## 4.3 Checkpoint

*Reread the poem "Dulce et Decorum Est" on page 283. Then complete the following open-response activity and answer the multiple-choice question.*

1. The most significant allusion in the poem is the Latin phrase that makes up the title and the last two lines of the poem. Consider the origin of the phrase, from the Roman poet Horace, who wrote:

> How sweet and fitting it is to die for one's country.
> Yet death chases after the soldier who runs,
> And it won't spare the cowardly back
> Or the limbs of peace-loving young men.

In a paragraph, explain how this origin reflects and affects a perspective on war as it is used in Owen's poem.

**2.** The allusion to a devil in line 20 ("His . . . sin;") primarily serves to suggest

    (A) the resemblance between gruesome death and the devil's face

    (B) moral ambiguity about sacrificing in war and living life to its fullest

    (C) the joy that evil finds in war and painful sacrifice

    (D) the absurdity of war since even a devil is sickened by the sin of such loss

    (E) the fear of being condemned in death for sacrificing one's life

**Creating on Your Own**

Revisit the writing you did earlier in the unit. Try adding one or more allusions. Consider a text, something from history, or even something from pop culture that you could reference in your poem to activate some knowledge and associations in your reader. Save your work.

# Part 4 Apply What You Have Learned

Read the poems in the Poetry Gallery of this unit (or Unit 2 or 8) and choose one to examine more closely. Write a paragraph or series of paragraphs in which you identify, examine, and explain figures of speech within it. Remember, it is never enough to simply identify them—always try to interpret their effect on the reader. Be certain to cite specific line numbers and explain your thinking to your reader.

> **Reflect on the Essential Question** Write a brief response that answers the essential question: *What is the function of a metaphor, personification, and allusion?* In your answer, correctly use the key terms listed on page 314.

# POETRY GALLERY

## AMORETTI XXX
### BY EDMUND SPENSER (1552–1599)

My Love is like to ice, and I to fire:
How comes it then that this her cold so great
Is not dissolved through my so hot desire,
But harder grows the more I her entreat?

5   Or how comes it that my exceeding heat
Is not allayed by her heart-frozen cold,
But that I burn much more in boiling sweat,
And feel my flames augmented manifold?

What more miraculous thing may be told,
10  That fire, which all things melts, should harden ice,
And ice, which is congeal'd with senseless cold,
Should kindle fire by wonderful device?

Such is the power of love in gentle mind,
That it can alter all the course of kind.

## LOVE AND FRIENDSHIP
### BY EMILY BRONTË (1818–1848), WRITTEN IN 1839

Love is like the wild rose-briar,
Friendship like the holly-tree—
The holly is dark when the rose-briar blooms
But which will bloom most constantly?

5   The wild rose-briar is sweet in spring,
Its summer blossoms scent the air;
Yet wait till winter comes again
And who will call the wild-briar fair?

Then scorn the silly rose-wreath now
10  And deck thee with the holly's sheen,
That when December blights thy brow
He still may leave thy garland green.

## ODE ON SOLITUDE
### BY ALEXANDER POPE (1688–1744), WRITTEN IN 1700

Happy the man, whose wish and care
  A few paternal acres bound,
Content to breathe his native air,
    In his own ground.

5     Whose herds with milk, whose fields with bread,
  Whose flocks supply him with attire,
Whose trees in summer yield him shade,
    In winter fire.

Blest, who can unconcernedly find
10   Hours, days, and years slide soft away,
In health of body, peace of mind,
    Quiet by day,

Sound sleep by night; study and ease,
  Together mixed; sweet recreation;
And innocence, which most does please,
    With meditation.

Thus let me live, unseen, unknown;
  Thus unlamented let me die;
Steal from the world, and not a stone
    Tell where I lie.

**Source:** Getty Images

## NUNS FRET NOT
### BY WILLIAM WORDSWORTH (1770–1850)

Nuns fret not at their convent's narrow room;
And hermits are contented with their cells;
And students with their pensive citadels;
Maids at the wheel, the weaver at his loom,

5    Sit blithe and happy; bees that soar for bloom,
High as the highest Peak of Furness-fells,[1]
Will murmur by the hour in foxglove bells:[2]
In truth the prison, into which we doom

Ourselves no prison is: and hence for me,
10   In sundry moods, 'twas pastime to be bound
Within the Sonnet's scanty plot of ground;

Pleased if some Souls (for such there needs must be)
Who have felt the weight of too much liberty,
Should find brief solace there, as I have found.

---

1 **Furness-fells:** A group of hills and mountains in Cumbria, England
2 **foxglove bells:** small bell-shaped flowers on the foxglove plant

## HOPE.
### BY EMILY DICKINSON (1830–1886), PUBLISHED IN 1891

Hope is the thing with feathers
That perches in the soul,
And sings the tune without the words,
And never stops at all,

5    And sweetest in the gale is heard;
And sore must be the storm
That could abash the little bird
That kept so many warm.

I've heard it in the chillest land,
10   And on the strangest sea;
Yet, never, in extremity,
It asked a crumb of me.

## IF WE MUST DIE
### BY CLAUDE MCKAY (1889–1948), PUBLISHED IN 1919

If we must die, let it not be like hogs
Hunted and penned in an inglorious spot,
While round us bark the mad and hungry dogs,
Making their mock at our accursèd lot.

5    If we must die, O let us nobly die,
So that our precious blood may not be shed
In vain; then even the monsters we defy
Shall be constrained to honor us though dead!

O kinsmen! we must meet the common foe!
10   Though far outnumbered let us show us brave,
And for their thousand blows deal one death-blow!
What though before us lies the open grave?

Like men we'll face the murderous, cowardly pack,
Pressed to the wall, dying, but fighting back!

## ELEGY FOR A WOMAN OF NO IMPORTANCE
### BY NAZIK AL-MALAIKA (1923–2007), PUBLISHED 1968

She died, but no lips shook, no cheeks turned white
no doors heard her death tale told and retold,
no blinds were raised for small eyes to behold
the casket as it disappeared from sight.
5    Only a beggar in the street, consumed
by hunger, heard the echo of her life—
the safe forgetfulness of tombs,
the melancholy of the moon.

The night gave way to morning thoughtlessly,
10   and light brought with it sound—boys throwing stones,
a hungry, mewling cat, all skin and bones,
the vendors fighting, clashing bitterly,
some people fasting, others wanting more,
polluted water gurgling, and a breeze
15   playing, alone, upon the door
having almost forgotten her.

## MEXICAN AMERICAN SONNET
### BY ILIANA ROCHA, PUBLISHED IN 2019

We have the same ankles, hips, nipples, knees—
our bodies bore the forks/tenedors
we use to eat. What do we eat? Darkness
from cathedral floors,

5      the heart's woe in abundance. Please let us
go through the world touching what we want,
knock things over. Slap & kick & punch
until we get something right. ¿Verdad?[1]

Isn't it true, my father always asks.
10     Your father is the ghost of mine & vice
versa. & when did our pasts
stop recognizing themselves? It was always like

us to first person: yo.[2] To disrupt a hurricane's
path with our own inwardness.
15     C'mon huracán, you watery migraine,
prove us wrong for once. This sadness

lasts/esta tristeza perdura. Say it both ways
so language doesn't bite back, but stays.

---

1   **¿Verdad?**: Spanish for "truth" or, with questions marks, "Right?"
2   **yo**: Spanish for "I"

## COMO TÚ / LIKE YOU / LIKE ME
### BY RICHARD BLANCO (1968–), PUBLISHED IN 2019

{for the D.A.C.A DREAMers and all our nation's immigrants}

> *. . . my veins don't end in me*
> *but in the unanimous blood*
> *of those who struggle for life . . .*
>
> *. . . mis venas no terminan en mí*
> *sino en la sangre unánime*
> *de los que luchan por la vida . . .*
>
> —*Roque Dalton, Como tú*[1]

Como tú,[2] I question history's blur in my eyes
each time I face a mirror. Like a mirror, I gaze
into my palm a wrinkled map I still can't read,
my lifeline an unnamed road I can't find, can't

5    trace back to the fork in my parents' trek
that cradled me here. Como tú, I woke up to
this dream of a country I didn't choose, that
didn't choose me—trapped in the nightmare
of its hateful glares. Como tú, I'm also from

10   the lakes and farms, waterfalls and prairies
of another country I can't fully claim either.
Como tú, I am either a mirage living among
these faces and streets that raised me here,
or I'm nothing, a memory forgotten by all

15   I was taken from and can't return to again.

Like memory, at times I wish I could erase
the music of my name in Spanish, at times
I cherish it, and despise my other syllables
clashing in English. Como tú, I want to speak

20   of myself in two languages at once. Despite
my tongues, no word defines me. Like words,
I read my footprints like my past, erased by
waves of circumstance, my future uncertain
as wind. Like the wind, como tú, I carry songs,

25   howls, whispers, thunder's growl. Like thunder,
I'm a foreign-borne cloud that's drifted here,
I'm lightning, and the balm of rain. Como tú,
our blood rains for the dirty thirst of this land.
Like thirst, like hunger, we ache with the need

30   to save ourselves, and our country from itself.

---

1 The lines in dark type are from the poem "Like You" by Roque Dalton.
2 **Como tú:** Spanish for "like you"

## TRIPLE SONNET FOR BLACK HAIR
### BY DOROTHY CHAN, PUBLISHED IN 2019

My mother warns me not to blow-dry my hair
    too hard, turning it from black to rust, and
I must wear my black hair proudly. Black,
    the color of clothing my grandmother hates,
5    because young women should always wear red
    or pink, the colors of luck and youth. Black,
the color of wedding dress the reality TV
    starlet circa 2006 wants, but she knows
walking down the aisle in black will break
10    her mother's heart, and fact: red is the color
of wedding dresses in Chinese culture—even
    if the bride wears white for the ceremony,
she'll change into red for the dinner—hello,
    ten course meal of my dreams that starts

15    with a meat platter of roasted pork, and how
guests go crazy for the abalone and swallow's
    nest soup with crab meat, and of course there's
a chicken, a pig, a fish, a duck, and a lobster—
    roll call. And fact: at Chinese funerals, relatives
20    of the deceased don't wear black, but white.
    And fact: eight's the lucky Chinese number,
not seven, and at dim sum, my grandmother
    makes sure she orders eight dishes, not seven,
but nine's alright too. Eight, like the number of
    legs on a spider—a spider, black, like my hair
25    that my mother warns me not to blow-dry
    too hard, turning it into rust, and I remember
my sixth-grade science experiment of lighting

a cigarette, watching how the smoke changed
30    the spider's web spinning. And black, because
it's hypnotic, like little black dresses on gorgeous
    women, or how I prefer my lingerie in black
over white, but red is probably the best, an ode
    to sexiness—an ode to the color of my culture
and history, and I want to feel like a million
35    dollars—be a million dollars. And black, the color
of my late dog, Buzzie, a Skye Terrier, twice as long
    as he was low, my mother once, joking, said he looked
like a giant rat. Or a licorice bunny. Or a furry snake.
    Or a dragon in some iterations of love, majestic in
40    dreams—how I miss him after these dream visits,
    black, the color of my wet hair in the morning

# Writing About Literature V

**Enduring Understanding and Skills**

## Part 5  Writing About Literature V

### Understand
Readers establish and communicate their interpretations of literature through arguments supported by textual evidence. (LAN-1)

### Demonstrate
Develop a thesis statement that conveys a defensible claim about an interpretation of literature and that may establish a line of reasoning. (7.B)

Develop commentary that establishes and explains relationships among textual evidence, the line of reasoning, and the thesis. (7.C)

Select and use relevant and sufficient evidence to both develop and support a line of reasoning. (7.D)

Demonstrate control over the elements of composition to communicate clearly. (7.E)

See also Units 1, 2, 3, 4, 6, 7, 8 & 9

**Source:** *AP* English Literature and Composition Course and Exam Description

**Essential Question:**  How can you communicate a written interpretation of a poem by expressing a thesis statement, using sufficient evidence and commentary to support your line of reasoning, and using transitional elements?

Is "Stopping by Woods on a Snowy Evening" a poem about a man who is tired of life and contemplates giving up in the "dark and deep" woods? Is it a poem about a man who wants to make the most of a mystical moment before moving on to the everyday obligations of life? Is it a poem about the thrill of creating a "reckless" rhyme scheme and trying to make it work? All of these interpretations, and many more, have been offered about Frost's famous poem. For many people, the pleasures of poetry are enhanced by opportunities to share them—and share interpretations—with others who love poetry as they do.

Most of the sharing of interpretations takes place through the written word in essays and articles. If you have completed previous units of this book, you will have had some practice in building a written interpretation or argument of a literary work. This section will provide more practice.

# 5.1 Thesis Statement and Line of Reasoning | LAN 1.D, LAN-1.E

You may not have realized it at the time, but with every reading and rereading of a poem, a unique position on the poem has gradually been coming into focus in your mind. Maybe it starts with an emotional response—why do those last two lines bring tears to your eyes? Maybe it starts with a pattern you hear when you read the poem aloud. Maybe you've puzzled and puzzled and puzzled over the meaning of the poem and finally see an interpretation that makes good sense to you. However you arrive at it, the **thesis statement** of a written argument lays out the interpretation of a literary text that you will defend through the use of textual evidence and a line of reasoning, both of which are explained in an essay through commentary.

## Goals of a Thesis Statement

The thesis statement is the overarching claim of your argument. A strong thesis statement is broad enough to frame the rest of your essay and to generate supporting claims that will help you defend your thesis. In fact, a thesis statement may even preview the claims and line of reasoning that will follow in your essay. Your **line of reasoning** is the logical sequence of claims that work together to defend the overarching thesis statement. Your line of reasoning shows how the evidence relates to your thesis and to other claims you may plan to make in the body of your essay.

Suppose, for example, your reading of "Dulce et Decorum Est" leads you to see a similarity between the wounded soldier and the narrator, as if just witnessing the horror has stolen any possible peace the surviving soldier might find after the war. You might write a working thesis statement such as the following:

> The horrors described in the first two stanzas of "Dulce et Decorum Est" take on an unending quality for the wounded soldier as well as for the haunted survivor who reports his dreams in the third and fourth stanzas.

This thesis presents an arguable position—some may disagree with the interpretation of the unending quality—and is broad enough to generate supporting claims that will form the basis of the paragraphs in the body of the essay. Further, it creates the expectation that the essay will move through the poem stanza by stanza with textual evidence for the details that make the experiences unending. In this way, it previews the line of reasoning of the essay. Not all thesis statements need to preview the line of reasoning. They also do not need to go into too much detail about the points of interpretation, literary elements, or specific evidence to be used in the argument.

 **Remember:** A thesis statement expresses an interpretation of a literary text and requires a defense through use of textual evidence and a line of reasoning, both of which are explained in an essay through commentary. A thesis statement may preview the development or line of reasoning of an interpretation. This is not to say that a thesis statement must list the points of an interpretation, literary elements to be analyzed, or specific evidence to be used in the argument. (LAN-1.D–G)

## 5.1 Checkpoint

Recall the route to a thesis statement (see Unit 4):

- Identify a big or universal idea in the text.
- Develop a general thematic statement related to that idea.
- Draft a thesis statement that ties the thematic statement directly to the text.

On separate paper, create a graphic organizer like the one below for "Dulce et Decorum Est," a poem from the Poetry Gallery, or another poem you are studying. Save your chart to add the supporting claims later, since you will return to this chart as you write your literary analysis.

| |
|---|
| **Text:** |
| **Big or Universal Ideas:** |
| **Thematic Statement:** |
| **Thesis Statement:** |
| **Supporting Claim 1:** |
| **Supporting Claim 2:** |
| **Supporting Claim 3:** |

**Composing on Your Own**

Evaluate your thesis statement. Does your thesis assert an arguable position that can be defended with evidence and commentary? Explain. Make any changes you believe will strengthen your thesis statement. Does it preview your line of reasoning? Write a brief explanation of your answer.

# 5.2 Line of Reasoning and Commentary | LAN-1.F, LAN-1.G

What might the line of reasoning look like to support the thesis statement about the unending horror of wars? Below is one example.

> The horrors described in the first two stanzas of "Dulce et Decorum Est" take on an unending quality for the wounded soldier as well as for the haunted survivor who reports his dreams in the third and fourth stanzas.
>
> **Supporting Claim 1:** The descriptions in the first stanza show constant though exhausted motion, with rest only "distant."
>
> **Supporting Claim 2:** The repeated use of the past progressive [-ing] form of the verbs in stanza 2 continues the unending feel.
>
> **Supporting Claim 3:** Stanzas 3 and 4 contain the most vivid horrors, which come to the narrator in his dreams which he cannot escape.

Typically, the claims that establish the line of reasoning frame the body of the essay, each claim forming the focus of at least one body paragraph and usually serving as a topic sentence. While it may be perfectly clear to the writer how the claims in the body support the thesis, readers need the line of reasoning spelled out clearly through **commentary**. Through commentary you show how you logically connect your overarching thesis statement and the claims and evidence within the body of your essay. Commentary becomes especially important in explaining how the textual evidence you provide defends the supporting claims as well as the thesis statement.

 **Remember:** A line of reasoning is the logical sequence of claims that work together to defend the overarching thesis statement. A line of reasoning is communicated through commentary that explains the logical relationship between the overarching thesis statement and the claims/evidence within the body of an essay. (LAN-1.F–G)

### 5.2 Checkpoint

Return to the chart you started in 5.1 Checkpoint. Sketch out your line of reasoning to support your thesis statement, and then take some time to word each supporting claim carefully to suggest its connection to the thesis statement. Save your completed chart for later use.

**Composing on Your Own**

Begin or continue gathering evidence to defend your supporting claims—your line of reasoning. You may use the template below for recording your evidence. Next to each piece of evidence, explain how it relates to your supporting claim. You may have more or fewer than three claims and three pieces of evidence for each one—adjust the chart accordingly.

| Claim | Evidence | Explanation |
|---|---|---|
| Supporting Claim 1 | 1. <br> 2. <br> 3. | 1. <br> 2. <br> 3. |
| Supporting Claim 2 | 1. <br> 2. <br> 3. | 1. <br> 2. <br> 3. |
| Supporting Claim 3 | 1. <br> 2. <br> 3. | 1. <br> 2. <br> 3. |

# 5.3 Effective Use of Evidence and Commentary

| LAN-1.H, LAN-1.I, LAN-1.J, LAN-1.K

Convincing arguments present sufficient high-quality evidence strategically and purposefully to illustrate, clarify, exemplify, associate, amplify, or qualify a point. However, without commentary to explain a logical relationship between the evidence and claim(s), even strategic and purposeful evidence cannot support a thesis alone.

## Strategic Evidence and Logical Connections

One way to evaluate the quality of your evidence is to assess how strategic and purposeful it is. (See Unit 3.)

Consider the evidence on "Dulce et Decorum Est" in the student draft on the following page. The sentences are numbered for reference.

(1) The horrors described in the first two stanzas of "Dulce et Decorum Est" take on an unending quality for the wounded soldier as well as for the haunted survivor who reports his dreams in the third and fourth stanzas.

(2) The descriptions in the first stanza show constant though exhausted motion, with rest only "distant." (3) The bent-over soldiers "cursed through sludge" until they decided to turn their backs on "the haunting flares," distress signals sent up by comrades in harm's way, and begin their "trudge" to "distant rest." (4) The soldiers march as if asleep. (5) Even the gas shells (the Five-Nines) are "tired and outstripped."

(6) The repeated use of the past progressive form of the verbs in stanza 2 continues the unending feel. (7) The terms accumulate: "fumbling," "fitting," "yelling," "stumbling," "flound'ring," "drowning." (8) The explosion of the gas shells causes the soldiers' desperate attempt to get their protective helmets on, accelerating the pace.

(9) Stanzas 3 and 4 contain the most vivid horrors, which come to the narrator in his dreams, which he cannot escape. (10) Adverbs describe how the man plunges at the narrator, "guttering, choking, drowning."

(11) Stanza 4 lays out several unending atrocities. (12) One is the wounded soldier, with his "white eyes writhing," his face "hanging," his blood "gargling" from his lungs. (13) The second unending atrocity is the "smothering dreams" the narrator suffers.

Recall the different strategic uses of evidence. The numbers show the sentences in which different strategic uses are employed.

| Strategic Uses of Evidence | |
|---|---|
| Illustrate | describe or explain (4) |
| Clarify | clear up ambiguities or contradictions (5) |
| Exemplify | provide examples (3) |
| Associate | draw comparisons (12–13) |
| Amplify | expand through additional evidence or examples (7, 10) |
| Qualify | acknowledge limitations |

**Table 5-7**

While the evidence *seems* to support the claims, the exact connection is not clear. In the revision below, the commentary (*in italic type*) adds clarity as it shows how the evidence supports the claims through logical connections. The sentence numbers are different since new sentences have been added.

(1) The horrors described in the first two stanzas of "Dulce et Decorum Est" take on an unending quality for the wounded soldier as well as for the haunted survivor who reports his dreams in the third and fourth stanzas.

(2) The descriptions in the first stanza show constant though exhausted motion, with rest only "distant." (3) The bent over soldiers "cursed through sludge" until they decide to turn their backs on "the haunting flares," the distress signals sent up by comrades in harm's way, and begin their "trudge" to "distant rest." (4) *The soldiers are always moving despite their pain and fatigue, marching as if asleep, but still moving.* (5) *There seems to be no rest*—even the gas shells (the Five-Nines) are "tired and outstripped."

(6) The repeated use of the past progressive form of the verbs in stanza 2 continues the unending feel. (7) *The progressive form of the verb expresses continuing action.* (8) The terms accumulate: fumbling, fitting, yelling, stumbling, flound'ring, drowning. (9) *The action is high in this stanza because of* the explosion of the gas shells and the soldiers' desperate attempt to get their protective helmets on, accelerating the pace. (10) *There is no more sleepwalking or limping with fatigue—the motion is intense.*

(11) Stanzas 3 and 4 contain the most vivid horrors, which come to the narrator in his dreams which he cannot escape. (12) *The second line of stanza 3 repeats the participial form of words, this time as adverbs describing how* the man plunges at the narrator, "guttering, choking, drowning." (13) *Once again, this form of the words conveys continuous motion.*

(14) Stanza 4 lays out several unending atrocities. (15) One is the wounded soldier, with his "white eyes writhing," his face "hanging," his blood "gargling" from his lungs. (16) *The soldier is portrayed as being in continuing misery, deprived of the rest that death could bring.* (17) The second unending atrocity is the "smothering dreams" the narrator suffers. (18) *Like the soldier, he seems deprived of rest; his rest would be dreamless sleep, not death.*

The figure below shows how the first body paragraph of a literary essay uses commentary to stitch together explanations of how the evidence supports the claim that supports the thesis.

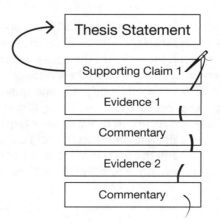

Figure 5-1

## Sufficient High-Quality Evidence

The quantity and quality of evidence and the strategic purposes for it are essential for defending your thesis statement and claims. There is no set amount for the right **quantity** of evidence required to support your thesis—use your judgment, as long as your evidence is **sufficient**, or enough, to convince readers it accurately reflects the poem. The **quality** of your evidence is determined by how effectively it supports your claim. Look for evidence that makes your point clearly.

Understanding the strategic purpose of your evidence (to illustrate, clarify, exemplify, associate, amplify, or qualify) will help you provide strong commentary, as the example below of one piece of evidence and its accompanying commentary illustrate.

| Claim | Evidence | Strategic Use of Evidence | Commentary |
|---|---|---|---|
| The repeated use of the past progressive form of the verbs in stanza 2 continues the unending feel. | The terms accumulate: "fumbling," "fitting," "yelling," "stumbling," "flound'ring," "drowning." | This statement exemplifies, providing a number of examples of the verb form. | The progressive form of the verb expresses continuing action. |

Table 5-8

As you write commentary to explain how your evidence supports the claims, you may find yourself adjusting your claims or thesis as you think about evidence in new ways. This **recursive** process may lead you to revise your thesis statement, your supporting claims, or your evidence, and you may then go back to look for more evidence to support your revised thesis.

Also, writers work in different ways. An interpretation can emerge from analyzing evidence and then forming a line of reasoning, or the interpretation can emerge from forming a line of reasoning and then identifying relevant evidence to support that line of reasoning.

**Remember:** Writers use evidence strategically and purposefully to illustrate, clarify, exemplify, associate, amplify, or qualify a point. Evidence is effective when the writer of the essay uses commentary to explain a logical relationship between the evidence and the claim. Evidence is sufficient when its quantity and quality provide apt support for the line of reasoning. Developing and supporting an interpretation of a text is a recursive process; an interpretation can emerge from analyzing evidence and then forming a line of reasoning, or the interpretation can emerge from forming a line of reasoning and then identifying relevant evidence to support that line of reasoning. (LAN-1.H–K)

### 5.3 Checkpoint

Look over your work from 5.2 Checkpoint. Identify the strategic purpose of each of the items of evidence you have included. Then read the poem again and look for other possible purposes of evidence. Add any you find to your chart of evidence and provide commentary on how it connects to the claims or thesis.

**Composing on Your Own**

Using your chart of claims, evidence, and commentary, write a draft of your essay. Refer to your big idea and thematic statement as possible ways to introduce your essay. Then use your notes to flesh out your draft.

# 5.4 Transitional Elements | LAN-1.Q

Just as commentary shows the connections between evidence and claims, **transitional elements** show the relationship between one idea and another as the essay progresses through its argument. By making those connections, transitional elements create **coherence**, a key quality in making writing logical and consistent.

## Levels of Coherence

Writers achieve coherence through words, phrases, clauses, sentences, and paragraphs when the arrangement and organization of reasons, evidence, ideas, or details is logical. Coherence through transitional words, phrases, clauses, and sentences is essential for readers to follow your argument.

**Transitional Words** Any word that creates a connection or establishes a relationship is a transitional word. They are very common, but they are also very powerful in clarifying relationships. The table below shows common transitional words and the relationship they establish.

| Transitional Words | | | |
|---|---|---|---|
| **Addition and Likeness** | **Contrast** | **Chronology** | **Cause** |
| and | or | first | unless |
| also | nor | next | when |
| too | yet | before | since |
| again | unlike | after | hence |
| similarly | although | later | while |
| like | instead | last | as |
| | however | when | whenever |

Table 5-9

**Transitional Phrases** Phrases can serve many of the same purposes as transitional words.

| Transitional Phrases | | | |
|---|---|---|---|
| Addition and Likeness | Contrast | Chronology | Cause |
| in addition to | in contrast | to begin | for the purpose of |
| equally important | on the contrary | after that | because of |
| in the same way | on the other hand | the next day | as a result |
| by the same token | even so | at the same time | in order to |
| in light of | even though | first of all | due to |
| | different from | in the meantime | if . . . then |

Table 5-10

**Transitional Clauses and Sentences** In literary analysis, transitional clauses are vital in identifying and expressing complexities and qualifying positions. They are especially useful in setting off your thesis statement from other possibly opposing or at least differing views. For example, in the following sentence, the subordinate clause (underlined) acknowledges a different point of view but then focuses attention on the writer's thesis statement by placing it in an independent clause.

> While some focus on the dark woods in "Stopping by Woods on a Snowy Evening" and argue that the narrator contemplates surrendering to the darkness, the diction and the imagery of the poem point to a more optimistic reading in which the narrator recognizes both the beauty of life and the obligations that connect him to others.

Transitional sentences, many of which begin with or include transitional words, phrases, or clauses, connect ideas within paragraphs and also between one paragraph and another. The draft on "Dulce et Decorum Est" could benefit from transitional sentences between paragraphs, although some (sentences 7, 10, and 14 in the previous draft) appeared when commentary was added. New transitional sentences are added in the version below, underlined.

> (1) The horrors described in the first two stanzas of "Dulce et Decorum Est" take on an unending quality for the wounded soldier as well as for the haunted survivor who reports his dreams in the third and fourth stanzas.

> (2) The constant unending motion first appears in stanza 1. (3) The descriptions in the first stanza show constant though exhausted motion, with rest only "distant." (4) The bent-over soldiers "cursed through sludge" until they decided to turn their backs on "the haunting flares," the distress signals sent up by comrades in harm's way, and begin their "trudge" to "distant rest." (5) *The*

*soldiers are always moving despite their pain and fatigue, marching as if asleep, but still moving.* (6) *There seems to be no rest*—even the gas shells (the Five-Nines) are "tired and outstripped."

(7) The repeated use of the past progressive form of the verbs in stanza 2 continues the unending feel. (8) *The progressive form of the verb expresses continuing action.* (9) The terms accumulate: fumbling, fitting, yelling, stumbling, flound'ring, drowning. (10) *The action is high in this stanza because of* the explosion of the gas shells and the soldiers' desperate attempt to get their protective helmets on, accelerating the pace. (11) *There is no more sleepwalking or limping with fatigue—the motion is intense.*

(12) <u>Most affecting, perhaps, is the relentlessness of the motion in the surviving soldier even after the war.</u> (13) Stanzas 3 and 4 contain the most vivid horrors, which come to the narrator in his dreams which he cannot escape. (14) *The second line of stanza 3 repeats the participial form of words, this time as adverbs describing how* the man plunges at the narrator, "guttering, choking, drowning." (15) *Once again, this form of the words conveys continuous motion.*

(16) Stanza 4 lays out several unending atrocities. (17) One is the wounded soldier, with his "white eyes writhing," his face "hanging," his blood "gargling" from his lungs. (18) *The soldier is portrayed as being in continuing misery, deprived of the rest that death could bring.* (19) The second unending atrocity is the "smothering dreams" the narrator suffers. (20) *Like the soldier, he seems deprived of rest; his rest would be dreamless sleep, not death.*

**Transitional Paragraphs** In long essays, articles, or books, sometimes entire paragraphs serve as transitions—to a new topic, or even a new aspect of a topic. Their purpose is the same as other transitional elements: to show relationships among ideas.

For a reminder of other tools of coherence, see Unit 4.

 **Remember:** Transitional elements are words or other elements (phrases, clauses, sentences, or paragraphs) that assist in creating coherence between sentences and paragraphs by showing relationships between ideas. (LAN-1.Q)

## 5.4 Checkpoint

Review your work from 5.3 Checkpoint. Identify any transitional words, phrases, clauses, or sentences you have used by underlining or italicizing them. Then evaluate your draft to see if additional transitional elements would be useful. If so, insert them in your draft. Save your work.

**Composing on Your Own**

Pulling together all you have learned about writing, prepare a second draft of your literary essay using the graphic organizer on page 267 in Unit 4 as a guide.

# Part 5 Apply What You Have Learned

Exchange drafts with a partner. Read your partner's essay and answer these questions in writing.

1. What is the thesis statement?

2. What claims support the thesis statement? In other words, what is the line of reasoning? Are the claims in a logical sequence?

3. Is the evidence relevant, sufficient, and of high quality? Explain your answer.

4. How effectively does commentary connect the evidence to the claims and thesis?

5. Identify five places where your partner achieved coherence and the tools used to achieve it.

6. What is one strength of this essay?

7. In what way might this essay be improved?

When your own essay is returned to you, carefully review your partner's evaluation and make revisions that you believe will improve your work.

**Reflect on the Essential Question** Write a brief response that answers the essential question: *How can you communicate a written interpretation of a poem by expressing a thesis statement, using sufficient evidence and commentary to support your line of reasoning, and achieve coherence?* In your answer, correctly use the key terms listed on page 332.

# Unit 5 Review

## Section I: Multiple Choice

## Section II: Free Response

## Section I: Multiple Choice

Questions 1-10. The following is an excerpt from a short story published in 1977 by a South African woman.

1　　Wedding days always started at the haunting, magical hour of early dawn when there was only a pale crack of light on the horizon. For those who were awake, it took the earth hours to adjust to daylight. The cool and damp of the night slowly arose in shimmering waves like water and even the forms of the people who bestirred themselves at this unearthly hour were distorted in the haze; they appeared to be dancers in slow motion, with fluid, watery forms. In the dim light, four men, the relatives of the bridegroom, Kegoletile, slowly herded an ox before them towards the yard of MmaKhudu, where the bride, Neo, lived. People were already astir in MmaKhudu's yard, yet for a while they all came and peered closely at the distorted fluid forms that approached, to ascertain if it were indeed the relatives of the bridegroom. Then the ox, who was a rather stupid fellow and unaware of his sudden and impending end as meat for the wedding feast, bellowed casually his early morning yawn. At this the beautiful ululating[1] of the women rose and swelled over the air like water bubbling rapidly and melodiously over the stones of a clear, sparkling stream. In between ululating all the while, the women began to weave about the yard in the wedding dance; now and then they bent over and shook their buttocks in the air. As they handed over the ox, one of the bridegroom's relatives joked:

2　　"This is going to be a modern wedding." He meant that a lot of the traditional courtesies had been left out of the planning for the wedding day; no one had been awake all night preparing diphiri or the traditional wedding breakfast of pounded meat and samp;[2] the bridegroom said he had no church and did not care about such things; the bride was six months pregnant and showing it, so there was just going to be a quick marriage ceremony at the police camp.

3　　"Oh, we all have our own ways," one of the bride's relatives joked back. "If the times are changing, we keep up with them." And she weaved away ululating joyously.

---

1　**ululating:** making loud, high-pitched, rhythmic sounds as an expression of strong emotion
2　**samp:** a hot cereal or porridge made from ground corn

4    Whenever there was a wedding the talk and gossip that preceded it were appalling, except that this time the relatives of the bride, Neo, kept their talk a strict secret among themselves. They were anxious to be rid of her; she was an impossible girl with haughty, arrogant ways. Of all her family and relatives, she was the only one who had completed her "O" levels[3] and she never failed to rub in this fact. She walked around with her nose in the air; illiterate relatives were beneath her greeting—it was done in a clever way, she just turned her head to one side and smiled to herself or when she greeted it was like an insult; she stretched her hand out, palm outspread, swung it down laughing with a gesture that plainly said: "Oh, that's you!" Only her mother seemed bemused by her education. At her own home Neo was waited on hand and foot. Outside her home nasty remarks were passed. People bitterly disliked conceit and pride.

5    "That girl has no manners!" the relatives would remark. "What's the good of education if it goes to someone's head so badly they have no respect for the people? Oh, she is not a person."

1. In paragraph 1, which adjective associated with the setting suggests that the wedding may not be what the people are used to?
   (A) "haunting" (sentence 1)
   (B) "pale" (sentence 1)
   (C) "shimmering" (line 3)
   (D) "distorted" (line 4)
   (E) "slowly" (line 4)

2. Which of the following best describes the effect of providing the information in the first paragraph before the rest of the narrative?
   (A) It establishes the relationship between MmaKhudi and Neo before explaining her relationship with her friends and relatives.
   (B) It establishes a peaceful setting before the ox discovers that he will "end as meat for the wedding feast."
   (C) On the surface, it creates the appearance of a regular traditional wedding day before the mention of the "quick marriage ceremony" in the next paragraph.
   (D) It defines the roles of men and women in the culture before moving on to narrate the wedding.
   (E) It demonstrates the relative ignorance of the people before introducing Neo and her outstanding education, regardless of her having "no manners."

---

3 **"O" Levels:** the exams taken at the end of high school education in the British educational system

3. The details in paragraph three and its position affect the relationship between which ideas in the passage?

   (A) Modern and traditional education

   (B) The modernity represented by Neo and the traditions of her relatives and family

   (C) Relationships between family and friends and marriage to someone

   (D) Fear of the modern world and comfort in local traditions

   (E) The commitment demonstrated by Kegoletile and Neo's impending wedding ceremony

Question 4 is covered in Unit 1.

4. The narrator's all-knowing, third-person point of view most evident because the narrator

   (A) is affected by the events of the passage

   (B) is directly involved in the events of the passage

   (C) delivers an opinion on Neo's behavior

   (D) offers details about multiple characters that would be difficult for one person to know

   (E) fails to provide enough information

Questions 5 and 6 are covered in Unit 2.

5. The comments and actions of the bride's relative in the third paragraph reveal her perspective most likely to be

   (A) angry at the disregard for tradition but thankful Neo will have a husband to help care for the child

   (B) saddened that Neo is pregnant on her wedding day

   (C) disappointed in Neo's complete ignorance of their shared culture

   (D) unconcerned with the unusual circumstances surrounding this marriage and happy for the event

   (E) ignorant of the gossip surrounding the wedding

6. In context, the simile "when she greeted it was like an insult" (paragraph 4, sentence 4) reveals what about Neo?

   (A) She practices social conventions without sincerity or respect toward others.

   (B) She is learning to care for those around her who have less education.

   (C) Her education does make her better than others.

   (D) She cannot tell the difference between being polite and insulting.

   (E) She will likely not be a good mother or wife.

Questions 7–9 are covered in Unit 3.

7.  What is revealed about the relatives in the final paragraph?
    (A) They distrust education.
    (B) They are stuck in the traditional ways.
    (C) They have little respect for Neo.
    (D) They think Kegoletile is making a mistake.
    (E) They are concerned about Neo and Kegoletile's future together.

8.  According to the passage, which of the following details most greatly affects Neo's character?
    (A) She has more formal education than the rest of her family and relatives.
    (B) She has "no manners."
    (C) She is going to have "a modern wedding."
    (D) She is marrying a man with "no church."
    (E) She will not eat traditional meals or have traditional food at her wedding.

9.  The narrator's perspective is most focused on
    (A) Neo's state of mind
    (B) how education changes people
    (C) the relationship between Neo and Kegoletile, her soon-to-be husband
    (D) how different genders prepare for wedding days
    (E) the traditions of the people and how Neo is different from them

Question 10 is covered in Unit 6.

10. Inclusion of details such as "she never failed to rub in this fact" (paragraph 4, sentence 3) and "'That girl has no manners!'" (paragraph 5, sentence 1) suggests the narrator is
    (A) fearful of Neo's relatives
    (B) cautious about Neo's future
    (C) concerned for Neo's unborn child
    (D) critical of Neo's treatment of others
    (E) accepting of Neo's immaturity

Questions 11–20. The following poem, published in 1921, is by a Jamaican poet.

## AMERICA

Although she feeds me bread of bitterness,
And sinks into my throat her tiger's tooth,
Stealing my breath of life, I will confess
I love this cultured hell that tests my youth!
5 Her vigor flows like tides into my blood,
Giving me strength erect against her hate.
Her bigness sweeps my being like a flood.
Yet as a rebel fronts a king in state,
I stand within her walls with not a shred
10 Of terror, malice, not a word of jeer,[1]
Darkly I gaze into the days ahead,
And see her might and granite wonders there,
Beneath the touch of time's unerring hand,
Like priceless treasures sinking in the sand

11. The metaphor of the tiger (lines 2–3) emphasizes which aspect of the poem?

(A) The natural feelings of the speaker

(B) The speaker attacking an idea in the poem

(C) The danger felt by the speaker

(D) The danger people like the speaker are in

(E) The speaker hunting for a home

12. The simile in line 5 ("flows like tides") illustrates what aspect of the speaker?

(A) Pain and loss

(B) Cyclical experiences

(C) Joy and optimism

(D) Lack of awareness

(E) Overwhelming feelings

13. The rhyming of *blood* and *flood* (lines 5 and 7) most likely contributes to the idea that

(A) the speaker has experienced arduous challenges

(B) blood is thicker than water, especially in the situation of this poem

(C) the speaker is inexperienced and lost in a strange place

(D) the speaker experiences all-consuming reactions

(E) the speaker longs for companions

---

1 **jeer:** mockery

14. In context, *granite* (line 12) can be seen as having multiple meanings relating to

(A) long-term strength and valuable riches

(B) heartache and inescapable pain

(C) eternal joy and strength

(D) complete acceptance and unexpected rejection

(E) enduring greatness and natural beauty

15. Which of the following best describes the complex perspective of the speaker?

(A) The speaker longed to go but now cannot wait to escape.

(B) The speaker loves the place but loathes the people.

(C) Despite experiencing mistreatment, the speaker still loves "her."

(D) Despite loving "her" dearly, the speaker is fearful of the days ahead.

(E) The speaker cannot accept things that are uncontrollable.

16. Which of the following lines best support the complexity of the speaker's perspective?

(A) "Although she feeds me bread of bitterness, / And sinks into my throat her tiger's tooth," (lines 1–2)

(B) "I stand within her walls with not a shred / Of terror, malice, not a word of jeer." (lines 9–10)

(C) "Giving me strength erect against her hate. / Her bigness sweeps my being like a flood." (line 6–7)

(D) "Beneath the touch of time's unerring hand, / Like priceless treasures sinking in the sand." (lines 13–14)

(E) "Her vigor flows like tides into my blood, / Giving me strength erect against her hate." (lines 5–6)

17. Use of the pronouns *she* and *her* throughout the poem are referents to

(A) "bread of bitterness" (line 1)

(B) America

(C) "time's unerring hand" (line 13)

(D) pain

(E) "breath of life" (line 3)

18. Which of the following best describes the speaker in this poem?

(A) A person returning to a loving home

(B) The last of a family leaving home

(C) An angry traveler lost in America

(D) A person lost and unable to find his way home

(E) An outsider in a place that is both frightening and inspiring

19. A central paradox of the poem is

(A) the pain that is caused by experiences that are meant to be fun

(B) the speaker's denial of experiencing something that has resulted in personal change

(C) the excitement and delight of the speaker despite such painful experiences

(D) the speaker's fear of doing something that will encourage resiliency

(E) the fear of dying despite the need to have experiences.

20. The situation of the poem might be best described as

(A) a traveler becomes lost in a land of people who mistreat him

(B) the speaker decides to accept the negative aspects of a place because of the overwhelmingly positive aspects

(C) the speaker refuses to accept the negative aspects of people, insisting on only seeing the good in people

(D) a king cannot rule his subjects and a rebellion is growing

(E) a great land is sinking into the desert because of the anger and bitterness of its people

## Section II: Free Response
### Question 1: Poetry Analysis

In the poem "America" (page 347) by Claude McKay (published 1921), the speaker addresses his new country. Read the poem carefully. Then, in a well-written essay, analyze how McKay uses poetic elements and techniques to develop the complex perspective of the speaker.

In your response you should do the following:

• Respond to the prompt with a thesis that presents a defensible interpretation.

• Select and use evidence to support your line of reasoning.

• Explain how the evidence supports your line of reasoning.

• Use appropriate grammar and punctuation in communicating your argument.

## Question 2: Prose Fiction Analysis

On pages 343-344 is an excerpt from the short story "Snapshots of a Wedding" published in 1977 by South African author Bessie Head. In the passage, the narrator describes the morning of the wedding day of Kegoletile and Neo.

Read the passage carefully. Then, in a well-written essay, analyze how Head uses literary elements and techniques to develop a complex perspective on Neo.

In your response you should do the following:

- Respond to the prompt with a thesis that presents a defensible interpretation.
- Select and use evidence to support your line of reasoning.
- Explain how the evidence supports your line of reasoning.
- Use appropriate grammar and punctuation in communicating your argument.

## Question 3: Literary Argument—Spoilers

A 2011 study by Nicholas Christenfeld and Jonathan Leavitt of University of California San Diego's psychology department seemed to indicate that people enjoy certain stories and books better when they have elements of the plot spoiled—that is, the researchers told them important aspects of the story (or even the endings) before the people had the chance to find them out on their own.

Choose a work of fiction that provides a significant piece of information early in the story. Then, in a well-written essay, analyze how the revelation of that significant information contributes to an interpretation of the work as a whole. Do not merely summarize the plot.

In your response you should do the following:

- Respond to the prompt with a thesis that presents a defensible interpretation.
- Provide evidence to support your line of reasoning.
- Explain how the evidence supports your line of reasoning.
- Use appropriate grammar and punctuation in communicating your argument.

# UNIT 6

# Disruption and Disparity

[Longer Fiction Or Drama II]

**Part 1:** Differences Between and Within Characters
**Part 2:** Plot Sequence and Contrasts
**Part 3:** Tone, Syntax, Perspective, and Bias
**Part 4:** The Role of Symbols
**Part 5:** Writing About Literature VI

---

**ENDURING UNDERSTANDINGS AND SKILLS:** Unit 6

## Part 1 Differences Between and Within Characters

**Understand**

Characters in literature allow readers to study and explore a range of values, beliefs, assumptions, biases, and cultural norms represented by those characters. (CHR-1)

**Demonstrate**

Identify and describe what specific textual details reveal about a character, that character's perspective, and that character's motives. (1.A)

Explain the function of contrasting characters. (1.C)

Explain how a character's own choices, actions, and speech reveal complexities in that character, and explain the function of those complexities. (1.E)

## Part 2 Plot Sequence and Contrasts

**Understand**

The arrangement of the parts and sections of a text, the relationship of the parts to each other, and the sequence in which the text reveals information are all structural choices made by a writer that contribute to the reader's interpretation of a text. (STR-1)

**Demonstrate**

Identify and describe how plot orders events in a narrative. (3.A)

Explain the function of a particular sequence of events in a plot. (3.B)

Explain the function of contrasts within a text. (3.D)

## Part 3 Tone, Syntax, Perspective, and Bias

### Understand

A narrator's or speaker's perspective controls the details and emphases that affect how readers experience and interpret a text. (NAR-1)

### Demonstrate

Identify and describe details, diction, or syntax in a text that reveal a narrator's or speaker's perspective. (4.C)

Explain how a narrator's reliability affects a narrative. (4.D)

## Part 4 The Role of Symbols

### Understand

Comparisons, representations, and associations shift meaning from the literal to the figurative and invite readers to interpret a text. (FIG-1)

### Demonstrate

Identify and explain the function of a symbol. (5.C)

## Part 5 Writing About Literature VI

### Understand

Readers establish and communicate their interpretations of literature through arguments supported by textual evidence. (LAN-1)

### Demonstrate

Develop a thesis statement that conveys a defensible claim about an interpretation of literature and that may establish a line of reasoning. (7.B)

Develop commentary that establishes and explains relationships among textual evidence, the line of reasoning, and the thesis. (7.C)

Select and use relevant and sufficient evidence to both develop and support a line of reasoning. (7.D)

Demonstrate control over the elements of composition to communicate clearly. (7.E)

Source: AP® English Literature and Composition Course and Exam Description

# Unit 6 Overview

No technology has had more impact on humans than the control of fire. It separates humans from all other creatures on Earth and, according to Greek mythology, it also separated humans from the gods—until Prometheus stole it from Zeus and gave it to humans. While countless anthropologists and other historians and scientists have reported on the effects of humans' control of fire, the mythological explanation retains an enduring appeal. Fiction, from mythology to longer fiction from any era, gives its creators a unique power to shine light on qualities of humanity by allowing readers to study and explore a range of values, beliefs, assumptions, biases, and cultural norms represented by characters with whom they identify through complex, textured plots, multiple perspectives, and powerful symbols. This unit will cover all these aspects of longer fiction—and focus on a tale of a modern Prometheus.

"I passed the summer of 1816 in the environs of Geneva,"[2] writes Mary Shelley in the preface to the 1831 edition of *Frankenstein*. "The season was cold and rainy, and in the evenings we crowded around a blazing wood fire, and occasionally amused ourselves with some German stories of ghosts, which happened to fall into our hands. These tales excited in us a playful desire of imitation. Two other friends . . . and myself agreed to write each a story, founded on some supernatural occurrence.

"The weather, however, suddenly became serene; and my two friends left me on a journey among the Alps, and lost, in the magnificent scenes which they present, all memory of their ghostly visions. The following tale is the only one which has been completed."

And so the story of Victor Frankenstein and his creature came to life.

As you may recall from Unit 4, Shelley tells the powerful story of Frankenstein through an unusual narrative structure. Three separate first-person narrators participate in the storytelling. The first is explorer Robert Walton, who writes letters to his sister Margaret in England about his efforts to discover a route to the "North Pacific Ocean through the seas which surround the pole." When he meets up with the haggard and half-frozen Victor Frankenstein, Walton turns the narrative over to him, and the reader learns about the young Victor and how in time he came to create a living being from nonliving parts. The next narrator is the Creature himself, well read and eloquent. After the Creature tells his story, the narrators reverse course, moving from the Creature to Victor Frankenstein and finally back to Robert Walton.

 **ROBERT WALTON, TO HIS SISTER MARGARET**

## From Letter I

2      I am already far north of London; and as I walk in the streets of Petersburgh,[3] I feel a cold northern breeze play upon my cheeks, which braces my nerves, and fills me with delight. Do you understand this feeling? This breeze, which has travelled from the regions towards which I am advancing, gives me a foretaste of those icy climes. Inspirited by this wind of promise, my day dreams become more fervent and vivid. I try in vain to be persuaded that the pole is the seat of frost and desolation; it ever presents itself to my imagination as the region of beauty and delight. There, Margaret, the sun is for ever visible; its broad disk just skirting the horizon, and diffusing a perpetual splendour. There . . . snow and frost are banished; and, sailing over a calm sea, we may be wafted to a land surpassing in wonders and in beauty every region hitherto discovered on the habitable globe. . . . What may not be expected in a country of eternal

---

1 You can read the entire 1831 edition of the novel for free at Project Gutenberg.
2 **Geneva:** a city in Switzerland
3 **Petersburgh:** St. Petersburg, Russia

light? . . . I shall satiate my ardent curiosity with the sight of a part of the world never before visited, and may tread a land never before imprinted by the foot of man. These are my enticements, and they are sufficient to conquer all fear of danger or death. . . .

## From Letter II

3    How slowly the time passes here, encompassed as I am by frost and snow! yet a second step is taken towards my enterprise. I have hired a vessel, and am occupied in collecting my sailors; those whom I have already engaged, appear to be men on whom I can depend, and are certainly possessed of dauntless courage.

4    But I have one want which I have never yet been able to satisfy; and the absence of the object of which I now feel as a most severe evil. I have no friend, Margaret: when I am glowing with the enthusiasm of success, there will be none to participate [in] my joy; if I am assailed by disappointment, no one will endeavour to sustain me in dejection. . . . You may deem me romantic, my dear sister, but I bitterly feel the want of a friend. . . .

## From Letter IV

5    So strange an accident has happened to us, that I cannot forbear recording it . . . .

6    Last Monday (July 31st), we were nearly surrounded by ice, which closed in the ship on all sides. . . . Our situation was somewhat dangerous, especially as we were compassed round by a very thick fog. We accordingly lay to,[4] hoping that some change would take place in the atmosphere and weather.

7    About two o'clock the mist cleared away, and we beheld, stretched out in every direction, vast and irregular plains of ice, which seemed to have no end. Some of my comrades groaned, and my own mind began to grow watchful with anxious thoughts, when a strange sight suddenly attracted our attention. . . . We perceived a low carriage, fixed on a sledge and drawn by dogs, pass on towards the north, at the distance of half a mile: a being which had the shape of a man, but apparently of gigantic stature, sat in the sledge, and guided the dogs. We watched the rapid progress of the traveller with our telescopes, until he was lost among the distant inequalities of the ice. . . .

8    About two hours after this occurrence . . . the ice broke, and freed our ship. We, however, lay to until the morning, fearing to encounter in the dark those large loose masses which float about after the breaking up of the ice. I profited of this time to rest for a few hours.

9    In the morning, however, as soon as it was light, I went upon deck, and found all the sailors busy on one side of the vessel, apparently talking to some one in the sea. It was, in fact, a sledge, like that we had seen

---

4 **lay to:** turn the ship toward the wind and hold it still

before, which had drifted towards us in the night, on a large fragment of ice. Only one dog remained alive; but there was a human being within it, whom the sailors were persuading to enter the vessel. He was not, as the other traveller seemed to be, a savage inhabitant of some undiscovered island, but an European. When I appeared on deck, the master said, "Here is our captain, and he will not allow you to perish on the open sea."

10    On perceiving me, the stranger addressed me in English, although with a foreign accent. "Before I come on board your vessel," said he, "will you have the kindness to inform me whither you are bound?"

11    You may conceive my astonishment on hearing such a question addressed to me from a man on the brink of destruction, and to whom I should have supposed that my vessel would have been a resource which he would not have exchanged for the most precious wealth the earth can afford. I replied, however, that we were on a voyage of discovery towards the northern pole.

12    Upon hearing this he appeared satisfied, and consented to come on board. Good God! Margaret, if you had seen the man who thus capitulated for his safety, your surprise would have been boundless. His limbs were nearly frozen, and his body dreadfully emaciated by fatigue and suffering. I never saw a man in so wretched a condition. . . .

13    When my guest was a little recovered, I had great trouble to keep off the men, who wished to ask him a thousand questions; but I would not allow him to be tormented by their idle curiosity, in a state of body and mind whose restoration evidently depended upon entire repose. Once, however, the lieutenant asked, Why he had come so far upon the ice in so strange a vehicle?

14    His countenance instantly assumed an aspect of the deepest gloom; and he replied, "To seek one who fled from me."

15    "And did the man whom you pursued travel in the same fashion?"

16    "Yes."

17    "Then I fancy we have seen him; for the day before we picked you up, we saw some dogs drawing a sledge, with a man in it, across the ice." . . .

18    My affection for my guest increases every day. He excites at once my admiration and my pity to an astonishing degree. How can I see so noble a creature destroyed by misery, without feeling the most poignant grief? He is so gentle, yet so wise; his mind is so cultivated; and when he speaks, although his words are culled with the choicest art, yet they flow with rapidity and unparalleled eloquence.

19    He is now much recovered from his illness, and is continually on the deck, apparently watching for the sledge that preceded his own. Yet, although unhappy, he is not so utterly occupied by his own misery, but that he interests himself deeply in the projects of others. He has frequently conversed with me on mine . . . . I was easily led by the sympathy which he evinced, to use the language of my heart; to give utterance to the burning ardour of my soul; and to say, with all the fervour that warmed me, how gladly I would sacrifice my fortune, my existence, my every hope, to the furtherance of my enterprise. One man's life or death were but a small

price to pay for the acquirement of the knowledge which I sought; for the dominion I should acquire and transmit over the elemental foes of our race. As I spoke, a dark gloom spread over my listener's countenance. At first I perceived that he tried to suppress his emotion; he placed his hands before his eyes; and my voice quivered and failed me, as I beheld tears trickle fast from between his fingers,—a groan burst from his heaving breast. I paused;—at length he spoke, in broken accents:—"Unhappy man! Do you share my madness? Have you drank also of the intoxicating draught? Hear me,—let me reveal my tale, and you will dash the cup from your lips!"

 **VICTOR FRANKENSTEIN, TO ROBERT WALTON**

*Victor Frankenstein takes over the narration in Chapters I–X. He begins in Chapter I recounting details of his parent's marriage and their adoption of Elizabeth, one year younger than himself. Through the next nine chapters he moves chronologically through his childhood to his entrance in the university at Ingolstadt[5] to his work on the Creature. This part of his story ends with a confrontation with the Creature after he has killed Victor's younger brother William and framed Justine, an innocent young woman, for the murder.*

*The following excerpt introduces readers to Henry Clerval, Victor's schoolmate and best friend, and presents Victor's perspective on his childhood.*

## From Chapter II

2      Henry Clerval was . . . a boy of singular talent and fancy. He loved enterprise, hardship, and even danger, for its own sake. He was deeply read in books of chivalry and romance. He composed heroic songs, and began to write many a tale of enchantment and knightly adventure. He tried to make us act plays, and to enter into masquerades, in which the characters were drawn from the heroes of Roncesvalles,[6] of the Round Table of King Arthur, and the chivalrous train who shed their blood to redeem the holy sepulchre[7] from the hands of the infidels.

3      No human being could have passed a happier childhood than myself. My parents were possessed by the very spirit of kindness and indulgence. . . .

4      My temper was sometimes violent, and my passions vehement; but by some law in my temperature they were turned, not towards childish pursuits, but to an eager desire to learn, and not to learn all things indiscriminately. . . . It was the secrets of heaven and earth that I desired to learn; and whether it was the outward substance of things, or the inner spirit of nature and the mysterious soul of man that occupied me, still my enquiries were directed to the metaphysical, or, in its highest sense, the physical secrets of the world.

---

5 **Ingolstadt:** a city in Bavaria
6 **Roncesvalles:** the site in Spain of a legendary battle in AD 778
7 **holy sepulchre:** tomb of Jesus in Jerusalem

5      Meanwhile Clerval occupied himself . . . with the moral relations of things. The busy stage of life, the virtues of heroes, and the actions of men, were his theme; and his hope and his dream was to become one among those whose names are recorded in story, as the gallant and adventurous benefactors of our species. The saintly soul of Elizabeth shone like a shrine-dedicated lamp in our peaceful home. Her sympathy was ours; her smile, her soft voice, the sweet glance of her celestial eyes, were ever there to bless and animate us. She was the living spirit of love to soften and attract: I might have become sullen in my study, rough through the ardour of my nature, but that she was there to subdue me to a semblance of her own gentleness. And Clerval—could aught ill entrench on the noble spirit of Clerval?—yet he might not have been so perfectly humane, so thoughtful in his generosity—. . . had she not unfolded to him the real loveliness of beneficence, and made the doing good the end and aim of his soaring ambition.

6      I feel exquisite pleasure in dwelling on the recollections of childhood, before misfortune had tainted my mind, and changed its bright visions of extensive usefulness into gloomy and narrow reflections upon self. Besides, in drawing the picture of my early days, I also record those events which led, by insensible steps, to my after tale of misery: for when I would account to myself for the birth of that passion, which afterwards ruled my destiny, I find it arise, like a mountain river, from ignoble and almost forgotten sources; but, swelling as it proceeded, it became the torrent which, in its course, has swept away all my hopes and joys.

## From Chapter V

*Victor, enthralled with his studies in the natural sciences and chemistry has spent two years studying corpses to determine how death progresses in hopes of discovering a way to reverse the process. He is successful. The following excerpt describes the Creature's first moments of life and Victor's reaction.*

1      It was on a dreary night of November, that I beheld the accomplishment of my toils. With an anxiety that almost amounted to agony, I collected the instruments of life around me, that I might infuse a spark of being into the lifeless thing that lay at my feet. It was already one in the morning; the rain pattered dismally against the panes, and my candle was nearly burnt out, when, by the glimmer of the half-extinguished light, I saw the dull yellow eye of the creature open; it breathed hard, and a convulsive motion agitated its limbs.

2      How can I describe my emotions at this catastrophe, or how delineate the wretch whom with such infinite pains and care I had endeavoured to form? His limbs were in proportion, and I had selected his features as beautiful. Beautiful!—Great God! His yellow skin scarcely covered the work of muscles and arteries beneath; his hair was of a lustrous black, and flowing; his teeth of a pearly whiteness; but these luxuriances only formed a more horrid contrast with his watery eyes, that seemed almost

of the same colour as the dun white[8] sockets in which they were set, his shrivelled complexion and straight black lips.

3          . . . I had worked hard for nearly two years, for the sole purpose of infusing life into an inanimate body. For this I had deprived myself of rest and health. I had desired it with an ardour that far exceeded moderation; but now that I had finished, the beauty of the dream vanished, and breathless horror and disgust filled my heart. Unable to endure the aspect of the being I had created, I rushed out of the room, and continued a long time traversing my bedchamber, unable to compose my mind to sleep. At length lassitude[9] succeeded to the tumult I had before endured; and I threw myself on the bed in my clothes, endeavouring to seek a few moments of forgetfulness. But it was in vain: I slept, indeed, but I was disturbed by the wildest dreams. . . . I started from my sleep with horror; a cold dew covered my forehead, my teeth chattered, and every limb became convulsed: when, by the dim and yellow light of the moon, as it forced its way through the window shutters, I beheld the wretch—the miserable monster whom I had created. He held up the curtain of the bed; and his eyes, if eyes they may be called, were fixed on me. His jaws opened, and he muttered some inarticulate sounds, while a grin wrinkled his cheeks. He might have spoken, but I did not hear; one hand was stretched out, seemingly to detain me, but I escaped, and rushed down stairs. I took refuge in the courtyard belonging to the house which I inhabited.

. . .

6          Morning, dismal and wet, at length dawned . . . and I issued into the streets, pacing them with quick steps, as if I sought to avoid the wretch whom I feared every turning of the street would present to my view. I did not dare return to the apartment which I inhabited, but felt impelled to hurry on, although drenched by the rain which poured from a black and comfortless sky.

## From Chapter IX

*Justine Moritz, a beloved servant in the Frankenstein household, is falsely accused of William Frankenstein's murder. Despite the Frankensteins' belief in her innocence, the circumstantial evidence is enough to convict her. Even though Victor knows the Creature killed William, he does not tell authorities. Before she is hanged, Justine tells Victor and Elizabeth that she falsely admitted to the murder to avoid excommunication and eternal damnation. The following excerpt gives readers insights into Elizabeth and Victor's responses to Justine's death.*

5          Often, after the rest of the family had retired for the night, I took the boat, and passed many hours upon the water. Sometimes, with my sails set, I was carried by the wind; and sometimes, after rowing into the middle

---

8 **dun white:** grayish white
9 **lassitude:** mental weariness

of the lake, I left the boat to pursue its own course, and gave way to my own miserable reflections. I was often tempted . . . to plunge into the silent lake, that the waters might close over me and my calamities for ever. But I was restrained, when I thought of the heroic and suffering Elizabeth, whom I tenderly loved, and whose existence was bound up in mine. I thought also of my father, and surviving brother: should I by my base desertion leave them exposed and unprotected to the malice of the fiend whom I had let loose among them?

6      At these moments I wept bitterly, and wished that peace would revisit my mind only that I might afford them consolation and happiness. But that could not be. Remorse extinguished every hope. I had been the author of unalterable evils; and I lived in daily fear, lest the monster whom I had created should perpetrate some new wickedness. . . . I ardently wished to extinguish that life which I had so thoughtlessly bestowed . . . .

7      Our house was the house of mourning. My father's health was deeply shaken by the horror of the recent events. Elizabeth was sad and desponding; she no longer took delight in her ordinary occupations; all pleasure seemed to her sacrilege toward the dead. . . . She was no longer that happy creature, who in earlier youth wandered with me on the banks of the lake, and talked with ecstasy of our future prospects. The first of those sorrows which are sent to wean us from the earth, had visited her, and its dimming influence quenched her dearest smiles.

8      "When I reflect, my dear cousin," said she, "on the miserable death of Justine Moritz, I no longer see the world and its works as they before appeared to me. Before, I looked upon the accounts of vice and injustice, that I read in books or heard from others, as tales of ancient days, or imaginary evils; at least they were remote, and more familiar to reason than to the imagination; but now misery has come home, and men appear to me as monsters thirsting for each other's blood. . . . William and Justine were assassinated, and the murderer escapes; he walks about the world free, and perhaps respected. But even if I were condemned to suffer on the scaffold for the same crimes, I would not change places with such a wretch."

9      I listened to this discourse with the extremest agony. I, not in deed, but in effect, was the true murderer.

## From Chapter X

*After Justine's execution, Victor leaves Geneva for the resort of Chamonix-Mont-Blanc in the French Alps. He hopes the beauty of the area will help restore his tortured mind. Instead, he encounters the Creature.*

4      It was nearly noon when I arrived at the top of the ascent. For some time I sat upon the rock that overlooks the sea of ice. . . . The sea, or rather the vast river of ice, wound among its dependent mountains, whose aerial summits hung over its recesses. Their icy and glittering peaks shone in the sunlight over the clouds. My heart, which was before sorrowful, now swelled with something like joy. . . .

5     ... I suddenly beheld the figure of a man, at some distance, advancing towards me with superhuman speed. He bounded over the crevices in the ice, among which I had walked with caution; his stature, also, as he approached, seemed to exceed that of man. ... I perceived, as the shape came nearer (sight tremendous and abhorred!) that it was the wretch whom I had created. I trembled with rage and horror, resolving to wait his approach, and then close with him in mortal combat. He approached; his countenance bespoke bitter anguish, combined with disdain and malignity, while its unearthly ugliness rendered it almost too horrible for human eyes. But I scarcely observed this; rage and hatred had at first deprived me of utterance, and I recovered only to overwhelm him with words expressive of furious detestation and contempt.

6     "Devil," I exclaimed, "do you dare approach me? and do not you fear the fierce vengeance of my arm wreaked on your miserable head? Begone, vile insect! or rather, stay, that I may trample you to dust! and, oh! that I could, with the extinction of your miserable existence, restore those victims whom you have so diabolically murdered!"

*The Creature tells Frankenstein that he wants a chance to explain himself. He says, "Believe me, Frankenstein: I was benevolent; my soul glowed with love and humanity: but am I not alone, miserably alone? You, my creator, abhor me; what hope can I gather from your fellow-creatures, who owe me nothing? They spurn and hate me." He begs Frankenstein to hear him out and grant his request to create a companion for him. He continues:*

15     "By the virtues that I once possessed, I demand this from you. Hear my tale; it is long and strange, and the temperature of this place is not fitting to your fine sensations; come to the hut upon the mountain. The sun is yet high in the heavens; before it descends to hide itself behind yon snowy precipices, and illuminate another world, you will have heard my story, and can decide. On you it rests, whether I quit for ever the neighbourhood of man, and lead a harmless life, or become the scourge of your fellow-creatures, and the author of your own speedy ruin."

16     As he said this, he led the way across the ice: I followed. My heart was full, and I did not answer him; but, as I proceeded, I weighed the various arguments that he had used, and determined at least to listen to his tale. I was partly urged by curiosity, and compassion confirmed my resolution. I had hitherto supposed him to be the murderer of my brother, and I eagerly sought a confirmation or denial of this opinion. For the first time, also, I felt what the duties of a creator towards his creature were, and that I ought to render him happy before I complained of his wickedness. These motives urged me to comply with his demand. We crossed the ice, therefore, and ascended the opposite rock. The air was cold, and the rain again began to descend: we entered the hut, the fiend with an air of exultation, I with a heavy heart, and depressed spirits. But I consented to listen; and, seating myself by the fire which my odious companion had lighted, he thus began his tale.

**THE CREATURE, TO VICTOR FRANKENSTEIN**

## From Chapter XI

*Chapters XI–XVI mainly present the Creature's account of what he did between his birth and his murder of William. He explains to Victor his initial attempts to make sense of his environment. He became accustomed to light, left the laboratory, encountered rain and cold, and looked for food and shelter.*

6    "One day, when I was oppressed by cold, I found a fire which had been left by some wandering beggars, and was overcome with delight at the warmth I experienced from it. In my joy I thrust my hand into the live embers, but quickly drew it out again with a cry of pain. How strange, I thought, that the same cause should produce such opposite effects! I examined the materials of the fire, and to my joy found it to be composed of wood . . . . When night came on, and brought sleep with it, I was in the greatest fear lest my fire should be extinguished. I covered it carefully with dry wood and leaves, and placed wet branches upon it; and then, spreading my cloak, I lay on the ground, and sunk into sleep.

7    "It was morning when I awoke, and my first care was to visit the fire. I uncovered it, and a gentle breeze quickly fanned it into a flame. I observed this also, and contrived a fan of branches, which roused the embers when they were nearly extinguished. When night came again, I found, with pleasure, that the fire gave light as well as heat; and that the discovery of this element was useful to me in my food. . . .

8    "Food, however, became scarce; and I often spent the whole day searching in vain for a few acorns to assuage the pangs of hunger. When I found this, I resolved to quit the place that I had hitherto inhabited, to seek for one where the few wants I experienced would be more easily satisfied. In this emigration, I exceedingly lamented the loss of the fire which I had obtained through accident, and knew not how to reproduce it. I gave several hours to the serious consideration of this difficulty; but I was obliged to relinquish all attempt to supply it; and, wrapping myself up in my cloak, I struck across the wood towards the setting sun. I passed three days in these rambles, and at length discovered the open country. A great fall of snow had taken place the night before . . . and I found my feet chilled by the cold damp substance that covered the ground.

9    "It was about seven in the morning, and I longed to obtain food and shelter; at length I perceived a small hut, on a rising ground, which had doubtless been built for the convenience of some shepherd. This was a new sight to me; and I examined the structure with great curiosity. Finding the door open, I entered. An old man sat in it, near a fire, over which he was preparing his breakfast. He turned on hearing a noise; and, perceiving me, shrieked loudly, and, quitting the hut, ran across the fields with a speed of which his debilitated form hardly appeared capable. His appearance, different from any I had ever before seen, and his flight, somewhat surprised me. But I was enchanted by the appearance of the

hut: here the snow and rain could not penetrate; the ground was dry . . . I greedily devoured the remnants of the shepherd's breakfast, which consisted of bread, cheese, milk, and wine; the latter, however, I did not like. Then, overcome by fatigue, I lay down among some straw, and fell asleep.

10    "It was noon when I awoke; and, allured by the warmth of the sun, which shone brightly on the white ground, I determined to recommence my travels; and, depositing the remains of the peasant's breakfast in a wallet[10] I found, I proceeded across the fields for several hours, until at sunset I arrived at a village. How miraculous did this appear! the huts, the neater cottages, and stately houses, engaged my admiration by turns. The vegetables in the gardens, the milk and cheese that I saw placed at the windows of some of the cottages, allured my appetite. One of the best of these I entered; but I had hardly placed my foot within the door, before the children shrieked, and one of the women fainted. The whole village was roused; some fled, some attacked me, until, grievously bruised by stones and many other kinds of missile weapons, I escaped to the open country, and fearfully took refuge in a low hovel, quite bare, and making a wretched appearance after the palaces I had beheld in the village. This hovel, however, joined a cottage of a neat and pleasant appearance; but, after my late dearly bought experience, I dared not enter it . . . .

11    "Here then I retreated, and lay down happy to have found a shelter, however miserable, from the inclemency of the season, and still more from the barbarity of man."

## From Chapter XII

*The following passage provides readers with the Creature's perceptions of himself and the family living in the nearby cottage.*

2    "The cottagers arose the next morning before the sun. The young woman arranged the cottage, and prepared the food; and the youth departed after the first meal.

3    "This day was passed in the same routine as that which preceded it. The young man was constantly employed out of doors, and the girl in various laborious occupations within. The old man, whom I soon perceived to be blind, employed his leisure hours on his instrument or in contemplation. Nothing could exceed the love and respect which the younger cottagers exhibited towards their venerable companion. They performed towards him every little office of affection and duty with gentleness; and he rewarded them by his benevolent smiles.

4    "They were not entirely happy. The young man and his companion often went apart, and appeared to weep. I saw no cause for their unhappiness; but I was deeply affected by it. If such lovely creatures were miserable, it was less strange that I, an imperfect and solitary being, should be wretched. . . .

---

10 **wallet:** a bag for holding provisions

5    "A considerable period elapsed before I discovered one of the causes of the uneasiness of this amiable family: it was poverty; and they suffered that evil in a very distressing degree. Their nourishment consisted entirely of the vegetables of their garden, and the milk of one cow, which gave very little during the winter, when its masters could scarcely procure food to support it. They often, I believe, suffered the pangs of hunger very poignantly, especially the two younger cottagers; for several times they placed food before the old man, when they reserved none for themselves.

6    "This trait of kindness moved me sensibly. I had been accustomed, during the night, to steal a part of their store for my own consumption; but when I found that in doing this I inflicted pain on the cottagers, I abstained, and satisfied myself with berries, nuts, and roots, which I gathered from a neighbouring wood.

7    "I discovered also another means through which I was enabled to assist their labours. I found that the youth spent a great part of each day in collecting wood for the family fire; and, during the night, I often took his tools, the use of which I quickly discovered, and brought home firing sufficient for the consumption of several days.

8    "I remember, the first time that I did this, the young woman, when she opened the door in the morning, appeared greatly astonished on seeing a great pile of wood on the outside. She uttered some words in a loud voice, and the youth joined her, who also expressed surprise. I observed, with pleasure, that he did not go to the forest that day, but spent it in repairing the cottage, and cultivating the garden."

*By watching the cottagers, the Creature discovers that people communicate with words. After three months of study, he had learned that names were given to familiar objects:*

9    . . . "I learned and applied the words, fire, milk, bread, and wood. I learned also the names of the cottagers themselves. The youth and his companion had each of them several names, but the old man had only one, which was father. The girl was called sister, or Agatha; and the youth Felix, brother, or son. I cannot describe the delight I felt when I learned the ideas appropriated to each of these sounds, and was able to pronounce them. I distinguished several other words, without being able as yet to understand or apply them; such as good, dearest, unhappy.

10    "I spent the winter in this manner. The gentle manners and beauty of the cottagers greatly endeared them to me: when they were unhappy, I felt depressed; when they rejoiced, I sympathised in their joys. . . . The old man, I could perceive, often endeavoured to encourage his children, as sometimes I found that he called them, to cast off their melancholy. He would talk in a cheerful accent, with an expression of goodness that bestowed pleasure even upon me. Agatha listened with respect, her eyes sometimes filled with tears, which she endeavoured to wipe away unperceived; but I generally found that her countenance and tone were more cheerful after having listened to the exhortations of her father. It was

not thus with Felix. He was always the saddest of the group; and, even to my unpractised senses, he appeared to have suffered more deeply than his friends. But if his countenance was more sorrowful, his voice was more cheerful than that of his sister, especially when he addressed the old man.

11    "I could mention innumerable instances, which, although slight, marked the dispositions of these amiable cottagers. In the midst of poverty and want, Felix carried with pleasure to his sister the first little white flower that peeped out from beneath the snowy ground. Early in the morning, before she had risen, he cleared away the snow that obstructed her path to the milk-house, drew water from the well, and brought the wood from the out-house, where, to his perpetual astonishment, he found his store always replenished by an invisible hand. In the day, I believe, he worked sometimes for a neighbouring farmer, because he often went forth, and did not return until dinner, yet brought no wood with him. At other times he worked in the garden; but, as there was little to do in the frosty season, he read to the old man and Agatha."

*The Creature, observing the reading, figured out the relationship between the marks on the page and speech. His understanding improved over time, but he wanted to master language before revealing himself to the cottagers, hoping that his knowledge might "make them overlook the deformity of [his] figure."*

13    "I had admired the perfect forms of my cottagers—their grace, beauty, and delicate complexions: but how was I terrified, when I viewed myself in a transparent pool! At first I started back, unable to believe that it was indeed I who was reflected in the mirror; and when I became fully convinced that I was in reality the monster that I am, I was filled with the bitterest sensations of despondence and mortification. Alas! I did not yet entirely know the fatal effects of this miserable deformity."

## From Chapter XV

*The Creature finds three abandoned books,* Paradise Lost, *an epic poem by John Milton that tells the story of Lucifer's fall from grace; a volume of* Plutarch's Lives; *and* The Sorrows of Young Werther *by Johann Wolfgang von Goethe. Since he has been abandoned by his creator, the Creature must self-instruct in the ways of the world. The books serve as a guide for him to understand the behaviors of others and his own emotions. In the following excerpt, the Creature reflects on the fallen angel Lucifer who becomes Satan after he rebels against God.*

4    "As I read . . . I applied much personally to my own feelings and condition. I found myself similar, yet at the same time strangely unlike to the beings concerning whom I read, and to whose conversation I was a listener. I sympathised with, and partly understood them, but I was unformed in mind; I was dependent on none, and related to none. . . . My person was hideous, and my stature gigantic. What did this mean? Who

was I? What was I? Whence did I come? What was my destination? These questions continually recurred, but I was unable to solve them.

5        "The volume of 'Plutarch's Lives,' which I possessed, contained the histories of the first founders of the ancient republics. This book had a far different effect upon me from '[The] Sorrows of [Young] Werter.' I learned from Werter's imaginations despondency and gloom: but Plutarch taught me high thoughts; he elevated me above the wretched sphere of my own reflections, to admire and love the heroes of past ages. . . . I read of men concerned in public affairs, governing or massacring their species. I felt the greatest ardour for virtue rise within me, and abhorrence for vice . . . .

6        "But 'Paradise Lost' excited different and far deeper emotions. I read it, as I had read the other volumes which had fallen into my hands, as a true history. It moved every feeling of wonder and awe, that the picture of an omnipotent God warring with his creatures was capable of exciting. I often referred the several situations, as their similarity struck me, to my own. Like Adam, I was apparently united by no link to any other being in existence; but his state was far different from mine in every other respect. He had come forth from the hands of God a perfect creature, happy and prosperous, guarded by the especial care of his Creator; he was allowed to converse with, and acquire knowledge from, beings of a superior nature: but I was wretched, helpless, and alone. Many times I considered Satan as the fitter emblem of my condition; for often, like him, when I viewed the bliss of my protectors, the bitter gall of envy rose within me.

7        "Another circumstance strengthened and confirmed these feelings. Soon after my arrival in the hovel, I discovered some papers in the pocket of the dress which I had taken from your laboratory. . . . It was your journal of the four months that preceded my creation. You minutely described in these papers every step you took in the progress of your work. . . . Every thing is related in them which bears reference to my accursed origin; the whole detail of that series of disgusting circumstances which produced it, is set in view. . . . Why did you form a monster so hideous that even you turned from me in disgust? God, in pity, made man beautiful and alluring, after his own image; but my form is a filthy type of yours, more horrid even from the very resemblance. Satan had his companions, fellow-devils, to admire and encourage him; but I am solitary and abhorred.

"These were the reflections of my hours of despondency and solitude; but when I contemplated the virtues of the cottagers, their amiable and benevolent dispositions, I persuaded myself that when they should become acquainted with my admiration of their virtues, they would . . . overlook my personal deformity. Could they turn from their door one, however monstrous, who solicited their compassion and friendship? I resolved, at least, not to despair, but in every way to fit myself for an interview with them which would decide my fate. . . ."

## From Chapter XVI

*The Creature decides to reveal himself to the cottagers. The father, who is blind, talks to him and offers his help. However, when the others return to the cottage, they react with horror to the Creature's appearance. Felix violently throws him out of the cottage, and once again, he is alone. The family moves away in fear of the Creature, who feels hatred and vengeance for the first time. He burns the cottage down and sets out for Geneva to find his maker. Along the way, he saves a drowning girl, but he is mistaken for a villain and shot in the shoulder, and his anguish increases. In an attempt to remedy his loneliness, the Creature captures a young boy walking in the woods, thinking that because he is so young, he might not yet have fear of or prejudice toward deformity.*

26     "I seized on the boy as he passed, and drew him towards me. As soon as he beheld my form, he placed his hands before his eyes, and uttered a shrill scream: I drew his hand forcibly from his face, and said, 'Child, what is the meaning of this? I do not intend to hurt you; listen to me.'

27     "He struggled violently. 'Let me go,' he cried; 'monster! ugly wretch! you wish to eat me, and tear me to pieces—You are an ogre—Let me go, or I will tell my papa.'

28     "'Boy, you will never see your father again; you must come with me.'

29     "'Hideous monster! let me go. My papa is a Syndic[11]—he is M. Frankenstein—he will punish you. You dare not keep me.'

30     "'Frankenstein! you belong then to my enemy—to him towards whom I have sworn eternal revenge; you shall be my first victim.'

31     "The child still struggled, and loaded me with epithets which carried despair to my heart; I grasped his throat to silence him, and in a moment he lay dead at my feet.

32     "I gazed on my victim, and my heart swelled with exultation and hellish triumph: clapping my hands, I exclaimed, 'I, too, can create desolation; my enemy is not invulnerable; this death will carry despair to him, and a thousand other miseries shall torment and destroy him.'

33     "As I fixed my eyes on the child, I saw something glittering on his breast. I took it; it was a portrait of a most lovely woman. In spite of my malignity, it softened and attracted me. For a few moments I gazed with delight on her dark eyes, fringed by deep lashes, and her lovely lips; but presently my rage returned: I remembered that I was for ever deprived of the delights that such beautiful creatures could bestow; and that she whose resemblance I contemplated would, in regarding me, have changed that air of divine benignity to one expressive of disgust and affright.

34     "Can you wonder that such thoughts transported me with rage? . . ."

---

11 **Syndic:** government official

**VICTOR FRANKENSTEIN, TO ROBERT WALTON**

## From Chapter XX

*The Creature has told Victor about his killing William and framing Justine. He extracted a promise from Victor to create a female mate for him. In exchange, he and his female companion would leave Europe and move to South America so Victor could marry Elizabeth and live in peace. Victor agrees.*

3    I trembled, and my heart failed within me; when, on looking up, I saw, by the light of the moon, the dæmon at the casement.[12] A ghastly grin wrinkled his lips as he gazed on me, where I sat fulfilling the task which he had allotted to me. Yes, he had followed me in my travels; he had loitered in forests, hid himself in caves, or taken refuge in wide and desert heaths; and he now came to mark my progress, and claim the fulfilment of my promise.

4    As I looked on him, his countenance expressed the utmost extent of malice and treachery. I thought with a sensation of madness on my promise of creating another like to him, and trembling with passion, tore to pieces the thing on which I was engaged. The wretch saw me destroy the creature on whose future existence he depended for happiness, and, with a howl of devilish despair and revenge, withdrew.

5    I left the room, and, locking the door, made a solemn vow in my own heart never to resume my labours; and then, with trembling steps, I sought my own apartment. I was alone; none were near me to dissipate the gloom, and relieve me from the sickening oppression of the most terrible reveries.

6    Several hours passed, and I remained near my window gazing on the sea; it was almost motionless, for the winds were hushed, and all nature reposed under the eye of the quiet moon. . . . I felt the silence, although I was hardly conscious of its extreme profundity, until my ear was suddenly arrested by the paddling of oars near the shore, and a person landed close to my house.

7    In a few minutes after, I heard the creaking of my door, as if some one endeavoured to open it softly. I trembled from head to foot; I felt a presentiment of who it was, and wished to rouse one of the peasants who dwelt in a cottage not far from mine; but I was overcome by the sensation of helplessness, so often felt in frightful dreams . . . .

8    Presently I heard the sound of footsteps along the passage; the door opened, and the wretch whom I dreaded appeared. Shutting the door, he approached me, and said, in a smothered voice—

9    "You have destroyed the work which you began; what is it that you intend? Do you dare to break your promise? I have endured toil and misery: I left Switzerland with you; I crept along the shores of the Rhine, among its willow islands, and over the summits of its hills. I have dwelt many months in the heaths of England, and among the deserts of Scotland. I have endured incalculable fatigue, and cold, and hunger; do you dare destroy my hopes?"

---

12 **casement:** window

10     "Begone! I do break my promise; never will I create another like yourself, equal in deformity and wickedness."

. . .

13     The monster saw my determination in my face, and gnashed his teeth in the impotence of anger. "Shall each man," cried he, "find a wife for his bosom, and each beast have his mate, and I be alone? I had feelings of affection, and they were requited by detestation and scorn. Man! you may hate; but beware! your hours will pass in dread and misery, and soon the bolt will fall which must ravish from you your happiness for ever. Are you to be happy, while I grovel in the intensity of my wretchedness? You can blast my other passions; but revenge remains—revenge, henceforth dearer than light or food! I may die; but first you, my tyrant and tormentor, shall curse the sun that gazes on your misery. Beware; for I am fearless, and therefore powerful. I will watch with the wiliness of a snake, that I may sting with its venom. Man, you shall repent of the injuries you inflict."

14     "Devil, cease; and do not poison the air with these sounds of malice. I have declared my resolution to you, and I am no coward to bend beneath words. Leave me; I am inexorable."

15     "It is well. I go; but remember, I shall be with you on your wedding-night."

## From Chapter XXIV

*On Victor and Elizabeth's wedding night, the Creature murders Elizabeth. Victor sets out to find and kill his creation. The two men engage in a cat-and-mouse chase through Russia to the North Pole. During the chase, the Creature leaves notes for Victor.*

12     My life, as it passed thus, was indeed hateful to me, and it was during sleep alone that I could taste joy. O blessed sleep! often, when most miserable, I sank to repose, and my dreams lulled me even to rapture. The spirits that guarded me had provided these moments, or rather hours, of happiness, that I might retain strength to fulfil my pilgrimage. Deprived of this respite, I should have sunk under my hardships. During the day I was sustained and inspirited by the hope of night: for in sleep I saw my friends, my wife, and my beloved country; again I saw the benevolent countenance of my father, heard the silver tones of my Elizabeth's voice, and beheld Clerval enjoying health and youth. Often, when wearied by a toilsome march, I persuaded myself that I was dreaming until night should come, and that I should then enjoy reality in the arms of my dearest friends. What agonising fondness did I feel for them! how did I cling to their dear forms, as sometimes they haunted even my waking hours, and persuade myself that they still lived! At such moments vengeance, that burned within me, died in my heart, and I pursued my path towards the destruction of the dæmon, more as a task enjoined by heaven, as the mechanical impulse of some power of which I was unconscious, than as the ardent desire of my soul.

13      What his feelings were whom I pursued I cannot know. Sometimes, indeed, he left marks in writing on the barks of the trees, or cut in stone, that guided me, and instigated my fury. "My reign is not yet over," (these words were legible in one of these inscriptions;) "you live, and my power is complete. Follow me; I seek the everlasting ices of the north, where you will feel the misery of cold and frost, to which I am impassive. You will find near this place, if you follow not too tardily, a dead hare; eat, and be refreshed. Come on, my enemy; we have yet to wrestle for our lives; but many hard and miserable hours must you endure until that period shall arrive."

14      Scoffing devil! Again do I vow vengeance; again do I devote thee, miserable fiend, to torture and death. Never will I give up my search, until he or I perish; and then with what ecstasy shall I join my Elizabeth, and my departed friends, who even now prepare for me the reward of my tedious toil and horrible pilgrimage!

15      As I still pursued my journey to the northward, the snows thickened, and the cold increased in a degree almost too severe to support. The peasants were shut up in their hovels, and only a few of the most hardy ventured forth to seize the animals whom starvation had forced from their hiding-places to seek for prey. The rivers were covered with ice, and no fish could be procured; and thus I was cut off from my chief article of maintenance.

16      The triumph of my enemy increased with the difficulty of my labours. One inscription that he left was in these words:—"Prepare! your toils only begin: wrap yourself in furs, and provide food; for we shall soon enter upon a journey where your sufferings will satisfy my everlasting hatred."

17      My courage and perseverance were invigorated by these scoffing words; I resolved not to fail in my purpose; and, calling on Heaven to support me, I continued with unabated fervour to traverse immense deserts, until the ocean appeared at a distance, and formed the utmost boundary of the horizon. Oh! how unlike it was to the blue seas of the south! Covered with ice, it was only to be distinguished from land by its superior wildness and ruggedness. The Greeks wept for joy when they beheld the Mediterranean from the hills of Asia, and hailed with rapture the boundary of their toils. I did not weep; but I knelt down, and, with a full heart, thanked my guiding spirit for conducting me in safety to the place where I hoped, notwithstanding my adversary's gibe, to meet and grapple with him.

 **ROBERT WALTON, TO HIS SISTER MARGARET**

August 26th, 17—.

1      You have read this strange and terrific story, Margaret; and do you not feel your blood congeal with horror, like that which even now curdles mine? Sometimes, seized with sudden agony, he could not continue his tale; at others, his voice broken, yet piercing, uttered with difficulty the words so replete with anguish. . . .

5    Thus has a week passed away, while I have listened to the strangest tale that ever imagination formed. My thoughts, and every feeling of my soul, have been drunk up by the interest for my guest, which this tale, and his own elevated and gentle manners, have created. I wish to soothe him; yet can I counsel one so infinitely miserable, so destitute of every hope of consolation, to live? Oh, no! the only joy that he can now know will be when he composes his shattered spirit to peace and death. . . .

8    Must I then lose this admirable being? I have longed for a friend; I have sought one who would sympathise with and love me. Behold, on these desert seas I have found such a one; but, I fear, I have gained him only to know his value, and lose him. I would reconcile him to life, but he repulses the idea.

September 2d.

10    I write to you, encompassed by peril. . . . I am surrounded by mountains of ice, which admit of no escape, and threaten every moment to crush my vessel. The brave fellows, whom I have persuaded to be my companions, lives of all these men are endangered through me. . . . If we are lost, my mad schemes are the cause. . . .

*Here Walton explains that his crew have demanded that if the ice melts and the ship is free to move again, they head south and return home. The ice does melt and Walton bitterly agrees to return home, believing his "hopes blasted by cowardice and indecision." Walton reports Frankenstein's final words.*

30    "That he should live to be an instrument of mischief disturbs me; in other respects, this hour, when I momentarily expect my release, is the only happy one which I have enjoyed for several years. The forms of the beloved dead flit before me, and I hasten to their arms. Farewell, Walton! Seek happiness in tranquillity, and avoid ambition, even if it be only the apparently innocent one of distinguishing yourself in science and discoveries. Yet why do I say this? I have myself been blasted in these hopes, yet another may succeed." . . .

32    Margaret, what comment can I make on the untimely extinction of this glorious spirit? What can I say, that will enable you to understand the depth of my sorrow? . . . But I journey towards England, and I may there find consolation.

*Walton then hears a noise in Frankenstein's cabin. He finds the Creature standing over Frankenstein's dead body. The Creature seems to want pardon for destroying all that was valuable to his maker. He says that after he killed Clerval he pitied Frankenstein, but when he learned Frankenstein had the love of Elizabeth, the kind of love he could never know, he felt an insatiable thirst for vengeance.*

42    ". . . Once my fancy was soothed with dreams of virtue, of fame, and of enjoyment. Once I falsely hoped to meet with beings, who, pardoning my outward form, would love me for the excellent qualities which I was

capable of unfolding. I was nourished with high thoughts of honour and devotion. But now crime has degraded me. . . .

43     "You, who call Frankenstein your friend, seem to have a knowledge of my crimes and his misfortunes. But, in the detail which he gave you of them, he could not sum up the hours and months of misery which I endured, wasting in impotent passions. For while I destroyed his hopes, I did not satisfy my own desires. They were for ever ardent and craving; still I desired love and fellowship, and I was still spurned. Was there no injustice in this? Am I to be thought the only criminal, when all human kind sinned against me? . . . Even now my blood boils at the recollection of this injustice. . . .

45     "Fear not that I shall be the instrument of future mischief. My work is nearly complete. . . . I shall quit your vessel on the ice-raft which brought me thither, and shall seek the most northern extremity of the globe; I shall collect my funeral pile, and consume to ashes this miserable frame, that its remains may afford no light to any curious and unhallowed wretch, who would create such another as I have been. I shall die. I shall no longer feel the agonies which now consume me, or be the prey of feelings unsatisfied, yet unquenched. He is dead who called me into being; and when I shall be no more, the very remembrance of us both will speedily vanish. I shall no longer see the sun or stars, or feel the winds play on my cheeks. Light, feeling, and sense will pass away; and in this condition must I find my happiness. Some years ago, when the images which this world affords first opened upon me, when I felt the cheering warmth of summer, and heard the rustling of the leaves and the warbling of the birds, and these were all to me, I should have wept to die; now it is my only consolation. Polluted by crimes, and torn by the bitterest remorse, where can I find rest but in death?. . ."

47     "But soon . . . these burning miseries will be extinct. I shall ascend my funeral pile triumphantly, and exult in the agony of the torturing flames. The light of that conflagration will fade away; my ashes will be swept into the sea by the winds. My spirit will sleep in peace; or if it thinks, it will not surely think thus. Farewell."

48     He sprung from the cabin-window, as he said this, upon the ice-raft which lay close to the vessel. He was soon borne away by the waves, and lost in darkness and distance.

 **What Do You Know?**

Before learning the new skills and information this unit presents, assess what you already know. Read the anchor text, *Frankenstein* by Mary Shelley. Then answer the following questions. Don't worry if you find these challenging. Answering questions on a subject before formally learning about it is one way to help you deepen your understanding of new concepts.

## CLOSE READING

1. How do the perspectives of Victor Frankenstein and the other characters differ? How do these different perspectives lead to different interpretations of the work as a whole?

2. What are some of the similarities and differences between characters? What is the significance of those similarities and differences?

3. Do any of the characters make inconsistent choices? What motivates those characters to make such choices?

4. Which excerpts have the most tension? How does the author create tension and suspense?

5. What contrasts did you notice? How did the contrasts affect your response to the text?

6. How do the narrators' tone, diction, and syntax differ from those of other narrators or characters?

## INTERPRETATION

1. What larger themes might the tensions and conflicts in the novel represent?

2. What evidence can you cite to support an interpretation of themes?

**Source:** Wikimedia Commons

Statue of Prometheus (1965) by Imre Varga, Budapest, Hungary

Prometheus not only brought fire to humanity (shown in the sculpture) but also, according to some myths, actually created humans from clay.

*What does the allusion to the Prometheus myth add to the story of Frankenstein and his creature?*

# Differences Between and Within Characters

## Part 1:  Differences Between and Within Characters

**Understand**

Characters in literature allow readers to study and explore a range of values, beliefs, assumptions, biases, and cultural norms represented by those characters. (CHR-1)

**Demonstrate**

Identify and describe what specific textual details reveal about a character, that character's perspective, and that character's motives. (1.A)

Explain the function of contrasting characters. (1.C)

Explain how a character's own choices, actions, and speech reveal complexities in that character, and explain the function of those complexities. (1.E)

See also Units 1, 2, 3, 4 & 9

**Source:** *AP® English Literature and Composition Course and Exam Description*

**Essential Question:**  How do differing perspectives, contrasting characters, and complexities within characters reveal values, beliefs, assumptions, and biases and influence the interpretation of a text?

Literary characters have their own unique perspective on events and on other characters, perspectives shaped by their backgrounds and biases. Contrasting characters highlight these different perspectives. Even within characters, inconsistencies between private thoughts and public behavior reveal tensions and complexities between private and professed values. These inconsistencies add complexity to a text.

---

**KEY TERMS**

---

perspective                    foil characters

# 1.1 Perspectives and Literary Interpretation | CHR-1.T

Open a detective novel and you expect that you will get conflicting accounts of what happened—from people with insufficient information or a poor view of the scene or even outright lies to cover their own guilt. In the end, however, you expect that the detective will sort through the accounts, gather some evidence of her own, get to the bottom of the crime, and find and bring to justice the perpetrator. The 1950 Japanese movie *Rashomon* takes a different, more complex approach to telling its crime story. Through flashbacks and other techniques, the movie tells the story of four different—and conflicting—eyewitness accounts of a crime without resolving which is the "true" one. To each of the eyewitnesses, his or her story is the truth. That story is true to the character's **perspective**—the understanding characters, narrators, and speakers have of their circumstances, which is influenced by their biases and backgrounds. Different character, narrator, or speaker perspectives often reveal different information, develop different attitudes, and influence different interpretations of a text and the ideas in it. Like the classic movie *Rashomon*, Shelley's novel *Frankenstein* employs several different accounts of the events of the plot through several narrative voices. To get a more complete picture of a work's complexity, readers analyze the perspectives of multiple characters and the narrator(s) and examine how those different perspectives allow multiple interpretations of the work as a whole.

## Different Information Revealed

Because of their differences in perspective, narrators, characters, or speakers often reveal different information. Near the end of *Frankenstein; or The New Prometheus*, the Creature even points that out:

> You, who call Frankenstein your friend, seem to have a knowledge of my crimes and his misfortunes. But, in the detail which he gave you of them, he could not sum up the hours and months of misery which I endured, wasting in impotent passions.

For another example, consider the novel *Kindred* by Octavia Butler, which includes a wide range of diverse characters: young and old, Black and White, and—because it includes time travel between the summer of 1976 and the days before the Civil War—modern and historic. In the following excerpt, Dana, the young Black protagonist, recounts to her husband Kevin, who is White, what happened during her first surprising time travel when she suddenly disappeared from their new home in California and found herself in the past in a muddy river where she saved a boy from drowning. Because of their different perspectives, only Kevin can provide information about what he witnessed when she was gone, and only Dana can provide information about what happened to her in the past: his facts, her facts.

"But it was real! I was there!" I caught myself, took a deep breath, and slowed down. "All right. If you told me a story like this, I probably wouldn't believe it either, but like you said, this mud came from somewhere."

"Yes."

"Look, what did you see? What do you think happened?"

He frowned a little, shook his head. "You vanished." He seemed to have to force the words out. "You were here until my hand was just a couple of inches from you. Then, suddenly, you were gone. I couldn't believe it. I just stood there. Then you were back again and on the other side of the room."

"Do you believe it yet?"

He shrugged. "It happened. I saw it. You vanished and you reappeared. Facts."

"I reappeared wet, muddy, and scared to death."

"Yes."

"And I know what I saw, and what I did—my facts. They're no crazier than yours."

"I don't know what to think." . . .

## Different Attitudes

The different perspectives of characters, narrators, and speakers also contribute to the development of different attitudes. For example, in *Kindred*, both Kevin and Dana are writers. Before they were married, Kevin asked Dana to type some stories for him. To Kevin, the request was just asking "a little favor." He was likely used to people, especially women, doing things for him. From Dana's perspective, however, the request touched on the restrictions she believed her aunt and uncle, who raised her, placed on her schooling when they urged her to study to be a secretary. Her attitude toward that kind of work is that it is demeaning, while Kevin's attitude is that it is just a little favor.

## Differing Interpretations

Dana in *Kindred* is the first-person narrator, so her perspective is the predominant one. After her first time travel, she experiences many more trips back in time and comes to see slavery first hand. Since hers is the main perspective, many readers would likely interpret the novel as a commentary on the long-lasting effects of slavery. However, two prominent White and male perspectives—those of Kevin and Tom Weylin, the father of the boy Dana saved and a plantation owner both Kevin and Dana come to know—suggest additional possible interpretations.

Kevin travels back in time at one point. He gets stuck in the past for five years, separated from Dana. When he finally returns, after Dana has been home for some time, he is mad at her.

90  I took his face between my hands and looked into his eyes, now truly cold. "I don't know what it was like for you," I said, "being gone so long, having so little control over whether you'd ever get back. I can't really know, I guess. But I do know . . . that I almost didn't want to be alive when I thought I'd left you behind for good. But now that you're back . . . ."

91       He pulled away from me and walked out of the room. The expression on his face was like something I'd seen, something I was used to seeing on Tom Weylin. Something closed and ugly.

Despite the genuine love between Kevin and Dana, Kevin was clearly shaken by his experience in the past when social norms were so different, and Dana's recognition of a "closed and ugly" look on Kevin's face like that on Tom Weylin's suggests that the power dynamics of race and gender, while greatly softened in the 20th century, still privileged White males. That observation could support an interpretation with a focus on gender as well as on race.

The chart below summarizes the different information, different attitudes, and influence on different interpretations that multiple perspectives can present.

| Character Perspectives | Dana | Kevin |
|---|---|---|
| Information Revealed | Can tell what happens when she returns to the past | Can tell what happens in the present during her absence |
| Attitudes | Resents being asked to type manuscripts, regarding it as menial work | Thinks that asking Dana to type manuscripts is just asking a small favor, suggesting an entitled stance |
| Influence on Interpretations | Recognizes some similarities between Kevin and Tom Weylin after expressing her love for Kevin | Behaves in a way that suggests the "closed and ugly" look of men in power in the past |

Table 6-1

In *Frankenstein*, two different first-person narrators—Victor Frankenstein and the creature he brought to life—are nested within the first-person frame of Robert Walton's letters to his sister. Each reveals different information, expresses different attitudes, and allows the reader to form different interpretations.

 **Remember:** Different character, narrator, or speaker perspectives often reveal different information, develop different attitudes, and influence different interpretations of a text and the ideas in it. (CHR-1.T)

## 1.1 Checkpoint

*Review the narrations of Victor Frankenstein and the Creature on pages 357–369. Then complete the open-response activities and answer the multiple-choice questions.*

1. Find textual evidence that shows the different information revealed, attitudes expressed, and influences on interpretations resulting from the different perspectives of Victor Frankenstein and the Creature. Then complete a chart like the one below.

| Character Perspectives | Frankenstein | The Creature |
|---|---|---|
| Information Revealed | | |
| Attitudes | | |
| Influence on Interpretations | | |

2. Using the information from your chart, write a paragraph with a claim, evidence, and commentary that explains the significance of the passage.

3. Which of the following best captures the complexity of Robert's perspective on Victor?

    (A) "His countenance instantly assumed an aspect of the deepest gloom" (Letter IV, paragraph 14)

    (B) "when he speaks, although his words are culled with the choicest art, yet they flow with rapidity and unparalleled eloquence." (Letter IV, paragraph 18)

    (C) "He excites at once my admiration and my pity" (Letter IV, paragraph 18)

    (D) "Yet, although unhappy, he is not so utterly occupied by his own misery, but that he interests himself deeply in the projects of others." (Letter IV, paragraph 19)

    (E) "As I spoke, a dark gloom spread over my listener's countenance." (Letter IV, paragraph 19)

4. Respectively, Elizabeth's and Victor's attitudes following the death of Justine (Chapter IX) are best described as

    (A) reluctant and arrogant

    (B) joyless and denying

    (C) lost and pitiful

    (D) hopeless and guilty

    (E) trusting and vain

**Creating on Your Own**

One way the story of Frankenstein and the Creature gets told is through the letters from Walton to his sister. Create a situation in which you find yourself far from home—maybe you are an exchange student in a foreign land, or maybe you have undertaken a solo wilderness trek—and you encounter a person with a remarkable story that you want to share with someone back home. Choose a person to whom you will write. In your first letter, establish your circumstances —your environment and purpose for being there. Then introduce the character with a remarkable story and provide a brief hint at what makes the story remarkable. Save your work.

# 1.2 The Function of Foils | CHR-1.U

Jewelers used to place gemstones on a backing of foil to make them shine more brightly. In a similar way, writers use **foil characters** (or foils) to illuminate, through contrast, another character's traits, attributes, or values. Often the foil is neither the protagonist nor the antagonist, but rather a character who helps reveal motivations and values of a major character. Whether friend or foe, the major character and the foil share some traits and differ on others. Foils can have a relatively minor role but still be significant to the story—they function mainly to broaden your understanding of the conflicts of another character.

## Contrasts in Foils

While the main character and the foil often share similarities that can highlight values and themes in the work, often the contrasts are even more revealing. They represent alternatives that allow readers to gain insight into the non-foil character's traits and values. For example, consider the character of Alice, a foil for Dana in *Kindred*. Alice is a Black woman from the past who is free at the beginning of the novel but later enslaved. A childhood friend of Rufus Weylin, the boy Dana saves on her first trip back in time, Alice is forced into a sexual relationship with him when they are grown. (Alice and Rufus turn out to be Dana's great-grandparents.) Alice feels powerless and depressed. In the end, she takes her own life. Rufus also becomes attached to Dana.

While they share some characteristics, the differences between Dana and Alice show the drastically different conditions and perspectives of a Black woman in 1976 and an enslaved Black woman before the Civil War. The diagram on the next page shows similarities and differences between the two women. The sadness and powerlessness of Alice highlight the freedom and vitality of Dana.

## Illuminating the Main Character

While Alice has other roles in the novel, her role as a foil to Dana shines a light on Dana's agency. The similarities between the women show that both held the same understanding of the unequal power in pre-Civil War times. However, it is through their varying responses to these power differences that Dana's confidence and vitality are displayed.

**Remember:** Foil characters (foils) serve to illuminate, through contrast, the traits, attributes, or values of another character. (CHR-1.U)

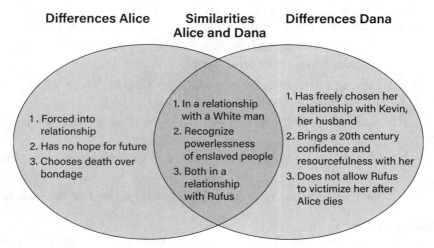

**Differences Alice**

1. Forced into relationship
2. Has no hope for future
3. Chooses death over bondage

**Similarities Alice and Dana**

1. In a relationship with a White man
2. Recognize powerlessness of enslaved people
3. Both in a relationship with Rufus

**Differences Dana**

1. Has freely chosen her relationship with Kevin, her husband
2. Brings a 20th century confidence and resourcefulness with her
3. Does not allow Rufus to victimize her after Alice dies

Figure 6-1

## 1.2 Checkpoint

*Review the excerpts from Robert Walton's letters on pages 353–356 and 369–371. Then complete the open-response activities and answer the multiple-choice questions.*

1. On separate paper, draw a Venn diagram like Figure 6-1 above but complete the diagram for Walton and Frankenstein.

2. In a few sentences, explain how the differences between Walton as a foil to Frankenstein help illuminate Frankenstein's character and the ideas in the work as a whole.

3. As a foil to Victor, Elizabeth highlights all of the following about his character EXCEPT

    (A) his self-centered ambition

    (B) a cautious and thoughtful kindness

    (C) a lack of empathy and compassion

    (D) his longing to change and control the world

    (E) his sense of entitlement and privilege

4. Which of the following best describes the difference between Henry Clerval and Victor based on information in the excerpt from Chapter II?

(A) Victor worries about how Elizabeth perceives him while Henry is not concerned about other people at all.

(B) Henry understands the effect Elizabeth has on Victor while Victor remains ignorant.

(C) Henry is more concerned with the general good of humanity than Victor.

(D) Victor cares more about the moralities and virtues of heroes than Henry.

(E) Henry cares for Victor while Victor cares for no one but himself.

**Creating on Your Own**

Review the letter you wrote in the last Creating on Your Own activity. As you begin to imagine the remarkable story your character will tell, think as well of a character you could introduce as a foil who would illuminate traits of your main character. Maybe the remarkable story your character tells concerns experiencing a close encounter with an alien creature. Maybe the foil you create for that character is a doubting astronomer you meet on your journey. Sketch out ideas—be imaginative! You can always refine and revise as you continue working on your series of letters. Save your work.

# 1.3 Inconsistencies | CHR-1.V, CHR-1.W

It's human nature: people want to be thought of favorably by authority figures, such as doctors, who ask them questions about their behaviors. "Do you have healthy eating habits? Do you limit screen time?" If asked those questions by their doctors, more than 80 percent of people either exaggerate or lie outright so they will not be judged harshly. The inconsistencies between what these patients report and their actual behavior reveal tensions and complexities between their private and professed values. For example, patients may know that limiting screen time is good for them, but they also value the social connections they get online and find it hard to unplug. In literature, these competing, conflicting, or inconsistent choices or actions in a character contribute to complexity in a text. They can also lead to puzzling and sometimes destructive choices and behaviors.

## Private Thoughts versus Public Actions

Many novels include inconsistent and complex characters. In E. M. Forster's *A Passage to India,* for example, the garrulous character Dr. Aziz often talks before he thinks, leaving him no choice but to revoke invitations and change plans. Also, he is aware of the prejudice against Indians during the British Raj (when Britain ruled India), yet he himself, a Hindu Indian, is prejudiced against Muslim Indians.

F. Scott Fitzgerald's *The Great Gatsby* is another novel with inconsistent and complex characters. It is narrated by Nick Carraway, a young man from a prominent Midwestern family who has gone to New York to learn the bond business. In the summer of 1922, he rents a bungalow between two mansions in the village of West Egg. Across the bay is the more fashionable village of East Egg. The "old money" residents of East Egg look down on the new millionaires of West Egg.

One of his neighbors is the enigmatic Jay Gatsby, who throws decadent parties attended by the newly rich and famous. Many of them have no idea who their host is, and rumors about him abound. Gatsby says, "I'll tell you God's truth. . . . I am the son of some wealthy people in the middle-west—all dead now. I was brought up in America but educated at Oxford because all my ancestors have been educated there for many years. It is a family tradition." Gatsby's story does not ring true to the "old money" people he meets. Indeed, after his death at the end of the book, Gatsby's father shows up for the funeral—not dead after all. He is proud of his son's accomplishments. Born James Gatz, Gatsby had set out on a course of self-improvement at an early age, one that would lead him to adopt a new name and a new persona to go with it, his private thoughts and public actions clearly at odds. His enormous mansion and lavish parties were attempts to impress Nick's cousin Daisy, with whom he had fallen in love five years earlier, but who had married one of Nick's Yale classmates, Tom Buchanan.

## Complex Choices and Behaviors

The competing, conflicting, or inconsistent choices and actions of a character contribute to complexity in a text. For example, tensions between what people are expected to do and their subconscious desires can coexist for a while. In *The Great Gatsby*, for example, Daisy Buchanan seems to be a traditional Southern belle transported to Long Island. She is married, has a young daughter, and turns a blind eye to her husband's infidelity. But she has carried a torch for the handsome soldier Jay Gatsby who had been stationed in Louisville before being shipped off to war five years before. The two are reunited at Nick's bungalow and begin to meet secretly. When Tom realizes what is going on, the two men fight a verbal duel for Daisy, who ends up choosing to stay with her husband. Her choices to meet secretly with Gatsby and yet stay with her husband show competing forces within Daisy and inconsistent actions that add complexity to her character and the text.

 **Remember:** Inconsistencies between the private thoughts of characters and their actual behavior reveal tensions and complexities between private and professed values. A character's competing, conflicting, or inconsistent choices or actions contribute to complexity in a text. (CHR-1.V–W)

## 1.3 Checkpoint

*Review the excerpts from Chapter XV on pages 364–365. Then complete the open-response activity and answer the multiple-choice question.*

1. Copy the following chart on separate paper. Based on the details in this selection, complete the chart with at least one example for each character. Then write a paragraph explaining how the inconsistencies add complexity to *Frankenstein*.

| Victor's Inconsistencies | The Creature's Inconsistencies |
|---|---|
| | |

2. Considering his later behavior, the Creature's statement "I felt the greatest ardour for virtue rise within me, an abhorrence for vice" (Chapter XV, paragraph 5) reveals a tension between his

   (A) arrogance and vulnerability

   (B) embarrassment and hostility

   (C) desires and upbringing

   (D) ignorance of morality and desire for vengeance

   (E) cruelty and power

### Creating on Your Own

Write your second letter to your chosen recipient. Add complexity by introducing internal conflicts that cause one of the characters to make choices that are inconsistent. If necessary, add more characters to your emerging epistolary (letter-based) story. Save your work.

## Part 1 Apply What You Have Learned

Carefully examine the excerpts from *Frankenstein* on pages 353–371 to gather textual evidence that reveals Frankenstein's perspective and motives. Determine how his perspective motivates him to make choices that are complex, conflicted, and inconsistent. Repeat the process for Robert Walton. Then write two paragraphs, one on each character, using evidence and commentary to explain how their perspectives provide different information and attitudes that can lead to multiple interpretations.

**Reflect on the Essential Question** Write a brief response that answers the essential question: *How do differing perspectives, contrasting characters, and complexities within characters reveal values, beliefs, assumptions, and biases?* In your answer, correctly use the key terms listed on page 373.

# Plot Sequence and Contrasts

---

**Enduring Understanding and Skills**

### Part 2  Plot Sequence and Contrasts

**Understand**

The arrangement of the parts and sections of a text, the relationship of the parts to each other, and the sequence in which the text reveals information are all structural choices made by a writer that contribute to the reader's interpretation of a text. (STR-1)

**Demonstrate**

Identify and describe how plot orders events in a narrative. (3.A)
Explain the function of a particular sequence of events in a plot. (3.B)
Explain the function of contrasts within a text. (3.D)
See also Units 1, 2, 4, 7 & 8

**Source:** *AP' English Literature and Composition Course and Exam Description*

---

**Essential Question:** How do chronological interruptions in the plot as well as characters' contradictions and inconsistencies affect readers' experiences?

When you write academic papers, you follow a logical line of reasoning. Point A leads logically to point B. Often the structures of such writing follow a chronological order. The 24-hour day and the 12-month calendar contribute to the idea that a sequential march through time is precisely measured, logical, and normal. Perhaps, however, you have experienced time slowing down or speeding up, or long stretches of time that are not as memorable as others. When you are bored, time drags. Conversely, when you are having fun, time moves quickly. In such cases perceived time is quite different from measured time. In *Exit West* by Mohsin Hamid (Unit 3), the narrator describes how the impact of rocket fire "accelerated time itself, a day's toll outpacing that of a decade." Authors of fiction, poetry, and drama manipulate time in order to replicate ways people perceive it.

---

**KEY TERMS**

| | | |
|---|---|---|
| flashback | in medias res | stream of |
| foreshadowing | | consciousness |

---

# 2.1 Interruptions in Chronology | STR-1.X, STR-1.Y

In the simplest plot structures, writers relate events in chronological order—that is, the order in which they occur. However, writers often introduce narrative structures that interrupt the plot's chronological order. Writers may choose not to begin at the beginning but in the thick of the action, or they may interrupt the story with a passage of stream of consciousness. These interruptive techniques help build anticipation in readers by creating suspense or heightening tension.

## Types, Purposes, and Effect of Interruptions

Authors have several options when they want to manipulate the narrative sequence of their work. All of these techniques are easy to identify, but thoughtful readers go beyond merely recognizing the device to consider its effect. Some of the major devices that control time are described below, along with some possible effects they have on readers.

**Flashback** This is one of the most common and easily identifiable narrative devices. A **flashback** is a device in which the narrator or speaker recounts an event that occurred earlier than the current narrative. Flashbacks can add complexity and depth by revealing information about characters, places, or things through memories or conversations.

**Possible purpose and effect of a flashback:**

- Fills in important background information after the reader has been hooked
- Provides a memory that explains character motivation

In *Kindred*, for example, several chapters begin with details of Kevin and Dana's lives before they were married. By the time readers get to those, they are hooked on the current story of time travel between the 19th and 20th centuries and interested in what motivated these two to marry.

**Foreshadowing** Another literary device that interrupts chronology hints at future events rather than recounting past events. **Foreshadowing** is a literary device that gives the audience a hint at future plot developments without revealing the final outcome. It may do this directly, by explicitly suggesting what may happen; indirectly, by providing subtle clues that hint at an outcome; through prophecy, as in the Old Testament and many classical Greek tragedies; or through symbols, such as a crow, which is often an omen of death.

**Possible purpose and effect of foreshadowing:**

- Alerts the reader to an impending event
- Builds suspense by giving only hints, not explicit details of what will happen later
- Creates curiosity in the reader to find out how the event will unfold

Mohsin Hamid often uses foreshadowing in *Exit West* (see Unit 3). For example, when Nadia and Saeed are taking leave of Saeed's father before going through their first door, Saeed's father quietly asks Nadia to stay by Saeed's side until he is out of danger: "and in the end she promised, and it was an easy promise to make because she had at that time no thoughts of leaving Saeed." The phrase "at that time" foreshadows that she later would have thoughts of leaving Saeed.

On the first few pages of *The Great Gatsby*, the narrator Nick Carraway foreshadows the end of the story: "Gatsby turned out all right at the end."

> Gatsby . . . represented everything for which I have an unaffected scorn. If personality is an unbroken series of successful gestures, then there was something gorgeous about him, some heightened sensitivity to the promises of life, as if he were related to one of those intricate machines that register earthquakes ten thousand miles away. This responsiveness had nothing to do with that flabby impressionability which is dignified under the name of "creative temperament"—it was an extraordinary gift for hope, a romantic readiness such as I have never found in any other person and which is not likely I shall ever find again. No—Gatsby turned out all right at the end; it is what preyed on Gatsby, what foul dust floated in the wake of his dreams that temporarily closed out my interest in the abortive sorrows and short-winded elations of men.

Also, in the final chapter of *Kindred*, Dana has returned from her fifth trip to antebellum Maryland. In order to come back to the 20th century, she has to fear for her life. During her fifth trip she slits her wrists in order to return home. As her husband Kevin notes, she could easily have died. He sees the danger in her going back to the past and says, "Then . . . it doesn't seem to me that you have such a difficult decision ahead of you," suggesting that she shouldn't go back. Dana responds, "But I do." Dana stays in 1976 for 15 days, but readers know she will return to the 19th century and again be in danger. Butler uses foreshadowing to keep the reader engaged by building suspense and creating curiosity about how the events will transpire.

Because Butler's story uses time travel, sometimes what may seem to be a flashback is not. For example, whenever Dana returns from her time in the past in Maryland, she returns to the present, not some distant time before the present, which would be characteristic of a flashback.

**In Medias Res** Sometimes a writer chooses to begin a story with a dramatic event that is the result of previous events. This practice, which is common in epics such as Homer's *Iliad* and *Odyssey*, is referred to as **in medias res**, a Latin phrase that means "in the midst of things." This narrative technique produces a dramatic effect intended to immediately grab the audience's attention. The events leading up to the opening scene are filled in later through flashbacks.

**Possible purposes and effect of in medias res:**

- Creates immediate interest in the reader to discover what led to the opening event
- Signals that the immediate event is the result of previous actions

For example, in the prologue to *Kindred,* Dana has lost her arm from above the elbow, and her husband Kevin has spent several days in jail under suspicion that he was responsible for her injuries. The rest of the novel explains the events that led up to the amputation in her final confrontation with Rufus. In addition, each time Dana goes back to 19th-century Maryland, she arrives in medias res, after some event that has endangered Rufus's life but in time to save him.

**Stream of Consciousness** Writers use various types of *interior monologue,* a technique that allows readers to eavesdrop on the innermost thoughts of a character. **Stream of consciousness** is an extreme form of interior monologue that attempts to replicate the actual thought process. It is a structural break in action to reveal a character's thoughts in a style that portrays nonlinear thinking patterns without objective commentary. The narrative can be in either first or third person. Both types of narrators may use signals such as "I/she thought," dashes, or italics to alert the reader to expect a shift from rational thoughts to thoughts that may be jumbled, incomplete, repetitive, divergent, or grammatically incorrect.

**Purpose and effect of stream of consciousness:**

- Attempts to replicate the way people's thoughts flow
- Gives readers insight into characters' personalities and motivations
- Signals a shift in character development
- Helps identify tensions between public actions and private thoughts

The 1922 novel *Ulysses* by James Joyce is one of the most famous examples of the stream of consciousness style. Told by a third-person omniscient narrator, the 900-page novel takes place in one day. The chief function of the narrator is to replicate the thoughts of Leopold Bloom, his wife Molly, and Stephen Dedalus, who is Joyce's literary alter ego.

Note how the following passage from *Ulysses* gives insight into the character Molly Bloom. In this passage she struggles to sleep and associates freely. These thoughts trigger further associations. She tries to get to sleep by counting, but her mind continues to wander. Molly's overactive mind is preventing her from sleeping.

> . . . a quarter after what an unearthly hour I suppose theyre just getting up in China now . . . well soon have the nuns ringing the angelus theyve nobody coming in to spoil their sleep except an odd priest or two for his night office the alarmclock next door at cockshout clattering the brains out of itself let me see if I can doze off 1 2 3 4 5 what kind of flowers are those they invented like the stars the wallpaper in Lombard street was much nicer the apron he gave me was like that something only I only wore it twice better lower this lamp and try again so that I can get up early . . . .

While many authors use interior monologue, only a few use actual stream of consciousness, and few use it as much as Joyce did in *Ulysses*. Marcel Proust, Virginia Woolf, and William Faulkner are three authors who used stream of consciousness extensively, while others use it much more sparingly.

 **Remember:** Some narrative structures interrupt the chronology of a plot; such structures include flashback, foreshadowing, in medias res, and stream of consciousness. Narrative structures that interrupt the chronology of a plot, such as flashback, foreshadowing, in medias res, and stream of consciousness, can directly affect readers' experiences with a text by creating anticipation or suspense or building tension. (STR-1.X–Y)

## 2.1 Checkpoint

*Review the excerpts from* Frankenstein *on pages 353–371. Then complete the following open-response activity and answer the multiple-choice questions.*

1. On separate paper, recreate the chart below. First, in your own words define each of the structural devices authors use to interrupt the events in a story. Then, using *Frankenstein* or another longer work that you are studying, find examples of these devices where possible and determine their effect on the story. One example is done for you, though you should be able to provide at least two more flashbacks from *Frankenstein*.

| Device | Definition | Purpose and Effect | Example |
|---|---|---|---|
| **Flashback** | A flashback is a scene that interrupts the chronology of a story to take readers back in time to an earlier event. | Flashbacks give insight into how a character came to be what he or she is. | Chapter II, paragraph 6<br><br>"Besides, in drawing the picture of my early days, I also record those events which led, by insensible steps, to my after tale of misery: for when I would account to myself for the birth of that passion, which afterwards ruled my destiny, I find it arise, like a mountain river, from ignoble and almost forgotten sources; but, swelling as it proceeded, it became the torrent which, in its course, has swept away all my hopes and joys."<br><br>2.<br><br>3. |
| **Foreshadowing** | | | |
| **In Medias Res** | . | | |

2. All of the following describe an effect of beginning this novel in medias res EXCEPT

    (A) to create empathy and understanding for the plight of both Victor and the Creature

    (B) to build suspense around the actions of the Creature

    (C) to establish a tension between the early events of the story and their (yet unknown) causes

    (D) to emphasize how shocking the events are as they are related to Walton's sister

    (E) to make the reader as curious and involved in the story as Robert Walton

3. The interruptions in chronology in *Frankenstein* serve primarily to

    (A) establish a clear background and setting for the events

    (B) create uncertainty about the various narrators' reliability

    (C) reflect the complexity of the story's themes and characters

    (D) provide a window into the characters' weaknesses

    (E) add variety to the pacing of the story

**Creating on Your Own**

What are the most complex events in your epistolary story? Experiment with ways you can interrupt the chronology of the narrative to do one or more of the following in your third letter, and then save your work.

- Fill in background information
- Build suspense
- Intensify readers' curiosity
- Emphasize the importance of a decision or event
- Replicate the thought process through stream of consciousness
- Provide insight into characters' personalities and motivations
- Signal a shift in character development
- Identify tensions between characters' public actions and private thoughts

# 2.2 Contrast and Complexity | STR-1.Z

You've read that contrasts between foil characters illuminate characteristics of the main character (Part 1). Structural contrasts can also add meaning and complexity. They often represent contradictions or inconsistencies that introduce nuance and ambiguity into a text.

## Structural Contrasts

Interruptions in chronology are a common type of structural contrast. Consider, for example, the complexity the flashbacks to the early days of Dana and Kevin's relationship add to the novel. While providing background information, they also create contrasting parallels between the 19th and 20th centuries. Dana works at a temp agency that she calls a modern-day "slave market." Kevin works in a warehouse but has just sold a book and can quit the job he hates. He offers to support Dana so she too can quit, but she refuses because she wants to remain independent. Readers also find out that Kevin has some chauvinist ideas as he wants Dana to be his secretary. Through these flashbacks readers see in 1976 remnants of 19th-century slavery and patriarchy.

The contrasts highlighted through the use of in medias res also texture the story with nuance and ambiguity. The novel begins with the line "I lost an arm on my last trip home," so readers know right away that Dana has done some kind of traveling and she has not come through it without serious harm. She explains in the prologue that the harm was her fault, but sheriffs suspect that Kevin may have hurt her.

As the story progresses, readers get more details about the relationship between Dana and Kevin as they are moving into their new house. Dana relates that while she is still unpacking, Kevin had quit "when he got his office in order," suggesting a selfishness or entitlement to take care of only his needs. But after a pleasant and teasing exchange with Dana, he begins helping again, showing some inconsistency in his behavior.

Also, after Dana returns from her first time travel, she says to Kevin, "I don't have a name for the thing that happened to me, but I don't feel safe anymore." As one critic noted, "what happened" to Dana was history—the legacy of slavery. Later Kevin asks if maybe she had dreamed it.

> "No! I know what I'm doing. I can see. I'm pulling away from it because it scares me so. But it was real."
> "Let yourself pull away from it." He got up and took the muddy towel from me. "That sounds like the best thing you can do, whether it was real or not. Let go of it."

In juxtaposition to the events of the prologue, this picture of the relationship between Dana and Kevin adds nuance and complexity to both their relationship and the legacy of history. Kevin, even as he tries to provide comfort, can imagine letting go of the experience, because he has never known anything like it. Dana, on the other hand, can not only not let go of it— she also feels, perhaps conditioned by the legacy she inherited, that it was somehow her fault, as she says in the prologue.

Of course contrasts appear in many forms—not just through structure. For example, contrasts between the time periods in the book (1807–1831 versus June 9 through July 4, 1976), the places in the book (Maryland versus California), the character foils, and the sets of relationships (Dana and Kevin/Alice and Rufus) all provide opportunity to examine ambiguities, contradictions, nuances, and complexity.

> **Remember:** Contrasts often represent contradictions or inconsistencies that introduce nuance, ambiguity, or contradiction into a text. As a result, contrasts make texts more complex. (STR-1.Z)

## 2.2 Checkpoint

*Review the excerpts from* Frankenstein *on pages 353–371. Then complete the following open-response activities and answer the multiple-choice questions.*

1. Choose one of the recurring contrasts from *Frankenstein* or another longer work you are studying. Identify and describe the contrast. Then analyze it to determine the impact of the contrast on the work's complexity. Does the contrast add nuance, ambiguity, or inconsistency? Explain your line of reasoning in answering that question.

2. Using your understanding of the contrast from question 1, write a claim about the role of the contrast in creating complexity.

3. The contrast created by Victor's broken promise and the Creature's decree that he "shall be with [Victor] on [his] wedding night" (Chapter 20, paragraph 15) develops nuance and complexity between the

   (A) joy of love and the pity of compassion

   (B) sense of loss and sense of loneliness felt by both characters

   (C) cruelty and compassion that stem from inherent kindness

   (D) complex beginnings represented by the wedding and the making of the Creature

   (E) ambiguous moralities represented by Victor and the Creature

4. In Robert Walton's letter dated August 26th, the Creature's comments in paragraphs 42-43 reveal his

   (A) recognition that he both loved Victor as a father and feared him as a creator

   (B) growing appreciation for morality problems faced by humankind

   (C) condemnation of humankind's contradictory morality and behavior

   (D) complex understanding of the relationship between creator and created

   (E) claim that only cruelty without regret can bring about change

**Creating on Your Own**

Identify any contrasts that you have in the story you are writing. Are there ways to intensify them to add complexity to characters or events? Perhaps you can add other contrasts. Consider sharpening your chronological interruptions to highlight contrasts. You may also want to add contrasting colors, settings, characters, or background events. Experiment with making contrasts more prominent to add nuance and ambiguity as you write one more letter in your story. Save your work.

# Part 2 Apply What You Have Learned

One of the best ways to think about structure in a novel is to diagram it in a nonlinguistic representation. The drawing doesn't have to be fancy. You can use stick figures and geometric shapes. You can draw by hand or using a computer. The important thing is to visualize the structure and then interpret its impact on your interpretation of the work.

Diagram the structure of *Frankenstein* or another longer work you are reading. Consider factors such as the author's manipulation of time, settings, and contrasts between events and characters. Below is one simple way to diagram the narrative structure of *Frankenstein*. After studying the diagram you create, write a paragraph that interprets the impact of structure on the work's meaning and on the reader's response.

### Time Disruptions in Frankenstein

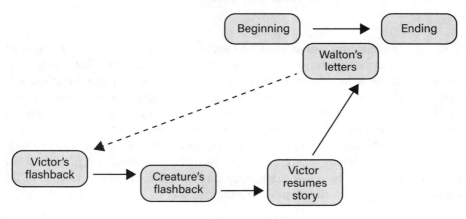

**Reflect on the Essential Question** Write a brief response that answers the essential question: *How do chronological interruptions in the plot as well as characters' contradictions and inconsistencies affect readers' experiences?* In your answer, correctly use the key terms listed on page 383.

# Narrative Perspective and Control

**Enduring Understanding and Skills**

### Part 3  Narrative Perspective and Control

**Understand**

A narrator's or speaker's perspective controls the details and emphases that affect how readers experience and interpret a text. (NAR-1)

**Demonstrate**

Identify and describe details, diction, or syntax in a text that reveal a narrator's or speaker's perspective. (4.C)

Explain how a narrator's reliability affects a narrative. (4.D)

See also Units 4, 7 & 9

**Source:** *AP® English Literature and Composition Course and Exam Description*

**Essential Question:** How do a narrator's tone, syntax, and perspective reveal biases and reliability?

Recall a conversation you recently had with your parents or friends. Because of voice inflections, determining the attitude of all parties was probably fairly easy. The task is more difficult with written texts. You read in Unit 4 that the attitude of narrators, characters, or speakers toward an idea, character, or situation emerges from their perspective. Since authors do not explicitly state their attitudes toward narrators, characters, or speakers, readers piece them together by examining word choice, the arrangement of words, perspectives, and details (or the lack of them). Which details narrators choose to include or omit can provide clues about the narrators' biases. Readers may find biased narrators unreliable. That unreliability may influence a reader's understanding of a character's motives.

| KEY TERMS | | |
|---|---|---|
| tone | syntax | bias |
| diction | motivations | reliability |

# 3.1 Syntax, Diction, Tone, and Details
| NAR-1.P, NAR-1.Q, NAR-1.R, NAR-1.S

Just as advertisers manipulate your response to their products, so too do narrators shape your response to the events they narrate and to the characters. The attitude of narrators, characters, or speakers toward an idea, character, or situation emerges from their perspective and may be referred to as **tone**. The narrator's or speaker's tone toward events or characters influences readers' interpretation of the ideas associated with those things. Tone is revealed through the author's viewpoint and **diction**, or choice of words. It is also often revealed by **syntax**, the arrangement of words and phrases.

## Syntax, Diction, and Tone

Writers consciously manipulate their sentence structure to produce desired effects. The goal of analyzing a writer's syntax is to understand its effect on meaning. Note that the placement of clauses and phrases within a sentence or paragraph shines a spotlight for readers on points of emphasis.

The following example is from the beginning of Chapter 2 of *The Great Gatsby*.

> (1) About half way between West Egg and New York the motor-road hastily joins the railroad and runs beside it for a quarter of a mile, so as to shrink away from a certain desolate area of land. (2) This is a valley of ashes—a fantastic farm where ashes grow like wheat into ridges and hills and grotesque gardens where ashes take the forms of houses and chimneys and rising smoke and finally, with a transcendent effort, of men who move dimly and already crumbling through the powdery air. (3) Occasionally a line of grey cars crawls along an invisible track, gives out a ghastly creak and comes to rest, and immediately the ash-grey men swarm up with leaden spades and stir up an impenetrable cloud which screens their obscure operations from your sight.
>
> (4) But above the grey land and the spasms of bleak dust which drift endlessly over it, you perceive, after a moment, the eyes of Doctor T. J. Eckleburg. (5) The eyes of Doctor T. J. Eckleburg are blue and gigantic—their retinas are one yard high. (6) They look out of no face but, instead, from a pair of enormous yellow spectacles which pass over a nonexistent nose. (7) Evidently some wild wag of an oculist set them there to fatten his practice in the borough of Queens, and then sank down himself into eternal blindness or forgot them and moved away. (8) But his eyes, dimmed a little by many paintless days under sun and rain, brood on over the solemn dumping ground.

Table 6-2 explores how some grammatical elements and their arrangement affect tone.

| Analysis of Diction and Syntax and Their Effect on Tone and Emphasis |
| --- |
| **DICTION (word choice)**<br>The diction of these two paragraphs is formal. The choice of descriptive words, such as *desolate, grotesque, crumbling, ghastly,* and *impenetrable*, sets a somber and depressing tone. |
| **MODIFIERS (placement of phrases and clauses that make meaning more specific and add emphasis)**<br>Sentence 2 begins with a simple independent clause: "This is a valley of ashes." After the dash, though, a series of subordinate clauses spins out to describe it, as if the ashes have a life of their own. The valley of ashes is<br><br>• a fantastic farm where ashes grow like wheat into ridges and hills and<br>• grotesque gardens where ashes take the forms of houses and chimneys and rising smoke and<br>• finally, with a transcendent effort, of men who move dimly and already crumbling through the powdery air<br><br>The sentence floats out almost like the ashes themselves, settling into an ashen landscape.<br><br>Sentence 4 also parallels the meaning through its structure and the placement of phrases and clauses. It could have been written like this: "You perceive after a moment the eyes of Doctor T. J. Eckleburg above the grey land and the spasms of bleak dust which drift endlessly over it." However, that more straightforward syntax, starting with a subject and verb, lacks the perspective of one trying to see through the ashes:<br><br>"But above the grey land and the spasms of bleak dust which drift endlessly over it, you perceive, after a moment, the eyes of Doctor T. J. Eckleburg."<br><br>Having the prepositional phrases and subordinate clause describing "the bleak dust" at the beginning of the sentence adds emphasis to it. Further, "you perceive, after a moment" suggests the difficulty of seeing things—it takes a moment to make out objects. This syntax reflects the narrator's perspective and the somewhat disdainful tone. |

Table 6-2

## Narrative Perspective and Details

Narrators are in complete control of everything the reader learns, including the details that are presented and those that are omitted. Details can help reveal characters' **motivations**, their reasons for behaving as they do. They can also reveal the narrator's **bias**, the inclination to like, dislike, or just have an opinion about something or someone based on experiences.

**Abundant Details** Consider the bias of the first-person narrator in *Kindred*. A Black woman from the 20th century, Dana knows what the 19th-century characters cannot know about the course of history and the official end of slavery. Dana gives the reader abundant details about her experiences with the Weylins and the enslaved people on their plantation. Readers learn about whippings Dana and others suffer and the effect on Dana of the selling of people enslaved by the Weylins, who are joined around the neck and made to walk in what was called a coffle. Through Dana's graphic descriptions of her experiences, the reader is guided to an understanding of slavery's horrors, something Dana has read about but never witnessed firsthand. But Dana also sees and reports on each character as a person—Sarah, the head of the cookhouse who appears to be compliant to her "owners" but whose actual motivation is fear; Alice who once was free but became a victim of Rufus's sexual assaults and retreated into profound sadness at the (untrue) news that Rufus had sold their children; the mute Carrie, Sarah's daughter, who provides strength for Dana. As a Black woman herself who has known freedom and independence, she sees the fullness and complex motivations of each Black character.

Dana is not the only 20th-century character transported to 19th-century Maryland. Her White husband Kevin manages to go with her on her third trip, and Dana is distraught when she returns to the present without him. Since Dana is in control of the narrative, she can't reveal as much about Kevin's reactions because she does not always know what they are, or even where he is. She does recognize, however, that both he and she fall too easily into something like comfort when they decide they would get fewer questions if they just pretend that Kevin is her owner.

**Withholding Information**  Dana reports some details about the Weylins that show their occasional humanity, but mainly she omits details that would paint them in a positive light.

Nick Carraway, the narrator of *The Great Gatsby*, hints at the outcome of the story through foreshadowing at the beginning (see page 384) but otherwise presents information as he gets it. He relates the official story of Gatsby's life and only later does he tell Gatsby's true story, which is closer to the rumors that surround him.

**First- and Third-Person Narrative Perspective and Details**  Discerning the perspective of characters is sometimes easier than discerning the perspective of narrators. Since the narrator gives background information and you see the character interacting with other characters, you learn factors that have shaped a character's perspective. If the narrator tells the story from a first-person perspective, you will have more details about that narrator's perspective than with a third-person narrator. Even though you may not know the background of a third-person narrator, you can still look at the words he or she uses to describe the characters and events.

Read the two passages below. The first is from *Kindred*, narrated by the novel's protagonist, Dana. The second is a passage of third-person narration from *Song of Solomon* by Toni Morrison.

In this passage from *Kindred*, Margaret Weylin, Rufus's mother and the mistress of the plantation, has just discovered that Dana has been sleeping in Kevin's room. Margaret thinks Dana is Kevin's slave, not his wife.

> She cornered me one day as I swept the library. If she had walked in two minutes earlier, she would have caught me reading a book.
>
> "Where did you sleep last night?" she demanded in the strident, accusing voice she reserved for slaves.

I straightened to face her, rested my hands on the broom. How lovely it would have been to say, *None of your business, b\*tch!* Instead, I spoke softly, respectfully. "In Mr. Franklin's room, ma'am." I didn't bother to lie because all the house servants knew. It might even have been one of them who alerted Margaret. So now what would happen?

Margaret slapped me across the face.

I stood very still, gazed down at her with frozen calm. She was three or four inches shorter than I was and proportionately smaller. Her slap hadn't hurt me much. It had simply made me want to hurt her. Only my memory of the whip kept me still.

**Interpretation:** Knowing Dana's thoughts is helpful in understanding her perspective. To survive in antebellum Maryland, she must pretend to accept a subservient position in society (when in the 20th century she would have been empowered to say "None of your business, b\*tch!"), but being privy to her thoughts, readers understand that her attitude toward Margaret Weylin is contemptuous. Readers will be pulled along with Dana's feelings and regard the slave-owning Margaret Weylin with the same contempt.

The following passage from *Song of Solomon* by Toni Morrison has a third-person narrator. The passage comes from the novel's beginning and describes a Black neighborhood in a fictional town in Michigan where Whites are in power.

Town maps registered the street as Mains Avenue, but the only colored doctor in the city had lived and died on that street, and when he moved there in 1896 his patients took to calling the street, which none of them lived in or near, Doctor Street. Later, when other Negroes moved there, and when the postal service became a popular means of transferring messages among them, envelopes from Louisiana, Virginia, Alabama, and Georgia began to arrive addressed to people at house numbers on Doctor Street. The post office workers returned these envelopes or passed them on to the Dead Letter Office. Then in 1918, when colored men were being drafted, a few gave their address at the recruitment office as Doctor Street. In that way, the name acquired a quasi-official status. But not for long. Some of the city legislators, whose concern for appropriate names and the maintenance of the city's landmarks was the principal part of their political life, saw to it that "Doctor Street" was never used in any official capacity. And since they knew that only Southside residents kept it up, they had notices posted in the stores, barbershops, and restaurants in that part of the city saying that the avenue . . . had always been and would always be known as Mains Avenue and not Doctor Street.

It was a genuinely clarifying public notice because it gave Southside residents a way to keep their memories alive and please the city legislators as well. They called it Not Doctor Street, and were inclined to call the charity hospital at its northern end No Mercy Hospital . . . .

**Interpretation:** The details and words in this passage show that the perspective of this narrator has been shaped by society's marginalization of

Blacks, who are not permitted to name their streets. The post office didn't recognize the street and sent letters with the street address to the "Dead Letter Office." Only when Blacks were needed for military service did the post office take the trouble to briefly recognize the street. *Not* in Not Doctor Street, and *Dead* in Dead Letter Office connect the narrator's perspective to a sardonic tone toward class stratification in the early 20th century. The narrator continues with carefully chosen words throughout the novel to lead readers to interpret events and characters in the same way. The surname of the protagonist, Milkman, is Dead. Even though his family has money and status in the Black community, they are dead in many respects.

 **Remember:** The narrator's or speaker's tone toward events or characters in a text influences readers' interpretation of the ideas associated with those things. The syntactical arrangement of phrases and clauses in a sentence can emphasize details or ideas and convey a narrator's or speaker's tone. Information included and/or not included in a text conveys the perspective of characters, narrators, and/or speakers. A narrator's or speaker's perspective may influence the details and amount of detail in a text and may reveal biases, motivations, or understandings. (NAR-1.P–S)

### *3.1 Checkpoint*

*Review the excerpts from* Frankenstein *on pages 353–371. Then complete the following open-response activities and answer the multiple-choice questions.*

1. Using *Frankenstein*, choose one of the three narrators and identify whether the narrator provides many details, few details, or no details on a character or event. Then offer an interpretation of the narrator's perspective, biases, or motivations. On separate paper, recreate the chart for your chosen work, adding as many rows as you can. An example has been provided for you using *The Great Gatsby*.

| Character or Event | Degree of Details | Interpretation of the Narrator's Perspective, Biases, or Motivations |
|---|---|---|
| Jordan Baker | Jordan Baker is a friend of Daisy Buchanan whom she knew in Louisville before Daisy's marriage. She is a professional golfer who is said to have cheated at the game, but she is beautiful, pragmatic, and a modern woman. | Nick says that Jordan is incurably dishonest, but that dishonesty in a woman doesn't bother him. He himself lies about his relationship with the Midwestern woman. He becomes mildly infatuated with Jordan. However, he decides he doesn't want to see her again, suggesting he is becoming motivated by a moral sense. |

2. Using the details from your chart in question 1, determine the narrator's tone toward the events and characters. Recreate the chart below on separate paper and fill it in, adding as many rows as necessary.

| Character or Event | Narrator's Tone |
|---|---|
|  |  |

3. Victor's tone in the excerpts from Chapter V alternates between
   (A) arrogance and fear
   (B) confusion and understanding
   (C) attraction and repulsion
   (D) dread and accomplishment
   (E) admiration and scorn

4. In the excerpt from Chapter IX, paragraph 6 serves to
   (A) add variety to the syntax of the surrounding paragraphs
   (B) provide the real reason for Victor's pain in the shadow of Justine's execution
   (C) illustrate the strength of Elizabeth when compared with Victor
   (D) contradict Victor's perspective on Elizabeth and her feelings toward Justine's execution
   (E) foreshadow Elizabeth's fate at the hands of the Creature

5. In context, the phrase "exult in the agony" from paragraph 47 of Robert Walton's final letter reveals which of the following about the Creature's perspective?
   (A) He finds more joy in dying than in continuing to live.
   (B) He fears the pain of dying.
   (C) He is curious about the role of death in making one live.
   (D) He rejects the concept of "resting in peace" when one dies.
   (E) He feels that continuing to live is impossible, so he accepts his death.

**Creating on Your Own**
Review the epistolary story you have been writing. What is your first-person narrator's perspective on the events and other characters? What shaped it? How might you revise your current draft to sharpen the narrator's perspective and make biases more apparent? Develop diction, syntax, and tone to sharpen and improve your story. Save your work.

# 3.2 Narrative Bias and Reliability | NAR-1.T, NAR-1.U, NAR-1.V

The narrator of a story influences readers' interpretations. Narrators' biases are revealed through the details they choose to include in their narrative as well as those they choose to leave out of it. For example, in *Kindred*, in which race is such a key issue, Dana never discusses whether she and Kevin talked about their racial difference. Readers see that both their families opposed the marriage but never learn if Kevin and Dana had thought or talked about it.

Readers may discover that narrators' biases affect their **reliability**, or the extent to which they can be believed, which in turn affects the readers' understanding of characters' motives. Reliable narrators try to stay objective and tell the story accurately. They tend to share the values of the author and readers. However, even the most objective reporter or a fully omniscient narrator cannot avoid a degree of subjectivity.

## Crossing the Line: From Bias to Unreliability

What are the qualities of a reliable narrator? The most important is having distance from the story. For this reason, first-person narrators are unreliable by nature since they are in the heart of the story. Their biases can become blind spots in their narration, causing readers to discount or mistrust the narrator. Unreliable narrators range from being completely untrustworthy to being untrustworthy in certain respects.

Narrators may be unreliable for several reasons.

- They may lie purposely out of self-interest, shaping the story to make themselves look better.
- Their knowledge of events may be limited so that they cannot accurately tell the story.
- They may have values that are different from those of the author and the readers.

Or they may even be sociopaths, as is the narrator in Anthony Burgess's 1962 novel *A Clockwork Orange*. Alex, a leader of an English gang, consciously lies to the readers as he and his followers steal, rape, and murder. Readers are aware that Alex's biases are magnified by drug and alcohol use. His amoral perspective of the world justifies his dishonesty in his mind. Readers are fascinated with his amoral behaviors while at the same time mistrusting of his accounts.

## Narrator Reliability and Character Motives

At the other end of the spectrum, Dana, the narrator in *Kindred*, is unaware of her blind spots. As a Black woman living in 1976, her perspective has been shaped by the civil rights movement of the 1960s. When she time travels to a 19th-century plantation, she views the earlier time through a more modern perspective. While she learns firsthand what slave life was like, her narration is skewed by her 1976 perspective. One of the earliest examples of her bias comes in the third chapter, when she first sees the Weylin plantation house. She expected the stereotypical plantation house, grand in size and white in color. She is shocked to see something quite different:

> The Weylin house surprised me too when I saw it in daylight. It wasn't white. It had no columns, no porch to speak of. I was almost disappointed. It was a red-brick Georgian Colonial, boxy but handsome in a quiet kind of way, two and a half stories high with dormered windows and a chimney on each end. It wasn't big or imposing enough to be called a mansion. In Los Angeles, in our own time, Kevin and I could have afforded it.

When Rufus refers to the cook who serves the master who has sold her children as "Aunt Sarah," Dana is horrified, observing that she might have been called "mammy" in other households. In Dana's day, Blacks chafed against the "mammy" stereotype for a Black woman taking care of White children while her own were enslaved. While modern readers likely share the disdain for racial stereotypes, they can recognize that for objective reporting on the attitudes and culture of antebellum Maryland, Dana's modern sensibility biases her views.

Dana's motives also stem from bias. At one point, Rufus asks Dana to persuade Alice to sleep with him. Dana has a vested interest in the survival of her bloodline—her own existence depends on it—so her motivation to persuade Alice to sleep with Rufus is self-interested and biased even while it is also true that Alice's fate is sealed and Dana wants to minimize the beating she would take if she refused.

 **Remember:** Readers can infer narrators' biases by noting which details they choose to include in a narrative and which they choose to omit. Readers who detect bias in a narrator may find that narrator less reliable. The reliability of a narrator may influence a reader's understanding of a character's motives. (NAR-1.T–V)

## The Writer's Craft: Parallel Contrasting Motives

What motivates Robert Walton to set out on his mission to the North Pole? What motivates Victor Frankenstein to create life? What motivates the Creature to interact with humans and learn language?

Both Walton and Frankenstein seem to be motivated by a desire to push the limits of human capability, to go beyond what other humans have been able to accomplish. Walton's bonds to his crew—to fellow humans—lead him to agree to turn back when the mission becomes too dangerous, suggesting that, despite blaming himself for cowardice and indecision, Walton values his own life and the lives of those who depend on him. For him, the cost of going beyond the normal limits of human capacity and risking lives is too high to pay.

Frankenstein, in contrast, devotes several years to his project to create life at the expense of his own health and is not held back by consideration of what the consequences might be of his stepping beyond the boundary of human capability. For someone who has given so much thought to the technicalities of sparking life, he seems to have given no thought at all to other qualities of humans—responsibility, compassion, nurture. What, after all, did he expect to do with his creation once he brought it to life? He was immediately repulsed by the Creature because of "its" appearance and abandoned it on the spot.

The Creature, instead of trying to surpass the limits of human capability, just wants to know the minimum requirements—what does he have to be or do to earn the benefits of humanity? His appearance seems to make fellowship with other humans impossible, so he learns to communicate eloquently, and still he is rejected. Accepting that he will never have the joys of human companionship, he requests a partner like himself and is once again spurned.

Through these parallel but contrasting character motivations, Shelley is, in effect, drawing the upper and lower limits of humanity, asking "When do people reach too high?" and "What separates people from other creatures?"

## Analyze the Writer's Craft

Write one or more paragraphs explaining the relationship of these motivations to each character's reliability. Is any one of the three the most reliable? Who is the least reliable, and why? Use details from the text to support your claims.

## 3.2 Checkpoint

*Review the excerpts from* Frankenstein *on pages 353–371. Then complete the following open-response activity and answer the multiple-choice questions.*

1. On separate paper, recreate the chart below. Then, using *Frankenstein* or another longer work you are reading, find three examples to illustrate how the narrator's perspective and biases affect the reliability of the account.

| Event | Unreliability |
|---|---|
|  |  |
|  |  |
|  |  |

2. Which of the following describes a reason why a given character may be an unreliable narrator in this novel?

   (A) Victor is concerned about his reputation and has reason to blame the Creature and deflect his own responsibility.

   (B) The Creature has nothing to lose and no reason to lie about the events of the story.

   (C) Robert Walton is trusted by the sailors under his command and shows clear concern for their well-being.

   (D) Victor is pursuing the Creature instead of the Creature pursuing him.

   (E) The Creature just wants to be treated as any regular person would be treated.

3. Robert's bias toward Victor is most clearly revealed in which line?

   (A) "He was not, as the other traveller seemed to be, a savage inhabitant of some undiscovered island" (Letter IV, paragraph 9)

   (B) "His limbs were nearly frozen, and his body dreadfully emaciated by fatigue and suffering" (Letter IV, paragraph 12)

   (C) "His countenance instantly assumed an aspect of the deepest gloom" (Letter IV, paragraph 14)

   (D) "He excites at once my admiration and my pity to an astonishing degree." (Letter IV, paragraph 18)

   (E) "He is so gentle, yet so wise; his mind is so cultivated;" (Letter IV, paragraph 18)

**Creating on Your Own**

As Shelley does in *Frankenstein* when Victor Frankenstein starts telling his own story, turn your first-person epistolary narration over to your character with the remarkable story. What details would this character add or leave out? Consider how their addition would affect a reader's interpretation. Also consider how their omission might create either bias or unreliability in your narrator. Determine the impact you want to have on readers and either add or delete details accordingly. Save your work.

# Part 3 Apply What You Have Learned

Choose a scene from *Frankenstein* or another longer work. Retell that scene from the perspective of another character. How do diction, syntax, details, and tone change? What biases emerge that weren't in the original version?

**Reflect on the Essential Question:** Write a brief response that answers the essential question: *How do a narrator's tone, syntax, and perspective reveal biases and reliability?* In your answer, correctly use the key terms listed on page 392.

**Source:** Wikimedia Commons

Frontispiece from the 1831 edition of *Frankenstein; or, The Modern Prometheus*

# Part 4

# The Role of Symbols

**Enduring Understanding and Skills**

**Part 4  The Role of Symbols**

**Understand**

Comparisons, representations, and associations shift meaning from the literal to the figurative and invite readers to interpret a text. (FIG-1)

**Demonstrate**

Identify and explain the function of a symbol. (5.C)

See also Units 7 & 8

**Source:** *AP' English Literature and Composition Course and Exam Description*

**Essential Question:** What is the function of a symbol?

As powerful as language is in shaping and defining the world, it has its limits. Sometimes ideas or concepts are so layered and multidimensional words can't capture their complexity. A **symbol** is a material object that comes to represent, or stand for, an idea or concept. Symbols can capture contradictions, subtleties, conflicts, and alternatives that elude words. When you encounter a symbol, pause and reflect on the context in which it appears. Chances are you will discover new meanings within the work as well as a deeper understanding of the culture in which it was written. Finally, analyzing symbols will help you see not only cultural implications but also universally shared experiences.

**KEY TERMS**

| | | |
|---|---|---|
| symbol | contextual symbol | archetypal symbol |
| common symbol | | |

## 4.1 Understanding Symbols | FIG-1.X, FIG-1.Y, FIG-1.Z, FIG-1.AA

Students often ask if too much is being read into symbols. Absolutely, it is possible to stretch too far. Sometimes a color is just a color. If, however, the color orange repeatedly appears, as it does in Yann Martel's *Life of Pi*, chances are it has symbolic meaning. In that novel, the Patel family decides to move from India to Canada. Mr. Patel is a zookeeper who loads his family and animals on a cargo ship bound for Canada to start a zoo. The boat sinks. Everyone dies except young Pi Patel who is stranded on the ocean in an orange lifeboat with an orange whistle, an orange life jacket, an orange buoy, and an orange tarpaulin. It doesn't take much thinking to realize the color orange in this early scene is associated with things necessary for Pi's survival, and therefore hope, but it represents even more ideas as it appears in different contexts throughout the novel. Several animals survive and join Pi on the boat. Two notable ones are an orange-and-black Bengal tiger named Richard Parker and an orangutan named Orange Juice. Richard Parker becomes Pi's companion, alleviating his loneliness. Orange Juice is associated with both motherhood and the Virgin Mary. Pi's emotional needs are met by these two orange animals. Pi practices three religions: Hinduism, Christianity, and Islam. Orange is symbolic in both Hinduism and Christianity, representing the intersection of heaven and earth.

When determining if an image becomes a symbol, ask the following two questions:

1. Does the image repeat three or more times?
2. Does the image shift into new or layered meanings within each occurrence?

If the answers are yes, you probably have an image functioning as a symbol. **Common symbols** are symbols that have been used so frequently that they are easily recognizable. Some common symbols include white for purity or innocence, red for blood or passion, spring for youth or new beginnings, winter for death, fog for confusion, storms for violent emotions, a dove for peace, or a lion for strength. Many have a dual nature. For example, water can signify a cleansing or rebirth but also death through floods and drowning.

## Multiple Meanings

Much of a symbol's power lies in its multiple meanings. As an individual reader, you will not get every possible meaning, nor should you expect to. Throughout these units you have been urged to value your responses to literature. Those responses are in part based on your life experiences. Honoring what you know when analyzing a symbol is the best place to start.

For example, at the end of Chapter 1 in *The Great Gatsby*, Nick Carraway sees Gatsby outside at night: "he stretched out his arms toward the dark water in a curious way, and, far as I was from him, I could have sworn he was trembling. Involuntarily I glanced seaward—and distinguished nothing except a single green light, minute and far away, that might have been the end of a dock." At this point, the only thing special about the green light is the fact that Gatsby appears to be reaching out toward it, but Nick doesn't yet realize its significance.

Of course, the green light is a universal symbol indicating that someone has permission to proceed. Green is also the color of hope and renewal. Table 6-3 identifies other occurrences of the green light in the novel and indicates how Fitzgerald gradually reveals its significance.

## The Green Light as Symbol in *The Great Gatsby*

| Passage | Meaning in Context | Meaning in Work as a Whole |
|---|---|---|
| "If it wasn't for the mist we could see your home across the bay," said Gatsby. "You always have a green light that burns all night at the end of your dock."<br><br>Daisy put her arm through his abruptly, but he seemed absorbed in what he had just said. Possibly it had occurred to him that the colossal significance of that light had now vanished forever. Compared to the great distance that had separated him from Daisy it had seemed very near to her, almost touching her. It had seemed as close as a star to the moon. Now it was again a green light on a dock. His count of enchanted objects had diminished by one.<br><br>(Chapter 5) | Gatsby tells Daisy—and the reader—why the green light was important to him. Now that he has her back in his life, however, he doesn't need it, and it ceases to be a symbol to him. | The green light had represented Gatsby's hopes for a reunion with Daisy after five years apart. |
| I thought of Gatsby's wonder when he first picked out the green light at the end of Daisy's dock. . . .<br><br>Gatsby believed in the green light, the orgastic [stimulating] future that year by year recedes before us. It eluded us then, but that's no matter—tomorrow we will run faster, stretch out our arms further . . . And one fine morning—<br><br>(Chapter 9) | Gatsby is now dead, and Nick is reflecting on him and on the significance of the green light for him. By the time of his death, Gatsby's hopes had been shattered. | Several different interpretations are possible.<br><br>• Nick does not give up hope in the dream that the green light symbolized. Sooner or later, he suggests, we may achieve fulfillment.<br>• People will never reach their desired goals; Nick is deceiving himself. |

**Table 6-3**

## Contextual Symbols

Paperweight or water? Which is a symbol? Did you choose water? It certainly is, but so too is a paperweight. In George Orwell's novel *1984*, a glass paperweight is a **contextual symbol**, with symbolic meaning only in this work. Some authors create their own symbols by repeatedly using objects in meaningful ways. For example, in *Lord of the Flies* William Golding uses a conch shell to represent order and governmental control. Orwell uses a paperweight to represent the doomed relationship between protagonists Julia and Winston. Winston buys the paperweight because it reminds him of better days before the ruling party seized power. Artifacts from the past as well as love-based relationships are illicit. When Julia and Winston's relationship is terminated by the Party, the paperweight falls to the floor and shatters. Both the conch shell and the glass paperweight are contextual symbols; while they may have symbolic value beyond these texts, it is likely not a universally understood value.

## Archetypal or Universal Symbols

**Archetypal symbols** are objects that have appeared in literature and ceremonies for centuries. While their meanings can vary, they share characteristics that readers associate with them. These symbols are useful for readers to decode what is happening and predict what is to come. There are several archetypal characters in *The Great Gatsby*. Gatsby is the tragic hero, a flawed character who sets out on a quest but ends up as a scapegoat, taking a bullet for the woman he loves. Nick Carraway, the narrator, is an outsider and a loner. Daisy, the woman Gatsby loves, is the temptress, and her husband Tom Buchanan is an archetypal narcissist. Knowing the patterns helps the reader make sense of the story's meanings. Additionally, archetypal symbols add to a work's complexity. The following list is not exhaustive but represents some of the more common archetypal characters: Hero (Epic, Classical, Romantic, Realistic, Anti-Hero), Outcast (or Outsider or Loner), Scapegoat, Trickster, Platonic Ideal, Monster, Narcissist, Devil, Temptress, Star-Crossed Lovers, Clown/Jester, and Prophet.

**Remember:** When a material object comes to represent, or stand for, an idea or concept, it becomes a symbol. A symbol is an object that represents a meaning, so it is said to be symbolic or representative of that meaning. A symbol can represent different things depending on the experiences of a reader or the context of its use in a text. Certain symbols are so common and recurrent that many readers have associations with them prior to reading a text. Other symbols are more contextualized and only come to represent certain things through their use in a particular text. When a character comes to represent, or stand for, an idea or concept, that character becomes symbolic; some symbolic characters have become so common they are archetypal. (FIG-1.X–AA)

## 4.1 Checkpoint

*Review the excerpts from* Frankenstein *on pages 353–371. Then complete the following open-response activity and answer the multiple-choice questions.*

1. Using *Frankenstein* or another longer work you are reading, choose an object that recurs often enough to become a symbol. Find at least three passages that contain the symbol. Try to find a passage from the beginning, middle, and end of the work. Interpret the symbol in the context of each passage, then consider them together. Answer as many of the questions below as you can. Then write a thesis statement that offers a defensible insight about the use of the symbol in the work.

## Questions to ask about symbols:

- Are any contextualized symbols used in the work? Any archetypal symbols? What are the symbols and their meanings?
- What settings or characters seem to have symbolic significance in addition to their literal meanings?
- How many levels of meaning can you extrapolate from each symbol? Do any contradictory meanings exist? If so, do the varied meanings help readers understand the psychology of the characters, their internal conflicts?
- In what ways do symbols add to plot structure?
- When looked at collectively, what theme might the symbols support? What is their effect on tone?
- Do the symbols seem to have a clear moral purpose, or do they raise more questions than they answer?

2. In the excerpt from Chapter XI, fire is represented as a complex symbol in that it
   - (A) represents all of the danger the Creature brings to humans
   - (B) provides the comfort of both warmth and light
   - (C) actually reflects humankind's fear of the Creature
   - (D) becomes associated with both comfort and pain
   - (E) fails to provide the comfort and safety it should have provided the Creature

3. Which of the following is the best interpretation of fire as a symbol in the excerpt from Chapter XI?
   - (A) It represents things in life that can be good in moderation but harmful in too great of a quantity.
   - (B) It represents how all good things are actually bad things seen from a different perspective.
   - (C) It represents the dangers of letting oneself become too comfortable and complacent.
   - (D) It represents how negative attitudes can spread and affect others in incendiary ways.
   - (E) It represents the significant progress that humankind has made since it first developed technology.

## Creating on Your Own

Return to the epistolary story you have been writing. Think of some objects that you might use to symbolize the complexity of the characters' evolution in response to the conflicts within the remarkable story. A good place to start is to ask what analogies you might draw. For instance, in *Frankenstein* you might see an analogy between *Paradise Lost* and the loss of innocence. Also consider whether one of the common archetypal symbols might fit into your story. If so, find a way to introduce it effectively.

Try to find a smooth way to take over the narration from the character who has been narrating as a way to bring your story to a conclusion, just as Robert Walton's narration wraps up the story of Frankenstein.

# Part 4 Apply What You Have Learned

Return to the thesis statement you wrote in the last Checkpoint, on page 407. Write three paragraphs, one on each passage that discusses the importance of the symbol. Tie each paragraph to the thesis. Save your work.

**Reflect on the Essential Question:** Write a brief response that answers the essential question: *What is the function of a symbol?* In your answer, correctly use the key terms listed on page 404.

**Source:** Getty Images

*Where is ice featured in* Frankenstein? *What symbolic meaning might it convey? How might its meaning be made more layered because of the symbolic use of fire as well?*

# Writing About Literature VI

## Part 5  Writing About Literature VI

### Understand

Readers establish and communicate their interpretations of literature through arguments supported by textual evidence. (LAN-1)

### Demonstrate

Develop a thesis statement that conveys a defensible claim about an interpretation of literature and that may establish a line of reasoning. (7.B)

Develop commentary that establishes and explains relationships among textual evidence, the line of reasoning, and the thesis. (7.C)

Select and use relevant and sufficient evidence to both develop and support a line of reasoning. (7.D)

Demonstrate control over the elements of composition to communicate clearly. (7.E)

See also Units 1, 2, 3, 4, 5, 7, 8 & 9

**Source:** *AP® English Literature and Composition Course and Exam Description*

**Essential Question:** How can you communicate in writing an interpretation of a work of literature that asserts a claim and supports it with evidence?

Think of writing a literary analysis as preparing for a debate. Everyone taking part in a debate knows all the different sides of the issue. The audience for your literary analysis will be other readers who are familiar with the work you are analyzing. You step into this group of thoughtful, well-read, and well-informed people and try to communicate your interpretation—to make *your* case. What do you need in order to succeed?

This unit will remind you of the fundamental tools debaters or writers of literary argument use to make their case. While others in the community of readers are eager to make their case, they are also colleagues and can help you make your case. Learning together through collaboration will help everyone's case become stronger.

| | | |
|---|---|---|
| thesis statement | evidence | subordination |
| commentary | coordination | punctuation |
| line of reasoning | | |

# 5.1 Developing a Thesis Statement and Commentary
| LAN-1.D, LAN-1.E

Your **thesis statement** is your overarching claim. Its job is to convey a defensible claim about an interpretation of literature and if possible establish a line of reasoning. Writers use **commentary** to establish and explain the relationship of the textual evidence to the line of reasoning and the thesis.

**A strong thesis statement:**

- Expresses an arguable interpretation of a literary text—others may disagree with it
- Requires a defense through use of textual evidence and a line of reasoning
- Uses commentary to connect interpretation and evidence
- Previews a line of reasoning that is logical

**Remember:** A thesis statement expresses an interpretation of a literary text and requires a defense through use of textual evidence and a line of reasoning, both of which are explained in an essay through commentary. A thesis statement may preview the development or line of reasoning of an interpretation. This is not to say that a thesis statement must list the points of an interpretation, literary elements to be analyzed, or specific evidence to be used in the argument. (LAN-1.D–E)

## 5.1 Checkpoint

Recognizing the mutual help you could provide your peers, begin to develop a checklist to use as you seek feedback from them on your literary analysis. Start with the thesis statement. Include not only the qualities of a thesis statement that would earn a point (as thesis statements are afforded on the College Board rubrics), but also the qualities that would *not* earn that point. Give examples of each kind.

**Composing on Your Own**

In the previous section you developed a thesis on symbols and wrote a draft of an essay. Now examine another aspect of the text you are studying and work toward developing a thesis statement about it. Before you can develop a thesis statement, of course, you need to have an idea for an interpretation of a text, the point you want to make about it and defend. Do some focused freewriting about *Frankenstein* or another longer work of fiction or drama you have been reading to explore your thoughts. Write about one or two of these points that were addressed in this unit:

- Multiple interpretations
- Foil characters
- Contrasts and inconsistencies
- Narrative structure and chronological interruptions
- Narrator or character perspective and style (diction, tone, details)

After freewriting, develop one or more working thesis statements. You can choose one and refine it based on your checklist criteria when you are further along in your essay. Save your work.

# 5.2 Developing a Line of Reasoning | LAN-1.F, LAN-1.G

The **line of reasoning** is the thought process a writer uses to connect the evidence to the thesis statement. To develop a line of reasoning, think about the main concept you introduced in your thesis statement, and focus on one literary element. It may be characterization, narrative structure, perspective, or figurative language. Begin by asking yourself how you know the author is doing what you claim. When you answer that question, you've developed your line of reasoning. Remember, your line of reasoning is an idea, not facts or evidence. Keep track of everything that leads you to believe that your claims are valid, and remember that your line of reasoning should lead to a logical conclusion.

**Criteria for effective line of reasoning and commentary:**

- Presents supporting claims to back up the thesis statement
- Orders the supporting claims logically
- Communicates through commentary that explains the logical sequence of ideas and their relationship to the thesis statement

The body paragraphs of a written argument develop the reasoning and justify claims using evidence and providing commentary that links the evidence to the overall thesis. Effective paragraphs are cohesive and often use topic sentences to state a claim and explain the reasoning that connects the various claims and evidence that make up the body of an essay.

**Remember:** A line of reasoning is the logical sequence of claims that work together to defend the overarching thesis statement. A line of reasoning is communicated through commentary that explains the logical relationship between the overarching thesis statement and the claims/evidence within the body of an essay. (LAN-1.F–G)

### 5.2 Checkpoint

Add criteria to your cumulative checklist to establish standards for a line of reasoning and commentary. You can refer to the rubric on the College Board website for key points but personalize your checklist to remind yourself of areas of particular challenge to you.

#### Composing on Your Own

Review the working thesis statements you developed and choose one to focus on for your literary essay. Develop your line of reasoning to explain why you believe your thesis is valid. What claims in the body paragraphs might you need to support your thesis? Go over your ideas with a peer to help you make sure you haven't strayed from your thesis or left out any key claims that would support it. Save your work.

## 5.3 Evidence | LAN-1.H, LAN-1.I, LAN-1.J, LAN-1.K

In literary analysis, **evidence** is any information from the text that supports the writer's claims. It may be in the form of specific details, a summary or paraphrase, or either a direct or indirect quotation. Evidence needs to be linked to the thesis and line of reasoning by commentary.

**Criteria for sufficient evidence:**

- Strategically and purposefully illustrates, clarifies, exemplifies, associates, amplifies, or qualifies a point
- Uses commentary to explain a logical relationship between the evidence and the claim
- Quantity and quality of evidence provides apt and sufficient support for the line of reasoning

### Recursive Process

Remember, developing and supporting an interpretation of a text is a recursive process. After you receive targeted feedback on your writing, decide how you want to use it. Which pieces of advice will help you improve your writing? Do you want to ignore some of it? Ultimately, you are in charge of revisions. Your reflection on feedback will help you to refine your thesis, interpretations, evidence, commentary, and line of reasoning. You may revise and then seek additional reviews, or you may decide you are finished.

**Remember:** Writers use evidence strategically and purposefully to illustrate, clarify, exemplify, associate, amplify, or qualify a point. Evidence is effective when the writer of the essay uses commentary to explain a logical relationship between the evidence and the claim. Evidence is sufficient when its quantity and quality provide apt support for the line of reasoning. Developing and supporting an interpretation of a text is a recursive process; an interpretation can emerge from analyzing evidence and then forming a line of reasoning, or the interpretation can emerge from forming a line of reasoning and then identifying relevant evidence to support that line of reasoning. (LAN-1.H–K)

### 5.3 Checkpoint

Add criteria to your cumulative checklist to establish standards for the use, quantity, and quality of evidence and for using commentary to effectively explain how the evidence supports the claims in your line of reasoning. Again, you may refer to the rubric on the College Board website for key points but personalize your checklist to remind yourself of areas of particular challenge to you.

**Composing on Your Own**

Return to the thesis statements and paragraphs you have been constructing in this unit. On separate paper, recreate the graphic organizer on page 267 in Unit 4 to plan an essay on the longer work you have been studying.

Then, using the graphic organizer you just completed, write a full essay with a thesis, claims, evidence, and commentary. Use the peer checklist you have developed to reflect on your first draft. Revise based on your own reflection. Then give a copy of your checklist and your essay to a peer for review. Repeat the process until you are satisfied with your essay.

## 5.4 Communicating Clearly with the Elements of Composition | LAN-1.R, LAN-1.S, LAN-1.T

Even the most original thesis and argument may still end up falling flat if it is not communicated with clarity and strength. With the same tools fiction writers use, however, academic writing can be engaging and clear, especially through strategic selection and placement of phrases and clauses that embody the relationships among ideas, showing which are more important and which less. Writers also use words that enhance the clarity of their interpretation and punctuation that shows relationships between and among parts of a sentence.

## Artful Syntax

What is a writer's style? How do writers develop a distinct style that readers can recognize as theirs? One of the most defining elements is syntax. In Part 3 of this unit you examined F. Scott Fitzgerald's syntax in Chapter 2 of *The Great Gatsby*. Among his many talents is the ability to arrange words in patterns that engage the reader and enhance his meaning.

**Coordination and Subordination** As you continue to refine your writing style, learn the power of coordination and subordination. **Coordination** illustrates a balance or equality between ideas. **Subordination** illustrates an imbalance or inequality. Expressing these relationships through grammatical constructions does a good share of the work of getting your ideas across.

Consider the following draft of a student essay on a symbol in *Frankenstein*.

(1) The archetypal symbol of fire has a rich history in Western culture. (2) The Greek myth of Prometheus is one of the earliest occurrences. (3) Prometheus was a Titan god who took fire from Zeus and the Olympian gods. (4) He took fire to Earth. (5) He gave it to humans. (6) Prometheus's gift to humans allowed them to forge their civilization. (7) Zeus punished Prometheus eternally by having his liver eaten by an eagle, only to have it regenerate and be eaten again in an endless cycle.

(8) Fire has contrasting meanings, as with most symbols. (9) It can represent knowledge and progress. (10) It can also symbolize hell and destruction. (11) Fire is a symbol in *Frankenstein* that provides the Creature relief from his harsh environment. (12) He comes to understand that fire gives "light as well as heat." (13) Victor uses "instruments of life" to "infuse a spark of life" into his creation. (14) Victor and the Creature see, on the other hand, the more sinister nature of fire. (15) The Creature touches embers and is burned. (16) Victor observes lightning striking an oak tree. (17) The resulting fire illuminates the sky, revealing an unnatural image of a burning lake. (18) The Creature burns the DeLacys' cottage, after being rejected by them, as he watches it being "enveloped by the flames, which clung to it, and licked it with their forked and destroying tongues." (19) Lightning reveals the Creature to Victor after William's murder. (20) Fire operates in Frankenstein in literal ways providing light, warmth, and destruction. (21) Fire and lightning symbolize both progress towards knowledge and its devastating repercussions.

You might note that the draft is somewhat choppy, that one thought moves right into another without much connection. Coordination and subordination can make a big difference in improving the writing.

Here are sentences 3–5 as originally written.

(3) Prometheus was a Titan god who took fire from Zeus and the Olympian gods. (4) He took fire to Earth. (5) He gave it to humans.

The writer does not suggest that any one of those actions of Prometheus is more important than the others, so they could be effectively expressed through coordination (three items in a series with the coordinating conjunction *and*). Below are the sentences combined into one sentence using coordination.

> Prometheus, a Titan god, took fire from Zeus and the Olympian gods, took it to Earth, and gave it to humans.

Now consider sentences 6 and 7 as written.

> (6) Prometheus's gift to humans allowed them to forge their civilization. (7) Zeus punished Prometheus eternally by having his liver eaten by an eagle, only to have it regenerate itself in an endless cycle of torture.

These sentences could also be joined with coordination, with the word *but* highlighting the contrast.

> From Prometheus's gift, humans were able to forge civilization, but Zeus punished Prometheus eternally by having his liver eaten by an eagle, only to have it regenerate itself in an endless cycle of torture.

To emphasize the negative effects of Prometheus's actions over the positive results of them—to show the imbalance or inequality of these ideas—these sentences can also be joined through subordination by making the first independent clause a subordinate or dependent clause. These clauses use subordinating conjunctions. In the following example, *because* is the conjunction that creates a subordinate or dependent clause.

> Because Prometheus's gift to humans allowed them to forge civilization, Zeus punished Prometheus eternally by having his liver eaten by an eagle, only to have it regenerate and be eaten again in an endless cycle.

Sentences 9 and 10 could be combined to show their relationship using the subordinating conjunction *while*.

> While it can represent knowledge and progress, fire can also symbolize hell and destruction.

Subordinate clauses are especially powerful to emphasize your thesis in contrast to possibly differing views. Here are sentences 20 and 21 as originally written, with 21 expressing the thesis statement.

> (20) Fire operates in Frankenstein in literal ways providing light, warmth, and destruction. (21) Fire and lightning symbolize both progress towards knowledge and its devastating repercussions.

Sentence 20 acknowledges that fire can be understood in a literal way in the story. Readers who believe that not everything has symbolic value may be tempted to raise that objection to your thesis. In these two sentences, the imbalance is between what people who disagree with you might think and what you not only think but are prepared to defend in your argument. In this case, making your position the independent clause gives it strength and puts opposing views somewhat off to the side. The subordinating conjunction *although* creates the dependent clause.

> Although they operate in literal ways providing light, warmth, and destruction, for Victor and the Creature, fire and lightning symbolize both progress towards knowledge and its devastating repercussions.

Rather than repeating the words *fire* and *lightning* in both clauses, using a pronoun in the first and saving the use of *fire* and *lightning* for the independent clause expressing your thesis adds even more strength to that clause.

**Positioning Phrases** The placement of phrases, such as prepositional phrases, affects the clarity of your message as well, sometimes simply because of what readers expect and sometimes because it provides sentence variety.

In the original draft, every sentence follows the same basic pattern: subject–verb. Some of the revisions made for coordination and subordination do add variety as well as clarify meaning, but the writer can get a better result with different placement of some phrases. For example, in the second sentence, moving the prepositional phrase from the end of the sentence to the beginning provides variety. It also meets the reader's expectations that an example will follow the claim made in the first sentence.

> **Original**: The Greek myth of Prometheus is one of the earliest occurrences.
>
> **Revised**: One of the earliest occurrences is the Greek myth of Prometheus.

Sentence 11 as originally written ("Fire is a symbol in *Frankenstein* that provides the Creature relief from his harsh environment.") also follows the subject–verb pattern. More important, though, is that it signals in the introduction a turn to the specific novel from the more general comments that precede it. For these reasons—providing sentence variety and clarifying the direction the argument is taking—starting the sentence with the prepositional phrase "In *Frankenstein*" is the stronger choice ("In *Frankenstein*, fire is a symbol that provides the Creature relief from his harsh environment.").

The following revised version of the draft puts coordination and subordination to use in clarifying meaning and emphasis and positions phrases effectively. Note that the sentence numbers have changed accordingly. The original was 21 sentences; the revision is 16.

> (1) The archetypal symbol of fire has a rich history in Western culture. (2) One of the earliest occurrences is the Greek myth of Prometheus. (3) Prometheus was a Titan god who took fire from Zeus and the Olympian gods, took it to Earth, and gave it to humans. (4) From Prometheus's gift, humans were able to forge civilization, but Zeus punished Prometheus eternally by having his liver eaten by an eagle, only to have it regenerate and be eaten again in an endless cycle.

(5) Fire, as with most symbols, has contrasting meanings. (6) While it can represent knowledge and progress, fire can also symbolize hell and destruction. (7) In *Frankenstein*, fire is a symbol that provides the Creature relief from his harsh environment. (8) He comes to understand that fire gives "light as well as heat." (9) Victor uses "instruments of life" to "infuse a spark of life" into his creation. (10) On the other hand, Victor and the Creature also see the more sinister nature of fire. (11) The Creature touches embers and is burned. (12) Victor observes lightning striking an oak tree. (13) The resulting fire illuminates the sky revealing an unnatural image of a burning lake. (14) After being rejected by them, the Creature burns the DeLacys' cottage, as he watches it being "enveloped by the flames, which clung to it, and licked it with their forked and destroying tongues." (15) After William's murder, lightning reveals the Creature to Victor. (16) Although they operate in literal ways providing light, warmth, and destruction, for Victor and the Creature, fire and lightning symbolize both progress towards knowledge and its devastating repercussions.

As you work on your essay, reflect on the following questions to evaluate how effectively you use various syntactical constructions.

| Syntactical Concept | Questions for Reflection |
|---|---|
| Independent Clause | • Do my independent clauses logically follow a line of reasoning that develops my thesis?<br>• Did I put my most important points in independent clauses? |
| Subordinate Clause | • Have I used subordinate clauses to provide qualifying information or address potential objections to my literary argument?<br>• Do my subordinate clauses add relevant information, or do they take away from the focus of the independent clause and thesis?<br>• Would the sentence be more powerful without the subordinate clause?<br>• What would be the impact if I move the subordinate clause to another position in the sentence? How would the emphasis shift? |
| Fragment | • Do I have a good reason for using any fragments that may be present?<br>• Do my fragments interrupt the flow of ideas?<br>• Do my fragments replicate confused or disjointed thinking?<br>• Do my fragments emphasize ideas? |
| Prepositional Phrase | • Can I reduce wordiness and clarify meaning by reducing my use of prepositional phrases?<br>• Did I place phrases in their most useful position to emphasize meaning and add sentence variety? |
| Repetition | • Have I used repetition to emphasize important ideas, or am I repetitive because I need to expand my argument? |
| Parallel Structure | • Have I used parallel structure to link important ideas in a balanced style?<br>• Have I reserved parallel structure for my most important points? |

**Table 6-4**

## The Power of Words

Every word has a story that adds layers of new meaning as time moves forward. Accomplished writers choose words whose stories and connotations match their purpose. Thoughtful word choices have the power to create pictures and leave lasting impressions in your readers' minds.

Look again at the revised student draft on pages 417–418. Read it and make a list of words you think could be replaced with stronger ones.

Which words did you identify as weak? Perhaps some of your choices match those in Table 6-7.

| Words and Phrases to Replace | Reason for Replacement | New Word or Phrase |
|---|---|---|
| took | Overused and general | stole |
| unnatural | Vague—unnatural to what degree? | horrifying |
| fire | Repeats too many times | conflagration |

Table 6-5

A revised draft might look like the one below. The wording changes are underlined.

(1) The archetypal symbol of fire has a rich history in western culture. 2) One of the earliest occurrences is the Greek myth of Prometheus. (3) Prometheus, a Titan god, <u>stole</u> fire from Zeus and the Olympian gods, took it to Earth, and gave it to humans. (4) From Prometheus's gift humans were able to forge civilization, but Zeus punished Prometheus eternally by having his liver eaten by an eagle, only to have it regenerate itself and be eaten again in an endless cycle.

(5) Fire, as with most symbols, has contrasting meanings. (6) While it can represent knowledge and progress, fire can also symbolize hell and destruction. (7) In *Frankenstein* fire is a symbol that provides the Creature relief from his harsh environment. (8) He comes to understand that fire gives "light as well as heat." (9) Victor uses "instruments of life" to "infuse a spark of life" into his creation. (10) On the other hand, Victor and the Creature see the more sinister nature of fire. (11) The Creature touches embers and is burned. (12) Victor observes lightning striking an oak tree. (13) The resulting <u>conflagration</u> illuminates the sky revealing a <u>horrifying</u> image of a burning lake. (14) After being rejected by them, the Creature burns the DeLacys' cottage, as he watches it being "enveloped by the flames, which clung to it, and licked it with their forked and destroying tongues." (15) After William's murder, lightning reveals the Creature to Victor. (16) Although they operate in literal ways providing light, warmth, and destruction, for Victor and the Creature, fire and lightning symbolize both progress towards knowledge and its devastating repercussions.

When you revise for diction, ask yourself:

- What are the connotations of the word I am choosing? Do those connotations match my purpose?
- Does my writing have the power to create a picture or leave a lasting impression in my readers' minds?
- Are most of my verbs active?
- Are my nouns concrete?
- Are my adjectives and adverbs specific? Can I replace overused words such as *very, really,* or *thing* with more meaningful words?
- Do I repeat certain words unnecessarily for emphasis?

## Punctuation and Meaning

**Punctuation** marks—the symbols such as commas and periods that writers use to structure and organize their writing—help readers understand the message being conveyed, but only if they are used properly. In Units 3 and 4 you focused on the need to use punctuation according to conventional usage. Following conventional usage helps you clearly and accurately communicate with your reader, but punctuation can also create meaning. Just as writers sometimes produce a fragment for an intended effect, they can also use punctuation to emphasize ideas and make clear the relationship among them.

Look at the image below. What possible meanings does the question mark bring to the word *Democracy*? What might be the artist's message?

**Source:** Getty Images

As you read works by professional writers, notice interesting or unusual punctuation and ask how it enhances meaning. For example, following are some lines from the beginning of *A Christmas Carol* by Charles Dickens.

> Marley was dead: to begin with. There is no doubt whatever about that.

And a few lines later, Dickens describes Scrooge.

> Oh! But he was a tight-fisted hand at the grindstone, Scrooge! a squeezing, wrenching, grasping, scraping, clutching, covetous, old sinner!

In the first sentence, which is in fact the first sentence of the novel, the colon is a surprise. A more common way to express that might have been: "To begin with, Marley was dead." The unusual punctuation may suggest to readers that a quirky narrator is going to tell an interesting story in an interesting way.

In the second excerpt, Dickens starts with an exclamation point after "Oh," a common enough pattern. However, he also uses an exclamation mark in the middle of the sentence. The punctuation adds liveliness to the narrator's description and again suggests a narrator with idiosyncrasies.

Try using punctuation rhetorically in your own writing. The following chart will give you some ideas on how to use punctuation to emphasize your ideas.

| Punctuation | Symbol | When to Use |
|---|---|---|
| period | . | • Closes a thought<br>• Causes the reader to pause |
| question mark | ? | • Causes the reader to pause<br>• Indicates uncertainty |
| exclamation mark | ! | • Causes the reader to pause<br>• Indicates excitement |
| comma | , | • Causes the reader to pause, but more briefly than the period, question mark, or exclamation mark<br>• Separates but does not close thoughts |
| dash | — | • Shows an abrupt break in thought |
| semicolon | ; | • Shows a close relationship between ideas |
| colon | : | • Creates anticipation that further information will follow |
| parentheses | ( ) | • Show a distant relationship between ideas |
| quotation marks | " " | • Indicate direct quotations<br>• Indicate titles of stories and poems<br>• Indicate that a writer is using a word or phrase in an ironic or other nonstandard sense |
| ellipsis | . . . | • Marks omission of related details |

**Table 6-6**

When you revise for punctuation ask yourself the following questions:

- Does the punctuation convey the relationship among ideas?
- Have I overused certain punctuation marks?
- Does my punctuation reflect the tone I want to convey?
- Can I change punctuation for effect and still retain clarity for my audience?

**Remember:** Writers convey their ideas in a sentence through strategic selection and placement of phrases and clauses. Writers may use coordination to illustrate a balance or equality between ideas or subordination to illustrate an imbalance or inequality. Writers use words that enhance the clear communication of an interpretation. Punctuation conveys relationships between and among parts of a sentence. (LAN-1.R–T)

### 5.4 Checkpoint

Complete your peer checklist by establishing standards for effective syntax, including coordination and subordination, diction, and punctuation. Save your checklist for reviewing your own work and exchanging papers with a peer to review.

### Composing on Your Own

Continue your essay revisions by closely examining syntax, diction, and punctuation. Use Tables 6-4, 6-5, and 6-6 to help you determine if you can revise for more artful syntax, precise words, or rhetorical use of punctuation. Revise your essay on a longer work you are reading and give it to a classmate or friend for a final peer review. Consider the feedback you receive and revise as you think best.

# Part 5 Apply What You Have Learned

The final stage of the writing process is editing. Make sure you clearly communicate to an academic audience by demonstrating control over the elements of composition. Do a final check of your essay for correct spelling, usage, and punctuation. Consider having someone else do a check for you as well.

**Reflect on the Essential Question** Write a brief response that answers the essential question: *How can you communicate in writing an interpretation of a work of literature that asserts a claim and supports it with evidence?* In your answer correctly use the key terms listed on page 411.

# Unit 6 Review

## Section I: Multiple Choice

Questions 1–13. Read the following passage carefully before you choose your answers.

1       1801—I have just returned from a visit to my landlord—the solitary neighbour that I shall be troubled with. This is certainly a beautiful country! In all England, I do not believe that I could have fixed on a situation so completely removed from the stir of society. A perfect misanthropist's[1] Heaven—and Mr. Heathcliff and I are such a suitable pair to divide the desolation between us. A capital fellow! He little imagined how my heart warmed towards him when I beheld his black eyes withdraw so suspiciously under their brows, as I rode up, and when his fingers sheltered themselves, with a jealous resolution, still further in his waistcoat,[2] as I announced my name.

2       "Mr. Heathcliff?" I said.

3       A nod was the answer.

4       "Mr. Lockwood, your new tenant, sir. I do myself the honour of calling as soon as possible after my arrival, to express the hope that I have not inconvenienced you by my perseverance in soliciting the occupation of Thrushcross Grange: I heard yesterday you had had some thoughts—"

5       "Thrushcross Grange is my own, sir," he interrupted, wincing. "I should not allow any one to inconvenience me, if I could hinder it—walk in!"

6       The "walk in" was uttered with closed teeth, and expressed the sentiment, "Go to the Deuce!" Even the gate over which he leant manifested no sympathising movement to the words; and I think that circumstance determined me to accept the invitation: I felt interested in a man who seemed more exaggeratedly reserved than myself.

7       When he saw my horse's breast fairly pushing the barrier, he did put out his hand to unchain it, and then sullenly preceded me up the causeway, calling, as we entered the court,—"Joseph, take Mr. Lockwood's horse; and bring up some wine."

---

1  **misanthropist:** a person who hates or distrusts humankind
2  **waistcoat:** vest

8      "Here we have the whole establishment of domestics, I suppose," was the reflection suggested by this compound order. "No wonder the grass grows up between the flags, and cattle are the only hedge-cutters."

9      Joseph was an elderly, nay, an old man, very old, perhaps, though hale and sinewy. "The Lord help us!" he soliloquised[3] in an undertone of peevish displeasure, while relieving me of my horse: looking, meantime, in my face so sourly that I charitably conjectured he must have need of divine aid to digest his dinner, and his pious ejaculation had no reference to my unexpected advent.

10      Wuthering Heights is the name of Mr. Heathcliff's dwelling. "Wuthering" being a significant provincial adjective, descriptive of the atmospheric tumult to which its station is exposed in stormy weather. Pure, bracing ventilation they must have up there at all times, indeed: one may guess the power of the north wind, blowing over the edge, by the excessive slant of a few stunted firs at the end of the house; and by a range of gaunt thorns all stretching their limbs one way, as if craving alms of the sun. Happily, the architect had foresight to build it strong: the narrow windows are deeply set in the wall, and the corners defended with large jutting stones.

11      Before passing the threshold, I paused to admire a quantity of grotesque carving lavished over the front, and especially about the principal door; above which, among a wilderness of crumbling griffins[4] and shameless little boys,[5] I detected the date "1500," and the name "Hareton Earnshaw." I would have made a few comments, and requested a short history of the place from the surly owner; but his attitude at the door appeared to demand my speedy entrance, or complete departure, and I had no desire to aggravate his impatience previous to inspecting the penetralium.[6]

12      One stop brought us into the family sitting-room, without any introductory lobby or passage: they call it here "the house" pre-eminently. It includes kitchen and parlour, generally; but I believe at Wuthering Heights the kitchen is forced to retreat altogether into another quarter: at least I distinguished a chatter of tongues, and a clatter of culinary utensils, deep within; and I observed no signs of roasting, boiling, or baking, about the huge fireplace; nor any glitter of copper saucepans and tin cullenders[7] on the walls. One end, indeed, reflected splendidly both light and heat from ranks of immense pewter dishes, interspersed with silver jugs and tankards, towering row after row, on a vast oak dresser, to the very roof. The latter had never been under-drawn: its entire anatomy lay bare to an inquiring eye, except where a frame of wood laden with oatcakes and clusters of legs of beef, mutton, and ham, concealed it. Above the

---

3  **soliloquised:** spoke his thoughts aloud, as in a soliloquy
4  **griffin:** a mythological creature with a lion's body and the head and wings of an eagle
5  **shameless little boys:** *putti*, or naked children (usually boys), especially in Renaissance art
6  **penetralium:** the innermost part of a building
7  **cullender:** an old form of colander, a bowl-shaped strainer

chimney were sundry villainous old guns, and a couple of horse-pistols: and, by way of ornament, three gaudily-painted canisters disposed along its ledge. The floor was of smooth, white stone; the chairs, high-backed, primitive structures, painted green: one or two heavy black ones lurking in the shade. In an arch under the dresser reposed a huge, liver-coloured bitch pointer,[8] surrounded by a swarm of squealing puppies; and other dogs haunted other recesses.

13      The apartment and furniture would have been nothing extraordinary as belonging to a homely, northern farmer, with a stubborn countenance, and stalwart limbs set out to advantage in knee-breeches and gaiters. Such an individual seated in his arm-chair, his mug of ale frothing on the round table before him, is to be seen in any circuit of five or six miles among these hills, if you go at the right time after dinner. But Mr. Heathcliff forms a singular contrast to his abode and style of living. He is a dark-skinned gipsy[9] in aspect, in dress and manners a gentleman: that is, as much a gentleman as many a country squire: rather slovenly, perhaps, yet not looking amiss with his negligence, because he has an erect and handsome figure; and rather morose. Possibly, some people might suspect him of a degree of under-bred pride; I have a sympathetic chord within that tells me it is nothing of the sort: I know, by instinct, his reserve springs from an aversion to showy displays of feeling—to manifestations of mutual kindliness. He'll love and hate equally under cover, and esteem it a species of impertinence to be loved or hated again. No, I'm running on too fast: I bestow my own attributes over-liberally on him. Mr. Heathcliff may have entirely dissimilar reasons for keeping his hand out of the way when he meets a would-be acquaintance, to those which actuate[10] me. Let me hope my constitution is almost peculiar: my dear mother used to say I should never have a comfortable home; and only last summer I proved myself perfectly unworthy of one.

14      While enjoying a month of fine weather at the sea-coast, I was thrown into the company of a most fascinating creature: a real goddess in my eyes, as long as she took no notice of me. I "never told my love" vocally; still, if looks have language, the merest idiot might have guessed I was over head and ears: she understood me at last, and looked a return— the sweetest of all imaginable looks. And what did I do? I confess it with shame—shrunk icily into myself, like a snail; at every glance retired colder and farther; till finally the poor innocent was led to doubt her own senses, and, overwhelmed with confusion at her supposed mistake, persuaded her mamma to decamp.

---

8   **pointer:** a breed of dog used for hunting game
9   **gipsy:** a term for a person of Roma or Romani descent, also known as Traveller or Tinker
10  **actuate:** cause to act

15     By this curious turn of disposition I have gained the reputation of deliberate heartlessness; how undeserved, I alone can appreciate.

16     I took a seat at the end of the hearthstone opposite that towards which my landlord advanced, and filled up an interval of silence by attempting to caress the canine mother, who had left her nursery, and was sneaking wolfishly to the back of my legs, her lip curled up, and her white teeth watering for a snatch. My caress provoked a long, guttural gnarl.[11]

17     "You'd better let the dog alone," growled Mr. Heathcliff in unison, checking fiercer demonstrations with a punch of his foot. "She's not accustomed to be spoiled—not kept for a pet."

1.  As a foil to Heathcliff, Mr. Lockwood calls the reader's attention to Heathcliff's
    (A) formal good manners
    (B) severely aloof nature
    (C) handsome cheerfulness
    (D) timid fearfulness
    (E) awkward shyness

2.  Mr. Lockwood's remarks in paragraph 1 reveal his perspective as a
    (A) social misfit
    (B) sociable farmer
    (C) nature lover
    (D) withdrawn introvert
    (E) passionate adventurer

3.  Mr. Lockwood's statement, "Mr. Heathcliff and I are such a suitable pair to divide the desolation between us" (paragraph 1) is contradicted by the statement
    (A) "I do myself the honour of calling as soon as possible after . . . the occupation of Thrushcross Grange." (paragraph 4)
    (B) "I should not allow any one to inconvenience me, if I could hinder it—walk in!"(paragraph 5)
    (C) "The 'walk in' was uttered with closed teeth, and expressed the sentiment, 'Go to the Deuce!'" (paragraph 6)
    (D) "When he saw my horse's breast fairly pushing the barrier, he did put out his hand to unchain it..." (paragraph 7)
    (E) "Joseph, take Mr. Lockwood's horse; and bring up some wine." (paragraph 7)

---

11 **gnarl:** growl

4. Paragraph 14 suggests that Mr. Lockwood
   (A) is openly flirtatious with most women
   (B) fears talking to people of greater stature
   (C) regrets that he lacks a comfortable home
   (D) possesses an unjustified sense of pride
   (E) prefers the idea of romance to actual romance

5. In context, the "reputation of deliberate heartlessness" mentioned in paragraph 15 most clearly reveals a tension between
   (A) Lockwood's motives as a tenant and Heathcliff's treatment of him as a landlord
   (B) Heathcliff and Lockwood's similar treatment of the people they meet
   (C) Lockwood's hopes for his future with the hopes of his mother
   (D) Lockwood's awareness of his public perception and his inner motivations
   (E) Lockwood's regrets about past actions and his hopes for future decisions

6. The inconsistencies of Lockwood's character are revealed by the contrast between his
   (A) stated preference for isolation and the prospect of Heathcliff's friendship
   (B) desire to live alone and his strong sentiments about his mother
   (C) lack of concern for his horses and affection for Heathcliff's dog
   (D) observant descriptions of the countryside and his apparent lack of interest in people
   (E) concern for behaving according to social customs and his hatred of people

7. The flashback to Lockwood's seaside experience in paragraph 14
   (A) establishes him as a dishonest narrator
   (B) foreshadows his eventual marriage to the girl
   (C) indicates his mother understood his weaknesses
   (D) suggests he is misunderstood by most people
   (E) parallels Lockwood's shyness with Heathcliff's

8. Contrasting descriptions of the house's exterior (paragraph 10) and its interior (paragraph 12) hint at the
   (A) complexities of the inhabitants of Wuthering Heights
   (B) contrast between Heathcliff's brusque nature and the friendlier features of Lockwood's
   (C) differences between Heathcliff and Lockwood's mother
   (D) Heathcliff's treatment of the horse versus his treatment of his dog
   (E) poverty of Heathcliff and the profound wealth of Lockwood

9. In stating that he bestows his own attributes over-liberally on Heathcliff (paragraph 13) Lockwood intimates that he
   (A) holds significantly different political beliefs from Heathcliff
   (B) tends to trust people who look like him
   (C) feels sorry for Heathcliff's dire poverty
   (D) pities those who are not as fortunate as he is
   (E) may not be fully reliable as a narrator

10. In describing Wuthering Heights as "A perfect misanthropist's Heaven" (paragraph 1), Lockwood suggests that he
    (A) wants peace and quiet
    (B) struggles socially
    (C) lacks a capacity to empathize with others
    (D) wishes to escape city life
    (E) feels a deep sense of shame

11. Lockwood's descriptions of Heathcliff and Wuthering Heights suggest that he is
    (A) prematurely judgmental
    (B) unnecessarily frightened
    (C) naïvely imperceptive
    (D) cautiously friendly
    (E) gratefully accommodating

12. Lockwood's descriptions of Heathcliff suggest which archetypal character?
    (A) Hero
    (B) Trickster
    (C) Spurned Lover
    (D) Devil
    (E) Scapegoat

Questions 13 is covered in Unit 8.

13. In the sentence "The 'walk in' was uttered with closed teeth, and expressed the sentiment "Go to the Deuce!" (paragraph 6), the narrator establishes a

   (A) flashback to the first meeting between Lockwood and Heathcliff

   (B) contrast between what is said and what is meant

   (C) shift in tone from aggressive to belligerent

   (D) foreshadowing of the tragic relationship between the two men

   (E) stream of consciousness approach revealing Lockwood's thoughts

Questions 14–19. Read the following poem carefully before you choose your answers.

### AFTER THE STORM

1   There are so many islands!
     As many islands as the stars at night
     on that branched tree from which meteors are shaken
     like falling fruit around the schooner *Flight*.[1]
5   But things must fall, and so it always was,
     on one hand Venus, on the other Mars;
     fall, and are one, just as this earth is one
     island in archipelagoes[2] of stars.
     My first friend was the sea. Now, is my last.
10  I stop talking now. I work, then I read,
     cotching[3] under a lantern hooked to the mast.
     I try to forget what happiness was,
     and when that don't work, I study the stars.
     Sometimes is just me, and the soft-scissored foam
15  as the deck turn white and the moon open
     a cloud like a door, and the light over me
     is a road in white moonlight taking me home.
     Shabine[4] sang to you from the depths of the sea.

14. The contrasts in lines 5–8 suggest

   (A) good and evil

   (B) division and unity

   (C) freedom and escape

   (D) life and death

   (E) cause and effect relationships

---

1  **schooner *Flight*:** a sailing ship named ***Flight***. "After the Storm" is the final section of the longer poem called "The Schooner *Flight*."
2  **archipelagoes:** groups of islands
3  **cotch:** stay or sleep somewhere temporarily
4  **Shabine:** the speaker in the poem; also a term for someone of mixed heritage

15. The main function of lines 6–8 is to show that
    (A) Venus and Mars are opposites
    (B) planets are islands in the galaxy
    (C) archipelagos are symbols for connectedness
    (D) the universe is an archipelago of stars
    (E) the earth will fall into the sea

16. The syntax in line 9 emphasizes the
    (A) insignificant passage of time
    (B) speaker's unabated sense of despair
    (C) friendship between the speaker and inanimate objects
    (D) sea's importance to the speaker
    (E) speaker's impending drowning

17. Line 18 primarily
    (A) conveys a sense of despair in the speaker
    (B) paraphrases the phrase "a road in white moonlight"
    (C) delivers a moral lesson
    (D) refers to a mythical god
    (E) shifts from present to past

18. The speaker provides the fewest details about the
    (A) storm
    (B) islands
    (C) effects of the storm
    (D) sea
    (E) archipelagos

19. The storm itself may act as a symbol for the
    (A) positive and negative effects of natural forces
    (B) questions and doubts the speaker has about the afterlife
    (C) strife caused by religious conflicts and wars
    (D) trials and tribulations of the speaker's life
    (E) unpredictability of changing weather patterns

## Section II: Free Response

### Question 1: Poetry Analysis

In "After the Storm," a poem by Derek Walcott, the speaker reflects on life after a storm. Read the poem carefully. Then, in a well-written essay, analyze how Walcott uses poetic techniques and elements to convey the speaker's complex response to the situation.

In your response you should do the following:

- Respond to the prompt with a thesis that presents a defensible interpretation.
- Select and use evidence to support your line of reasoning.
- Explain how the evidence supports your line of reasoning.
- Use appropriate grammar and punctuation in communicating your argument.

### Question 2: Prose Fiction Analysis

On pages 423–426 is the opening of the first chapter of *Wuthering Heights*, an 1847 novel by Emily Brontë. In the passage, the narrator, Mr. Lockwood, describes the first time he met Mr. Heathcliff, his reclusive landlord, in a remote part of England. Read the passage carefully. Then, in a well-written essay, analyze how Brontë uses literary elements and techniques to create the complex tensions at this first meeting.

In your response you should do the following:

- Respond to the prompt with a thesis that presents a defensible interpretation.
- Select and use evidence to support your line of reasoning.
- Explain how the evidence supports your line of reasoning.
- Use appropriate grammar and punctuation in communicating your argument.

## Question 3: Literary Argument—Symbolism

"All struggles are essentially power struggles. Who will rule? Who will lead? Who will define, refine, confine, design? Who will dominate?"

*Octavia Butler*

Using *Frankenstein* or another longer work of fiction you have read, choose a symbol in the work that represents power struggles. Then, in a well-written essay, explain how the symbol reveals the complex nature of the power struggles and contributes to an interpretation of the work as a whole. Do not merely summarize the plot.

In your response you should do the following:

- Respond to the prompt with a thesis that presents a defensible interpretation.
- Provide evidence to support your line of reasoning.
- Explain how the evidence supports your line of reasoning.
- Use appropriate grammar and punctuation in communicating your argument.

# UNIT 7

# Deepening Complexity

[Short Fiction III]

**Part 1: Changing and Unchanging Characters**
**Part 2: Settings and Characters**
**Part 3: Plot and Pacing**
**Part 4: Narrative Emphasis**
**Part 5: Function of Symbols and Motifs**
**Part 6: Writing About Literature VII**

---

**ENDURING UNDERSTANDINGS AND SKILLS:** Unit 7

## Part 1 Changing and Unchanging Characters

**Understand**

Characters in literature allow readers to study and explore a range of values, beliefs, assumptions, biases, and cultural norms represented by those characters. (CHR-1)

**Demonstrate**

Explain the function of a character changing or remaining unchanged. (1.B)

Describe how textual details reveal nuances and complexities in characters' relationships with one another. (1.D)

## Part 2 Settings and Characters

**Understand**

Setting and the details associated with it not only depict a time and place, but also convey values associated with that setting. (SET-1)

**Demonstrate**

Explain the function of setting in a narrative. (2.B)

Describe the relationship between a character and a setting. (2.C)

## Part 3 Plot and Pacing

**Understand**

The arrangement of the parts and sections of a text, the relationship of the parts to each other, and the sequence in which the text reveals information are all structural choices made by a writer that contribute to the reader's interpretation of a text. (STR-1)

**Demonstrate**

Identify and describe how the plot orders events in a narrative. (3.A)

Explain the function of a particular sequence of events in a plot. (3.B)

## Part 4 Narrative Emphasis

**Understand**

A narrator's or speaker's perspective controls the details and emphases that affect how readers experience and interpret a text. (NAR-1)

**Demonstrate**

Explain how a narrator's reliability affects a narrative. (4.D)

## Part 5 Function of Symbols and Motifs

**Understand**

Comparisons, representations, and associations shift meaning from the literal to the figurative and invite readers to interpret a text. (FIG-1)

**Demonstrate**

Identify and explain the function of a symbol. (5.C)

Identify and explain the function of an image or imagery. (5.D)

Identify and explain the function of a simile. (6.A)

Identify and explain the function of personification. (6.B)

## Part 6 Writing About Literature VII

**Understand**

Readers establish and communicate their interpretations of literature through arguments supported by textual evidence. (LAN-1)

**Demonstrate**

Develop a thesis statement that conveys a defensible claim about an interpretation of literature and that may establish a line of reasoning. (7.B)

Develop commentary that establishes and explains relationships among textual evidence, the line of reasoning, and the thesis. (7.C)

Select and use relevant and sufficient evidence to both develop and support a line of reasoning. (7.D)

Demonstrate control over the elements of composition to communicate clearly. (7.E)

Source: *AP® English Literature and Composition Course and Exam Description*

# Unit 7 Overview

Suppose two people—one who has read literary fiction and one who has not—are placed in separate situations in which each is with a person whose background is different from their own who feels offended by something the person said. Which person—the one who reads fiction or the one who does not—is more likely to understand the point of view of the other person in the room? Researchers have found that people who read literary fiction performed better than those who did not on psychological tests measuring their ability to recognize that others as well as themselves have certain beliefs and desires and that they might be different. The conclusion: literary fiction draws readers into a world with multiple perspectives and with unfamiliar characters, and seeing how characters navigate that world may make readers better able to discern the thinking and feeling of others who are different from them in the real world.

In this final unit of short fiction—in fact in all the remaining units—the emphasis will be on multiple perspectives and complexity, aspects of literature that may explain its potential social benefit. Of course readers do not pick up a book and think to themselves, "I will read this so I am better able to navigate a complex world." They are much more likely to think, "This looks like a book or story or poem I will enjoy and that will pay me back for the time I invest in it." That in itself is enough.

---

⚓ **Short Story**
**"Interpreter of Maladies" by Jhumpa Lahiri**

The following is a short story published in 1999 by American author Jhumpa Lahiri. In this story, an American family, visiting parents who have returned to their homeland of India, goes on a sightseeing day trip. The day's events reveal complex relationships within the family.

1    At the tea stall, Mr. and Mrs. Das bickered about who should take Tina to the toilet. Eventually Mrs. Das relented when Mr. Das pointed out that he had given the girl her bath the night before. In the rearview mirror Mr. Kapasi watched as Mrs. Das emerged slowly from his bulky white Ambassador, dragging her shaved, largely bare legs across the back seat. She did not hold the little girl's hand as they walked to the rest room.

2    They were on their way to see the Sun Temple at Konarak. It was a dry, bright Saturday, the mid-July heat tempered by a steady ocean breeze, ideal weather for sightseeing. Ordinarily Mr. Kapasi would not have stopped so soon along the way, but less than five minutes after he'd picked up the family that morning in front of Hotel Sandy Villa, the little girl had complained. The first thing Mr. Kapasi had noticed when he saw Mr. and Mrs. Das, standing with their children under the portico of the hotel, was that they were very young, perhaps not even thirty. In addition to Tina they had two boys, Ronny and Bobby, who appeared very close in age and had teeth covered in a network of flashing silver wires. The family looked Indian but dressed as foreigners did, the children in stiff, brightly colored clothing and caps with translucent visors. Mr. Kapasi was accustomed to foreign tourists; he was assigned to them regularly because he could speak English. Yesterday he had driven an elderly couple from Scotland, both with spotted faces and fluffy white hair so thin it exposed their sunburnt scalps. In comparison, the tanned, youthful faces of Mr. and Mrs. Das were all the more striking. When he'd introduced himself, Mr. Kapasi had pressed his palms together in greeting, but Mr. Das squeezed hands like an American so that Mr. Kapasi felt it in his elbow. Mrs. Das, for her part, had flexed one side of her mouth, smiling dutifully at Mr. Kapasi, without displaying any interest in him.

3    As they waited at the tea stall, Ronny, who looked like the older of the two boys, clambered suddenly out of the back seat, intrigued by a goat tied to a stake in the ground.

4    "Don't touch it," Mr. Das said. He glanced up from his paperback tour book, which said "INDIA" in yellow letters and looked as if it had been published abroad. His voice, somehow tentative and a little shrill, sounded as though it had not yet settled into maturity.

5    "I want to give it a piece of gum," the boy called back as he trotted ahead.

6    Mr. Das stepped out of the car and stretched his legs by squatting briefly to the ground. A clean-shaven man, he looked exactly like a magnified version of Ronny. He had a sapphire blue visor, and was dressed in shorts, sneakers, and a T-shirt. The camera slung around his neck, with an impressive telephoto lens and numerous buttons and markings, was the only complicated thing he wore. He frowned, watching as Ronny rushed toward the goat, but appeared to have no intention of intervening. "Bobby, make sure that your brother doesn't do anything stupid."

7    "I don't feel like it," Bobby said, not moving. He was sitting in the front seat beside Mr. Kapasi, studying a picture of the elephant god taped to the glove compartment.

8    "No need to worry," Mr. Kapasi said. "They are quite tame." Mr. Kapasi was forty-six years old, with receding hair that had gone completely silver, but his butterscotch complexion and his unlined brow, which he treated in spare moments to dabs of lotus-oil balm, made it easy to imagine what he must have looked like at an earlier age. He wore gray trousers and a matching jacket-style shirt, tapered at the waist, with short sleeves and a large pointed collar, made of a thin but durable synthetic material. He had specified both the cut and the fabric to his tailor—it was his preferred uniform for giving tours because it did not get crushed during his long hours behind the wheel. Through the windshield he watched as Ronny circled around the goat, touched it quickly on its side, then trotted back to the car.

9    "You left India as a child?" Mr. Kapasi asked when Mr. Das had settled once again into the passenger seat.

10    "Oh, Mina and I were both born in America," Mr. Das announced with an air of sudden confidence. "Born and raised. Our parents live here now. They retired. We visit them every couple years." He turned to watch as the little girl ran toward the car, the wide purple bows of her sundress flopping on her narrow brown shoulders. She was holding to her chest a doll with yellow hair that looked as if it had been chopped, as a punitive measure, with a pair of dull scissors. "This is Tina's first trip to India, isn't it, Tina?"

11    "I don't have to go to the bathroom anymore," Tina announced.

12    "Where's Mina?" Mr. Das asked.

13    Mr. Kapasi found it strange that Mr. Das should refer to his wife by her first name when speaking to the little girl. Tina pointed to where Mrs. Das was purchasing something from one of the shirtless men who worked at the tea stall. Mr. Kapasi heard one of the shirtless men sing a phrase

from a popular Hindi love song as Mrs. Das walked back to the car, but she did not appear to understand the words of the song, for she did not express irritation, or embarrassment, or react in any other way to the man's declarations.

14    He observed her. She wore a red-and-white-checkered skirt that stopped above her knees, slip-on shoes with a square wooden heel, and a close-fitting blouse styled like a man's undershirt. The blouse was decorated at chest-level with a calico appliqué in the shape of a strawberry. She was a short woman, with small hands like paws, her frosty pink fingernails painted to match her lips, and was slightly plump in her figure. Her hair, shorn only a little longer than her husband's, was parted far to one side. She was wearing large dark brown sunglasses with a pinkish tint to them, and carried a big straw bag, almost as big as her torso, shaped like a bowl, with a water bottle poking out of it. She walked slowly, carrying some puffed rice tossed with peanuts and chili peppers in a large packet made from newspapers. Mr. Kapasi turned to Mr. Das.

15    "Where in America do you live?"

16    "New Brunswick, New Jersey."

17    "Next to New York?"

18    "Exactly. I teach middle school there."

19    "What subject?"

20    "Science. In fact, every year I take my students on a trip to the Museum of Natural History in New York City. In a way we have a lot in common, you could say, you and I. How long have you been a tour guide, Mr. Kapasi?"

21    "Five years."

22    Mrs. Das reached the car. "How long's the trip?" she asked, shutting the door.

23    "About two and a half hours," Mr. Kapasi replied.

24    At this Mrs. Das gave an impatient sigh, as if she had been traveling her whole life without pause. She fanned herself with a folded Bombay film magazine written in English.

25    "I thought that the Sun Temple is only eighteen miles north of Puri," Mr. Das said, tapping on the tour book.

26    "The roads to Konarak are poor. Actually it is a distance of fifty-two miles," Mr. Kapasi explained.

27    Mr. Das nodded, readjusting the camera strap where it had begun to chafe the back of his neck.

28    Before starting the ignition, Mr. Kapasi reached back to make sure the cranklike locks on the inside of each of the back doors were secured. As soon as the car began to move the little girl began to play with the lock on her side, clicking it with some effort forward and backward, but Mrs. Das said nothing to stop her. She sat a bit slouched at one end of the back seat, not offering her puffed rice to anyone. Ronny and Tina sat on either side of her, both snapping bright green gum.

29    "Look," Bobby said as the car began to gather speed. He pointed with his finger to the tall trees that lined the road. "Look."

30    "Monkeys!" Ronny shrieked. "Wow!"

31      They were seated in groups along the branches, with shining black faces, silver bodies, horizontal eyebrows, and crested heads. Their long gray tails dangled like a series of ropes among the leaves. A few scratched themselves with black leathery hands, or swung their feet, staring as the car passed.

32      "We call them the hanuman,"[1] Mr. Kapasi said. "They are quite common in the area."

33      As soon as he spoke, one of the monkeys leaped into the middle of the road, causing Mr. Kapasi to brake suddenly. Another bounced onto the hood of the car, then sprang away. Mr. Kapasi beeped his horn. The children began to get excited, sucking in their breath and covering their faces partly with their hands. They had never seen monkeys outside of a zoo, Mr. Das explained. He asked Mr. Kapasi to stop the car so that he could take a picture.

34      While Mr. Das adjusted his telephoto lens, Mrs. Das reached into her straw bag and pulled out a bottle of colorless nail polish, which she proceeded to stroke on the tip of her index finger.

35      The little girl stuck out a hand. "Mine too. Mommy, do mine too."

36      "Leave me alone," Mrs. Das said, blowing on her nail and turning her body slightly. "You're making me mess up."

37      The little girl occupied herself by buttoning and unbuttoning a pinafore on the doll's plastic body.

38      "All set," Mr. Das said, replacing the lens cap.

39      The car rattled considerably as it raced along the dusty road, causing them all to pop up from their seats every now and then, but Mrs. Das continued to polish her nails. Mr. Kapasi eased up on the accelerator, hoping to produce a smoother ride. When he reached for the gearshift the boy in front accommodated him by swinging his hairless knees out of the way. Mr. Kapasi noted that this boy was slightly paler than the other children. "Daddy, why is the driver sitting on the wrong side in this car, too?" the boy asked.

40      "They all do that here, dummy," Ronny said.

41      "Don't call your brother a dummy," Mr. Das said. He turned to Mr. Kapasi. "In America, you know . . . it confuses them."

42      "Oh yes, I am well aware," Mr. Kapasi said. As delicately as he could, he shifted gears again, accelerating as they approached a hill in the road. "I see it on *Dallas*, the steering wheels are on the left-hand side."

43      "What's *Dallas*?" Tina asked, banging her now naked doll on the seat behind Mr. Kapasi.

44      "It went off the air," Mr. Das explained. "It's a television show."

45      They were all like siblings, Mr. Kapasi thought as they passed a row of date trees. Mr. and Mrs. Das behaved like an older brother and sister, not parents. It seemed that they were in charge of the children only for the day; it was hard to believe they were regularly responsible for anything other than themselves. Mr. Das tapped on his lens cap, and his tour book,

---

1  **hanuman:** in Hindu mythology, the monkey that commanded an army of monkeys to help the gods, especially Rama

dragging his thumbnail occasionally across the pages so that they made a scraping sound. Mrs. Das continued to polish her nails. She had still not removed her sunglasses. Every now and then Tina renewed her plea that she wanted her nails done, too, and so at one point Mrs. Das flicked a drop of polish on the little girl's finger before depositing the bottle back inside her straw bag.

46    "Isn't this an air-conditioned car?" she asked, still blowing on her hand. The window on Tina's side was broken and could not be rolled down.

47    "Quit complaining," Mr. Das said. "It isn't so hot."

48    "I told you to get a car with air-conditioning," Mrs. Das continued. "Why do you do this, Raj, just to save a few stupid rupees. What are you saving us, fifty cents?"

49    Their accents sounded just like the ones Mr. Kapasi heard on American television programs, though not like the ones on *Dallas*.

50    "Doesn't it get tiresome, Mr. Kapasi, showing people the same thing every day?" Mr. Das asked, rolling down his own window all the way. "Hey, do you mind stopping the car. I just want to get a shot of this guy."

51    Mr. Kapasi pulled over to the side of the road as Mr. Das took a picture of a barefoot man, his head wrapped in a dirty turban, seated on top of a cart of grain sacks pulled by a pair of bullocks. Both the man and the bullocks were emaciated. In the back seat Mrs. Das gazed out another window, at the sky, where nearly transparent clouds passed quickly in front of one another.

52    "I look forward to it, actually," Mr. Kapasi said as they continued on their way. "The Sun Temple is one of my favorite places. In that way it is a reward for me. I give tours on Fridays and Saturdays only. I have another job during the week."

53    "Oh? Where?" Mr. Das asked.

54    "I work in a doctor's office."

55    "You're a doctor?"

56    "I am not a doctor. I work with one. As an interpreter."

57    "What does a doctor need an interpreter for?"

58    "He has a number of Gujarati patients. My father was Gujarati, but many people do not speak Gujarati in this area, including the doctor. And so the doctor asked me to work in his office, interpreting what the patients say."

59    "Interesting. I've never heard of anything like that," Mr. Das said.

60    Mr. Kapasi shrugged. "It is a job like any other."

61    "But so romantic," Mrs. Das said dreamily, breaking her extended silence. She lifted her pinkish brown sunglasses and arranged them on top of her head like a tiara. For the first time, her eyes met Mr. Kapasi's in the rearview mirror: pale, a bit small, their gaze fixed but drowsy.

62    Mr. Das craned to look at her. "What's so romantic about it?"

63    "I don't know. Something." She shrugged, knitting her brows together for an instant. "Would you like a piece of gum, Mr. Kapasi?" she asked brightly. She reached into her straw bag and handed him a small square

wrapped in green-and-white-striped paper. As soon as Mr. Kapasi put the gum in his mouth a thick sweet liquid burst onto his tongue.

64    "Tell us more about your job, Mr. Kapasi," Mrs. Das said.

65    "What would you like to know, madame?"

66    "I don't know," again she shrugged, munching on some puffed rice and licking the mustard oil from the corners of her mouth. "Tell us a typical situation." She settled back in her seat, her head tilted in a patch of sun, and closed her eyes. "I want to picture what happens."

67    "Very well. The other day a man came in with a pain in his throat."

68    "Did he smoke cigarettes?"

69    "No. It was very curious. He complained that he felt as if there were long pieces of straw stuck in his throat. When I told the doctor he was able to prescribe the proper medication."

70    "That's so neat."

71    "Yes," Mr. Kapasi agreed after some hesitation.

72    "So these patients are totally dependent on you," Mrs. Das said. She spoke slowly, as if she were thinking aloud. "In a way, more dependent on you than the doctor."

73    "How do you mean? How could it be?"

74    "Well, for example, you could tell the doctor that the pain felt like a burning, not straw. The patient would never know what you had told the doctor, and the doctor wouldn't know that you had told the wrong thing. It's a big responsibility."

75    "Yes, a big responsibility you have there, Mr. Kapasi," Mr. Das agreed.

76    Mr. Kapasi had never thought of his job in such complimentary terms. To him it was a thankless occupation. He found nothing noble in interpreting people's maladies, assiduously translating the symptoms of so many swollen bones, countless cramps of bellies and bowels, spots on people's palms that changed color, shape, or size. The doctor, nearly half his age, had an affinity for bell-bottom trousers and made humorless jokes about the Congress party. Together they worked in a stale little infirmary where Mr. Kapasi's smartly tailored clothes clung to him in the heat, in spite of the blackened blades of a ceiling fan churning over their heads.

77    The job was a sign of his failings. In his youth he'd been a devoted scholar of foreign languages, the owner of an impressive collection of dictionaries. He had dreamed of being an interpreter for diplomats and dignitaries, resolving conflicts between people and nations, settling disputes of which he alone could understand both sides. He was a self-educated man. In a series of notebooks, in the evenings before his parents settled his marriage, he had listed the common etymologies of words, and at one point in his life he was confident that he could converse, if given the opportunity, in English, French, Russian, Portuguese, and Italian, not to mention Hindi, Bengali, Oriya, and Gujarati. Now only a handful of European phrases remained in his memory, scattered words for things like saucers and chairs. English was the only non-Indian language he spoke fluently anymore. Mr. Kapasi knew it was not a remarkable talent.

Sometimes he feared that his children knew better English than he did, just from watching television. Still, it came in handy for the tours.

78    He had taken the job as an interpreter after his first son, at the age of seven, contracted typhoid—that was how he had first made the acquaintance of the doctor. At the time Mr. Kapasi had been teaching English in a grammar school, and he bartered his skills as an interpreter to pay the increasingly exorbitant medical bills. In the end the boy had died one evening in his mother's arms, his limbs burning with fever, but then there was the funeral to pay for, and the other children who were born soon enough, and the newer, bigger house, and the good schools and tutors, and the fine shoes and the television, and the countless other ways he tried to console his wife and to keep her from crying in her sleep, and so when the doctor offered to pay him twice as much as he earned at the grammar school, he accepted. Mr. Kapasi knew that his wife had little regard for his career as an interpreter. He knew it reminded her of the son she'd lost, and that she resented the other lives he helped, in his own small way, to save. If ever she referred to his position, she used the phrase "doctor's assistant," as if the process of interpretation were equal to taking someone's temperature, or changing a bedpan. She never asked him about the patients who came to the doctor's office, or said that his job was a big responsibility.

79    For this reason it flattered Mr. Kapasi that Mrs. Das was so intrigued by his job. Unlike his wife, she had reminded him of its intellectual challenges. She had also used the word "romantic." She did not behave in a romantic way toward her husband, and yet she had used the word to describe him. He wondered if Mr. and Mrs. Das were a bad match, just as he and his wife were. Perhaps they, too, had little in common apart from three children and a decade of their lives. The signs he recognized from his own marriage were there—the bickering, the indifference, the protracted silences. Her sudden interest in him, an interest she did not express in either her husband or her children, was mildly intoxicating. When Mr. Kapasi thought once again about how she had said "romantic," the feeling of intoxication grew.

80    He began to check his reflection in the rearview mirror as he drove, feeling grateful that he had chosen the gray suit that morning and not the brown one, which tended to sag a little in the knees. From time to time he glanced through the mirror at Mrs. Das. In addition to glancing at her face he glanced at the strawberry between her breasts, and the golden brown hollow in her throat. He decided to tell Mrs. Das about another patient, and another: the young woman who had complained of a sensation of raindrops in her spine, the gentleman whose birthmark had begun to sprout hairs. Mrs. Das listened attentively, stroking her hair with a small plastic brush that resembled an oval bed of nails, asking more questions, for yet another example. The children were quiet, intent on spotting more monkeys in the trees, and Mr. Das was absorbed by his tour book, so it seemed like a private conversation between Mr. Kapasi and Mrs. Das. In this manner the next half hour passed, and when they stopped for

lunch at a roadside restaurant that sold fritters and omelette sandwiches, usually something Mr. Kapasi looked forward to on his tours so that he could sit in peace and enjoy some hot tea, he was disappointed. As the Das family settled together under a magenta umbrella fringed with white and orange tassels, and placed their orders with one of the waiters who marched about in tricornered caps, Mr. Kapasi reluctantly headed toward a neighboring table.

81      "Mr. Kapasi, wait. There's room here," Mrs. Das called out. She gathered Tina onto her lap, insisting that he accompany them. And so, together, they had bottled mango juice and sandwiches and plates of onions and potatoes deep-fried in graham-flour batter. After finishing two omelette sandwiches Mr. Das took more pictures of the group as they ate.

82      "How much longer?" he asked Mr. Kapasi as he paused to load a new roll of film in the camera.

83      "About half an hour more."

84      By now the children had gotten up from the table to look at more monkeys perched in a nearby tree, so there was a considerable space between Mrs. Das and Mr. Kapasi. Mr. Das placed the camera to his face and squeezed one eye shut, his tongue exposed at one corner of his mouth. "This looks funny. Mina, you need to lean in closer to Mr. Kapasi."

85      She did. He could smell a scent on her skin, like a mixture of whiskey and rosewater. He worried suddenly that she could smell his perspiration, which he knew had collected beneath the synthetic material of his shirt. He polished off his mango juice in one gulp and smoothed his silver hair with his hands. A bit of the juice dripped onto his chin. He wondered if Mrs. Das had noticed.

86      She had not. "What's your address, Mr. Kapasi?" she inquired, fishing for something inside her straw bag.

87      "You would like my address?"

88      "So we can send you copies," she said. "Of the pictures." She handed him a scrap of paper which she had hastily ripped from a page of her film magazine. The blank portion was limited, for the narrow strip was crowded by lines of text and a tiny picture of a hero and heroine embracing under a eucalyptus tree.

89      The paper curled as Mr. Kapasi wrote his address in clear, careful letters. She would write to him, asking about his days interpreting at the doctor's office, and he would respond eloquently, choosing only the most entertaining anecdotes, ones that would make her laugh out loud as she read them in her house in New Jersey. In time she would reveal the disappointment of her marriage, and he his. In this way their friendship would grow, and flourish. He would possess a picture of the two of them, eating fried onions under a magenta umbrella, which he would keep, he decided, safely tucked between the pages of his Russian grammar. As his mind raced, Mr. Kapasi experienced a mild and pleasant shock. It was similar to a feeling he used to experience long ago when, after months of translating with the aid of a dictionary, he would finally read a passage from a French novel, or an Italian sonnet, and understand the words, one

after another, unencumbered by his own efforts. In those moments Mr. Kapasi used to believe that all was right with the world, that all struggles were rewarded, that all of life's mistakes made sense in the end. The promise that he would hear from Mrs. Das now filled him with the same belief.

90     When he finished writing his address Mr. Kapasi handed her the paper, but as soon as he did so he worried that he had either misspelled his name, or accidentally reversed the numbers of his postal code. He dreaded the possibility of a lost letter, the photograph never reaching him, hovering somewhere in Orissa, close but ultimately unattainable. He thought of asking for the slip of paper again, just to make sure he had written his address accurately, but Mrs. Das had already dropped it into the jumble of her bag.

91  They reached Konarak at two-thirty. The temple, made of sandstone, was a massive pyramid-like structure in the shape of a chariot. It was dedicated to the great master of life, the sun, which struck three sides of the edifice as it made its journey each day across the sky. Twenty-four giant wheels were carved on the north and south sides of the plinth.[2] The whole thing was drawn by a team of seven horses, speeding as if through the heavens. As they approached, Mr. Kapasi explained that the temple had been built between A.D. 1243 and 1255, with the efforts of twelve hundred artisans, by the great ruler of the Ganga dynasty, King Narasimhadeva the First, to commemorate his victory against the Muslim army.

92     "It says the temple occupies about a hundred and seventy acres of land," Mr. Das said, reading from his book.

93     "It's like a desert," Ronny said, his eyes wandering across the sand that stretched on all sides beyond the temple.

94     "The Chandrabhaga River once flowed one mile north of here. It is dry now," Mr. Kapasi said, turning off the engine.

95     They got out and walked toward the temple, posing first for pictures by the pair of lions that flanked the steps. Mr. Kapasi led them next to one of the wheels of the chariot, higher than any human being, nine feet in diameter.

96     "'The wheels are supposed to symbolize the wheel of life,'" Mr. Das read. "'They depict the cycle of creation, preservation, and achievement of realization.' "Cool." He turned the page of his book. "'Each wheel is divided into eight thick and thin spokes, dividing the day into eight equal parts. The rims are carved with designs of birds and animals, whereas the medallions in the spokes are carved with women in luxurious poses, largely erotic in nature.'"

97     What he referred to were the countless friezes of entwined naked bodies, making love in various positions, women clinging to the necks of men, their knees wrapped eternally around their lovers' thighs. In addition to these were assorted scenes from daily life, of hunting and trading, of

---

2  plinth: base

deer being killed with bows and arrows and marching warriors holding swords in their hands.

98      It was no longer possible to enter the temple, for it had filled with rubble years ago, but they admired the exterior, as did all the tourists Mr. Kapasi brought there, slowly strolling along each of its sides. Mr. Das trailed behind, taking pictures. The children ran ahead, pointing to figures of naked people, intrigued in particular by the Nagamithunas, the half-human, half-serpentine couples who were said, Mr. Kapasi told them, to live in the deepest waters of the sea. Mr. Kapasi was pleased that they liked the temple, pleased especially that it appealed to Mrs. Das. She stopped every three or four paces, staring silently at the carved lovers, and the processions of elephants, and the topless female musicians beating on two-sided drums.

99      Though Mr. Kapasi had been to the temple countless times, it occurred to him, as he, too, gazed at the topless women, that he had never seen his own wife fully naked. Even when they had made love she kept the panels of her blouse hooked together, the string of her petticoat knotted around her waist. He had never admired the backs of his wife's legs the way he now admired those of Mrs. Das, walking as if for his benefit alone. He had, of course, seen plenty of bare limbs before, belonging to the American and European ladies who took his tours. But Mrs. Das was different. Unlike the other women, who had an interest only in the temple, and kept their noses buried in a guidebook, or their eyes behind the lens of a camera, Mrs. Das had taken an interest in him.

100     Mr. Kapasi was anxious to be alone with her, to continue their private conversation, yet he felt nervous to walk at her side. She was lost behind her sunglasses, ignoring her husband's requests that she pose for another picture, walking past her children as if they were strangers. Worried that he might disturb her, Mr. Kapasi walked ahead, to admire, as he always did, the three life-sized bronze avatars of Surya, the sun god, each emerging from its own niche on the temple facade to greet the sun at dawn, noon, and evening. They wore elaborate headdresses, their languid, elongated eyes closed, their bare chests draped with carved chains and amulets. Hibiscus petals, offerings from previous visitors, were strewn at their gray-green feet. The last statue, on the northern wall of the temple, was Mr. Kapasi's favorite. This Surya had a tired expression, weary after a hard day of work, sitting astride a horse with folded legs. Even his horse's eyes were drowsy. Around his body were smaller sculptures of women in pairs, their hips thrust to one side.

101     "Who's that?" Mrs. Das asked. He was startled to see that she was standing beside him.

102     "He is the Astachala-Surya," Mr. Kapasi said. "The setting sun."

103     "So in a couple of hours the sun will set right here?" She slipped a foot out of one of her square-heeled shoes, rubbed her toes on the back of her other leg.

104     "That is correct."

105     She raised her sunglasses for a moment, then put them back on again. "Neat."

106     Mr. Kapasi was not certain exactly what the word suggested, but he had a feeling it was a favorable response. He hoped that Mrs. Das had understood Surya's beauty, his power. Perhaps they would discuss it further in their letters. He would explain things to her, things about India, and she would explain things to him about America. In its own way this correspondence would fulfill his dream, of serving as an interpreter between nations. He looked at her straw bag, delighted that his address lay nestled among its contents. When he pictured her so many thousands of miles away he plummeted, so much so that he had an overwhelming urge to wrap his arms around her, to freeze with her, even for an instant, in an embrace witnessed by his favorite Surya. But Mrs. Das had already started walking.

107     "When do you return to America?" he asked, trying to sound placid.

108     "In ten days."

109     He calculated: A week to settle in, a week to develop the pictures, a few days to compose her letter, two weeks to get to India by air. According to his schedule, allowing room for delays, he would hear from Mrs. Das in approximately six weeks' time.

110     The family was silent as Mr. Kapasi drove them back, a little past four-thirty, to Hotel Sandy Villa. The children had bought miniature granite versions of the chariot's wheels at a souvenir stand, and they turned them round in their hands. Mr. Das continued to read his book. Mrs. Das untangled Tina's hair with her brush and divided it into two little ponytails.

111     Mr. Kapasi was beginning to dread the thought of dropping them off. He was not prepared to begin his six-week wait to hear from Mrs. Das. As he stole glances at her in the rear-view mirror, wrapping elastic bands around Tina's hair, he wondered how he might make the tour last a little longer. Ordinarily he sped back to Puri using a shortcut, eager to return home, scrub his feet and hands with sandalwood soap, and enjoy the evening newspaper and a cup of tea that his wife would serve him in silence. The thought of that silence, something to which he'd long been resigned, now oppressed him. It was then that he suggested visiting the hills at Udayagiri and Khandagiri, where a number of monastic dwellings were hewn out of the ground, facing one another across a defile. It was some miles away, but well worth seeing, Mr. Kapasi told them.

112     "Oh yeah, there's something mentioned about it in this book," Mr. Das said. "Built by a Jain king or something."

113     "Shall we go then?" Mr. Kapasi asked. He paused at a turn in the road. "It's to the left."

114     Mr. Das turned to look at Mrs. Das. Both of them shrugged.

115     "Left, left," the children chanted.

116     Mr. Kapasi turned the wheel, almost delirious with relief. He did not know what he would do or say to Mrs. Das once they arrived at the hills. Perhaps he would tell her what a pleasing smile she had. Perhaps he would

compliment her strawberry shirt, which he found irresistibly becoming. Perhaps, when Mr. Das was busy taking a picture, he would take her hand.

117    He did not have to worry. When they got to the hills, divided by a steep path thick with trees, Mrs. Das refused to get out of the car. All along the path, dozens of monkeys were seated on stones, as well as on the branches of the trees. Their hind legs were stretched out in front and raised to shoulder level, their arms resting on their knees.

118    "My legs are tired," she said, sinking low in her seat. "I'll stay here."

119    "Why did you have to wear those stupid shoes?" Mr. Das said. "You won't be in the pictures."

120    "Pretend I'm there."

121    "But we could use one of these pictures for our Christmas card this year. We didn't get one of all five of us at the Sun Temple. Mr. Kapasi could take it."

122    "I'm not coming. Anyway, those monkeys give me the creeps."

123    "But they're harmless," Mr. Das said. He turned to Mr. Kapasi. "Aren't they?"

124    "They are more hungry than dangerous," Mr. Kapasi said. "Do not provoke them with food, and they will not bother you."

125    Mr. Das headed up the defile with the children, the boys at his side, the little girl on his shoulders. Mr. Kapasi watched as they crossed paths with a Japanese man and woman, the only other tourists there, who paused for a final photograph, then stepped into a nearby car and drove away. As the car disappeared out of view some of the monkeys called out, emitting soft whooping sounds, and then walked on their flat black hands and feet up the path. At one point a group of them formed a little ring around Mr. Das and the children. Tina screamed in delight. Ronny ran in circles around his father. Bobby bent down and picked up a fat stick on the ground. When he extended it, one of the monkeys approached him and snatched it, then briefly beat the ground.

126    "I'll join them," Mr. Kapasi said, unlocking the door on his side. "There is much to explain about the caves."

127    "No. Stay a minute," Mrs. Das said. She got out of the back seat and slipped in beside Mr. Kapasi. "Raj has his dumb book anyway." Together, through the windshield, Mrs. Das and Mr. Kapasi watched as Bobby and the monkey passed the stick back and forth between them.

128    "A brave little boy," Mr. Kapasi commented.

129    "It's not so surprising," Mrs. Das said.

130    "No?"

131    "He's not his."

132    "I beg your pardon?"

133    "Raj's. He's not Raj's son."

134    Mr. Kapasi felt a prickle on his skin. He reached into his shirt pocket for the small tin of lotus-oil balm he carried with him at all times, and applied it to three spots on his forehead. He knew that Mrs. Das was watching him, but he did not turn to face her. Instead he watched as the figures of Mr. Das and the children grew smaller, climbing up the steep

path, pausing every now and then for a picture, surrounded by a growing number of monkeys.

135    "Are you surprised?" The way she put it made him choose his words with care.

136    "It's not the type of thing one assumes," Mr. Kapasi replied slowly. He put the tin of lotus-oil balm back in his pocket.

137    "No, of course not. And no one knows, of course. No one at all. I've kept it a secret for eight whole years." She looked at Mr. Kapasi, tilting her chin as if to gain a fresh perspective. "But now I've told you."

138    Mr. Kapasi nodded. He felt suddenly parched, and his forehead was warm and slightly numb from the balm. He considered asking Mrs. Das for a sip of water, then decided against it.

139    "We met when we were very young," she said. She reached into her straw bag in search of something, then pulled out a packet of puffed rice. "Want some?"

140    "No, thank you."

141    She put a fistful in her mouth, sank into the seat a little, and looked away from Mr. Kapasi, out the window on her side of the car. "We married when we were still in college. We were in high school when he proposed. We went to the same college, of course. Back then we couldn't stand the thought of being separated, not for a day, not for a minute. Our parents were best friends who lived in the same town. My entire life I saw him every weekend, either at our house or theirs. We were sent upstairs to play together while our parents joked about our marriage. Imagine! They never caught us at anything, though in a way I think it was all more or less a setup. The things we did those Friday and Saturday nights, while our parents sat downstairs drinking tea . . . I could tell you stories, Mr. Kapasi."

142    As a result of spending all her time in college with Raj, she continued, she did not make many close friends. There was no one to confide in about him at the end of a difficult day, or to share a passing thought or a worry. Her parents now lived on the other side of the world, but she had never been very close to them anyway. After marrying so young she was overwhelmed by it all, having a child so quickly, and nursing, and warming up bottles of milk and testing their temperature against her wrist while Raj was at work, dressed in sweaters and corduroy pants, teaching his students about rocks and dinosaurs. Raj never looked cross or harried, or plump as she had become after the first baby.

143    Always tired, she declined invitations from her one or two college girlfriends, to have lunch or shop in Manhattan. Eventually the friends stopped calling her, so that she was left at home all day with the baby, surrounded by toys that made her trip when she walked or wince when she sat, always cross and tired. Only occasionally did they go out after Ronny was born, and even more rarely did they entertain. Raj didn't mind; he looked forward to coming home from teaching and watching television and bouncing Ronny on his knee. She had been outraged when Raj told her that a Punjabi friend, someone whom she had once met but did not

remember, would be staying with them for a week for some job interviews in the New Brunswick area.

144    Bobby was conceived in the afternoon, on a sofa littered with rubber teething toys, after the friend learned that a London pharmaceutical company had hired him, while Ronny cried to be freed from his playpen. She made no protest when the friend touched the small of her back as she was about to make a pot of coffee, then pulled her against his crisp navy suit. He made love to her swiftly, in silence, with an expertise she had never known, without the meaningful expressions and smiles Raj always insisted on afterward. The next day Raj drove the friend to JFK. He was married now, to a Punjabi girl, and they lived in London still, and every year they exchanged Christmas cards with Raj and Mina, each couple tucking photos of their families into the envelopes. He did not know that he was Bobby's father. He never would.

145    "I beg your pardon. Mrs. Das, but why have you told me this information?" Mr. Kapasi asked when she had finally finished speaking, and had turned to face him once again.

146    "For God's sake, stop calling me Mrs. Das. I'm twenty-eight. You probably have children my age."

147    "Not quite." It disturbed Mr. Kapasi to learn that she thought of him as a parent. The feeling he had had toward her, that had made him check his reflection in the rearview mirror as they drove, evaporated a little.

148    "I told you because of your talents." She put the packet of puffed rice back into her bag without folding over the top.

149    "I don't understand." Mr. Kapasi said.

150    "Don't you see? For eight years I haven't been able to express this to anybody, not to friends, certainly not to Raj. He doesn't even suspect it. He thinks I'm still in love with him. Well, don't you have anything to say?"

151    "About what?"

152    "About what I've just told you. About my secret, and about how terrible it makes me feel. I feel terrible looking at my children, and at Raj, always terrible. I have terrible urges, Mr. Kapasi, to throw things away. One day I had the urge to throw everything I own out the window, the television, the children, everything. Don't you think it's unhealthy?"

153    He was silent.

154    "Mr. Kapasi, don't you have anything to say? I thought that was your job."

155    "My job is to give tours, Mrs. Das."

156    "Not that. Your other job. As an interpreter."

157    "But we do not face a language barrier. What need is there for an interpreter?"

158    "That's not what I mean. I would never have told you otherwise. Don't you realize what it means for me to tell you?"

159    "What does it mean?"

160    "It means that I'm tired of feeling so terrible all the time. Eight years, Mr. Kapasi, I've been in pain eight years. I was hoping you could help me feel better, say the right thing. Suggest some kind of remedy."

161    He looked at her, in her red plaid skirt and strawberry T-shirt, a woman not yet thirty, who loved neither her husband nor her children, who had already fallen out of love with life. Her confession depressed him, depressed him all the more when he thought of Mr. Das at the top of the path, Tina clinging to his shoulders, taking pictures of ancient monastic cells cut into the hills to show his students in America, unsuspecting and unaware that one of his sons was not his own. Mr. Kapasi felt insulted that Mrs. Das should ask him to interpret her common, trivial little secret. She did not resemble the patients in the doctor's office, those who came glassy-eyed and desperate, unable to sleep or breathe or urinate with ease, unable, above all, to give words to their pains. Still, Mr. Kapasi believed it was his duty to assist Mrs. Das. Perhaps he ought to tell her to confess the truth to Mr. Das. He would explain that honesty was the best policy. Honesty, surely, would help her feel better, as she'd put it. Perhaps he would offer to preside over the discussion, as a mediator. He decided to begin with the most obvious question, to get to the heart of the matter, and so he asked, "Is it really pain you feel, Mrs. Das, or is it guilt?"

162    She turned to him and glared, mustard oil thick on her frosty pink lips. She opened her mouth to say something, but as she glared at Mr. Kapasi some certain knowledge seemed to pass before her eyes, and she stopped. It crushed him; he knew at that moment that he was not even important enough to be properly insulted. She opened the car door and began walking up the path, wobbling a little on her square wooden heels, reaching into her straw bag to eat handfuls of puffed rice. It fell through her fingers, leaving a zigzagging trail, causing a monkey to leap down from a tree and devour the little white grains. In search of more, the monkey began to follow Mrs. Das. Others joined him, so that she was soon being followed by about half a dozen of them, their velvety tails dragging behind.

163    Mr. Kapasi stepped out of the car. He wanted to holler, to alert her in some way, but he worried that if she knew they were behind her, she would grow nervous. Perhaps she would lose her balance. Perhaps they would pull at her bag or her hair. He began to jog up the path, taking a fallen branch in his hand to scare away the monkeys. Mrs. Das continued walking, oblivious, trailing grains of puffed rice. Near the top of the incline, before a group of cells fronted by a row of squat stone pillars, Mr. Das was kneeling on the ground, focusing the lens of his camera. The children stood under the arcade, now hiding, now emerging from view.

164    "Wait for me," Mrs. Das called out. "I'm coming."

165    "Great," Mr. Das said without looking up. "Just in time. We'll get Mr. Kapasi to take a picture of the five of us."

166    Mr. Kapasi quickened his pace, waving his branch so that the monkeys scampered away, distracted, in another direction.

167    "Where's Bobby?" Mrs. Das asked when she stopped.

168    Mr. Das looked up from the camera. "I don't know. Ronny, where's Bobby?"

169    Ronny shrugged. "I thought he was right here."

170    "Where is he?" Mrs. Das repeated sharply. "What's wrong with all of you?"

171    They began calling his name, wandering up and down the path a bit. Because they were calling they did not initially hear the boy's screams. When they found him, a little farther down the path under a tree, he was surrounded by a group of monkeys, over a dozen of them, pulling at his T-shirt with their long black fingers. The puffed rice Mrs. Das had spilled was scattered at his feet, raked over by the monkeys' hands. The boy was silent, his body frozen, swift tears running down his startled face. His bare legs were dusty and red with welts from where one of the monkeys struck him repeatedly with the stick he had given to it earlier.

172    "Daddy, the monkey's hurting Bobby," Tina said.

173    Mr. Das wiped his palms on the front of his shorts. In his nervousness he accidentally pressed the shutter on his camera; the whirring noise of the advancing film excited the monkeys, and the one with the stick began to beat Bobby more intently. "What are we supposed to do? What if they start attacking?"

174    "Mr. Kapasi." Mrs. Das shrieked, noticing him standing to one side. "Do something, for God's sake, do something!"

175    Mr. Kapasi took his branch and shooed them away, hissing at the ones that remained, stomping his feet to scare them. The animals retreated slowly, with a measured gait, obedient but unintimidated. Mr. Kapasi gathered Bobby in his arms and brought him back to where his parents and siblings were standing. As he carried him he was tempted to whisper a secret into the boy's ear. But Bobby was stunned, and shivering with fright, his legs bleeding slightly where the stick had broken the skin. When Mr. Kapasi delivered him to his parents, Mr. Das brushed some dirt off the boy's T-shirt and put the visor on him the right way. Mrs. Das reached into her straw bag to find a bandage which she taped over the cut on his knee. Ronny offered his brother a fresh piece of gum. "He's fine. Just a little scared, right Bobby?" Mr. Das said, patting the top of his head.

176    "God, let's get out of here." Mrs. Das said. She folded her arms across the strawberry on her chest. "This place gives me the creeps."

177    "Yeah. Back to the hotel, definitely," Mr. Das agreed.

178    "Poor Bobby," Mrs. Das said. "Come here a second. Let Mommy fix your hair." Again she reached into her straw bag, this time for her hairbrush, and began to run it around the edges of the translucent visor. When she whipped out the hairbrush, the slip of paper with Mr. Kapasi's address on it fluttered away in the wind. No one but Mr. Kapasi noticed. He watched as it rose, carried higher and higher by the breeze, into the trees where the monkeys now sat, solemnly observing the scene below. Mr. Kapasi observed it too, knowing that this was the picture of the Das family he would preserve forever in his mind.

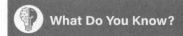
This unit will explore a variety of complexities in short fiction. Before you learn new skills and information, assess what you already know. Read the anchor text on pages 435–450 and answer the following questions. Don't worry if you find these challenging. Answering questions on a subject before formally learning about it is one way to help you deepen your understanding of new concepts.

## CLOSE READING

1. To what extent are characters at the beginning of the story different from how they are at the end? What causes any changes?

2. Are any of the characters outsiders of a group? What evidence led you to your answer?

3. What do the changes in setting and the characters' response to them reveal about the characters?

4. In what part does the tempo or pace of the story slow down and in what part does it speed up?

5. What do symbols and motifs contribute to the meaning of the story?

## INTERPRETATION

1. What bigger ideas are being developed in this story? What might be the meaning of the work as a whole?

2. What are the most important pieces of information in the text that would support a claim about the story (that is, your interpretation)?

**Source:** Wikimedia Commons

*How does the behavior of the characters at Konarak, the sun temple, contribute to your understanding of their perspectives?*

# Part 1

# Changing and Unchanging Characters

**Essential Question:** How and why do characters change?

Think back to your first day of high school. Did the thought of it create excitement or dread? Have your feelings about high school changed? If so, what caused the change, and did your change happen gradually or quickly?

In this part you will examine characters who experience changes because of a shift in their values and/or circumstances. Sometimes their change happens gradually, and you are not surprised at the end result. Other times the change happens quickly, producing a moment of sudden realization called an **epiphany.** Some people call this an "Aha! moment, " such as when you finally figure out a puzzle or realize that someone you distrusted is actually telling the truth. An epiphany allows a character to see things in a new light and is often directly related to a central conflict of the narrative. These sudden realizations are not as easily anticipated by the reader as are gradual changes.

---

**KEY TERM**

epiphany

---

# 1.1 Character Change: Values, Circumstances, and Epiphanies | CHR-1.X, CHR-1.Y, CHR-1.Z, CHR-1.AA

Some writers refer to the changes a character goes through as an inner journey. How a character gets from the beginning of that journey to the end varies, but there are several common routes.

- A character can experience change as a result of a conflict of values that emerges in the narrative.
- A character's circumstances may change and lead to inner changes in the character.
- A character can change gradually through the narrative.
- A character can make a sudden change after a moment of new realization—an epiphany—and act on that realization, providing a turn in the plot.

Conflict is the guiding hand of characters' journeys no matter what route they follow. Watching for changes in characters is a key part of literary analysis.

## Conflicting Values and Circumstances

The short story "Cell One" by Nigerian author Chimamanda Ngozi Adichie shows both conflicting values and a change in circumstances as forces that lead a character to change. The story is set in the university town of Nsukka, Nigeria. The unnamed narrator is the sister of the protagonist, Nnamabia, a handsome and charming young man getting ready to enter the university where their father is a professor. The family lives a comfortable middle-class lifestyle. The story begins:

> The first time our house was robbed, it was our neighbor Osita who climbed in through the dining-room window and stole our TV and VCR, and the "Purple Rain" and "Thriller" videotapes that my father had brought back from America. The second time our house was robbed, it was my brother Nnamabia, who faked a break-in and stole my mother's jewelry. It happened on a Sunday. My parents had travelled to their home town to visit our grandparents, so Nnamabia and I went to church alone. He drove my mother's green Peugeot 504. We sat together in church as we usually did, but we did not have time to nudge each other and stifle giggles about somebody's ugly hat or threadbare caftan, because Nnamabia left without a word after ten minutes. He came back just before the priest said, "The Mass is ended, go in peace." I was a little piqued. I imagined that he had gone off to smoke or to see some girl, since he had the car to himself for once; but he could at least have told me. We drove home in silence, and when he parked in our long driveway I stayed back to pick some ixora flowers while Nnamabia unlocked the front door. I went inside to find him standing in the middle of the parlor.
>
> "We've been robbed!" he said.

Nnamabia's sister notices a "theatrical quality to the ways the drawers had been flung open" and knows that her brother had done the break-in and stolen their mother's jewelry. His parents also know he did it, but Nnamabia says "with wounded eyes" that "he may have done horrible things in the past" that caused pain to his parents but that he had nothing to do with the break-in. He leaves the house and returns two weeks later, "gaunt, smelling of beer, crying," apologizing, and explaining he had sold all the jewelry and used up all the money.

The story then jumps to three years later, when Nnamabia is in his third year at the university. The "cults" are becoming active. "The Black Axe, the Buccaneers, and the Pirates were the best known. They had once been benign fraternities, but they had evolved, and now eighteen-year-olds who had mastered the swagger of American rap videos were undergoing secret initiations that sometimes left one or two of them dead on Odim Hill." Violence spread on campus. Nnamabia's parents worry that he has become a cult member—he is very popular, as were cult members. "Boys yelled out his nickname—'The Funk!'—and shook his hand whenever he passed by, and girls, especially the popular ones, hugged him for too long when they said hello. He went to all the parties, the tame ones on campus and the wilder ones in town . . . ." He laughs at the attempts of the police, with their inferior guns, to bring the cults under control. He denies being a cult member but is nonetheless arrested for belonging to a cult.

His family visits him in prison. He tells the story of one of his cellmates, an ill old man who is imprisoned because of something his son did. The police hope that the old man will tell them where his son is. His sister narrates:

> [One day] Nnamabia barely touched his rice. He said that the policemen had splashed soapy water on the floor and walls of the cell, as they usually did, and that the old man, who had not bathed in a week, had yanked his shirt off and rubbed his frail back against the wet floor. The policemen started to laugh when they saw him do this, and then they asked him to take all his clothes off and parade in the corridor outside the cell; as he did, they laughed louder and asked whether his son the thief knew that Papa's buttocks were so shrivelled. Nnamabia was staring at his yellow-orange rice as he spoke, and when he looked up his eyes were filled with tears, my worldly brother, and I felt a tenderness for him that I would not have been able to describe if I had been asked to.

Some time after his arrest, Nnamabia is found innocent of being in a cult and is set to be released. When his family comes to get him, they discover he has been sent to another location. Before being relocated, he was sent to Cell One, a place where prisoners are tortured and often die. In the excerpt below after his release, Nnamabia tells his family about the episode that got him in trouble with the guards. He recounts the story about the old man and the policemen and the story ends.

7     "I shouted at the policeman. I told him the old man was innocent and ill, and if they kept him here it wouldn't help them find his son, because the man did not even know where his son was. They said that I should shut up immediately, that they would take me to Cell One. I didn't care. I didn't shut up. So they pulled me out and slapped me and took me to Cell One."

8     Nnamabia stopped there, and we asked him nothing else. Instead, I imagined him calling the policeman a stupid idiot, a spineless coward, a sadist, a bastard, and I imagined the shock of the policemen—the chief staring openmouthed, the other cellmates stunned at the audacity of the boy from the university. And I imagined the old man himself looking on with surprised pride and quietly refusing to undress. Nnamabia did not say what had happened to him in Cell One, or what happened at the new site. It would have been so easy for him, my charming brother, to make a sleek drama of his story, but he did not.

The chart below will help you trace changes in values or circumstances and their effect on a character. You can use the chart for any character in any work. To help you draw meaning from the changes, write a claim that captures the significance of the changes you note. The examples below outline Nnamabia's change in values and circumstances. The claim is one possible interpretation of Nnamabia's transformation.

| Character: Nnamabia | | |
|---|---|---|
| Text | Competing Values/Changing Circumstances | Impact of Competing Values and Changing Circumstances on the Character |
| [Beginning]<br><br>Nnamabia steals his mother's jewelry when he was supposed to be in church and then lies about it when confronted by his father. He confesses to pawning the jewelry after he has spent the money he received and says he is sorry. | Nnamabia's actions show the competing values between the law against stealing and the church's mandate to honor his father and mother and his desire to show himself to be a fearless rebel like his neighbor. He does not respect his family and will take advantage of them to get what he wants. | Even though he says he is sorry, he has not changed. The details of his "gaunt" appearance and "smelling of beer" imply his remorse is only because he is out of money and needs to return home. |
| [Middle]<br><br>While it is not clear if Nnamabia is a cult member, he associates with them. He smokes and drinks and is popular with both males and females. Partying is a priority. | The description of violence and Nnamabia's acceptance of it as normal shows a young man becoming even more amoral than he was when he stole his mother's jewelry. He continues to show disrespect for law enforcement and disregard for his parents' concern. | Nnamabia has progressed from seeing nothing wrong with stealing to seeing nothing wrong with murder. He is a college student who cares more about his social life than his education. |

*continued*

| Text | Competing Values/Changing Circumstances | Impact of Competing Values and Changing Circumstances on the Character |
|---|---|---|
| [Ending]<br><br>Nnamabia still has no respect for law enforcement and challenges police authority, but now he does it for someone besides himself and his inflated ego. He feels sympathy for the old man who is being punished for a crime his son committed. | Both values and circumstances change for Nnamabia. His prison environment and treatment worsen, and he no longer wants to be popular. | Nnamabia has shifted from a morally ambiguous protagonist to an admirable one. While the reader isn't privy to details of Nnamabia's internal struggle, it is clear that his values have changed from self serving to caring. His indignation over the old man's treatment outweighs his fear of Cell One. Furthermore, his flair for the dramatic is replaced with a matter of fact telling of the story. He no longer needs to impress others. |

**Claim:** Nnamabia remains defiant to authority throughout the story, but his motivation to challenge those in charge changes from self-aggrandizement to concern for others.

Table 7-1

## Epiphanies and Central Conflicts

Characters can change gradually or quickly. An epiphany, or sudden realization usually about the central conflict, often triggers a deeper and more profound understanding than the character had previously. For example, Nnamabia in "Cell One" has an epiphany at the end of the story. The narrative takes place over a three-year period. For most of that time, Nnamabia exhibits careless disregard for the law and the feelings of others. He becomes increasingly repugnant as he worries his parents, parties with wild abandon, and fraternizes with murderers.

His incarceration lasts only two weeks of the story. During the first week he is his old self, ridiculing the police and presenting himself as a long-suffering hero to his family. His sister observes: "He seemed to enjoy his new role as the sufferer of indignities, and he did not understand how lucky he was that the policemen allowed him to come out and eat our food, or how stupid he'd been to stay out drinking that night, and how uncertain his chances were of being released." It seems that even prison could not change his arrogant attitude.

During the second week of imprisonment his circumstances change and so does his self-assured attitude. When the police abuse and ridicule the innocent old man, Nnamabia begins a quick transformation. His sister now notices he is growing more somber with each visit: "The following days, he was more subdued. He spoke less, and mostly about the old man: how he could not afford bathing water, how the others made fun of him or accused him of hiding his son, how the chief ignored him, how he looked frightened and so terribly small." Within a week's time Nnamabia's values have changed from putting himself above all others to compassion and sympathy for the old man, possibly because he reflects on his behavior toward his own father. He now cares more about the old man's feelings than his own and challenges the guards: "They said that I should shut up immediately, that they would take me to Cell One. I didn't care. I didn't shut up."

**Epiphanies and Action** The deeper understanding of a conflict that comes with an epiphany can cause a character to change behavior as well as values. Nnamabia's decision to defend the old man at the risk of personal harm to himself brings the plot to an end and earns him the respect of his sister, who has criticized his behavior throughout the story. The story ends with her noting: "Nnamabia did not say what had happened to him in Cell One, or what happened at the new site. It would have been so easy for him, my charming brother, to make a sleek drama of his story, but he did not." His behavior has changed as a result of his epiphany. The central conflict centering on Nnamabia's selfish sense of entitlement is resolved.

> **Remember:** Often the change in a character emerges directly from a conflict of values represented in the narrative. Changes in a character's circumstances may lead to changes in that character. While characters can change gradually over the course of a narrative, they can also change suddenly as the result of a moment of realization, known as an epiphany. An epiphany allows a character to see things in a new light and is often directly related to a central conflict of the narrative. An epiphany may affect the plot by causing a character to act on his or her sudden realization. (CHR-1.X–1.AA)

## 1.1 Checkpoint

*Review "Interpreter of Maladies" on pages 435–450. Then complete the following open-response activities and answer the multiple-choice questions.*

1. Recreate the chart on pages 455–456 with all the bold words copied, and replace Nnamabia with Mr. Kapasi. Trace the competing values and changing circumstances of Mr. Kapasi and analyze the impact on his changing character and final epiphany. Find at least three passages from the beginning, middle, and end, but add as many as you can find. After analyzing his changes, write a claim that captures the significance of those changes.

2. What is Mr. Kapasi's epiphany and how does it fit the criteria for one?

3. What competing values contributed to the epiphany?

4. Did any change in circumstances lead to the epiphany? If so, how and why? How does the epiphany affect the plot?

5. The epiphany Mr. Kapasi experiences in paragraph 162 ("She turned to him and glared . . . their velvety tails dragging behind.") is a sudden realization that

   (A) he is being punished for not following his moral obligations

   (B) he fantasized about Mrs. Das when she showed interest in him

   (C) his desire for approval was futile

   (D) his family was more important than he had realized

   (E) Mrs. Das loved her family more than she showed

6. Which of the following textual details shows a consistency in Mrs. Das's character?

   (A) "Always tired, she declined invitations from her one or two college girlfriends, to have lunch or shop in Manhattan" (paragraph 143)

   (B) "He was married now, to a Punjabi girl, . . . and every year they exchanged Christmas cards with Raj and Mina" (paragraph 144)

   (C) "'I feel terrible looking at my children, and at Raj, always terrible. I have terrible urges, Mr. Kapasi, to throw things away.'" (paragraph 152)

   (D) "Mrs. Das continued walking, oblivious, trailing grains of puffed rice." (paragraph 163)

   (E) "'Poor Bobby,' Mrs. Das said. 'Come here a second. Let Mommy fix your hair.'" (paragraph 178)

7. The reaction of Mr. Kapasi to Mrs. Das's confession in paragraph 161 ("He looked at her, in her red plaid skirt and strawberry T-shirt . . .") suggests his

   (A) obligation to help despite the nature of her problem

   (B) disgust that he is involved in Mrs. Das's secret

   (C) remorse for his lustful thoughts

   (D) anger at Mrs. Das's selfishness

   (E) helplessness to help Mrs. Das

**Creating on Your Own**

Suppose on your own personal journey you come to a fork in the road. The sign pointing to one road reads "The Thing You Want to Do." The sign pointing to the road going in the other direction reads "The Thing You Ought to Do." Think of conflicts you have had with competing values or changing circumstances (that you are comfortable writing about) that have led you to choose one of those directions, and write a memoir, or literary autobiography. How did you resolve the tensions? What insights did you gain through the struggles to reconcile the conflicts? Write a draft of a brief memoir that communicates your struggles to an audience. Save your work.

**Source:** Getty Images

# 1.2 Characters and Groups | CHR-1.AB, CHR-1.AC, CHR-1.AD

On a character's journey, you can expect that character to experience conflict with another character along the way. However, a group of people or a social or natural force can also function as a character either aiding a character or presenting a barrier on the journey. How a character interacts with other characters, groups, or forces may reveal important insights into the character. Further, whether a character is an insider in a group or an outsider reveals the attitude of the group toward the character as well as the character's attitude toward the group.

## Groups and Character Interactions

Authors create groups to contribute to ideas and values central to a work's conflict. For example, a group may represent some sort of rebellion. In "Cell One," the cults that terrorize the Nsukka university campus rebel against the authority of local laws as well as their parents. The cults become a collective character in the story. Only one member, Aboy, is referred to briefly by his given name. One other boy who is murdered is referred to as a professor's son. Otherwise they are referred to as members of one of the cults, "Buccaneers," "Black Axes," or "Pirates." Adichie characterizes these young men by their collective actions and their opposition to such authority figures as the police or their parents. The cults' actions highlight several of the short story's conflicts. First, the cults are a product of overindulgent middle-class parents. They also highlight the broken law enforcement system. Even though the police crack down on the gangs, the reader sees their abuse of power as they take bribes and physically abuse innocent people. The reasons for the groups' existence are complex. Certainly they are morally wrong to kill without remorse, but their parents and law enforcement share in the blame.

Not all groups are rebellious. In George Orwell's 1948 novel, *1984*, a group called the proletariat represents that society's lower class. They are oppressed by those in power. Not one prole, a member of the proletariat, receives a name. They are not considered important enough for individual identities by those in power. Rather, Orwell characterizes this group by their blind acceptance of food rations and bombings in their neighborhoods. They are easily tranquilized by promises of lottery winnings. Of course, no one ever wins the jackpot. Characters from higher classes largely ignore the proles. This group illustrates how easily those who wield power can control those who don't. When you encounter groups that serve as characters, interpret their collective characterization as you would an individual character and analyze what the interactions between the group and individual characters reveal about each.

## Forces and Character Interactions

In Shakespeare's play *Hamlet,* Hamlet and his friends see the ghost of Hamlet's dead father. Horatio, Hamlet's good friend and fellow scholar, tries to explain the supernatural appearance using conventional teachings ranging from indigestion, to a warning, to trickery by the devil. Hamlet, however, responds, "There are more things in heaven and earth, Horatio, / Than are dreamt of in your philosophy." Hamlet correctly knows that there are unseen and unnatural forces at work that defy easy explanation.

Authors often use nature as a force to convey mysterious and complex realities. In Joseph Conrad's 1899 novella *Heart of Darkness,* the Congo jungle becomes a character that wields its force on those, particularly European invaders, who don't understand its natural laws. The Europeans who journey to Africa in the 19th century operate under a lie. Publicly they maintain their reason for being in Africa is to bring improvements to the indigenous people, when in reality they are there to profit from the continent's rich natural resources. The jungle punishes them with disease and death. One character, a French doctor, observes that no one he sends into the jungle comes back.

Another notable example of an unseen force as a character is the standard of beauty based on whiteness in Toni Morrison's novel *The Bluest Eye*. Pecola Breedlove, the young Black girl who is the story's protagonist, is obsessed with having blue eyes, blonde hair, and white skin, because everywhere she turns in the prevailing culture, whiteness is held up as the epitome of beauty. It is celebrated in the movies; it is represented in the dolls girls play with; and it exerts its force powerfully in the excerpts from the "Dick and Jane" stories that were so popular in the 1940s, excerpts from which Morrison weaves throughout the book. Dick and Jane and their happy White family were the subjects of books with which a whole generation of children were taught to read. Pecola prays every night for blue eyes, which she believes will help her finally be recognized and loved.

## Character and Group Attitudes

Can you think of a time that you have been excluded from a group? Conversely, have you ever excluded someone from your group? If a person holds values antithetical to yours, you might have good reason for not wanting to associate with that person, but often the reasons for exclusion are based on prejudices and biases. Literature, like life, reflects a myriad of reasons for exclusion and inclusion of characters by groups. For example, Percival Everett's short story "The Appropriation of Cultures" (see Unit 1) offers a complex example of Blacks in the South being excluded by White society. Although Daniel is rich and cultured, the White fraternity boys want to exert their superiority when they shout for Daniel, who is Black, to "Play *Dixie* for us." Their intent seems to be to put Daniel in his place by having him play a song closely associated with slavery. Daniel's reaction is unexpected. He plays "the song he had grown up hating, the song the whites had always pulled out to remind themselves and those other people just where they were." However, he decides it is *his* song and puts emphasis on words that take away the glory of slavery's past: *Old times there are not forgotten . . . Look away, look away, look away, Dixieland.* This incident reveals both the exclusionary attitude of the fraternity boys as well as Daniel's passive aggression toward the group.

 **Remember:** A group or force can function as a character. When readers consider a character, they should examine how that character interacts with other characters, groups, or forces and what those interactions may indicate about the character. The relationship between a character and a group, including the inclusion or exclusion of that character, reveals the collective attitude of the group toward that character and possibly the character's attitude toward the group. (CHR-1.AB–AD)

### 1.2 Checkpoint

*Review "Interpreter of Maladies" on pages 435–450. Then complete the following open-response activities and answer the multiple-choice questions.*

The forces and groups in "Interpreter of Maladies" are not as obvious as a jungle or social groups, but they are present and influential nonetheless. Answer the following questions to understand their significance in the story.

1. What force(s) led to Mr. Kapasi's job with the doctor, which he regards as "a sign of his failings"?

2. Which character is an outsider, and how is that exclusion shown in the story?

3. What is the significance to the story of the character's exclusion?

4. Which of the following statements by Mr. Das best conveys his attitude toward the people of India?

    (A) "Oh, Mina and I were both born in America. . . Born and raised." (paragraph 9)

    (B) "In a way we have a lot in common, you could say, you and I." (paragraph 19)

    (C) "It went off the air. . . . It's a television show." (paragraph 43)

    (D) "Oh, yeah, there's something . . . in this book . . . built by a Jain king or something." (paragraph 112)

    (E) "But we could use one of these pictures for our Christmas card this year." (paragraph 121)

**Creating on Your Own**

Return to the memoir you have begun. What groups or forces complicated your conflict? Revise your memoir characterizing groups or forces with which you interacted. Save your work.

# Part 1   Apply What You Have Learned

Carefully review "Interpreter of Maladies." As you review, gather evidence that shows the impact society's expectations and the interactions with other characters have on the behaviors of Mrs. Das and Mr. Kapasi. Write a paragraph that interprets the similarities and differences in how the two characters respond.

**Reflect on the Essential Question** Write a brief response that answers the essential question: *How and why do characters change?* In your answer, correctly use the key term listed on page 452.

# Part 2

# Settings and Characters

**Enduring Understanding and Skills**

## Part 2

### Understand
Setting and the details associated with it not only depict a time and place, but also convey values associated with that setting. (SET-1)

### Demonstrate
Explain the function of setting in a narrative. (2.B)

Describe the relationship between a character and a setting. (2.C)

See also Unit 4

**Source:** *AP® English Literature and Composition Course and Exam Description*

**Essential Question:** How does a change in setting relate to a change in character?

Setting helps ground readers in the context of the plot by placing them in the world of the characters. Homer's Odysseus goes on a journey as does Frodo Baggins in *The Lord of the Rings*. Their journeys share many general traits, such as tests of strength and descents into dangerous situations, yet readers will encounter two different worlds through setting. In addition to creating the characters' worlds, the setting also creates atmosphere, establishes mood, and provides context for why characters may behave as they do in their environments. (See Unit 4.) Finally, settings can provide layers of metaphoric meaning. The hole Alice falls through in *Alice in Wonderland* not only grounds the reader in Alice's world, but also serves as a metaphor for Alice's subconscious thoughts. The focus on setting in this unit will build on what you have previously learned by asking you to find patterns in setting throughout a work and analyze the key elements. You will note changes within those patterns and interpret their impact on mood, atmosphere, characters, and meaning.

## 2.1 Changing and Contrasting Settings | SET-1.E, SET-1.F

When a setting changes, the change may suggest other movements, changes, or shifts in the narrative. These changes may shift the mood, atmosphere, or tone. Settings can also be contrasted to highlight differences in values.

## Setting Changes

Setting, character, and plot are inextricably linked. For example, "The Sanctuary Desolated" has two settings, Grandma's farm and that of her daughter's family (See Unit 4). When Grandma moves into her daughter's house, the plot takes very unexpected turns and Grandma's mood goes from contented to miserable and her character acquires an almost supernatural sense. In "Cell One," Nnamabia's character undergoes a major transformation when he is moved to Cell One. In each setting change in *Exit West* (see Unit 3), Nadia and Saeed learn more about each other and themselves and gradually change.

## Contrasting Settings

In some cases, including "The Sanctuary Desolated," settings are purposefully contrasted. Grandma's place has old oak and hickory trees, mature shrubs and roses, a moss-covered roof, a broken gate, and a water well over 85 years old. Her daughter's farm, by contrast, has young apple trees, tall rye grass for fertilizing the young trees, and a water well less than 25 years old. Each setting carries metaphoric significance. Grandma's farm represents her values, her connections with the past, while that of her daughter and son-in-law represents theirs, a growing family looking toward the future.

Katherine Mansfield's 1920 short story "Miss Brill" also highlights contrasting settings. It recounts the details of one day in the life of an English teacher living in France. Miss Brill is an older, unmarried woman who lives alone in a small room. One of her greatest pleasures is a Sunday visit to the public park where she eavesdrops on people and imagines what they are thinking. Miss Brill lives vicariously through others, not by talking to them, but by pretending they are all characters in a play in which she, too, is a participant. Her illusions are shattered when she overhears a young couple making fun of her looks, age, and prize possession, a fox stole.

**Source:** Getty Images

A picture of a typical early to mid-20th-century fox stole

*Why might the fox stole play such a big role in the story of Miss Brill?*

The story begins on a Sunday in early spring. Miss Brill is in a public park located somewhere in France. From other works, songs, or movies, you might associate France in spring with romance and beauty. She was wearing her beloved fox stole.

> She had taken it out of its box that afternoon, shaken out the moth-powder, given it a good brush, and rubbed the life back into the dim little eyes. "What has been happening to me?" said the sad little eyes. Oh, how sweet it was to see them snap at her again from the red eiderdown![1] But the nose, which was of some black composition, wasn't at all firm.[2] It must have had a knock, somehow. Never mind—a little dab of black sealing-wax when the time came—when it was absolutely necessary . . . Little rogue! Yes, she really felt like that about it. Little rogue biting its tail just by her left ear. She could have taken it off and laid it on her lap and stroked it.

Certainly spring is a time connected with new life. The atmosphere is charged with lively activity as the band plays and an increased number of people visit the park. When Miss Brill arrives at the "Jardins Publiques," the blue sky is clear, "powdered with gold and great spots of light like white wine." Even though the band plays year round, it sounded "louder and gayer . . . because the Season had begun." Miss Brill listens to the "flutey" music and decides it is "very pretty!—a little chain of bright drops." Despite the festive setting, however, the temperature had "a faint chill, like a chill from a glass of iced water before you sip." Nonetheless, Miss Brill doesn't mind the brisk air and her mood remains joyful because she has her fur to keep her warm. The second paragraph of the story ends with "she smiled."

At the story's end, although it is still Sunday, the setting has shifted to evening, indicating an ending rather than a beginning. Instead of enjoying her usual Sunday "slice of honey-cake" that she picks up from a bakery on the way home, she sits alone in "her little dark room" before she quickly returns her beloved fur to its storage box, and when she "put the lid on she thought she heard something crying." This is in marked contrast to the description of her lovingly removing it to wear to the park. The story's joyful mood and bustling atmosphere change to a somber mood and isolated atmosphere. She realizes the fur can no longer take away the chill. Instead of smiling, someone now is crying, perhaps Miss Brill. Miss Brill's world contracts from the beautiful park full of people, music, and possibility to a small dark room that resembles a "cupboard" and a life of limited options.

 **Remember:** When a setting changes, it may suggest other movements, changes, or shifts in the narrative. Settings may be contrasted in order to establish a conflict of values or ideas associated with those settings. (SET-1.E–F)

### 2.1 Checkpoint

*Review "Interpreter of Maladies" on pages 435–450. Then complete the following open-response activities and answer the multiple-choice questions.*

1. On separate paper, recreate the following chart to organize your thinking about the significance of the different settings and their relationship to one another in "Interpreter of Maladies." After you finish, write a claim that captures the significance of changes and contrasts in the setting.

| Setting Details | Impact on the Narrative |
|---|---|
| Hotel Sandy Villa and Tea Stall: | Hotel Sandy Villa and Tea Stall: |
| Car Ride: | Car Ride: |
| Roadside Cafe: | Roadside Cafe: |
| Sun Temple at Konarak: | Sun Temple at Konarak: |
| Hills of Udayagiri and Khandagiri: | Hills of Udayagiri and Khandagiri: |
| Claim: | |

2. The significance of the change from the car ride to the roadside cafe with a magenta umbrella described in paragraph 89 ("The paper curled …") is that

   (A) Mr. Das has a chance for more pictures

   (B) The children can find more monkeys

   (C) They needed a break from the bumpy car ride

   (D) Mr. Kapasi finds joy thinking about the future

   (E) Mrs. Das is beginning to enjoy herself

**Creating on Your Own**
Return to your memoir in progress. What effect did your surroundings have on your struggles? Revise your memoir, adding and emphasizing details from your environment that will illuminate the conflicts with values, other people, or groups. Save your work.

# 2.2 Insights from Interactions of Characters with Their Setting | SET-1.G, SET-1.H

Psychologist B. F. Skinner theorized that the environment in which people live shapes their behaviors. At the very least, characters' interactions with and attitudes toward their surroundings will provide insights into their development. In "Interpreter of Maladies," Mr. Das interacts with the Indian setting as he would his native American one. He dresses as an American in a "sapphire blue visor" and "shorts, sneakers, and a T-shirt." Rather than immersing himself in India's culture as fully as he might, Mr. Das first goes to a foreign-published tour book on India for his information on historic sites he plans to visit. He spends much of the time at those sites reading from the book or taking pictures with his camera that has "an impressive telephoto lens and numerous buttons and markings." His attitude indicates he feels more comfortable with his American environment than the current one. He is afraid for Bobby to get near a goat and when Mr. Kapasi asks, "You left India as a child?" Mr. Das replies, "Oh, Mina and I were both born in America." He proclaims his birthplace "with an air of sudden confidence. 'Born and raised.' " He continues to be a tourist throughout the story, interacting with his environment at arm's length.

## Attitudes Revealed by Character Interactions with Their Surroundings

You can learn much about characters' attitudes toward the environment by examining how they describe or behave in it.

> "I told you to get a car with air-conditioning," Mrs. Das continued. "Why do you do this, Raj, just to save a few stupid rupees. What are you saving us, fifty cents?"
>
> Their accents sounded just like the ones Mr. Kapasi heard on American television programs, though not like the ones on *Dallas*.
>
> "Doesn't it get tiresome, Mr. Kapasi, showing people the same thing every day?" Mr. Das asked, rolling down his own window all the way. "Hey, do you mind stopping the car. I just want to get a shot of this guy."
>
> Mr. Kapasi pulled over to the side of the road as Mr. Das took a picture of a barefoot man, his head wrapped in a dirty turban, seated on top of a cart of grain sacks pulled by a pair of bullocks. Both the man and the bullocks were emaciated.

To Mr. Das, the emaciated man and the steers pulling the cart were nothing more than a photo opportunity. Even though his lens is supposed to be able to capture great detail, Mr. Das seems to miss entirely the hard life this man must have. This detail combines with others to reveal that his attitude toward his surroundings is that they are inferior to what he is used to, not even worth the empathy that the man on the cart deserves. Further, this detail is juxtaposed with Mrs. Das's complaint about the air conditioning in the car—a luxury the man on the cart could never even imagine. Together, the details of Mr. Das's interactions with his surroundings contribute to the development of his character and the reader's interpretation of him as somewhat self-absorbed and detached.

**Remember:** The way characters interact with their surroundings provides insights about those characters and the setting(s) they inhabit. The way characters behave in or describe their surroundings reveals an attitude about those surroundings and contributes to the development of those characters and readers' interpretations of them. (SET-1.G–H)

## 2.2 Checkpoint

Review "Interpreter of Maladies" on pages 435–450. Then complete the following open-response activities and answer the multiple-choice questions.

1. The T-Chart below will help you organize your understanding about the role of setting in "Interpreter of Maladies." Using the first two examples that have been completed for you as a model, finish the other elements of setting. Interpret the impact of the two settings on mood, atmosphere, and character development. Be sure to include specific evidence from the story to support your interpretations. After reflecting on the impact of setting, develop a thesis statement that asserts a claim about how these details of the two settings come together to suggest movements, changes, shifts, and a clash of values or ideas. Do not summarize the plot.

| Setting and Characters in "Interpreter of Maladies" ||
| --- | --- |
| Setting 1—Paragraphs 1–3 and 22–52 | Setting 2—Paragraphs 110–125 and 162–178 |
| **Time and Place:**<br>Paragraphs 1–2: The story begins with American family, the Dases. They are at a tea stall in India. There is a goat tied to a stake. They are on their way to see the Sun Temple at Konarak with their guide, Mr. Kapasi. It is a dry, bright Saturday, the mid-July heat tempered by a steady ocean breeze, ideal weather for sightseeing.<br><br>Paragraphs 22–52: After they leave the tea stall, they head to the Sun Temple which is a 2½-hour, 52-mile drive on bumpy roads. As they leave town, they see monkeys in trees.<br><br>**Atmosphere:**<br>While the dry, bright, comfortable weather indicates the trip should be pleasant, the following details create an uncomfortable atmosphere: unairconditioned car, bumpy and dusty road, long drive.<br><br>**Mood:**<br><br><br>**Character Development and the Environment:** | **Time and Place:**<br>Paragraphs 110–125: "A little past four-thirty" after visiting the Sun Temple, Mr. Kapasi suggests going to the "hills at Udayagiri and Khandagiri, where a number of monastic dwellings were hewn out of the ground, facing one another across a defile. It was some miles away, but well worth seeing, Mr. Kapasi told them."<br><br>Paragraphs 162–178: The hills to the monastic caves are steep and Mr. Das leads the children up a "defile," which is a narrow pass or gorge between mountains. Mrs. Das and Mr. Kapasi join the rest of the family climbing the mountain. Mrs. Das drops puffed rice that attracts monkeys who aren't dangerous unless provoked by food.<br><br>**Atmosphere:**<br>Late afternoon creates a feeling of closure as opposed to the bright sunny beginning. The monastic caves embedded in steep mountains and narrow passageways convey an atmosphere of spirituality but also danger.<br><br>**Mood:**<br><br><br>**Character Development and the Environment:** |
| **Thesis Statement:** ||

2. Which of the following statements best describes the main role of the monkeys in "Interpreter of Maladies?"

    (A) They amuse the Das children.

    (B) They show Mr. Kapasi's comfort with the environment.

    (C) They present a contrast to the goat at the tea stall.

    (D) They serve as a symbol of Indian culture.

    (E) They signal the Dases' oblivious naivete to their surroundings.

**Creating on Your Own**

Return to your memoir in progress. What do your interactions with the surroundings reveal about your attitude toward them? Revise your memoir, adding and emphasizing details from your environment that will illuminate your attitude toward the surroundings. Save your work.

# Part 2   Apply What You Have Learned

Carefully examine "Interpreter of Maladies" to gather textual evidence that reveals the role of setting in characterization and the development of ideas. Reflect on the evidence for new insights and revise the thesis statement you wrote with the T-Chart activity. Write a draft of a multiparagraph essay that develops the thesis with a logical line of reasoning.

**Reflect on the Essential Question** Write a brief response that answers the essential question: *How does a change in setting relate to a change in character?*

# Plot and Pacing

## Part 3

### Understand

The arrangement of the parts and sections of a text, the relationship of the parts to each other, and the sequence in which the text reveals information are all structural choices made by a writer that contribute to the reader's interpretation of a text. (STR-1)

### Demonstrate

Identify and describe how the plot orders events in a narrative. (3.A)

Explain the function of a particular sequence of events in a plot. (3.B)

See also Units 1, 4 & 6

**Source:** *AP® English Literature and Composition Course and Exam Description*

**Essential Question:** How does narrative pacing affect readers' experiences?

Have you read a book that seemed to drag? Perhaps the book had a problem with narrative **pacing,** the manipulation of time in a text that affects the tempo or speed at which the plot moves. Accomplished authors know they need to vary their pacing. If the pace is too slow, readers lose interest, but if it is too rapid they don't have time to process the significance of the plot's events.

---

**KEY TERM**

---

pacing

---

## 3.1 Narrative Pacing | STR-1.AA

In Unit 6 you read that authors interrupt chronology and control pace through flashbacks, foreshadowing, in medias res, and stream of consciousness. Interrupting chronology is only one method of controlling pace. Others involve adjusting the density of details and actions and varying the use of dialogue and description.

## Techniques for Controlling Pace

Looking at the overall narrative structure is a good place to begin when analyzing narrative pace. That will give you a map of the story's tempo. Once you have an overview, consider looking more microscopically at techniques the author uses to control pace.

One of the more common techniques is the use of dialogue. When authors want to speed the pace, they often have characters rather than narrators speak. When authors want to slow the pace, they have narrators speak. The number of details and amount of description provided by the narrator will determine how slowly the passage moves—the more detail and description, the slower the pace.

In addition to dialogue and narration, writers have other options to control tempo.

- arrangement of details
- frequency of events
- narrative structures
- syntax
- tempo or speed at which events occur
- shifts in tense and chronology

Sometimes authors will divide a text into chapters or parts. These structural cues will allow you to think about each part and determine how and why the writer controls pace. For example, author Percival Everett separates "The Appropriation of Cultures" (Unit 1) into ten sections by inserting a short, dashed line between them. If you consider the sections together, you might notice this map of the story's tempo: the pace quickens throughout the story, especially during and after Daniel's and Sarah's visit to Travis and Barb. The longest section is in the middle of the story; paragraph lengths shorten and the pace quickens as the actions related to Daniel's "appropriation" multiply and the story draws to a close. In the first part of the story, there are relatively infrequent events—mainly the one that sets the story in motion. By the end of the story, more events are happening, and they are happening at a quicker pace.

Table 7-2 identifies the pacing in the first section of the story in more detail.

| Pacing Techniques in Section 1 of "The Appropriation of Cultures" |
| --- |
| **Pacing:** Paragraph 1 quickly gives the reader relevant information about Daniel's background. It begins with short sentences in rapid succession that declare what Daniel "had": money, a nice house, a fancy car, an Ivy League education. What he had is followed by what he did: played in a jazz band and drove a fancy car. The repetition of "had" and the relatively short sentences move the exposition quickly to the conflict he has with the White fraternity boys, who shout for him to play "Dixie." |
| **Techniques:** <br> • Syntax—short sentences <br> • Relatively few details |

*continued*

| | |
|---|---|
| **Pacing:** Everett picks up the narrative pace and introduces the conflict by quoting the boys, "Play *Dixie* for us." | |
| **Technique:**<br>• Narrative structure—introducing conflict | |
| **Pacing:** He then slows the narrative in paragraph 3 with longer sentences that show Daniel processing the boys' "beer-shiny eyes stuck into puffy, pale faces, hovering over golf shirts and chinos" and the uncomfortable body language of other patrons. Daniel will not be rushed and the narrative pace reflects his measured response. | |
| **Techniques:**<br>• Syntax—longer sentences<br>• Placement of details about the boys and the scene | |
| **Pacing:** The pace of paragraphs 4 and 7 is the slowest in this section. Everett wants the reader to understand that 23 years of anger had erupted and Daniel was "at ease" with it. The long sentences cause the reader to slow and process Daniel's perspective on "Dixie." | |
| **Techniques:**<br>• Syntax—longer sentences | |
| **Pacing:** The final paragraph of the section shifts to active verbs: Daniel drives home, makes tea, and reads about a Confederate general, Pickett, who lost at Gettysburg. This quickened pace foreshadows Daniel's future actions. In a mere eight paragraphs Everett has provided enough information that the reader is aware of Daniel's conflict and his deliberate, reflective personality. | |
| **Techniques:**<br>• Shift in verb tense | |

Table 7-2

The pace of the three of the final sections shows a clear speeding up and slowing down.

| **Pacing Techniques in the Final Three Sections of<br>"The Appropriation of Cultures"** |
|---|
| **Section 7:** *Paragraphs 86–99 (Confrontation with two White men and the four Black teenagers)*<br>The pace continues to quicken as the confrontation between Daniel and Whites turns physical. In a short space Everett has used simple dialogue and the recurring image of the flag to show both the deep prejudice of Whites and Daniel's effort to turn the ownership of the Confederate flag around. It takes only a few lines for the four young Black men to understand why they need to fly the Confederate flag proudly. |
| **Section 8:** *Paragraphs 100–103 (Exchange with Ahmad Wilson, an attorney driving a BMW)*<br>The pace quickens even more as it takes only three paragraphs of mainly dialogue to show that Daniel's effort to claim his place in the South is making a point. People who can afford to drive BMWs and are professionals are noticing his flag. The reader has enough details and description from earlier sections to understand the significance of the events. |
| **Last two paragraphs:**<br>These mark a return to a slower pace. Dialogue is replaced with longer sentences and polysyllabic words. The slower pace gives readers time to reflect on the accomplishments Daniel has achieved. |

Table 7-3

"The Appropriation of Cultures" does not interrupt chronology with flashbacks as a way to manipulate pace, though it does present a brief backstory at the beginning and uses many other techniques to provide both movement and time for reflection.

 **Remember:** Pacing is the manipulation of time in a text. Several factors contribute to the pace of a narrative, including arrangement of details, frequency of events, narrative structures, syntax, the tempo or speed at which events occur, or shifts in tense and chronology in the narrative. (STR-1.AA)

## 3.1 Checkpoint

*Review "Interpreter of Maladies" on pages 435–450. Then complete the following open-response activity and answer the multiple-choice questions.*

1. Reread paragraphs 52–90. Identify places where the writer uses techniques that speed up or slow down the tempo. You can use a chart like the following to record your findings. Add as many rows as you need.

| Paragraph Numbers | Technique | Effect on Pacing |
|---|---|---|
|  |  |  |
|  |  |  |
|  |  |  |

2. Which best describes how the structure of "Interpreter of Maladies" affects pacing?

   (A) Narration alternates equally with dialogue.

   (B) Descriptions of American culture alternate with descriptions of Indian culture.

   (C) Tension slowly builds in Mrs. Das's confession, which contrasts with the fast-paced ending.

   (D) Conversations between Mr. Das and Mr. Kapasi slow the pace by adding description.

   (E) Pacing accelerates when first Mr. Kapasi and Mrs. Das reflect on their problems.

**3.** Paragraph 7 ("No need to worry. . . trotted back to the car") uses which technique to control pacing?

   (A) Providing narrative description

   (B) Adding exposition to set up the conflict

   (C) Referring to previous events through flashbacks

   (D) Alternating between monosyllabic and polysyllabic words

   (E) Alternating between simple and compound sentences

**Creating on Your Own**

Return to your memoir in progress. Read over your memoir and analyze the pacing you have now. Is it as suitable to the parts of the story as it can be? If not, use some of the techniques to manipulate time to make your pacing more effective. Save your work.

# 3.2 Emotional Impact of Pacing | STR-1.AB

As you have been reminded about every literary technique mentioned in this book, simply identifying it does not deepen your understanding of a text. The question is always, "What is the effect on the reader?" The same is true with pacing. Narrative pacing may evoke an emotional response in readers in at least three ways:

- the order in which information is revealed

- the relationships between the information, when it is provided, and other parts of the narrative

- the significance of the revealed information to other parts of the narrative

For example, most readers would probably agree that the emotional center of the narrative is Mr. Kapasi's backstory about how he came to be an interpreter for a doctor. Leading up to that, some feelings seem to be building in Mrs. Das for Mr. Kapasi and vice versa, and when she calls his job "romantic" they make eye contact in the rearview mirror for the first time (paragraph 61). Yet that accelerating exchange is stalled when narration explains how Mr. Kapasi came to take that job, the grief and disappointment associated with it, and the distant relationship he has with his wife. The tone of that revealed information contrasts with that of the conversation that precedes it and the narration that follows it, raising sympathy in the reader for Mr. Kapasi.

After you note pacing techniques in what you read, ask yourself the following questions.

| Questions to Ask When Analyzing Pacing |
| --- |
| 1. What is the overall narrative structure and at what pace do the different parts move? |
| 2. What are the techniques the author uses to vary tempo? |
|     a. Which portions increase suspense or anticipation? |
|     b. Which portions prompt you to slow down to process and reflect on larger meanings? |
|     c. Which portions create mood and atmosphere? |
|     d. Which portions fill a backstory or hint at future developments? |
| 3. Why does the author vary tempo? |
| 4. What impact does the varied pace have on the reader? |

Table 7-4

 **Remember:** Narrative pacing may evoke an emotional reaction in readers by the order in which information is revealed; the relationships between the information, when it is provided, and other parts of the narrative; and the significance of the revealed information to other parts of the narrative. (STR-1.AB)

### 3.2 Checkpoint

*Review paragraphs 126–163 in "Interpreter of Maladies" on pages 446–449. Then write answers to the questions in Table 7-4.*

**Creating on Your Own**

Return to your memoir. Do you have enough explanatory details for your audience to understand the situation? Do you have some details that are unnecessary to convey your message? Add and delete as necessary. Using what you have learned about narrative pacing, determine how you can structure the memoir to effectively alter the tempo. Save your work.

## Part 3 Apply What You Have Learned

Review "Interpreter of Maladies." You have already analyzed the story by shifts in setting. Use the different settings from Part 1 (page 466 of this unit) to analyze how and why Lahiri alters the narrative pace both among the settings and within them.

**Reflect on the Essential Question** Write a brief response that answers this essential question: *How does narrative pacing affect readers' experiences?* In your answer, correctly use the key term listed on page 470.

# Narrative Emphasis

**Enduring Understanding and Skill**

### Part 4

**Understand**

A narrator's or speaker's perspective controls the details and emphases that affect how readers experience and interpret a text. (NAR-1)

**Demonstrate**

Explain how a narrator's reliability affects a narrative. (4.D)
See also Unit 6

**Source:** *AP® English Literature and Composition Course and Exam Description*

**Essential Question:** How does a narrator's reliability affect the narrative?

In Unit 6 you read that narrators, in particular first-person narrators, can be unreliable because of biases. For example, Shan, the young narrator in "The Sanctuary Desolated" (see Unit 4), is biased. He admits, "I didn't want Grandma to come and stay with us." He wants to be able to visit Grandma in her big old house where he can do as he pleases. His bias affects how readers view characters who have a different perspective, such as Mom and Pa. Readers only learn about those characters through speech. This part will explore how speakers other than the narrator affect the reliability of not only the narrator but also of the narrative. It will also examine whether speakers add information supporting the narrator's account or contradictory details that raise the question of the **reliability**, or believability, of the narrative.

---

**KEY TERMS**

reliability
first-person narrator
omniscient narrator

limited omniscient narrator
speakers

---

# 4.1 Limitations of Narrators | NAR-1.W

All narrators have limitations in what they can or will reveal. For instance, a **first-person narrator,** a character involved in the plot, cannot possibly know all the details of a situation, such as what is going on in the heads of other characters or what is happening in other settings. **Omniscient narrators** do have the ability to know all information but choose which thoughts to reveal and events to include. A story told by a **limited omniscient narrator** reports the thoughts of only a few characters and emphasizes events that focus on those characters. Authors can augment a narrator's reporting by having other **speakers,** characters who speak to others or themselves, add additional information and details. A speaker may provide additional information and details that either support or contradict the narrator or other speakers. Mary Shelley's *Frankenstein* demonstrates the contradictions of narrators. (See Unit 4, Part 4 and Unit 6, Parts 1 and 3).

## Supporting Details and Information

The third-person limited omniscient narrator in "Interpreter of Maladies" reveals the thoughts of only Mr. Kapasi, not those of any other character. The narrator also provides physical descriptions and reports events. Much of what readers learn is from the speech of the characters, which reinforces and adds to details and information from the narrator. In the following excerpt, the narrator describes the initial meeting between Mr. Das and Mr. Kapasi.

> When he'd introduced himself, Mr. Kapasi had pressed his palms together in greeting, but Mr. Das squeezed hands like an American so that Mr. Kapasi felt it in his elbow. Mrs. Das, for her part, had flexed one side of her mouth, smiling dutifully at Mr. Kapasi, without displaying any interest in him.

The narrator implies that, although Mr. Das looks Indian, he is American and unaware of Indian customs. In the following speech by Mr. Das, that implication is made explicit. When asked if the Dases immigrated to America, he replies: "Oh, Mina and I were both born in America . . . Born and raised. Our parents live here now. They retired. We visit them every couple years."

## Contradictory Details and Information

Sometimes information added from speakers contradicts rather than reinforces that provided by the narrator. "Miss Brill" provides such an example. This story is also told from a third-person limited omniscient narrator's point of view, but rather than just revealing some of the character's thoughts, this narrator spends most of the story revealing Miss Brill's thoughts about her surroundings. As you've read in Part 2, Miss Brill enjoys going to the park to watch people and eavesdrop on their conversations. As she sits on her special bench, she invents stories about people in the park. These types of thoughts predominate the narrator's storytelling until the very end. The excerpt below comes from the end of the story. This is the only time another speaker adds to the narrative. Read the passage and note how the couple's speech contradicts the information the narrator has presented.

> The band had been having a rest. Now they started again. And what they played was warm, sunny, yet there was just a faint chill—a something, what was it?—not sadness—no, not sadness—a something that made you want to sing. The tune lifted, lifted, the light shone; and it seemed to Miss Brill that in another moment all of them, all the whole company, would begin singing. The young ones, the laughing ones who were moving together, they would begin, and the men's voices, very resolute and brave, would join them. And then she too, she too, and the others on the benches—they would come in with a kind of accompaniment— something low, that scarcely rose or fell, something so beautiful—moving. . . . And Miss Brill's eyes filled with tears and she looked smiling at all the other members of the company. Yes, we understand, we understand, she thought—though what they understood she didn't know.
>
> Just at that moment a boy and girl came and sat down where [an] old couple had been. They were beautifully dressed; they were in love. The hero and heroine, of course, just arrived from his father's yacht. And still soundlessly singing, still with that trembling smile, Miss Brill prepared to listen.
>
> "No, not now," said the girl. "Not here, I can't."
>
> "But why? Because of that stupid old thing at the end there?" asked the boy. "Why does she come here at all—who wants her? Why doesn't she keep her silly old mug at home?"
>
> "It's her fu-ur which is so funny," giggled the girl. "It's exactly like a fried whiting."
>
> "Ah, be off with you!" said the boy in an angry whisper. Then: "Tell me, ma petite chére—"[1]
>
> "No, not here," said the girl. "Not *yet*."

The conversation of the two lovers contradicts Miss Brill's thoughts that she was a vital part of the cast of characters in the park. She realizes that she is as old and odd as the other older people on the benches.

## Multiple Speakers, Multiple Contradictions

The more speakers in a work, the greater the chance they will contradict one another or the narrator. In Adichie's story "Cell One" (see Part 1), the father contradicts the narrator's assessment of her mother and brother. When Nnamabia steals his mother's gold and pawns it for beer money, his mother asks, "How much did they give you for my gold?" When he tells her, she responds, "Oh! Oh! Chi m egbuo m! My God has killed me!" The father and daughter give contradictory responses to this scene. The narrator is disgusted with her mother: "It was as if she felt that the least he could have done was get a good price. I wanted to slap her." On the other hand, her father defends his

---

1  **ma petite chére:** French for "my little love"

wife: "That he could hurt his mother like this," indicating her hurt went beyond losing her jewelry. The narrator's reliability is called into question again when Nnamabia is arrested. When his mother, father, and sister first visit him, he describes his jail experience.

> "If we ran Nigeria like this cell," he said, "we would have no problems in this country. Things are so organized. Our cell has a chief called General Abacha and he has a second in command. Once you come in, you have to give them some money. If you don't, you're in trouble."
> "And did you have any money?" my mother asked.
> Nnamabia smiled, his face even more beautiful with a new pimple-like insect bite on his forehead, and said in Igbo that he had [hidden his money] shortly after the arrest at the bar. He knew the policemen would take it if he didn't hide it and he knew he would need it to buy his peace in the cell. He bit into a fried drumstick and switched to English. "General Abacha was impressed with how I hid my money. I've made myself amenable to him. I praise him all the time. When the men asked all of us newcomers to hold our ears and frog-jump to their singing, he let me go after ten minutes. The others had to do it for almost thirty minutes."

On their way home Nnamabia's father says, "This is what I should have done when he broke into the house. I should have had him locked up in a cell." When the narrator asks, "Why?" her father replies, "Because this has shaken him for once." The narrator, however, has a contradictory response, "I couldn't see it. Not that day. Nnamabia seemed fine to me . . . ." The result of these differing responses calls the narrator's or speaker's reliability into question. When speakers contradict the narrator or each other, the reader must decide who is the most trustworthy.

 **Remember:** Some narrators or speakers may provide details and information that others do not or cannot provide. Multiple narrators or speakers may provide contradictory information in a text. (NAR-1.W)

## 4.1 Checkpoint

*Review "Interpreter of Maladies" on pages 435–450. Then complete the following open-response activity and answer the multiple-choice questions.*

1. On separate paper, copy the chart on the next page. In column one, identify the page ranges of three brief passages in which either the narrator or other characters speak. In column two, identify the page range of a corresponding passage that adds more details or contradicts existing information. In column three, explain the relationship between the two and decide which is more reliable.

| Passage One | Passage Two | Relationship Between Passages |
|---|---|---|
|  |  |  |
|  |  |  |
|  |  |  |

2. Mr. Das's response in paragraph 62 to the use of the word *romantic* in paragraph 61 has what effect on the development of the story?

    (A) It establishes Mrs. Das as a romantic character.

    (B) It highlights Mr. and Mrs. Das's dysfunctional marriage.

    (C) It reveals Mrs. Das's changing mood toward the trip.

    (D) It signifies the subjective nature of the word.

    (E) It calls into question the narrator's reliability.

3. The third-person narrator's shift from Mrs. Das's speech to Mr. Kapasi's thoughts in paragraph 161 ("He looked at her . . . is it guilt?") primarily creates the effect of

    (A) illuminating Mrs. Das's childlike naivete

    (B) creating sympathy for Mr. Das

    (C) juxtaposing values of marriage and infidelity

    (D) challenging Mr. Kapasi's romantic feelings

    (E) showing Mr. Kapasi's shift from fantasy to reality

**Creating on Your Own**

Return to your memoir. Add dialogue that reflects what other people involved might say about the situation. What information or perspective might some of those involved have that is different from yours? What might they say to you or to one another? Does the dialogue enhance your memoir? If so, revise it to your liking. If not, delete it. Save your work.

# Part 4  Apply What You Have Learned

Using your chart from 4.1 Checkpoint above as a starting point, write a paragraph that explains the function of narrators and speakers on the reliability of the narrative of "Interpreter of Maladies."

**Reflect on the Essential Question** Write a brief response that answers the essential question: *How does a narrator's reliability affect the narrative?* In your answer, correctly use the key terms listed on page 476.

## The Writer's Craft: Interpreter of Characters

After Mrs. Das turns to Mr. Kapasi for what she hopes will be a comforting interpretation of her "pain," he compares her problem to those of the patients whose symptoms he translates:

> Mr. Kapasi felt insulted that Mrs. Das should ask him to interpret her common, trivial little secret. She did not resemble the patients in the doctor's office, those who came glassy-eyed and desperate, unable to sleep or breathe or urinate with ease, unable, above all, to give words to their pains.

Despite the life-or-death ailments Mr. Kapasi mentions, he puts "above all" the patients' inability "to give words to their pains."

Difficulty communicating is a thread that runs through the story. The children don't listen to their parents; Mr. and Mrs. Das barely communicate except through bickering; Mr. Kapasi has lost his ability to understand a number of foreign languages and has grown accustomed to the silence between him and his wife; and the fluttering away of his address at the end forecloses any possibility of the imagined conversations he and Mrs. Das would carry on through letters.

Yet Mr. Kapasi offers a suggestion for the only meaningful communication that will relieve Mrs. Das's misery—identifying it for what it is, guilt, and being honest with her husband about it—advice readers have no reason to believe she will follow.

"Interpreter of Maladies" is the title of the collection of short stories by Jhumpa Lahiri in which this story appears. While readers may first assume that the title refers to Mr. Kapasi, it may also refer to the author herself, who through her craft "gives words" to her characters' pains.

## Analyze the Writer's Craft

Lahiri paints Mr. Kapasi and Mrs. Das as characters with similarities. In the only two places in the story with flashbacks, each character's backstory is revealed. Read these passages carefully. Then write a paragraph comparing

- how the couples came to be married
- what precipitated the separation each feels from his or her spouse
- how Lahiri "interprets" each character's pain—that is, which is portrayed as deeper, which raises more sympathy in the reader
- the literary techniques Lahiri uses to convey these two stories

# The Function of Symbols and Motifs

**Essential Question:** How can setting function as a symbol, and how do imagery and figurative detail emphasize ideas?

If you read fairy tales when you were young or had them read to you, your heart may have started beating faster when the young people in the story entered the woods. It was there that Little Red Riding Hood encountered the wolf, Hansel and Gretel were abandoned by their parents and lured to the gingerbread house, Snow White lived with her dwarf roommates and was visited by the jealous queen in the form of a witch, and Rumpelstiltskin made his home. The woods are dark at night and they provide many hiding places for dangers.

Settings convey and arouse emotions and are a powerful tool for authors to emphasize ideas. Recurring images can have a similar effect, sometimes foreshadowing impending problems. Sometimes setting, images, and figurative language can be so effective that you find yourself in their spell. As a close reader, though, stand back and consider their effect on the text to appreciate the author's skill in using them.

# 5.1 Setting as Symbol | FIG-1.AB, FIG-1.AC

At what point do settings become symbolic and when do they merely enhance plot development, characterization, and ideas? At the very least a setting should always contextualize time and place for the reader. A well-planned setting can contribute to a text's meaning in multiple ways by establishing mood, creating atmosphere, reinforcing character traits, and illuminating conflicts. For setting to become symbolic, however, it must reach a new threshold of being associated with abstract emotions, ideologies, and beliefs. In some cases, settings can resemble archetypal characters you learned about in Unit 4. Over time they have developed universal associations with emotions, ideologies, or beliefs that readers will understand symbolically. For example, forests often represent danger or refuge; water, death and rebirth; gardens, fertility and sin. Like characters, archetypal settings have multilayered meanings. A river may symbolize a journey, or it may indicate boundaries, or possibly both. When readers encounter symbolic settings, they look for evidence of whether the universal associations fit with the other elements of the story.

## Abstract Emotions, Ideologies, and Beliefs

Most of the settings in Adichie's short story "Cell One" are not symbolic. The town of Nsukka merely provides a contrast between what one would expect from a university town with educated citizens and the brutal murders committed by cults comprised of many professors' sons. Even the Enugu jail isn't symbolic. It serves to highlight the diminished influence of Nnamabia's family, his continued defiance of authority, and the corruption of the police, but it doesn't rise to the level of symbol. Within the jail, however, the actual Cell One becomes a **symbol**. It embodies emotions, beliefs, and ideologies. Read the passages below that describe Cell One, noting the abstractions it comes to symbolize.

> Nnamabia's first shock was seeing a Buccaneer sobbing. The boy was tall and tough, rumored to have carried out one of the killings and likely to become Capone next semester, and yet there he was in the cell, cowering and sobbing after the chief gave him a light slap on the back of the head. Nnamabia told me this in a voice lined with both disgust and disappointment; it was as if he had suddenly been made to see that the Incredible Hulk was really just painted green. His second shock was learning about the cell farthest away from his, Cell One. He had never

seen it, but every day two policemen carried a dead man out of Cell One, stopping by Nnamabia's cell to make sure that the corpse was seen by all.

Nnamabia's first experience with Cell One starts the symbolic association between the actual place and several abstract associations. Clearly Cell One is associated with death by torture and the police's belief they had the right to instill fear and obedience in their prisoners. One incident, however, is not enough for symbolic status. Adichie continues to thread references to Cell One throughout the latter part of the story. Read the second mention of it and determine if the initial meanings are still present.

> Even the chief of his cell seemed afraid of Cell One. When Nnamabia and his cell mates, those who could afford to buy bathing water in the plastic buckets that had once held paint, were let out to bathe in the open yard, the policemen watched them and often shouted, "Stop that or you are going to Cell One now!" Nnamabia had nightmares about Cell One. He could not imagine a place worse than his cell, which was so crowded he often stood pressed against the cracked wall. Tiny kwalikwata lived inside the cracks and their bites were vicious, and when he yelped his cell mates called him Milk and Banana Boy, University Boy, Yeye Fine Boy.

The scared cult chief, the public baths, and insect bites provide specific details about Nnamabia's current cell and continue to build Cell One into a symbol of torture and corrupt power. The symbolism of Cell One remains multilayered through the end of the story. Despite his nightmares about Cell One, Nnamabia defies authority and is sent there after he is beaten. The reader never learns what happens in Cell One because Nnamabia refuses to discuss it. In the end Cell One remains a symbol for nightmarish fear and the police's belief that they have the right to instill that fear at will.

## Universal Symbols

As you learned in Unit 6, contextual symbols have meaning only in a specific work. The horrifying Cell One in Adichie's short story is a contextual symbol. Other symbols are readily apparent, such as the setting in "Miss Brill." The translation of "Jardins Publiques" is "public gardens." The name of this park suggests that it isn't an ordinary park, but a garden, a symbol of fertility and life. To reinforce the symbolic associations with the park, Mansfield set the story in early spring, a universal symbol for new life. Readers might bring these symbolic associations to the story. Miss Brill certainly does. She is excited that the spring season has arrived and feels part of the teeming life that surrounds her. The story, however, has two settings—the gardens and Miss Brill's one-room apartment that is compared to a cupboard. As she is enjoying the gardens and spring weather, she overhears a couple refer to her as old and worthless. Instead of finding renewed life, she returns to the confines of her cupboardlike room. The contrast between the symbolic garden and Miss Brill's room serves to subvert the reader and Miss Brill's expectations. When you encounter archetypal settings, be sure to test your expectations against the events of the story.

**Remember:** A setting may become symbolic when it is, or comes to be, associated with abstractions such as emotions, ideologies, and beliefs. Over time, some settings have developed certain associations such that they almost universally symbolize particular concepts. (FIG-1.AB–AC)

## 5.1 Checkpoint

*Review the passage below from* Wuthering Heights. *Then complete the following open-response activity and answer the multiple-choice question.*

1. The following passage is the first description of setting from the beginning of *Wuthering Heights*, a novel written by Emily Brontë in 1847. The house is located in Northern England on top of a hill.

   In the first column of the chart that follows it, you will see potentially symbolic characteristics of hills. In the second column list details or information that are associated with abstractions such as emotions, ideologies, and beliefs. Examine the details in both columns and write a paragraph explaining the possible symbolic significance that begins to emerge in this early description of setting.

   > Wuthering Heights is the name of Mr. Heathcliff's dwelling. "Wuthering" being a significant provincial adjective, descriptive of the atmospheric tumult to which its station is exposed in stormy weather. Pure, bracing ventilation they must have up there at all times, indeed: one may guess the power of the north wind blowing over the edge, by the excessive slant of a few stunted firs at the end of the house; and by a range of gaunt thorns all stretching their limbs one way, as if craving alms of the sun. Happily, the architect had foresight to build it strong: the narrow windows are deeply set in the wall, and the corners defended with large jutting stones.
   >
   > Before passing the threshold, I paused to admire a quantity of grotesque carving lavished over the front, and especially about the principal door; above which, among a wilderness of crumbling griffins and shameless little boys, I detected the date "1500," and the name "Hareton Earnshaw."
   >
   > I would have made a few comments, and requested a short history of the place from the surly owner; but his attitude at the door appeared to demand my speedy entrance, or complete departure, and I had no desire to aggravate his impatience previous to inspecting the penetralium [innermost part].
   >
   > One stop brought us into the family sitting-room, without any introductory lobby or passage: they call it here "the house" pre-eminently. It includes kitchen and parlour, generally; but I believe at Wuthering Heights the kitchen is forced to retreat altogether into another quarter: at least I distinguished a chatter of tongues, and a clatter of culinary utensils, deep within; and I observed no signs of roasting, boiling, or baking, about

the huge fireplace; nor any glitter of copper saucepans and tin [colanders] on the walls. One end, indeed, reflected splendidly both light and heat from ranks of immense pewter dishes, interspersed with silver jugs and tankards, towering row after row, on a vast oak dresser, to the very roof. The latter had never been under-drawn: its entire anatomy lay bare to an inquiring eye, except where a frame of wood laden with oatcakes and clusters of legs of beef, mutton, and ham, concealed it. Above the chimney were sundry villainous old guns, and a couple of horse-pistols: and, by way of ornament, three gaudily-painted canisters disposed along its ledge. The floor was of smooth, white stone; the chairs, high-backed, primitive structures, painted green: one or two heavy black ones lurking in the shade. In an arch under the dresser reposed a huge, liver-coloured bitch pointer, surrounded by a swarm of squealing puppies; and other dogs haunted other recesses.

| Universal Associations with Hills | Details Associated with Emotions, Beliefs, Ideologies |
|---|---|
| Hills can symbolize any of the following ideas:<br>• Spirituality<br>• Knowledge<br>• Constancy<br>• Firmness<br>• Achievement<br>• Life<br>• Death<br>• Danger<br>• Isolation | |
| Write a paragraph that explains the possible symbolic significance of the setting: | |

2. As a whole the initial setting description of Wuthering Heights functions as a symbol of

   (A) joy and warmth

   (B) oppression and darkness

   (C) adversity and survival

   (D) turmoil and anguish

   (E) isolation and danger

**Creating on Your Own**

Return to your memoir. What are the features of your setting? Do you have water, mountains, valleys, caves, cities, countryside, or does the story mostly take place indoors in a home or school or church? Do any of the setting details or information have associations that would enhance your narrative? Revise your story to help readers associate elements of setting with emotions, beliefs, or ideologies that you want to convey. Save your work.

# 5.2 Motifs | FIG-1. AD

What is the difference between a motif and a symbol? Both add concrete images to a work's abstract ideas. Both can evoke emotional responses from readers and can illuminate beliefs and ideologies. The difference between a symbol and a motif lies in repeated patterns.

## Function of Motifs

A symbol is typically one image—the fox stole in "Miss Brill," for example, or Cell One in Adichie's story. A **motif**, in contrast, can be a category of images that tend to appear numerous times throughout a work. The repeated imagery throughout a text can help emphasize a theme of the story or a trait of a character.

While the fox stole is a single symbol in "Miss Brill," clothing more generally is a motif in the story. Miss Brill comments on the appearance, especially clothing, of everyone she sees.

- "Wasn't the conductor wearing a new coat, too?"

- "fine old man in a velvet coat"

- "An Englishman and his wife, he wearing a dreadful Panama hat and she button boots"

- "little boys with big white silk bows under their chins, little girls, little French dolls, dressed up in velvet and lace"

- "Two young girls in red came by and two young soldiers in blue met them"

- "And now an ermine toque [a hat, usually with upturned brim—made from the fur of a white short-tailed weasel] and a gentleman in grey met just in front of her"

- "Just at that moment a boy and girl came and sat down where the old couple had been. They were beautifully dressed; they were in love."

Miss Brill attaches great importance to the clothing people wear, using it as a way to judge their social standing and vitality. The repeated clothing images support the main symbol of the fox stole and how it stands for Miss Brill in the story. It also may suggest the poverty of her human connections since it represents such a superficial aspect of the people in the park.

 **Remember:** A motif is a unified pattern of recurring objects or images used to emphasize a significant idea in large parts of or throughout a text. (FIG-1.AD)

## 5.2 Checkpoint

*Review "Interpreter of Maladies" on pages 435–450. Then complete the following open-response activities and answer the multiple-choice questions.*

1. Reflect on Mrs. Das's eating throughout the story. How do the repeated scenes of her eating puffed rice, chewing gum, and having lunch convey significant ideas throughout the narrative? Copy the chart below to guide your reflection on each scene's significance, adding as many rows as needed. You might also want to trace the motif related to "seeing"—camera, visors, sunglasses, mirrors, windows—and explain its significance.

| Paragraph Numbers | Significance of the Motif |
|---|---|
| | |

2. The reference to Mr. Das's camera in paragraph 6 functions primarily as
   (A) a motif related to his inability to connect with the culture
   (B) a metaphor for his dedication to his students
   (C) an emblem of his desire to preserve the experience
   (D) a symbol of his American values
   (E) a commentary on American tourists

### Creating on Your Own
Reflect on the central message of your memoir. Jot down some images or objects that you could add throughout the narrative to emphasize significant ideas. Decide where they might best fit and add them to your story if you choose. Save your work.

# 5.3 Similes and Personification | FIG-1.AE, FIG-1.AF

Sometimes mere facts will not serve a writer's purpose or clearly convey complex ideas. **Figurative language,** word choice that goes beyond literal meanings, allows writers to appeal to readers' emotions and provide a frame of reference for new or complex ideas. Two of the more common types of figurative language are similes (see Unit 2) and personification (see Unit 5). As you read and encounter figurative language that draws comparisons between unlike objects or ideas, slow down and unpack the qualities being compared and ask yourself how the comparisons develop characters, affect tone or attitude, or contribute to larger ideas of the text.

## Similes
In Unit 2 you learned that **similes** use the words *like* or *as* to compare objects and transfer qualities of the comparison subject to the main subject. Writers strive to select comparison subjects that are easy for readers to understand

because readers must be able to mentally transfer the traits of the comparison subject to the main subject. In the following passage from "Interpreter of Maladies," the narrator uses three similes to describe Mrs. Das's appearance.

> He observed her. She wore a red-and-white-checkered skirt that stopped above her knees, slip-on shoes with a square wooden heel, and a <u>close-fitting blouse styled like a man's undershirt</u>. The blouse was decorated at chest-level with a calico appliqué in the shape of a strawberry. She was a short woman, with <u>small hands like paws,</u> her frosty pink fingernails painted to match her lips, and was slightly plump in her figure. Her hair, shorn only a little longer than her husband's, was parted far to one side. She was wearing large dark brown sunglasses with a pinkish tint to them, and carried <u>a big straw bag, almost as big as her torso, shaped like a bowl</u>, with a water bottle poking out of it.

The traits being transferred in each of the three comparison subjects—a man's undershirt, paws, and a bowl are readily understood and transferred. Readers will get a mental picture of Mrs. Das as a small woman whose clothing attracts attention, but why did the narrator choose those particular comparison subjects? Writers choose comparison subjects for the way in which they function. The tight shirt reveals Mrs. Das's sensuality, the paws liken her to an animal, and the big bowl-shaped purse reinforces the eating motif that runs throughout the story. All of these qualities are part of her characterization and the plot development.

## Personification

Authors characterize nonhuman objects, entities, or ideas through **personification** by assigning them human characteristics. For example, "The Rocking-Horse Winner" (1926) by English writer D. H. Lawrence is a story about a family living above their means whose house whispers to them "There must be more money! There must be more money!" Just as they do with similes, readers transfer human traits, in this case the ability to whisper, to the nonhuman object (the house) or to an idea. One effect of this personification is to create a vivid image for readers experiencing the dysfunctions of this family. The house, standing for their excesses, haunts the family relentlessly.

For another example, read the description below of the kitchen at Wuthering Heights. The personification is underlined. Ask yourself the following two questions.

1. What image is created by the personification?

2. What tone does the narrator convey about the setting?

> One stop brought us into the family sitting-room, without any introductory lobby or passage: they call it here 'the house' pre-eminently. It includes kitchen and parlour, generally; but I believe at Wuthering Heights <u>the kitchen is forced to retreat altogether into another quarter</u>: at least I distinguished a chatter of tongues, and a clatter of culinary utensils,

deep within; and I observed no signs of roasting, boiling, or baking, about the huge fireplace; nor any glitter of copper saucepans and tin [colanders] on the walls.

The personification creates images of war and discord. People facing hostile situations, not kitchens, "retreat." The narrator's personification of the hidden kitchen indicates his attitude toward this environment. Kitchens are a place where people gather, and nourishment is created. The narrator at the very least feels unwelcome and perhaps even threatened, and the reader is left to wonder why the people in the kitchen had to retreat.

Writers at times reverse personification. **Inverted personification** assigns nonhuman traits to humans. Read the following poem by St. Lucian poet Derek Walcott. It contains both personification in lines 1–11 and inverted personification in lines 16–20. Examples of personification are underlined and inverted personification is in boldface type. As you read the poem, ask yourself the following questions.

1. What images are created by personification and inverted personification?

2. What tone does the speaker convey about the setting and Sidone?

## XIV

With the frenzy of an old snake shedding its skin,
the speckled road, scored with ruts, smelling of mold,
twisted on itself and reentered the forest
where the dasheen¹ leaves thicken and folk stories begin.
5   Sunset would threaten us as we climbed closer
to her house up the asphalt hill road, whose yam vines
wrangled over gutters with the dark reek of moss,
the shutters closing like the eyelids of that mimosa²
called Ti-Marie; then—lucent as paper lanterns,
10  lamplight glowed through the ribs, house after house—
there was her own lamp at the black twist of the path.
There's childhood, and there's childhood's aftermath.
She began to remember at the minute of the fireflies,
to the sound of pipe water banging in kerosene tins,
15  stories she told to my brother and myself.
**Her leaves were the libraries of the Caribbean.**
**The luck that was ours, those fragrant origins!**
**Her head was magnificent, Sidone. In the gully of her voice**
**Shadows stood up and walked, her voice travels my shelves.**
20  **She was the lamplight in the stare of two mesmerized boys**
Still joined in one shadow, indivisible twins.

---

1  **dasheen:** tropical plant with large leaves
2  **mimosa:** tropical plant whose leaves close or droop when touched or shaken

While metaphors and similes abound in the first 11 lines and add to the effect of personification, the actual examples of personification are on the road that "twisted on itself and reentered the forest." The boys' journey will not be easy. A threatening sun, wrangling yam vines, and shutters appearing to close on their own add images of danger. The sense of danger lessens with the personified lamplight glowing "through the ribs of house after house." Still the reader gets a sense of ghosts as the houses have ribs, not wood. The speaker's tone in these lines is one of trepidation.

The inverse personification in lines 16–20 helps relieve the fear and uneasiness the boys felt. Sidone is given nonhuman traits of lamplight and book leaves or pages filled with stories. Her light becomes knowledge for the boys that will help guide them through "childhood's aftermath" or into their adult lives. With Sidone's guidance the speaker's tone has shifted from wariness in the first 11 lines to confidence in the last six lines.

 **Remember:** The function of a simile relies on the selection of the objects being compared as well as the traits of the objects. By assigning the qualities of a nonhuman object, entity, or idea to a person or character, the narrator, character, or speaker communicates an attitude about that person or character. (FIG-1.AE–AF)

## 5.3 Checkpoint

*Review "Interpreter of Maladies" on pages 435–450. Then complete the following open-response activities and answer the multiple-choice questions.*

1. Copy the chart below. Find at least six examples of similes in "Interpreter of Maladies." Choose examples from the beginning, middle, and end of the story. One example has been provided for you. Add at least six more rows.

| Example of Simile | Traits Being Compared | Function of the Simile |
|---|---|---|
| "They [monkeys] were seated in groups along the branches, with shining black faces, silver bodies, horizontal eyebrows, and crested heads. <u>Their long gray tails dangled like a series of ropes among the leaves.</u>" | Ropes secure objects. The monkeys' tails secure them in their environment. | The simile implies that the monkeys are secure in their environment. It is their natural habitat. |

2. The simile in paragraph 2—"Mr. Das squeezed hands like an American so that Mr. Kapasi felt it in his elbow"—chiefly

    (A) criticizes American manners

    (B) shows that Mr. Das looks Indian but is American in culture

    (C) portrays Mr. Das's strength and dominance

    (D) contrasts Mrs. Das's indifference in the paragraph

    (E) introduces a conflict in cultures

3. The inverted personification of Mrs. Das's "small hands like paws" in paragraph 14

    (A) characterizes her as a woman with animalistic qualities

    (B) mocks her appearance

    (C) illustrates her inability to care for her children

    (D) explains why she drops pieces of puffed rice

    (E) reflects a discrepancy with her other physical features

**Creating on Your Own**
Return to your memoir. Consider the tone you want to convey for each character and idea. Add at least one simile and one personification to create images for your reader that make your message and tone clearer. Save your work.

# Part 5  Apply What You Have Learned

Review the analysis of figurative language you completed in Part 5. Return to the multiparagraph essay you began in Part 2. Revise the essay, inserting examples of figurative language to support your line of reasoning. Save your work.

> **Reflect on the Essential Question**  Write a brief response that answers the essential question: *How can setting function as a symbol, and how do imagery and figurative detail emphasize ideas?* In your answer, correctly use the key terms listed on page 483.

# Part 6

# Writing About Literature VII

**Enduring Understanding and Skills**

## Part 6

### Understand
Readers establish and communicate their interpretations of literature through arguments supported by textual evidence. (LAN-1)

### Demonstrate
Develop a thesis statement that conveys a defensible claim about an interpretation of literature and that may establish a line of reasoning. (7.B)

Develop commentary that establishes and explains relationships among textual evidence, the line of reasoning, and the thesis. (7.C)

Select and use relevant and sufficient evidence to both develop and support a line of reasoning. (7.D)

See also Units 3, 4, 5, 6, 8 & 9

**Source:** *AP® English Literature and Composition Course and Exam Description*

**Essential Question:** How can you communicate a written interpretation of a work of literature by expressing a thesis statement; using reasoning, commentary, and sufficient evidence to support your line of reasoning; and creating a level of sophistication?

In this unit you have spent considerable time uncovering multidimensional meanings for several texts. As you thought specifically about epiphanies, group forces as characters, changes in settings, arrangement of details, and figurative language, your understanding of the text deepened and perhaps even changed. Perhaps you realized that alternative interpretations can exist. In addition to rereading and reflecting on texts, circumstances in which people read a text can influence their interpretation. A 16th-century interpretation of *Hamlet* could differ from a 21st-century interpretation. A person of color reading Toni Morrison's works might have a different interpretation from that of a White person. As long as you have sufficient evidence to support your interpretation and line of reasoning, your interpretation is valid. British author William Golding said the following about his popular novel *Lord of the Flies*:

There have been so many interpretations of the story that I am not going to choose between them. Make your own choice. They contradict each other, the various choices. The only choice that really matters, the only interpretation of the story, if you want one, is your own.

Of course, not all interpretations are equal. As you have read in Units 3–6, when you write a literary argument, you are defending your interpretation through a strong thesis statement, claims that develop the thesis, sufficient evidence to support your claims, and commentary that explains and persuades your audience to accept your interpretation as valid. To do so you must have a solid line of reasoning with sufficient evidence, using the accepted conventions of written English.

---

**KEY TERMS**

| | | |
|---|---|---|
| thesis statement | recursive | alternative |
| line of reasoning | revision | interpretations |
| commentary | broader context | relevant analogies |
| evidence | | sufficient evidence |

---

# 6.1 Overview of the Process of Literary Analysis

| LAN-1.D, LAN-1.E, LAN-1.F, LAN-1.G, LAN-1.H, LAN-1.I, LAN-1.J, LAN-1.-K, LAN.1-V

Study the chart below to review what you have learned in previous units.

| Review of Elements of a Literary Argument | |
|---|---|
| **Thesis Statement** | An overarching claim that expresses an interpretation of a literary text that you can defend with textual evidence. It may preview your line of reasoning, but it does not have to. |
| **Line of Reasoning** | A logical sequence of supporting claims that help you defend your thesis statement and show your thinking |
| **Commentary** | Explanations of your logical reasoning. Commentary shows clearly how evidence ties supporting claims and how supporting claims tie to your thesis statement. |
| **Evidence** | Textual details strategically and purposefully used to illustrate, clarify, exemplify, associate, amplify, or qualify a point<br><br>Effective evidence is:<br><br>• explained well through commentary that shows the logical connections between the evidence and the claims<br>• sufficient in quantity and quality to support your line of reasoning |

Table 7-5

## Revision and Recursion

Chances are good that all of those readers who developed an interpretation of *The Lord of the Flies* did not just sit down and produce each element in Table 7-5 and call their interpretation done. Most probably reread the book to check for further evidence. In the process, they may have discovered some evidence that refuted their position or that led them in a different direction. That discovery may in turn have led them to revise their thesis statement, and the hunt for sufficient and high-quality evidence was on again. Writing is a **recursive** process. Each discovery helps you refine your position and strengthen your evidence. **Revision** is a key step in making your argument the best it can be.

For example, an initial reading of "Interpreter of Maladies" might leave a reader thinking Mr. Kapasi fantasizes that Mrs. Das will leave her husband and he will leave his wife. While he does have thoughts of a relationship with Mrs. Das, the evidence for divorce is not present in the text. He merely thinks they will admit to "unhappy" marriages and continue their relationship through letters. Revision may reveal places where you went beyond what the text was actually saying and drew conclusions that do not hold up under scrutiny.

## Collaboration

Talking about your interpretation with other readers is one of the best ways to sharpen your thinking and the clarity of your argument. In small face-to-face study groups or in online conversations, test your ideas with others who are developing interpretations and listen to feedback. Be open to hearing an idea in someone else's interpretation that makes you rethink your position.

Also use collaboration by sharing your drafts with others. By the time you have a draft, you will have given much thought to your thesis, line of reasoning, evidence, and commentary, and without another set of eyes, you might not be aware of a hole in your reasoning or a piece of unconvincing evidence. Most effective peer reviews make a point of stating what is well done in an essay as well as making suggestions for ways to improve it. You have the final say in your interpretation, but remaining open to ideas that challenge some of yours is a good habit of mind to refine your arguments.

## Elements of Composition

During the revising stage, once you are satisfied with your revised thesis statement and argument, you should review the elements of composition that clarify relationships and add polish to your writing. These include

- correct use of key conventions of grammar and mechanics
- coherence at the sentence, paragraph, and whole-text level through devices that link ideas
- syntax, including selection and placement of phrases and clauses and subordination and coordination
- well-chosen words
- effective punctuation that clarifies relationships among ideas

**Remember:** A thesis statement, line of reasoning, evidence, and commentary are the backbone of literary argument. Control over the elements of composition helps you convey your meaning clearly. Revision of your evidence and thesis may be needed as you review your work under scrutiny. (LAN-1.D–K, LAN-1.V)

### Composing on Your Own

Return to the essay you have been developing in the Apply What You Have Learned activities. Review it and revise it to improve the essay. Then exchange essays with a peer, using Table 7-5 and the bullet points on the previous page as a basis for evaluating your peer's work. When your essay is returned, review your peer's comments and make revisions as you see fit.

## 6.2 Complex Reasoning | LAN-1.U

Even after you have completed all of the above, you can still improve your literary argument by challenging your thinking to develop more complex reasoning. Steps you can take to add complexity to your argument include putting the text in a **broader context**, discussing **alternative interpretations** of a text, and using **relevant analogies** to help an audience better understand your interpretation. For this revision process, you will use the close reading skills you practiced in this unit and others to make sure you have sufficient and convincing evidence. Asking the following questions will help you write a sophisticated literary argument.

1. Have characters changed because of shifts in values or circumstances?
2. Have I examined all the characters' interactions with other characters or group forces?
3. Have I examined the relationship between setting and characters?
4. Have I considered why pacing slows or speeds up?
5. Do various narrators or speakers provide contradictory information? If so, how does that affect my interpretation?
6. Have I unpacked figurative language? How does it function and affect my interpretation?

The third category of the AP˚ Literature rubric is "Sophistication," described in Row C. Sophistication is the most difficult point to earn. To receive this point you must demonstrate sophistication of thought and/or develop a complex literary argument. In other words, your interpretation must show deep and complex thinking. You will be expected to write with sophistication throughout college. Three ways you might demonstrate sophisticated and complex thinking are to put your argument about the text in a broader context, acknowledge alternative interpretations, and use analogies.

## Broader Context

While the focus of your literary argument should be on the text being analyzed, connecting it to other works, events, or people may help readers see the relevance of your argument. For example, "Interpreter of Maladies" is written by an American born to Indian immigrants. You could briefly connect the immigrant experience of Lahiri to a broader context with a statement such as the following:

> While America might be considered a melting pot of cultures, children born in America to immigrant parents often feel torn between American culture and that of their parents. Writers such as Chinese-American Amy Tan and Indian-American Jhumpa Lahiri explore the real tensions of being loyal to their parents' culture and assimilating into the new one.

## Alternative Interpretations

Who is to blame for Mrs. Das's brief extramarital affair? You might say it is her fault for not stopping the house guest's advances. Someone else might blame the ungrateful house guest or Mr. Das for being oblivious to his wife's loneliness. All three are valid. Suppose you choose to focus on Mr. Das as a negligent husband. You can make your argument more complex by acknowledging the role the others play. The acknowledgment should be brief, perhaps merely a subordinate clause, but you will have increased your credibility with the reader.

Another way you might incorporate alternative interpretations is to offer different critical perspectives. These perspectives could come from different time periods. This approach is especially good for older works. Jane Austen's novels, published in the 19th century, were largely viewed as realistic portrayals of aristocratic and gentry life. In the 1940s, criticism shifted and viewed her works as ironic commentary on those socioeconomic groups. In the 1960s, feminists began debating whether Austen satirizes or promotes the patriarchy of her day.

You could also look at favorable and unfavorable reviews of a work. Decide which camp you most agree with and offer a summary of the opposing view. If you decide to include critical responses as alternative interpretations, be certain to explain why you agree and disagree with each one.

## Analogies

**Analogies**, like similes and metaphors, compare unlike objects in order to illustrate shared traits. Similes and metaphors show concepts without explanation. Readers must unpack the shared traits or differences and infer their meaning. With analogies, on the other hand, writers explain their intended point. When writers use analogies in literary analysis, typically they have noticed a pattern in the text that brings to mind other texts with a similar pattern. They then try to map the new text with the other texts and build an analogy from there.

For example, many readers might put "Interpreter of Maladies" in the broad category of immigrant stories. A typical arc of an immigrant story is

- the arrival of a young person in a new country
- the clash that person feels between cultural traditions upheld by parents and family and the norms and expectations of the new country
- a struggle to resolve that clash
- a new identity formed as a result of the mix of cultures OR a rejection of one of the cultures in favor of the other

While "Interpreter of Maladies" does center on a clash of cultures, it does not map neatly to the typical arc. Explaining how it does not is one good way to add complexity to your analysis though analogy. For example, you might map the two in this way:

> Many immigrant stories focus on the arrival of a young person in a new country and the struggle that person faces to balance the traditions of the culture left behind with the expectations and norms of the culture in the new country. "Interpreter of Maladies," however, looks at a later stage of the immigrant experience. Mr. Das's parents have chosen to return to India at retirement. Their son and daughter-in-law were born in the United States, and in a variation of the typical immigrant story, "Interpreter of Maladies" examines a culture clash of Americans of Indian descent seeming distant and even unaware of the culture of their parents. Further, the reader might conclude that Mr. and Mrs. Das do not undergo a struggle to resolve the clash. Instead they seem unchanged by their encounter with their parents' culture except by their desire to return to familiar ground as soon as possible.

A well-constructed analogy is a mini argument in itself. It has a claim: ("'Interpreter of Maladies' is a variation on a typical immigrant story"), followed by evidence ("the clash of cultures arises when the offspring of first generation immigrants return to the country of their parents' birth"), and finally by commentary that connects the evidence to the claim ("In this model there does not even seem to be a struggle—the travelers do not seem open to absorbing Indian culture in a meaningful way").

Other analogies could be made between this story and Lahiri's other works, this story and works by other Indian American writers, and this story and the trope of "American tourists abroad," to name a few. In each case, a familiar pattern, or "schema," becomes the base for comparison to the text being analyzed.

Constructing analogies requires complex and deep thinking, but they can serve to make your literary argument more sophisticated.

**Remember:** More sophisticated literary arguments may explain the significance or relevance of an interpretation within a broader context, discuss alternative interpretations of a text, or use relevant analogies to help an audience better understand an interpretation. (LAN-1.U)

**Composing on Your Own**
Return to the essay you have been developing.
1.  Place your literary argument in a broader context by inserting outside connections to make your message more relevant and easily understood for your reader.
2.  Acknowledge alternative interpretations and note their strengths and weaknesses, but explain why your stance is the best.
3.  Insert analogies to works that are similar in some key ways to the work you are analyzing.

# Part 6   Apply What You Have Learned

Choose a short story to read. You might consider another story in Jhumpa Lahiri's collection *Interpreter of Maladies*, or since you are somewhat familiar with "Cell One" and "Miss Brill," you might choose one of them. Both are available online. Write an essay in which you apply all you have learned about writing a literary argument.

- Constructing a defensible thesis
- Making arguable claims that develop the thesis in a logical line of reasoning
- Providing sufficient evidence to support each claim
- Explaining the connection among claims, line of reasoning, and evidence with commentary

After writing your initial draft, revise to make your thinking more complex and sophisticated by using one or more of the three techniques outlined in Composing on Your Own above.

**Reflect on the Essential Question** Write a brief response that answers the essential question: *How can you communicate a written interpretation of a work of literature by expressing a thesis statement; using reasoning, commentary, and sufficient evidence to support your line of reasoning; and creating a level of sophistication?* In your answer, correctly use the key terms listed on page 494.

# Unit 7 Review

## Section I: Multiple-Choice

## Section II: Free Response

## Section I: Multiple Choice

Questions 1–11. Read the following passage carefully before you choose your answers.

1   *Dearly Beloved,*

2   She dreams; dragging herself across the world. A small girl in her mother's white robe and veil, knee raised waist high through a bowl of quicksand soup. The man who stands beside her is against this standing on the front porch of her house, being married to the sound of cars whizzing by on highway 61.

3   *we are gathered here*

4   Like cotton to be weighed. Her fingers at the last minute busily removing dry leaves and twigs. Aware it is a superficial sweep. She knows he blames Mississippi for the respectful way the men turn their heads up in the yard, the women stand waiting and knowledgeable, their children held from mischief by teachings from the wrong God. He glares beyond them to the occupants of the cars, white faces glued to promises beyond a country wedding, noses thrust forward like dogs on a track. For him they usurp the wedding.

5   *in the sight of God*

6   Yes, open house. That is what country black folks like. She dreams she does not already have three children. A squeeze around the flowers in her hands chokes off three and four and five years of breath. Instantly she is ashamed and frightened in her superstition. She looks for the first time at the preacher, forces humility into her eyes, as if she believes he is, in fact, a man of God. She can imagine God, a small black boy, timidly pulling the preacher's coattail.

7   *to join this man and this woman*

8    She thinks of ropes, chains, handcuffs, his religion. His place of worship. Where she will be required to sit apart with covered head. In Chicago, a word she hears when thinking of smoke, from his description of what a cinder was, which they never had in Panther Burn. She sees hovering over the heads of the clean neighbors in her front yard black specks falling, clinging, from the sky. But in Chicago. Respect, a chance to build. Her children at last from underneath the detrimental wheel. A chance to be on top. What a relief, she thinks. What a vision, a view, from up so high.

9    *in holy matrimony.*

10    Her fourth child she gave away to the child's father who had some money. Certainly a good job. Had gone to Harvard. Was a good man but weak because good language meant so much to him he could not live with Roselily. Could not abide TV in the living room, five beds in three rooms, no Bach except from four to six on Sunday afternoons. No chess at all. She does not forget to worry about her son among his father's people. She wonders if the New England climate will agree with him. If he will ever come down to Mississippi, as his father did, to try to right the country's wrongs. She wonders if he will be stronger than his father. His father cried off and on throughout her pregnancy. Went to skin and bones. Suffered nightmares, retching and falling out of bed. Tried to kill himself. Later told his wife he found the right baby through friends. Vouched for, the sterling qualities that would make up his character.

11    It is not her nature to blame. Still, she is not entirely thankful. She supposes New England, the North, to be quite different from what she knows. It seems right somehow to her that people who move there to live return home completely changed. She thinks of the air, the smoke, the cinders. Imagines cinders big as hailstones; heavy, weighing on the people. Wonders how this pressure finds its way into the veins, roping the springs of laughter.

12    *If there's anybody here that knows a reason why*

13    But of course they know no reason why beyond what they daily have come to know. She thinks of the man who will be her husband, feels shut away from him because of the stiff severity of his plain black suit. His religion. A lifetime of black and white. Of veils. Covered head. It is as if her children are already gone from her. Not dead, but exalted on a pedestal, a stalk that has no roots. She wonders how to make new roots. It is beyond her. She wonders what one does with memories in a brand-new life. This had seemed easy, until she thought of it. "The reasons why . . . the people who" . . . she thinks, and does not wonder where the thought is from.

14    *these two should not be joined*

1. The pacing of the narrative is set by
   (A) memorable events that happened in the past
   (B) short staccato sentences
   (C) lengthy descriptions
   (D) focused action from the onlookers
   (E) current events juxtaposed with memories

2. Paragraph 13 primarily reveals that the bride
   (A) is worried about her children's future
   (B) realizes for the first time the consequences of her marriage
   (C) is determined to be happy in her new life
   (D) wonders what will become of her Mississippi family
   (E) is afraid of both her new husband and his family

3. In paragraph 4 the reference to the "occupants of the cars" serves
   (A) as a distraction from the wedding ceremony
   (B) to reveal the groom's dislike of White southerners
   (C) to highlight the bride's confusion and nervousness
   (D) as a symbol for southern segregation
   (E) to create a chaotic atmosphere

4. The contrasting settings in paragraphs 4 and 8 primarily function to represent
   (A) the south and the north
   (B) happiness and sorrow
   (C) freedom and enslavement
   (D) socialization and isolation
   (E) acquiescence and resistance

5. In paragraphs 10 and 11, which of the following does the narrator do to control the narrative pace?
   (A) Alternates long and short sentences to keep the reader guessing what comes next
   (B) Slows the pace with analogies that cause the reader to reflect on the implications
   (C) Slows the pace through a flashback to fill in expository details
   (D) Constricts time through a flash forward
   (E) Creates suspense by comparing a failed marriage with the current one

6.  For the bride, Chicago predominantly symbolizes
    (A) a new beginning for her children
    (B) an escape from rural Mississippi
    (C) a way to reconcile giving away her fourth child
    (D) a chance to grow new roots and form new memories
    (E) a frightening and harsh environment

Question 7 is covered in Unit 1.

7.  Which best describes the bride's attitude toward her marriage?
    (A) Regret for her decision to get married
    (B) Dread at the thought of leaving Mississippi
    (C) Trepidation and hope for the future
    (D) Anger at her circumstances
    (E) Dislike for her husband

Question 8 is covered in Unit 2.

8.  The simile "Like cotton to be weighed" in paragraph 4 primarily serves to
    (A) compare the light weight of cotton to the bride's values
    (B) highlight the judgmental nature of the groom
    (C) represent the values of the old south
    (D) liken the color of cotton to the bride's traditional dress
    (E) reflect the bride's desire to "sweep away" the debris of her life

Question 9 is covered in Unit 4.

9.  The description of the groom's thoughts in paragraph 4 ("Like cotton to be weighed.") serves to
    (A) show the groom's impatience
    (B) reveal the bride's nervousness
    (C) suggest she doesn't want the marriage
    (D) indicate the preacher's hypocrisy
    (E) contrast his values with the bride's

Questions 10 and 11 are covered in Unit 6.

10. The wedding ceremony fragments have what effect on the narrative?

    (A) Provide a frame for the bride and groom's thoughts

    (B) Create a competing speaker with the narrator

    (C) Foreshadow a doomed and failed marriage along with other life challenges

    (D) Show a conflict between the marriage vows and the bride's thoughts

    (E) Provide a critique of marriage expectations

11. Together the italicized lines from the marriage ceremony followed by the bride's thoughts suggest that she

    (A) does not believe in God

    (B) is afraid of her husband's God

    (C) wants to escape

    (D) has a growing awareness of the difficulties ahead

    (E) hopes her children's lives will be better than hers

## QUARANTINE

In the worst hour of the worst season
   of the worst year of a whole people
a man set out from the workhouse with his wife.
He was walking—they were both walking—north.

5  She was sick with famine fever and could not keep up.
   He lifted her and put her on his back.
He walked like that west and west and north.
Until at nightfall under freezing stars they arrived.

In the morning they were both found dead.
10    Of cold. Of hunger. Of the toxins of a whole history.
But her feet were held against his breastbone.
The last heat of his flesh was his last gift to her.

Let no love poem ever come to this threshold.
   There is no place here for the inexact
15  praise of the easy graces and sensuality of the body.
There is only time for this merciless inventory:

Their death together in the winter of 1847.
   Also what they suffered. How they lived.
And what there is between a man and woman.
20  And in which darkness it can best be proved.

12. The poem as a whole can best be described as

(A) a commentary on the cruelty of humanity

(B) a hypothetical situation about the power of love

(C) objective narration of tragic deaths

(D) a historical account of an 1847 famine

(E) a cautionary tale about the sacrifices of marriage

13. The speaker's command in line 13 ("Let no love poem ever come to this threshold.") interrupts the pacing in order to

(A) slow the pace to become more descriptive

(B) shift from the narrative situation to the meaning of it

(C) move from description to action

(D) emphasize the importance of setting to events

(E) reflect on the futility of seeking happiness

14. In line 7 ("He walked like that west and west and north.") the setting serves to

    (A) suggest they are walking to their deaths
    (B) situate the reader in the poem's location
    (C) highlight the challenge of the difficult journey
    (D) emphasize the man's love for his wife
    (E) imply they are looking for the north star for direction

15. "Of the toxins of a whole history" in line 10 does which of the following?

    (A) Creates a simile to compare the current famine to historical ones
    (B) Broadens the impact of this famine
    (C) Continues the motif of suffering and loss
    (D) Personifies history to show an unchanging harmful environment
    (E) Provides a stark image to illuminate meaning

16. The pacing shift from stanza 3 to stanza 4 is intended to

    (A) provide descriptive details of the couple's death
    (B) begin the quickening pace in the last two stanzas
    (C) desensitize the reader to the horrors of the couple's deaths
    (D) move the reader from facts to an emotional response
    (E) convey the meaning of the situation and quickly provide evidence

17. The speaker's use of prepositional phrases in line 10 ("Of cold. Of hunger. Of the toxins of a whole history.") helps to emphasize

    (A) society's role in the couple's death
    (B) the couple's blind acceptance of their plight
    (C) the narrator's sympathy for the couple
    (D) the couple's devotion to one another
    (E) the harsh conditions of the workhouse

18. When the setting changes between stanzas 1 and 2, the tone changes from

    (A) hopeful to cautiously optimistic
    (B) dreadful to bleak
    (C) hope to despair
    (D) depressed to somber
    (E) denial to acceptance

19. The speaker's description of the setting suggests

   (A) the woman was doomed before she left the workhouse

   (B) the man was aware of the hazards

   (C) the people in the workhouse were unhelpful

   (D) the man's love for his wife transcended harsh conditions

   (E) society could have prevented the tragic outcome

Question 20 is covered in Unit 5.

20. The image of "freezing stars" (line 8) most clearly serves to evoke

   (A) a sense of time

   (B) a tactile response from the reader

   (C) a feeling of loneliness

   (D) a vision of the couple's love

   (E) hope through the star's light

## Section II: Free Response

### Question 1: Poetry Analysis

In the poem on page 505, "Quarantine" by Eavan Boland, published in 2008, the speaker tells the story of a poor couple who can't survive an 1847 famine.

Read the poem carefully. Then, in a well-written essay, analyze how Boland uses poetic techniques and elements to portray the husband's complex response to their situation.

In your response you should do the following:

• Respond to the prompt with a thesis that presents a defensible interpretation.

• Select and use evidence to support your line of reasoning.

• Explain how the evidence supports your line of reasoning.

• Use appropriate grammar and punctuation in communicating your argument.

## Question 2: Prose Fiction Analysis

On pages 500–501 is the opening from "Roselily," a 1973 short story by Alice Walker. In the passage, the narrator reports the events of a rural Mississippi wedding along with thoughts of the bride.

Read the passage carefully. Then, in a well-written essay, analyze how Walker uses literary elements and techniques to create the complex tensions at the wedding.

In your response you should do the following:

- Respond to the prompt with a thesis that presents a defensible interpretation.
- Select and use evidence to support your line of reasoning.
- Explain how the evidence supports your line of reasoning.
- Use appropriate grammar and punctuation in communicating your argument.

## Question 3: Literary Argument—Culture Clash

Sociologist Jonathon H. Turner defines cultural conflict as a conflict caused by "differences in cultural values and beliefs that place people at odds with one another." All societies experience cultural conflicts. Sometimes known as "culture clash," such conflicts may lead to changes and even merging of the cultures involved or to widening gaps and greater conflict.

Choose a work of fiction that presents or represents a clash in cultural values. Then, in a well-written essay, analyze how the culture clash reveals the complex nature of characters or cultures in the work and contributes to an interpretation of the work as a whole. Do not merely summarize the plot.

In your response you should do the following:

- Respond to the prompt with a thesis that presents a defensible interpretation.
- Provide evidence to support your line of reasoning.
- Explain how the evidence supports your line of reasoning.
- Use appropriate grammar and punctuation in communicating your argument.

# UNIT 8

# Language and Ambiguity

[Poetry III]

**Part 1: Subtleties of Structure and Contrasts**
**Part 2: Ambiguity and Symbols**
**Part 3: The Power of Comparisons**
**Part 4: Writing Review I: Literary Analysis**

---

**ENDURING UNDERSTANDINGS AND SKILLS: Unit 8**

## Part 1 Subtleties of Structure and Contrasts

**Understand**

The arrangement of the parts and sections of a text, the relationship of the parts to each other, and the sequence in which the text reveals information are all structural choices made by a writer that contribute to the reader's interpretation of a text. (STR-1)

**Demonstrate**

Explain the function of structure in a text. (3.C)
Explain the function of contrasts within a text. (3.D)

## Part 2 Ambiguity and Symbols

**Understand**

Comparisons, representations, and associations shift meaning from the literal to the figurative and invite readers to interpret a text. (FIG-1)

**Demonstrate**

Explain the function of specific words and phrases in a text. (5.B)
Identify and explain the function of a symbol. (5.C)

## Part 3 The Power of Comparisons

**Understand**

Comparisons, representations, and associations shift meaning from the literal to the figurative and invite readers to interpret a text. (FIG-1)

**Demonstrate**

Identify and explain the function of a metaphor. (6.B)
Identify and explain the function of an allusion. (6.D)

**Understand**

Readers establish and communicate their interpretations of literature through arguments supported by textual evidence. (LAN-1)

**Demonstrate**

Develop a thesis statement that conveys a defensible claim about an interpretation of literature and that may establish a line of reasoning. (7.B)

Develop commentary that establishes and explains relationships among textual evidence, the line of reasoning, and the thesis. (7.C)

Select and use relevant and sufficient evidence to both develop and support a line of reasoning. (7.D)

Demonstrate control over the elements of composition to communicate clearly. (7.E)

**Source:** *AP* ® *English Literature and Composition Course and Exam Description*

# Unit 8 Overview

"Every game ever invented by [hu]mankind is a way of making things hard for the fun of it," writes poet John Ciardi. He mentions chess and juggling as examples. In the Middle Ages, for example, the queen became the most powerful chess piece, and its ability to move in any direction greatly complicated the game. And what's the fun in juggling two balls when you can, as comedian and juggler Michael Davis does, add a bowling ball and egg into the juggling pattern? (You can see Davis's routines on YouTube.) He set himself a challenge—created a problem for himself—and then figured out a way to solve it.

Ciardi continues: "The great fun, of course, is in making the hard look easy. . . . Learning to experience poetry is not a radically different process from that of learning any other kind of play. The way to develop a poetic sense is by using it. And one of the real joys of the play-impulse is in the sudden discovery that one is getting better at it . . . ."

Mention poets to most people and what might come to mind are images of struggling artists living in cramped, dank garrets waiting for their muse to inspire them to create poetry of everlasting beauty. Closer to the truth, though, would be images of everyday people with a nagging thought and persistent image and a playful challenge to connect the two and express something whose meaning is just out of reach.

Some of the most obvious "playthings" poets use are rhythm—the pattern of stressed and unstressed syllables—and rhyme. Others are

- structure—the relationship of the parts to one another and to the whole

- sequence—the order in which ideas and imagery are presented

- contrasts—differences expressed through juxtapositions

- ambiguity—multiple possible meanings and interpretations
- symbols—objects that stand for something else
- metaphors—direct comparisons between two essentially dissimilar things
- allusions—references to other books or shared knowledge

This unit will explore how poets play with these elements to create effect and meaning—and to challenge themselves in their craft.

 **Poem**
**"An Autumn Sunset" by Edith Wharton**

In the following poem published in 1894 by American writer Edith Wharton (1862–1937), the speaker describes an experience watching a sunset and the thoughts that come to mind. This poem challenges the reader as it no doubt challenged the poet herself. Take your time reading the poem. Understand the meanings of words you don't know by checking the footnotes for definitions.

### AN AUTUMN SUNSET

**I**

Leaguered[1] in fire
The wild black promontories[2] of the coast extend
Their savage silhouettes;
The sun in universal carnage[3] sets,
5  And, halting higher,
The motionless storm-clouds mass their sullen threats,
Like an advancing mob in sword-points penned,
That, balked, yet stands at bay.
Mid-zenith[4] hangs the fascinated day
10  In wind-lustrated[5] hollows crystalline,
A wan Valkyrie[6] whose wide pinions[7] shine
Across the ensanguined[8] ruins of the fray,
And in her hand swings high o'erhead,
Above the waste of war,
15  The silver torch-light of the evening star
Wherewith to search the faces of the dead.

---

1  **leaguered:** laid siege to by the military
2  **promontories:** points of high land that jut out into a large body of water
3  **carnage:** bloody slaughter
4  **mid-zenith:** the midpoint in the sky or celestial sphere directly above an observer
5  **wind-lustrated:** ceremonially purified
6  **wan Valkyrie:** In Norse mythology, a female figure who chose those who would die in battle and then took them into the afterlife. She is described here as wan, or pale and weak.
7  **pinions:** wings
8  **ensanguined:** stained or covered with blood

## II

Lagooned in gold,
Seem not those jetty[9] promontories rather
The outposts of some ancient land forlorn,
20  Uncomforted of morn,
Where old oblivions gather,
The melancholy[10] unconsoling fold
Of all things that go utterly to death
And mix no more, no more
25  With life's perpetually awakening breath?
Shall Time not ferry me to such a shore,
Over such sailless seas,
To walk with hope's slain importunities[11]
In miserable marriage? Nay, shall not
30  All things be there forgot,
Save the sea's golden barrier and the black
Close-crouching promontories?
Dead to all shames, forgotten of all glories,
Shall I not wander there, a shadow's shade,
35  A spectre[12] self-destroyed,
So purged of all remembrance and sucked back
Into the primal void,
That should we on the shore phantasmal[13] meet
I should not know the coming of your feet?

 **What Do You Know?**

This unit will explore how poets play with structure and language and ideas. Before you learn new skills and information, assess what you already know. Read the anchor text on pages 511–512 and answer the following questions. Don't worry if you find these challenging. Answering questions on a subject before formally learning about it is one way to help you deepen your understanding of new concepts.

### CLOSE READING

1. What is the most significant single line in the poem and why?

2. If you were to title part I (page 511) and part II (page 512) of the poem separately, how would you title them? What might your title choices

---

9  **jetty:** breakwater; a structure extending into the water to influence the flow of water
10  **melancholy:** a feeling of pensive sadness, typically with no obvious cause
11  **importunities:** entreaties, acts of begging
12  **spectre:** ghost
13  **phantasmal:** of or related to a figment of the imagination

suggest about the ideas in the poem? What might they suggest about the relationship between the two stanzas?

3. What ideas or images are provided that seem to contradict one another?

4. What remains unclear or uncertain in the poem?

5. Are there expressions that could have more than one meaning? Could all of those meanings be "in play" at the same time? How might those multiple meanings affect the way you read the poem and think about its ideas?

6. What objects in the text carry meaning? What meaning do they carry? What might the use of those objects say about the speaker's perspective?

7. What comparisons are used in the poem? What do these comparisons reveal about the ideas in the poem?

## INTERPRETATION

1. What bigger ideas are being developed in this poem? What ideas beyond the poem may they suggest?

2. What are the most important pieces of information in the text that you could use to support a claim about the poem (that is, your interpretation)?

**Source:** Getty Images

In Norse mythology, a valkyrie, from Old Norse "chooser of the slain," is one of a host of female figures who choose those who die in battle and those who live.

*The Valkyrie in "Autumn Sunset" is described as "wan," in contrast to the Valkyrie shown in this 1899 painting. What does that adjective add to the tone of the poem?*

# Subtleties of Structure and Contrasts

---

## Part 1  Subtleties of Structure and Contrasts

### Understand

The arrangement of the parts and sections of a text, the relationship of the parts to each other, and the sequence in which the text reveals information are all structural choices made by a writer that contribute to the reader's interpretation of a text. (STR-1)

### Demonstrate

Explain the function of structure in a text. (3.C)

Explain the function of contrasts within a text. (3.D)

See also Units 2, 4, 5 & 6

**Source:** *AP\* English Literature and Composition Course and Exam Description*

---

**Essential Question:**  How do structure and contrast in poetry create and convey meaning?

**Source:** National Gallery of Art

*Sunset Over a Pond* c. 1880 by François-Auguste Ravier

*How do structure and contrast help create and convey meaning in this painting?*

Look closely at the watercolor painting on the previous page. How would you describe the structure of the painting? Maybe you would note that the painting seems to have a mainly horizontal orientation and that there may be three main horizontal slices—the ground level, the lighter part of the sky, and the cloud layer on top. Where are the contrasts in the painting? You might say they are between the darker ground and the lighter sky or between the dark, flat land and the darker, swirly cloud layer. Where else might there be contrast? And in this sunset picture, where exactly is the sun? Does the sunlight extend beyond a single point in the sky?

As you explore structure and contrasts in poetry in Part 1, you will be asking similar questions about poetry. Remember their effect in this painting and the strength of their impact on your understanding of the scene.

---

**KEY TERMS**

| | | |
|---|---|---|
| structural patterns | punctuation marks | verbal irony |
| line | juxtapositions | situational irony |
| stanza | antithesis | paradox |

---

## 1.1 Ideas, Punctuation, and Interruptions of Patterns | STR-1.AC, STR-1.AD, STR-1.AE

As in painting, structure and contrast in poetry are key building blocks in the entire composition. Poets establish structure—through lines, stanzas, and punctuation—and raise expectations in readers about how that structure will continue. However, they also interrupt **structural patterns** to create points of emphasis. Ideas and images in a poem may extend beyond a single line or stanza. While brushstroke, color, and light are critical to understanding a painting, punctuation is often crucial to the understanding of a text.

### Extended Ideas and Images

One of the key differences between poetry and prose is that poems can be broken into lines. Both the **line**—a basic structural unit of poetry—and the sentence are units of meaning in a poem. Often ideas and images extend beyond a single line or even a single **stanza**—a verse or group of related lines—of a poem.

Read the poem on the following page written in 1650 by Welsh poet Henry Vaughan (1621–1695). Reading the poem aloud—always a good idea—may help you hear the way ideas extend beyond lines.

# THE RETREAT

Happy those early days! when I
Shined in my angel infancy.
Before I understood this place
Appointed for my second race,
5      Or taught my soul to fancy aught[1]
But a white, celestial thought;
When yet I had not walked above
A mile or two from my first love,
And looking back, at that short space,
10    Could see a glimpse of His[2] bright face;
When on some gilded[3] cloud or flow'r
My gazing soul would dwell an hour,
And in those weaker glories spy
Some shadows of eternity;
15    Before I taught my tongue to wound
My conscience with a sinful sound,
Or had the black art to dispense
A several sin to every sense,
But felt through all this fleshly dress
20    Bright shoots of everlastingness.
        O, how I long to travel back,
And tread again that ancient track!
That I might once more reach that plain
Where first I left my glorious train,
25    From whence th' enlightened spirit sees
That shady city of palm trees.
But, ah! my soul with too much stay
Is drunk, and staggers in the way.
Some men a forward motion love;
30    But I by backward steps would move,
And when this dust falls to the urn,[4]
In that state I came, return.

This poem has five sentences broken into thirty-two lines across two parts (not really stanzas because there is no line space between the parts). It also presents almost all of those lines with eight syllables and a repetitive pattern of stressed and unstressed syllables known as *iambs*.

Although identifying the structure is a necessary first step, the heart of poetry analysis is examining how the structure helps convey possible meanings. The following approaches may help you in your analysis of how all the parts fit together.

---

1  **aught:** anything at all
2  **His:** "His" with a capital "H" often refers to the Christian God in poetry of this era.
3  **gilded:** covered or tinged with gold or a golden color
4  **urn:** a vessel containing the ashes of a person's body

**Follow the Grammar** Because ideas extend over lines, to get a clear understanding of the literal meaning of the poem, identify the grammatical elements and the punctuation that marks them so you know where the complete sentences are (if there are any). Below is the poem broken into grammatical elements. The original line breaks are shown by a slash.

> Happy those early days! when I / Shined in my angel infancy.

The first two lines form a complete sentence, especially since the word *were* in the first part is understood: "Happy [were] those early days when I shined in my angel infancy."

From there, though, a series of subordinate clauses appears to refer back to "my angel infancy" with the subordinating conjunctions *before, when yet, when,* and *before* again (underlined below). These dependent clauses describe what the narrator's life was like before his "second race," his life on Earth, when he was still a heavenly angel. All those dependent clauses seem to suggest he is being pulled back to that innocent time.

> Before I understood this place / Appointed for my second race, / Or taught my soul to fancy aught / But a white, celestial thought; / When yet I had not walked above / A mile or two from my first love, / And looking back, at that short space, / Could see a glimpse of His bright face; / When on some gilded cloud or flow'r / My gazing soul would dwell an hour, / And in those weaker glories spy / Some shadows of eternity; / Before I taught my tongue to wound / My conscience with a sinful sound, / Or had the black art to dispense / A several sin to every sense, / But felt through all this fleshly dress / Bright shoots of everlastingness.

The beginning of the second part starts with a complete sentence, as did the first part.

> O, how I long to travel back, / And tread again that ancient track!

Once again, the lines that follow are subordinate clauses.

> That I might once more reach that plain / Where first I left my glorious train, / From whence th' enlightened spirit sees / That shady city of palm trees.

The final lines, however, are complete sentences.

> But, ah! my soul with too much stay / Is drunk, and staggers in the way. / Some men a forward motion love; / But I by backward steps would move, / And when this dust falls to the urn, / In that state I came, return.

By following the grammar, you can see the simple, literal meaning:

I was happy in my angel infancy. (sentence)
[This is what I was like in my angel infancy.] (dependent clauses)
I want to go back to that state. (sentence)
[Why I want to go back] (dependent clauses)
My soul is too tarnished to go back. (sentence)
Some men like to go forward. (independent clause)
I want to move backwards. (independent clause)
When I die, I want to go back to my angel infancy. (end of compound-complex sentence)

**Blocking/Chunking the Text** Another way to express this structure and meaning is by blocking, or chunking, the text.

| Block/Chunks of Related Texts | Label or Ideas |
|---|---|
| **Title**: "The Retreat" | Moving away or withdrawing from |
| **Part 1**<br>Happy those early days! when I<br>Shined in my angel infancy. | Happy as an infant |
| Before I understood this place<br>Appointed for my second race,<br>5  Or taught my soul to fancy aught<br>But a white, celestial thought;<br>When yet I had not walked above<br>A mile or two from my first love,<br>And looking back, at that short space,<br>10  Could see a glimpse of His bright face;<br>When on some gilded cloud or flow'r<br>My gazing soul would dwell an hour,<br>And in those weaker glories spy<br>Some shadows of eternity;<br>15  Before I taught my tongue to wound<br>My conscience with a sinful sound,<br>Or had the black art to dispense<br>A several sin to every sense,<br>But felt through all this fleshly dress<br>20  Bright shoots of everlastingness. | Before sin |
| **Part 2**<br>O, how I long to travel back,<br>And tread again that ancient track!<br>That I might once more reach that plain<br>Where first I left my glorious train,<br>25  From whence th' 'lightened spirit sees<br>That shady city of palm trees. | Longing for a return to innocence |
| But, ah! my soul with too much stay<br>Is drunk, and staggers in the way. | But I have fallen too far. |
| Some men a forward motion love; | Some want to move forward. |
| 30  But I by backward steps would move,<br>And when this dust falls to the urn,<br>In that state I came, return. | I want to go back and return to innocence. |

Table 8-1

**Unpack the Imagery** Imagery, like ideas, often extends beyond a single line. Grouping the lines according to how the imagery extends can help you see other divisions within the text. Paraphrasing may help ground you to the literal meaning while you explore the figurative. The words that suggest the imagery are in italic type.

| Lines of Poetry (Part 1) | Paraphrase | Imagery |
|---|---|---|
| 1) Happy those early days! when I / *Shined* in my *angel infancy.* (lines 1–2) | I was so happy as a (heavenly) baby. | brightness; angelic innocence |
| 2) Before I understood this place / Appointed for my second race, / Or taught my soul to fancy aught / But a *white, celestial* thought; (lines 3–6) | Before I understood the world and taught myself to value heavenly purity | purity (white) and heavenly (celestial) |
| 3) When yet I had not *walked* above/ A mile or two from my *first love,* / And looking back, at that short space, / Could see a glimpse of *His bright face*; (lines 7–10) | When I had not yet wandered too far from God | The image of traveling away from his "first love," God, but looking back, still close enough to be able to see His brightness |
| 4) When on some *gilded cloud or flow'r* / My gazing soul would dwell an hour, / And in those *weaker glories* spy / Some *shadows of eternity*; (lines 12–14) | When I would think about the world, I could dimly see the greatness of eternity/heaven. | *Gilded* means "thinly covered" rather than solid," which is why these earthly things were "weaker glories," or shadows, that contrast with "eternity" as a greater glory. Things on earth are at most a shadow of heaven. |
| 5) Before I taught my tongue to *wound* / My conscience with a *sinful sound,* / Or had the *black art* to dispense / A several sin to every sense, / But felt through all this *fleshly dress* / *Bright shoots* of everlastingness. (lines 15–20) | Before my words could hurt me or before I sinned all the time, I sensed something bright and eternal beyond my body. | The imagery of wounding and sinning labeled as the "black art" and connected to the flesh and contrasted with the "bright" light imagery of eternity/heaven again |

Table 8-2

*Part 2 appears in the next table.*

| Lines of Poetry (Part 2) | Paraphrase | Imagery |
|---|---|---|
| 6) O, how I long to travel back, / And *tread again* that *ancient track!* (lines 21–22) | I want to go back there and do it over. | Explicitly stating he wants to go back in time and walk the track of his innocent life |
| 7) That I might once more reach that *plain* / Where first I left my *glorious train,* / From whence *th' enlightened spirit* sees / That *shady city of palm trees.* (lines 23–26)) | So I could stop myself from sinning and doing wrong and abandoning the path to glory (heaven) | Imagery of that first plain before he struck out on his own, leaving the "glorious train." From that plain, enlightened spirits can see paradise (city of shady palm trees). |
| 8) But, ah! my soul with *too much stay* / Is *drunk,* and *staggers* in the way. (lines 27–28) | But I have gone too far, and my soul is damaged and gets in the way of paradise. | The "but" counters all of his hopes and longing. Imagery suggests he has stayed distant from God too long and his soul is "drunk and staggering," keeping him from the return to paradise. |
| 9) Some men a *forward motion* love; (line 29) | Some people love moving through life. | The image of "forward motion" indicates movement through time and also away from innocence. |
| 10) But I by *backward steps* would move, / And when this *dust falls to the urn,* / In that state I came, return. (lines 30–32) | But I would rather go back and start all over when I die. | Again, the "but" contrasts with what other men may want and emphasizes his desire to do it all over again. The image of the "dust in the urn"—death—gives way to the reference to the "state" in which he "came," suggesting that when he dies he wants to return to the state of innocence. |

Table 8-3

## Punctuation and Enjambment

Most **punctuation marks** act as road signs on your trip through a poem as well as indicators of pauses and stops. *Enjambment* is a term used to describe a line of poetry that has no punctuation and therefore propels the reader to the next line. Enjambment can increase the tempo of a poem and provide unexpected shifts. Punctuation (or its absence) is critical to a poem's rhythm and meaning.

Consider the first two lines of the poem (the first sentence):

> Happy [were] those early days! when I
> Shined in my angel infancy.

Immediately, the exclamation point stands out. You can tell the next part isn't really a complete thought because the "when" that follows is not capitalized to indicate the beginning of another sentence. So this punctuation, the exclamation mark, stands only to emphasize the happiness of those early days, but the entire thought is not complete until the end of the next line where a period marks the end.

Consider another example from lines 5 and 6:

> Or taught my soul to fancy aught
> But a white, celestial thought;

Line 5 is enjambed, so when you take it to say something like "my soul came to enjoy everything," the line initially feels positive and the speaker appears to be enjoying life and all it has to offer. However, because of the enjambment, you are forced fairly quickly to the next line and its *but*, which always serves to counter whatever came before it. In this case, you learn that the speaker fancied only those things that were "white" and "celestial," or good and godly.

Contrast this with lines 21 and 22, which are, importantly, also the first lines of the second part:

> O, how I long to travel back,
> And tread again that ancient track!

As in the first line of the poem, you see the exclamation point, but here it is the ending of a complete thought. The comma at the end of the first line prevents you from being forced too abruptly into the second line. This pause allows the speaker's desire to "travel back" to stand somewhat alone, a point that will shape the entire part of the poem. Still part of the same complete thought, but not a contrasting qualifier as in lines 5 and 6, the second of these lines simply expands on the same idea as the preceding line.

## Setting and Breaking Patterns

"The Retreat" has a regular eight-syllable line structure and even a regular pattern of stressed and unstressed syllables. Consider the lines from above:

> O, **how** I **long** to **trav**-el **back**,
> And **tread** a-**gain** that **an**-cient **track!**

Each boldfaced word or syllable gets a little more stress than the syllables in plain type.

Another pattern throughout this poem is the rhyming of pairs of lines (called *rhyming couplets*). Of course, poetry doesn't have to rhyme, but in well-written rhyming poems, the rhyming words often relate to one another and contribute meaning and style to the poem.

Consider both syllables and rhymes as you look at these last lines (the last sentence) from the poem.

> Some **men** a **for**-ward **mo**-tion **love**;
> But **I** by **back**-ward **steps** would **move**,
> And **when** this **dust** falls **to** the **urn**,
> **In** that **state** I **came**, re-**turn.**

Looking at the two different couplets reveals some rhymes that may help in understanding the poem. The first two lines are joined by both a semicolon (that separates complete thoughts) and a "but," which indicates a contrast between "Some men" and the speaker's "I." The rhyming of *love* and *move* could further emphasize that contrast. Some men love moving through life, but the speaker wants to move backward to prebirth innocence. Similarly, the rhyming of *urn* with *return* emphasizes the speaker's desire to return to a state of innocence after dying.

In a somewhat parallel way, the patterns of syllables and stresses in the first two lines of this sentence are almost identical.

> Some **men** a **for**-ward **mo**-tion **love**;
> But **I** by **back**ward **steps** would **move**,

Just as the content of those lines aligns, so, too, does the meter—the syllables and patterns of stress and unstress.

The last two lines of the poem, however, break that pattern.

> And **when** this **dust** falls **to** the **urn**,
> **In** that **state** I **came**, re-**turn**.

The regularity and predictability of the pattern in the previous lines seem to be followed at first; however, in the last line, a syllable is missing at the beginning of the line. The pattern of stresses is interrupted, suggesting an emphatic shift—that line expresses something more definite, more finite, than the previous lines, as it signals the end of the speaker's life.

*NOTE: Studying poetry in depth will include knowing the names for the patterns of stressed and unstressed syllables. Because this course focuses on the understanding and interpretation of the language and larger structures of poetry, those aspects of poetry are not addressed at length in this book, nor are they covered on the exam.*

---

 **Remember:** Ideas and images in a poem may extend beyond a single line or stanza. Punctuation is often crucial to the understanding of a text. When structural patterns are created in a text, any interruption in the pattern creates a point of emphasis. (STR-1.AC–AE)

---

## 1.1 Checkpoint

*Reread the poem "An Autumn Sunset" on pages 511–512. Then complete the following open-response activity and answer the multiple-choice questions.*

1. Use one or more of the reading and analysis techniques you read about in this section to help you understand the poem by Edith Wharton.

   - Following the Grammar
   - Blocking/Chunking
   - Unpacking the Imagery
   - Reading the Punctuation
   - Looking for Patterns

You may wish to recreate Tables 8-1 and/or 8-2/8-3 to record your analysis.

2. Which of the following best describes the development of the poem as a whole?

    (A) The losses predicted in the first stanza are realized in the second.

    (B) The imagery of darkness and "universal carnage" (line 4) develops into imagery of light and life across the remainder of the poem.

    (C) The imagery progresses from that associated with battle to that associated with surrender.

    (D) Each stanza enhances the images provided in the other.

    (E) Each line provides additional details to the light imagery of the poem.

3. Which of the following best describes the relationship between the first lines of each stanza?

    (A) They are structurally similar but contradict one another to illustrate the contrast between the two stanzas.

    (B) They are structurally similar because they reflect the observation of the same promontories later in the sunset.

    (C) Though they are structurally similar, the first line in the second stanza represents hope that is missing in the first stanza.

    (D) They are structurally similar and their imagery is identical to illustrate how time has stood still for the speaker.

    (E) That they are structurally similar does not matter since the imagery of the two lines and the ideas of the two stanzas completely differ.

4. The pattern of syllables and rhyme in the last two lines (reproduced below) breaks the pattern of the rest of the poem in order to emphasize

> That should we on the shore phantasmal meet
> I should not know the coming of your feet?

    (A) that the speaker now only exists as a ghost without memory

    (B) how lost the speaker is without the presence of the addressee

    (C) the effect of the speaker's loss of memory on a reunion with the addressee

    (D) the speaker's fear of memories and their effect on the addressee

    (E) a relationship between the setting sun and the memories of the speaker

**Creating on Your Own**

Select one of the following subjects or another of your choice. Take five to ten minutes to just write, filling each line of your paper or computer all the way to the end. Don't try to be "poetic" or "accurate"—just write what you see and what you know.

- An event or a place (or both together) that may seem normal to others but is important to you
- The time when you believe your childhood ended
- A time when you wanted to give up but didn't
- A "first" and how it changed you

After writing, go back and create the line breaks that will make this the first draft of your poem. Consider the following suggestions, and save your work.

1. Maybe you can begin to play with how the sentences break up.

2. Look at how your ideas are arranged in blocks, or chunks. Maybe move some around to create a contrast or some other effect.

3. Revise some of your punctuation and/or line endings so one idea runs over into a contrasting idea to create complexity or ambiguity.

4. Play with your syllables and/or rhymes (but don't sacrifice meaning or ideas for the sake of rhyme).

# 1.2 Juxtaposition, Irony, and Paradox
| STR-1.AF, STR-1.AG, STR-1.AH

A key tool in conveying shades of meaning in poetry is structure. Through contrasts and opposites, poets also play with readers' expectations, sometimes creating inconsistencies and contradictions that complicate and enrich a poem's layers of meaning. Irony and paradox are forms of contrasts and opposites and also add richness to a text.

## Juxtaposition and Antithesis

Just as a poem may present a pattern and then emphasize ideas by breaking that pattern, so, too, can it emphasize ideas by placing contrasting ideas next to each other in a parallel grammatical construction, a technique called **juxtaposition**. Sometimes juxtaposition creates or demonstrates the exact opposite of a person or thing or idea—an **antithesis**—also in parallel grammatical construction ("It was the best of times, it was the worst of times . . ."). Antithesis requires two statements expressing opposite meanings in parallel construction. Antithesis emphasizes the quality of the main subject by showing it in sharp contrast to an opposite quality.

Review lines 29–30 of "The Retreat."

> Some men a forward motion love;
> But I by backward steps would move,

As you saw, these lines are structurally similar. That structural similarity actually emphasizes the differences between what they are conveying, since you might expect similar constructions to convey similar ideas. For this reason, "some men" and the speaker could be said to be juxtaposed in these two lines. In fact, by structuring those lines in a similar way and placing them one after the other, the poet could also be said to be making the speaker antithetical to those other men. Along with other textual evidence, such as the shift in meter in the last line, this antithesis supports the reading of these lines as clearly separating the desire of this speaker to move backward from the desire of "some" people to move forward.

## Irony

Irony is usually understood as the effect of saying one thing while meaning the opposite, often for comic purposes or emphasis. For example, if on a miserable rainy day a friend offers you a ride to school and you say, "No, thanks—gorgeous day for walk!" you would be speaking ironically. The core trait of irony is that it goes against expectations. Without an expectation, there is no irony.

**Verbal Irony** Irony in literature can take several forms. **Verbal irony** is a literary device in which a character, speaker, or narrator makes statements that intentionally contradict intended meanings—that are often even opposite intended meanings—and that are inconsistent with expectations.

For example, the poem called "The Lanyard" by Billy Collins begins with the speaker's recollection of being at summer camp, where he braided a lanyard with long red and white plastic strips as a gift for his mother, and then continues:

> She gave me life and milk from her breasts,
> and I gave her a lanyard.
> She nursed me in many a sick room,
> lifted spoons of medicine to my lips,
> laid cold face-cloths on my forehead,
> and then led me out into the airy light
>
> and taught me to walk and swim,
> and I, in turn, presented her with a lanyard.
> Here are thousands of meals, she said,
> and here is clothing and a good education.
> And here is your lanyard, I replied,
> which I made with a little help from a counselor.

When the speaker responds to the many motherly gifts offered over the years with, "and I gave her a lanyard" or "and I, in turn, presented her with a lanyard," the speaker is using verbal irony, intentionally equating the product of a bored summer camper to the countless gifts parents give their children when he knows nothing can repay a parent's love.

**Situational Irony** Another type of irony, **situational irony,** is a literary device in which events are inconsistent with expectations, or even the opposite happens. For example, in the poem "Handsome Man" by Rebecca Hazelton, the speaker addresses "Handsome man who rides in to save me" and tells him she is ready to "swoon into your arms like this, / see how limp?" so he can save her from a dragon. She practices her "helpless cries" and tells him "how good I damsel." As he approaches, though, she begins to see him for what he is, noting "that witch / who wanted you to be kind to old women but you showed her / what was what." The more she learns about him, the less flowery her language becomes, and at the end, the outcome is the opposite of a rescue.

> You know what,
>
> handsome man who rides in to save me? I think I'm just going to stay here. Yeah. With the dragon. . . .
>
> That's right. Ride away. That's what you're good at. Ride away!

In "The Retreat" by Henry Vaughan, situational irony occurs in lines 27–28 when the speaker explains:

> But, ah! my soul with too much stay
> Is drunk, and staggers in the way.

A reader might expect that the soul of a person would long for eternal life in paradise ("That shady city of palm trees"), but in this case the soul gets in his way because it is "drunk" by having been on Earth too long. This situational irony makes the point that being on Earth seems to have made the soul—a spiritual part of a person—be held back by earthly pleasures typically associated with the body.

## Paradox

*Paradox* is another term you sometimes hear used in different ways to describe interesting or perplexing situations. Often, the word refers to self-contradictory statements, such as "This sentence is a lie." That statement cannot be true nor can it be false, because if it is one, then it is also the other. Statements like these are fun word games, but a paradox in literature goes further.

A **paradox** in literature may at first seem absurd and self-contradictory, but on closer look, it actually reveals a meaningful idea. Consider these lines, the last two from the sonnet "Death, Be Not Proud" by John Donne, a 16th-century English poet. This poem is part of his series of poems called "Holy Sonnets."

> One short sleep past, we wake eternally
> And death shall be no more; Death, thou shalt die.

"Death, thou shalt die" is self-contradictory, and yet for a person who believes in eternal life with God, it makes a kind of sense—when our bodies die in a "short sleep," our souls will "wake eternally."

The last two lines of the Henry Vaughan poem also present a paradox, also about death.

> And when this dust falls to the urn,
> In that state I came, return.

Death is juxtaposed with rebirth in these lines. The first line's image ("dust falls to the urn") refers to the dust of the cremated body falling into the urn used to store ashes. That image is set directly against the second line's statement that the speaker will "return" from death. These conflicting images could be seen as more than simply antithetical because the idea that death can lead to life seems absurd and self-contradictory. As a paradox, these lines reveal the speaker's desire to do the impossible—to go backward to his prebirth innocence.

Consider another example from "Song from a Reedless Flute" by Sara Littlecrow-Russell on page 548:

> You are the love song
> Played on a reedless flute
> That only spirits hear.

This is a single sentence broken into enjambed lines, and it stands as its own stanza in the poem. The three individual lines provide pieces of information that build and accumulate until the sentence is complete. The addressee (the person the speaker is addressing) is being compared to a love song, but it is played on a flute without a reed, so there is no sound—only spirits can hear it. The idea of a song that doesn't have sound could be seen as paradoxical: its deeper meaning might be that the person compared to the love song cannot communicate with the speaker.

**Remember:** Juxtaposition may create or demonstrate an antithesis. Situational or verbal irony is created when events or statements in a text are inconsistent with either the expectations readers bring to a text or the expectations established by the text itself. Paradox occurs when seemingly contradictory elements are juxtaposed, but the contradiction—which may or may not be reconciled—can reveal a hidden or unexpected idea. (STR-1.AF–AH)

## 1.2 Checkpoint

*Reread the poem "An Autumn Sunset" on pages 511–512. Then complete the following open-response activity and answer the multiple-choice questions.*

1. Review your reading and analysis techniques from 1.1 Checkpoint (Following the Grammar, Blocking/Chunking, Unpacking the Imagery, Reading the Punctuation, and Looking for Patterns) and use your work to help you recognize and interpret the devices on the following page.

   - juxtaposition/antithesis
   - irony
   - paradox

Write a few sentences identifying where in the poem you see these literary devices and what effect they have on the reader's interpretation of the poem.

2. Which of the following describes an antithetical relationship?

(A) the speaker and the reader

(B) fear of loss and desire for love

(C) the desires of living men and the desires of the ghosts that surround them

(D) different perspectives on loss and rebirth

(E) the varying light of the sun and the different darkness that appear at sunset

3. Lines 17–20 (reproduced below) might be described as

> Lagooned in gold,
> Seem not those jetty promontories rather
> The outposts of some ancient land forlorn,
> Uncomforted of morn

(A) contradictory in their use of light imagery

(B) ironic in that morning light brings no comfort or hope

(C) antithetical to the first four lines of the previous stanza

(D) paradoxical as they address finding joy in what is lost

(E) juxtaposing the comfort of morning with the losses felt at sunset

4. In the context of lines 33–39 (reproduced below), the paradox "a shadow's shade" (line 34) most likely means that

> Dead to all shames, forgotten of all glories,
> Shall I not wander there, a shadow's shade,
> A spectre self-destroyed,
> So purged of all remembrance and sucked back
> Into the primal void,
> That should we on the shore phantasmal meet
> I should not know the coming of your feet?

(A) ghosts have better memories than the living people they are meant to represent

(B) memories all fall into shadow and darkness at the end of the day

(C) the shadows ultimately win over the light

(D) one without memory is not even a shadow but the emptiness that makes the shadow

(E) only memories can provide the comfort of shade

5. In the context of "An Autumn Sunset," rhyming "death" (line 23) with "breath" (line 25) is most likely meant to

    (A) represent the struggle to stay alive

    (B) reflect the inevitably of death

    (C) emphasize the antithesis of life and death

    (D) demonstrate the irony of death and life

    (E) juxtapose the real and imagined worlds of the speaker

**Creating on Your Own**

Review your writing from the previous Creating on Your Own activity and examine the relationships between the structural parts of your poem. Try revising your poem in these ways, and save your work.

- Devising a stark juxtaposition of ideas or images or speakers to create an antithesis

- Going against any expectations you may have created for your reader (or for yourself)

- Playing with language and statements to create some paradoxes that align with your ideas. Consider looking up some literary paradoxes for more ideas. Ask yourself what sort of complex truth these absurd statements might reveal.

# Part 1 Apply What You Have Learned

Read the poems in the Poetry Gallery of this unit (or Unit 2 or 5) and choose one to examine closely. Write a paragraph or series of paragraphs that identifies structural aspects of the poem, examines the effect of those structures, and explains how those structures and their effect relate to meanings beyond the poem. Cite specific line numbers and explain your thinking to your reader.

**Reflect on the Essential Question** Write a brief response that answers the essential question: *How do structure and contrast in poetry create and convey meaning?* In your response, correctly use the key terms listed on page 515.

# Ambiguity and Symbols

## Part 2  Ambiguity and Symbols

### Understand

Comparisons, representations, and associations shift meaning from the literal to the figurative and invite readers to interpret a text. (FIG-1)

### Demonstrate

Explain the function of specific words and phrases in a text. (5.B)

Identify and explain the function of a symbol. (5.C)

See also Units 2, 5, 6 & 7

**Source:** *AP® English Literature and Composition Course and Exam Description*

---

**Essential Questions:**  How can a text support multiple interpretations? How do symbols contribute to an attitude or perspective in a text?

---

*Retreat (v.)* "to move back or withdraw"; *retreat (n.)* "a quiet place for spiritual reflection." Which of these meanings does the title of the poem by Henry Vaughan convey? Probably both. You read at the beginning of this unit that poets play with various elements of poetry. **Ambiguity**—the quality of allowing for different readings and understandings by different readers—is an especially important example of how poets can make their work more difficult for the joy of conveying more than one meaning. Especially in poetry, in which the words are few and dense, being able to ascribe more than one meaning to words, phrases, or situations allows poets to add layers of meaning elegantly and economically.

**Symbols**—images or objects that stand for something else—provide another way for poets to convey multiple meanings. The way symbols are used in a text may also imply that a narrator, character, or speaker has a particular attitude or perspective.

---

**KEY TERMS**

ambiguity                                  symbols

---

# 2.1 Ambiguity | FIG-1.AG

Read this poem by American poet Archibald MacLeish (1892–1982), first published in 1926.

### ANCESTRAL

The star dissolved in evening—the one star
The silently
         and night O soon now, soon
And still the light now
5                and still now the large
Relinquishing
        and through the pools of blue
Still, still the swallows
        and a wind now
10              and the tree
Gathering darkness:
        I was small. I lay
Beside my mother on the grass, and sleep
Came—

15      slow hooves and dripping with the dark
The velvet muzzles, the white feet that move
In a dream water
        and O soon now soon
Sleep and the night.

20        And I was not afraid.
Her hand lay over mine. Her fingers knew
Darkness,—and sleep—the silent lands, the far
Far off of morning where I should awake.

In the first line of the poem, the speaker refers to a star that "dissolved in evening." The first image that might come to mind is a star as a small point of light in an evening sky. However, that star dissolving in the evening could also be the sun. The phrase "the one star" bolsters this interpretation.

Trying to decide which is the "right" reading may deprive you of the benefit of the ambiguity of the beginning. If you think of both meanings—the setting sun and the rising star—you will more clearly see the image of the day passing gradually through evening into nighttime. This imagery creates a continuity of light, which is supported by lines 3 and 4 in which the night soon comes yet there is "still the light." Then comes the "large" light of line 5 that, while "relinquishing," is described as "pools of blue"—maybe the remaining blue in the sky, maybe the moon. In this reading, there is always some light, despite the "gathering darkness" (line 11).

In that reading, you can see how the ambiguity of the word *star* and of the phrase "dissolved in evening" creates different possibilities for the poem and how those possibilities rely on other parts of the poem to be supported in a way that makes sense to the meaning of the poem.

Another poem with enriching ambiguity is "Sunday Morning," published in 1937, by American poet Louis MacNeice (1907–1963). You can read the whole poem on page 549. Following are two lines from the second stanza.

> Take corners on two wheels until you go so fast
> That you can clutch a fringe or two of the windy past,

The poem mentions (among other things) cars and driving in relation to passing time on a Sunday morning. In this context, the word *clutch* and the phrase "windy past" take on multiple possible meanings. *Clutch* can mean grabbing hold of something—in this case, something in the past—but it can also refer to using the clutch on a car, something you would do when shifting gears.

The phrase "windy past" can also take on multiple meanings:

- the winding or "windy" road on which one would often use a clutch to shift gears

- a suggestion that the past is not a straight line but rather winds and weaves and is hard to hold onto, or "clutch"

- the possibility that "windy" refers to blowing wind. That gives the word a different pronunciation, but the meaning still makes sense when you consider both the wind moving over the "fast" car and the past as uncertain and difficult to "clutch" because it is windy and not still.

The implication of these different possible readings is that the past is slippery and hard to hold on to—with lots of turbulent curves and changes in direction, and the faster you move through time, the harder it is to get hold of the past.

**Source:** Getty Images

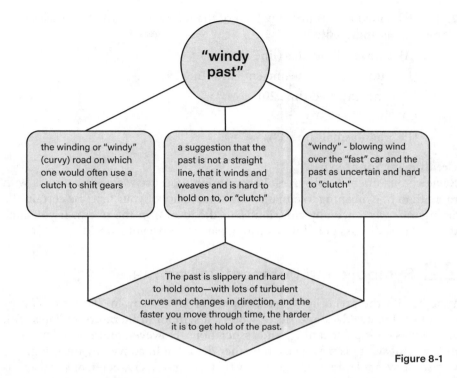

**Figure 8-1**

The ambiguity of these words and phrases opens the entire poem to several possible readings. When you also consider other aspects of the poem—the structure, the sentences, the fact that *fast* and *past* are rhymed—you can begin to see how a number of different techniques throughout the poem relate to one another to enrich interpretation.

 **Remember:** Ambiguity allows for different readings and understandings of a text by different readers. Symbols in a text and the way they are used may imply that a narrator, character, or speaker has a particular attitude or perspective. (FIG-1.AG–AH)

## 2.1 Checkpoint

*Reread the poem "An Autumn Sunset" on pages 511–512. Then complete the following open-response activity and answer the multiple-choice question.*

1. Identify possible ambiguity in the language of the poem. Then explain in a few sentences how those different possible meanings might affect the ideas presented in the poem.

2. In the context of this poem, which of the following words or phrases can be read as ambiguous?

   (A) savage silhouettes (line 3)

   (B) outposts of some ancient land (line 19)

   (C) Uncomforted (line 20)

   (D) fold (line 23)

   (E) phantasmal (line 38)

**Creating on Your Own**

Review your poem in progress. Where might you use a word or phrase with more than one meaning to enhance the complexity of your text? Be certain the ambiguous word actually contributes to the idea(s) in the poem. If you can't think of any, discuss possibilities with a partner. Save your work.

# 2.2 Symbols and Perspective | FIG-1.AH

Whether it's the green light that beckons to Jay Gatsby in *The Great Gatsby* or Robert Frost's "dark and deep" woods, a symbol in literature radiates with and invites multiple meanings and associations. However, more complex, more meaningful symbols may go even further than that in conveying meaning. The way some symbols are used may imply that a narrator, character, or speaker has a particular attitude or perspective.

For example, consider how symbolism is used in the poem "Arise, Go Down" by American poet Li-Young Lee on pages 544–545. In that poem, the speaker, standing in his dead father's rose garden, feels a wasp on his face and stands still to keep it from stinging him. In that stillness, he contemplates the opposing or cancelling forces at work in the world (lines 18–30):

> Here, I stand among my father's roses
>
> and see that what punctures outnumbers what
> 20    consoles, the cruel and the tender never
> make peace, though one climbs, though one descends
>
> petal by petal to the hidden ground
> no one owns. I see that which is taken
> away by violence or persuasion.
>
> 25    The rose announces on earth the kingdom
> of gravity. A bird cancels it.
> My eyelids cancel the bird. Anything
>
> might cancel my eyes: distance, time, war.
> My father said, *Never take your both eyes*
> 30    *off of the world*, before he rocked me.

In lines 34–39, the speaker recalls waiting in terror for an all-clear sign so the family could escape from political and religious persecution, but the signal never came. In the final stanzas, he begins by quoting his father:

> *I didn't make the world I leave you with*,
> 35     he said, and then, being poor, he left me
> only this world, in which there is always
>
> a family waiting in terror
> before they're rended, this world wherein a man
> might arise, go down, and walk along a path
>
> 40     and pause and bow to roses, roses
> his father raised, and admire them, for one moment
> unable, thank God, to see in each and
> every flower the world cancelling itself.

Roses are a common symbol in literature and often stand for beauty or dangerous beauty because of their thorns. The use of roses as a symbol in this poem, however, reveals the speaker's perspective on the "cancelling" nature of life itself and the gift, for one moment, to be able to see a more unified view.

The speaker concludes that the punctures, possibly a reference to a rose's thorns, outnumber what consoles, possibly the beauty of a rose, and that "the cruel and the tender never make peace" (lines 19–21). From there the speaker builds on the tensions of opposing forces. Roses announce gravity, as their petals fall to the ground. Birds "cancel" gravity by being able to fly. The speaker's closed eyes cancel the birds by removing them from sight (lines 25–28).

In the final stanzas, the speaker continues the theme of opposing realities: This is a world in which families wait in terror before being broken apart and also a world in which a man might bow to and admire his father's roses and, for just a moment, see them in their wholeness.

In this poem, then, the way the symbol of the rose is used reveals the speaker's complex attitude or perspective on all of life itself.

 **Remember:** Symbols and the way they are used in a text may imply that a narrator, character, or speaker has a particular attitude or perspective. (FIG-1.AH)

### 2.2 Checkpoint

*Reread the poem "An Autumn Sunset" on pages 511–512. Then complete the following open-response activity and answer the multiple-choice question.*

1. Look for objects that may bring certain associations to mind or that may reveal attitudes or perspectives of the speaker. In a few sentences, write about how those symbols may affect different possible meanings of the poem.

2. In the context of the poem, things related to darkness ("silhouettes" [line 3], "storm-clouds" [line 6], "black" [line 31], "shadow's shade" [line 34], and "primal void" [line 37]) can be seen as symbolizing

    (A) nighttime as the vengeance of the gods

    (B) unavoidable death

    (C) the loss of hope and joy

    (D) the fear of emptiness without memory

    (E) the pity one feels for those who have lost someone they love

**Creating on Your Own**

Review your poem in progress. Focus on an object or related set of objects that you have introduced in the poem. If you have not introduced an object that could symbolize something, brainstorm to think of some objects that could relate to the ideas and your attitude toward them. Revise your poem to integrate these objects as symbols. Save your work.

# Part 2 Apply What You Have Learned

Read the poems in the Poetry Gallery of this unit (or Unit 2 or 5) and choose one to examine more closely. Write a paragraph or series of paragraphs in which you identify, examine, and explain a symbol or set of symbols and what they reveal about the attitude or the perspective of the speaker.

> **Reflect on the Essential Questions** Write a brief response that answers these essential questions: *How can a text support multiple interpretations? How do symbols contribute to an attitude or perspective in a text?* In your answer, correctly use the key terms listed on page 530.

# The Power of Comparisons

## Part 3 The Power of Comparisons

### Understand
Comparisons, representations, and associations shift meaning from the literal to the figurative and invite readers to interpret a text. (FIG-1)

### Demonstrate
Identify and explain the function of a metaphor. (6.B)
Identify and explain the function of an allusion. (6.D)
See also Units 2 and 5

**Source:** *AP® English Literature and Composition Course and Exam Description*

**Essential Question:** How can complex comparisons and allusions contribute to the overall complexity of a text?

Although all poets likely delight in wordplay, some have stretched the boundaries by looking for witty and startling extended comparisons, called **conceits**. In responding to some of the 17th-century poetry he read that included many of these devices, the 18th-century critic Samuel Johnson complained about conceits because of their power to "violent[ly] bring together 'heterogeneous' [different] ideas." Yet many of the poets who engaged in this wordplay left behind poems that have resonated through the centuries for their delightful and challenging ways of inviting readers to look with fresh eyes on old ideas through compelling extended comparisons that reflect life's complexities.

The complexity of poetry and other literature is also enriched by indirect references to a person, place, event, or thing (including a text) that has some cultural significance. Such a reference is called an **allusion**. Every quality of the subject alluded to will transfer to the subject of the text.

---

**KEY TERMS**

conceits                                        allusion

---

# 3.1 Conceits | FIG-1.AI, FIG-1.AJ, and FIG-1.AK

The strength of love between two lovers who must be apart might be compared to the pull between the moon and the tides, and readers would easily understand. But what if the relationship between two parted lovers were compared to a compass, the kind you might use in geometry class? You would probably have to stop and think about how that comparison worked.

That comparison of the parted lovers is an example of a conceit, probably the most famous example of a conceit in English poetry. Poets have often used conceits to describe subjects that are generally indefinable and unknowable. Sometimes these subjects are referred to as *metaphysical*—literally, beyond the physical—including such abstract concepts as being, knowing, substance, cause, identity, time, and space. The poets often included references to scientific knowledge and expressed their ideas almost as a logical argument.

The use of these especially complex, often extended comparisons is not unique to the so-called metaphysical poets. These clever comparisons have been used by many poets on many different topics. Conceits also make comparisons that may be surprising or ironic.

Read this poem by English metaphysical poet John Donne (1572–1631), published posthumously in 1633. It is the one that contains the compass conceit, among others.

## A VALEDICTION: FORBIDDING MOURNING

As virtuous men pass mildly away,
   And whisper to their souls to go,
Whilst some of their sad friends do say
   The breath goes now, and some say, No:

5  So let us melt, and make no noise,
   No tear-floods, nor sigh-tempests move;
'Twere profanation of our joys
   To tell the laity[1] our love.

Moving of th' earth[2] brings harms and fears,
10  Men reckon what it did, and meant;
But trepidation of the spheres,[3]
   Though greater far, is innocent.

Dull sublunary[4] lovers' love
   (Whose soul is sense) cannot admit
15  Absence, because it doth remove

---

1  **laity:** ordinary people; also, congregants as opposed to the clergy
2  **moving of th' earth:** earthquakes
3  **spheres:** stars and planets and other heavenly bodies
4  **sublunary:** existing below the moon (i.e., on Earth)

Those things which elemented it.
But we by a love so much refined,
    That our selves know not what it is,
Inter-assured of the mind,
20    Care less, eyes, lips, and hands to miss.

Our two souls therefore, which are one,
    Though I must go, endure not yet
A breach, but an expansion,
    Like gold to airy thinness beat.

25  If they be two, they are two so
    As stiff twin compasses[5] are two;
Thy soul, the fixed foot, makes no show
    To move, but doth, if the other do.

And though it in the center sit,
30    Yet when the other far doth roam,
It leans and hearkens after it,
    And grows erect, as that comes home.

Such wilt thou be to me, who must,
    Like th' other foot, obliquely run;
35  Thy firmness makes my circle just,
    And makes me end where I begun.

In lines 25–36, you will see an extended comparison related to "stiff twin compasses." These refer to the "two souls" in line 20. The speaker is setting up an extended metaphor between the two souls and the two legs of a compass.

To examine a conceit, look for parts of the poem that connect with it to examine them separately from the poem itself. Consider the table below.

| Original Lines of the Conceit | Explanation of the Conceit |
| --- | --- |
| If they be two, they are two so<br>  As stiff twin compasses are two;<br>Thy soul, the fixed foot, makes no show<br>  To move, but doth, if the other do. | One soul (the addressee's) stays put as the sharp point of a compass stays in one place. It doesn't appear to move but does if the other does. |
| And though it in the center sit,<br>  Yet when the other far doth roam,<br>It leans and hearkens after it,<br>  And grows erect, as that comes home. | Your soul is at the center, but when the other soul moves far away, your soul remains but leans toward the other, as if calling it back home. When the other comes closer, your soul stands tall as if proud. |
| Such wilt thou be to me, who must,<br>  Like th' other foot, obliquely run;<br>Thy firmness makes my circle just,<br>  And makes me end where I begun. | You (the addressee) will be the one who stays put because I (the speaker) must go, but because you stand firm and don't move, you make me stay attached and cause me to come back to the center. |

Table 8-4

---

5 **compass:** device used for making arcs and circles in mathematics such as geometry

The compass as a metaphor comparing two very different subjects is extended as it plays out across multiple lines and even stanzas. With little romantic imagery associated with a compass, this comparison seems odd and almost surprising. Yet with it Donne captures a quality of love that is difficult to describe—the attachment that crosses time and space, the part of love that, even though people may be separated, keeps them attached and eventually brings them back together.

The poem also contains other startling comparisons. Consider how they relate to one another and affect one another throughout the poem. For example, the stanza just before the compass comparison contains this comparison:

> Our two souls therefore, which are one,
>     Though I must go, endure not yet
> A breach, but an expansion,
>     Like gold to airy thinness beat.

The simile at the end of the stanza likens the lovers' two souls to gold that has been beaten so thin that it almost floats on air (an actual property of gold). This comparison is explained in the previous stanza, where the speaker describes the lovers' leaving not a "breach" or a break "but an expansion." Like the beaten gold, this couple may be apart in distance but their souls remain together. This comparison is similar to the conceit of the compass, which suggests the endurance of this couple's love and the more universal idea that love endures across time and distance.

> **Remember:** A conceit is a form of extended metaphor that often appears in poetry. Conceits develop complex comparisons that present images, concepts, and associations in surprising or paradoxical ways. Often, conceits are used to make complex comparisons between the natural world and an individual. Multiple comparisons, representations, or associations may combine to affect one another in complex ways. (FIG-1.AI–AK)

### 3.1 Checkpoint

*Reread the poem "An Autumn Sunset" on pages 511–512. Then complete the following open-response activity and answer the multiple-choice question.*

1. Look for unconventional or surprising comparisons used to demonstrate a complex idea (for example, the day as a "wan Valkyrie" or Time as a ferry across "sailless seas"). Examine the nature of those comparisons, the ideas they capture about the poem, and their relationship to one another. Write a few sentences explaining your interpretation.

2. Which of the following lines includes a comparison that may be considered a conceit?

(A) "The wild black promontories of the coast extend
    Their savage silhouettes;" (lines 2–3)

(B) "The motionless storm-clouds mass their sullen threats,
    Like an advancing mob in sword-points penned,
    That, balked, yet stands at bay." (lines 6–8)

(C) "Mid-zenith hangs the fascinated day
    In wind-lustrated hollows crystalline,
    A wan Valkyrie whose wide pinions shine
    Across the ensanguined ruins of the fray," (lines 9–12)

(D) "Seem not those jetty promontories rather
    The outposts of some ancient land forlorn," (lines 18–19)

(E) "The melancholy unconsoling fold
    Of all things that go utterly to death
    And mix no more, no more
    With life's perpetually awakening breath?" (lines 22–25)

## Creating on Your Own

Once again review your poem in progress. What complex idea are you trying to capture? Consider what makes it complex and how you might craft a striking or surprising metaphor to explain it. You might try watching some comedians because comedy often relies on surprising and shocking comparisons.

Likewise, how do different comparisons across your draft work together? How could you revise to help them better fit with and affect one another? Make changes that suit you and save your work.

# 3.2 Allusions | FIG-1.AL

Just as an author may choose certain comparisons because of a reader's familiarity or association with them, so, too, might an author refer to certain subjects about which they may share knowledge with the reader. Such references or allusions are ways of awakening certain associations and understandings in the reader. Mentioning the terrorist attacks of 9/11/2001, for example, allows an author to engender certain feelings of loss or fear that many—even those not alive at the time—associate with that event.

Most allusions fall into one or more of the following types:

- Historical: a reference to events from the past, such as 9/11 or the first moon landing

- Mythological/Religious: a reference to some story or character from traditions of faith or mythology, such as mentioning the Trojan Horse as an example from Greek mythology that suggests deception and distrust

- Literary: a reference to a character or event from other works of literature, such as calling a problem an "albatross around your neck" in reference to the famous Samuel Taylor Coleridge poem "The Rime of the Ancient Mariner," in which the title character is plagued with bad luck after killing an albatross
- Cultural: a reference to some aspect of shared culture or pop culture (politics, science, music, art, or film, for example), such as referring to the famous line in the movie *Jaws*—"you're going to need a bigger boat"—to express a point about how big a problem is

Simply identifying allusions can be satisfying, but examining their role in a possible interpretation of the poem is the real task. For example, Henry Vaughan's poem "The Retreat" on page 516 could be seen as making a religious (specifically, a biblical) allusion to the garden of Eden or to heaven (or, ambiguously, both):

> That I might once more reach that plain
> Where first I left my glorious train,
> 25  From whence th' enlightened spirit sees
> That shady city of palm trees.

Vaughan's allusion likely brings to mind the reward of paradise that awaits those who have "enlightened" spirits, reinforcing the speaker's longing for a return to a state of innocence.

If a reader does not have knowledge of the subject to which the author is alluding, the allusion will have little meaning. No one can know allusions to every possible source. But if something stands out as a likely allusion, research it to learn more.

Sara Littlecrow-Russell's "Song from a Reedless Flute" on page 548 has many allusions to Native American culture that can be researched for a deeper understanding of the poem. For example, the speaker refers in line 5 to a "bear claw necklace." Many Native American cultures regard bears as embodying the Great Spirit. When a bear was killed, its death was seen as a sacrifice to replenish the Earth, and a bear claw necklace was a way to gain the protection of that powerful spirit. In line 17, the speaker refers to a star blanket, a cherished item in any home because it represents the "eye of the creator." In line 19, the speaker refers to "a stubborn braid of *wiingashk*." If you look up the word *wiingashk*, you can learn that it is sweetgrass that some Native American culture groups regard as the hair of Grandmother Earth. The three braided strands represent mind, body, and spirit.

Simply tracing the source of an allusion will not add much meaning to a poem. However, once you have a basic understanding, you can analyze how the allusions are used in the poem. In "Song from a Reedless Flute," for example, in isolation each allusion has a positive association. As they are used in the poem, though, the allusions take on a limited or inadequate nature: the bear claw necklace no longer caresses, the star blanket is sliding off the bed, and the *wiingashk* is stubborn.

**Remember:** Because of shared knowledge about a reference, allusions create emotional or intellectual associations and understandings. (FIG-1.AL)

### 3.2 Checkpoint

*Reread the poem "An Autumn Sunset" on pages 511–512. Then complete the following open-response activity and answer the multiple-choice question.*

1. Look closely at the poem for allusions made to mythology. In a few sentences, explain the associations these allusions bring to the poem and how those associations affect the reading of the rest of the poem.

2. In context, the allusion to "A wan Valkyrie" (line 11) most likely does which of the following in the poem?

   (A) Establishes the poem as part of Norse folklore

   (B) Contrasts with the innately masculine qualities of the poem

   (C) Distinguishes between the earthly and the heavenly

   (D) Brings to mind our lack of control of death but hope for the afterlife

   (E) Affirms the speakers' perspective on death while still allowing doubt about the nature of living in service of others

**Creating on Your Own**
Review your poem in progress. What allusion(s) could you make related to your subject and ideas that might enrich a reader's interpretation? Revise your draft in an attempt to insert this allusion. Save your work.

## Part 3 Apply What You Have Learned

Read the poems in the Poetry Gallery of this unit (or Unit 2 or 5) and choose one to examine more closely. Write a paragraph or series of paragraphs in which you identify, examine, and explain conceits and allusions in the poem and how they relate to an interpretation. Be certain to cite specific line numbers and explain your thinking to your reader.

**Reflect on the Essential Question** Write a brief response that answers this essential question: *How can complex comparisons and allusions contribute to the overall complexity of a text?* In your answer, correctly use the key terms listed on page 537.

# POETRY GALLERY

## ARISE, GO DOWN
### BY LI-YOUNG LEE (1957–), PUBLISHED IN 1990

It wasn't the bright hems of the Lord's skirts
that brushed my face and I opened my eyes
to see from a cleft in rock His backside;

it's a wasp perched on my left cheek. I keep
5    my eyes closed and stand perfectly still
in the garden till it leaves me alone,

not to contemplate how this century
ends and the next begins with no one
I know having seen God, but to wonder

10   why I get through most days unscathed, though I
live in a time when it might be otherwise,
and I grow more fatherless each day.

For years now I have come to conclusions
without my father's help, discovering
15   on my own what I know, what I don't know,

and seeing how one cancels the other.
I've become a scholar of cancellations.
Here, I stand among my father's roses

and see that what punctures outnumbers what
20   consoles, the cruel and the tender never
make peace, though one climbs, though one descends

petal by petal to the hidden ground
no one owns. I see that which is taken
away by violence or persuasion.

25  The rose announces on earth the kingdom
of gravity. A bird cancels it.
My eyelids cancel the bird. Anything

might cancel my eyes: distance, time, war.
My father said, *Never take your both eyes*
30  *off of the world*, before he rocked me.

All night we waited for the knock
that would have signalled, *All clear, come now*;
it would have meant escape; it never came.

*I didn't make the world I leave you with*,
35  he said, and then, being poor, he left me
only this world, in which there is always

a family waiting in terror
before they're rended, this world wherein a man
might arise, go down, and walk along a path

40  and pause and bow to roses, roses
his father raised, and admire them, for one moment
unable, thank God, to see in each and
every flower the world cancelling itself.

# DUENDE[1]
## BY TRACY K. SMITH (1972–), PUBLISHED IN 2007

### 1.

The earth is dry and they live wanting.
Each with a small reservoir
Of furious music heavy in the throat.
They drag it out and with nails in their feet
5    Coax the night into being. Brief believing.
A skirt shimmering with sequins and lies.
And in this night that is not night,
Each word is a wish, each phrase
A shape their bodies ache to fill—

10        *I'm going to braid my hair*
        *Braid many colors into my hair*
          *I'll put a long braid in my hair*
        *And write your name there*

They defy gravity to feel tugged back.
15    The clatter, the mad slap of landing.

### 2.

And not just them. Not just
The ramshackle family, the *tíos*,[2]
*Primitos*,[3] not just the *bailaor*[4]
Whose heels have notched
20    And hammered time
So the hours flow in place
Like a tin river, marking
Only what once was.
Not just the voices of scraping
25    Against the river, nor the hands
Nudging them farther, fingers
Like blind birds, palms empty,
Echoing. Not just the women
With sober faces and flowers
30    In their hair, the ones who dance
As though they're burying
Memory—one last time—
Beneath them.

And I hate to do it here.
35　To set myself heavily beside them.
Not now that they've proven
The body a myth, a parable
For what not even language
Moves quickly enough to name.
40　If I call it pain, and try to touch it
With my hands, my own life,
It lies still and the music thins,
A pulse felt for through garments.
If I lean into the desire it starts from—
45　If I lean unbuttoned into the blow
Of loss after loss, love tossed
Into the ecstatic void—
It carries me with it farther,
To chords that stretch and bend
50　Like light through colored glass.
But it races on, toward shadows
Where the world I know
And the world I fear
Threaten to meet.

3.

55　There is always a road,
The sea, dark hair, *dolor*.[5]

Always a question
Bigger than itself—

*They say you're leaving Monday*
60　*Why can't you leave on Tuesday?*

---

1　**Duende:** the creative force, first used in relation to Flamenco dancers
2　**tíos:** uncles
3　**primitos:** cousins
4　**bailaor:** flamenco dancer
5　**dolor:** pain

## SONG FROM A REEDLESS FLUTE
### BY SARA LITTLECROW-RUSSELL (1969–),
### PUBLISHED IN 2006

You are beadwork woven by a broken Indian woman
That I mend with cautious, needle-pricked fingers.
You are raw sweetness of burning *chaga*[1]
Scraping my lungs and startling tears.
5    You are the bear claw necklace
No longer caressing
The space between my breasts.
You are cigarettes
That I quit years ago,
10   But sometimes smoke anyways.

You are maple syrup on snow
Melting on my tongue
Until I ache from the cold.
You are the cedar tree
15   Sheltering my childhood
From unwanted caresses.
You are the star blanket
Sliding off the bed on autumnal nights.
You are a stubborn braid of *wiingashk*[2]
20   That must be relit with a dozen matches
Before it releases thin streamers of sweetness.

You are the love song
Played on a reedless flute
That only spirits hear.

---

1 *chaga:* a mushroom with many uses, including burning for incense
2 *wiingashk:* sweetgrass thought by some to be the hair of Grandmother Earth

## SUNDAY MORNING
### BY LOUIS MACNEICE (1907–1963), PUBLISHED IN 1936

Down the road someone is practising scales,
The notes like little fishes vanish with a wink of tails,
Man's heart expands to tinker with his car
For this is Sunday morning, Fate's great bazaar;
5    Regard these means as ends, concentrate on this Now,

And you may grow to music or drive beyond Hindhead
    anyhow,
Take corners on two wheels until you go so fast
That you can clutch a fringe or two of the windy past,
That you can abstract this day and make it to the week
    of time
10   A small eternity, a sonnet self-contained in rhyme.

But listen, up the road, something gulps, the church spire
Open its eight bells out, skulls' mouths which will not tire
To tell how there is no music or movement which secures
Escape from the weekday time. Which deadens and
    endures.

## HARLEM
### BY LANGSTON HUGHES (1902–1967), PUBLISHED IN 1951

What happens to a dream deferred?

Does it dry up
like a raisin in the sun?
Or fester like a sore—
5    And then run?
Does it stink like rotten meat?
Or crust and sugar over—
like a syrupy sweet?

Maybe it just sags
10   like a heavy load.

*Or does it explode?*

## THE COLLAR
## BY GEORGE HERBERT (1593–1633), PUBLISHED IN 1633

I struck the board, and cried, "No more;
      I will abroad!
What? shall I ever sigh and pine?
My lines and life are free, free as the road,
5    Loose as the wind, as large as store.
      Shall I be still in suit?
Have I no harvest but a thorn
To let me blood, and not restore
What I have lost with cordial fruit?
10      Sure there was wine
Before my sighs did dry it; there was corn[1]
   Before my tears did drown it.
   Is the year only lost to me?
   Have I no bays[2] to crown it,
15   No flowers, no garlands gay? All blasted?
      All wasted?
Not so, my heart; but there is fruit,
   And thou hast hands.
Recover all thy sigh-blown age
20   On double pleasures: leave thy cold dispute
Of what is fit and not. Forsake thy cage,
      Thy rope of sands,
Which petty thoughts have made, and made to thee
Good cable, to enforce and draw,[3]
25      And be thy law,
While thou didst wink and wouldst not see.
      Away! take heed;
      I will abroad.
Call in thy death's-head[4] there; tie up thy fears;
30      He that forbears
      To suit and serve his need
      Deserves his load."
But as I raved and grew more fierce and wild
      At every word,
35   Methought I heard one calling, *Child*!
      And I replied *My Lord.*

---

1 **corn:** in British English, any kind of grain, especially wheat
2 **bays:** laurel; a wreath or crown of laurel was a symbol of honor
3 **draw:** pull
4 **death's-head:** human skull, representing death

## SONNET 97
## BY WILLIAM SHAKESPEARE (1564–1616), PUBLISHED IN 1609

How like a winter hath my absence been
From thee, the pleasure of the fleeting year!
What freezings have I felt, what dark days seen!
What old December's bareness everywhere!

5    And yet this time remov'd was summer's time,
The teeming autumn, big with rich increase,
Bearing the wanton burthen[1] of the prime,
Like widow'd wombs after their lords' decease:

Yet this abundant issue[2] seem'd to me
10   But hope of orphans and unfather'd fruit;
For summer and his pleasures wait on thee,
And thou away, the very birds are mute;

Or if they sing, 'tis with so dull a cheer
That leaves look pale, dreading the winter's near.

---

1  **burthen:** burden
2  **issue:** offspring

**Source:** Getty Images

*What is the conceit in* Sonnet 97?

### The Critic's Craft: Joining the Conversation

Before moving into Part 4, take a moment to think about the community of readers and writers you join when you develop a written literary analysis or argument. It's a centuries-long community of critics evaluating and analyzing the works of literature that generate interest in their time—or were rejected in their time and possibly later reevaluated and seen more favorably through a different lens. Reading critical reviews of a poem is, of course, not needed to appreciate, understand, and respond to it. But it can help you see how other people think about poetry and other literature and the process they use to make the best sense they can of a poetic work.

One way to join the conversation of poetry critics is to participate in the Modern American Poetry Site (MAPS) (modernamericanpoetry.org), which is attempting to gather criticism of American poetry in one place. On that site, you can choose among a number of poets and poems to see what criticism has been collected on a certain poet or body of work. For example, you can search for Langston Hughes's "Harlem" and find a piece that analyzes the unusual structure of the poem and offers an explanation of what the structure contributes to the meaning of the poem. There are a number of pieces discussing Hughes's poem "The Negro Speaks of Rivers," which he wrote when he was 17 years old. Each addresses the poem from a different angle, and together they form an interesting prism of views on the poem. Many of the critical essays are excerpts from books that are cited so you can follow up for more information.

One of the tabs at the top of the page is Education, and in a drop-down menu you can find a Student's Guide to MAPS that will help you get the most out of the site. You can even submit your own critical essays and join the conversation of scholars and students sharing their ideas about poetry.

### Use the Critic's Craft

Visit MAPS and explore the site. While the site does not have critical essays on all the poets and poems you might be interested in, it does have quite a few and continually adds new essays and excerpts. Find the piece on "Harlem" as a way to practice navigating the site and to get a perspective on a critical piece that focuses on structure. Then explore the site for poems you especially like to see what other readers have said about them. Consider contributing your own critical essay to the site.

# Writing Review I: Literary Analysis

## Part 4  Writing Review I: Literary Analysis

### Understand
Readers establish and communicate their interpretations of literature through arguments supported by textual evidence. (LAN-1)

### Demonstrate
Develop a thesis statement that conveys a defensible claim about an interpretation of literature and that may establish a line of reasoning. (7.B)

Develop commentary that establishes and explains relationships among textual evidence, the line of reasoning, and the thesis. (7.C)

Select and use relevant and sufficient evidence to both develop and support a line of reasoning. (7.D)

Demonstrate control over the elements of composition to communicate clearly. (7.E)

See also Units 3, 4, 5, 6 & 7

**Source:** *AP® English Literature and Composition Course and Exam Description*

**Essential Question:** How can you communicate in writing an interpretation of a poem that asserts a claim, supports it with evidence, and acknowledges the words and ideas of others?

Throughout this course, you have had many opportunities to write about literature—in small activities within the units, in the final section of each unit devoted to writing, and in the unit review in the free-response questions. Each unit also reminded you of the recursive process of writing (see page 59), pointing out the continuing process of reevaluating your evidence and possibly your overarching claim or thesis. Each unit also added a new skill or understanding, so gradually you have been "upgrading" your written literary analyses.

# 4.1 Reviewing the Literary Analysis Process | LAN-1.A–V

The chart below shows the progression of skills you have developed. The words in bold show the key changes in the four main categories of written literary analysis:

- Thesis Statement
- Commentary
- Evidence
- Elements of Composition

| Unit | Written Product |
|---|---|
| **Unit 1, Part 5**<br>(pp. 53–66)<br>Graphic organizer, p. 60 | • A **paragraph** of literary analysis about a work of literature that defends a **claim** (LAN-1.A–B) with<br>• **textual evidence** to support the claim (LAN-1.C) |
| **Unit 2, Part 5**<br>(pp. 115–126)<br>Graphic organizer, p. 122 | • A **paragraph** of literary analysis about a poem that defends a **claim** (LAN-1.A–B) with<br>• **textual evidence** to support the claim (LAN-1.C) |
| **Unit 3, Part 4**<br>(pp. 186–200)<br>Graphic organizer, p. 192 | **Thesis Statement**<br>• A **paragraph** of literary analysis with a full **thesis statement** expressing an interpretation of a longer literary text that may preview the line of reasoning and that requires defense through textual evidence and a line of reasoning (LAN-1.D-E)<br>**Commentary**<br>• a **logical sequence of claims** that work together to defend the overarching thesis statement (LAN-1.F)<br>• **commentary** that explains the relationships among the evidence, line of reasoning, and thesis (LAN-1.G)<br>**Evidence**<br>• **relevant and sufficient evidence** that strategically and purposefully illustrates, clarifies, exemplifies, associates, amplifies, or qualifies a point; evidence reviewed and reconsidered through **recursive process** (LAN-1.H–K)<br>**Elements of Composition**<br>• correct use of **key conventions** of grammar and mechanics (LAN-1.L) |

| Unit 4, Part 5<br>(pp. 255–268)<br>Graphic organizer, p. 267 | **Thesis Statement**<br>- An **essay** of literary analysis about a longer work with a full thesis statement that may preview the line of reasoning and that guides the reader through evidence and a line of reasoning that connects the evidence to the thesis. (LAN-1.D, E)<br>**Commentary**<br>- a **logical sequence of claims** that work together to defend the overarching thesis statement (LAN-1.F)<br>- **commentary** that explains the relationships among the evidence, line of reasoning, and thesis (LAN-1.G)<br>- **body paragraphs** that develop the reasoning and justify claims using evidence and commentary linking the evidence to the overarching thesis (LAN-1.M)<br>- **cohesive body paragraphs** that often use topic sentences to state a supporting claim and explain the reasoning connecting the various claims and evidence that make up the body of the essay (LAN-1.N)<br>**Evidence**<br>- **high-quality and sufficient evidence** used strategically and purposefully to illustrate, clarify, exemplify, associate, amplify, or qualify a point (LAN-1.H–J)<br>**Elements of Composition**<br>- **coherence** at the sentence, paragraph, and whole text levels through devices that link ideas (LAN-1.O)<br>- coherence is reflected by a **logical arrangement** of reasons, evidence, and ideas and through such **linking techniques** as transitions, repetition, synonyms, pronoun references, and parallel structure (LAN-1.P) |
| Unit 5, Part 5<br>(pp. 331–342)<br>Graphic organizer, p. 335 | All of the above in Unit 4 plus:<br>**Elements of Composition**<br>- **enhancement of coherence** through phrases, clauses, sentences, or paragraphs that show relationships among ideas (LAN-1.Q) |
| Unit 6, Part 5<br>(pp. 407–421)<br>Elements of Composition<br>(pp. 411–421) | All of the above in Unit 5 plus:<br>**Elements of Composition**<br>- strategic **selection and placement of phrases and clauses**, including use of **coordination and subordination** to clarify relationship of ideas (LAN-1.R)<br>- **well-chosen words** (LAN-1.S)<br>- **punctuation** that clearly conveys relationships among ideas (LAN-1.T) |
| Unit 7, Part 6<br>(pp. 493–499) | All of the above in Unit 6 plus:<br>**Commentary**<br>- added **sophistication** through the explanation or relevance of an interpretation within a **broader context**, discussion of **alternative interpretations**, or use of **relevant analogies** for clarity (LAN-1.U)<br>**Evidence**<br>- **revision** of interpretation and line of reasoning if the evidence does not sufficiently support the initial interpretation or line of reasoning (LAN-1.V) |

This unit will add a further upgrade—integrating the ideas of others and acknowledging intellectual property. The final unit will provide guidance in adding an introduction and conclusion that broaden the scope of your essay.

## 4.1 Checkpoint

Each of the items in the chart on pages 554–555 is followed by its code from the College Board Course and Exam Description (CED). Take some time to review your previous essays and the constructive comments your teacher and peers made. Make a chart identifying the categories into which they tend to fall and indicate the code from the CED that best describes the issue. To give you an idea of how to complete your chart, the following provides an example if you had challenges with

- having your thesis statement guide your readers
- using topic sentences to state supporting claims
- using sufficient evidence
- using coordination and subordination effectively

| Inventory of Areas I Can Improve in My Literary Analyses | | |
|---|---|---|
| Category | Specific Code | Strategies for Improving |
| Thesis Statement | LAN-1.E | Carefully think through my supporting claims and try to find a way to suggest or imply them in my thesis statement or to state them outright. |
| Line of Reasoning | LAN-1.N | Review the examples in Unit 4. Pull out my thesis statement and supporting claims so I can see only them and determine how each supporting claim can become the topic sentence of a body paragraph. |
| Evidence | LAN.1-H-J | Evaluate whether I just haven't used enough evidence present in the text or if there isn't sufficient evidence in the text to support my thesis. If the former, find the best place in the essay to insert the additional evidence. If the latter, revise my thesis statement to assert a claim for which there is ample evidence in the text. |
| Elements of Composition | LAN.1–R | Review Unit 6 on coordination and subordination. Be sure I understand what each type of clause is. If using subordination, identify my main point and make sure I express it in the independent clause. |

Save your work so you can check future essays using your chart to be sure you have made improvements.

**Composing on Your Own**

Use the processes you have learned through Units 3–7 to develop an essay of literary analysis on "An Autumn Sunset," a poem from the Poetry Gallery in this unit or in Unit 2 or 5, or another poem you are reading.

1. Make the poem "yours."
   - Read the text closely, following the grammar, blocking/chunking, unpacking imagery, or reading punctuation to ground yourself in the literal meaning and structure of the poem.
   - Look for contrasts and shifts. Note any juxtaposition, irony, or paradox.
   - Identify places where words or phrases could have multiple meanings.
   - Look for symbols and think about their meanings.
   - Identify comparisons, including complex comparisons such as conceits.
   - Note any allusions.

2. Review your work from #1, looking for patterns and breaks in patterns, and thoughtfully examine how the parts of the poem work together to convey meaning.

3. Develop a working thesis based on the evidence you gathered and the analysis you have done in #2.

4. Develop supporting claims that will form the basis of your line of reasoning in your body paragraphs.

5. Organize your textual evidence according to the claims they support. Use your textual evidence strategically and purposefully.

6. Weave together your evidence and line of reasoning to make clear how they support the claims and overarching thesis.

7. If you come to see your evidence in a new light or find more evidence that puts your thesis in question, revise your thesis and adjust your essay.

8. Strive for coherence within and between sentences and paragraphs. Save your work for future use.

# 4.2 Acknowledging the Words and Ideas of Others
## | LAN-1.W

Whether you are sharing your ideas in discussions with classmates or reading criticism of the sort you might find on the Modern American Poetry Site (MAPS), you are bound to bump into ideas that support yours, improve on yours, or disagree with yours. You may wish to use some of them in your essay to bolster your thesis by showing that others agree with you or by acknowledging some merit to other, possibly opposing views but showing why yours is superior. Any time you use others' words, ideas, images, texts, or other **intellectual property**, works that the creators own and can copyright, you must acknowledge their source. Failing to do so will make you guilty of plagiarism, a serious offense that carries significant consequences. Three common ways to acknowledge sources are attribution, reference, and citation.

## Attribution

**Attribution** is the act of acknowledging the source of an idea, statistic, fact, observation, image, or other intellectual property by ascribing, or attributing, it to its creator. Writers use attribution by including the author's name and any other pertinent information in their commentary.

Suppose, for example, you are writing a literary analysis of Langston Hughes's "Harlem" (see page 549). You are developing a thesis about the structure of the poem and what that contributes to the meaning. So far, you have the following working thesis statement and sketch of supporting claims.

> **Working Thesis Statement:** Every aspect of the structure of "Harlem" by Langston Hughes contributes to the poem's condemnation of racial injustices.
>
> **Supporting Claim 1:** Framing the poem with a beginning and ending question, spaced from the rest of the poem, emphasizes the final question as a powerful answer.
>
> **Supporting Claim 2:** The progression of questions in the middle of the poem establishes a pattern of two-line questions which is disrupted in line 6, conveying disunity and reflecting the fractures in American society.
>
> **Supporting Claim 3:** The single declarative sentence in lines 9 and 10 adds to the disjointed feel of the poem but leads forcefully to the final line as its meaning shifts in relation to that final question.

You might be curious when you get to this stage what other critics have to say about the poem, so you go to MAPS (or to any other resource your library may have for scholarship on Hughes) and find that piece by Tom Hansen referred to in The Critic's Craft. You find many interesting ideas in Hansen's essay, some going in a somewhat different direction from yours, but you also find a succinct statement of something you were thinking yourself. After reviewing some of the elements of the poem he has already discussed, he concludes that they "result in a poem in conflict with itself, pulled in different directions by some of its most basic constituent elements. Yet this surely calculated failure is the measure of the poem's success." At some point in your essay, maybe in your first paragraph or maybe in the paragraphs addressing Supporting Claim 2, you may want to refer to this idea. A good way to do so would be to weave it into your own writing but attribute the idea to its creator. For example, you might write the following in your first paragraph. The attribution is in italic type.

Every aspect of the structure of "Harlem" by Langston Hughes contributes to the poem's condemnation of racial injustices. Its unusual and disjointed structure and its anger shielded by the question format create and reflect a tension about how to understand the consequences of a dream deferred. *As Tom Hansen writes in his essay "On Harlem,"* the poem is "pulled in different directions by some of its most basic constituent elements."

By using quotation marks around Hansen's words and by preceding them with an attribution, you have ethically and usefully built on the ideas of others.

Even if you are not quoting a source directly but are still using original ideas from the source, be sure to acknowledge them, as in the following example.

Every aspect of the structure of "Harlem" by Langston Hughes contributes to the poem's condemnation of racial injustices. Its unusual and disjointed structure and its anger shielded by the question format create and reflect a tension about how to understand the consequences of a dream deferred. *Tom Hansen notes in his essay "On Harlem" that the poem's tensions and inconsistencies are actually what make it such an effective expression.*

In this example, ideas are paraphrased but credit is still given to the original creator.

## Citation

Attributions are usually included within the body of a text, as above, to identify the source of such material. A **citation** is a more formal documentation of another's work, research, or words and often appears as a footnote or endnote. For example, if you wanted to include enough information for the reader to be able to find the source and check it independently, you could prepare a footnote or endnote such as the following.

1. Tom Hansen, "On Harlem" (modernamericanpoetry.org/criticism/ -tom-hansen-harlem) paragraph 6.

Or you might cite the original source listed at the end of the online essay.

Tom Hansen, "On Harlem," *The Explicator* 58.2 (Winter 2000), pp. 106–107.

*NOTE: You are not expected to use a specific attribution style (like MLA) within the timed essays on the AP© exam. However, you should follow the style your teacher wants you to use on extended papers you develop in class through multiple revisions.*

## Reference

A **reference** is like a citation, but it does not refer to a specific page or chapter number in a source. Instead, it provides the basic publishing information about a source. References to all the works an author has consulted often appear at the end of an essay or a book in a list called a bibliography.

Hansen includes references at the end of his essay.

**WORKS CITED**

Hughes, Langston. "Harlem." *The Panther and the Lash*. New York: Knopf, 1951.

Olson, Charles. "Projective Verse." *The New American Poetry*. Ed. Donald M. Allen. New York: Grove, 1960.

Thrall, William Flint, et al. *A Handbook to Literature*. New York: Odyssey, 1960.

Acknowledging others' intellectual property through attribution, citation, and/or reference is a useful step for validating your evidence, including diverse perspectives, and adding credibility to your own position. These acknowledgments will often be standard requirements in essays you write in college.

**Remember:** Writers must acknowledge words, ideas, images, texts, and other intellectual property of others through attribution, citation, or reference. (LAN-1. W)

## 4.2 Checkpoint

Explore the resources for literary criticism available through your library's databases. EBSCO, ProQuest, Gale, JSTOR, and InfoTrac are databases commonly found in school libraries. Google Scholar is a web-based search engine for scholarly articles that can point you to useful resources but does not include full texts.

Search for scholarly articles on the poem that is the subject of your essay. Read as many as possible, at least three if they are available. Take notes on ideas, phrases, and sentences that are so well expressed that you may want to use or quote them as they appear in the source. Note the bibliographic information of each source as well and save your work.

### Composing on Your Own

Review the draft of the essay you began in the previous Composing on Your Own activity. Look for opportunities to include the ideas, words, and phrases or sentences you found in your research to support and add credibility to your position. Weave them in carefully, being sure to acknowledge them through attribution, citation, or reference and place quotation marks around any words or phrases taken directly from the source. At this stage, revise for artful syntax, effective word choice, and clear punctuation. Then give it to a classmate or friend for a final peer review. Consider the feedback you receive and revise as you think best.

# Part 4 Apply What You Have Learned

The final stage of the writing process is editing. Make sure you clearly communicate to an academic audience by demonstrating control over the elements of composition. Do a final check of your essay for correct spelling, usage, and punctuation. Consider having someone else do a check for you as well.

**Reflect on the Essential Question** Write a brief response that answers this essential question: *How can you communicate in writing an interpretation of a poem that asserts a claim, supports it with evidence, and acknowledges the words and ideas of others?* In your answer correctly use the key terms listed on page 554.

# Unit 8 Review

## Section I: Multiple Choice

## Section II: Free Response

## Section I: Multiple Choice

Questions 1–10. Read the following passage carefully before you choose your answers.

1    Veiling as it did the dirt, the mud, and the darkness, the snow would continue to speak to Ka of purity, but after his first day in Kars it no longer promised innocence. The snow here was tiring, irritating, terrorizing. It had snowed all night. It continued snowing all morning, while Ka walked the streets playing the intrepid reporter—visiting coffeehouses packed with unemployed Kurds,[1] interviewing voters, taking notes—and it was still snowing later, when he climbed the steep and frozen streets to interview the former mayor and the governor's assistant and the families of the girls who had committed suicide. But it no longer took him back to the white-covered streets of his childhood; no longer did he think, as he had done as a child standing at the windows of the sturdy houses of Nisantas,[2] that he was peering into a fairy tale; no longer was he returned to a place where he could enjoy the middle-class life he missed too much even to visit in his dreams. Instead, the snow spoke to him of hopelessness and misery.

2    Early that morning, before the city woke up and before he had let the snow get the better of him, he took a brisk walk through the shantytown below Atatürk Boulevard to the poorest part of Kars, to the district known as Kalealt. The scenes he saw as he hurried under the ice-covered branches of the plane trees and the oleanders—the old decrepit Russian buildings with stovepipes sticking out of every window, the thousand-year-old Armenian church towering over the wood depots and the electric generators, the pack of dogs barking at every passerby from a five-hundred-year-old stone bridge as snow fell into the half-frozen black waters of the river below, the thin ribbons of smoke rising out of the tiny shanty houses of Kalealt sitting lifeless under their blanket of snow—made him feel so melancholy that tears welled in his eyes. On the opposite bank were two children, a girl and a boy who'd been sent out early to buy bread, and as they danced along, tossing the warm loaves back and forth or

---

1 **Kurds:** mainly Islamic ethnic group living in a region overlapped by the countries of Turkey, Iran, Iraq, and Syria
2 **Nisantas:** a neighborhood in Istanbul

clutching them to their chests, they looked so happy that Ka could not help smiling. It wasn't the poverty or the helplessness that disturbed him; it was the thing he would see again and again during the days to come—in the empty windows of photography shops, in the frozen windows of the crowded teahouses where the city's unemployed passed the time playing cards, and in the city's empty snow-covered squares. These sights spoke of a strange and powerful loneliness. It was as if he were in a place that the whole world had forgotten, as if it were snowing at the end of the world.

3      Ka's luck stayed with him all morning, and when people asked him who he was they wanted to shake his hand; they treated him like a famous journalist from Istanbul; all of them, from the governor's assistant to the poorest man, opened their doors and spoke to him. He was introduced to the city by Serdar Bey, the publisher of *Border City News* (circulation three hundred and twenty), who sometimes sent local news items to the *Republican* [newspaper] in Istanbul (mostly they didn't print them). Ka had been told to visit "our local correspondent" first thing in the morning, as soon as he left the hotel, and no sooner had he found this old journalist ensconced in his office than he realized this man knew everything there was to know in Kars. It was Serdar Bey who was the first to ask him the question he would hear again hundreds of times during his three-day stay.

4      "Welcome to our border city, sir. But what are you here for?"

---

1.  Throughout the passage, the snow functions as a symbol of
    (A) pain and the unjust consequences of poverty
    (B) repressed loss and joyless memories
    (C) inescapable and all-encompassing misery and poverty
    (D) overwhelming commitment to a place that holds memories
    (E) cold and oppressive memories

2.  Sentence 5 in paragraph 1 ("But it . . . dreams.") illustrates and reiterates the differences between Ka's memories of the city and the realities he now observes by
    (A) providing a detailed explanation of Ka's current perspective alongside his childhood perspective
    (B) repeating what Ka used to think to contrast it with what he thinks now
    (C) using punctuation to include certain parts of text that a reader may find particularly interesting all in one sentence
    (D) establishing a contrast and then using punctuation to combine several related independent clauses to demonstrate how Ka has changed
    (E) failing to address the differences portrayed in the independent clauses that have been joined by punctuation in that sentence

3. Allusions to "old decrepit Russian buildings" and the "thousand-year-old Armenian church" serve primarily to

   (A) reveal the degradation of the city

   (B) demonstrate the ancient mix of cultures in the city

   (C) illustrate the failures of the city government

   (D) display the importance of faith to the people of the city

   (E) show the different sections and neighborhoods of the city

4. In paragraph 2, sentence 3 ("On the opposite . . . help smiling.") the imagery surrounding the girl and boy "who'd been sent out early to buy bread" juxtaposes

   (A) imagery of degradation and decay used to describe the city

   (B) Ka's experiences as a child

   (C) "Ka's luck" as mentioned in the following paragraph

   (D) the symbolism of the snow and its multiple connotations

   (E) "crowded teahouses" mentioned later in the paragraph

Question 5 is covered in Unit 4.

5. In the first sentence, the detail that the snow is "[v]eiling as it did the dirt, the mud, and the darkness," functions primarily in the setting to

   (A) contrast the seeming purity and innocence created by the snow with the reality of the city

   (B) demonstrate Ka as a naive outsider

   (C) illustrate the loss the people of the city feel

   (D) create a complex relationship between Ka and the snow t

   (E) portray the city s better than Ka and many others expect

Questions 6–8 are covered in Unit 7.

6. The statement set off by dashes in paragraph 2, sentence 2 ("The scenes ... in his eyes.") serves primarily to

 (A) contrast Ka's experiences as a child with the things that he is observing now

 (B) illustrate the contrast Ka feels between the longevity of his culture and the degradation of the city around him

 (C) compare the city covered by snow with the city when it is not covered by snow

 (D) reveal Ka's insecurities stemming from the anxieties and uncertainties he experienced as a child growing up in the city

 (E) expose that Ka's real reason for returning to Kars was to face his past

7. In paragraph 2, sentence 2 ("The scenes ... in his eyes."), the detail that "tears welled in his eyes" reveals which of the following about Ka?

 (A) His childhood means more to him than he understood.

 (B) He does not know what to expect upon his return to the city.

 (C) He has higher expectations upon his return home.

 (D) He has a deeply personal association with the city.

 (E) He fails to understand the reality of how the city has changed.

8. How the reader sees others interact with Ka at the beginning of paragraph 3 might best be described as

 (A) ironic, because he was treated with such excitement after having been so saddened by the state of the city in the previous paragraph

 (B) pitiful, given the decaying state of the city

 (C) understated, since they were clearly excited about the visit from someone living in the big city

 (D) hyperbolic, given he was from Kars and was only returning home for a visit

 (E) ambiguous, since the people of the town do not know how to react to him

Questions 9 and 10 are covered in Unit 9.

9.  The syntax of sentence 3 in paragraph 1 ("But it . . . dreams.") combines a number of independent clauses primarily to

   (A) maintain a consistent structure so as not to emphasize something and take away from the main narrative

   (B) assure that the reader understands who Ka was as a child and how his childhood affects his perspective

   (C) emphasize the complexity of Ka's "fairy tale" perspective

   (D) shift the reader from a focus on the city to a focus on Ka's "hopelessness and misery"

   (E) reveal Ka's changing and complex perspective on his hometown

10. Serdar Bey's question of Ka in the final sentence of the excerpt does which of the following?

   (A) contrasts with Serdar Bey knowing "everything there was to know in Kars" with his uncertainty about Ka's visit to Kars

   (B) establishes Serdar Bey as the dominant personality in their relationship, as the man who knows "everything there was to know in Kars"

   (C) reveals Serdar Bey's true intentions for inviting Ka to the city

   (D) suggests that Ka's visit will only bring trouble on himself, Serdar Bey, and the other people of the city

   (E) emphasizes the reasons why Ka has not visited since he was a small child

Questions 11–19. Read the following poem carefully before you choose your answers.

## MORNING SONG

Love set you going like a fat gold watch.
The midwife[1] slapped your footsoles, and your bald cry
Took its place among the elements.

Our voices echo, magnifying your arrival. New statue.
5    In a drafty museum, your nakedness
Shadows our safety. We stand round blankly as walls.

I'm no more your mother
Than the cloud that distills a mirror to reflect its own slow
Effacement[2] at the wind's hand.

10    All night your moth-breath
Flickers among the flat pink roses. I wake to listen:
A far sea moves in my ear.

One cry, and I stumble from bed, cow-heavy and floral
In my Victorian nightgown.
15    Your mouth opens clean as a cat's. The window square

Whitens and swallows its dull stars. And now you try
Your handful of notes;
The clear vowels rise like balloons.

11. All of the following are possible readings of the phrase "moth-breath / Flickers" (lines 10–11) EXCEPT

(A) breath so faint that it is barely noticeable

(B) breath like the flutter of a moth's wings

(C) breath as light as a moth landing

(D) breath that starts and stops as a flame flickers

(E) breath that will only last through the night

---

1  **midwife:** a person (typically a woman) trained to assist women in childbirth
2  **effacement:** the act of wiping out, erasing, or doing away with something; it also relates to childbirth as the effacement of the cervix that holds the yet unborn child inside of the womb

12. The contrast between stanza 4 (lines 10–12) and stanza 5 (lines 13–15) is primarily created by
    (A) juxtaposing floral imagery with domestic imagery
    (B) shifting between primary speakers
    (C) juxtaposing quiet imagery with noisy imagery
    (D) contradictory comparisons
    (E) shifting attitudes about the addressee

13. In the context of the poem as a whole, "cow-heavy" in line 13 could best be said to both represent and symbolize
    (A) the attitude of the new mother toward her own physical image and her rejection of the child
    (B) the animalistic nature of childbirth and the idea that the mother feels less than human
    (C) the new mother ready to nurse and the burdens felt by a new mother caring for her child
    (D) the midwife's brutal treatment of the mother and the mother now feeling closer to nature
    (E) the new mother's painful, aching body and her new role as caregiver for the child

14. Breaking the sentence "The window . . . dull stars" (lines 15–16) across two stanzas allows
    (A) the speaker to communicate how loudly the child cries while also already aging as time passes between stanzas
    (B) for imagery of both the child exploring the world and already aging as time passes across the stanzas
    (C) the author to shift attention away from the newborn and onto the passage of time across the stanzas
    (D) the image of the window to represent the newborn's mouth as an opening to the world and establish the passage of time across stanzas
    (E) the window to become a metaphor for how the newborn observes his or her new world

15. The last sentence of the poem in lines 16–18 relies on punctuation and line breaks to

(A) emphasize the speaker's attitude toward the child and the role of a new parent

(B) contrast the imagery related to both quiet and noise

(C) characterize the newborn as disruptive to the speaker's lifestyle

(D) contrast the pain and joy of a newborn's cries

(E) emphasize the simile in the last line and the attitude that it reveals

Question 16 is covered in Unit 4.

16. The statement "One cry, and I stumble from my bed" reveals which of the following about the speaker?

(A) She is alert and attentive as a mother.

(B) She focuses too much on herself.

(C) She cares too greatly and will not care for herself.

(D) She is haphazard and clumsy around the newborn.

(E) She fears the child will wake others.

Question 17 is covered in Unit 5.

17. As a metaphor, the "New statue" (line 4) reveals which of the following about the perspective of the speaker?

(A) The newborn is a physical work of art.

(B) The newborn is unreal and only represents what could be.

(C) The newborn cannot meet the expectations of others.

(D) The newborn cannot speak but can only be seen.

(E) The newborn represents something more than just a baby.

Questions 18 and 19 are covered in Unit 7.

18. The simile used in line 1 ("Love . . . gold watch") can be best interpreted as the speaker saying the addressee

    (A) is worth his or her weight in gold
    (B) is valuable and all parts working according to design
    (C) can only be compared to things with great material value
    (D) is like clockwork and valuable because the addressee works so well and so hard
    (E) can only be measured according to material wealth

19. In the context of the poem, the image in line 6 ("We stand round blankly as walls") reveals which of the following about the speaker and others in the poem?

    (A) They no longer care about anything.
    (B) They are incapable of describing what they see.
    (C) They remain silently reverential of the speaker.
    (D) They are unable to understand what they see.
    (E) They are in awe of what they see.

## Section II: Free Response

### Question 1: Poetry Analysis

In the poem on page 567, "Morning Song" by Sylvia Plath (published in 1960), the speaker addresses her newborn child. Read the poem carefully. Then, in a well-written essay, analyze how Plath uses poetic elements and techniques to develop the complex reactions of the speaker.

In your response you should do the following:

- Respond to the prompt with a thesis that presents a defensible interpretation.
- Select and use evidence to support your line of reasoning.
- Explain how the evidence supports your line of reasoning.
- Use appropriate grammar and punctuation in communicating your argument.

### Question 2: Prose Fiction Analysis

On pages 562–563 is an excerpt from the novel *Snow* written in 2004 by Nobel Prize-winning Turkish author Orhan Pamuk. In the passage, the narrator describes the experiences of the poet and journalist Ka as he walks through the city of Kars, where he had grown up and to which he has recently returned.

Read the passage carefully. Then, in a well-written essay, analyze how Pamuk uses literary elements and techniques to develop the complex relationship between Ka and the setting.

In your response you should do the following:

- Respond to the prompt with a thesis that presents a defensible interpretation.
- Select and use evidence to support your line of reasoning.
- Explain how the evidence supports your line of reasoning.
- Use appropriate grammar and punctuation in communicating your argument.

## Question 3: Literary Argument—Ambiguity

The Merriam-Webster dictionary defines *ambiguous* as "doubtful or uncertain, especially from obscurity or indistinctness."

Choose a work of fiction that leaves some aspect doubtful or uncertain in the end. Then, in a well-written essay, analyze how that ambiguity contributes to an interpretation of the work as a whole. Do not merely summarize the plot.

In your response you should do the following:

- Respond to the prompt with a thesis that presents a defensible interpretation.
- Provide evidence to support your line of reasoning.
- Explain how the evidence supports your line of reasoning.
- Use appropriate grammar and punctuation in communicating your argument.

# UNIT 9

# Interactions of Elements

[Longer Fiction and Drama III]

## Part 1: Character Development
## Part 2: Tension and Resolution
## Part 3: Multiple and Changing Perspectives
## Part 4: Writing Review II: Literary Analysis

---

**ENDURING UNDERSTANDINGS AND SKILLS:** Unit 9

## Part 1  Character Development

**Understand**

Characters in literature allow readers to study and explore a range of values, beliefs, assumptions, biases, and cultural norms represented by those characters. (CHR-1)

**Demonstrate**

Explain the function of a character changing or remaining unchanged. (1.B)

Explain how a character's own choices, actions, and speech reveal complexities in that character, and explain the function of those complexities. (1.E)

## Part 2  Tension and Resolution

**Understand**

The arrangement of the parts and sections of a text, the relationship of the parts to each other, and the sequence in which the text reveals information are all structural choices made by a writer that contribute to the reader's interpretation of a text. (STR-1)

**Demonstrate**

Explain the function of a significant event or related set of significant events in a plot. (3.E)

Explain the function of conflict in a text. (3.F)

## Part 3  Multiple and Changing Perspectives

**Understand**

A narrator's or speaker's perspective controls the details and emphases that affect how readers experience and interpret a text. (NAR-1)

**Demonstrate**

Identify and describe details, diction, or syntax in a text that reveal a narrator's or speaker's perspective. (4.C)

## Part 4  Writing Review II: Literary Analysis

**Understand**

Readers establish and communicate their interpretations of literature through arguments supported by textual evidence. (LAN-1)

**Demonstrate**

Develop a thesis statement that conveys a defensible claim about an interpretation of literature and that may establish a line of reasoning. (7.B)

Develop commentary that establishes and explains relationships among textual evidence, the line of reasoning, and the thesis. (7.C)

Select and use relevant and sufficient evidence to both develop and support a line of reasoning. (7.D)

**Source:** *AP® English Language and Composition Course and Exam Description*

# Unit 9 Overview

If you have read the anchor texts in previous units, you have met a wide variety of characters in a wide variety of dramatic situations.

You've met Daniel Barkley in "The Appropriation of Cultures" (Unit 1), whose challenge to play "Dixie" by frat boys with "puffy, pale faces" caused him to take a turn in his life. You've met the White woman in "On the Subway" (Unit 2) whose perspective about the Black youth riding the subway with her changes, introducing complexity to the poem. You've shared the stories of Nadia and Saeed in *Exit West* (Unit 3) as their competing values help them grow and develop during significant events. You met young Shan and his stubborn Grandma in "The Sanctuary Desolated" (Unit 4) and may still remain perplexed at the unseen forces at work in moving Grandma back to her home. You've suffered with the narrator in "Dulce et Decorum Est" and noted that his perspective changes at the end of the poem from the haunted soldier to the critic of patriotic poems. You saw multiple perspectives and chronology disruptions in *Frankenstein; or, The Modern Prometheus* (Unit 6) and the accumulating and colliding tension and conflicts between the Creature's creator and the abandoned Creature himself. You've watched as the Das family interacts with the settings they tour with Mr. Kapasi in "Interpreter of Maladies" (Unit 7). You've studied the rich and careful language of nuance and ambiguity as the speaker contemplates the nature of death in "An Autumn Sunset" (Unit 8).

Although they have been separated out for purposes of building understanding, all the elements of poetry and prose fiction—characters, structure, setting, events, narrators, and language—interact in all literary works, their interactions strengthening and supporting multiple possible interpretations. These interwoven relationships among literary elements bring nuance and complexity to the work. This final unit, more than others, will focus on the textures of the inconsistencies and complexities of literary works that help give them both depth and wide and lasting appeal among readers.

*"What I really lack is to be clear in my mind what I am to do, not what I am to know, except in so far as a certain knowledge must precede every action."*

In 1835, twenty-two-year-old Søren Kierkegaard wrote this line in his personal journal. Over the next twenty years until his death at age 42, the Danish Kierkegaard would become one of the most influential philosophers in the world, a key influence in how people think about "being," what it means to exist, and why we do what we do. These ideas became the root of a philosophy that continues to shape contemporary thought—Existentialism.

Existentialism is a philosophy concerned with questions about existence itself. Who am I? What do I do with life? What is the meaning of life? Is there a purpose? Is there a god or gods? What is death? How do I take responsibility for my actions?

*No Exit*, a one-act play by French philosopher and author Jean-Paul Sartre (pronounced saar-truh), originally published in French in 1943, explores these questions. The three main characters arrive one at a time to a room in the afterlife. The characters never met while they were alive.[1]

**Note:** *As it depicts the consequences in the afterlife of wrongdoing while alive, this play mentions such acts as infidelity, infanticide, and suicide.*

CHARACTERS:

- GARCIN
- ESTELLE
- INEZ
- A VALET

1   *SCENE*: A drawing-room[2] in Second Empire style.[3] A massive bronze ornament stands on the mantelpiece.

2   GARCIN: [*enters, accompanied by the ROOM-VALET, and glances around him*] Hm! So here we are?

3   VALET: Yes, Mr. Garcin.

4   GARCIN: And this is what it looks like?

5   VALET: Yes.

6   GARCIN: Second Empire furniture, I observe . . . Well, well, I dare say one gets used to it in time.

7   VALET: Some do. Some don't.

8   GARCIN: Are all the other rooms like this one?

---

1   A number of videos of performances of this play are available online. Since plays are meant to be seen and not just read, consider watching the play as you read along (and fill in the gaps in the excerpts). Pause along the way to make notes of events or developments.

2   **drawing room:** a room in a large private house in which guests can be received and entertained

3   **Second Empire style:** a highly ornamental style popular when Napoleon III ruled France (1848–1870), first as president and then as emperor

9    VALET: How could they be? We cater for all sorts: [Chinese] and Indians, for instance. What use would they have for a Second Empire chair?

10   GARCIN: And what use do you suppose I have for one? Do you know who I was? . . . Oh, well, it's no great matter. . . .

11   VALET: And you'll find that living in a Second Empire drawing-room has its points.

12   GARCIN: Really? . . . Yes, yes, I dare say. . . . [*He takes another look around.*] Still, I certainly didn't expect—this! You know what they tell us down there?[4]

13   VALET: What about?

14   GARCIN: About [*makes a sweeping gesture*] this—er—residence.

15   VALET: Really, sir, how could you believe such cock-and-bull stories?[5] Told by people who'd never set foot here. For, of course, if they had—

16   GARCIN: Quite so. [*Both laugh. Abruptly the laugh dies from GARCIN'S face.*] But, I say, where are the instruments of torture?

17   VALET: The what?

18   GARCIN: The racks and red-hot pincers and all the other paraphernalia?

19   VALET: Ah, you must have your little joke, sir!

20   GARCIN: My little joke? Oh, I see. No, I wasn't joking. [*A short silence. He strolls round the room.*] No mirrors, I notice. No windows. Only to be expected. And nothing breakable. [*Bursts out angrily.*] But, damn it all, they might have left me my toothbrush!

21   VALET: That's good! So you haven't yet got over your—what-do-you-call-it?—sense of human dignity? Excuse me smiling.

22   GARCIN: [*thumping ragefully the arm of an armchair*] I'll ask you to be more polite. I quite realize the position I'm in, but I won't tolerate . . .

23   VALET: Sorry, sir. No offense meant. But all our guests ask me the same questions. Silly questions, if you'll pardon me saying so. Where's the torture-chamber? That's the first thing they ask, all of them. They don't bother their heads about the bathroom requisites, that I can assure you. But after a bit, when they've got their nerve back, they start in about their toothbrushes and whatnot. Good heavens, Mr. Garcin, can't you use your brains? What, I ask you, would be the point of brushing your teeth?

24   GARCIN: [*more calmly*] Yes, of course you're right. [*He looks around again.*] And why should one want to see oneself in a looking-glass? But that bronze contraption on the mantelpiece, that's another story. I suppose there will be times when I stare my eyes out at it. Stare my eyes out—see what I mean? . . . All right, let's put our cards on the table. I assure you I'm quite conscious of my position. Shall I tell you what it feels like? A man's drowning, choking, sinking by inches, till only his eyes are just above water. And what does he see? A bronze atrocity by—what's the fellow's name?—Barbedienne.[6] A collector's piece. As in a nightmare. That's their idea, isn't it? . . . No, I suppose you're under orders not to answer questions; and I won't

---

4 **down there:** on Earth with living people
5 **cock-and-bull stories:** fanciful stories
6 **Ferdinand Barbedienne:** French metalworker who created bronze miniatures of statues

insist. But don't forget, my man, I've a good notion of what's coming to me, so don't you boast you've caught me off my guard. I'm facing the situation, facing it. [*He starts pacing the room again.*] So that's that; no toothbrush. And no bed, either. One never sleeps, I take it?

25 VALET: That's so.

26 GARCIN: Just as I expected. Why should one sleep? A sort of drowsiness steals on you, tickles you behind the ears, and you feel your eyes closing—but why sleep? You lie down on the sofa and—in a flash, sleep flies away. Miles and miles away. So you rub your eyes, get up, and it starts all over again.

27 VALET: Romantic, that's what you are.

28 GARCIN: Will you keep quiet, please! . . . I won't make a scene, I shan't be sorry for myself, I'll face the situation, as I said just now. Face it fairly and squarely. I won't have it springing at me from behind, before I've time to size it up. And you call that being "romantic"! . . . So it comes to this; one doesn't need rest. Why bother about sleep if one isn't sleepy? That stands to reason, doesn't it? Wait a minute, there's a snag somewhere; something disagreeable. Why, now, should it be disagreeable?. . . Ah, I see; it's life without a break.

29 VALET: What do you mean by that?

30 GARCIN: What do I mean? [*Eyes the VALET suspiciously.*] I thought as much. That's why there's something so beastly, so damn bad-mannered, in the way you stare at me. They're paralyzed.

31 VALET: What are you talking about?

32 GARCIN: Your eyelids. We move ours up and down. Blinking, we call it. It's like a small black shutter that clicks down and makes a break. Everything goes black; one's eyes are moistened. You can't imagine how restful, refreshing, it is. Four thousand little rests per hour. Four thousand little respites—just think! . . . So that's the idea. I'm to live without eyelids. Don't act the fool, you know what I mean. No eyelids, no sleep; it follows, doesn't it? I shall never sleep again. But then—how shall I endure my own company? Try to understand. You see, I'm fond of teasing, it's a second nature with me—and I'm used to teasing myself. Plaguing myself, if you prefer; I don't tease nicely. But I can't go on doing that without a break. Down there I had my nights. I slept. I always had good nights. By way of compensation, I suppose. And happy little dreams. There was a green field. Just an ordinary field. I used to stroll in it. . . . Is it daytime now?

33 VALET: Can't you see? The lights are on.

34 GARCIN: Ah yes, I've got it. It's your daytime. And outside?

35 VALET: Outside?

36 GARCIN: Damn it, you know what I mean. Beyond that wall.

37 VALET: There's a passage.

38 GARCIN: And at the end of the passage?

39 VALET: There's more rooms, more passages, and stairs.

40 GARCIN: And what lies beyond them?

41 VALET: That's all.

42    GARCIN: But surely you have a day off sometimes. Where do you go?

43    VALET: To my uncle's place. He's the head valet here. He has a room on the third floor.

44    GARC1N: I should have guessed as much. Where's the light-switch?

45    VALET: There isn't any.

46    GARCIN: What? Can't one turn off the light?

47    VALET: Oh, the management can cut off the current if they want to. But I can't remember their having done so on this floor. We have all the electricity we want.

48    GARCIN: So one has to live with one's eyes open all the time?

49    VALET: To live, did you say?

50    GARCIN: Don't let's quibble over words. With one's eyes open. Forever. Always broad daylight in my eyes—and in my head. [*Short silence.*] And suppose I took that contraption on the mantelpiece and dropped it on the lamp—wouldn't it go out?

51    VALET: You can't move it. It's too heavy.

52    GARC1N: [*seizing the bronze ornament and trying to lift it*] You're right. It's too heavy. [*A short silence follows.*]

53    VALET: Very well, sir, if you don't need me anymore, I'll be off.

54    GARCIN: What? You're going? [*The VALET goes up to the door.*] Wait. [*VALET looks round.*] That's a bell, isn't it? [*VALET nods.*] And if I ring, you're bound to come?

55    VALET: Well, yes, that's so—in a way. But you can never be sure about that bell. There's something wrong with the wiring, and it doesn't always work. [*GARCIN goes to the bell-push and presses the button. A bell purrs outside.*]

56    GARCIN: It's working all right.

57    VALET: [*looking surprised*] So it is. [*He, too, presses the button.*] But I shouldn't count on it too much if I were you. It's—capricious.[7] Well, I really must go now. [*GARCIN makes a gesture to detain him.*] Yes, sir?

58    GARCIN: No, never mind. [*He goes to the mantelpiece and picks up a paper-knife.[8]*] What's this?

59    VALET: Can't you see? An ordinary paper-knife.

60    GARCIN: Are there books here?

61    VALET: No.

62    GARCIN: Then what's the use of this? [*VALET shrugs his shoulders.*] Very well. You can go.

63    [*VALET goes out.*]

64    [*GARCIN is by himself. He goes to the bronze ornament and strokes it reflectively. He sits down; then gets up, goes to the bell-push, and presses the button. The bell remains silent. He tries two or three times, without success. Then he tries to open the door, also without success. He calls the*

---

**7 capricious:** given to sudden and unaccountable changes of mood or behavior
**8 paper-knife:** an object like a letter opener used to cut through the folds of uncut pages in books that were printed, folded, and assembled by hand

VALET several times, but gets no result. He beats the door with his fists, still calling. Suddenly he grows calm and sits down again. At the same moment the door opens and INEZ enters, followed by the VALET.]

65 VALET: Did you call, sir?

66 GARCIN: [on the point of answering "Yes"—but then his eyes fall on INEZ] No.

67 VALET: [turning to INEZ] This is your room, madam. [INEZ says nothing.] If there's any information you require—? [INEZ still keeps silent, and the VALET looks slightly huffed.] Most of our guests have quite a lot to ask me. But I won't insist. Anyhow, as regards the toothbrush, and the electric bell, and that thing on the mantel shelf, this gentleman can tell you anything you want to know as well as I could. We've had a little chat, him and me. [VALET goes out.]

68 [GARCIN refrains from looking at INEZ, who is inspecting the room. Abruptly she turns to GARCIN.]

69 INEZ: Where's Florence? [GARCIN does not reply.] Didn't you hear? I asked you about Florence. Where is she?

70 GARCIN: I haven't an idea.

71 INEZ: Ah, that's the way it works, is it? Torture by separation. Well, as far as I'm concerned, you won't get anywhere. Florence was a tiresome little fool, and I shan't miss her in the least.

72 GARCIN: I beg your pardon. Who do you suppose I am?

73 INEZ: You? Why, the torturer, of course.

74 GARCIN: [looks startled, then bursts out laughing] Well, that's a good one! Too comic for words. I, the torturer! So you came in, had a look at me, and thought I was—er—one of the staff. Of course, it's that silly fellow's fault; he should have introduced us. A torturer indeed! I'm Joseph Garcin, journalist and man of letters by profession. And as we're both in the same boat, so to speak, might I ask you, Mrs.—?

75 INEZ: [testily]: Not "Mrs." I'm unmarried.

76 GARCIN: Right. That's a start, anyway. Well, now that we've broken the ice, do you really think I look like a torturer? And, by the way, how does one recognize torturers when one sees them? Evidently you've ideas on the subject.

77 INEZ: They look frightened.

78 GARCIN: Frightened! But how ridiculous! Of whom should they be frightened? Of their victims?

79 INEZ: Laugh away, but I know what I'm talking about. I've often watched my face in the glass.[9]

80 GARCIN: In the glass? [He looks around him.] How beastly of them! They've removed everything in the least resembling a glass. [Short silence.] Anyhow, I can assure you I'm not frightened. Not that I take my position lightly; I realize its gravity only too well. But I'm not afraid.

---

9 glass: mirror

81     INEZ: [*shrugging her shoulders*] That's your affair. [*Silence.*] Must you be here all the time, or do you take a stroll outside, now and then?

82     GARCIN: The door's locked.

83     INEZ: Oh! . . . That's too bad.

84     GARCIN: I can quite understand that it bores you having me here. And I, too—well, quite frankly, I'd rather be alone. I want to think things out, you know; to set my life in order, and one does that better by oneself. But I'm sure we'll manage to pull along together somehow. I'm no talker, I don't move much; in fact I'm a peaceful sort of fellow. Only, if I may venture on a suggestion, we should make a point of being extremely courteous to each other. That will ease the situation for us both.

85     INEZ: I'm not polite.

86     GARCIN: Then I must be polite for two. [*A longish silence. GARCIN is sitting on a sofa, while INEZ paces up and down the room.*]

87     INEZ: [*fixing her eyes on him*]: Your mouth!

88     GARCIN: [*as if waking from a dream*] I beg your pardon.

89     INEZ: Can't you keep your mouth still? You keep twisting it about all the time. It's grotesque.

90     GARCIN: So sorry. I wasn't aware of it.

91     INEZ: That's just what I reproach you with. [*GARCIN'S mouth twitches.*] There you are! You talk about politeness, and you don't even try to control your face. Remember you're not alone; you've no right to inflict the sight of your fear on me.

92     GARCIN: [*getting up and going towards her*] How about you? Aren't you afraid?

93     INEZ: What would be the use? There was some point in being afraid before; while one still had hope.

94     GARCIN: [*in a low voice*] There's no more hope—but it's still "before." We haven't yet begun to suffer.

95     INEZ: That's so. [*A short silence.*] Well? What's going to happen?

96     GARCIN: I don't know. I'm waiting.

97     [*Silence again. GARCIN sits down and INEZ resumes her pacing up and down the room. GARCIN'S mouth twitches; after a glance at INEZ he buries his face in his hands. Enter ESTELLE with the VALET. ESTELLE looks at GARCIN, whose face is still hidden by his hands.*].

98     ESTELLE: [*to GARCIN*] No. Don't look up. I know what you're hiding with your hands. I know you've no face left. [*GARCIN removes his hands.*] What! [*A short pause, then, in a tone of surprise*] But I don't know you!

99     GARCIN: I'm not the torturer, madam.

100    ESTELLE. I never thought you were. I—I thought someone was trying to play a rather nasty trick on me. [*To the VALET*] Is anyone else coming?

101    VALET: No madam. No one else is coming.

102    ESTELLE: Oh! Then we're to stay by ourselves, the three of us, this gentleman, this lady, and myself. [*She starts laughing.*]

. . . . .

111    ESTELLE: . . . Well, as we're to live together, I suppose we'd better introduce ourselves. My name's Rigault. Estelle Rigault. [*GARCIN bows and is going to announce his name, but INEZ steps in front of him.*]

112    INEZ: And I'm Inez Serrano. Very pleased to meet you.

113    GARCIN: [*bowing again*] Joseph Garcin.

114    VALET: Do you require me any longer?

115    ESTELLE: No, you can go. I'll ring when I want you. [*Exit VALET, with polite bows to everyone.*]

116    INEZ: You're very pretty. I wish we'd had some flowers to welcome you with.

117    ESTELLE: Flowers? Yes, I loved flowers. Only they'd fade so quickly here, wouldn't they? It's so stuffy. Oh, well, the great thing is to keep as cheerful as we can, don't you agree? Of course, you, too, are—

118    INEZ: Yes. Last week. What about you?

119    ESTELLE: I'm—quite recent. Yesterday. As a matter of fact, the ceremony's not quite over.

*At this point, Estelle begins to describe what she sees happening in real time at her own funeral. She tells the others she died of pneumonia and keeps describing the funeral and her husband's grief, though she notes that her sister Olga could try harder to get a few more tears out. Inez tells the others she died by the gas stove; Garcin reports he got 12 bullets through his chest. He reports that he left his wife "down there," and, like Estelle, he describes what he sees in real time—his wife doesn't yet know he's dead and she comes to the barracks every day looking for him. He expresses annoyance at her "big tragic eyes" and says that she got on his nerves.*

*They all continue to talk about what they see back among the living. Inez sees her room being sealed up. Garcin sees the men he's worked with at the newspaper office smoking cigars. Estelle said she expected to be put with old friends, and Inez asks if she means the man with the hole in the middle of his face. Estelle recalls that he danced the tango divinely.*

*The three try to figure out why they have been put together in this room. They decide it must have been deliberate, and Inez presses them to tell the truth about what they've done to land them in hell. Estelle is convinced it must have been some mistake. She explains that she married an older man but then two years ago met a younger man and fell in love. She refused to run away with him, got pneumonia, and died. Garcin goes next and explains that all he did was stand for his pacifist principles by refusing to fight in the war, for which he was shot. Inez presses him about his wife, and he says that he rescued her from the gutter.*

197    INEZ: Yes, I see. [*A pause.*] Look here! What's the point of play-acting, trying to throw dust in each other's eyes? We're all tarred with the same brush.

198    ESTELLE: [*indignantly*] How dare you!

199    INEZ: Yes, we are criminals—murderers—all three of us. We're in hell, my pets; they never make mistakes, and people aren't damned for nothing.

200   ESTELLE: Stop! For heaven's sake—

201   INEZ: In hell! Damned souls—that's us, all three!

202   ESTELLE: Keep quiet! I forbid you to use such disgusting words.

203   INEZ: A damned soul—that's you, my little plaster saint. And ditto our friend there, the noble pacifist. We've had our hour of pleasure, haven't we? There have been people who burned their lives out for our sakes—and we chuckled over it. So now we have to pay the reckoning.

204   GARCIN: [*raising his fist*] Will you keep your mouth shut, damn it!

205   INEZ: [*confronting him fearlessly, but with a look of vast surprise*] Well, well! [*A pause.*] Ah, I understand now. I know why they've put us three together.

206   GARCIN: I advise you to—to think twice before you say any more.

207   INEZ: Wait! You'll see how simple it is. Childishly simple. Obviously there aren't any physical torments—you agree, don't you? And yet we're in hell. And no one else will come here. We'll stay in this room together, the three of us, for ever and ever. . . . In short, there's someone absent here, the official torturer.

208   GARCIN: [*sotto voce*[10]] I'd noticed that.

209   INEZ: It's obvious what they're after—an economy of man-power—or devil-power, if you prefer. The same idea as in the cafeteria, where customers serve themselves.

210   ESTELLE: Whatever do you mean?

211   INEZ: I mean that each of us will act as torturer of the two others. [*There is a short silence while they digest this information.*]

212   GARCIN: [*gently*] No, I shall never be your torturer. I wish neither of you any harm, and I've no concern with you. None at all. So the solution's easy enough; each of us stays put in his or her corner and takes no notice of the others. You here, you here, and I there. Like soldiers at our posts. Also, we mustn't speak. Not one word. That won't be difficult; each of us has plenty of material for self-communings. I think I could stay ten thousand years with only my thoughts for company.

213   ESTELLE: Have I got to keep silent, too?

214   GARCIN: Yes. And that way we—we'll work out our salvation. Looking into ourselves, never raising our heads. Agreed?

215   INEZ: Agreed.

216   ESTELLE [*after some hesitation*]: I agree.

217   GARCIN: Then—goodbye. [*He goes to his sofa and buries his head in his hands. There is a long silence; then INEZ begins singing to herself*]

Here Inez sings a song about public executions.

219   [*Meanwhile ESTELLE has been plying her powderpuff and lipstick. She looks round for a mirror, fumbles in her bag, then turns towards GARCIN.*]

220   ESTELLE: Excuse me, have you a glass? [*GARCIN does not answer*]. Any sort of glass, a pocket-mirror will do. [*GARCIN remains silent.*] Even if you

---

**10** *sotto voce:* in a quiet voice, as if not to be overheard

won't speak to me, you might lend me a glass. [*His head still buried in his hands, GARCIN ignores her.*]

221 INEZ: [*eagerly*] Don't worry. I've a glass in my bag. [*She opens her bag. Angrily.*] It's gone! They must have taken it from me at the entrance.

222 ESTELLE: How tiresome! [*A short silence. ESTELLE shuts her eyes and sways, as if about to faint. Inez runs forward and holds her up.*]

223 INEZ: What's the matter?

224 ESTELLE: [*opens her eyes and smiles*] I feel so queer. [*She pats herself*] Don't you ever get taken that way? When I can't see myself I begin to wonder if I really and truly exist. I pat myself just to make sure, but it doesn't help much.

225 INEZ: You're lucky. I'm always conscious of myself—in my mind. Painfully conscious.

226 ESTELLE: Ah yes, in your mind. But everything that goes on in one's head is so vague, isn't it? It makes one want to sleep. [*She is silent for a while.*] I've six big mirrors in my bedroom. There they are. I can see them. But they don't see me. They're reflecting the carpet, the settee,[11] the window—but how empty it is, a glass in which I'm absent! When I talked to people I always made sure there was one nearby in which I could see myself. I watched myself talking. And somehow it kept me alert, seeing myself as the others saw me. . . Oh dear! My lipstick! I'm sure I've put it on all crooked. No, I can't do without a looking-glass for ever and ever. I simply can't.

227 INEZ: Suppose I try to be your glass? Come and pay me a visit, dear. Here's a place for you on my sofa.

228 ESTELLE: But—[*Points to GARCIN.*]

229 INEZ: Oh, he doesn't count.

230 ESTELLE. But we're going to—to hurt each other. You said it yourself.

231 INEZ: Do I look as if I wanted to hurt you?

232 ESTELLE: One never can tell.

233 INEZ: Much more likely you'll hurt me. Still, what does it matter? If I've got to suffer, it may as well be at your hands, your pretty hands. Sit down. Come closer. Closer. Look into my eyes. What do you see?

234 ESTELLE: Oh, I'm there! But so tiny I can't see myself properly.

235 INEZ: But I can. Every inch of you. Now ask me questions. I'll be as candid as any looking glass. [*ESTELLE seems rather embarrassed and turns to GARCIN, as if appealing to him for help.*]

236 ESTELLE: Please, Mr. Garcin. Sure our chatter isn't boring you? [*GARCIN makes no reply.*]

237 INEZ: Don't worry about him. As I said, he doesn't count. We're by ourselves. . . . Ask away.

238 ESTELLE: Are my lips all right?

239 INEZ: Show! No, they're a bit smudgy.

---

11 **settee:** sofa

240 ESTELLE: I thought as much. Luckily [*throws a quick glance at GARCIN*] no one's seen me. I'll try again.

241 INEZ: That's better. No. Follow the line of your lips. Wait! I'll guide your hand. There. That's quite good.

242 ESTELLE: As good as when I came in?

243 INEZ: Far better. Crueler. Your mouth looks quite diabolical that way.

244 ESTELLE: Good gracious! And you say you like it! How maddening, not being able to see for myself! You're quite sure, Miss Serrano, that it's all right now?

245 INEZ: Won't you call me Inez?

246 ESTELLE: Are you sure it looks all right?

247 INEZ: You're lovely, Estelle.

248 ESTELLE: But how can I rely upon your taste? Is it the same as my taste? Oh, how sickening it all is, enough to drive one crazy!

249 INEZ: I have your taste, my dear, because I like you so much. Look at me. No, straight. Now smile. I'm not so ugly, either. Am I not nicer than your glass?

250 ESTELLE: Oh, I don't know. You scare me rather. My reflection in the glass never did that; of course, I knew it so well. Like something I had tamed . . . I'm going to smile, and my smile will sink down into your pupils, and heaven knows what it will become!

251 INEZ: And why shouldn't you "tame" me? [*The women gaze at each other, ESTELLE with a sort of fearful fascination.*] Listen! I want you to call me Inez. We must be great friends.

252 ESTELLE: I don't make friends with women very easily.

253 INEZ: Not with postal clerks, you mean? Hullo, what's that—that nasty red spot at the bottom of your cheek? A pimple?

254 ESTELLE: A pimple? Oh, how simply foul! Where!

255 INEZ: There. . . . You know the way they catch larks[12]—with a mirror? I'm your lark-mirror, my dear, and you can't escape me. . . . There isn't any pimple, not a trace of one. So what about it? Suppose the mirror started telling lies? Or suppose I covered my eyes—as he is doing—and refused to look at you, all that loveliness of yours would be wasted on the desert air. No, don't be afraid, I can't help looking at you. I shan't turn my eyes away. And I'll be nice to you, ever so nice. Only you must be nice to me, too. [*A short silence.*]

256 ESTELLE: Are you really—attracted by me?

257 INEZ: Very much indeed. [*Another short silence.*]

258 ESTELLE: [*indicating GARCIN by a slight movement of her head*] But I wish he'd notice me, too.

259 INEZ: Of course! Because he's a Man! [*To GARCIN*] You've won. [*GARCIN says nothing.*] But look at her, damn it! [*Still no reply from GARCIN*] Don't pretend. You haven't missed a word of what we've said.

---

**12 larks:** small ground-dwelling songbirds; they were often hunted by attracting them with reflected light from a mirror.

260 GARCIN: Quite so; not a word. I stuck my fingers in my ears, but your voices thudded in my brain. Silly chatter. Now will you leave me in peace, you two? I'm not interested in you.

261 INEZ: Not in me, perhaps—but how about this child? Aren't you interested in her? Oh, I saw through your game; you got on your high horse just to impress her.

262 GARCIN: I asked you to leave me in peace. There's someone talking about me in the newspaper office and I want to listen. And, if it'll make you any happier, let me tell you that I've no use for the "child," as you call her.

263 ESTELLE: Thanks.

264 GARCIN: Oh, I didn't mean it rudely.

265 ESTELLE: You cad! [*They confront each other in silence for some moments.*]

266 GARCIN: So that's that. [*Pause.*] You know I begged you not to speak.

267 ESTELLE: It's her fault; she started. I didn't ask anything of her and she came and offered me her—her glass.

268 INEZ: So you say. But all the time you were making up to him, trying every trick to catch his attention.

269 ESTELLE: Well, why shouldn't I?

270 GARCIN: You're crazy, both of you. Don't you see where this is leading us? For pity's sake, keep your mouths shut. [*Pause.*] Now let's all sit down again quite quietly; we'll look at the floor and each must try to forget the others are there.

271 [*A longish silence. GARCIN sits down. The women return hesitantly to their places. Suddenly INEZ swings round on him.*]

272 INEZ: To forget about the others? How utterly absurd! I feel you there, in every pore. Your silence clamors in my ears. You can nail up your mouth, cut your tongue out—but you can't prevent your being there. Can you stop your thoughts? I hear them ticking away like a clock, tick-tock, tick-tock, and I'm certain you hear mine. It's all very well skulking on your sofa, but you're everywhere, and every sound comes to me soiled, because you've intercepted it on its way. Why, you've even stolen my face; you know it and I don't! And what about her, about Estelle? You've stolen her from me, too; if she and I were alone do you suppose she'd treat me as she does? No, take your hands from your face, I won't leave you in peace— that would suit your book too well. You'd go on sitting there, in a sort of trance, like a yogi, and even if I didn't see her I'd feel it in my bones—that she was making every sound, even the rustle of her dress, for your benefit, throwing you smiles you didn't see. . . . Well, I won't stand for that, I prefer to choose my hell; I prefer to look you in the eyes and fight it out face to face.

273 GARCIN: Have it your own way. I suppose we were bound to come to this; they knew what they were about, and we're easy game. If they'd put me in a room with men—men can keep their mouths shut. But it's no use wanting the impossible. [*He goes to ESTELLE and lightly fondles her neck.*] So I attract you, little girl? It seems you were making eyes at me?

274 ESTELLE: Don't touch me.

275 GARCIN: Why not? We might, anyhow, be natural.... Do you know, I used to be mad about women? And some were fond of me. So we may as well stop posing, we've nothing to lose. Why trouble about politeness, and decorum, and the rest of it? We're between ourselves. And presently we shall be naked as—as newborn babes.

276 ESTELLE: Oh, let me be!

277 GARCIN: As newborn babes. Well, I'd warned you, anyhow. I asked so little of you, nothing but peace and a little silence. I'd put my fingers in my ears. Gomez [back among the living] was spouting away as usual, standing in the center of the room, with all the pressmen listening. In their shirt-sleeves. I tried to hear, but it wasn't too easy. Things on earth move so quickly, you know. Couldn't you have held your tongues? Now it's over, he's stopped talking, and what he thinks of me has gone back into his head. Well, we've got to see it through somehow.... Naked as we were born. So much the better; I want to know whom I have to deal with.

278 INEZ: You know already. There's nothing more to learn.

279 GARCIN: You're wrong. So long as each of us hasn't made a clean breast of it—why they've damned him or her—we know nothing. Nothing that counts. You, young lady, you shall begin. Why? Tell us why. If you are frank, if we bring our specters into the open, it may save us from disaster. So— out with it! Why?

280 ESTELE: I tell you I haven't a notion. They wouldn't tell me why.

281 GARCIN: That's so. They wouldn't tell me, either. But I've a pretty good idea.... Perhaps you're shy of speaking first? Right. I'll lead off. [A short silence.] I'm not a very estimable person.

282 INEZ: No need to tell us that. We know you were a deserter.

Here Garcin explains that he treated his wife badly for five years, coming home "blind drunk, stinking of wine and women." He says his wife admired him too much. He goes on to say that he brought a girl to stay in their house and he stayed with the girl while his wife slept upstairs. She even brought them coffee in the morning.

Next Inez tells her story. She had an affair with a woman, Florence, who was married to her cousin. She left him to be with Inez, and then her husband was killed when a tram hit him.

306 INEZ: Then that tram did its job. I used to remind her every day: "Yes, my pet, we killed him between us." [A pause.] I'm rather cruel, really.

307 GARCIN: So am I.

308 INEZ: No, you're not cruel. It's something else.

309 GARCIN: What?

310 INEZ: I'll tell you later. When I say I'm cruel, I mean I can't get on without making people suffer. Like a live coal. A live coal in others' hearts. When I'm alone I flicker out. For six months I flamed away in her heart, till there was nothing but a cinder. One night she got up and turned on the gas while I was asleep. Then she crept back into bed. So now you know.

*Estelle is next to tell her story. At first she skirts the real story but finally admits she got pregnant by Roger, the man she fell in love with, who wanted her to have the baby even though she didn't want to. They went to Switzerland for five months and after the baby daughter was born, Estelle drowned her by throwing her off a balcony into a lake. She returned to Paris, and Roger shot and killed himself.*

*Inez looks back on the people "down there" and sees that her apartment is being rented and a man and a woman say that it's noon and the sun is shining. However, Inez can see only black and realizes she has had her last contact with earth. Garcin tries to offer some comforting words, but Inez rejects his attempts.*

*Estelle can still see what's going on. She sees her sister Olga taking a young man, Peter, to a cabaret. A love interest after Estelle returned from Switzerland, Peter used to call her "my glancing stream, my crystal girl." Estelle makes fun of Olga's clumsiness on the dance floor. Then she realizes that Olga is telling Peter about Switzerland and the baby, and Estelle recognizes "the crystal's shattered into bits." She says she'd like to be back on earth and dance again, but the music gets soft and finally disappears, and her ties, like those of Inez, are cut off.*

*Estelle turns to Garcin, asking him to pay attention to her and take her in his arms. Garcin, though, is distracted by what he hears on earth about himself. He then asks Estelle to trust him.*

448  GARCIN: They shot me.

449  ESTELLE: I know. Because you refused to fight. Well, why shouldn't you?

450  GARCIN: I—I didn't exactly refuse. [*In a far-away voice*] [Here he is listening in on "down there."] I must say he talks well, he makes out a good case against me, but he never says what I should have done instead. Should I have gone to the general and said: "General, I decline to fight"? A mug's game; they'd have promptly locked me up. But I wanted to show my colors, my true colors, do you understand? I wasn't going to be silenced. [*To ESTELLE*] So I—I took the train. . . . They caught me at the frontier.

451  ESTELLE: Where were you trying to go?

452  GARCIN: To Mexico. I meant to launch a pacifist newspaper down there. [*A short silence.*] Well, why don't you speak?

453  ESTELLE: What could I say? You acted quite rightly, as you didn't want to fight. [*GARCIN makes a fretful gesture.*] But, darling, how on earth can I guess what you want me to answer?

454  INEZ: Can't you guess? Well, I can. He wants you to tell him that he bolted like a lion. For "bolt" he did, and that's what's biting him.

455  GARCIN: "Bolted," "went away"—we won't quarrel over words.

456  ESTELLE: But you had to run away. If you'd stayed they'd have sent you to jail, wouldn't they?

457  GARCIN: Of course. [*A pause.*] Well, Estelle, am I a coward?

458  ESTELLE: How can I say? Don't be so unreasonable, darling. I can't put myself in your skin. You must decide that for yourself.

459  GARCIN: [*wearily*] I can't decide.

460   ESTELLE: Anyhow, you must remember. You must have had reasons for acting as you did.

461   GARCIN: I had.

462   ESTELLE: Well?

463   GARCIN: But were they the real reasons?

464   ESTELLE: You've a twisted mind, that's your trouble. Plaguing yourself over such trifles!

465   GARCIN: I'd thought it all out, and I wanted to make a stand. But was that my real motive?

466   INEZ: Exactly. That's the question. Was that your real motive? No doubt you argued it out with yourself, you weighed the pros and cons, you found good reasons for what you did. But fear and hatred and all the dirty *little* instincts one keeps dark—they're motives too. So carry on, Mr. Garcin, and try to be honest with yourself—for once.

467   GARCIN: Do I need you to tell me that? Day and night I paced my cell, from the window to the door, from the door to the window. I pried into my heart, I sleuthed myself like a detective. By the end of it I felt as if I'd given my whole life to introspection. But always I harked back to the one thing certain—that I had acted as I did, I'd taken that train to the frontier. But why? Why? Finally I thought: My death will settle it. If I face death courageously, I'll prove I am no coward.

468   INEZ: And how did you face death?

469   GARCIN: Miserably. Rottenly. [*INEZ laughs.*] Oh, it was only a physical lapse—that might happen to anyone; I'm not ashamed of it. Only everything's been left in suspense forever. [*To ESTELLE*] Come here, Estelle. Look at me. I want to feel someone looking at me while they're talking about me on earth. . . . I like green eyes.

470   INEZ: Green eyes! Just hark to him! And you, Estelle, do you like cowards?

471   ESTELLE: If you knew how little I care! Coward or hero, it's all one—provided he kisses well.

472   GARCIN: There they are, slumped in their chairs, sucking at their cigars. Bored they look. Half-asleep. They're thinking: "Garcin's a coward." But only vaguely, dreamily. One's got to think of something. "That chap Garcin was a coward." That's what they've decided, those dear friends of mine. In six months' time they'll be saying: "Cowardly as that skunk Garcin." You're lucky, you two; no one on earth is giving you another thought. But I—I'm long in dying.

473   INEZ: What about your wife, Garcin?

474   GARCIN: Oh, didn't I tell you? She's dead.

475   INEZ: Dead?

476   GARCIN: Yes, she died just now. About two months ago.

477   INEZ: Of grief?

478   GARCIN: What else should she die of? So all is for the best, you see; the war's over, my wife's dead, and I've carved out my place in history. [*He gives a choking sob and passes his hand over his face. ESTELLE catches his arm.*]

479 ESTELLE: My poor darling! Look at me. Please look. Touch me. Touch me. [*She takes his hand and puts it on her neck.*] There! Keep your hand there. [*GARCIN makes a fretful movement.*] No, don't move. Why trouble what those men are thinking? They'll die off one by one. Forget them. There's only me, now.

480 GARCIN: But they won't forget me, not they! They'll die, but others will come after them to carry on the legend. I've left my fate in their hands.

481 ESTELLE: You think too much, that's your trouble.

482 GARCIN: What else is there to do now? I was a man of action once. . . . Oh, if only I could be with them again, for just one day—I'd fling their lie in their teeth. But I'm locked out; they're passing judgment on my life without troubling about me, and they're right, because I'm dead. Dead and done with. [*Laughs.*] A back number. [*A short pause.*]

483 ESTELLE: [*gently*] Garcin.

484 GARCIN: Still there? Now listen! I want you to do me a service. No, don't shrink away. I know it must seem strange to you, having someone asking you for help; you're not used to that. But if you'll make the effort, if you'll only will it hard enough, I dare say we can really love each other. Look at it this way. A thousand of them are proclaiming I'm a coward; but what do numbers matter? If there's someone, just one person, to say quite positively I did not run away, that I'm not the sort who runs away, that I'm brave and decent and the rest of it—well, that one person's faith would save me. Will you have that faith in me? Then I shall love you and cherish you forever. Estelle—will you?

485 ESTELLE: [*laughing*] Oh, you dear silly man, do you think I could love a coward?

486 GARCIN: But just now you said—

487 ESTELLE: I was only teasing you. I like men, my dear, who're real men, with tough skin and strong hands. You haven't a coward's chin, or a coward's mouth, or a coward's voice, or a coward's hair. And it's for your mouth, your hair, your voice, I love you.

488 GARCIN: Do you mean this? Really mean it?

489 ESTELLE: Shall I swear it?

490 GARCIN: Then I snap my fingers at them all, those below and those in here. Estelle, we shall climb out of hell. [*INEZ gives a shrill laugh. He breaks off and stares at her.*] What's that?

491 INEZ: [*still laughing*] But she doesn't mean a word of what she says. How can you be such a simpleton? "Estelle, am I a coward?" As if she cared a damn either way.

492 ESTELLE: Inez, how dare you? [*To GARCIN*] Don't listen to her. If you want me to have faith in you, you must begin by trusting me.

493 INEZ: That's right! That's right! Trust away! She wants a man—that far you can trust her—she wants a man's arm 'round her waist, a man's smell, a man's eyes glowing with desire. And that's all she wants. She'd assure you you were God Almighty if she thought it would give you pleasure.

494 GARCIN: Estelle, is this true? Answer me. Is it true?

495 ESTELLE: What do you expect me to say? Don't you realize how maddening it is to have to answer questions one can't make head or tail of? [*She stamps her foot.*] You do make things difficult . . . Anyhow, I'd love you just the same, even if you were a coward. Isn't that enough? [*A short pause.*]

496 GARCIN: [*to the two women*] You disgust me, both of you. [*He goes towards the door.*]

497 ESTELLE: What are you up to?

498 GARCIN: I'm going.

499 INEZ: [*in a quiet voice, as if not to be overheard.*] You won't get far. The door is locked.

500 GARCIN: I'll make them open it. [*He presses the bell-push. The bell does not ring.*]

501 ESTELLE: Please! Please!

502 INEZ: [*to ESTELLE*] Don't worry, my pet. The bell doesn't work.

503 GARCIN: I tell you they shall open. [*Drums on the door.*] I can't endure it any longer, I'm through with you both. [*ESTELLE runs to him; he pushes her away.*] Go away. You're even fouler than she. I won't let myself get bogged in your eyes. You're soft and slimy. Ugh! [*Bangs on the door again.*] Like an octopus. Like a quagmire.

504 ESTELLE: I beg you, oh, I beg you not to leave me. I'll promise not to speak again, I won't trouble you in any way—but don't go. I daren't be left alone with Inez, now she's shown her claws.

505 GARCIN: Look after yourself. I never asked you to come here.

506 ESTELLE: Oh, how mean you are! Yes, it's quite true you're a coward.

507 INEZ: [*going up to ESTELLE*] Well, my little sparrow fallen from the nest, I hope you're satisfied now. You spat in my face—playing up to him, of course—and we had a tiff on his account. But he's going, and a good riddance it will be. We two women will have the place to ourselves.

508 ESTELLE: You won't gain anything. If that door opens, I'm going, too.

509 INEZ: Where?

510 ESTELLE: I don't care where. As far from you as I can. [*GARCIN has been drumming on the door while they talk.*]

511 GARCIN: Open the door! Open, blast you! I'll endure anything, your red-hot tongs and molten lead, your racks and prongs and garrotes[13]—all your fiendish gadgets, everything that burns and flays and tears—I'll put up with any torture you impose. Anything, anything would be better than this agony of mind, this creeping pain that gnaws and fumbles and caresses one and never hurts quite enough. [*He grips the door-knob and rattles it.*] Now will you open? [*The door flies open with a jerk, and he just avoids falling.*] Ah! [*A long silence.*]

512 INEZ: Well, Garcin? You're free to go.

513 GARCIN: [*meditatively*] Now I wonder why that door opened.

514 INEZ: What are you waiting for? Hurry up and go.

---

**13 garrotes:** wire cords used to strangle someone

515   GARCIN: I shall not go.

516   INEZ: And you, Estelle? [*ESTELLE does not move. INEZ bursts out laughing.*] So what? Which shall it be? Which of the three of us will leave? The barrier's down, why are we waiting? . . . But what a situation! It's a scream! We're—inseparables! [*ESTELLE springs at her from behind.*]

517   ESTELLE: Inseparables? Garcin, come and lend a hand. Quickly. We'll push her out and slam the door on her. That'll teach her a lesson.

518   INEZ: [*struggling with ESTELLE*] Estelle! I beg you, let me stay. I won't go, I won't go! Not into the passage.

519   GARCIN: Let go of her.

520   ESTELLE: You're crazy. She hates you.

521   GARCIN: It's because of her I'm staying here. [*ESTELLE releases INEZ and stares dumbfoundedly at GARCIN.*]

522   INEZ: Because of me? [*Pause.*] All right, shut the door. It's ten times hotter here since it opened. [*GARCIN goes to the door and shuts it.*] Because of me, you said?

523   GARCIN: Yes. You, anyhow, know what it means to be a coward.

524   INEZ: Yes, I know.

525   GARCIN: And you know what wickedness is, and shame, and fear. There were days when you peered into yourself, into the secret places of your heart, and what you saw there made you faint with horror. And then, next day, you didn't know what to make of it, you couldn't interpret the horror you had glimpsed the day before. Yes, you know what evil costs. And when you say I'm a coward, you know from experience what that means. Is that so?

526   INEZ: Yes.

527   GARCIN: So it's you whom I have to convince; you are of my kind. Did you suppose I meant to go? No, I couldn't leave you here, gloating over my defeat, with all those thoughts about me running in your head.

528.   INEZ: Do you really wish to convince me?

529   GARCIN: That's the one and only thing I wish for now. I can't hear them any longer, you know. Probably that means they're through with me. For good and all. The curtain's down, nothing of me is left on earth—not even the name of coward. So, Inez, we're alone. Only you two remain to give a thought to me. She—she doesn't count. It's you who matter; you who hate me. If you'll have faith in me I'm saved.

530   INEZ: It won't be easy. Have a look at me. I'm a hard-headed woman.

531   GARCIN: I'll give you all the time that's needed.

532   INEZ: Yes, we've lots of time in hand. All time.

533   GARCIN: [*putting his hands on her shoulders*] Listen! Each man has an aim in life, a leading motive; that's so, isn't it? Well, I didn't give a damn for wealth, or for love. I aimed at being a real man. A tough, as they say. I staked everything on the same horse. . . . Can one possibly be a coward when one's deliberately courted danger at every turn? And can one judge a life by a single action?

534 INEZ: Why not? For thirty years you dreamt you were a hero, and condoned a thousand petty lapses—because a hero, of course, can do no wrong. An easy method, obviously. Then a day came when you were up against it, the red light of real danger—and you took the train to Mexico.

535 GARCIN: I "dreamt," you say. It was no dream. When I chose the hardest path, I made my choice deliberately. A man is what he wills himself to be.

536 INEZ: Prove it. Prove it was no dream. It's what one does, and nothing else, that shows the stuff one's made of.

537 GARCIN: I died too soon. I wasn't allowed time to—to do my deeds.

538 INEZ: One always dies too soon—or too late. And yet one's whole life is complete at that moment, with a line drawn neatly under it, ready for the summing up. You are—your life, and nothing else.

539 GARCIN: What a poisonous woman you are! With an answer for everything.

540 INEZ: Now then! Don't lose heart. It shouldn't be so hard, convincing me. Pull yourself together, man, rake up some arguments. [*GARCIN shrugs his shoulders.*] Ah, wasn't I right when I said you were vulnerable? Now you're going to pay the price, and what a price! You're a coward, Garcin, because I wish it. I wish it—do you hear?—I wish it. And yet, just look at me, see how weak I am, a mere breath on the air, a gaze observing you, a formless thought that thinks you. [*He walks towards her, opening his hands.*] Ah, they're open now, those big hands, those coarse, man's hands! But what do you hope to do? You can't throttle thoughts with hands. So you've no choice, you must convince me, and you're at my mercy.

541 ESTELLE: Garcin!

542 GARCIN: What?

543 ESTELLE: Revenge yourself.

544 GARCIN: How?

545 ESTELLE: Kiss me, darling—then you'll hear her squeal.

546 GARCIN: That's true, Inez. I'm at your mercy, but you're at mine as well. [*He bends over ESTELLE. INEZ gives a little cry.*]

547 INEZ: Oh, you coward, you weakling, running to women to console you!

548 ESTELLE: That's right, Inez. Squeal away.

549 INEZ: What a lovely pair you make! If you could see his big paw splayed out on your back, rucking up your skin and creasing the silk. Be careful, though! He's perspiring, his hand will leave a blue stain on your dress.

550 ESTELLE: Squeal away, Inez, squeal away! . . . Hug me tight, darling; tighter still—that'll finish her off, and a good thing too!

551 INEZ: Yes, Garcin, she's right. Carry on with it, press her to you till you feel your bodies melting into each other; a lump of warm, throbbing flesh. . . . Love's a grand solace, isn't it, my friend? Deep and dark as sleep. But I'll see you don't sleep.

552 ESTELLE: Don't listen to her. Press your lips to my mouth. Oh, I'm yours, yours, yours.

553 INEZ: Well, what are you waiting for? Do as you're told. What a lovely scene: coward Garcin holding baby-killer Estelle in his manly arms! Make

your stakes, everyone. Will coward Garcin kiss the lady, or won't he dare? What's the betting? I'm watching you, everybody's watching, I'm a crowd all by myself. Do you hear the crowd? Do you hear them muttering, Garcin? Mumbling and muttering. "Coward! Coward! Coward! Coward!"—that's what they're saying. . . . It's no use trying to escape, I'll never let you go. What do you hope to get from her silly lips? Forgetfulness? But I shan't forget you, not I! "It's I you must convince." So come to me. I'm waiting. Come along, now. . . . Look how obedient he is, like a well-trained dog who comes when his mistress calls. You can't hold him, and you never will.

554 GARCIN: Will night never come?

555 INEZ: Never.

556 GARCIN: You will always see me?

557 INEZ: Always. [*GARCIN moves away from ESTELLE and takes some steps across the room. He goes to the bronze ornament.*]

558 GARCIN: This bronze. [*Strokes it thoughtfully.*] Yes, now's the moment; I'm looking at this thing on the mantelpiece, and I understand that I'm in hell. I tell you, everything's been thought out beforehand. They knew I'd stand at the fireplace stroking this thing of bronze, with all those eyes intent on me. Devouring me. [*He swings round abruptly.*] What? Only two of you? I thought there were more; many more. [*Laughs.*] So this is hell. I'd never have believed it. You remember all we were told about the torture-chambers, the fire and brimstone, the "burning marl."[14] Old wives' tales! There's no need for red-hot pokers. Hell is—other people!

559 ESTELLE: My darling! Please—

560 GARCIN: [*thrusting her away*] No, let me be. She is between us. I cannot love you when she's watching.

561 ESTELLE Right! In that case, I'll stop her watching. [*She picks up the paper-knife from the table, rushes at INEZ and stabs her several times.*]

562 INEZ [*struggling and laughing*]: But, you crazy creature, what do you think you're doing? You know quite well I'm dead.

563 ESTELLE: Dead? [*She drops the knife. A pause. INEZ picks up the knife and jabs herself with it regretfully.*]

564 INEZ: Dead! Dead! Dead! Knives, poison, ropes—all useless. It has happened already, do you understand? Once and for all. So here we are, forever. [*Laughs.*]

565 ESTELLE: [*with a peal of laughter*]: Forever. My God, how funny! Forever.

566 GARCIN: [*looks at the two women, and joins in the laughter*] For ever, and ever, and ever. [*They slump onto their respective sofas. A long silence. Their laughter dies away and they gaze at each other.*]

567 GARCIN: Well, well, let's get on with it. . . .

568 *CURTAIN*

THE END

---

14 **burning marl:** a mixture of clay and carbonate of lime that, when burned, produces a dust that's irritating to skin.

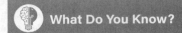
Try to answer the following questions even if they seem challenging to you. Asking and trying to answer questions before formally studying a subject is a good way to learn.

## CLOSE READING

1. Which character seems to undergo the most significant change throughout the story?

2. Select one character whose choices reveal a particularly complex or ambiguous personality and discuss how that complexity/ambiguity affects your perception of that character.

3. Identify and discuss the most significant event in the plot of the play. It could be something that happens to the characters in the room or something that happened in one of the character's lives.

4. What is the most significant conflict in the play? How do the perspectives of the characters contribute to this conflict?

## INTERPRETATION

1. What bigger ideas are being developed in the play? What might it be saying about those ideas beyond the play itself?

2. What are the most important pieces of information in the text that would support a claim about the ideas in the play (that is, your interpretation)?

**Source:** Munch Museum

Edvard Munch, 1910, *The Scream*, tempera on panel

*What ideas do the imagery and composition of this work of art convey? If the screaming figure were a character in a story, what would you assume about that character? What story elements do you think are in this work of art?*

# Character Development

## Part 1 Character Development

### Understand
Characters in literature allow readers to study and explore a range of values, beliefs, assumptions, biases, and cultural norms represented by those characters. (CHR-1)

### Demonstrate
Explain the function of a character changing or remaining unchanged. (1.B)

Explain how a character's own choices, actions, and speech reveal complexities in that character, and explain the function of those complexities. (1.E)

See also Units 3, 6 & 7

**Source:** *AP® English Language and Composition Course and Exam Description*

**Essential Question:** How do a character's changes and choices affect a reader's interpretation?

In Unit 3, you may have explored how you have changed as a result of going through metaphorical doors (see Creating on Your Own throughout that unit). But what if there had been no doors, or you had chosen not to go through them, or you went through them but returned to your starting point unchanged? In literature, how and why characters change or don't change reveals much about the characters and your response to them.

---

**KEY TERMS**

changing characters          minor characters          resolution

---

## 1.1 Interpreting Changes | CHR-1.AE, CHR-1.AF

In literature, **changing characters** reflect the development of the story and sometimes represent the evolution of their values throughout the story. Their changes affect the way you read the story and respond to that character, other characters, and the events of the story.

Some characters don't change. Their failure to change might result from their inability to adapt to events in the story, and some characters just play supporting roles and aren't developed enough by the author for you to know how they respond to events in the story. **Minor characters**, for example, often exist just to help the major characters develop or to help move the plot along. Readers' interpretations of a text are often affected by a character's changing— or not—and the meaning conveyed by such changes or lack of change.

## Minor Characters

Minor characters are easy to ignore. They often say very little or appear in small parts of the text so readers rarely pay much attention to them. They are minor, after all, and don't demand much attention. But how minor characters interact with major characters and affect the events of the narrative often reveals insights about the story and the major characters that otherwise would remain unseen.

Most minor characters remain unchanged only because they aren't developed enough for you to see a change in them. Yet minor characters are essential to a narrative for a few reasons.

1. *They move the story forward* through what they say and do in relation to the rest of the characters.

2. *They expose information or offer insight* on major characters and events. They may have knowledge about characters or events that the reader needs to know, knowledge that will affect how the reader interprets those characters and events.

3. *They help establish the mood.* What they say (or don't say) or do (or don't do) contributes to development of the setting.

Take, for example, Lorraine Hansberry's masterpiece *A Raisin in the Sun* (1958). In this play, a multigenerational Black family—the Youngers—live in a small, two-bedroom apartment known as a "kitchenette" where all the residents on the same floor had to share a bathroom. Living together in the small apartment are Walter Lee, Ruth (his wife), Lena (his mother), Beneatha (his sister), and his son, Travis. Recently, Walter Lee and Beneatha's father has died and the family will soon receive a $10,000 life insurance check.

**Source:** Library of Congress

On once wealthy streets, landlords broke up apartments into tiny units called "kitchenettes" and rented them to Black tenants.

*What conflicts might ripen from living in such close quarters? How could these conflicts affect or be affected by other characters?*

Mama has decided to use the check to buy a house outside of their neighborhood so the family can leave their crowded circumstances. Walter Lee, though, wants to use the money to open a liquor store, setting up a key conflict in the play.

Mama is finally able to put a down payment on a house, but she chooses a house in a White neighborhood instead of a Black neighborhood because the houses in the Black neighborhood "cost twice as much as other houses."

Audiences watching the play when it was first performed would understand why houses were more expensive in Black neighborhoods. Because of the practice of breaking up buildings into tiny units, real estate ownership was hugely profitable for White investors in Black neighborhoods. Blacks trying to buy a property in those neighborhoods had to compete with those investors, who drove up the prices there or would simply refuse to sell. Further, unscrupulous investors drove down the prices of some homes owed by White families, preying on the fear that if Blacks moved into their neighborhoods, their home values would plunge. These investors then offered low down payments to Black families moving into such areas but charged impossibly high monthly payments. When the new owners could not meet the payments, the houses went back into the possession of the investors, leaving the home buyers with nothing.

Because of the decision to buy in a White neighborhood, the Youngers soon meet Mr. Lindner, a representative of the neighborhood they intend to move to, who visits them on moving day. Politely, he explains to the Youngers that the Clybourne Park Improvement Association—which in the play stands for the segment of White society trying to maintain residential segregation—believes everybody would be happier if the Youngers chose a different neighborhood, and to make that possible, the association would even like to make an offer to buy the house at a price that would provide financial gain for Mama. Walter Lee angrily tells the man to leave. On his way out, Lindner says to Walter, "You just can't force people to change their hearts, son."

Mr. Lindner will return later in the play when he is told to keep his money and that nothing he can do will stop the Youngers from moving into their new house in their new neighborhood. It is a triumphant moment for the family, and especially for Walter Lee, who has changed and grown, but Lindner is not changed.

Though he is described as "a gentle man; thoughtful and somewhat labored in his manner" and he can simply say that he is a "representative of the Clybourne Park Improvement Association," Lindner, in representing the members, also represents their bigoted values. When he later explains that he is also the chairman of the association, he then becomes directly aligned with what the members believe.

## Excerpt 1 (Act II, Scene Three)

> LINDNER: . . . the overwhelming majority of our people out there feel that people get along better, take more of a common interest in the life of the community, when they share a common background. I want you to believe me when I tell you that race prejudice simply doesn't enter into it. It is a matter of the people of Clybourne Park believing, rightly or wrongly, as I say, that for the happiness of all concerned that our Negro families are happier when they live in their own communities."

Lindner represents certain ideas that the Youngers resist, including segregation enforced by money, influence, and ignorance. Lindner continues to stand for these values when Walter Lee calls him to return at the end of the play so they can all reject his offer in person.

If Lindner shows up twice only to finally be rejected, then what is his purpose in the play? He is a minor character who doesn't change. He doesn't realize the errors of his prejudice. Instead, he only reiterates his prejudice and even seems to threaten the family at the end when he says "I sure hope you people know what you're getting into."

But the story is not about Lindner—it is about the Youngers and what they face as they attempt to make their dream a reality. While there are other issues they have to face during the course of the play, a central conflict is between racism, as embodied in Mr. Lindner, and this one Black family trying to fulfill the promise of the American Dream.

When Walter Lee calls Mr. Lindner to invite him back to the house, he even says he has called

> The Man. Like the guys in the streets say—The Man. Captain Boss—Mistuh Charley . . . Old Cap'n Please Mr. Bossman . . .

These names come from the long tradition of a system that was meant to oppress and repress, and in using those names to refer to Lindner, Walter Lee equates him to other oppressors. His use of those names indicates Walter Lee's depths of despair after being betrayed by a "friend" (see page 617) and failing his family so profoundly. He is ready to be the subservient character everyone in Clybourne Park believes him to be, which is a betrayal of everything his father had taught him.

Reflecting on what minor characters do in a text, consider the table on the next page that examines Mr. Lindner's role.

| Text: *A Raisin in the Sun* | Minor Character: Mr. Lindner |
|---|---|
| What minor characters do . . . | How this character does that . . . |
| 1. They move the story forward. | He provides something for the family to rally against and to defeat together. |
| 2. They expose information or offer insight on major characters and events. | His words and his offer expose the pride of the family and motivate them to fulfill their dream regardless of setbacks. |
| 3. They establish the mood. | His treatment of the family establishes the tension that comes with insincerity and passive aggression and the eventual triumphant feeling when the family rejects him. |

Table 9-1

Without the minor character of Mr. Lindner, there would be no one for the family members to interact with who would demonstrate the values in conflict. He seems kind and demure, but he is the face of prejudice and ignorance. In these ways, he advances the plot and allows you to see the Youngers—once split by events earlier in the play—come together as a family.

## Changing Characters

In the second half of Act II of *A Raisin in the Sun*, Walter Lee talks to his mother. As you read the next few excerpts, pay particular attention to the underlined and boldfaced portions that emphasize Walter's childish characteristics. Also note details that might suggest Mama's domineering character.

### Excerpt 2 (Act I, Scene Two)

SCENE: MAMA and RUTH are in the apartment. The check has come, but MAMA hesitated to open it because, as a life insurance check, it represents the death of her husband. Soon after opening it . . . .]

[*WALTER enters in great excitement*]

WALTER: Did it come?

MAMA: [*Quietly*] Can't you give people a Christian greeting before you start asking about money?

WALTER: [*To RUTH*] Did it come? [*RUTH unfolds the check and lays it quietly before him, watching him intently with thoughts of her own. WALTER sits down and grasps it close and counts off the zeros*] Ten thousand dollars—[*He turns suddenly, frantically to his mother and draws some papers out of his breast pocket*] Mama—look. Old Willy Harris put everything on paper—

MAMA: Son—I think you ought to talk to your wife . . . I'll go on out and leave you alone if you want—

WALTER: I can talk to her later—Mama, look—

MAMA: Son—

WALTER: <u>WILL SOMEBODY PLEASE LISTEN TO ME TODAY!</u>

MAMA: [*Quietly*] I don't 'low no yellin' in this house, Walter Lee, and you know it—[*WALTER stares at them in frustration and starts to speak several times*] And there ain't going to be no investing in no liquor stores.

WALTER: But, Mama, you ain't even looked at it.

MAMA: I don't aim to have to speak on that again. [*A long pause*]

WALTER: You ain't looked at it and you don't aim to have to speak on that again? You ain't even looked at it and you have decided—[*Crumpling his papers*] Well, you tell that to my boy tonight when you put him to sleep on the living-room couch . . . [*Turning to MAMA and speaking directly to her*] Yeah—and tell it to my wife, Mama, tomorrow when she has to go out of here to look after somebody else's kids. And tell it to me, Mama, every time we need a new pair of curtains and I have to watch you go out and work in somebody's kitchen. Yeah, you tell me then! [*WALTER starts out*]

RUTH: Where you going?

WALTER: I'm going out!

RUTH: Where?

WALTER: Just out of this house somewhere—

RUTH: [*Getting her coat*] I'll come too.

WALTER: I don't want you to come!

RUTH: I got something to talk to you about, Walter.

WALTER: That's too bad.

MAMA: [*Still quietly*] Walter Lee—[*She waits and he finally turns and looks at her*] Sit down.

WALTER: I'm a grown man, Mama.

MAMA: Ain't nobody said you wasn't grown. But you still in my house and my presence. And as long as you are—you'll talk to your wife civil. Now sit down.

RUTH: [*Suddenly*] Oh, let him go on out and drink himself to death! He makes me sick to my stomach! [*She flings her coat against him and exits to bedroom*]

WALTER: [*Violently flinging the coat after her*] And you turn mine too, baby! [*The door slams behind her*] That was my biggest mistake—

MAMA: [*Still quietly*] Walter, what is the matter with you?

WALTER: Matter with me? Ain't nothing the matter with me!

MAMA: Yes there is. Something eating you up like a crazy man. Something more than me not giving you this money. The past few years I been watching it happen to you. You get all nervous acting and kind of wild in the eyes—[*WALTER jumps up impatiently at her words*] I said sit there now, I'm talking to you!

Mama tells Walter that every time he gets upset about something he won't talk about it—he just wants to leave the house and go drinking. Walter settles down a little and tells his mother how bleak his future looks to him: "The future, Mama. Hanging over there at the edge of my days. Just waiting for me—a big, looming blank space—full of nothing. Just waiting for me." His mother tells him that he's got a good wife and a job and he shouldn't think so much about money. He tells her it's all about money. Although she feels out of place telling him, Mama informs Walter that his wife is pregnant and that she is thinking of not having the baby. Walter Lee, of course, does not know this in the previous scene on pages 599–600. Once again, note details suggesting how Mama treats Walter as if he is a child.

> MAMA: . . . this ain't for me to be telling—but you ought to know. [*She waits*] I think Ruth is thinking 'bout getting rid of that child.
> WALTER: [*Slowly understanding*] No—no—Ruth wouldn't do that.
> MAMA: When the world gets ugly enough—a woman will do anything for her family. The part that's already living.
> WALTER: You don't know Ruth, Mama, if you think she would do that.
> [*RUTH opens the bedroom door and stands there a little limp*]
> RUTH: [*Beaten*] Yes I would too, Walter. [*Pause*] I gave her a five-dollar down payment [on an abortion].
> [*There is total silence as the man stares at his wife and the mother stares at her son.*]
> MAMA: [*Presently*] Well—[*Tightly*] Well—son, I'm waiting to hear you say something . . . [*She waits*] **I'm waiting to hear how you be your father's son. Be the man he was** . . . [*Pause. The silence shouts*] Your wife say she going to destroy your child. And I'm waiting to hear you talk like him and say we a people who give children life, not who destroys them—[*She rises*] I'm waiting to see you stand up and look like your daddy and say we done give up one baby to poverty and that we ain't going to give up nary another one . . . I'm waiting.
> WALTER: Ruth—[*He can say nothing*]
> MAMA: If you a son of mine, tell her! [*WALTER picks up his keys and his coat and walks out. She continues, bitterly*] You . . . you are a disgrace to your father's memory. Somebody get me my hat!
>     [Curtain]

Significantly, a number of lines and stage directions seem to show or describe Walter Lee as a child and establish who he is as a character—someone who declares "I'm a grown man, Mama" but who storms about the apartment childishly. Hansberry even plants an opportunity for Walter Lee to prove everyone wrong when Mama explains (in the boldfaced font) to him how she is "waiting to hear how you be your father's son. Be the man he was." When she calls for him to be the man his father was, he fails the test. Yet Mama is an influence on Walter's behavior: She *treats* him like a child and takes away his agency by telling him *how* to be a man like his father. He may be a grown man, but he is not the man he will become—yet.

Later in the play, Mama makes the down payment on the house and gives the rest of the money to Walter for his family. After Walter gets conned out of that money by a dishonest friend, Mr. Lindner appears again.

At this moment, Walter Lee is at his lowest. The despair he feels drives him to sell out his family's dreams, perhaps realizing that moving to a new house will not suddenly make life better for the Youngers in a society that blocks off roads to success for Blacks. Walter's despair prompts Beneatha to ask (Act III, Scene One):

> "Oh, God! Where is the bottom! Where is the real honest-to-God bottom so he can't go any farther!"

Mama quickly and without equivocation states her perspective on taking Lindner's money:

> "nobody in my family never let nobody pay 'em no money that was a way of telling us we wasn't fit to walk the earth. We ain't never been that poor."

But as you know from having studied narratives and characters, once at the bottom, many characters make their turn. Consider this excerpt and pay particular attention to the underlined and boldfaced portions.

## Excerpt 3 (Act III, Scene One)

> SCENE: At the moment that Lindner arrives to sign the papers and write the check, Walter Lee and Ruth's son, Travis, walk in the door announcing that the moving men have arrived.]
>
> [*TRAVIS bursts into the room at the end of the speech, leaving the door open*]
>
> TRAVIS: Grandmama—the moving men are downstairs! The truck just pulled up.
>
> MAMA: [*Turning and looking at him*] Are they, baby? They downstairs?
>
> [*She sighs and sits. LINDNER appears in the doorway. He peers in and knocks lightly, to gain attention, and comes in. All turn to look at him*]
>
> LINDNER: [*Hat and briefcase in hand*] Uh—hello . . . [*RUTH crosses mechanically to the bedroom door and opens it and lets it swing open freely and slowly as the lights come up on WALTER within, still in his coat, sitting at the far corner of the room. He looks up and out through the room to LINDNER*]
>
> RUTH: He's here.
>
> [*A long minute passes and WALTER slowly gets up*]
>
> LINDNER: [*Coming to the table with efficiency, putting his briefcase on the table and starting to unfold papers and unscrew fountain pens*] Well, I certainly was glad to hear from you people. [*WALTER has begun the trek out of the room, slowly and awkwardly, rather like a small boy, passing the back of his sleeve across his mouth from time to time*] Life can really be so much simpler than people let it be most of the time. Well—with whom do I negotiate? You, Mrs. Younger, or your son here? [*MAMA sits with her hands folded on her lap and her eyes closed as WALTER advances. TRAVIS goes closer to LINDNER and looks at the papers curiously*] Just some official papers, sonny.

RUTH: Travis, you go downstairs—

MAMA: [*Opening her eyes and looking into WALTER'S*] No. Travis, you stay right here. And you make him understand what you doing, Walter Lee. You teach him good. Like Willy Harris taught you. You show where our five generations done come to. [*WALTER looks from her to the boy, who grins at him innocently*] Go ahead, son—[*She folds her hands and closes her eyes*] Go ahead.

WALTER: [*At last crosses to LINDNER, who is reviewing the contract*] Well, Mr. Lindner. [*BENEATHA turns away*] We called you—[*There is a profound, simple groping quality in his speech*]—because, well, me and my family [*He looks around and shifts from one foot to the other*] Well—we are very plain people . . .

LINDNER: Yes—

WALTER: I mean—I have worked as a chauffeur most of my life—and my wife here, she does domestic work in people's kitchens. So does my mother. I mean—we are plain people . . .

LINDNER: Yes, Mr. Younger—

WALTER [*Really like a small boy, looking down at his shoes and then up at the man*] And—uh—well, my father, well, he was a laborer most of his life . . . .

LINDNER: [*Absolutely confused*] Uh, yes—yes, I understand.

[*He turns back to the contract*]

**WALTER: [*A beat;[1] staring at him*] And my father—[*With sudden intensity*] My father almost beat a man to death once because this man called him a bad name or something, you know what I mean?**

**LINDNER: [*Looking up, frozen*] No, no, I'm afraid I don't—**

**WALTER: [*A beat. The tension hangs; then WALTER steps back from it*] Yeah. Well—what I mean is that we come from people who had a lot of pride. I mean—we are very proud people. And that's my sister over there and she's going to be a doctor—and we are very proud—**

LINDNER: Well—I am sure that is very nice, but—

WALTER: What I am telling you is that we called you over here to tell you that we are very proud and that this—[*Signaling to TRAVIS*] Travis, come here. [*TRAVIS crosses and WALTER draws him before him facing the man*] This is my son, and he makes the sixth generation our family in this country. And we have all thought about your offer—

LINDNER: Well, good . . . good—

WALTER: And we have decided to move into our house because my father—my father—he earned it for us brick by brick. [*MAMA has her eyes closed and is rocking back and forth as though she were in church, with her head nodding the Amen yes*] We don't want to make no trouble for nobody or fight no causes, and we will try to be good neighbors. And that's all we got to say about that. [*He looks the man absolutely in the eyes*] We don't want your money. [*He turns and walks away*]

---

**1 beat:** a pause signaling a change in direction in the character's thoughts

LINDNER: [*Looking around at all of them*] I take it then—that you have decided to occupy . . .

BENEATHA: That's what the man said.

LINDNER: [*To MAMA in her reverie*] Then I would like to appeal to you, Mrs. Younger. You are older and wiser and understand things better I am sure . . .

MAMA: <u>I am afraid you don't understand. My son said we was going to move and there ain't nothing left for me to say</u>. [*Briskly*] You know how these young folks is nowadays, mister. Can't do a thing with 'em! [*As he opens his mouth, she rises*] Good-bye.

LINDNER: [*Folding up his materials*] Well—if you are that final about it . . . there is nothing left for me to say. [*He finishes, almost ignored by the family, who are concentrating on WALTER LEE. At the door LINDNER halts and looks around*] I sure hope you people know what you're getting into. [*He shakes his head and exits.*]

Although in agony about the decision, Walter Lee undergoes a shift here. Mama had declared that she was waiting for him to be a man like his father. When Walter Lee has to face the decision in front of his son and face what the decision would mean for his family, he recalls how his own father had once reacted to an insult and then had changed as a result. Mr. Lindner's check is as much an insult to the family, and Walter Lee will not accept it.

When examining characters and how they have changed, recognize how they were before they changed and after they changed and then look for the point or points at which they shift. Some characters change gradually over several different events in the narrative. Some characters change more than once. Some characters seem to change but really don't. Every change—no matter how small—demands your attention.

So Walter Lee has changed: He has grown into the man he needed to be for the sake of his family. When set against the static, unchanging Mr. Lindner, Walter Lee's change is emphasized even more. The Walter Lee who had behaved in childish ways now can stand on his own against what Lindner represents.

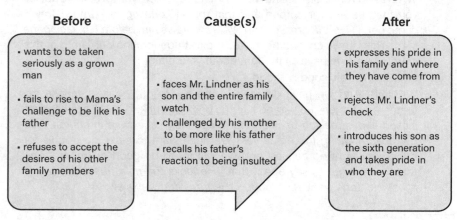

| Before | Cause(s) | After |
|---|---|---|
| • wants to be taken seriously as a grown man <br><br> • fails to rise to Mama's challenge to be like his father <br><br> • refuses to accept the desires of his other family members | • faces Mr. Lindner as his son and the entire family watch <br> • challenged by his mother to be more like his father <br> • recalls his father's reaction to being insulted | • expresses his pride in his family and where they have come from <br><br> • rejects Mr. Lindner's check <br><br> • introduces his son as the sixth generation and takes pride in who they are |

**Figure 9-1**

Walter Lee's change and Lindner's lack of change affect how you think about the play, how you think about Walter Lee, and how you think about the big ideas the play communicates. If Lindner weren't a character and his position were expressed only in a letter sent to the family or a voice on the other end of a phone line, then you would never see Walter Lee confront the conflict head on. The changing and unchanging characters allow you to see the values of those characters, how those values affect them, and how the face-off ultimately shapes them and the outcome of the play.

**Remember:** Minor characters often remain unchanged because the narrative doesn't focus on them. They may only be part of the narrative to advance the plot or to interact with major characters CHR-1.AE. Readers' interpretations of a text are often affected by a character changing—or not—and the meaning conveyed by such changes or lack thereof. (CHR-1.AE–AF)

## 1.1 Checkpoint

*Review* No Exit *or another work of longer fiction or drama you are studying. Then complete the following open-response activities and answer the multiple-choice questions.*

1. Identify and examine a minor character in the work. In *No Exit,* that character may be the Valet or possibly one of the unseen characters mentioned by the three main characters. You might use the table below.

| Text: | Minor Character: |
|---|---|
| What minor characters do . . . | How this character does that . . . |
| 1. They move the story forward. | |
| 2. They expose information or offer insight on major characters and events. | |
| 3. They establish the mood. | |

2. Review the text you are studying. Where do you see a character change from the way he or she was originally portrayed? What caused the character to reveal that? Examine how the character was before and after the change, and then explain the cause of the character's change. On separate paper, recreate Figure 9-1 to record your thoughts.

**3.** In the context of the play as a whole, the detail that Garcin's wife comes to the barracks everyday wondering about him emphasizes which of the following about his character?

    (A) He took every opportunity to avoid her because of all that she represented about what he had done wrong in his life.

    (B) He had a number of affairs and disregarded her emotions completely, even failing to respect their home.

    (C) He took advantage of a person who was clearly devoted to him regardless of what he did wrong and treated that person terribly.

    (D) He claimed to be a pacifist, but by being in the barracks, he sent the message that he was supporting the war effort and the soldiers fighting in it.

    (E) He disregarded the judgment of others and was only concerned with how she felt and how she cared about him because of her unending devotion to him.

**4.** Of the major characters, the one who appears to change the least as a result of what he or she reveals is

    (A) Garcin, because he admits to being a pacifist early in the play and knows that is why he has been condemned

    (B) Estelle, because she is clearly vain and self-centered from the time she arrives in the room

    (C) Inez, because she knows she is cruel to people and takes pleasure in being cruel to the others in the room

    (D) Inez, because she is able to see through the lies the others tell and eventually causes them to recall their painful memories

    (E) Garcin, because he continually wants to be liked and to avoid conflict with the others

## Creating on Your Own

Both *No Exit* and *A Raisin in the Sun* show characters in very close quarters. Think of any situation in which a group of very different people are forced into a circumstance of close quarters. That could be seats on a plane; kids at an adult party where they hardly know one another, but the adults keep telling them to "go play with one another"; new college roommates; two people who were friends in elementary school but not since then who are stuck in the school elevator; two people who met on the Internet now meeting face-to-face in a coffee shop for the first time—anything you can think of.

Write the conversation as a play script. Take five to ten minutes to just write, filling each line of your paper or computer all the way to the end. Maybe consider adding some stage directions that contribute to what you are telling. Save your work.

# 1.2 Interpreting Choices | CHR-1.AG, CHR-1.AH

Everything a character does or says reflects that character's values. However, as you just read, characters often change over the course of a narrative. By the time the conflict in the narrative is resolved, a character's response may seem to suggest a shift in values. Such inconsistencies and unexpected developments in a character shape how you interpret that character; other characters; events in the plot; conflicts; the perspective of the narrator, character, or speaker; and/or the setting.

## Responses to Resolution

The **resolution** to any story is where you expect or at least hope to have all of the loose ends tied. How characters respond to the resolution also gives you new insight into them.

In *A Raisin in the Sun*, for example, the resolution of the play is Walter's proclamation of pride in his family and the rejection of Mr. Lindner's offer. However, the story is not over, as these final lines show.

## Excerpt 4 (Act III, Scene One)

RUTH: [*Looking around and coming to life*] Well, for God's sake—if the moving men are here—LET'S GET THE HELL OUT OF HERE!

MAMA: [*Into action*] Ain't it the truth! Look at all this here mess. Ruth, put Travis' good jacket on him . . . Walter Lee, fix your tie and tuck your shirt in, you look like somebody's hoodlum! Lord have mercy, where is my plant? [*She flies to get it amid the general bustling of the family, who are deliberately trying to ignore the nobility of the past moment*] You all start on down . . . Travis child, don't go empty-handed . . . Ruth, where did I put that box with my skillets in it? I want to be in charge of it myself . . . I'm going to make us the biggest dinner we ever ate tonight. . . Beneatha, what's the matter with them stockings? Pull them things up, girl . . . [*The family starts to file out as two moving men appear and begin to carry out the heavier pieces of furniture, bumping into the family as they move about*]

. . .

[*WALTER and BENEATHA go out yelling at each other vigorously and the anger is loud and real till their voices diminish. RUTH stands at the door and turns to MAMA and smiles knowingly*]

MAMA: [*Fixing her hat at last*] Yeah—they something all right, my children . . .

RUTH: Yeah—they're something. Let's go, Lena.

MAMA: [*Stalling, starting to look around at the house*] Yes—I'm coming. Ruth—

RUTH: Yes?

MAMA: [*Quietly, woman to woman*] **He finally come into his manhood today, didn't he? Kind of like a rainbow after the rain . . .**

RUTH: [*Biting her lip lest her own pride explode in front of MAMA*] **Yes, Lena.**

[*WALTER'S voice calls for them raucously*]

WALTER: [*Off stage*] Y'all come on! These people charges by the hour, you know!

MAMA: [*Waving RUTH out vaguely*] All right, honey—go on down. I be down directly.

**[RUTH hesitates, then exits. MAMA stands, at last alone in the living room, her plant on the table before her as the lights start to come down. She looks around at all the walls and ceilings and suddenly, despite herself, while the children call below, a great heaving thing rises in her and she puts her fist to her mouth to stifle it, takes a final desperate look, pulls her coat about her, pats her hat and goes out.** The lights dim down. The door opens and she comes back in, grabs her plant, and goes out for the last time]

[Curtain]

The boldfaced portions of the text show how Mama's words and actions reveal something more about her character as the play comes to an end. Her perspective on Walter has evolved as a result of his resolute behavior with Mr. Lindner. And despite her dream to leave the apartment, she chokes during her last look at the place. The stage directions offer no hints about why she is choked up, and the adjective "desperate" could be read a number of ways, including foreboding at the unwelcome reception they likely face.

In this scene, Mama's character develops a bit more and you know her a bit better. Importantly, you see her accept Walter Lee as a man like his father and you see how the change coming to the family affects her emotionally.

**Source:** Wikimedia Commons

This photo is of the final scene from the original 1959 Broadway performance of *A Raisin in the Sun*.

*How does the staging of the scene affect your perspective on the scene and the characters? How might that perspective change if the characters were positioned in a different way?*

## Unexpected and Inconsistent Characters

Beneatha, Walter Lee's younger sister, is a college student. She provides a strong, independent, feminist perspective in the play. Throughout, however, she searches for her identity.

Beneatha dates two very different men, George and Asagai, who represent choices she has to make in her life. These choices also reflect tensions within the African American community at the time. George is an affluent black man who stands for capitalism and thinks it important to assimilate into White culture. Asagai is from Nigeria and represents the anti-colonial movement—he encourages Beneatha to connect with her African heritage. She prefers Asagai, even though he tells her that, on the one hand, she is too independent for not wanting to marry, but on the other hand, she is too dependent because she refuses to leave America to be with him.

Near the end of the play, though, you see what appears to be unexpected behavior from Beneatha. The following section was omitted from Excerpt 4 at the point of the ellipses (…).

### Excerpt 5 (Act III, Scene One)

> BENEATHA: Mama, Asagai asked me to marry him today and go to Africa—
>
> MAMA: [*In the middle of her getting-ready activity*] He did? **You ain't old enough to marry nobody—**[*Seeing the moving men lifting one of her chairs precariously*] Darling, that ain't no bale of cotton, please handle it so we can sit in it again! I had that chair twenty-five years . . . [*The movers sigh with exasperation and go on with their work*]
>
> BENEATHA: [*Girlishly and unreasonably trying to pursue the conversation*] **To go to Africa, Mama—be a doctor in Africa . . .**
>
> MAMA: [*Distracted*] Yes, baby—
>
> WALTER: Africa! What he want you to go to Africa for?
>
> BENEATHA: To practice there . . .
>
> WALTER: <u>Girl</u>, **if you don't get all them silly ideas out your head!** You better marry yourself a man with some loot . . .
>
> BENEATHA: [*Angrily, precisely as in the first scene of the play*] What have you got to do with who I marry?
>
> WALTER: Plenty. Now I think George Murchison—
>
> BENEATHA: George Murchison! I wouldn't marry him if he was Adam and I was Eve!

Beneatha seems to be seriously considering accepting Asagai's offer of marriage. Further, she appears excited about the prospect of moving to Africa to practice medicine. As a character established as proud and independent, she now seems to stumble in the presence of her mother. Beneatha is now being treated like the child. Mama calls out her age, the stage directions describe her behaving "girlishly and unreasonably," and even Walter Lee—having established himself finally as a grown man in this same scene—calls her a "girl" and "silly" in the same breath.

Like Walter Lee, Beneatha ("Beneath her") has been dominated by her mother. While Walter Lee exerts his own strength at the end, Beneatha is no longer acting like the proud, independent character she was earlier in the play.

 **Remember:** A character's responses to the resolution of the narrative—in their words or in their actions—reveal something about that character's own values; these responses may be inconsistent with the previously established behaviors or perspectives of that character. Inconsistencies and unexpected developments in a character affect readers' interpretation of that character; other characters; events in the plot; conflicts; the perspective of the narrator, character, or speaker; and/or setting. (CHR-1.AG–AH)

## 1.2 Checkpoint

*Review the section of* No Exit *starting at 540. Then complete the following open-response activity and answer the multiple-choice questions.*

1. Examine how the characters respond to the resolution following Inez's speech at 553. What does their response reveal about their real values? Is this behavior consistent or inconsistent with the perspective you may have had about them earlier in the play? Answer these questions in a few sentences.

2. The characters' collective laughter at the end of the play can be best explained as a reaction to

    (A) teasing one another as they torture one another

    (B) accepting their role as torturers

    (C) realizing the absurdity of trying to avoid the inevitable

    (D) responding to the emotional pain they can feel and the physical pain they cannot feel

    (E) recognizing the futility of the bell-push that doesn't always work

3. At section 511, when the door swings open, Garcin's reaction to it in subsequent lines can be best explained as

   (A) directly influenced by Inez's poor treatment of him both before and after the door opens

   (B) consistent with his need to protect Estelle because he does not want to leave her alone with Inez

   (C) inconsistent with the supposed reasons for finding himself condemned in the room

   (D) inconsistent with his behavior in the room but consistent with what he reveals about his life

   (E) a fearful response consistent with his treatment of his wife and the treatment of the others in the room with him

**Creating on Your Own**

Review the writing you did in the previous Creating on Your Own activity. Examine the nature of the relationships you created between different characters in your script.

1. What could one or more of the characters do that is unexpected or inconsistent with what they have said or done and that would also reveal something interesting about who they really are? Experiment with some possibilities.

2. If you have not already, draft or write a resolution to your scene. How do the characters act in response to the way the scene ends? What can you include in their words and actions (stage directions) that reveals something more about their character? Again, experiment to see what you might come up with.

# Part 1   Apply What You Have Learned

For one of the characters in the play, examine:

1. How he or she changes or doesn't change

2. How his or her behaviors are consistent or inconsistent with what has been established earlier in the play

3. How he or she responds to the resolution of the play

4. How his or her interaction with any minor character (the Valet or any of the mentioned characters) might reveal something about the major character

You may want to record your answers in a chart like the one below.

| Advanced Character Analysis of [insert character] | |
|---|---|
| 1. how he or she changes or doesn't change | |
| 2. how his or her behaviors are consistent or inconsistent with what has been established earlier in the play | |
| 3. how he or she responds to the resolution of the play | |
| 4. how his or her interaction with any minor character might reveal something about the major character | |

Once you have recorded evidence, choose the most valuable information and evidence and then write two or three paragraphs that explain and support an interpretation of that character and any new revelations about that character.

**Reflect on the Essential Question**   Write a brief response that answers this essential question: *How do a character's changes and choices affect a reader's interpretation?* In your answer, correctly use the key terms listed on page 595.

# Part 2

# Tension and Resolution

**Enduring Understanding and Skills**

## Part 2 Tension and Resolution

### Understand
The arrangement of the parts and sections of a text, the relationship of the parts to each other, and the sequence in which the text reveals information are all structural choices made by a writer that contribute to the reader's interpretation of a text. (STR-1)

### Demonstrate
Explain the function of a significant event or related set of significant events in a plot. (3.E)

Explain the function of conflict in a text. (3.F)

See also Unit 3

**Source:** *AP® English Literature and Composition Course and Exam Description*

**Essential Question:** How does rising tension from colliding events affect the reader's experience?

Maybe you've experienced this progression of thoughts when you've read a novel or watched a play.

Stage 1: "Hmm. I don't really know what's going on or who anybody is. I'm not sure I'm going to get into this."

Stage 2: "Ok, now I get what's going on and I can see how some problems and conflicts are starting to develop. I'm starting to care about the characters."

Stage 3: "Wow, these colliding conflicts make me feel anxious about how the main character is going to get through them. I'm going to keep reading for just *one* more chapter to find out."

Stage 4: "Oh, thank goodness it worked out ok." *OR* "Wow, I didn't expect the ending to be so up in the air."

Stage 3 has attracted a lot of attention from people in the entertainment industry as well as writers of popular fiction. Studies show that when watching films, especially thrillers, people have a physiological reaction—changes detected by electrodes on the skin and those that measure emotional sweating. These studies conclude that when fictional characters face dangers, the "fight or flight" response that people feel when they are in danger themselves is aroused. Emotional conflict may evoke similar responses. Even though readers or viewers have willingly "suspended their disbelief" and recognize that what they are experiencing is fictional, they still have strong reactions in their sympathetic nervous system, and, further, they *enjoy* that experience and those feelings, and they re-experience them even if they already know the outcome.

---

**KEY TERMS**

| | | |
|---|---|---|
| value systems | anticipation | unresolved ending |
| catharsis | unseen character | suspense |
| preceding action | | |

---

# 2.1 Competing Values, Suspense, and Catharsis
## | STR-1.AI, STR-1.AJ, STR-1.AK

The structure of most literary works makes the kind of progression outlined above nearly unavoidable. Once you know the characters, you get caught up in the conflicts that often result from competing value systems. Tension continues to build as events in a plot collide and accumulate to create a sense of anticipation and suspense. When the resolution of the anticipation, suspense, or central conflicts finally happens, readers often feel a moment of emotional release.

Not all works provide that moment of emotional release, however. Some works have unresolved endings, and the up-in-the-air quality may contribute to the interpretation of the text. Readers or viewers may interpret such works as conveying a complex worldview in which right may not always triumph over wrong or right may not even be discernible from wrong. Such worldviews may make readers question their own values and sense of right and wrong and feel the moral ground crumbling beneath their feet.

## Competing Values

How different characters react when significant events occur in a text creates contrasts and comparisons for readers to examine as they explore the development and values of the characters. Comparing these reactions often reveals distinct, competing **value systems** represented by those characters. These value systems include the established values, norms, or goals of a group of people, a culture, or a society.

For example, Mama Younger wants the house in Clybourne Park. Certainly she values the comforts the house would bring for her family—more room to spread out. She also values the right to make her own decisions about where to live. The house also represents a dream deferred (as expressed in the poem "Harlem" by Langston Hughes on page 549 from which the title of the play comes) because she and her late husband had been planning on buying a house when they first married.

## Excerpt 6 (Act I, Scene One)

> MAMA: We was going to set away [money], little by little, don't you know, and buy a little place out in Morgan Park. We had even picked out the house. [*Chuckling a little*] Looks right dumpy today. But Lord, child, you should know all the dreams I had 'bout buying that house and fixing it up and making me a little garden in the back—[*She waits and stops smiling*] And didn't none of it happen.

Mama's goals contrast with Walter Lee's. He thinks that investing in a liquor store will solve the family's money problems.

## Excerpt 7 (Act I, Scene One)

> WALTER: Yeah. You see, this little liquor store we got in mind cost seventy-five thousand and we figured the initial investment on the place be 'bout thirty thousand, see. That be ten thousand each. Course, there's a couple of hundred you got to pay so's you don't spend your life just waiting for them clowns to let your license get approved. . . .
>
> RUTH: [*Softly*] Walter, that ain't none of our money.
>
> WALTER: [*Not listening at all or even looking at her*] This morning, I was lookin' in the mirror and thinking about it . . . I'm thirty-five years old; I been married eleven years and I got a boy who sleeps in the living room—[*Very, very quietly*]—and all I got to give him is stories about how rich white people live . . .

Walter Lee values the liquor store for what it represents—wealth. The conflict between Mama and Walter Lee, then, is not about money but about values. She places greater value on trying to fulfill the dream she has for her family, while Walter values getting more money so the family has more options. The table below compares these competing values.

| Character Conflicts and Values | | | |
|---|---|---|---|
| **Character: Mama** | | **Character: Walter Lee** | |
| **Perspective** | **Value(s)** | **Value(s)** | **Perspective** |
| Buy a house with the life insurance money | Dreams<br>Right to choose where she lives | Money | Open a liquor store with the life insurance money |
| Take family away from the city | Safety<br>Comfort<br>Health | Money<br>Comfort | Make more money to support the family |
| Opposes liquor store | Morality | Money | Favors liquor store |
| Do what she thinks best for family | Family | Family | Do what he thinks best for family |

Table 9-2

Mama makes it clear that her values also reject a liquor store as immoral because of what liquor can drive people to do. As Mama explains, she "don't want that on [her] ledger this late in life." So, ultimately, the conflict is one not just of values, but also of morality, what each sees as right and wrong.

The organization of the plot leads to the build-up of tension as readers await the eventual confrontation between Mama and Walter Lee. Walter Lee talks to Ruth about it. Ruth talks to Mama about it. Walter Lee talks to Beneatha about. All of these conversations take place to establish the different perspectives and values for the audience to compare. They also build **anticipation**—suspenseful expectation and waiting—in readers or viewers as the main conflict has been made clear and they await the clash between the conflicting characters. Anticipation is more than just expectation, though. Anticipation is often something you can feel physically and mentally, as those studies about films have shown—almost an excitement at what is to come. On the day the check comes, the tension is thick and you find yourself excited not for the clash of mother and son but to learn how the conflict will play out.

When Mama has the last word in this exchange, you know who has won this conflict and whose values will prevail in the family. So there is no surprise for the reader when Mama, having put money down on the house, comes to tell young Travis and the rest of the family.

## Excerpt 9 (Act II, Scene One)

> MAMA: [*Holding out her arms to her grandson*] Well—at least let me tell him something. I want him to be the first one to hear . . . Come here, Travis. [*The boy obeys, gladly*] Travis—[*She takes him by the shoulder and looks into his face*]—you know that money we got in the mail this morning?
>
> TRAVIS: Yes'm—
>
> MAMA: Well—what you think your grandmama gone and done with that money?
>
> TRAVIS: I don't know, Grandmama.
>
> MAMA: [*Putting her finger on his nose for emphasis*] She went out and she bought you a house! [**The explosion comes from WALTER at the end of the revelation and he jumps up and turns away from all of them in a fury. MAMA continues, to TRAVIS**] You glad about the house? It's going to be yours when you get to be a man.
>
> TRAVIS: Yeah—I always wanted to live in a house.
>
> MAMA: All right, gimme some sugar then—[*TRAVIS puts his arms around her neck as she watches her son over the boy's shoulder. Then, to TRAVIS, after the embrace*] Now when you say your prayers tonight, you thank God and your grandfather—'cause it was him who give you the house—in his way.

Notice Walter Lee's reaction in boldfaced text, despite having been told her decision already. This clash of perspectives lays bare the differences between the two characters.

When Mama eventually gives the remaining money to Walter to save, he gives it to Willy Harris to invest in the liquor store and it appears that maybe he and Mama will both get what they want. But when Willy Harris disappears with the money, Walter Lee hits his low point—his fortunes have fallen and he and the family have hit rock bottom.

By this point, they had already met Karl Lindner with his offer to keep the family from moving into the house, so readers once again feel the anticipation of a clash of values. Now the clash is among three sets of values: Lindner's, Mama's, and Walter's. The tension has risen from an anticipated clash to **suspense**, beyond just excitement to almost anxiety about what will happen.

| Colliding and Accumulating Events | | |
|---|---|---|
| Events that Relate to One Another in the Plot | | What Is the Tension, and How Does It Get Resolved? |
| Event 1: Mama makes the down payment on the house. | → | The tension is between Mama and her values and Walter Lee and his, but it also involves Lindner and whether Walter will take the check. In the end, the down payment stands and Walter Lee refuses to accept Mr. Lindner's check. |
| Event 2: Lindner offers the family money to NOT move into the house. | → | |
| Event 3: Willy Harris runs off with Walter Lee's money. | → | |
| Event 4: Walter Lee calls Lindner and invites him over to take the check and not move. | → | |

Table 9-3

Despite their contrasting values, Mama and Walter Lee share common ground: the family. When people or characters in conflict share common ground for their reasoning, they often can work through the conflict and reach a compromise or come to a reasonable resolution, as is demonstrated at the end of the play when Walter Lee rejects Mr. Lindner and what he represents.

## Catharsis

Near the end of a story or play, readers or audience members are usually so invested in the characters or the plot that they feel driven to know what will happen. How will things be resolved? Will the main character(s) be okay? What will happen to the evil characters? That suspense and tension build to keep you interested, and when you finally learn how it all ends and you no longer have to wonder about where things are going, then you have reached the moment of **catharsis** (from the Greek word meaning "to cleanse" or "to purge"). The catharsis comes when you release and feel relief from strong or repressed emotions. This feeling occurs when you encounter a story that draws you in and gets you emotionally invested.

Review Excerpt 3 from *A Raisin in the Sun* (pages 601–603) in which the tension between Mama and Walter Lee is finally resolved and released. At that moment, readers or viewers of the play are released from emotional investment with one of the play's major problems.

**Remember:** Significant events often illustrate competing value systems that relate to a conflict present in the text. Events in a plot collide and accumulate to create a sense of anticipation and suspense. The resolution of the anticipation, suspense, or central conflicts of a plot may be referred to as the moment of catharsis or emotional release. (STR-1.AI–AK)

## 2.1 Checkpoint

*Review* No Exit *or another longer work you are studying. Then complete the following open-response activities and answer the multiple-choice questions.*

1. Pay special attention to a conflict between two of the characters. On separate paper, recreate a table like 9-2. Use the information in the table to help you write a brief explanation of how these values are in conflict and how that conflict may relate to a bigger idea in the text.

2. As you review *No Exit* or another work, this time focus on the events that happen that build anticipation and suspense. On separate paper, create an organizer similar to 9-3 to examine those events, how they relate, and how that tension gets resolved.

3. In the scene running from 226–250, Inez offers to be Estelle's "glass," or mirror. Which of the following best represent the values and characteristics in conflict in this scene?

   (A) Pity and shame
   (B) Vanity and cruelty
   (C) Honesty and reliability
   (D) Commitment and acceptance
   (E) Joy and honesty

4. Which of the following best describes the catharsis in relation to the play as a whole?

   (A) Inez experiences catharsis as she taunts Garcin and Estelle.
   (B) Estelle experiences catharsis as she gives in and stabs Inez.
   (C) Catharsis for the audience comes earlier in the play, once the characters have revealed their true selves.
   (D) There is no catharsis in the play as the audience feels the tension of these three spending eternity together.
   (E) There is no catharsis as the audience cannot truly become invested in characters who are no longer living.

**Creating on Your Own**

Review the writing you did in earlier Creating on Your Own activities. Examine the nature of the relationships you created between different characters in your script. Then complete the following activities.

1. Think about the values in conflict within each character. Are the actions and statements of the characters consistent with those values? If the relationship between values and actions is not the way you want it to be, revise it until you are happy with it.

2. Consider the plot that is developing with your story. What multiple events might build upon one another? How do or can they lead to one another and build some anticipation or suspense? Experiment with ways to have them interact. You might want to sketch them out on a storyboard before drafting in writing.

# 2.2 Unseen Characters and Unresolved Endings
## | STR-1.AL, STR-1.AM

Since you have been reading stories or watching films, you have become accustomed to thinking about and maybe even analyzing the characters in the story or the events in the plot. As you improve your ability to think about stories in different ways, you may find that some of the most interesting forces or people to examine are those that remain unseen.

## Evidence of Things Unseen

Walter Lee—or the hopeless context in which he finds himself, including social injustice and a domineering mother—is one source of his problems. Willy, however, is the instigator of most of the problems in Walter Lee's life as you see them in the play. But you never see Willy himself in the play.

Willy is an **unseen character**. While many characters in the world of the story may be unseen, characters like Willy are important because they have a direct effect on the events of the story. Willy intensifies conflict for Walter Lee.

The same is true for Big Walter, Walter Lee's father, or, rather, for his death. If not for Big Walter's death before the play, there would be no check, no thought of a house or a liquor store, and no Mr. Lindner. In short, without the death of Big Walter, there would be no play. An event like this occurring before the story begins is called a **preceding action**. Preceding actions tie directly to the action of the plot and often affect and are mentioned in the story.

Understanding how unseen characters and preceding actions affect the story helps you understand the full context. Willy runs off with the money because he is probably in desperate circumstances similar to those of the Younger family. Seeing what Willy represents—the liquor store and then the theft of the money—may help the reader understand these feelings of desperation. The money coming from the death of Big Walter is also in a context that shapes characters' attitudes toward it. For example, Mama knows the money comes from the decades of hard work Big Walter had done, so she wants to spend it on something she feels is worth those decades of work: the house.

## Unresolved Ending

You've reached the last page or heard the last line on stage and still there are some unanswered questions. Something hasn't been resolved or something new has recently come up but has not been addressed by the ending. Maybe it's not the entire ending of a story that remains unresolved but only one out of multiple conflicts. Maybe there will be a sequel but, if not, then what are you to make of such an **unresolved ending**? Just as you have learned to notice when patterns break or when expected events don't happen or unexpected ones do, you need to think closely about what an unresolved conflict may mean at the end of a story.

*A Raisin in the Sun* provides resolution to a major conflict within the family, but Karl Lindner's final line reminds the audience of a looming problem still remaining: "I sure hope you people know what you're getting into." This line foreshadows future problems once the family moves.

That this potential problem is not addressed in the play means that it remains unresolved. Though the audience may assume or at least hope for the happily-ever-after narrative at the end, Mr. Lindner's line clearly forecloses that option. In fact, leaving this issue unresolved highlights the idea that the family's struggles are not over—nor is the struggle against segregation and prejudice more generally.

**Source:** Seattle Municipal Archives

In cities across the country, protesters—both Blacks and Whites—held demonstrations in an effort to end unfair real estate practices. This demonstration took place in Seattle, Washington, in 1964.

**Remember:** Sometimes things not actually shown in a narrative, such as an unseen character or a preceding action, may be in conflict with or result in conflict for a character. Although most plots end in resolution of the central conflicts, some have unresolved endings, and the lack of resolution may contribute to interpretations of the text. (STR-1.AL–AM)

## 2.2 Checkpoint

*Review* No Exit *or another work of longer fiction or drama you are studying. Then complete the following open-response activities and answer the multiple-choice question.*

1. In this review, pay special attention to events that happen before the beginning of the story and characters who are mentioned but not seen in the play. Examine how those preceding actions and unseen characters affect what happens in the main body of the text (e.g., in the room in *No Exit*) and write a few sentences explaining your conclusions.

2. Now look at the ending and determine which conflicts are or are not resolved. Examine why a conflict may not be resolved and what its lack of resolution could mean for the bigger ideas of the text as a whole. Write a few sentences to explain.

3. Now focus on the end of *No Exit* or another longer work you are studying. Is there a real resolution to the play? If so, what is it? If not, why may there be no resolution presented? How does your perspective on the resolution contribute to bigger ideas in the work as a whole? Write a few sentences to explain your answers.

4. The preceding actions of this play can all be categorized as

   (A) excuses the characters make for their terrible behavior while alive

   (B) things that were unfortunate yet unavoidable

   (C) behavior that shows why these characters have been condemned

   (D) well-intentioned, despite the horrific outcomes

   (E) unavoidable twists of fate

### Creating on Your Own

Review the writing you did in earlier Creating on Your Own activities and consider revising some of your work, taking the following questions into account.

1. What character or characters are not present in your draft that could be used to create some kind of effect? How might the seen characters mention the unseen character(s) to establish their importance to the plot? Experiment with introducing unseen characters.

2. If you have not yet written a resolution, consider how you could do so and how you might leave some aspect of it up in the air. Again, experiment to see what might work by revising your draft.

# Part 2   Apply What You Have Learned

For one of the characters in *No Exit* or another play or work of longer fiction you are studying, examine and jot notes about the following:

1. What the character values that drives the conflict in the story

2. How the character's behavior contributes to the anticipation/suspense

3. How the character's relationship with an unseen character contributes to the story

4. How preceding actions contribute to the story

   Then choose the most valuable information and evidence from your examination and write two or three paragraphs that explain and support your thinking about that character's values and life choices and how they all affect the meaning of the work as a whole.

**Reflect on the Essential Question**  Write a brief response that answers the essential question: *How does rising tension from colliding events affect the reader's experience?* In your answer, correctly use the key terms listed on page 614.

**Source:** Florida Grand Opera, photograph by Brittany Mazzurco

*What kind of music would you expect in this operatic version of* No Exit? *View the Florida Grand Opera production on YouTube to see if your expectation was correct.*

# Part 3

# Multiple and Changing Perspectives

**Enduring Understanding and Skill**

## Part 3  Multiple and Changing Perspectives

**Understand**

A narrator's or speaker's perspective controls the details and emphases that affect how readers experience and interpret a text. (NAR-1)

**Demonstrate**

Identify and describe details, diction, or syntax in a text that reveal a narrator's or speaker's perspective. (4.C)

See also Units 2, 5 & 8

**Source:** *AP® English Literature and Composition Course and Exam Description*

**Essential Question:**  How do multiple, contrasting, and changing perspectives affect a reader's understanding?

At the 1968 Olympics in Mexico City, U.S. athlete Tommie Smith set a new world record when he completed the 200-meter race in 19.83 seconds. Close behind him in a surprising silver finish was Australian Peter Norman at 20.06 seconds. John Carlos of the United States finished third with a time of 20.10 seconds.

However, the athletes became even more famous for something they did on the winner's platform when receiving their medals. During the playing of "The Star-Spangled Banner," Smith and Carlos, each wearing a black glove on one hand, bowed their heads and raised their gloved fists. Some have called this gesture the Black Power salute. Smith and Carlos, along with Peter Norman— whose religious faith led him to believe that all people were equal and who protested Australia's immigration policy that limited the entry of people of color—referred to the gesture as a human rights salute.

In some respects, what happened that day depended on the perspectives of those telling the story. Onlookers from the International Olympic Committee told a story about "a deliberate and violent breach of the fundamental principles of the Olympic spirit" and expelled the American athletes for politicizing an event that was supposed to be above politics. *Time* magazine told the story of "a public display of petulance that sparked one of the most unpleasant controversies in Olympic history." Up-and-coming sports journalist Brent Musburger described the participants as "a couple of black-skinned storm troopers" who were "ignoble," "juvenile," and "unimaginative."

What story did the participants in the event, the three athletes, tell? Tommie Smith explained soon after the event that since protesters were not being heard, they needed to be seen, so he took the moment when the world was watching to make a point. John Carlos said that they "were standing for something. We were standing for humanity." Second-place winner Peter Norman, the only White winner, had said to Smith and Carlos, "I will stand with you." Decades later, Norman summarized the story to the *New York Times*. "I won a silver medal. But really, I ended up running the fastest race of my life to become part of something that transcended the Games."

A narrator's **perspective**, the way a narrator perceives his or her circumstances, directly affects the details included in the story, and it influences how the reader reacts to the story. For example, Olympic committee members saw their circumstances as a duty to uphold the long-standing nonpolitical traditions of the Olympics. The athletes on the winners' platform saw their circumstances as allowing them a chance to make a statement that was otherwise not being heard.

Perspective depends on experiences and context. With an infinite combination of experiences, there can be an infinite number of perspectives, ranging from only slightly different to significantly different.

As you live, your perspective changes based on more and more experiences. For example, although Brent Musberger never apologized, a major sports network, ESPN, gave Smith and Carlos its Arthur Ashe Courage Award in 2008, saying "They were right." In the 40 years since the event, the perspective of many sports reporters had changed.

The same kind of change can happen with the narrators and speakers in a text. As the stories develop, the perspectives in the text often change along with the characters who have those perspectives. With all of these different ways of viewing events and characters in a text, myriad different possible perspectives significantly affect the way readers will interact with the text and interpret its bigger ideas.

---

**KEY TERMS**

perspective          complexity          irony

---

# 3.1 Multiple Perspectives of Narrators or Speakers
| NAR-1.X, NAR-1.Y, and NAR-1.Z

Narrators and speakers in a text have unique roles relative to readers: They control what the readers see and hear, what they know, and what they don't know. When there are multiple speakers in a text—in a play, for example—each speaker has a different and unique perspective on the story. Changing characters—and therefore perspectives—make for an even more complex text with several layers of possible meanings and ideas. As in the Olympics example, multiple perspectives may often be at odds with one another.

Rarely is there just one reason for a perspective and the actions that emerge from that perspective. For example, think about reasons why Walter Lee in *A Raisin in the Sun* refused Mr. Lindner's check. Here are just a few:

- the influence of layers of history with his father and his upbringing
- his mother's dream
- his treatment as less than a man by the society around him
- the desire for his own son to see that the family was proud and able to support itself

These layered perspectives add **complexity** for readers or viewers as they consider their own perspectives and how to interpret the ideas provided in the text.

Despite the layers of complexity to Walter Lee's perspective, Mr. Lindner clearly had a contrasting perspective informed by layers of his own experiences, though the play does not reveal those. The only perspective associated with Mr. Lindner in the play is that Black people and White people are not meant to live together. He does what he does based strictly on his perspective on the race of the Youngers, so his motivations are racist and bigoted.

## Changing Perspectives

German philosopher, cultural critic, composer, poet, and writer Friedrich Nietzsche made an observation that many people today have heard and take for granted: What does not kill me makes me stronger.

This sentiment has been echoed in a number of songs and poems and books ever since. The point is that your experiences often change you in some positive way, even if you may not recognize it. For example, Walter Lee's father dies, his mother is upset with him, and his friend runs off with his money all within a relatively short period of time. Though he would have likely chosen for none of these events to happen, they are the circumstances and events that lead him to making a change for the better.

For a majority of the play, Walter Lee is treated as puerile and ineffective. Even he knows that no one listens to him. His perspective is shaped by his experiences of being treated as a child by many around him.

His perspective changes when he has an epiphany about his role in the family—the moment when Mama challenges him to accept Lindner's check in front of his own child and demean himself before Mr. Lindner. At that moment, Walter Lee comes into his own. His interactions with Mama and his treatment by Willy all led to this change.

## Irony and Inconsistency

As you get to know the people in your life, you come to expect certain behavior from them. When someone in your life then does something unexpected or inconsistent, you may wonder what has changed or what has happened to that person. If a person behaves in the opposite way of those expectations, that situation is called **irony**—it is inconsistent with established expectations.

Characters are no different. When they behave inconsistently, you are forced to consider what has changed. Maybe an event or an interaction in the text affected them much more severely than you may have recognized. Maybe something has happened outside of the narrative that you will learn about later.

Again, consider Walter Lee's inconsistent behavior when he surprises everyone—even the audience—and rejects Mr. Lindner's check. Suddenly, his character is more complex and you have reason to think about how the interactions with other characters in the play have affected him in such a way as to change him.

Also consider Mama's final lines to Mr. Lindner. "I am afraid you don't understand. My son said we was going to move, and there ain't nothing left for me to say. . . . You know how these young folks is nowadays, mister. Can't do a thing with 'em!" These lines are ironic, since they are not consistent with Mama's domineering attitude toward her children.

 **Remember:** Multiple, and even contrasting, perspectives can occur within a single text and contribute to the complexity of the text. A narrator or speaker may change over the course of a text as a result of actions and interactions. Changes and inconsistencies in a narrator's or speaker's perspective may contribute to irony or the complexity of the text. (NAR-1.X–Z)

## 3.1 Checkpoint

*Review* No Exit *or another work of longer fiction or drama you are studying. Then complete the following open-response activities and answer the multiple-choice question.*

1. Examine two characters who have different perspectives on a similar or related subject. Explain in a few sentences how those perspectives contribute to some complexity in the text.

2. Explain in a few sentences how one of the major characters changes (not just when he or she reveals his or her true self) as a result of interactions in the room and how those changes may be consistent or inconsistent with his or her established character.

3. Which of the following best describes the relationship between the multiple perspectives presented by the three characters in *No Exit*?

    (A) A bitter, abused woman taunts a murderer in denial and a foolish pacifist as they attempt to ignore their earthly deeds.

    (B) A failed newspaper editor is mocked by a murdered beauty and an abuser of people who collaborate in their counterattack on him.

    (C) A cruel user and abuser of people taunts a vain, selfish murderer and an insecure coward who each try to find comfort in the other.

    (D) An angry but passive socializer confronts the fear of a bitter working-class woman and exploits that fear to abuse a coward.

    (E) A coward begs for and gets affirmation and approval from a disowned abuser and an immature, beautiful social climber.

## Creating on Your Own

Review the writing you did in previous Creating on Your Own activities. Consider revising your work to take the following questions into account:

1. What perspectives are developing in your writing? Are they different enough to be interesting? Consider revising to provide more contrast and contribute to more complexity in your writing.

2. How has a character's or narrator's perspective changed over the course of the text? Consider revising to include some inconsistent or ironic actions and perspectives.

# Part 3 Apply What You Have Learned

For one of the characters in *No Exit* or another play or work of longer fiction you are studying, examine the following:

1. The perspective the character displays in contrast with others

2. Interactions and behaviors in the text that may cause the character to change

3. Changes and inconsistencies in the character's perspectives that are ironic or that contribute to complexity

You may want to record your discoveries in a chart like the one on the next page.

| Changes and Perspectives of [insert character] | |
|---|---|
| 1. Character's perspective in contrast with others | |
| 2. Interactions and behaviors in the text that may cause the character to change | |
| 3. Changes and inconsistencies in the character's perspectives that are ironic or that contribute to complexities | |

Then choose the most valuable information and evidence from your examination and write two to three paragraphs that explain and support your thinking about that character's perspective and the development of that perspective throughout the text.

**Reflect on the Essential Question** Write a brief response that answers the essential question: *How do multiple, contrasting, and changing perspectives affect a reader's understanding?* In your answer, correctly use the key terms listed on page 624.

**Source:** Sarahszloboda
A scene from The Electric Company's 2009 production of *No Exit*
*How does the positioning of the characters express the characters' environment and relationships?*

# Part 4

# Writing Review II: Literary Analysis

**Enduring Understanding and Skills**

## Part 4  Writing Review II: Literary Analysis

### Understand
Readers establish and communicate their interpretations of literature through arguments supported by textual evidence. (LAN-1)

### Demonstrate
Develop a thesis statement that conveys a defensible claim about an interpretation of literature and that may establish a line of reasoning. (7.B)

Develop commentary that establishes and explains relationships among textual evidence, the line of reasoning, and the thesis. (7.C)

Select and use relevant and sufficient evidence to both develop and support a line of reasoning. (7.D)

See also Units 3, 4, 5, 6, 7 & 8

**Source:** *AP® English Literature and Composition Course and Exam Description*

**Essential Question:** How can you communicate in writing an interpretation of a play or longer work of fiction that asserts a claim, supports it with evidence, and connects it to a broader context with sophistication?

Mastering the writing techniques presented in Units 1–8 will prepare you well for the writing portions of the AP® examination. As you can review in the chart on the next page, those units covered

- a strong and defensible thesis statement
- quality evidence in sufficient quantities to support your thesis
- a line of reasoning with specific claims supported by the evidence
- clear commentary that explains how the evidence supports the line of reasoning
- sophisticated arguments that explain the significance of an interpretation within a broader context, discuss alternative interpretations, or use relevant analogies

This final unit will focus on the last bullet point and how to use an introduction and conclusion to help achieve a sophisticated argument.

complexities and tensions
broader context
introduction

alternative interpretations
vivid and persuasive style
conclusion

# 4.1 Reviewing the Literary Analysis Process

| LAN-1.A–W

The chart below shows the progression of skills you have developed. The words in bold show the key changes in the four main categories of written literary analysis:

- Thesis statement
- Commentary
- Evidence
- Elements of Composition

| Unit | Written Product |
|---|---|
| **Unit 1, Part 5** (pp. 53–66) Graphic organizer, p. 60 | • A **paragraph** of literary analysis about a work of literature that defends a **claim** (LAN-1.A–B), with<br>• **Textual evidence** to support the claim (LAN-1.C) |
| **Unit 2, Part 5** (pp. 115–126) Graphic organizer, p. 122 | • A **paragraph** of literary analysis about a poem that defends a **claim** (LAN-1.A–B), with<br>• **Textual evidence** to support the claim (LAN-1.C) |
| **Unit 3, Part 4** (pp. 186–200) Graphic organizer, p. 192 | **Thesis Statement**<br>• A **paragraph** of literary analysis with a full **thesis statement** expressing an interpretation of a longer literary text that may preview the line of reasoning and that requires defense through textual evidence and a line of reasoning (LAN-1.D–E)<br><br>**Commentary**<br>• a **logical sequence of claims** that work together to defend the overarching thesis statement (LAN-1.F)<br>• **commentary** that explains the relationships among the evidence, line of reasoning, and thesis (LAN-1.G)<br><br>**Evidence**<br>• **relevant and sufficient evidence** that strategically and purposefully illustrates, clarifies, exemplifies, associates, amplifies, or qualifies a point; **recursive process** used (LAN-1.H–K)<br><br>**Elements of Composition**<br>• correct use of **key conventions** of grammar and mechanics (LAN-1.L) |

*continued*

| | |
|---|---|
| **Unit 4, Part 5**<br>(pp. 255–268)<br>Graphic organizer,<br>p. 267 | **Thesis Statement**<br>• An **essay** of literary analysis about a longer work with a full thesis statement that may preview the line of reasoning and that guides the reader through evidence and a line of reasoning that connects the evidence to the thesis (LAN-1.D, E)<br>**Commentary**<br>• a **logical sequence of claims** that work together to defend the overarching thesis statement (LAN-1.F)<br>• **commentary** that explains the relationships among the evidence, line of reasoning, and thesis (LAN-1.G)<br>• **body paragraphs** that develop the reasoning and justify claims using evidence and commentary linking the evidence to the overarching thesis (LAN-1.M)<br>• **cohesive body paragraphs** that often use topic sentences to state a supporting claim and explain the reasoning connecting the various claims and evidence that make up the body of the essay (LAN-1.N)<br>**Evidence**<br>• **high-quality and sufficient evidence** used strategically and purposefully to illustrate, clarify, exemplify, associate, amplify, or qualify a point (LAN-1.H–J)<br>**Elements of Composition**<br>• **coherence** at the sentence, paragraph, and whole text level through devices that link ideas (LAN-1.O)<br>• coherence is reflected by a **logical arrangement** of reasons, evidence, and ideas and through such **linking techniques** as transitions, repetition, synonyms, pronoun references, and parallel structure (LAN-1.P) |
| **Unit 5, Part 5**<br>(pp. 331–342)<br>Graphic organizer,<br>p. 335 | All of the above in Unit 4 plus:<br>**Elements of Composition**<br>• **enhancement of coherence** through phrases, clauses, sentences, or paragraphs that show relationships among ideas (LAN-1.Q) |
| **Unit 6, Part 5**<br>(pp. 407–421)<br>Elements of<br>Composition | All of the above in Unit 5 plus:<br>**Elements of Composition**<br>• strategic **selection and placement of phrases and clauses**, including use of **coordination and subordination** to clarify relationship of ideas (LAN-1.R)<br>• **well-chosen words** (LAN-1.S)<br>• **punctuation** that clearly conveys relationships among ideas (LAN-1.T) |
| **Unit 7, Part 6**<br>(pp. 493–499) | All of the above in Unit 6 plus:<br>**Commentary**<br>• added **sophistication** through the explanation or relevance of an interpretation within a **broader context**, discussion of **alternative interpretations**, or use **of relevant analogies** for clarity (LAN-1.U)<br>**Evidence**<br>• **revision** of interpretation and line of reasoning if the evidence does not sufficiently support the initial interpretation or line of reasoning (LAN-1.V) |
| **Unit 8, Part 4**<br>(pp. 553–561) | All of the above in Unit 7 plus:<br>**Commentary**<br>• **acknowledgment** of words, ideas, images, texts, and other intellectual property of others through **attribution, citation, and reference** (LAN-1.W) |

**Table 9-4**

## 4.1 Checkpoint

Choose one of the essays you have written that you are most proud of or that you especially enjoyed working on. Evaluate how effectively it

- explores complexities or tensions in the text
- situates the argument in a broader context
- explores alternative interpretations
- uses vivid and persuasive language

Think about how you might improve in each area. Write notes to yourself for each bullet point to return to when you revise your essay. Save your work.

### Composing on Your Own

Use library or Internet resources to find two or three critical articles on the work that is the subject of the essay you decided to revise in the Checkpoint above. Complete a chart like the following to keep track of your sources and what you learn. One row of a chart based on *A Raisin in the Sun* is modeled below.

| **Work:** *A Raisin in the Sun* | | |
| --- | --- | --- |
| **My working thesis:** The failure of Walter Lee's dream to materialize has as its cause enduring racism and oppression, rather than flaws in the angry man's character. | | |
| **Source 1** | **Relation to My Thesis** | **Ideas and Quotes I Could Use** |
| Washington, J. Charles. "A Raisin in the Sun Revisited." *Black American Literature Forum* 22.1, Black Women Writers Issue (1988): 109–24. | This presents an opposing view, so I will explain why it is less sound than my interpretation. | "Walter's dream remains only that not because of defects in the American system but because of basic flaws in his own character" (120). |

*What power dynamics between Mama and Walter Lee seem to show in this scene from a 1959 production of* A Raisin in the Sun?

## The Critic's Craft: Conversations Through Literary Texts

Shakespeare's Sonnet 130 ("My mistress' eyes are nothing like the sun") is a response to and parody of the frequent depictions of ideal beauty in Elizabethan poetry. Wilfred Owen's haunting World War I poem "Dulce et Decorum Est" was in part a response to popular poems told with "high zest" to encourage young men to fight for their countries. The two dramatists featured in this unit, Jean-Paul Sartre and Lorraine Hansberry, represent two very different philosophies of human agency, and although *A Raisin in the Sun* is not a direct response to *No Exit*, Hansberry's final play, *Les Blancs* (The Whites) was a direct response to the work of another French existential dramatist, the play *Les Nègres* (The Blacks) by Jean Genet. Hansberry disputed the existentialists' focus on nothingness and despair and the absurdity of life that dominated intellectual thought after World War II. She believed that the plays and other literary works that grew out of existentialism were racist and sexist and lacked a moral center. She believed they ignored the historical circumstances that led to oppression and the possibilities of humans to bring about social change. When she herself was criticized for not adopting "the vogue of despair" in her work, she responded that "Attention must be paid in equal and careful measure to the frequent triumph of [humans], if not nature, *over* the absurd."

## Use the Critic's Craft

Write a review of *No Exit* through the lens of someone like Hansberry, or write a review of *A Raisin in the Sun* through the lens of an existentialist. Compare your reviews with those of your classmates.

**Source:** Dutch National Archives

Jean-Paul Sartre, 1965

# 4.2 Developing Sophistication in Critical Analysis

| LAN-1.U, LAN-1.V, LAN-1.W

The four bullet points in 4.1 Checkpoint come from the College Board's rubric and describe some of the features readers look for in essays when awarding the point for sophistication. Such sophistication will also be expected in your college writing. To earn the point, such essays should meet at least one of those requirements, though not necessarily all of them.

Suppose you have gotten this far in writing a draft supporting your working thesis on *A Raisin in the Sun*.

(1) The failure of Walter Lee's dream to materialize has as one of its causes enduring racism, not just flaws in the angry man's character.

(2) Walter Lee's dream for a business of his own is not unreasonable. In Act I, Scene One, Ruth tells Walter that Willy Harris, who wants to buy a liquor store with Walter, is "a good-for-nothing loudmouth." Walter responds by reminding her of another person she called "a good-for-nothing loudmouth," Charlie Atkins, who wanted Walter to go into his dry-cleaning business and is now earning $100,000 a year. This detail supports the idea that Walter could have a chance at success in business—that it is not an irresponsible dream. His earlier dream for this, with Charlie Atkins, was deferred but not unreasonable. He is tired of being a chauffeur for a rich White man with only stories of how rich White men live to pass on to his son Travis.

(3) The insurance money belongs to Lena, and no one in the family thinks Walter would not share any success in business with the entire family. Walter's dream is another path out of the stifling living circumstances the family finds itself in, just as is Beneatha's dream of becoming a doctor, though her path out does not as clearly include the family. Ruth comes around to supporting Walter when she is alone with Mama.

MAMA: We ain't no business people, Ruth. We just plain working folks.

RUTH: Ain't nobody business people till they go into business. Walter Lee say colored people ain't never going to start getting ahead till they start gambling on some different kinds of things in the world—investments and things.

Walter's desire to start a business is not a character flaw that needs overcoming but rather another reasonable way to plan a path toward some kind of financial security.

(4) Finally, in the scene leading up to the emotional climax of the play, Walter tells his family that there are always takers and those who get "tooken." He says he thanks Willy, the man who stole the money that was to go toward buying the liquor store and Beneatha's education, for teaching him the lesson that he has to keep his eyes on "what

counts in this world." He says he is going to take the money from Mr. Lindner while he's got the chance. After his sister turns on him for this decision, Mama reminds her that now more than ever they need to love Walter. "When you starts measuring somebody, measure him right, child, measure him right. Make sure you done taken into account what hills and valleys he come through before he got to wherever he is." When Walter actually refuses the money instead, his Mama and Ruth agree that he had come into himself as a man by doing so.

(5) But how, exactly, did that decision make him more of a man than he was? Mama said that the family never let anyone pay them anything as a way of telling them they "wasn't fit to walk the earth." What message, though, is being sent by the people who have hired Ruth and Mama and Walter to drive their cars or clean their clothes or houses and paid them in wages so low that the whole family cannot afford to live in anything more than a two-bedroom kitchenette apartment? How is the family better off because of Walter's decision? They are moving into a neighborhood where they will be unwelcome and possibly threatened; Walter will still be a chauffeur; they will still have to work hard to pay the mortgage. Ruth says, "I'll work twenty hours a day in all the kitchens in Chicago . . . I'll strap my baby on my back if I have to and scrub all the floors in America and wash all the sheets in America if I have to—but we got to MOVE!"

This draft uses evidence to support a line of reasoning that, in turn, justifies the claim in the thesis statement. But it can do more by working in the following considerations.

## Complexities and Tensions

The draft above already includes **complexities and tensions**, specifically Mama's reaction to Beneatha when she writes off Walter for his decision and the consequences of Walter's final decision in tension with the pride the family feels. However, more explicit language would help bring theses complexities and tensions to the fore.

Consider the effect the explicit language would have if it were added to this section of paragraph 4. The new wording is in italic type.

> He says he is going to take the money from Mr. Lindner while he's got the chance. After his sister turns on him for this decision, Mama, *who herself has been critical of Walter and his focus on money,* reminds her that now more than ever they need to love Walter, *adding complexity to her character.*

Or consider how the tension of values might be highlighted if the following sentences were added to paragraph 5.

> *Yet no one can doubt that Walter has made the right decision. He has not groveled to Mr. Lindner in exchange for money, just as Rosa Parks did not give up her seat to a White person in exchange for not being arrested. He stood with his family.*

## Situating in a Broader Context

Recall the path to a thesis statement: big (or universal) idea → thematic statement → thesis statement. To situate your argument in a **broader context**, think back to the big ideas and themes that you associate with this work and your thesis. Ask yourself how what you are writing helps explain or illuminate some aspect of the broader world.

Chances are the thinking that might have brought you to this working thesis statement relates to the growing awareness people have of racial injustice that is so pervasive that a single individual's choices may have little effect in combating it. Situating your argument about Walter in this context, which is already expressed in your working thesis statement, might best be done in an **introduction**, typically a first paragraph in an essay that establishes the context for the argument and often leads up to the thesis statement as the final sentence. Here's how you might situate the argument about Walter in an introductory paragraph.

> Lorraine Hansberry's play *A Raisin in the Sun* was the first play by a Black woman to appear on Broadway (1959). It was described by James Baldwin as the first time "so much of the truth of black people's lives [had] been seen on the stage." In the more than 50 years since its debut, conversations about race have gone through many changes. The most recent focuses on racism so deeply ingrained in American life that escaping from it can seem impossible. Although many viewers and critics see Walter Lee's choices as he comes into manhood as the high point of the play, through the lens of racism, a different interpretation is possible. The failure of Walter Lee's dream to materialize has as one of its causes enduring racism, not just flaws in the angry man's character.

## Alternative Interpretations

Including and responding to **alternative interpretations** also adds sophistication to a literary argument. You can refer to alternative interpretations generally, as in "While some viewers may feel . . . ." You can also refer to interpretations by specific critics. For example, you may include the information you found in the article by J. Charles Washington referred to above (see page 632). He wrote "Walter's dream remains only that not because of defects in the American system but because of basic flaws in his own character." You might work that into the introduction, as shown on the next page.

> Many viewers and critics see Walter Lee's choices as he comes into manhood as the high point of the play, with his previous choices as the source of the problem. For example, J. Charles Washington writes in *Black American Literature Forum* (1988) that "Walter's dream remains only that not because of defects in the American system but because of basic flaws in his own character." However, through the lens of racism, a different interpretation is possible. The failure of Walter Lee's dream to materialize has as one of its causes enduring racism, which is evident throughout the play, not just flaws in the angry man's character.

# Vivid and Persuasive Style

Precise word choice, effective use of subordination and coordination, and smooth transitions will contribute to a **vivid and persuasive style**. The following draft has been revised with these features in mind. The additions and changes are underlined. Some, like the more precise word *catharsis* or the phrase *subtle shifts in focus*, strengthen your credibility in literary analysis. Other changes, such as in the first sentences of paragraphs 1 and 3, combine sentences with the use of phrases and clauses. The first sentence of paragraph 2 provides a stronger transition between paragraphs.

(1) Lorraine Hansberry's play *A Raisin in the Sun*, the first play by a Black woman to appear on Broadway (1959), was described by James Baldwin as the first time "so much of the truth of black people's lives [had] been seen on the stage." In the more than 50 years since its debut, conversations about race have gone through many subtle shifts in focus. The most recent focus is on racism so deeply ingrained in American life that extricating from it can seem impossible. Many viewers and critics see Walter Lee's choices as he comes into manhood as the catharsis of the play, with his choices as the source of the problem. For example, J. Charles Washington writes in *Black American Literature Forum* (1988) that "Walter's dream remains only that not because of defects in the American system but because of basic flaws in his own character." However, through the lens of racism a different interpretation is possible. The failure of Walter Lee's dream to materialize has as one of its causes enduring racism, which is evident throughout the play, not just flaws in the angry man's character.

(2) Walter has good reason to be angry. His dream for a business of his own is not unreasonable. In Act I, Scene One, Ruth tells Walter that Willy Harris, who wants to buy a liquor store with Walter, is "a good-for-nothing loudmouth." Walter responds by reminding her of another person she called "a good-for-nothing loudmouth," Charlie Atkins, who wanted Walter to go into his dry-cleaning business and is now earning $100,000 a year. This detail supports the idea that Walter could have a chance at success in business—that it is not an irresponsible dream. His earlier dream for this was deferred but not unreasonable. He is tired of being a chauffeur for a rich White man with only stories of how rich White men live to pass on to his son Travis.

(3) Further, while it is true that the insurance money belongs to Lena, no one in the family thinks Walter would not share any success in business with the entire family. Walter's dream is another path out of the stifling living circumstances the family finds itself in, just as is Beneatha's dream of becoming a doctor, though her path out does not as clearly include the family. Ruth comes around to supporting Walter when she is alone with Mama. . . .

## Conclusion

A final paragraph, or **conclusion**, can pull the pieces of your literary analysis together for a strong and clear ending. In some cases, the conclusion refers back to ideas in the introduction to create a sense of closing a "full circle." One possible conclusion for the essay above is the following.

> (4) Yet Mama, who felt "some awful pain inside her" earlier when Walter announced his intention to accept Lindner's offer, takes a softer tone toward Walter when Beneatha says Walter has brought death to the family. Mama says, "Child, when do you think is the time to love somebody the most? When they done good and made things easy for everybody? Well then, you ain't through learning—because that ain't the time at all. It's when he's at his lowest and can't believe in hisself 'cause the world done whipped him so!" Through these words, Mama seems to recognize that pervasive oppression faces Black people and that the responsibility to relieve that oppression lies with those in the world who have done the whipping. Yet Walter's decision to say no, especially in front of his son, is a necessary step to believing in himself.

*NOTE: Introductions and conclusions are not required on the AP® Exam as long as the other elements are present, though they will become standard requirements in college.*

**Remember:** More sophisticated literary arguments may explain the significance or relevance of an interpretation within a broader context, discuss alternative interpretations of a text, or use relevant analogies to help an audience better understand an interpretation. Writers must acknowledge words, ideas, images, texts, and other intellectual property of others through attribution, citation, or reference. (LAN-1.U–W)

### 4.2 Checkpoint

Return to the essay you chose to revise and your notes on the bullet points. Using the strategies above, revise your essay to add sophistication to your argument and language.

**Composing on Your Own**

Share your work with a peer and ask for feedback, especially on the points related to sophistication. Make revisions as you see fit based on your peer's comments.

# Part 4 Apply What You Have Learned

The final stage of the writing process is editing. Make sure you clearly communicate to an academic audience by demonstrating control over the elements of composition. Do a final check of your essay for correct spelling, usage, and punctuation. Consider having someone else do a check for you as well.

**Reflect on the Essential Question** Write a brief response that answers the essential question: *How can you communicate in writing an interpretation of a play or longer work of fiction that asserts a claim, supports it with evidence, and connects it to a broader context with sophistication?* In your answer, correctly use the key terms listed on page 630.

# Unit 9 Review

## Section I: Multiple Choice

## Section II: Free Response

---

## Section I: Multiple Choice

Questions 1–10. Read the following passage carefully before you choose your answers.

1    *HEDDA enters from the left through the inner room. Her face and figure show refinement and distinction. Her complexion is pale and opaque. Her steel-grey eyes express a cold, unruffled repose. Her hair is of an agreeable brown, but not particularly abundant. She is dressed in a tasteful, somewhat loose-fitting morning gown.*

2    MISS TESMAN: [*Going to meet HEDDA.*] Good morning, my dear Hedda! Good morning, and a hearty welcome!

3    HEDDA: [*Holds out her hand.*] Good morning, dear Miss Tesman! So early a call! That is kind of you.

4    MISS TESMAN: [*With some embarrassment.*] Well—has the bride slept well in her new home?

5    HEDDA: Oh yes, thanks. Passably.

6    GEORGE: [*Laughing.*] Passably! Come, that's good, Hedda! You were sleeping like a stone when I got up.

7    HEDDA: Fortunately. Of course one has always to accustom one's self to new surroundings, Miss Tesman—little by little. [*Looking towards the left.*] Oh, there the servant has gone and opened the veranda door, and let in a whole flood of sunshine.

8    MISS TESMAN: [*Going towards the door.*] Well, then we will shut it.

9    HEDDA: No no, not that! Tesman, please draw the curtains. That will give a softer light.

10   GEORGE: [*At the door.*] All right—all right.—There now, Hedda, now you have both shade and fresh air.

11   HEDDA: Yes, fresh air we certainly must have, with all these stacks of flowers—. But—won't you sit down, Miss Tesman?

12   MISS TESMAN: No, thank you. Now that I have seen that everything is all right here—thank heaven!—I must be getting home again. My sister is lying longing for me, poor thing.

13    GEORGE: Give her my very best love, Auntie; and say I shall look in and see her later in the day.

14    MISS TESMAN: Yes, yes, I'll be sure to tell her. But by-the-by, George—[*Feeling in her dress pocket*]—I had almost forgotten—I have something for you here.

15    GEORGE: What is it, Auntie? Eh?

16    MISS TESMAN: [*Produces a flat parcel wrapped in newspaper and hands it to him.*] Look here, my dear boy.

17    GEORGE: [*Opening the parcel.*] Well, I declare!—Have you really saved them for me, Aunt Julia! Hedda! Isn't this touching—eh?

18    HEDDA: [*Beside the whatnot on the right.*] Well, what is it?

19    GEORGE: My old morning-shoes! My slippers.

20    HEDDA: Indeed. I remember you often spoke of them while we were abroad.

21    GEORGE: Yes, I missed them terribly. [*Goes up to her.*] Now you shall see them, Hedda!

22    HEDDA: [*Going towards the stove.*] Thanks, I really don't care about it.

23    GEORGE: [*Following her.*] Only think—ill as she was, Aunt Rina embroidered these for me. Oh you can't think how many associations cling to them.

24    HEDDA: [*At the table.*] Scarcely for me.

25    MISS TESMAN: Of course not for Hedda, George.

26    GEORGE: Well, but now that she belongs to the family, I thought—

27    HEDDA: [*Interrupting.*] We shall never get on with this servant, Tesman.

28    MISS TESMAN: Not get on with Berta?

29    GEORGE: Why, dear, what puts that in your head? Eh?

30    HEDDA: [*Pointing.*] Look there! She has left her old bonnet lying about on a chair.

31    GEORGE: [*In consternation, drops the slippers on the floor.*] Why, Hedda—

32    HEDDA: Just fancy, if any one should come in and see it.

33    GEORGE: But Hedda—that's Aunt Julia's bonnet.

34    HEDDA: Is it!

35    MISS TESMAN: [*Taking up the bonnet.*] Yes, indeed it's mine. And, what's more, it's not old, Madam Hedda.

36    HEDDA: I really did not look closely at it, Miss Tesman.

37    MISS TESMAN: [*Trying on the bonnet.*] Let me tell you it's the first time I have worn it—the very first time.

38    GEORGE: And a very nice bonnet it is too—quite a beauty!

39    MISS TESMAN: Oh, it's no such great thing, George. [*Looks around her.*] My parasol—? Ah, here. [*Takes it.*] For this is mine too—[*mutters*]—not Berta's.

40    GEORGE: A new bonnet and a new parasol! Only think, Hedda.

41    HEDDA: Very handsome indeed.

42  GEORGE: Yes, isn't it? Eh? But Auntie, take a good look at Hedda before you go! See how handsome she is!

43  MISS TESMAN: Oh, my dear boy, there's nothing new in that. Hedda was always lovely.

44  GEORGE: [*Following.*] Yes, but have you noticed what splendid condition she is in? How she has filled out on the journey?

45  HEDDA: [*Crossing the room.*] Oh, do be quiet—!

46  MISS TESMAN: [*Who has stopped and turned.*] Filled out?

47  GEORGE: Of course you don't notice it so much now that she has that dress on. But I, who can see—

48  HEDDA: [*At the glass door, impatiently.*] Oh, you can't see anything.

49  GEORGE: It must be the mountain air in the Tyrol—

50  HEDDA: [*Curtly, interrupting.*] I am exactly as I was when I started.

51  GEORGE: So you insist; but I'm quite certain you are not. Don't you agree with me, Auntie?

52  MISS TESMAN: [*Who has been gazing at her with folded hands.*] Hedda is lovely—lovely—lovely. [*Goes up to her, takes her head between both hands, draws it downwards, and kisses her hair.*] God bless and preserve Hedda Tesman—for George's sake.

53  HEDDA: [*Gently freeing herself.*] Oh—! Let me go.

54  MISS TESMAN: [*In quiet emotion.*] I shall not let a day pass without coming to see you.

55  GEORGE: No you won't, will you, Auntie? Eh?

56  MISS TESMAN: Good-bye—good-bye!

57  [*She goes out by the hall door. GEORGE accompanies her. The door remains half open. GEORGE can be heard repeating his message to Aunt Rina and his thanks for the slippers.*]

58  [*In the meantime, HEDDA walks about the room, raising her arms and clenching her hands as if in desperation. Then she flings back the curtains from the glass door, and stands there looking out.*]

---

1.  The statement "So early a call!" in Hedda's first lines in line 3 ("Good morning . . . kind of you.") most clearly serves to introduce Hedda and a series of her subsequent comments in the excerpt as

   (A) doting and dutiful to her husband and his family

   (B) kind and naive as a young newlywed

   (C) suffering at the will of her emotionally unavailable husband

   (D) impatient with others, distant and cold in her relationships

   (E) persistent in her attempts to be liked by her new family

2. The conflict emerging between Hedda and Miss Tesman most likely represents which of the following conflicting values?

   (A) education and liberation of women vs. commitment to domestic obligations

   (B) appearances and how others perceive you vs. devotion to family at all costs

   (C) the care and well-being of children vs. concern about the world into which children are being born

   (D) marriage for love vs. marriage for practicality

   (E) acceptance of extended family vs. stubborn dedication to parents and siblings

3. Hedda's behavior at the end of the excerpt at line 53 ("In the meantime . . . stands there looking out.") indicates which of the following about her perspective?

   (A) She feels powerless and is already looking for an escape.

   (B) She cannot contain her anger toward Miss Tesman.

   (C) She wants nothing more than to be alone with her husband.

   (D) She fears that which she cannot control.

   (E) She can find escape only in the peace of nature.

4. Which of the following best describes the significance of the statement following the dash in paragraph 37?

   (A) It demonstrates the judgment and bitterness of Miss Tesman toward Hedda.

   (B) It illustrates George's concern about the relationship between Hedda and his aunt.

   (C) It shows how Miss Tesman cannot maintain a line of reasoning.

   (D) It reiterates the foolishness of Hedda's comments about Miss Tesman's bonnet.

   (E) It supports Hedda's feelings toward Miss Tesman.

5.  Which of the following is a complex, defensible claim that could be made about Hedda based on this passage?

    (A)  Despite lacking tact and respect in her interactions with Miss Tesman, Hedda is very happy in her marriage.

    (B)  As a newlywed, Hedda has much to learn about the interactions between family members.

    (C)  Though she appears happy, what Hedda says and her actions when she is alone reveal unhappiness and discontent.

    (D)  Whenever possible, Hedda will escape her marriage.

    (E)  Miss Tesman can see beyond her beauty to the person Hedda really is.

Question 6 is covered in Unit 3.

6.  In the context of the passage, all of the following are significant aspects of the setting EXCEPT

    (A)  the curtains

    (B)  the time of day

    (C)  the veranda door

    (D)  the furniture

    (E)  the hallway

Questions 7 and 8 are covered in Unit 6.

7.  Which of the following best describes how the structure of paragraph 11 ("Yes . . . Miss Tesman.") functions in the passage?

    (A)  It shows the level of detail about which Hedda is concerned.

    (B)  It shows the concern that George and Miss Tesman have for Hedda's comfort.

    (C)  It shows how Hedda cares first about her own comfort and then about the comfort of others.

    (D)  It shows how Miss Tesman has sought to make Hedda uncomfortable in her new surroundings.

    (E)  It shows how sensitive Hedda is to all of the attention she is receiving.

8. The bonnet and the slippers can both be seen as symbolic of
    (A) George's ignorance about Hedda's situation
    (B) Miss Tesman's commitment to her family
    (C) George's unreturned love and affection for Hedda
    (D) Hedda's disconnect from the people around her
    (E) Hedda's dislike of Miss Tesman and her treatment

Questions 9 and 10 are covered in Unit 7.

9. In paragraphs 27–28, Miss Tesman's reaction to Hedda's comment that she and Tesman "shall never get on with this servant" suggests that
    (A) Miss Tesman knows the servant and is surprised by this
    (B) Hedda is being vindictive because she wants to hurt the family
    (C) Miss Tesman did not know they had a servant
    (D) George feels the servant is part of the family, like Hedda
    (E) Berta must be more careful in her interactions with Hedda

10. Miss Tesman's bringing George his slippers (paragraphs 14–24) is significant because it
    (A) illustrates her and George's commitment to family and tradition
    (B) proves Hedda's foolishness in how she treats Miss Tesman
    (C) confirms that Miss Tesman seeks to be more important than Hedda
    (D) establishes the conflict between George and Hedda
    (E) contrasts with Miss Tesman's treatments of Hedda

Questions 11–20. Read the following poetic speech from a drama carefully before you choose your answers.

> The quality of mercy is not strained.
> It droppeth as the gentle rain from heaven
> Upon the place beneath. It is twice blest:
> It blesseth him that gives and him that takes.
> 5    'Tis mightiest in the mightiest; it becomes
> The thronèd monarch better than his crown.
> His scepter shows the force of temporal power,
> The attribute to awe and majesty
> Wherein doth sit the dread and fear of kings;
> 10   But mercy is above this sceptered sway.
> It is enthronèd in the hearts of kings;
> It is an attribute to God Himself;
> And earthly power doth then show likest God's

When mercy seasons justice. Therefore, Jew,[1]
15    Though justice be thy plea, consider this:
That in the course of justice none of us
Should see salvation. We do pray for mercy,
And that same prayer doth teach us all to render
The deeds of mercy. I have spoke thus much
20    To mitigate[2] the justice of thy plea,
Which, if thou follow, this strict court of Venice
Must needs give sentence 'gainst the merchant there.

11. In the direct address of the speaker to the "Jew" (lines 14–23), the values in conflict are

    (A) mercy and salvation

    (B) religion and mercy

    (C) mercy and justice

    (D) victory and justice

    (E) vengeance and justice

12. Which of the following best characterizes the speech as a whole?

    (A) a contrast between the results of mercy and the consequences of focusing only on justice

    (B) an argument that mercy is nothing when someone in power cannot guarantee it

    (C) an explanation of what makes justice valuable in the face of mercy and vengeance

    (D) an explanation of the results of mercy when used in a compassionate way

    (E) an argument that showing mercy makes someone greater than having power

Questions 13 and 14 are covered in Unit 2.

13. Repetition of the pronoun *it* throughout most of the speech refers to

    (A) "The quality of mercy" (line 1)

    (B) "the gentle rain from heaven" (line 2)

    (C) "The thronèd monarch" (line 6)

    (D) "the hearts of kings" (line 11)

    (E) "the course of justice" (line 16)

---

1  **Jew:** short for *Jewish*; someone whose religion is Judaism
2  **mitigate:** make less severe, serious, or painful

**14.** Which of the following best describes the effect of line 8 ("The attribute of awe and majesty") standing alone and with no punctuation?

    (A) It contrasts the role of the monarch with that of the merchant.

    (B) It contrasts mercy with the consequences of power.

    (C) It emphasizes the consequences of vengeance.

    (D) It emphasizes the greatness of mercy.

    (E) It defines the role of the monarch in handing out mercy.

Question 15 is covered in Unit 4.

**15.** In context, the word *becomes* (line 5) means "looks good on or suits." Which of the following best explains how this definition functions in the speech?

    (A) It explains the role of mercy in determining who has power and how best to use that power.

    (B) It pleads to the reader to consider how being merciful looks to others and how that can be used to gain power.

    (C) It makes a claim that mercy makes a powerful person look better than the symbols that signify power.

    (D) It denies the importance of one's image in favor of what one actually does and says.

    (E) It defines the role power plays in determining when one can or cannot be merciful.

Question 16 is covered in Unit 5.

**16.** In the context of the speech, all of the following images relate to imagery of power EXCEPT

    (A) "The thronèd monarch" (line 6)

    (B) "awe and majesty" (line 8)

    (C) "sceptered sway" (line 10)

    (D) "enthronèd in the hearts of kings" (line 11)

    (E) "the course of justice" (line 16)

Question 17 is covered in Unit 6.

**17.** In the context of the speech, the "scepter" (line 7) symbolizes

(A) the power of the monarch

(B) the value of mercy

(C) the permanence of justice

(D) the struggle against tyranny

(E) the loss of faith in salvation

Questions 18–20 are covered in Unit 7.

**18.** The shift that begins at the end of line 14 (". . . Therefore, Jew") can best be described as between

(A) the condition of mercy and the value of justice as part of that mercy

(B) the speaker's reasoning about mercy and plea to the Jew as the audience

(C) the definition of mercy by itself and how it is viewed as part of justice

(D) the Jew's understanding of mercy and the speaker's understanding of it

(E) the failure of the justice system and the need for mercy because of those failures

**19.** The comparison in lines 13–14 ("And Earthly ... Jew") demonstrates the speaker's perspective that

(A) mercy relies on religion

(B) only kings can show mercy

(C) mercy comes only from power

(D) showing mercy is godlike

(E) only God can show mercy

**20.** In the context of the speech as a whole, the simile in lines 2–3 ("It droppeth . . . twice blest") suggests that mercy is both gentle and

(A) vengeful

(B) generous

(C) pitiful

(D) nourishing

(E) divine

## Section II: Free Response
### Question 1: Poetry Analysis

In the poetic speech on page 646 from Shakespeare's *The Merchant of Venice*, the speaker, a woman named Portia, asks another character, Shylock, to show mercy to someone who has wronged him. Read the poetic speech carefully. Then, in a well-written essay, analyze how Shakespeare uses poetic elements and techniques to develop the complex perspective of the speaker.

In your response you should do the following:

- Respond to the prompt with a thesis that presents a defensible interpretation.
- Select and use evidence to support your line of reasoning.
- Explain how the evidence supports your line of reasoning.
- Use appropriate grammar and punctuation in communicating your argument.

### Question 2: Prose Fiction Analysis

On pages 640–642 is an excerpt from the play *Hedda Gabler* written in 1891 by Norwegian playwright Henrik Ibsen. In the passage, George Tesman's aunt visits the home of the newlywed George and his wife Hedda, who have just returned from a long honeymoon.

Read the passage carefully. Then, in a well-written essay, analyze how Ibsen uses literary elements and techniques to reveal the complex perspective of Hedda.

In your response you should do the following:

- Respond to the prompt with a thesis that presents a defensible interpretation.
- Select and use evidence to support your line of reasoning.
- Explain how the evidence supports your line of reasoning.
- Use appropriate grammar and punctuation in communicating your argument.

## Question 3: Literary Argument—Differing Perspectives

In Act 2, Scene Two of the play *Hamlet*, the title character explains that "there is nothing either good or bad, but thinking makes it so."

Choose a work of fiction with characters or narrators whose perspectives view the good or bad of a situation in different ways. Then, in a well-written essay, analyze how the different perspectives contribute to an interpretation of the work as a whole. Do not merely summarize the plot.

In your response you should do the following:

- Respond to the prompt with a thesis that presents a defensible interpretation.
- Provide evidence to support your line of reasoning.
- Explain how the evidence supports your line of reasoning.
- Use appropriate grammar and punctuation in communicating your argument.

# AP® English Literature Practice Exam

## Section I

### TIME—1 HOUR

**Directions:** *This section consists of selections from literary works and questions on their content, form, and style. After reading each passage or poem, choose the best answer to each question and then fill in the corresponding circle on the answer sheet.*

**Note:** Pay particular attention to the requirements of questions that contain the words NOT, LEAST, or EXCEPT.

**Questions 1-13. Read the following passage carefully before you choose your answers.**

1      Cayetana greeted that dawn with a concoction made with coffee beans and burned corn kernels. As the light poured out of the eastern sea and splashed into windows from coast to coast, Mexicans rose and went to their million kitchens and cooking fires to pour their first rations of coffee. A tidal wave of coffee rushed west across the land, rising and falling from kitchen to fire ring to cave to ramada.[1] Some drank coffee from thick glasses. Some sipped it from colorful gourds, rough clay pots that dissolved as they drank, cones of banana leaf. Café negro.[2] Café with canela.[3] Café with goat's milk. Café with a golden-brown cone of piloncillo[4] melting in it like a pyramid engulfed by a black flood. Tropical café with a dollop of sugarcane rum coiling in it like a hot snake. Bitter mountaintop café that thickened the blood. In Sinaloa,[5] café with boiled milk, its burned milk skin floating on top in a pale membrane that looked like the flesh of a peeled blister. The heavy-eyed stared into the round mirrors of their cups and regarded their own dark reflections. And Cayetana Chávez, too, lifted a cup, her coffee reboiled from yesterday's grounds and grits, sweet with spoons of sugarcane syrup, and lightened by thin blue milk stolen with a few quick squeezes from one of the patrón's cows.

2      On that long westward morning, all Mexicans still dreamed the same dream. They dreamed of being Mexican. There was no greater mystery.

---

1 **ramada:** porch
2 **Café negro:** Spanish for "black coffee"
3 **canela:** Spanish for "cinnamon"
4 **piloncillo:** unrefined cane sugar
5 **Sinaloa:** Mexican state on the west coast

3    Only rich men, soldiers, and a few Indians had wandered far enough from home to learn the terrible truth: Mexico was too big. It had too many colors. It was noisier than anyone could have imagined, and the voice of the Atlantic was different from the voice of the Pacific. One was shrill, worried, and demanding. The other was boisterous, easy to rile into a frenzy. The rich men, soldiers, and Indians were the few who knew that the east was a swoon of green, a thick-aired smell of ripe fruit and flowers and dead pigs and salt and sweat and mud, while the west was a riot of purple. Pyramids rose between llanos[6] of dust and among turgid jungles. Snakes as long as country roads swam tame beside canoes. Volcanoes wore hats of snow. Cactus forests grew taller than trees. Shamans ate mushrooms and flew. In the south, some tribes still went nearly naked, their women wearing red flowers in their hair and blue skirts, and their breasts hanging free. Men outside the great Mexico City ate tacos made of live winged ants that flew away if the men did not chew quickly enough.

4    So what were they? Every Mexican was a diluted Indian, invaded by milk like the coffee in Cayetana's cup. Afraid, after the Conquest and the Inquisition, of their own brown wrappers, they colored their faces with powder, covered their skins in perfumes and European silks and American habits. Yet for all their beaver hats and their lace veils, the fine citizens of the great cities knew they had nothing that would ever match the ancient feathers of the quetzal.[7] No cacique[8] stood atop any temple clad in jaguar skins. Crinolines,[9] waistcoats. Operas, High Mass, café au lait[10] in demitasse cups in sidewalk patisseries.[11] They attempted to choke the gods with New York pantaloons, Parisian petticoats. But still the banished spirits whispered from corners and basements. In Mexico City, the great and fallen Tenochtitlán,[12] among streets and buildings constructed with the stones of the Pyramid of the Sun, gentlemen walked with their heads slightly tilted, cocked as if listening to this puzzling murmur of wraiths.[13]

5    They still spoke a thousand languages—Spanish, too, to be sure, but also a thicket of songs and grammars. Mexico—the sound of wind in the ruins. Mexico—the waves rushing the shore. Mexico—the sand dunes, the snowfields, the steam of sleeping Popocatépetl.[14] Mexico—across marijuana fields, tomato plants, avocado trees, the agave[15] in the village of Tequila.

---

6 **llanos:** plains
7 **quetzal:** an ornately colored bird found in central America; the plumage of the feathered serpent, a major Mexican god before the Spanish conquest
8 **cacique:** originally a name for a native chief, it came to refer to a local political boss after the Spanish conquest
9 **Crinolines:** structures designed to be worn under skirts to hold them away from the body; hoop skirts
10 **café au lait::** French for "coffee with hot milk"
11 **patisseries:** French for "pastry shops"
12 **Tenochtitlán:** capital of the Aztec empire at the time of the Spanish conquest; the Spanish built Mexico City on and with its ruins.
13 **wraiths:** ghosts or ghostlike images
14 **Popocatépetl:** a volcano in central Mexico
15 **agave:** a succulent plant whose leaves yield a sweetener

1. The details provided in paragraph 1, sentence 14 ("And Cayetana . . . cows.") could suggest all of the following about Cayetana EXCEPT that she
   (A) may not be able to afford fresh coffee and milk on a daily basis
   (B) chooses not to spend money on fresh coffee and milk on a daily basis
   (C) finds ways to save small amounts of money wherever she can
   (D) steals from others merely for the excitement it provides
   (E) does not have her own access to fresh coffee or fresh milk

2. Within the context of the passage, paragraph 1 serves primarily to
   (A) establish the diversity of the cultures across Mexico through coffee imagery and symbolism
   (B) suggest an antagonistic relationship between Cayetana and the general setting in which she lives
   (C) juxtapose the dream and the mystery of being Mexican mentioned in paragraph 2
   (D) illustrate the drastic differences between the varied people of Mexico to characterize Cayetana as a distinct outcast
   (E) convey the jovial atmosphere in which the rest of the passage takes place

3. The adjective "noisier" in paragraph 3, sentence 3 ("It was . . . Pacific.") figuratively means
   (A) a unified voice of one people and one culture
   (B) the cry of the native Mexican for justice
   (C) a single culture demanding recognition among the sea of others
   (D) the bustling and expanding Mexican economy
   (E) a confusing jumble of people and cultures and languages

4. Which of the following best describes how the details provided in paragraph 3 establish the setting of the passage?

(A) They contrast those who are wealthy enough to afford foreign goods with those who continue to live off the land.

(B) They describe the daily challenges indigenous Mexican people face in their daily lives.

(C) They provide images that emphasize the economic value of the country's natural resources.

(D) They create a sense that the people of Mexico ignore the violence and pain of their shared history.

(E) They illustrate the vast geographic, historical, economic, and social diversity of the country.

5. In relation to the third paragraph, the fourth paragraph represents a shift from

(A) the history of the Mexican people to a portrait of the everyday Mexican's life

(B) an examination of the myriad differences that divide Mexicans to a reflection of the commonalities that bond all Mexicans

(C) a geographical description of Mexico to an analysis of its people and their histories

(D) a description of common traits that make Mexicans a cultural group today to descriptions of how Mexicans attempt to distance themselves from their cultural past

(E) a history of the invasion and conquest of Mexico to a critique of Mexico's influence on other nations as a result

6. The simile in paragraph 4, sentence 2 ("Every Mexican ... cup.") functions to

(A) criticize the way some Mexicans prefer to embrace their European heritage and neglect their native Mexican identities

(B) elaborate on the way coffee is a common experience for most Mexicans

(C) describe how native Mexicans and their culture were diminished after white Spaniards occupied Mexico

(D) suggest that contemporary Mexico has a shared culture among all the diverse people who live there

(E) illustrate the diversity of each Mexican person's heritage, similar to the diverse ways people make their coffee in paragraph 1

7. Which of the following best describes the image of "their own brown wrappers" in paragraph 4, sentence 3 ("Afraid . . . habits.")?

   (A) It creates a contrast between the Mexican people's positive self-image and the Spanish invader's negative perspective on the Mexican people.

   (B) It highlights how Mexican people grew suspicious of Spanish culture over time.

   (C) It understates the importance of skin color in the way the Mexican people identify themselves and others.

   (D) It emphasizes the role of race in determining who has power and influence in Mexican society.

   (E) It functions as a metaphor for the Mexican people's skin and their cultural identity.

8. In each sentence of paragraph 5, the statements following the dashes (—) serve to

   (A) compare the various regions of Mexico with one another

   (B) emphasize the cultural and geographic diversity of Mexico

   (C) illustrate Mexico as a uniform nation that is home to a proud people

   (D) emphasize the differences of the people across Mexico

   (E) compare the eastern and western regions of Mexico

9. Which of the following best describes the narrator's perspective on the Mexican people?

   (A) They can be seen as one character with a number of nuances and complexities to their personality.

   (B) They are so different from one another they cannot be compared.

   (C) They are isolated from the outside world and unable to understand the complexities of modern society.

   (D) They do not have a national identity because they are too different from one another.

   (E) They treat people poorly when they are different from the rest of Mexican society.

10. Throughout the passage, coffee (or café) best serves as

   (A) an extended metaphor comparing the Mexican people's rich native history to the richness of coffee

   (B) a symbol of the Mexican people's enthusiastic pride in their single national identity, which is a result of their common life experiences

   (C) a complex symbol that first unites the people in a common experience and then distinguishes the people in their unique and nuanced differences

   (D) a detail revealing Cayetana's perspective on the people surrounding her and her bitter attitude toward them

   (E) an image that represents the Mexican people's desire to form separate nations because of their irreconcilable differences

11. According to the descriptions and details provided throughout the passage, the attitude of the narrator toward the people of Mexico can best be described as

   (A) concerned about their treatment at the hands of their Spanish conquerors

   (B) prejudiced against their language and unfamiliar traditions

   (C) confused by a history that is both tragic and proud

   (D) respectful of both their history and numerous differences

   (E) disinterested in the details of their history but worried about their future

12. Which of the following best explains the function of the third-person point of view narration in this passage?

   (A) It sympathizes with the Mexican people by having Cayetana's narrate her private thoughts and feelings about her own Mexican identity.

   (B) It provides seemingly objective information about Cayetana and the Mexican people.

   (C) It represents a perspective from outside of the Mexican culture and conveys how an outsider might define Cayetana's cultural identity.

   (D) It reflects the voice of the "rich men, soldiers, and a few Indians" but not others in Mexican society.

   (E) It displays a bias against the Mexican people due to its reliance on information from Spanish conquerors.

13. The passage as a whole can be best understood as
   (A) a description of the people with whom Cayetana must interact daily.
   (B) a metaphor for the evils of invasion and conquest of other people
   (C) an argument for the evils of economic divisions
   (D) a meditation on the diversity of Mexico and its people
   (E) an explanation for why Mexico has an uncomplicated national identity

**Questions 14-24. Read the following poem carefully before you choose your answers.**

### BEFORE THE BIRTH OF ONE OF HER CHILDREN

All things within this fading world hath end,
Adversity doth still our joys attend;
No ties so strong, no friends so dear and sweet,
But with death's parting blow are sure to meet.
5    The sentence past is most irrevocable,
A common thing, yet oh, inevitable.
How soon, my Dear, death may my steps attend,
How soon't may be thy lot to lose thy friend,
We both are ignorant, yet love bids me
10   These farewell lines to recommend to thee,
That when the knot's untied that made us one,
I may seem thine, who in effect am none.
And if I see not half my days that's due,
What nature would, God grant to yours and you;
15   The many faults that well you know I have
Let be interred in my oblivious grave;
If any worth or virtue were in me,
Let that live freshly in thy memory
And when thou feel'st no grief, as I no harms,
20   Yet love thy dead, who long lay in thine arms,
And when thy loss shall be repaid with gains
Look to my little babes, my dear remains.
And if thou love thyself, or loved'st me,
These O protect from stepdame's[1] injury.
25   And if chance to thine eyes shall bring this verse,
With some sad sighs honor my absent hearse;
And kiss this paper for thy dear love's sake,
Who with salt tears this last farewell did take.

---

1 **stepdame's:** stepmother's

14. Considering the order of the phrases in line 3 ("No ties . . . sweet,"), which of the following best describes what is revealed about the speaker's attitude?

    (A) Bitterness that death seems to come only to those we love the most

    (B) Acceptance that all relationships are subject to death, even the best friendships

    (C) Optimism that the relationships we have with others will help us live forever in their memories

    (D) Questioning whether any relationships are worthwhile if they are end when death comes

    (E) Pity for those without close relationships to help their memory live beyond death

15. By using the phrase "sentence past" in line 5, the speaker is referring both to how people are figuratively sentenced to death and

    (A) the certainty of pain and suffering in life that may ironically lead to joy and comfort

    (B) the contrast of death being a part of everyone's future yet also a source of pain in everyone's past

    (C) the previous sentence in the poem in which the speaker asserts that all things end and nothing escapes death

    (D) the decree by God in the Abrahamic religions that all people will die because of Adam and Eve's original sin

    (E) the actual sentence in the poem in which the phrase is used, which creates an emphasis on the inevitability of death

16. In line 9 ("We both . . . me"), personification portrays love as

    (A) ignorant of the fate of people and relationships

    (B) certain that it can outlast and overcome death

    (C) natural and irrevocable, just like death

    (D) a friend who is lost when a person dies

    (E) encouraging the speaker to write this poem

17. In the context of the poem, the "knot's untied" (line 11) most likely describes

 (A) the umbilical cord connecting mother and child

 (B) a conflicted relationship that remained unresolved when one of the people died

 (C) a mystery buried in the lines of the poem

 (D) the speaker and addressee's spousal relationship ending because of death

 (E) the metaphorical cord that ties all humans to life

18. The descriptive language in lines 15–19 ("The many faults . . . memory") suggests that the speaker's perspective includes

 (A) confession of the speaker's personal failings but also hope that her virtues will be remembered

 (B) rejection of physical death due to religious salvation and the promise of eternal life

 (C) acceptance that death has no memory and joy in the memory of the living

 (D) hope that the speaker's virtues will save her from death but acceptance of what is inevitable

 (E) disappointment in a God that would use death to rob a child of its mother

19. In the context of the poem, the rhyming lines 21–22 ("yet . . . remains.") likely emphasizes

 (A) that her children who live past her will benefit the person she left behind

 (B) that she would rather stay behind with the one she loves than give birth to any more children

 (C) the significant loss she feels even imagining that she may leave her children and loved one behind

 (D) the security she feels from the loved ones she will leave behind

 (E) the enormous debt she owes to the ones who loved her while she was alive

20. Which of the following best describes the speaker's perspective on her children as revealed in line 22 ("Look . . . remains.")?

    (A) She would willingly give her own life for them.

    (B) They are too young to lose their mother.

    (C) They are the best of what she will leave behind after her death.

    (D) Death may just as easily and unpredictably take them as well.

    (E) They are the rewards she has earned for a virtuous and religious life.

21. Alliteration of the "s" sound in line 26 ("With . . . hearse;") functions to emphasize

    (A) the cruelty of death in taking a loved one in the prime of life

    (B) the value of memory to comfort those who are dying

    (C) the emptiness felt when a child loses a parent

    (D) the fond memory of the speaker that this poem hopes to evoke

    (E) the unexplainable sadness felt when a close relation dies

22. Which of the following most strongly influences the speaker's perspective?

    (A) The speaker's relationship with her yet unborn child

    (B) The speaker's personal doubts and fears about death

    (C) The speaker's memories of dead people with whom she has had relationships

    (D) The speaker's religious affiliation

    (E) The speaker's relationship with the person to whom the poem is addressed

23. Details throughout the poem reveal that the speaker values

    (A) escaping death completely

    (B) being remembered after her death

    (C) sacrificing herself for the life of her unborn child

    (D) prioritizing her own life above any relationships with others

    (E) ensuring that her children follow in her religious faith if she were to die

24. The dramatic situation of the poem establishes which of the following contrasts?

    (A) Death and Childbirth

    (B) Hatred and Love

    (C) Religion and Unbelief

    (D) Forgetfulness and Memory

    (E) Grief and Celebration

25. The poem as a whole can be best described as

    (A) an argument for the speaker to be remembered after her death

    (B) an appeal by the speaker to her God to save her child's life

    (C) a letter to her husband in case she should die in childbirth

    (D) instructions for how the speaker should be memorialized if she should die

    (E) an extended metaphor for the relationship between nature and religion

**Questions 26-34. Read the passage carefully before choosing your answers.**

1    This is too near the first hours of my life for me to relate anything of myself but by hearsay; it is enough to mention, that as I was born in such an unhappy place, I had no parish to have recourse to for my nourishment in my infancy; nor can I give the least account how I was kept alive, other than that, as I have been told, some relation of my mother's took me away for a while as a nurse, but at whose expense, or by whose direction, I know nothing at all of it.

2    The first account that I can recollect, or could ever learn of myself, was that I had wandered among a crew of those people they call gypsies, or Egyptians; but I believe it was but a very little while that I had been among them, for I had not had my skin discoloured or blackened, as they do very young to all the children they carry about with them; nor can I tell how I came among them, or how I got from them.

3    It was at Colchester, in Essex, that those people left me; and I have a notion in my head that I left them there (that is, that I hid myself and would not go any farther with them), but I am not able to be particular in that account; only this I remember, that being taken up by some of the parish officers of Colchester, I gave an account that I came into the town with the gypsies, but that I would not go any farther with them, and that so they had left me, but whither they were gone that I knew not, nor could they expect it of me; for though they send round the country to inquire after them, it seems they could not be found.

4    I was now in a way to be provided for; for though I was not a parish charge upon this or that part of the town by law, yet as my case came to be known, and that I was too young to do any work, being not above three

years old, compassion moved the magistrates[1] of the town to order some care to be taken of me, and I became one of their own as much as if I had been born in the place.

5    In the provision they made for me, it was my good hap to be put to nurse, as they call it, to a woman who was indeed poor but had been in better circumstances, and who got a little livelihood by taking such as I was supposed to be, and keeping them with all necessaries, till they were at a certain age, in which it might be supposed they might go to service or get their own bread.

6    This woman had also had a little school, which she kept to teach children to read and to work; and having, as I have said, lived before that in good fashion, she bred up the children she took with a great deal of art, as well as with a great deal of care.

7    But that which was worth all the rest, she bred them up very religiously, being herself a very sober, pious woman, very house-wifely and clean, and very mannerly, and with good behaviour. So that in a word, expecting a plain diet, coarse lodging, and mean clothes, we were brought up as mannerly and as genteelly as if we had been at the dancing-school.

8    I was continued here till I was eight years old, when I was terrified with news that the magistrates (as I think they called them) had ordered that I should go to service.[2]

26. In providing the details about having been "born in such an unhappy place" (paragraph 1), the narrator establishes

   (A) pity for her circumstances

   (B) anger for her mistreatment

   (C) anguish for her entirely miserable childhood

   (D) disgust for the mother who abandoned her

   (E) resentment for lost opportunities despite her potential

27. The semicolons in paragraph 2 serve to

   (A) emphasize the narrator's loving, vivid memories she recounts about her time living with the "gypsies"

   (B) contrast the narrator's unfortunate life before encountering the "gypsies" with her improved life afterwards

   (C) arrange the narrator's explanation of the origin of "gypsies"

   (D) combine the narrator's hazy memories of her time with the "gypsies" and her reflections about that time

   (E) distinguish between the narrator's time wandering and her coming to Colchester

---

1 **magistrates:** civil officers or judges who administer the law
2 **service:** some sort of employment

28. The details that the narrator provides about her time with the "gypsies" in paragraphs 2 and 3 are significant because they suggest

   (A) the "gypsies," like the narrator's family, rejected and abandoned her for unknown reasons

   (B) the narrator's story about the "gypsies" may not be true or that some details may be fabricated

   (C) the people of Colchester cared more about finding the "gypsies" than caring for the narrator

   (D) the narrator had no means for discovering where she came from

   (E) the people of Colchester would be reluctant to care for a child with dark "gypsie" skin

29. In context, all of the following details from paragraphs 6–7 suggest the values of the woman who cared for the narrator EXCEPT

   (A) "had also had a little school" (paragraph 6)

   (B) "she bred up the children she took with a great deal of art" (paragraph 6)

   (C) "plain diet, coarse lodging, and mean clothes" (paragraph 7)

   (D) "she bred them up very religiously" (paragraph 7)

   (E) "we were brought up as mannerly and as genteelly as if we had been at the dancing-school" (paragraph 7)

30. The woman who raised the narrator (paragraphs 5–7) is a minor character who contributes to the narrator's development by

   (A) contrasting the narrator's true character with the persona the narrator attempts to establish

   (B) providing further reasons why the narrator is justified in feeling self-pity for her unfortunate childhood

   (C) illustrating that the narrator had a decent upbring despite her tumultuous beginnings

   (D) explaining the skills that narrator had been trained to do while in the woman's care

   (E) emphasizing that the narrator's early upbringing had no effect on her at all

31. The comparison of the narrator's time with the woman (paragraphs 5–7) to a "dancing-school" illustrates a contrast between

    (A) an expectation of how orphans would be cared for and the reality of the narrator's situation

    (B) the privileged upbringing of girls who attended dance school and the narrator's upbringing

    (C) orphans who spent time with "gypsies" and those who grew up in Colchester

    (D) how the woman treated the boy orphans and how she treated the girl orphans

    (E) attending a private school focused on arts education and attending a public school focused on work training

32. Which of the following best describes what the narrator reveals by following "magistrates" in paragraph 8 with the statement in parentheses but not doing the same in paragraph 4?

    (A) The narrator continues to be confident in the accuracy of her memory.

    (B) The narrator remains uncertain and unsure of herself.

    (C) The narrator cannot maintain a consistent line of reasoning.

    (D) The narrator provides details only when they are necessary.

    (E) The narrator has a thorough understanding of her past and present circumstances.

33. Considering the passage as a whole, which of the following best describes the narrator's perspective on her situation?

    (A) The narrator's identity is rooted in the experiences she had with the "gypsies."

    (B) Despite learning manners and taking care of herself, the narrator is doomed to a life of poverty.

    (C) The narrator is capable of achieving much more than the magistrates and others think possible.

    (D) Though the narrator was well cared for, she is angry at the mother who abandoned her.

    (E) Despite an early life of uncertainty, the narrator came to be well cared for.

34. Which of the following is the most reasonable statement about the passage as a whole?

(A) It illustrates the problem of relying on community leaders to take care of individuals in need.

(B) It provides an argument for not allowing outsiders access to communities and their resources.

(C) It shows that children cannot be trusted to care for themselves or improve their circumstances.

(D) It demonstrates how good will and charity can improve the lives of those in even the worst circumstances.

(E) It explains how hopeless children are when they do not have their family to support them.

## AND THEN IT WAS LESS BLEAK BECAUSE WE SAID SO
Today there has been so much talk of things exploding

into other things, so much that we all become curious, that we
all run outside into the hot streets
and hug. Romance is a grotto[1] of eager stones
5     anticipating light, or a girl whose teeth
you can always see. With more sparkle and pop
is the only way to live. Your confetti tongue explodes
into acid jazz.[2] Small typewriters
that other people keep in their eyes
10    click away at all our farewell parties. It is hard
to pack for the rest of your life. Someone is always
eating cold cucumber noodles. Someone will drop by later
to help dismantle some furniture. A lot can go wrong
if you sleep or think, but the trees go on waving
15    their broken little hands.

35. In lines 1–2 ("Today . . . that we"), the word "things" lacks a clear reference and suggests the speaker believes that

   (A) anything could happen at any point to make people feel as though things are getting worse

   (B) individuals can prevent impending disaster by observing warning signs and then acting

   (C) the only thing people can rely on is their own curiosity and that others will spread rumors when they are uncertain

   (D) the worst that can possibly happen and the best possible outcome are both possible at the same time

   (E) people fear only the things that they cannot predict

36. The use and repetition of "so much" in lines 1–2 ("Today . . . that we") conveys the speaker's perspective that the talk

   (A) is indescribable

   (B) controls society in general

   (C) has become overwhelming

   (D) causes fear in others

   (E) creates no real cause for concern

---

1 **grotto:** a small picturesque cave, especially an artificial one in a park or garden
2 **acid jazz:** music genre that combines jazz with elements of funk, soul, hip hop, and disco

37. The combination of the comma and the word "or" in line 5 ("anticipating . . . teeth") emphasizes

   (A) the combined imagery of the two different metaphors used to describe romance

   (B) the emptiness of the grotto from line 4

   (C) the separation between the two different metaphors used to describe romance

   (D) the way the second of the two metaphors used to describe romance enhances the first

   (E) the sense of anticipation referenced in line 5

38. In lines 2–4 ("into . . . stones"), breaking line 2 at "we," having line 3 stand on its own without any punctuation, and then resolving the sentence in line 4 with the words "and hug" has the effect of

   (A) increasing the level of curiosity felt by all people, including the speaker and reader

   (B) minimizing an individual's need for connecting with others

   (C) contrasting the experiences of the speaker and reader from all other people

   (D) emphasizing the speaker and reader's shared experiences and perspectives

   (E) distinguishing the perspectives of the speaker from those of the reader

39. Which of the following best explains the perspective suggested by the personification of the "grotto" and "stones" in the metaphor in lines 4–5 ("and hug . . . teeth")?

   (A) Enlightenment is possible only through romance.

   (B) Romance is always waiting to be realized and fulfilled.

   (C) Romance seems attainable but sometimes ends unexpectedly.

   (D) Emptiness defines romance.

   (E) Romance is something that simply happens rather than something that is created.

40. The shift in the final sentence of the poem—lines 13–15 ("to . . . hands")—creates a contrast between

(A) the human mind and the physical world

(B) the inevitability of nature and the hopes of people

(C) the isolation of crowds and the social experience of nature

(D) the emotions of people and the realities of the natural world

(E) the concerns of people and the continuity of nature

41. Which of the following best describes the effect of the numerous shifts in the speaker's point of view?

(A) It conveys uncertainty about whether the reader will accept the speaker's insights as true.

(B) It creates a sense of togetherness by having the reader follow along with the speaker's musings.

(C) It emphasizes the speaker's failure to create a perspective to which the reader can relate.

(D) It suggests the speaker's feelings of chaos and isolation in a society others reject.

(E) It contrasts the confidence the speaker has in understanding his or her world with the chaos occurring all around.

42. All of the following contribute to the ambiguity of the poem EXCEPT

(A) "Today" (line 1)

(B) "so much talk" (line 1)

(C) "things" (lines 1 and 2)

(D) "other people" (line 9)

(E) "Someone" (lines 11 and 12)

43. All of the following examples of figurative language contribute to a motif of overwhelming sound in the poem EXCEPT

(A) "things exploding into other things" (lines 1–2)

(B) "sparkle and pop"

(C) "Small typewriters / that other people keep in their eyes / click away" (lines 8–10)

(D) "run outside into the hot streets / and hug." (lines 4–5)

(E) "confetti tongue explodes / into acid jazz" (lines 7–8)

44. Which of the following best characterizes the poem as a whole?

    (A) A collection of statements about trying to retain individuality in contemporary society

    (B) An argument about nature regulating the social conditions of contemporary society

    (C) A commentary on the tension between friendship and romance in contemporary society

    (D) An examination of social situations and individuality in contemporary society

    (E) A collection of observations about social interaction in contemporary society

1    The youth was filled with terror. He stared in pain and wonder. The fight was lost. The army was going to be eaten. War, the red animal—war, the blood-drinking god—would have what it wanted.

2    Within him something wanted to cry out. He had the desire to make a speech, to shout, but he could only get his tongue to call into the air: "Why—why—what—what's the matter?"

3    Soon he was in the middle of the mob. They were leaping and running all about him. Their pale faces shone in the weakening sunlight. They seemed, most of them, to be very big men. The youth turned from one to another of them as they came along. His senseless questions were not heard. The men gave no attention to his appeals. They did not seem to see him.

4    The youth, after rushing about and asking questions, finally caught a man by the arm. They swung around face to face.

5    "Why—why—" started the youth, struggling with his tongue.

6    The man screamed, "Let me go! Let me go!" His face was ashy pale and his eyes were rolling uncontrolled. He was breathing with difficulty. He still grasped his rifle, perhaps having forgotten to let go of it. He pulled away, and the youth was dragged several paces.

7    "Let me go! Let me go!"

8    "Why—why—" repeated the youth.

9    "No!" shouted the man. In his mad anger he fiercely swung his rifle. It crushed upon the youth's head; The man ran away.

10    The youth's fingers had turned to water upon the other's arm. The energy was struck from his muscles. He saw flaming wings of lightning flash before his eyes; there was a vast roar of thunder within his head.

11    Suddenly his legs seemed to die. He sank to the ground. He tried to get up. In his efforts against the pain he was like a man fighting with a creature made of air. There was a cruel struggle.

12    At last, with a forceful movement, he got upon his hands and knees, and from there, like a baby trying to walk, to his feet. Pressing his hands to his head, he went, struggling to stay straight, over the grass. He went like the tall soldier.

13    Once he put his hand to the top of his head and carefully touched the wound. The sudden pain made him draw a long breath through his teeth. His fingers were covered with blood. He regarded them with a glassy stare.

14    He hurried on. The day had turned to darkness and he could hardly see where to put his feet.

15    His wound now pained him very little. He was afraid to move rapidly, however, for fear of hurting it. He held his head very still and took great care not to fall. He was filled with worry and fear that any sudden mistake of his feet in the dark would bring more pain.

16    His thoughts, as he walked, were completely upon his hurt. There was a cool, liquid feeling about it and he imagined blood moving slowly down under his hair. His head seemed to be swelling to a size that made him think his neck would be too small.

17    He began to think about things of the past. He thought of certain meals his mother had cooked at home, in which foods he particularly liked had been served. He saw the loaded table. The pine walls of the kitchen glowed in the warm light from the stove. Also, he remembered how he and his friends would go from the schoolhouse to a shaded pool. He saw his clothes thrown upon the grass. He felt the waves of the water upon his body. The branches of the overhanging trees softly sang in the wind of youthful summer.

45. Setting the youth "in the middle of the mob" (paragraph 3) establishes a mood of

   (A) reflection

   (B) loss

   (C) victory

   (D) curiosity

   (E) desperation

46. In the interaction between the youth and the soldier (paragraphs 4–9), holding onto the soldier clearly demonstrates that the youth values

   (A) the success of the entire army more than the life of any one individual soldier

   (B) avoiding pain more than causing others pain

   (C) providing comfort to others more than having to face his own fear

   (D) having his questions answered more than the desperation of the soldier

   (E) his own safety and security more than the safety and security of his fellow soldiers

47. The simile in paragraph 11 illustrates the youth's struggle to
    (A) escape the pain
    (B) stop the other soldier
    (C) drive off the attacking vultures
    (D) understand the evils of war
    (E) fulfill his role in society

48. In the context of this passage, the stark contrast in settings provided between paragraphs 16 and 17 emphasizes the
    (A) mistrust of other soldiers that the youth must carry with him now
    (B) romantic belief that the war is a justified battle of ideals
    (C) pity the youth feels for other soldiers and their families
    (D) naive idealism the youth still carries with him
    (E) carefree innocence that the war has taken from the youth

49. Which of the following best describes the attitude of the youth toward this situation?
    (A) eager and confident
    (B) uncertain and pained
    (C) hesitant and suspicious
    (D) pitiless and determined
    (E) apathetic and accepting

50. In the context of this passage, the third-person point of view narration
    (A) allows the reader to more easily empathize with the youth's situation
    (B) helps the character of the youth to develop apart from the narration
    (C) provides a less biased, more factual account of the events
    (D) creates a more detailed description of the youth's encounter with the soldier
    (E) encourages a critical examination of the characters apart from the narrator's influence

51. The narrator's tone toward the youth and the situation of the passage can be best described as

    (A) matter-of-fact and candid
    (B) critical and dismissive
    (C) insincere and flippant
    (D) affectionate and concerned
    (E) idealistic and nostalgic

52. In the context of the passage, all of the following images contribute to the imagery of suffering EXCEPT

    (A) "flaming wings of lightning flash before his eyes" (paragraph 10)
    (B) "draw a long breath through his teeth" (paragraph 13)
    (C) "He held his head very still" (paragraph 15)
    (D) "cool, liquid feeling" (paragraph 16)
    (E) "glowed in the warm light" (paragraph 17)

53. Which of the following best describes the situational irony represented in the interactions between the youth and the soldiers?

    (A) The youth respects his fellow soldiers but decides to part ways with them when they fail to show courage in the midst of battle.
    (B) The youth fails to recognize that the fleeing soldiers are from the other army.
    (C) The inexperienced youth does not flee from the war and is instead more curious about what is happening, while the experienced soldiers flee.
    (D) The soldier who harms the youth merely wanted to return to the war and not be held back.
    (E) The youth wants to let go after he caught the man by the arm, but his fear prevents him from letting go.

54. The interaction between the youth and the soldier (paragraphs 5-10), represents a conflict between which of the following values?

    (A) innocence and success
    (B) respect and maturity
    (C) faith and certainty
    (D) curiosity and self-preservation
    (E) loss and salvation

55. Which of the following is a defensible claim that could be made about the youth based on this passage?

(A) Despite his troubling experiences, the youth remains committed to his fellow soldiers and their survival.

(B) Due to his experiences on the battlefield, the youth fears how those at home will now view him.

(C) The older, experienced soldiers underestimate the youth because of his age and inexperience.

(D) Even though the youth is injured, he remains committed to the war and the cause for which the war is being fought.

(E) While the youth's inexperience and age may seem to be disadvantages, they prevent the youth from fearing the war like the other soldiers.

# Section II: Free Response

## Question 1

**(This question counts as one-third of the total essay section score.)**

### SUGGESTED TIME—40 MINUTES

In the following poem by Spanish philosopher and poet George Santayana (published in 1896), the speaker considers the mind and the outside world.

Read the poem carefully. Then, in a well-written essay, analyze how Santayana uses poetic elements and techniques to convey the speaker's complex perspective on the mind.

In your response you should do the following:

- Respond to the prompt with a thesis that presents a defensible interpretation.
- Select and use evidence to support your line of reasoning.
- Explain how the evidence supports your line of reasoning.
- Use appropriate grammar and punctuation in communicating your argument.

### THERE MAY BE CHAOS STILL AROUND THE WORLD

There may be chaos still around the world,
This little world that in my thinking lies;
For mine own bosom is the paradise
Where all my life's fair visions are unfurled.
5   Within my nature's shell I slumber curled,
Unmindful of the changing outer skies,
Where now, perchance, some new-born Eros[1] flies,
Or some old Cronos[2] from his throne is hurled.
I heed them not; or if the subtle night
10  Haunt me with deities I never saw,
I soon mine eyelid's drowsy curtain draw
To hide their myriad faces from my sight.
They threat in vain; the whirlwind cannot awe
A happy snow-flake dancing in the flaw.

---

1  **Eros:** Greek god of love; to the Romans this was Cupid
2  **Cronos:** Greek god of time and king of the Titans, a race of beings defeated by the other Greek gods

# Question 2
## (This question counts as one-third of the total essay section score.)

### SUGGESTED TIME—40 MINUTES

In the following excerpt from the novel *Sing, Unburied, Sing*, written in 2017 by Jesmyn Ward, the narrator, Joseph (Jojo), describes a scene with several of his family members on the occasion of his birthday.

Read the passage carefully. Then, in a well-written essay, analyze how Ward uses literary elements and techniques to portray the lively scene and the complexities of the family's conflicts.

In your response you should do the following:

- Respond to the prompt with a thesis that presents a defensible interpretation.
- Select and use evidence to support your line of reasoning.
- Explain how the evidence supports your line of reasoning.
- Use appropriate grammar and punctuation in communicating your argument.

1   Usually, the singing is my favorite part of my birthday, because the candles make everything look gold, and they shine in Mam's and Pop's faces and make them look young as Leonie and Michael. Whenever they sing to me, they smile. I think it's Kayla's favorite part, too, because she sings stutteringly along. Kayla's making me hold her, because she cried and pushed at Leonie's collarbone and reached for me until Leonie frowned and held her out to me, said: "Here." But this year, the song is not my favorite part of my birthday because instead of being in the kitchen, we're all crowded into Mam's room, and Leonie's holding the cake like she held Kayla earlier, out and away from her chest, like she going to drop it. Mam's awake but doesn't really look awake, her eyes half open, unfocused, looking past me and Leonie and Kayla and Pop. Even though Mam's sweating, her skin looks pale and dry, like a muddy puddle dried to nothing after weeks of no rain in the summer. And there's a mosquito buzzing around my head, dipping into my ear, veering out, teasing to bite.

2   When the happy birthday song starts, it's only Leonie. She has a pretty voice, the kind of voice that sounds good singing low but sort of cracks on the high notes. Pop is not singing; he never sings. When I was younger, I didn't know because I'd have a whole family singing to me: Mam, Leonie, and Michael. But this year, when Mam can't sing because she's sick and Kayla makes up words to the melody and Michael's gone, I know Pop isn't singing because he's just moving his lips, lip-synching, and there's no noise coming out. Leonie's voice cracks on *dear Joseph*, and the

light from the thirteen candles is orange. No one but Kayla looks young. Pop is standing too far out of the light. Mam's eyes have closed to slits in her chalky face, and Leonie's teeth look black at the seams. There's no happiness here.

3    "Happy birthday, Jojo," Pop says, but he's not looking at me when he says it. He's looking at Mam, at her hands loose and open at her sides. Palms up like something dead. I lean forward to blow out my candles, but the phone rings, and Leonie jumps, so the cake jumps with her. The flames waver and feel hotter under my chin. Pearls of wax drip onto the baby shoes. Leonie turns away from me with the cake, looking to the kitchen, to the phone on the counter.

4    "You going to let the boy blow out his candles, Leonie?" Pop asks.

5    "Might be Michael," Leonie says, and then there is no cake because Leonie's taken it with her to the kitchen, set it on the counter next to the black-corded phone. The flames are eating the wax. Kayla shrieks and throws her head back. So I follow Leonie into the kitchen, to my cake, and Kayla smiles. She's reaching for the fire. The mosquito that was in Mam's room has followed us, and he's buzzing around my head, talking about me like I'm a candle or a cake. *So warm and delicious*. I swat him away.

6    "Hello?" Leonie says.

7    I grab Kayla's arm and lean into the flames. She struggles, transfixed.

8    "Yes."

9    I blow.

10    "Baby."

11    Half the candles gutter out.

12    "This week?"

13    The other half eating wax to the nub.

14    "You sure?"

15    I blow again, and the cake goes dark. The mosquito lands on my head. *So scrumptious*, he says, and bites. I swat him, and my palm comes away smeared with blood. Kayla reaches.

16    "We'll be there."

17    Kayla has a handful of frosting, and her nose is running. Her blond afro curls high. She sticks her fingers in her mouth, and I wipe.

18    "Easy, baby. Easy."

19    Michael is an animal on the other end of the telephone behind a fortress of concrete and bars, his voice traveling over miles of wire and listing, sun-bleached power poles. I know what he is saying, like the birds I hear honking and flying south in the winter, like any other animal. I'm coming home.

# Question 3
## (This question counts as one-third of the total essay section score.)

### SUGGESTED TIME—40 MINUTES

"God himself could not sink this ship."—Cal Hockley, *Titanic*

"Dramatic irony" occurs when the audience members or readers have knowledge before the characters learn it, creating a situation in which the characters' words and actions take on a different—often contradictory—meaning for the audience than they have for the characters.

Choose a work of fiction in which the characters' awareness of their situation differs substantially from that of the audience. Then, in a well-written essay, analyze how these different levels of awareness contribute to an interpretation of the work as a whole. Do not merely summarize the plot.

In your response you should do the following:

- Respond to the prompt with a thesis that presents a defensible interpretation.
- Provide evidence to support your line of reasoning.
- Explain how the evidence supports your line of reasoning.
- Use appropriate grammar and punctuation in communicating your argument.

# Acknowledgments

"XIV" from "Midsummer" from MIDSUMMER by Derek Walcott. Copyright © 1984 by Derek Walcott. Reprinted by permission of Farrar, Straus & Giroux. All Rights Reserved.

"After the Storm" from "The Schooner *Flight*" from THE STAR-APPLE KINGDOM by Derek Walcott. Copyright © 1979 by Derek Walcott. Reprinted by permission of Farrar, Straus & Giroux. All Rights Reserved.

*Agnes Grey* by Anne Brontë, originally published by Thomas Cautley Newby, London, 1847. This work is in the public domain.

"America" by Claude McKay from *Liberator* (December 1921). This work is in the public domain.

"Amoretti XXX" by Edmund Spenser at poetryfoundation.org. This work is in the public domain.

"Autumn Sunset" by Willa Cather from *American Poetry: The Nineteenth Century* (The Library of America, 1993). This work is in the public domain.

"Ancestral" from COLLECTED POEMS 1917-1982 by Archibald MacLeish. Copyright © 1985 by The Estate of Archibald MacLeish. Reprinted by permission of Houghton Mifflin Harcourt Publishing Company. All rights reserved.

"And Then It Was Less Bleak Because We Said So" from *You Are Not Dead* by Wendy Xu. Copyright © 2013 by Wendy Xu. Reprinted with the permission of The Permissions Company, LLC, on behalf of the Cleveland State University Poetry Center, csupoetrycenter.com.

"The Ant of the Self" by ZZ Packer from *Drinking Coffee Elsewhere*, Penguin Publishing Group. *Copyright © 2003* by ZZ Packer.

"The Appropriation of Cultures" by Percival Everett. Published in *Callaloo* 19:1 (1996), 24-30. © 1996 Johns Hopkins University Press. Reprinted with permission of Johns Hopkins University Press.

"Arise, Go Down" from *The City In Which I Love You* by Li-Young Lee. Copyright © 1990 by Li-Young Lee. Reprinted with the permission of The Permissions Company, LLC on behalf of BOA Editions, Ltd., www.boaeditions.org.

"As I Walked Out One Evening" by W. H Auden from *Another Time* by W. H. Auden, published by Random House. Copyright © 1940 W. H. Auden, renewed by the Estate of W. H. Auden.

"At Black River" from *Why I Wake Early* by Mary Oliver. Published by Beacon Press, Boston. Copyright © 2004 by Mary Oliver. Reprinted by permission of The Charlotte Sheedy Literary Agency Inc.

"A Barred Owl" from *MAYFLIES: New Poems and Translations* by Richard Wilbur. Copyright © 2000 by Richard Wilbur. Reprinted by permission of Houghton Mifflin Harcourt Publishing Company. All rights reserved.

"Before the Birth of One of Her Children" by Anne Bradstreet. This work is in the public domain.

"BETWEEN THE ROCKETS AND SONGS: New Year's Eve 2003" by Martín Espada was first published in THE REPUBLIC OF POETRY, copyright © 2006 by Martín Espada. Permission to reprint granted by author.

"Cell One" from THE THING AROUND YOUR NECK by Chimamanda Ngozi Adichie. Copyright © 2009 Chimamanda Ngozi Adichie, used by permission of The Wylie Agency LLC.

"The Children's Moon from *Mrs. Nelson's Class* by Marilyn Nelson. Reprinted by permission of author.

"Como Tú / Like You / Like Me" from *How to Love a Country: Poems by Richard Blanco*. Copyright © 2019 by Richard Blanco. Reprinted by permission of Beacon Press, Boston.

"Death Be Not Proud" by John Donne, first published in 1633 and one of the "Holy Sonnets." This work is in the public domain.

"Duende" from *Duende: Poems, by Tracy K. Smith*. Copyright © 2007 by Tracy K. Smith. Reprinted with the permission of The Permissions Company, LLC on behalf of Graywolf Press, Minneapolis, Minnesota, USA, www.graywolfpress.org.

"Dulce Et Decorum Est" by Wilfred Owen from *Poems* 1920, published by Chatto & Windus in London. This work is in the public domain.

"Elegy for a Woman of No Importance" from *Revolt Against the Sun: The Selected Poetry of Nazik al-Mala'ika* by Nazik al-Mala'ika. *A Bilingual Reader*, translated by Emily Drumsta (Saqi Books, 2020).

"Enemies" from *ENTRIES: POEMS* by Wendell Berry, copyright © 1994 by Wendell Berry. Used by permission of Pantheon Books, an imprint of the Knopf Doubleday Publishing Group, a division of Penguin Random House LLC. All rights reserved.

Excerpt(s) from *EXIT WEST: A NOVEL* by Mohsin Hamid, copyright © by Margo Jefferson. Used by permission of Riverhead, an imprint of Penguin Publishing Group, a division of Penguin Random House LLC. All rights reserved.

"Fire and Ice" by Robert Frost, first published in *Harper's Magazine*, December 1920. This work is in the public domain.

*Frankenstein; or. The Modern Prometheus* by Mary Shelley, first published in 1818 by Lackington, Hughes, Harding, Mavor & Jones with a revised edition published in 1831. Both versions are in the public domain.

*The Grapes of Wrath* by John Steinbeck, Viking Press, New York, 1939.

*Great Expectations* by Charles Dickens, first published in book form in 1861 by Chapman & Hall. This work is in the public domain.

*The Great Gatsby* by F Scott Fitzgerald, first published in 1925 by Charles Scribner's and Sons. This work is in the public domain.

*Hamlet* by William Shakespeare

"Handsome Man" by Rebecca Hazelton in *Waxwing, issue XXIII. waxwingmag.org*

*"Harlem" from The Collected Works of Langston Hughes. Copyright © 2002 by Langston Hughes.*

*Hedda Gabler* by Henrik Ibsen, first staged on 1891 in Munich, Germany. This work is in the public domain.

"Hope." by Emily Dickinson from *Poems* published in 1891 by Thomas Wentworth Higginson and Mabel Loomis Todd. This work is in the public domain.

From "The Hummingbird's Daughter" by Luis Alberto Urrea, copyright © 2005. Reprinted by permission of Little, Brown, an imprint of Hachette Book Group, Inc.

"I Wandered Lonely as a Cloud" by William Wordsworth from *Poems, in Two Volumes*, first published in 1807. This work is in the public domain.

"If We Must Die" by Claude McKay published in the July 1919 issue of *The Liberator*. This work is in the public domain.

"INTERPRETER OF MALADIES" by JHUMPA LAHIRI From *INTERPRETER OF MALADIES* by Jhumpa Lahiri. Copyright © 1999 by Jhumpa Lahiri. Reprinted by permission of Houghton Mifflin Harcourt Publishing Company. All rights reserved.

"Keep Going" by Edgar Guest, first appeared in "Public Opinion," Chambersburg, Pennsylvania, 03 Mar 1921, page 8. This work is in the public domain.

From *Kindred* by Octavia Butler. Copyright © 1979 by Octavia Butler. Reprinted by permission of Writers House LLC acting as agent for the author/illustrator.

"The Kiss" by Kate Chopin, first published in 1895. This work is in the public domain.

"The Man He Killed" by Thomas Hardy, first published in *Harper's Weekly*, Nov. 8 1902 and then reprinted in *Time's Laughingstocks and Other Verses*, London: Macmillan, 1909. This work is in the public domain

"The Metamorphosis" by Franz Kafka, first published in German by Kurt Wolff Verlag, Leipzig, 1915. This work is in the public domain.

"Mexican American Sonnet" by Iliana Rocha, originally published in Poem-a-Day on September 19, 2019, by the Academy of American Poets. Reprinted by permission of author.

"La Migra" by Pat Mora from *Agua Santo*, Beacon Press © 1993.

"Miss Brill" by Katherine Mansfield first published in *Athenaeum* on 26 November 1920, and later reprinted in *The Garden Party and Other Stories*. This work is in the public domain.

*Moll Flanders* by Daniel Defoe, first published in 1722 by William Rufus Chetwood in England. This work is in the public domain.

"Mother to Son" by Langston Hughes, first published in 1922 in *Crisis*. This work is in the public domain.

*The Name of the Wind* by Patrick Rothfuss, published in 2007 by DAW Books.

"The New Colossus" by Emma Lazarus, written in 1883 to raise money for a pedestal for the Statue of Liberty, first published in *New York World* and *The New York Times*. It is inscribed on bronze plaque on statue's pedestal. This work is in the public domain.

Excerpt(s) from NO EXIT AND THE FLIES by Jean-Paul Sartre, translated by Stuart Gilbert, copyright © 1946 by Stuart Gilbert, copyright renewed 1974, 1975 by Maris Agnes Mathilde Gilbert. Used by permission of Alfred A. Knopf, an imprint of the Knopf Doubleday Publishing Group, a division of Penguin Random House LLC. All rights reserved.

"Nuns Fret Not" by William Wordsworth from *Poems Volume II* (1815) by William Wordsworth. This work is in the public domain.

"Ode on Solitude " by Alexander Pope (at the age of 12), published in1700.

"On the Subway" from THE GOLD CELL by Sharon Olds, copyright © 1987 by Sharon Olds. Used by permission of Alfred A. Knopf, an imprint of the Knopf Doubleday Publishing Group, a division of Penguin Random House LLC. All rights reserved.

"Ozymandias" by Percy Bysshe Shelley, first published in the January 1818 issue of *The Examiner* of London. This work is in the public domain.

"Persephone, Falling" by Rita Dove from *Mother Love*, W. W. Norton © 1996.

*A Portrait of the Artist as a Young Man* by James Joyce, first published as a book in 1916 by B. W. Huebsch of New York. This work is in the public domain.

"Quality of mercy" from *The Merchant of Venice* by William Shakespeare, first published in 1600. This work is in the public domain.

"Quarantine" by Eavan Boland from *New Collected Poems*, W. W. Norton © 2005.

A Raisin in the Sun Lorraine Hansberry

*The Red Badge of Courage* by Stephen Crane, first published in 1895. This work is in the public domain.

*The Rise of David Levinsky* by Abraham Cahan, published in 1917. This work is in the public domain.

*Romeo and Juliet* by William Shakespeare

"Roselily" from IN LOVE & TROUBLE: Stories of Black Women by Alice Walker. Copyright © 1973, and renewed 2001 by Alice Walker. Reprinted by permission of Houghton Mifflin Harcourt Publishing Company. All rights reserved.

"The Sanctuary Desolated" by Jesse Stuart from TALES FROM THE PLUM GROVE HILLS. Copyright © 1997 Jesse Stuart Foundation. Used by permission of the Jesse Stuart Foundation.

"Sonnet 22" by William Shakespeare, first published in 1609 as part of the Fair Youth series. This work is in the public domain.

From SING, UNBURIED, SING by Jesmyn Ward. Copyright © 2017 by Jesmyn Ward. Reprinted with the permission of Scribner, a division of Simon & Schuster, Inc. All rights reserved.

Excerpt from "Snapshots of a Wedding" by Bessie Head from *The Collector of Treasures and Other Botswana Village Tales*, Waveland Press © 2013.

Excerpt(s) from SNOW by Orhan Pamuk, translated by Maureen Freely, translation copyright © 2004 by Penguin Random House LLC. Originally published in Turkey as KAR by İletisim, Istanbul, in 2002; copyright © 2002 by İletisim Yayinciltk A.S.. Used by permission of Alfred A. Knopf, an imprint of the Knopf Doubleday Publishing Group, a division of Penguin Random House LLC. All rights reserved

"Snowflakes" from *Trying conclusions: New and Selected Poems, 1961-1991* by Howard Nemerov. Reprinted by permission of the University of Chicago Press.

"Song from a Reedless Flute" by Sara Littlecrow-Russell from *The Secret Powers of Naming*, by Sara Littlecrow-Russell. © 2006 Sara Littlecrow-Russell. Reprinted by permission of the University of Arizona Press.

# Index

# E

EBSCO, 560
"Elegy for a Woman of No Importance"
    (Nazik Al-Malaika), 288, 327
Emotional
    conflict, 614
    investment, 246
Emphasis, 296–297
Encounters, 176
"Enemies" (Wendell Berry), 296–297
Enjambment, 520–521
Environment
    and character, 230–232
Epiphany(ies)
    and action, 457
    and central conflicts, 456–457
    defined, 452–453, 457
Espada, Martín, 133
    "Between the Rockets and the Songs,"
        129, 133
Event(s)
    defined, 177
    that develop characters or themes, 177
    that introduce or develop plot, 176
Everett, Percival, 4
    "The Appropriation of Cultures," 4–11,
        15, 17–19, 23, 29–31, 38, 41, 43, 47,
        51, 53, 57–58, 60, 220–221, 230,
        250, 461, 471–473
Evidence, 494, 554–555, 630–631
    criteria for sufficient, 413
    defined, 413
    effective use of, 335–337
    quality of, 263
    quantity of, 263
    recursive process, 413
    relevant, 263
    strategic, 194–195, 335–336
    sufficient high-quality, 194–195, 263,
        338
    supporting claim with, 120–121
    of things unseen, 619
    use by writers, 196, 264, 338
Exaggerations/exaggerating, 304–307
*Exit West* (Mohsin Hamid), 136–152,
    155–159, 161, 163, 165–166, 168, 170,
    175, 177, 179–183, 188, 190–191, 193,
    383, 385, 464, 574
Expectations, 281–282
Exposition, 33, 39–41
Extended metaphor, 314, 317

External conflict, 178, 180

# F

Faulkner, William, 386
Figurative language, 105, 282, 310, 314, 488
Figures of speech, 105
"Fire and Ice" (Robert Frost), 307
Fitzgerald, F. Scott
    *The Great Gatsby,* 381, 385, 393–395, 397,
        405–407, 534
Flashback
    defined, 384
    effect of, 384
    possible purpose of, 384
Foil or foil characters
    functions of
        contrasts in foils, 378
        illuminating main character, 378
Foreshadowing
    defined, 384
    effect of, 384
    possible purpose of, 384
Forster, E. M., 380
    *A Passage to India,* 380
Foster, Tom, 290
Fragment, 418
*Frankenstein; or, the Modern Prometheus*
    (Mary Shelley), 225, 246–247, 254,
    353–371, 477
Frost, Robert, 92, 300, 534
    "Fire and Ice," 307
    "The Road Not Taken," 92
    "Stopping by Woods on a Snowy
        Evening," 301–302, 310–311

# G

Genet, Jean, 633
    *Les Nègres* ("The Blacks"), 633
Golding, William, 406, 493
    *Lord of the Flies,* 406, 493–494
Google Scholar, 560
Gozzi, Carlo, 238
*Grapes of Wrath, The* (John Steinbeck),
    163–165, 168–169
*Great Expectations* (Charles Dickens),
    201–202, 205
*Great Gatsby, The* (F. Scott Fitzgerald), 381,
    385, 393–395, 397, 405–407, 534
Group attitudes, 461
Guest, Edgar, 286
    "Keep Going," 286–289, 293

Phrases
 positioning, 417
 transitional, 339–340
Physical distance, 246
Plath, Sylvia, 571
 "Morning Song," 567, 571
Plot
 artful arrangement of incidents
  connected, 33–34
  dramatic situation, 34–35
  sequenced events, 33–34
 cause-and-effect relationship, 33, 36
 defined, 32–33, 35, 39
 dramatic situation, 33
 events that introduce or develop, 176
Poe, Edgar Allan, 290
 "The Raven," 290
 "The Tell-Tale Heart," 224
Poem, 95
 defined, 85
 origin of, 85
 structure of, 86–88
 writing a paragraph of literary argument
  about, 123–124
Poetry, 281
 characters in, 78
 communicates through figurative
  language, 105
 defined, 75, 79
 open form of, 295–296
Poets (known as shapers), 85, 90, 101
 establish structure, 515
 pay close attention to words, 95
 signal shifts through structural
  conventions, 92
Poet's Craft, The
 breaking patterns, 291–293
Point of view, 48
 contribution of, 51
 defined, 45
 function of, 50–51
Pollard, Wayne E., 96
 Bo's Café Life, 96
Polti, Georges, 238
 The Thirty-Six Dramatic Situations, 238
Pope, Alexander
 "Ode on Solitude," 325
Positioning phrases, 417
Portrait of the Artist as a Young Man, A
 (James Joyce), 249
Power of words, 419–420

Preceding action, 619
Prepositional phrase, 418
Pride and Prejudice (Jane Austen), 497
Property, intellectual, 558
ProQuest, 560
Protagonist(s). See also Character
 ambiguous, 225
 and antagonists, distinction between, 224
 defined, 224
 internal conflicts of, 224–225
 values, 226
Proust, Marcel, 247, 386
 Remembrance of Things Past, 247
 Swann's Way, 247
Punctuation
 blocking or chunking the text, 518
 defined, 420
 and enjambment, 520–521
 extended ideas and images, 515–516
 follow the grammar, 517–518
 setting and breaking patterns, 521–522
 symbols for, 421
 unpack the imagery, 519–520

## Q

"Quarantine" (Eavan Boland), 504, 507

## R

Raisin in the Sun, A (Lorraine Hansberry),
 596–605, 607–610, 614–618, 619–621,
 625–626, 632, 633, 634–638
Rashamon (movie), 373
"Raven, The" (Edgar Allan Poe), 290
reader response theory (Louise Rosenblatt),
 154
Readers
 get to know characters
  descriptions, 155–157
  expectations of readers, 155–157
Reasoning, complex
 alternative interpretations, 497
 broader context, 496–497
 defined, 496
 relevant analogies, 496–498
Recursive process, 195–196, 338
Reference
 defined, 560
Referents
 and ambiguity, 96–99
 clause as, 96
 defined, 96